A Beckett Canon

THEATER: Theory/Text/Performance

Enoch Brater, Series Editor

Recent Titles:

Trevor Griffiths: Politics, Drama, History by Stanton B. Garner Jr.

Memory-Theater and Postmodern Drama by Jeanette R. Malkin

Performing America: Cultural Nationalism in American Theater
edited by Jeffrey D. Mason and J. Ellen Gainor

Space in Performance: Making Meaning in the Theatre by Gay McAuley

Mirrors of Our Playing: Paradigms and Presences in Modern Drama
by Thomas R. Whitaker

Brian Friel in Conversation edited by Paul Delaney

Sails of the Herring Fleet: Essays on Beckett by Herbert Blau

On Drama: Boundaries of Genre, Borders of Self by Michael Goldman

Contours of the Theatrical Avant-Garde: Performance and Textuality
edited by James M. Harding

The Painted Word: Samuel Beckett's Dialogue with Art
by Lois Oppenheim

*Performing Democracy: International Perspectives on Urban
Community-Based Performance* edited by Susan C. Haedicke
and Tobin Nellhaus

A Beckett Canon by Ruby Cohn

A Beckett Canon

Ruby Cohn

Ann Arbor

THE UNIVERSITY OF MICHIGAN PRESS

2004   2003   2002   2001   4   3   2   1

A CIP catalog record for this book is available from the British Library.

Library of Congress Cataloging-in-Publication Data

Cohn, Ruby.
    A Beckett canon / Ruby Cohn.
        p.   cm. — (Theater—theory/text/performance)
    Includes bibliographical references and index.
    ISBN 0-472-11190-6
    1. Beckett, Samuel, 1906—Criticism and interpretation. 2.
Beckett, Samuel, 1906—Bibliography. 3. Beckett, Samuel, 1906—
Authorship. 4. Beckett, Samuel, 1906—Chronology. I. Title. II.
Series.
PR6003.E282 Z6184   2001
848'.91409—dc21   00-12319

For appreciators of the writings of Samuel Beckett
(1906–1989)

Acknowledgments: Manifold Gratitudes

The unsung heroes of literary scholarship are the curators of research libraries, and I am most grateful to Susan E. Rainville at the Burns Library of Boston College; Geoff Smith of the Ohio State University Library; Mike Botts, Frances Miller, and especially Julian Garforth at the Beckett Archive of the University of Reading; Linda Ashton, Sally Leach, and Pat Fox at the Harry Ransom Humanities Research Center at the University of Texas; and Felicity O'Mahoney and Stuart O. Seanoir at Trinity College, Dublin. This summary listing is inadequate to express my gratitude to them.

In the matter of chronology, I am grateful to the following: the manuscript study of Richard Admussen; the bibliography of Raymond Federman and John Fletcher; Edith Fournier in *Revue d'esthétique;* J. C. C. Mays in *Beckett avant Beckett;* Eoin O'Brien in *The Beckett Country;* and consultation with Martha Fehsenfeld, Lois Overbeck, and especially James Knowlson and John Pilling.

For the nitty-gritty of publication details, I am most grateful to Breon Mitchell, who interrupted his own work to correct mine, but residual errors are mine alone.

For un-Beckettian ebullience and publishing reassurance I thank Enoch Brater. For photocopying far-flung pieces and for stimulating discussion, I thank Daniela Caselli and Diane Sol, respectively. For shared enthusiasms from different perspectives I thank Peter Gidal. For matters Irish and Trinitarian I thank Anna McMullan and Gerry Dukes. For matters French and literary I thank Michèle Praeger. For recondite publications and information I thank Rick Praeger. For entrance to, and rescue from, the mysteries of cyberspace I thank Brit Pyland. For the few quotations from unpublished Beckett materials I thank Jérôme Lindon of Les Editions de Minuit. For helpful suggestions I thank the anonymous reader of the University of Michigan Press. Specific scholarly debts are acknowledged in my notes.

Contents

	Abbreviations and Conventions	xi
1929–31	*Rather Too Self-Conscious*	1
1932–33	*Intricate Festoons of Words*	33
1934–36	*These Demented Particulars*	64
1937–40	*No Trifle Too Trifling*	88
1941–45	*Semantic Succour*	108
1946	*J'Ouvre la Série*	127
1947–49	*Mais la Réalité, Trop Fatigué Pour Chercher le Mot Juste*	152
1950–52	*Rien à faire*	184
1953–58	*Then These Flashes, or Gushes*	209
1959–61	*Fresh Elements and Motifs*	244
1962–69	*A Little Rush, Then Another*	276
1970–76	*Soudain ou Peu à Peu*	308
1977–89	*Comment Dire*	345
	Appendix 1: Beckett and Performance	385
	Appendix 2: Beckett's Self-Translations	387
	Notes	389
	Works Cited	407
	Index	415

Abbreviations and Conventions

Abbreviations are listed for works, catalogs, archives, and two Beckett periodicals.

Beckett Editions

	Catastrophe et autres dramaticules. Paris: Minuit, 1982.
CDW	*Complete Dramatic Works*. London: Faber, 1986.
Comédie	*Comédie et actes divers*. Paris: Minuit, 1972.
	Comment c'est. Paris: Minuit, 1961.
	Collected Poems in English and French. London: Calder, 1977.
CSP	*Complete Short Prose, 1929–1989*. New York: Grove, 1995.
	Le Dépeupleur. Paris: Minuit, 1970.
	Disjecta. London: Calder, 1983.
Dream	*Dream of Fair to Middling Women*. London: Calder, 1993.
	Eleutheria. Paris: Minuit, 1995.
	Fin de partie et Acte sans paroles. Paris: Minuit, 1957.
Godot	*En attendant Godot*. Paris: Minuit, 1954.
	L'Image. Paris: Minuit, 1988.
	L'Innommable. Paris: Minuit, 1953.
	Malone meurt. Paris: Minuit, 1951.
	Mal vu mal dit. Paris: Minuit, 1981.
	Mercier et Camier. Paris: Minuit, 1970.
	Molloy. Paris: Minuit, 1951.
MPTK	*More Pricks Than Kicks*. New York: Grove, 1972.
	Murphy. New York: Grove, 1957.
	Nohow On. New York: Grove, 1996 (referenced by paragraph number).
Nouvelles	*Nouvelles et textes pour rien*. Paris: Minuit, 1955.
Poems	*Collected Poems, 1930–1978*. London: Calder, 1984.

Pour finir encore et autres foirades. Paris: Minuit, 1975.
Proust. New York: Grove, 1957.
Têtes-Mortes. Paris: Minuit, 1991.
The Theatrical Notebooks of Samuel Beckett. Vol. IV.
1999. S. E. Gontarski, ed. London: Faber and Faber. New
York: Grove.
Three Novels. New York: Grove-Weidenfeld, 1991.
Watt. New York: Grove, 1959.

The page numbers in the text refer to these editions. Titles of all Beckett's publications are italicized, except for poems, which are enclosed in quotation marks, as are unpublished works.

Libraries, Catalogs, and Periodicals

BatR	*Beckett at Reading: Catalogue of the Beckett Manuscript Collection at the University of Reading*, Whiteknights Press and the Beckett International Foundation, 1998
BC	Burns Library, Boston College
HRC	Harry Ransom Humanities Research Center, University of Texas
ICU	The University of Chicago Library, Chicago, Illinois
JOBS	*Journal of Beckett Studies*
	McMaster University Library, Hamilton, Ontario, Canada
MoSW	Washington University Library, St. Louis, Missouri
NhD	Dartmouth College Library, Hanover, New Hampshire
OSU	The Ohio State University Library, Columbus, Ohio
RUL	Beckett Archive, University of Reading Library, Reading, United Kingdom
SBT	*Samuel Beckett Today*
TCD	Trinity College Library, Dublin, Ireland

Except as indicated otherwise, all citations of Knowlson are to his biography *Damned to Fame: The Life of Samuel Beckett* (New York: Simon and Schuster, 1996).

Unless otherwise designated, translations from foreign languages are mine. Beckett's self-translations are followed by page numbers except for title-headings, which are translated within parentheses.

1929–31

Rather Too Self-Conscious

Having read nothing by Beckett, I fell in love with his *En attendant Godot* in 1953, when it was performed at the short-lived Théâtre de Babylone in Paris. That passion spurred me to read Beckett's few publications, and I continued to read as he wrote through the decades—magnetized by his unique depth and originality. I published an article on Beckett in 1959, after a prior rejection: "We like your criticism, but we don't feel your author merits publishing space." Emphatically disagreeing, I continued to appreciate "your author" until there was a book (my doctoral dissertation). Then another book. Then still another. I have not, however, written on the whole Beckett canon—now complete, although still not completely published—and that is my present point of embarkation. In undertaking this journey, I hope to share my renewed sense of the immediacy of Beckett's individual works, while I try to elucidate some of their difficulties.

Of the hundred-odd books I have read about Beckett's oeuvre, none moves in quite the way I now intend. Venturing into meaning, skirting the biography so scrupulously investigated by James Knowlson, I will not impose coherence upon the many threads of Beckett's tapestry—autobiographical, dramatic, eschatological, essentialist, existential, inter- and intratextual, metaliterary, mythic, performative, philosophic, psychological, rhythmic, stylistic, thematic. Writing on Beckett's work once again, I flaunt the label that has sometimes been scornfully affixed to me—humanist.

During these years of work on *A Beckett Canon* I have tried to envision my reader, and I imagine her/him as one who has been drawn to Beckett in print or performance, and who is curious about other facets of his oeuvre. I therefore summarize contents more fully than is usual in Beckett criticism, but I also comment on that content, as is quite usual in Beckett criticism. Lucky enough to be among the early Beckett critics, I am also lucky to *enjoy* learning from other critics. Without a thesis to uphold, I will wend my way chronologically through Beckett's works, gliding as he did from one genre to another, from one theme to another, from one wordscape to another. What-ever the limitations of a chronological survey, it does bear testimony to Beck-ett's writerly energy over a period of sixty years, even though he was para-doxically attracted to Dante's slothful Belacqua. In my chronology, I limit myself to Beckett's works in their originary language, for the most part ignoring his extraordinary translations. I aim to be inclusive, but I realize that other readers will construct a different Beckett canon, and I therefore use the indefinite article in the title of my book (and I willfully ignore the fashionable suspicion about the very word *canon*).

My task is daunting, for Beckett is prolific, difficult, and self-critical. It is daunting above all because Beckett's work is so *personal* a possession for his readers, and my words will inevitably be an encroachment on such pos-session. I plead that my reading is also personal, after long immersion.

However readers may react to my approach, I should forewarn them about the problems of chronology. Beckett is sometimes meticulous about dating his manuscripts, but at other times he neglects to do this, and at still other times he misremembers dates. Occasionally, Beckett began one work while another was still incomplete, and he sometimes revised his plays when he directed them. I nevertheless try to choose the date of emergent concep-tion in the originary language. When I am guessing at a date, I marshal my evidence or confess the guess. John Pilling has painstakingly dated Beckett's works to 1940, and I am indebted to his *Beckett before Godot,* to his *Beck-ett's Dream Notebook,* and to his generous advice.[1]

My chronological approach compels me to begin anticlimactically. Beckett is not Rimbaud, or even Chatteron. As Lawrence Harvey pointed out in a most informative book of 1970, creation did not well up ineluctably in the young Beckett. We who love to read Beckett can scarcely imagine that his writerly destiny was not early apparent. Although the mature Beckett told me that there must have been "execrable juvenilia" in his schooldays, they have not come to light, and I therefore begin with a twenty-three-year-old Irishman, on a two-year fellowship at the Ecole Normale Supérieure in Paris, where his compatriot Thomas MacGreevy introduced him to the expatriate Irish writer James Joyce.

1929

Dante . . . Bruno . Vico . . Joyce

Given Beckett's skepticism about critics, and the abusive term "Crrritic!" in *Waiting for Godot,* it is ironic that his first extant publication should be a

---

No manuscript of *Dante . . . Bruno . Vico . . Joyce* is extant. Unless my notes men-tion manuscripts, it can be assumed that I know of none. HRC holds both the *trans*

piece of criticism. Beckett has credited James Joyce with choosing the subject, outlining the themes, and arranging for the publication of his disquisition: "The subject was suggested to me by Joyce. He had no part in the writing. The texts were available in the library of the Ecole Normale. He found me short on Bruno."[2] Composed during the second year of Beckett's fellowship, the essay was the last to be commandeered by Joyce for a volume of self-homage, *Our Exagmination Round His Factification for Incamination of Work in Progress.* Beckett chose the title not of the whole book, but of his essay, which embraces four writers, who are separated by several centuries. Accordingly, each dot in Beckett's title approximates a century, so that Joyce emerges at the apex of a distinguished Italian lineage, which is not examined chronologically in the essay itself.

Beckett begins peremptorily: "The danger is in the neatness of identifications." His second sentence, rarely quoted, is embarrassing: "The conception of Philosophy and Philology as a pair of nigger minstrels out of the Teatro dei Piccoli is soothing, like the contemplation of a carefully folded ham-sandwich." The young man means his images to startle, but he seems unaware of the offensiveness of his vocabulary. Airily, he proceeds to pontificate: "Literary criticism is not book-keeping" (*Disjecta,* 19). "Here form *is* content, content *is* form. . . . [Joyce's] writing is not *about* something; *it is that something itself*" (27). "No language is so abstracted as English. It is abstracted to death" (28). At times Beckett verbally pummels his readers: "You complain that this stuff is not written in English. It is not written at all. It is not to be read—or rather it is not only to be read. It is to be looked at and listened to" (27). These dicta have been quoted and requoted as keys to Beckett's own work, and indeed they are. At the time he composed this essay, however, Beckett's creative work was barely a gleam in his scholarly eye. His fellowship at the Ecole Normale was expected to encompass academic research on the subject of his choice in French literature—unanimism in general, and in particular the poet Pierre-Jean Jouve (1887–1976).[3]

Instead, Beckett submerged himself in the eighteenth-century Italian philosopher Giovanni Battista Vico. Occasionally, Beckett's prose reads like notes upon the lecture of a mentor: "a mountain, the coincidence of contraries, the inevitability of cyclic evolution, a system of Poetics, and the prospect of self-extension in the world of Mr Joyce's *Work in Progress*" (19). The mountain is both landscape and character in its dominance of what will become *Finnegans Wake,* but the other subjects are Viconian, however idiosyncratically interpreted by Beckett.[4] The young scholar outlines Vico's cycli-

---

ition and the book versions of Beckett's article, which differ slightly. Federman and Fletcher date the book publication in May and the *transition* 16–17 publication in June.

cal theory of history, his view of the identity of contraries (which, Beckett notes, he borrows without acknowledgment from Bruno), and especially his poetics, wherein myth and language are seen to develop along parallel lines. Although Beckett summarizes Vico with verve, he rarely quotes him. Joyce himself acknowledged that Vico was a *structural* convenience for *Work in Progress,* and this is duly noted by other contributors to the *Exagmination* volume, but Beckett is also sensitive to the *texture* of Vico's poetics, especially the concreteness of his imagery. For all Beckett's haughty stance, he is wryly self-deflating about his own criticism: "Such is a painful exposition of Vico's dynamic treatment of Language, Poetry and Myth" (26).

Halfway through his essay, Beckett virtually abandons Vico for gratuitous reflection on how the sounds of words in different languages can enhance their sense, and on how Joyce creates an idiom where words "elbow their way on to the page, and glow and blaze and fade and disappear" (28). Almost as an afterthought, Beckett credits Vico for Joyce's "reduction of various expressive media to their primitive economic directness" (29). Having reported creditably on Joyce's forbears, Beckett moves on to the Italian author he most admires: "Basta! Vico and Bruno [barely mentioned] are here, and more substantially than would appear from this swift survey of the question. . . . To justify our title, we must move North" (29–30)—to Dante, whose *Divina Commedia* Beckett had studied with the help of a private teacher, Bianca Esposito.[5]

Dante was to remain Beckett's most durable literary allegiance. Undated notecards (RUL ms. 4123) testify to his fascination with the smiles, prayers, violence, and chronology of the *Commedia.* As late as 1986 Beckett declared: "Dante created a new language that was not used before. Dante was a Joycean writer" (Rabinovitz 1992, 107). In this early essay Beckett paired the great Florentine poet with the new Irish acquaintance, whom he was always to address as "Mr. Joyce." Beckett rationalizes this juxtaposition: "It is reasonable to admit that an international phenomenon might be capable of speaking [Joyce's English], just as in 1300 none but an inter-regional phenomenon could have spoken the language of the Divine Comedy" (31). More incidentally, Beckett also couples Dante and Joyce in their preoccupation with the significance of numbers. He finds them similar, too, in their anticlericalism. Indeed, Beckett's own agnosticism—"On this earth that is Purgatory"—causes him to dilute the diverse religious leanings of Vico, Dante, and Joyce.

For all the erudition and arrogance of Beckett's essay, it does illuminate Joyce's *Work in Progress.* It also offers information about what Beckett was reading during his Paris fellowship, but it does not reveal that the twenty-three-year-old scholar yearned to be an imaginative writer. In later years Beckett would often remark that Joyce was an ethical ideal for him.

Dante . . . Bruno . Vico . . Joyce pays *aesthetic* homage to the Irish self-exile, but the reference to ethics is puzzling. My totally unconfirmed guess is that the ethics were aesthetic. That is to say, Joyce by example convinced Beckett that writing could be a kind of mission, to which all other activities or alliances are ancillary. Beckett told James Knowlson: "That's what it was, epic, heroic, what [Joyce] achieved." He added: "But I realised that I couldn't go down that same road" (Knowlson, 111). The realization may have been delayed, however, for only in 1938 did Beckett admit in a January 5 letter to his friend Tom MacGreevy that he no longer felt the danger of the association with Joyce: "He is just a very lovable human being."

Beckett would later deride himself at this period as a young man with nothing to say and the itch to write (Harvey, 305). The itch nevertheless brought quick scratches within a year—a short story *Assumption,* a school-boy joke *Che Sciagura,* and a handful of poems that share the mannered intellectualism of Beckett's homage to Joyce. (The order of composition is uncertain, but I follow Pilling, who has brooded harder than I over the scant evidence.)

Assumption

Assumption is constructed in three page-long paragraphs, followed by a short climactic fourth paragraph, and concluding with a one-sentence fifth paragraph. The opening sentence is arresting in its seeming contradiction: "He could have shouted and could not" (*CSP*, 3). It leads to longer sentences of description or of editorial comment about the unnamed "he." The narrator begins at some distance from the anonymous protagonist, but the second paragraph focuses on his feelings, in a covert plea for reader sympathy: "Still he was silent, in silence listening for the first murmur of the torrent that must destroy him" (5). Midstory an anonymous Woman is introduced, and she is seen (with distaste) only through the eyes of the protagonist. His metaphysical propensity is contrasted with her physicality, but we are not offered a single word of their respective idioms.

Beckett's first published story is slenderly plotted, focusing on the protagonist's conflict between silence and the voice within him: "he dreaded lest his prisoner should escape, he longed that it might escape" (5). This might be a prophecy of Beckett's later ambivalence about his own writing—at once compulsive and unsatisfactory. Listening for his voice, the central character is so disturbed by the Woman's visits "that he hungers to be irretrievably engulfed in the light of eternity, one with the birdless cloudless colourless

---

Assumption was first published (with some half dozen typos) along with *Dante . . . Bruno . Vico . . Joyce* in the June 1929 issue of *transition*. It is reprinted in *CSP*, with typos corrected. Peter Murphy is virtually alone in viewing it as a key Beckett text.

skies, in infinite fulfilment" (7). When his voice does burst forth, it "shak[es] the very house with its prolonged, triumphant vehemence, climbing in a dizzy, bubbling scale, until, dispersed, it fused into the breath of the forest and the throbbing cry of the sea." The concluding sentence is briefer but also cliché-drenched: "They found her caressing his wild dead hair." The narrator's romantic extravagance is reminiscent of such Shelleyan excesses as "I pant, I sink, I tremble, I expire!" ("Epipsychidion") or "I fall upon the thorns of life! I bleed!" ("Ode to the West Wind").

Assumption has aroused little enthusiasm among Beckett critics. However, Lawrence Harvey confusingly pays tribute to its clarity: "In 'Assumption' the relationship between love, mysticism and artistic creation becomes clear. . . . It seems fairly certain that the tale told is of the making of an artist" (287). Although Mary Bryden does not use the adjective *clear* about the story, she sees it as a clear paradigm of Beckett's early fiction: "Male artist pursues quest in seclusion; Woman intrudes, male colludes 'in spite of himself'; disaster and fragmentation result" (1993, 42). There is no necessary disparity between these readings. Nor does Pilling demur: "*Assumption* had enabled Beckett to dramatize and melodramatize, at least some of his deeper feelings, confused and turbulent as they obviously were" (1997, 32). In fiction, however, feelings are only as deep as the words that convey them, and Beckett's words are shallow through staleness, however they may echo Joyce (Murphy, 1999).

Although the title-word *assumption* is not found in the story itself, it may be a guide to Beckett's intentions. The voice of the anonymous protagonist parallels the glorious ascent of the Virgin Mary, even though he yearns for obliteration in a colorless cosmos bordering on a void. Also relevant is the meaning of assumption as usurpation, for the Woman has usurped the man's quest, and she does so with an assumption of her own importance. Physical and trivial, she is oblivious of the man's power to "whisper . . . the turmoil down." Beckett's artless artist husbands his voice while reluctantly receiving the visitations of the Woman. After thinly veiled nightly orgasms— "a timeless parenthesis"—the protagonist falls prey to his own voice that becomes the agent of his immolation. The final sentence, as Pilling notes, shows "the couple unwittingly composing a bizarre Beckettian equivalent of a *Pietà*" (1997, 32). Beckett's protagonist cannot serve woman *and* art. Or even self and art. Expression becomes a form of suicide in this very short story, whose title announces Beckett's taste for encapsulation.

This early Beckett story often digresses from its thin plot—with learned nods to chess, aesthetics, Robert Browning, unanimism, George Meredith, the physical appearance of the woman, and the mystical yearning of the protagonist. The point of view shifts without warning from the aloof narrator to the suffering hero. Beckett's convoluted syntax, erudite reference, and snobbery toward his readers are (unintentionally) amusing. After accusing English of being "abstracted" (in the Joyce essay), Beckett himself indulges in such abstractions as Beauty, pain, Power, infinite fulfillment, and he wallows in a stale romanticism embedded in such words as *wild, violent, dreaming, throbbing, twilight, hopeless,* and the many repetitions of *silence.* As Robert Cochran appreciates: "It is in every way a young man's story, a young artist's story, a young intellectual's story, brimming with suffering and apotheosis and determinedly transcendent sexuality" (5). *Assumption* is a laborious composition, and yet it reveals that twenty-three-year-old Beckett was indulging in composition—when he was supposed to be engaged in academic research. Not that the two are mutually exclusive.

Beckett was also amusing himself.

Che Sciagura (What a misfortune)

Perhaps Paris publication whetted Beckett's appetite for Irish print. At home on summer holiday he wrote a witty but arcane dialogue for publication in the Trinity College weekly newspaper. In Voltaire's *Candide* a eunuch who is confronted with a nude woman exclaims (in Italian in the French novel): "O che sciagura d'essere senza coglioni!" [O what a misfortune to be without balls!]. Beckett suppresses the "O," conscripts the first two Italian words for his title, and pilfers the first letters of the last four words—D.E.S.C.—for the authorial signature to a veiled conversation about the embargo on contraceptives into Ireland—so veiled that it is virtually undecipherable. Beckett's hermetic title is ironic, since the thrust of the brief piece implies that it is a misfortune to be *with* balls, when contraception is forbidden. The dialogue is spirited if enigmatic, and it is noteworthy as the first example of dialogue in Beckett's publications, even if the two circumlocutory speakers speak in the same studied style.

It is uncertain when Beckett began writing verse, but I follow John Pilling's dates as to the order of the poems of the 1930s.

"For Future Reference"

Beckett's title "For Future Reference" hints at prospective authorship that may draw upon that poem. Harvey describes the verse as "raw material for

---

Che Sciagura was first published (unsigned) in *T.C.D.: A College Miscellany* 36 (November 14, 1929) 42, and is reprinted in *Disjecta.*

Dated 1929 in Harvey's notes (301 n. 91), "For Future Reference" was first published in *transition* in June 1930, but Beckett never included it in collections of his poems. It is reprinted by Harvey, on whom I am often dependent for interpretation of Beckett's verse. Gross's dissertation offers more ample glosses than those of Harvey, but her interpretations are marred by insensitivity to the tone of particular poems.

poetry" or "pre-poem," and he summarizes its biographical background: an antipathetic chemistry teacher at Portora Royal School, a paternal diving lesson to the six-year-old Beckett. "Fear of the teacher is associated in the poem with fear of high places" (298). However, the narrative progression of the seventy-four-line poem is more fragmented than Harvey indicates.

The first of the four irregular stanzas dramatizes a horrifying science lesson (chemistry and anatomy), and the long second stanza revolves around a terrified plunge into deep water. The voice of "the Mutilator" reaches the floating persona, who is also assailed by a "red-faced rat of a pure mathematician." Then the persona is back on the diving board, looking down on "him" in the water below. The brief third stanza conflates the inimical *hes*— would-be tutors all; it conflates them and hopes to dissolve them in the persona's desire for oblivion—"he might forget me / they all might."

The three-line final stanza contains the neologism "palaiate," which means "parrotlike," but also suggests *palate* and *palliate* (Gross, 31). The implication is that the whole poem is a parrotlike repetition of a nightmare. As in a nightmare, one image floats into another. As in a nightmare, contradictory images jostle one another; the "*snowy* floor of the parrot's cell / *burn*[s] at dawn" (emphasis added). The poem's speaker finally possesses a "strange mouth" that has uttered these four stanzas. For all the confusion of imagery, the free verse ripples through internal rime, alliteration, and repetition. Thematically, the several instructors will not actually serve Beckett "for future reference," but the high dive will recur sporadically in his work. (Victor Krap of *Eleutheria* and Estragon of *Waiting for Godot* will suffer from this nightmare. Watt will dream of "dives from dreadful heights into rocky waters," and the narrator of *Company* will recall his father's urging him to dive: "Be a brave boy.")

1930

In spite of the quasi-dramatic dialogue form of *Che Sciagura,* Beckett zigzagged during the 1930s between verse and fiction. Pilling believes it probable that 1930 saw the beginning of Beckett's untitled notebook that supplied many phrases for both genres. Pilling himself has excavated some two dozen major sources (and as many minor ones) of Beckett's notes, which ultimately fed his first novel, and which scholars therefore call the *Dream* Notebook. The range is astonishing: the Bible, Dante, Shakespeare, Chaucer, and Tennyson are almost predictable. In addition, however, are books on flagellation, onanism, Napoleon, music, mysticism, physics, philosophy, and fairy tales. Nearly three hundred entries are dedicated to Robert Burton's *Anatomy of Melancholy*. In Pilling's words: "The *Dream* notebook contains those [notes] Beckett called to his help between 1930 and 1932, whom he could still call on, more sparingly, for the rest of his writing life" (1999a, xxi).

Beckett's poems of the 1930s are cogently described by Patricia Coughlan as "clogged, obscure exercises in multiple allusiveness, often furiously choleric in tone and jagged with awkward movements which seem aimed at undermining the lyric speaker even at the very moment he [or she] is being constituted" (187). Often autobiographical in inspiration, the poems are distanced through Beckett's adoption of the dramatic monologue form. Although this early verse predates Beckett's published translations of surrealist poets, he may well have begun to read their work. John Fletcher has summarized what Beckett's verse shares with surrealism: "metric anarchy, the precedence of the image over the sense, lines of greatly varying length within the same stanza, and a tendency to construct poems on the basis not of syntactical coherence but of associated imagery, the association usually existing only in the mind of the poet" (1967, 25). In spite of arcane associations, the power of the imagery attracts readers to the lyrics of Aragon, Breton, Eluard, Peret, whereas it is unlikely that Beckett's early verse would be admired, without the magnet of his later drama or fiction. Even in 1970 Harvey's title for his book was surprising—*Samuel Beckett: Poet and Critic,* rather than *Samuel Beckett: Playwright and Fabulist.*

As Beckett's two-year Paris fellowship neared termination, he composed his most ambitious poem, "Whoroscope." On June 15, 1930, Beckett was visited by his friend Thomas MacGreevy, who informed him that the Paris-based Hours Press (owned by a wealthy Englishwoman, Nancy Cunard) was offering a prize of ten pounds for the best poem under one hundred lines, on the subject of time. It is reasonable to suppose that MacGreevy brought this news to Beckett because he knew that the young scholar was dabbling in verse, like himself. It is probable that several of Beckett's poems predate "Whoroscope," which, although written on the night of June 15–16, may have been "worked toward over some months" (Pilling, personal communication).

"Return to the Vestry"
Beckett's title announces clerical renunciation of eroticism, as in "Magie" by the sixteenth-century French poet Pierre de Ronsard. Unlike the frankly

---

"Return to the Vestry" was first published in the *New Review* (August–October 1931), but Pilling dates it late 1929 or very early 1930. The poem is reprinted by Harvey but is not elsewhere published. The narrator of Beckett's *Dream* would recall: "We have a little note somewhere on Anteros we do believe, in fact we seem to remember we once wrote a poem . . . on him or to him cogged from the liquorish laypriest's Magic Ode" (68). In the poem "the liquorish laypriest" is the sixteenth-century French poet Pierre de Ronsard, whose "Magie, ou délivrance d'amour" is the source of Beckett's imagery.

autobiographical persona of Ronsard's long poem, however, Beckett's free-verse lines waver between commands to a lover and regrets of a persona who renounces love. The poem opens on Beckett's memory of his 1926 visit to Ronsard's grave in the Loire valley (Harvey, 308). It then distills the ingredients of Ronsard's intricate purification ritual in "Magie," only to parody them. The line—"Mumps and a orchid to Fraulein Miranda"—enfolds Shakespeare's heroine into Beckett's cousin, Peggy Sinclair, who spoke German better than English, and with whom he had been in love. The tone then shifts abruptly to a lyrical prayer to "gentle Anteros," "noble Anteros," the antierotic deity. A single residual first-person subject juxtaposes the image of a quarry (at once a tomb and a mine) against a fluid snakelike movement. Although the image is difficult to visualize, the lyrical lines hint at an anti-aubade; relief rather than regret greets the end of a night of love. The final line invites Anteros to mock impurity.

"Casket of Pralinen for a Daughter of a Dissipated Mandarin"

The traditional box of candy for a beloved is subverted by the word "casket." Rather than a lover offering sweetmeats to his beloved, the speaker of the poem is unidentifiable. "Casket" consists of thirteen irregular stanzas, which vary in length from two to thirteen lines. Despite the number of stanzas, Gross suggests that the poem divides into three disjunctive parts: stanzas 1 through 3, redemption through Christ; stanzas 4 through 11, celebration of beauty; stanzas 12 and 13, death and its aftermath. Beckett's erudition is foisted on the persona, who refers to paintings by Montegna and Dahlberg, Beaumarchais's *Marriage of Figaro,* Matthew Arnold's *Thyrsis,* Milton's *Lycidas,* Proust, the Bible, several poems by Wordsworth, and at least three plays by Shakespeare (*Lear, Macbeth,* and *All's Well That Ends Well*). Beckett's poem does not end well, since it implies that the slaughter of the innocents (Matt. 2:16) and the devil-driven men who are turned to swine (Matt. 8:28) meet comparable fates. Spoken in stage Irish—"me little timid Rosinette, Now me boy"—the sardonic tone escapes at midpoint from its moorings. Stanza 4 reads: "Oh I am ashamed / of all clumsy artistry / I am ashamed of presuming / to arrange words / of everything but the ingenuous fibres / that suffer honestly." Although honest suffering might be a rhetorical strategy, the very lack of imagery in these lines conveys an impression of sincerity, especially since this stanza is followed by an explosive self-address: "Fool! do you hope to untangle / the knot of God's pain?" Then, donning his mask again, the persona returns to habitual cynicism: "Melancholy Christ

Published in the 1931 *European Caravan,* "Casket of Pralinen" has been reprinted only in Harvey. A variant version is found in the Leventhal papers in HRC.

that was a soft one! / Oh yes I think that was perhaps just a very little inclined to be rather too self-conscious." I have borrowed Beckett's last three words as a global comment on his writing during this period. Whatever therapeutic purpose "Casket" may have served, the wavering tones fail to fuse or to justify the scatological puns, the borrowed phrases, and the occasionally striking images.

"Text"

This blandly titled poem is summarized by Harvey: "Pity given and pity withheld are the twin themes that unify the poem" (287), but "unify" is a strong verb for the rambling free verse, divided into eight stanzas of approximately equal length. Gross titles her analysis "What Tiresias Says," and she should be credited for discovering the identity of the persona of this recondite dramatic monologue, which relies on "Ovid's *Metamorphoses* III by way of Dante's *Inferno* XX . . . Proust's *Remembrance of Things Past*, Apollinaire's *The Dugs of Tiresias*, and Freud's *Interpretation of Dreams*" (Gross, 80). Tiresias is not immediately evident in the first stanza, which accords a line to the passions at Troy, before focusing on Proust's cook who is preoccupied with the Virgin Mary's "abstract belly" rather than the suffering of the pregnant maidservant. The second stanza reveals the bisexuality of Tiresias, who nurses the newborn infant. The third stanza turns to Psalm 51, whose seventh line reads: "O Lord, open Thou my lips: and my mouth shall spew forth thy praise." Instead of praise, however, Beckett's Tiresias spews forth blame of divinity, conflating the sorcerers' punishment in the *Inferno* with Job's complaints to God. With his head "arsy-versy," moreover, Tiresias cannot find his nether parts. The fourth stanza pays mocking homage to Dante, without mentioning him by name, thus paralleling Dante's refusal to mention Christ's name in hell. The fifth stanza returns to Dante's Tiresias of the twisted body and to the compassion of "the piteous pelican." The sixth stanza constitutes a flashback to the pitiless divinities who were responsible for the blindness and the bisexuality of Tiresias. The seventh stanza abruptly introduces a plural or editorial "we" who implicitly contradict Dante's "ingenious damnation," for Beckett's lines confer a "dark pride" and "bitter dignity" upon the damned companions of Tiresias.

In conclusion, Tiresias returns to the Bible; as Gross notes, the source of the opening line of the final stanza is Hos. 1:6: "And God said unto him, Call her name Lo-Ruhamah: for I will have no more mercy upon the house of Israel." God's mercy having been absent throughout Beckett's poem, the

---

One of four poems published in the 1931 *European Caravan*, "Text" was republished in the winter 1931–32 issue of the *New Review*. A similar version is found in the Leventhal papers in HRC. The poem is republished only by Harvey.

speaker then quotes the words of Dante's Virgil (in translation), although he is not named. Beckett offers a remarkably condensed and oxymoronic version of Dante's line 28 of Canto XX of the *Inferno*—"Qui vive la pietà quand è ben morta"—"pity is quick with death." The last four lines of Beckett's poem paraphrase Virgil's admonition to Dante to refrain from showing sympathy for "the sad maimed shades," since human pity has threaded irregularly through the poem, in spite of its neutral title—"Text." Dante's line 28 will haunt Beckett for many years to come.[6]

"Hell Crane to Starling"

Canto V of Dante's *Inferno* damns as birds those who indulged in illicit eroticism. In spite of the Dantesque title, however, Beckett's twenty-five-line poem rests precariously on the Bible. Gross heads her discussion of the poem "Rachel Crying for Her Children," naming the persona concealed behind a sprinkling of first-person pronouns. Gross further reads "Oholiba" as "Jacob's various procreative visits to Rachel and Leah and their maid servants, Zilpah and Bilhah" (63). Those names sound like "Aholibah," the biblical whore, who was corrupted by her sister Aholah (Ezek. 23:2–13). Another pair of sisters enter biblical Zoar or Tsoar in the company of their father Lot (Gen. 19:30). Gross interprets these seemingly confused references: "the human and divine, like the donkey and ass, the titular birds, and the sisters, Rachel and Leah, Aholah and Aholibah, Lot's two daughters . . . are also but different species of the same genre and . . . Jehovah is really only an imaginary projection of Jacob-Israel" (68). It remains only to note "two of Jacob's sons emerge as one with their human father like, presumably, Jacob himself and his divine one" (71). Gross marvels at Beckett's powers of encapsulation, where his twenty-five lines condense many verses of Genesis and Ezekiel, under a Dantean title. Annotation notwithstanding, however, the biblical freight sinks the poem.

As already mentioned, Beckett's friend Thomas MacGreevy brought Beckett news of a poetry contest—on the very day (June 15) that submissions were due. Beckett therefore labored through the night of June 15–16, with only a short break for "a guzzle of salad and Chambertin at the Cochon de Lait . . . About three in the morning it was done, and I walked down to the Rue Guénégaud and put it in [Cunard's] box" (Cunard, 111). On Bloomsday, as it happens, the date in Joyce's *Ulysses*. The judges, Richard Aldington and Nancy Cunard, were jubilant at the late entry, to which they awarded the prize. It was they who suggested the addition of explanatory

---

"Hell Crane to Starling" was first published in *European Caravan* (1931). A variant version is found in the Leventhal papers at HRC. It is republished only by Harvey. Knowlson discusses the biographical background.

notes to the published version of the poem, in the manner of T. S. Eliot's *Waste Land*. "Whoroscope" is Beckett's earliest surviving manuscript, and it became his first individual publication.

"Whoroscope"

The poem has been of exceptional interest to Lawrence Harvey, who devotes over sixty printed pages to Beckett's "first important work"; to Johannes Hedberg, who annotates the poem in some thirty pages; and to William Bysshe Stein, who consecrates some thirty pages to Beckett's "paradoxical love and scorn of [Descartes's] modes of thought" (125). More modestly, Francis Doherty in twenty pages calls attention to a hitherto unnoticed source for Beckett's erudite poem, putatively spoken by René Descartes, Seigneur du Perron. Harvey and Hedberg have indefatigably plumbed the seventeenth-century Baillet biography of Descartes as Beckett's source, but Doherty traces several details of Beckett's poem to a 1901 monograph by J. P. Mahaffy, a professor at Beckett's own university, Trinity College, Dublin.[7]

Beckett's "Whoroscope" has ninety-eight lines, just under the designated limit of one hundred. His notes divide into three global remarks and seventeen glosses of specific lines. In spite of the mocking tone, the global entries are indeed useful:

> René Descartes, Seigneur du Perron, liked his omelette made of eggs hatched from eight to ten days; shorter or longer under the hen and the result, he says, is disgusting.
>
> He kept his own birthday to himself so that no astrologer could cast his nativity.
>
> The shuttle of a ripening egg combs the warp of his days.

Time, the requisite subject of the Hours Press contest, takes the form of "days" in Beckett's notes, but it enters into the poem in a smaller unit—hours. Beckett's title plays on *horo,* which is Greek for "hour," and his final line contains English *hour*—"starless inscrutable hour." Within its ninety-eight lines, however, the poem secretes a life*time,* that of René Descartes, Seigneur du Perron, who is named only in part, and only in the antepenultimate line.

Evidently short of writing paper, or too pressed for time to buy any, Beckett composed (or copied?) "Whoroscope" on five sides of stationery of Hotel Bristol, Carcassonne (now in HRC). The leaves lack revision or the doodles to which Beckett resorts when hesitating. The poem was individually published by the Hours Press in 1930; it has often been republished, and it is found in *Poems*. On the verso of leaf 3 of the holograph is the sonnet later published in *Sedendo et Quiescendo,* and still later incorporated (with variants) into *Dream of Fair to Middling Women,* which begins, "At last I find in my confused soul . . ." Admussen (21) misreads the first line: "At last since in my confused soul. . . ."

Descartes's odd taste in eggs is dramatized by Beckett as his protagonist's repeated demands for his breakfast, but the young poet's main strategy is encompassed in the third global note: "The shuttle of a ripening egg combs the warp of his days." The weaver is Samuel Beckett, however he may borrow fact or phrase from Adrien Baillet and J. P. Mahaffy. "[T]he affinity between the mind of Descartes and the mind of Beckett, so different in other ways," Harvey remarks, "may lie in this need to know through the personal experience of meditation" (37). Hedberg argues convincingly against Beckett's own later disparagement of the poem. Stein reads the poem as a riddle that is both recreational and ritualistic in its argument that "the logic of philosophy, science, mathematics, and theology, all with their special, insulated premises, is not compatible with the nature of individual human experience" (126). Although two scholars differ somewhat in their views of Beckett's opus—that of Harvey seeking "to break up the illusory patterns that give life an apparent order" (66), that of Stein dancing scatologically and eschatologically on the grave of rationalism—they both stress the poem's commitment to Descartes's experience.

I hear the poem as a dramatic monologue, which cries out to be read aloud. (It is curious that Hedberg does not mention this, sensitive as he is to the poem's rhythms, puns, and sound play.) Opening with a question—"What's that?"—the speaker asks four times for his breakfast eggs. After each of these imperious requests, he meanders associationally through events and people of his life. His speech is sharp and colloquial, rhythmed not only by questions, but also by exclamations, imprecations, and repetitions. Even the intimidating roster of proper names—the Boot brothers, Galileo father and son, Copernicus, Faulhaber, Beeckman, Peters the Red and the Bruiser, Gassendi, Hals, Harvey, Hobbes, Bacon, Rahab—is musical. Read aloud, an un-Cartesian tune sounds through alliteration, assonance, apophony, and interplay of metrical feet. Harvey is appreciative of the melody: "In *Whoroscope,* rhythm is fractured, not annihilated. As we read through the poem attentive to its cadence, we are aware again and again of beginnings that never develop, of metric feet that fail to stretch out into metric lines. The strands of rhythm are severed just as the pattern begins to emerge. Here again the poet expresses being that remains *in ovo*" (63). The Latin pun belongs to Harvey, who too easily hears the poem's rhythmic variety as an echo of life's emotional variety. I am rather inclined to see the rhythms as young Beckett flexing his verbal muscles.

Irregularly, the dramatic monologist zigzags between the immediacy of his breakfast requests and the involuntary surge of people from his past. The avalanche of proper names pounds the speaker with hostility, but in each half of the poem, arcane references culminate in an emotional burden. The series of scientists and their quarrels melt into the speaker's distress at the death of his six-year-old daughter. Comparably, the scholastics, Augustine, bluestockings, and Queen Christina of Sweden wither into the speaker's final prayer—not to a deity, but to an enemy physician. It is a rending prayer in which refusal is immanent: "Oh Weulles spare the blood of a Frank / who has climbed the bitter steps, / (René du Perron. . . !) / and grant me my second / starless inscrutable hour" (*perron* is French for steps). The poem has not alluded to the first rare hour, which may be Descartes's dream or his birth. Between the beginning and the end of the poem, the speaker wanes from his high-handed breakfast commands, implying the start of the day, to his pitiful last request, retrospectively coloring the whole poem with the advent of death. Descartes's memories have assaulted him while he is on his deathbed—in the poem of a twenty-four-year-old poet.

Despite the mortal end, the poem is not solemn. Beckett skillfully intertwines the colloquial and the erudite, achieving a comic incongruity. The heart as a "cracked beater" and Augustine's garden as "shrubbery" illustrate his iconoclastic approach to "noble" subjects. Moreover, he ignores Baillet and Doherty to present Descartes as a virtual agnostic—in Beckett's traces, as it were—by reducing transubstantiation to Beaune (wine) and Hovis (bread), and especially by obscene reference to "His jigging self."

Although the poem progresses through the life of Descartes, it also circles back to its beginning, in a pattern that Beckett will often repeat. The first brief stanza introduces an egg that "stinks fresh"; the last stanza opens on one that "smells . . . rich." The second stanza quotes Galileo: "We're moving," and Descartes comments: "That's not moving, that's *moving*." In the last stanza Descartes predicts that he will eat his breakfast, "Then I will rise and move moving." He moves to his death, and yet the phrasing of that death, with its susurrant "s" sounds, hints at peace after a life of conflict— "starless inscrutable hour."

The holograph of "Whoroscope" also contains a sonnet, presumably of the same vintage.

"Sonnet—At last I find . . ."

Although Beckett is fond of the sonnet form, this is the only example in English of his strict adherence to its tenets—Shakespearean as opposed to Petrarchan. The lover yearns for fusion with his beloved "Conjoined in the One and in the Infinite." It is difficult to tell whether parody is the intention of Beckett's imperfect rhymes (cypresses, unless; skies, die; bright, infinite)

As mentioned in the preceding footnote, "Sonnet—At last I find" is found in the holograph of "Whoroscope" and is presumably of the same year. It is mentioned by Federman and Fletcher and is quoted in *Dream*, but it is absent from collections of Beckett's verse.

and of his inept repetitions (at last, dark, bright, one). There is no evidence that Beckett ever sought to publish the sonnet under his own name, but in his first novel, *Dream of Fair to Middling Women,* he foisted it on his fictional Belacqua, as one of a "Night of May hiccupsobs" (70). The sonnet wavers in tone between a typical romantic vocabulary and (perhaps) mockery of that romanticism. Although it lacks the energy of his dramatic monologues, Beckett shows some skill in composing the sonnet as a single sinuous sentence.

Through "Whoroscope" Beckett was befriended by the judges of his poem—Richard Aldington, the British editor-novelist, and Nancy Cunard, writer, editor, adventurer, and espouser of left-wing causes. The former not only recommended to the London publishers Chatto and Windus that Beckett be assigned a critical monograph on Proust, but he also subsidized the project with a loan. The latter invited Beckett to share cafe evenings with her and her lover, Henry Crowder, an African-American jazz pianist.[8] Beckett translated articles from the French for Cunard's *Negro Anthology* (published in 1934), and he also offered a poem for what proved to be the last publication of her Hours Press—*Henry-Music,* a handsome volume of six differently authored poems, with music by Henry Crowder, published in December 1930.

"From the Only Poet to a Shining Whore: for Henry Crowder to sing"

Beckett's poem contains seventeen lines without notes, and yet it resembles the more ambitious "Whoroscope" in its opaque erudition, irregular rhythms, and dramatic quality. Like other Beckett poems of the early 1930s, it draws upon Dante, but it is the only one in which Dante is the speaker of a dramatic monologue. There seems to be a joke in the very title, where the definite article modifies "poet," and the indefinite article precedes "whore." In the poem itself, however, Beckett's poetic shadow hovers over Dante, and Rahab the biblical whore is paired with Dante's celestial Beatrice.

Gross traces Beckett's sources: for Rahab she cites the biblical Joshua and Canto IX of the *Paradiso;* for Beatrice she cites Canto XXIII of the *Paradiso.* As monologist, Dante contrasts the two women—the Hebrew harlot Rahab and the Florentine lady Beatrice. The poem's drama lies not in the unnamed poet of the title, but in a speaker's direct address to two very different heavenly women, Beatrice and Rahab. The harlot of Jericho concealed the spies of Israel—"You hid them happy in the high flax"—and was therefore spared when her city was destroyed. Beatrice, in contrast, triumphed effortlessly, with "bloodless fingers," and the speaker equates her with

---

"From the Only Poet" was first published in 1930 in the Hours Press *Henry-Music.* It is republished only in Harvey. A variant version is found in the Leventhal papers at HRC.

"mother, sister, daughter, belovèd." Harvey reads the poem as "a gentle reproach on the part of the Irish poet to loved ones in Ireland who fear for him in his descent through . . . the Parisian inferno" (306), but he ignores the *drama* of pitting the dynamic harlot against a bland matron. Since both women are described as "pale," however, there is also an implied equation in the seeming contrast. The traditional jazz appreciation of "loose" women may have appealed to Crowder, who sang Beckett's song often, even recording it (Bair, 111). In Beckett's own writerly growth, Dante has moved from a critical essay through incidental references in verse to the persona of a contemporary poem.

Verse may have offered Beckett a temporary escape from his two serious pensums of the summer. At the termination of his fellowship in June 1930, he had hoped to travel, but he felt obligated to produce a monograph on Proust for the London publishers, Chatto and Windus, even though he did not actually receive a contract till October. At the same time Beckett acceded to Joyce's request to translate into French the "Anna Livia Plurabelle" section of his *Work in Progress.* Uncertain that his French was adequate to this Herculean task, Beckett enlisted the aid of his friend Alfred Péron, who had been an exchange student at Trinity College. Beckett's summer was busy but ungratifying. Ousted from his room at the Ecole Normale, he lived in quarters of vacationing friends—MacGreevy and Aldington. Feeling alone in Paris, Beckett twice read through Proust's *A la recherche du temps perdu* in "the abominable edition of the *Nouvelle Revue Française,* in sixteen volumes" (*Proust,* 1), and he also summoned to his aid Schopenhauer's *The World as Will and Representation* and Arnaud Dandieu's *Marcel Proust,* the latter published that very year. Beckett's letters to MacGreevy complain about his self-imposed task of criticism, but in late September 1930, he delivered *Proust* to his London publisher, on his way home to Foxrock, Ireland—still intending to pursue an academic career. His *Proust* is both a literary appreciation and a compass on his own writerly path. As Edith Fournier felicitously phrases it: "*Proust* est un acte de compréhension où se révèlent à la fois l'oeuvre comprise et celui que la comprend" (15) [*Proust* is an act of comprehension that simultaneously reveals the work comprehended and the one who comprehends it]. It is that rare work of criticism that is a pleasure to read.

Proust

Beckett's monograph shows an affinity with the work of the French author who had died eight years earlier, and yet he rejects its basic premise of

The London firm Chatto and Windus published Beckett's monograph *Proust* on March 5, 1931. Not until 1957 was it republished—by Grove Press. Beckett resisted translation into French, but it was done after his death, by Edith Fournier, whose notes are invaluable.

redeeming time through art. Considerably longer than the Joyce essay, Beckett's criticism abounds in description, summary, interpretation, and quotation in Beckett's own translation, although the Scott-Moncrieff *Remembrance of Things Past* had been available since 1922. Beckett does not number the seven sections of his treatise, but he organizes them thematically: (1) Time, (2) Habit, (3) Memory, (4) Involuntary Memory, (5) The Albertine Tragedy, (6) The Epiphany in the Guermantes Library, (7) Art. Despite many extra-Proustian references (Baudelaire, Calderón, Dante, Dostoyevsky, Leopardi, Racine, among others), Beckett hews to his main line of argument about the transformation of the personality under the onslaught of time. Like Proust himself, Beckett summons considerable erudition to subvert an intellectual approach to art or experience. It may be true, as Zurbrugg charges in *Beckett and Proust,* that Beckett emphasizes the negative aspects of Proust's vision, notably the impossibility of love and friendship, but he does not invent them. Beckett himself later admitted: "Perhaps I overstated Proust's pessimism a little" (qtd. in McQueeny, 148). Overstated perhaps, but Beckett threaded his way lucidly and lyrically through the plot-strands of *A la recherche.*

Beckett's opening gambit resembles the end of the first paragraph of his Joyce essay:

Joyce essay: Literary criticism is not bookkeeping.
Proust: The Proustian equation is never simple.

A few of Beckett's other apothegms would later be applied to his own work. It is hard to exaggerate the importance of this early nugget, with its implied uncertainty principle: "The observer infects the observed with his own mobility" (*Proust,* 6). Also relevant to his work to come are such kernels as "wisdom consists not in the satisfaction but in the ablation of desire" (7); "The mortal microcosm cannot forgive the relative immortality of the macrocosm" (10); "the heart of the cauliflower or the ideal core of the onion would represent a more appropriate tribute to the labours of poetical excavation than the crown of bay" (16–17);[9] "And art is the apotheosis of solitude" (47); "The only fertile research is excavatory, immersive, a contraction of the spirit, a descent" (48); "The tragic figure represents the expiation of original sin . . . the sin of having been born" (49); "[Proust] deplores his lack of will until he understands that will, being utilitarian, a servant of intelligence and habit, is not a condition of the artistic experience" (69). In Pilling's words: "The temptation to read *Proust* as a kind of template constituted by ideas which Beckett would thereafter seek either to dispel or to disguise [or to reformulate] is, it must be admitted, a very difficult one to resist" (1997, 49). Having quoted pertinent passages in that respect, I will try to resist further prediction.

Beckett intersperses epigrams with flowing clauses that imitate the style of their subject. Early in the essay, we read: "The periods of transition that separate consecutive adaptations (because by no expedient of macabre transubstantiation can the grave-sheets serve as swaddling-clothes) represent the perilous zones in the life of the individual, dangerous, precarious, painful, mysterious and fertile, when for a moment the boredom of living is replaced by the suffering of being" (8). (One might contrast this sentence with the rapid exchanges on the same subject in *Godot*.) Perhaps Beckett's most convoluted sentence is his grand finale:

> The narrator—unlike Swann who identifies the "little phrase" of the Sonata with Odette, spatialises what is extraspatial, establishes it as the national anthem of his love—sees in the red phrase of the Septuor, trumpeting its victory in the last movement like a Mantegna archangel clothed in scarlet, the ideal and immaterial statement of the essence of a unique beauty, a unique world, the invariable world and beauty of Vinteuil, expressed timidly, as a prayer, in the Sonata, imploringly, as an aspiration, in the Septuor, the "invisible reality" that damns the life of the body on earth as a pensum and reveals the meaning of the word: "defunctus."

To parse the sentence, one has to decide which of the many phrases constitute the object of the verb "sees," and which constitute mere modifiers. It is fitting that Beckett's conclusion about music in Proust should itself ramble musically through its provocative grammar. Moreover, the final Latin word "defunctus" (borrowed from Schopenhauer) is a pun that embraces completion, perfection, and death. Somewhat abrupt as a conclusion to *Proust*, the sentence nevertheless shows a mastery of convoluted syntax for a complex view of art.

Beckett never explicitly compares Proust to Joyce (as did Marcel Brion in the *Exagmination*), but the young critic approves of both writers for fusing form and content, and for scorning realism, with its "vulgarity of a plausible concatenation." Beckett finds that Proust and Joyce share a dedication, even a martyrdom to art. This is only implied in the Joyce essay, but it is explicit in *Proust*: "In Time creative and destructive Proust discovers himself as an artist. . . . Now he sees . . . the work of art as neither created nor chosen, but discovered, uncovered, excavated, pre-existing within the artist, a law of his nature" (64). Less than half of Beckett's Joyce essay focuses on Joyce, but the whole Proust monograph is centered on Proust, including frequent paraphrase and nearly forty quotations. Sensitive to Proust's language, Beckett declares: "For Proust the quality of language is more important than any system of ethics or aesthetics" (67).

In spite of that sentence, Beckett accords more attention to the thematics than to the style of Proust's long novel, however he insists upon the union of form and content. Although the twenty-four-year-old critic registers scorn of experience, he nevertheless grapples with death through the figure of Marcel's grandmother; and he grapples with love through the figure of Marcel's Albertine. Beckett admires Proust for elevating art above experience, and yet his monograph reveals how absorbed he was in the intensity of the fictionalized experience. He sees in Proust's Marcel a volatile self at the mercy of time, and the instability of the self will haunt Beckett throughout his writing career.

The last division of Beckett's seven-part analysis, which I have labeled "Art," is a catchall. It is almost as though Beckett gathered up a series of disconnected notes. He argues that Proust is an impressionist and not an allegorist; he then pins other labels on Proust, defining them for his immediate purposes. His three pages on Proust's style are less revealing of that style than incidental phrases nominally treating content. Astutely, however, he points to Proust's predilection for botanical images, and he ends the monograph abruptly on the importance of music to Proust. Beckett has rendered homage to a long novel about the creation of a writer.

If Beckett plunged into his own microcosm in quest of an artist, that figure was only slowly discovered. In *Proust* the young academic still functioned as a critic, who praises Proust, for creating "an art that is perfectly intelligible and perfectly inexplicable"—after seventy-two printed pages of his own explication. In letters to MacGreevy Beckett expressed distaste for his most painstaking critical enterprise. For a short while, he contemplated revising it, but he never did; nor did he translate it into French. Yet his *Proust* remains talismanic reading for those interested in either Beckett or Proust.

Perhaps his plunge into Proust tempted Beckett to try his hand at writing in French. An unpublished sonnet exhibits ambivalence toward love and lust, desire and its sublimation.

"Tristesse Janale"

The poem is a regular sonnet, whose strict form encouraged Beckett to summarize the opposition of sensuality and spirituality. The sonnet displays the two faces, but not the sadness named in the title, and these two faces are evidenced in the contradictions of phenomena—Kant versus Bilitis, the wound-cure property of the sabers of Telephus, the same word "greffe" meaning a graft or a written record, according to its gender, and, finally, a crest versus a crater. The final couplet hopes, traditionally, for resolution:

Unpublished, the sonnet "Tristesse Janale" is found in the Leventhal papers at HRC, where it is entitled "Lamentation Janale." Although it is undated, Pilling, in a personal communication, deduces from Beckett's correspondence that it cannot be later than November 1930.

Et co-ordonne enfin, lacustre conifère,
Tes tensions ambigues de crête et de cratère.

[And finally, lakeside conifer, coordinate
Your ambiguous tensions between crest and crater.]

It would take time for Beckett to immerse himself in, rather than to coordinate, contradictions. Although Beckett's French sonnet is less skillful syntactically than its English predecessor, the ambivalent tone is more controlled.

Le Concentrisme or Jean du Chas

In Ireland Beckett perpetrated an academic prank. In November 1930, Beckett read a paper on concentrism (his neologism) to the Modern Language Society of Trinity College.[10] A. J. Cronin (155–56) believes that Beckett's paper was taken seriously in the Modern Language Society, but Beckett told me and others that it was recognized as the hoax it was. What purports to be literary criticism is actually fiction. In a parody of academic scholarship, the literary movement concentrism is said to be founded by Jean du Chas, who designates a fellow Toulousain as his literary heir.

The typescript of three and one-third pages is preceded by a one-page letter from an unnamed native of Toulouse, presumably in reply to Beckett's question about the provenance of the journal of Jean du Chas. The anonymous correspondent reviews the circumstances whereby the founder of concentrism bequeathed his notebooks to a total stranger, on the eve of his death, perhaps by suicide. The sulky tone of the letter from Toulouse, in which Chas is called an idiot and an imbecile, mocks scholarly exhilaration at the fortuitous discovery of documents, as in Henry James's The Aspern Papers or Tom Stoppard's Arcadia. The complimentary closing of the letter mocks the courtesies of French correspondence, since it requests the recipient "d'agréer ma sympathie et mon plus profond mépris" [to accept my sympathy and my deepest scorn].

Without transition, an academic narrator—presumably Beckett himself—takes up the report. Although the device of a fictitious scholarly introduction is at least as old as Don Quijote, Beckett compounds it in prefacing the erudite report by the irritated letter from Toulouse. The anonymous scholar zigzags through Chas's incongruous characteristics and his slender biography. Sharing Beckett's birthdate—April 13, 1906—Jean du Chas died

---

I list alternate titles, used by different libraries. Read in November 1930 to the Modern Language Society of Trinity College, Le Concentrisme was in 1961 given by Beckett to Lawrence Harvey, who deposited it in NhD. Another typescript was given by Nuala Costello to RUL. The spoof was first published in Disjecta (with four sentences inadvertently omitted and brought to my attention by James Knowlson).

in January 1928 (while Beckett himself was still a student at Trinity). Although the nameless scholar mentions Chas's obsession with concierges, his taste for crepuscular light and for several of his literary contemporaries, only a few comments on and quotations from his putative work are offered, notably his self-command: "va t'embêter ailleurs" [go be bored elsewhere, although Beckett suggested: "Feck off" to me]. Even though Chas boasts of his invention of concentrism, and of his pseudo-Cartesian composition "Discours de la Sortie," he is portrayed as an antiacademic, who nevertheless ventures to quote Proust on sneezing. Beckett's spurious lecture concludes with a nod toward Kant, Labiche, and Mozart.

Academic spoof though it is, the biography and beliefs of Chas obliquely predict the later Beckett. The very neologism concentrism puns on "concentric" and "concentrated," both relevant to Beckett, as are the following sentences: Chas's life is horizontal, "sans sommet, tout en longueur, un phénomène de mouvement, sans possibilité d'accélération ni de ralentissement, déclenché, sans être inauguré, par l'accident d'une naissance, terminé, sans être conclu, par l'accident d'une mort. Et vide, creuse, sans contenu, abstraction faite des vulgarités machinales de l'épiderme, celles qui s'accomplissent sans que l'âme en prenne connaissance" (*Disjecta,* 38) [without a summit, but stretched out in length, a phenomenon of movement, without the possibility of acceleration or slowing down; beginning without being inaugurated, by the accident of birth, terminating, without conclusion, by the accident of death. And empty, hollow, contentless, with the exception of mechanical vulgarities of the epidermis, which happen without the soul being aware of them]. Jean du Chas, who experiences "crises de négation," is an individual who cannot explain himself, but who nevertheless creates an art that is "parfaitement intelligible et parfaitement inexplicable"—Beckett's translation into French of his own phrase in praise of Proust. Chas is not quite an alter ego for the academic Beckett, but he is not so distant as his mocking tone implies. Yet one should not exaggerate the significance of a *canular* perpetrated by Beckett after his residence at the Ecole Normale Supérieure, where such hoaxes are said to abound.

1931

Academic mockery also took another form. With the French exchange student Georges Pelorson, Beckett composed *Le Kid,* a parody of Corneille's *Le Cid*—"a Cornelian nightmare."[11] Knowlson describes the action: "Don Fernand, the King of Castile, treated as a mild, harmless geriatric, spent the entire play in a Bath chair; a silent Infanta drifted twice across the stage to the music of Ravel's Pavane. . . ; all the men wore modern dress, with the Kid himself sporting flannel trousers; and Don Diègue (played by Beckett in a long white beard à la Old Father Time) carried an umbrella instead of a sword and . . . an alarm clock" (126). Beckett skipped the rehearsals of *Le Kid,* but he nevertheless assumed his role in the three performances. When after the first night his respected French professor Rudmose-Brown berated the authors of the travesty, Beckett was embarrassed by the whole enterprise and stumbled drunkenly through the remaining two performances (but Cronin writes of two sober Beckett performances, followed by the debacle on the third night). Macmillan and Fehsenfeld give a fuller account than either biographer.

The Possessed

Presumably sober, Beckett replied in writing (but without signature) to the lukewarm review of the production, whose editors aver: "We are given to understand that the following is a reply to our reporter's criticism of the M.L.S. Plays; as such we publish it." The petulance of the editors is understandable in view of the obscurity of *The Possessed.* Beckett stages his riposte as a duel between two learned critics, in a prevision of Stoppard's *The Real Inspector Hound.* Beckett's critics, the Marquis of Stanfor and Professor Allcon, are caricatures of the student editors, W. B. Stanford and John Allcon. Although one of them is armed with an umbrella and the other with a caduceus, their styles are indistinguishable in their sprightly rhymes, Joycean puns, snide topicalities, and recondite references. Stanfor, "postponing inarticulation," briefly denigrates the production, but most of their dialogue ignores it completely. Breathes there a student with soul so dead as never to have burlesqued Shakespeare, Corneille, Goethe, or another classic?

Marooned temporarily in Dublin academe, Beckett escaped on vacations to Paris and to Kassel, Germany, where he had friends or family, although he was no longer in love with his cousin Peggy Sinclair. Uncertain of his vocation, he expressed his plight indirectly, in verse or fiction. Since manuscript evidence is lacking, only the odd letter dates poems of this period, which are invariably personal, allusive, and elusive of interpretation. Even for Beckett scholars, they make laborious reading. In plodding through them chronologically, we should recall a quotation from Beckett's (television) Joe: "The best's to come"—after many years. In Paris in March 1931, Beckett arranged for the publication of four poems in *The European Caravan*—"Hell Crane to Starling," "A Casket of Pralinen for a Daughter of a Dissipated Mandarin," "Yoke of Liberty," and "Text." Harvey has argued

---

The Possessed was published anonymously in *T.C.D.: A College Miscellany* (March 12, 1931) 138. It is republished in McMillan and Fehsenfeld, 21–22.

exhaustively that these poems share a common theme—the conflict between a young man's erotic desire and his puritan upbringing. However, that conflict changes complexion with genre; that is to say, it is fairly explicit in the novel of this period, *Dream of Fair to Middling Women*, but the theme is only sporadically discernible in the opaque free verse of the early 1930s.[12]

"Yoke of Liberty"

The oxymoronic title phrase from Dante's *De Monarchia* was already noted by Beckett in his essay on Joyce: "History [is] the result of a Necessity that is not Fate, of a Liberty that is not Chance (compare Dante's 'yoke of liberty')" (*Disjecta*, 22). For Dante, however, as Gross notes (94), the yoke of liberty is love of God's order, whereas Beckett changes the context to a victory over the lure of an erotic female. Formally, "Yoke of Liberty" is a truncated sonnet, which encloses three sentences within thirteen unrhyming lines of varying length. The first quatrain images the temptress, and the second quatrain cites her dangers for "sensitive wild things." Only in the shortened sextet (of five lines) does the persona introduce the first-person pronoun, to predict his "tamed and watchful sorrow" at her death into "a pitiful crescent." Although the images are surrealistically associative, rather than graphically precise, their erotic charge is unmistakable. Coughlan perceptively reads the images as "a chain of displaced metaphoric terms for the female genitals: 'lips,' 'loop,' 'wound,' 'snare,' 'crescent'" (193). Regaining liberty from them is accepting a yoke of restraint.

Harvey speaks of Beckett's early poems as those of "a young man at a crossroads, torn between Phoebus and Narcissus, temptation and knighthood, Eros and Anteros" (314). Harvey is illuminating on the three poems that are based on medieval Provençal genres—the two enuegs and "Alba." Beckett subsequently discarded his sporadically published poems; yet he continued to cherish "Alba," which dates from the same year and is similar in theme.

"Alba"

A troubadour genre (listed by Beckett in the *Dream* Notebook), an alba features a persona who greets the dawn reluctantly because it terminates a night

---

A variant of "Yoke of Liberty," entitled "Moly," is found in the Morton Dauwen Zabel papers at ICU. Published in the 1931 *European Caravan*, "Yoke of Liberty" has been reprinted by Harvey. Knowlson writes that Beckett thought of including it in *Echo's Bones*. Although he finally decided against it, he did try to publish it separately—in vain.

A variant version of "Alba" is found in the Leventhal papers at HRC. Beckett has annotated this poem in the copy of *Echo's Bones* at HRC: "39 Trinity College

of love. This night of love is, however, imaginary in a poem that consists, according to Gross, of "a single sentence held together by connectives ('and,' in particular, being repeated eight times) and spaced out through the repetition of certain key words like 'stoop'" (203). Fragile though the poem's structure may be, its sensuality is strong.

Beckett divides his alba into three stanzas, each with its own rhythm. The opening five-line stanza begins and ends with the phrase "before morning," and the stanza's last line is related to the first by chiasmus. The repetition of "you shall . . . here" concretizes the imaginary presence of the loved one. The nocturnal "you" will establish a synesthetic "white plane of music" that can banish the troubling ideas aroused by Dante, the Logos, the branded moon, and other mysteries. The second stanza, whose three lines are typographically indented, displays an oriental aura in such words as "silk," "areca," "bamboos," and "willows."[13] Each line lingers longer than its predecessor, enriched with internal rhyme and consonance, which enhance the eroticism of the night.

Not until the final stanza (of nine lines of varying length) does the first-person persona enter the scene. The beloved seems to blend into the unnamed Christ-figure, both of whom are said to "stoop." Bounty is balanced by beauty in a sheet that can banish "the tempest of emblems." A sense of regret trembles through three negatives—"no sun, no unveiling, no host." The poem ends heavily on "bulk dead." Rich sonically, "Alba" displays Beckett's lyricism, undiluted by his usual irony. In the words of Patricia Coughlan: "'Alba' is the nearest Beckett comes [in the early poems] to a capacity to represent the erotic as a route to, rather than away from, the ideal" (192).

"Enueg II"

Like the alba, the enueg appears in Beckett's *Dream* Notebook list of troubadour forms. He used the title twice for poems, finally numbering them in inverse order of composition. "Enueg II" was written in Ireland during the summer of 1931, whereas "Enueg I" looks back at Ireland from Paris, later that year. Harvey defines an enueg as a witty but discontinuous catalog of

Dublin," which implies that it was written in his room there. First published in *Dublin Magazine* (October–December 1931), the poem (revised) is fourth of the thirteen in *Echo's Bones,* and it is republished in *Poems.* Alone among Beckett's early poems, it was translated into French and published by Beckett's friend, Alfred Péron in *Soutes* (May, 1938). Beckett did not assist with the translation and thought it "not very good" (Federman and Fletcher, 38).

"Enueg II" is the third poem in *Echo's Bones* and was reprinted in *transition* (June 1936). It is found in *Poems.*

vexations.[14] In the order of publication (but not of writing) the first enueg describes very specific vexations, whereas the second implies a vexatious world.

Written in free verse, "Enueg II" is an unusual Beckett poem in containing punctuation. In spite of its seven stanzas, the poem is brief. Without the arcane knowledge (supplied by Gross) that Beckett's poem is a riposte to "Veronica's Napkin" by W. B. Yeats, one can still forge a link between the persona's grief at the four-times repeated "world" and a face that appears in stanzas 1, 3, and 7. Perhaps a dramatic monologue, the poem limits its first-person pronoun to the sarcastic refrain line "doch I assure thee," where the archaic English pronoun clashes with the colloquial German.

The speaker is troubled by almost everything he sees. The entire second verse is an incomplete Latin quotation: "de morituris nihil nisi." The "bonum" is omitted, for nothing can be said about the moribund. The human body (especially its face) is juxtaposed against the sky. Musically, the poem thrives on repetitions: too late, veronica, tired, marmalade, heart, shining, and the final "doch doch I assure thee." Discontinuity characterizes the Provençal enueg, but Beckett's poem is continuous in its focus on the human body. A face hovers over the suffering persona who sweats and goggles, as if his feet and heart were immersed in marmalade. Early in the poem the anonymous face crumbles "too late to darken the sky"; late in the poem the face appears "too late to brighten the sky." The human head is thus out of kilter with the cosmos. Compassionate veronicas can accomplish no redemption, as they did in Christian legend.

"Enueg I"

Rather than the traditional enueg's miscellaneous catalog of vexations, a journey structure is imposed upon Beckett's "Enueg I" of seventy-four lines, grouped in nine irregular stanzas. Although nine months is the period of human gestation, the poem is steeped in death, rather than birth. Then again, nine is the number of circles in Dante's inferno, and Beckett's poem subsumes that hell into his contemporary walk around Dublin. Gross has glossed "its secret things" of Beckett's first stanza as Dante's "le segrete cose" of *Inferno* III, where we also find "una insegna" or the bright stiff banner of those who cannot die ("Questi non hanno speranza di morte").

Although the manuscript of the *Echo's Bones* version of "Enueg I" is not extant, two variant versions exist. One, in TCD, was rejected for *Dublin Magazine* in November 1931. The other is included in a submission to *Poetry* magazine in November 1934. In the HRC copy of *Echo's Bones* Beckett annotates: "Canal Dublin at Portobello Bridge/ and thence west one day that—" which implies the poem's autobiographical origin. The poem was first published as the second in *Echo's Bones* and is reprinted in *Poems*.

Paradoxically, Beckett opens his poem on an exit—"Exeo." The speaker then moves through Dublin by verbs and adverbs—"Exeo in a spasm, toil to the crest, lapse down, I trundle, I splashed, I stopped and climbed, so on, next, next." Everywhere the speaker registers pain, penury, and exclusion. In his own skull the speaker hears the cruel wind that numbs his mind. Swiftly and vividly, the persona sketches those who live miserably in a moribund city—a scuttling cripple, a fidgeting child, verminous hens, sweaty heroes, vigilant gulls. Begun in the present tense, the account lapses into the past, and then into gerundive phrases. In the final stanza the banner image returns, reinforced by translation of phrases from Rimbaud's "Barbare": "the banner of meat bleeding / on the silk of the seas and the arctic flowers / that do not exist" [Le pavillon en viande saignante sur la soie des mers et des fleurs arctiques: (elles n'existent pas)]. Inexistence of redemptive images is literally parenthetical for Rimbaud; it is final for Beckett.

In Harvey's telling summary, the poem reflects "a dying world populated by putrid flora, verminous fauna, moribund human beings" (99). Ann Lecercle reads "Enueg I" as a series of loops, where the end circles around to the beginning, death through birth back to death, fluids of microcosm (blood) and macrocosm (water), old man and boy, male and female. She is sensitive to the functionality of sound play and line length as they confer pattern on a seeming labyrinth. "Ce poème est donc un roman picaresque embryonnaire ou plutô avorté parce qu'il se transforme, à chaque nouveau départ, en voyage à travers les cercles de l'Enfer'" (Rabaté, 78) [This poem is thus an embryonic picaresque novel, or rather an aborted one, because it embarks, at every new departure, on a voyage through the circles of "hell"].

"Enueg I" was a poem that Beckett apparently cherished above others of this period; he sent a variant version to MacGreevy, and he made several vain attempts at publication between 1931 and 1935, when "Enueg I" was printed second in the collection Echo's Bones. The "Enuegs" are a diptych that reveals a Beckett despondent about the state of the world, beyond his own fate. After vainly attempting to publish his poems separately (and enumerating twenty-seven poems in a note to his friend Con Leventhal), Beckett winnowed them down to thirteen for the 1935 collection Echo's Bones. Seven of these thirteen poems are titled for troubadour genres, and, despite the contemporary settings, Beckett's poems resemble those of the medieval troubadours in being centered on the emotions of the persona, rather than on the lady to whom the poems are addressed.

It is probable that Beckett also dabbled in fiction at this time, and one of his slightest poems may have been written for the fiction. Ascribed to a French character in Dream of Fair to Middling Women, "Ce n'est au Pélican" may be Beckett's second French poem.

"Ce n'est au pélican"

Beckett's character Lucien implies that the poem is improvised while he writes. Opening on the phrase that later became the title, the poem is composed of a single sentence of twelve short, irregular lines, rhythmed by rhyme and assonance. The speaker addresses his plea not to the pelican (who devours its own heart) nor to the pure Egyptian (perhaps Cleopatra), but to two local women who could offer him solace. Each woman inspires a punning neologism: Lucie is a *peaussière,* or silken-skinned; Jude's remains have been *adororé,* or gilded with adoration. The light verse closes on an octosyllabic couplet that summarizes the frustration of the speaker. Without overvaluing the brief poem, one might nevertheless observe its sonic and syntactical skill.

Sedendo et Quiescendo

It is uncertain where Beckett's Belacqua was born, but my guess is *Sedendo et Quiescendo.* Pilling thinks that that story was begun in Kassel at the end of 1930 and was continued in Dublin in the first half of 1931. A May 29, 1931, letter to MacGreevy mentions "writing the German comedy . . . on and off." Pilling observes: "There is no way of knowing whether 'the German comedy' in the May letter comprises *only* the text 'Sedendo et Quiescendo' as subsequently (in March 1932) published in *transition,* or the whole of the portion of *Dream* section 'TWO' " (1999a, x). Inconclusive as the evidence is, I think it probable that Beckett's first novel, *Dream of Fair to Middling Women,* was kindled in the story *Sedendo et Quiescendo.*

The title derives from an anonymous fifteenth-century Florentine commentator on Dante, who ascribes an Aristotelian sentence to the slothful Belacqua of Canto IV of the *Purgatorio:* "Sedendo et quiescendo anima efficitur sapiens" [Being seated and keeping quiet, the soul acquires wisdom]. To which, the note goes on, Dante replied: "Per certo, se per sedere si diventa savio, niuno fu mai piu savio di te" [Surely, if one becomes wise by sitting, no one was ever wiser than you]. Dante's retort mocks its victim, and indeed the lazy Belacqua arouses a rare laugh from the grave Florentine pilgrim. The

---

Occurring on page 21 of *Dream,* the twelve-line "Ce n'est au pélican" is found only in that typescript, although Beckett mentions it among the twenty-seven poems listed for Con Leventhal.

Several scholars label *Sedendo et Quiescendo* as an excerpt from *Dream of Fair to Middling Women,* whose typescript is in NhD (with a copy at RUL). However, the story probably precedes that novel (as well as the 1931 *The Smeraldina's Billet-Doux* and *Walking Out*), as affirmed in Pilling's *Beckett's Dream Notebook. Sedendo's* first publication (with the misspelling "Quiesciendo") was in *transition* (March 1932). The story is republished in *CSP,* with the title correctly spelled. Daniela Caselli has analyzed the Dantean elements (1996).

protagonist of Beckett's story acquires no wisdom, even though he sits—perhaps quietly—for some "29 hours third-class," on trains between Paris and Hesse. Nevertheless, Beckett endows his protagonist with the Dantean name Belacqua.

Even thinner in plot than *Assumption, Sedendo et Quiescendo* turns on a single event, the meeting of its protagonist with the woman of his "waning lust-affair." Beckett's opening paragraph establishes the disjunctive mode, which will follow a first-person narrator as he moves from Frankfort (*sic*) to Perpignan to Hesse, from Shakespeare to Shelley to a pornographic joke: "Cosi fan tutte with the magic flute." Only on the second page does the narrator deign to christen his lovers: "BELACQUA we'll call him" and "what shall we call her . . . SMERALDINA-RIMA and anything that comes in handy for short" (10). The narrator names these characters with an offhand air, failing to mention the Dantean source for his twentieth-century Dubliner. In Canto IV of Dante's *Purgatorio*, Virgil encourages the weary poet up the steep Mountain of Purgatory. Suddenly, a voice remarks cynically: "Forse che di sedere in prima avrai distretta" [Perhaps you may first need to sit down]. The voice belongs to Belacqua, a Florentine lute-maker who is "più negligente che se pigrizia fosse sua sirocchia" [more indolent than if sloth were his sister]. Sitting outside the purgatorial traffic, Belacqua adopts a fetal position to meditate. While alive, Belacqua had been too lazy to repent, and he is therefore condemned to spend the equivalent of his lifetime in Antepurgatory. Indolent in life, he is indolent after death, sitting motionless in the shade of a rock (as Botticelli pictured him and as Beckett will visualize him).[15]

On unparagraphed pages, Beckett shifts without warning between Belacqua's thoughts and the narrator's description: "Oh did I do right to leave my notes at home! So then after another little bit he came back through the leaves and stood looking with his tongue in his cheek instead of" (15). At the end of *Sedendo et Quiescendo* the narrator leaps from Belacqua's illness on the train to his arrival at the home of the Smeraldina, which resembles a busy inferno, rather than a meditative purgatory.

Beckett's narrator often mocks Belacqua, even calling him Bollocky, but more relentless is his derision of the Smeraldina—her clothes, her venery, her Germanic English, her hilarity, but mainly her body, for which he enlists the help of the sculptor Gozzi-Epstein—an early example of Beckett's allusion to visual artists. The Smeraldina and Belacqua are not an idyllic couple, and they serve as a fulcrum for the narrator's frequent digressions. In Dantesque fashion, this narrator addresses a "gentle reader" and calls attention to his narrative: "what [do] you think of my erotic sostenutino," which he identifies "as a kind of contapuntal [*sic*] compensation" for an unquoted Anteros poem. Beckett reveals his own name—"(thank you Mr Beckett)"—but he ascribes to Belacqua his own overwrought sonnet, which he quotes in full. Beckett retrieves the romantic phrase, "strange exalted death" of line 12 of that sonnet, in order to apply it to Belacqua in the story, after he is revealed as a Peeping Tom. Aside from his sonnet, Belacqua is a recalcitrant lover, but he is a busy voyeur of the fornications of others.

The narrator rambles digressively before returning to his protagonist: "perhaps I let my pen run away with me, don't for a moment imagine Bollocky's down the drain" (16). After its circumlocutions, *Sedendo et Quiescendo* terminates swiftly. Short peremptory phrases render the arrival of Belacqua and the Smeraldina at the "Same old Wohnung" where the narrator shifts suddenly to scatological German: "Beschissenes Dasein beschissenes Dasein Augenblick bitte beschissenes Dasein Augenblickchen bitte beschissenes" (16). Puns, macaronics, double entendres, allusions to music, painting, and literature overwhelm the brief encounter of Belacqua and the Smeraldina. The narrator ostentatiously displays—and digresses from—his narrative.

A letter of August 1931 from Charles Prentice, the editor of Chatto and Windus, praises Beckett's "love letters" that were submitted to him, although he does not accept them for publication. *Dream* of 1932 contains two love letters, which were both salvaged for *More Pricks Than Kicks*. The one, purportedly written by a mindless athlete, is a brief address to a Dublin woman named Alba. The other, *The Smeraldina's Billet-Doux*, is longer and more ambitious. The story evidently exploits the imperfect English of Beckett's cousin Peggy Sinclair, who lived (and died) in Kassel, Germany. "A mixture of fact and fiction," Beckett told Knowlson (144). Fiction involved the Smeraldina, in love with Belacqua.

The Smeraldina's Billet-Doux

Self-contained, the story at once adheres to and mocks the old form of epistolary fiction. Even older is the literary depiction of a woman as lusty and vulgar, in the mode of Chaucer's Wife of Bath. Beckett is therefore quite traditional in his epistolary portrait—and laboriously comic in its execution. Analyzing the story, Anthony Farrow calls attention to the literary quality of the lady's love: "Whatever her inclinations towards a more conventional form of bliss with Belacqua in the flesh, the Smeraldina . . . demonstrates her capacity for accepting a substitute in the form of a written equivalent" (166). Trying his hand at a female protagonist, Beckett has the Smeraldina woo Belacqua from afar, by means of writing. He exploits her for facile comedy of the foreigners-are-funny variety.

Since *The Smeraldina's Billet-Doux* was not published before it was salvaged for *Dream,* it is found in that typescript at NhD, and in the transcription at RUL. It is republished unrevised as the eighth story of *MPTK.*

Walking Out

Beckett returns to his male protagonist in what may have been his next story to be written, probably in an earlier version. The Smeraldina has been displaced by Lucy, now Belacqua's fiancée, whom he has tried in vain to persuade "to establish their married life on this solid basis of a cuckoldry" (*MPTK*, 103). One might see the influence of Joyce's *Exiles* on this plot strand, except that Belacqua seems indifferent to the identity of his replacement, and he feels no sexual titillation from it. Rather, that pleasure is derived from the voyeurism, of which he keeps Lucy ignorant.

One fine spring day Belacqua takes his dog for a "walk out." Enjoying his solitude, he is overtaken by Lucy on horseback. Although he claims to be wax in Lucy's hands, he convinces her to continue on her solitary way, momentarily "walking out" on her, but making an appointment to meet at the gate to the wood. Belacqua keeps his rendezvous, but Lucy fails him because she has been run over by a drunken lord in a Daimler. Unaware of the accident, Belacqua waits no longer, for he is impatient to peep at a romantic couple, but, inadvertently revealing his presence, he is thrashed by the watched lover. Lucy is so incapacitated by her accident that cuckoldry is out of the question, but her marriage to Belacqua is nevertheless a happy one, for the wedded pair listen to the gramophone in their home, especially "An die Musik."

Overloaded with unromantic irony, *Walking Out* opens in Belacqua's mind, but the narrator soon moves us to the mind of his dog. Then, after describing Lucy's beauty, the narrator asks whether such detail is ridiculous. He warns us of Belacqua's falsehoods, and he introduces a gratuitous tinker to watch the parting of Lucy and Belacqua. The narrator admits us to Lucy's suspicions about Belacqua's voyeurism, but after her accident we are barred from her mind, to concentrate on Belacqua's misadventure. Only at the last does the narrator inform us that Belacqua finds "in [Lucy's] big eyes better worlds than this" (113). Eyes have been noted throughout the story, and yet the optic imagery does not cohere. In this (probably revised) version of *Walking Out* Beckett has produced an atypical happy ending. "Walking out" in springtime changes into "walking out" on his fiancée, but Belacqua nonetheless marries Lucy in a happy union. Yet Beckett's story is not a happy literary effort.

Despite his preoccupation with verse and fiction, Beckett received his Trinity M.A. degree in December 1931. The end of the year was also the end of his academic career. Fleeing Dublin for Kassel, Germany, where he had

---

Walking Out was probably revised by Beckett before inclusion as the sixth item in *MPTK*. I comment on that version.

spent the last three Christmas vacations, Beckett sent his resignation to Trinity. Although there were no melodramatic announcements, and although he had only two independent publications—"Whoroscope" and *Proust*—he might henceforth be a writer.

1932–33

Intricate Festoons of Words

1932

Beckett's new career began modestly with a short poem. Beckett told Harvey that the title came from the name of a beer, in which he indulged copiously while on Christmas vacation in Kassel, Germany. However, Pilling (1999a) has shown that the poem is nourished by Beckett's study of the French troubadour poets.

"Dortmunder"

This poem resembles an alba or aubade in its appreciation of erotic joys of the night. The beloved is a lute-playing bawd in a brothel, and the lover, through biblical reference, becomes a scribe—"Habbakuk, mard of all sinners." Structurally, the poem is a free-form, unrhymed sonnet, like the earlier "Yoke of Liberty." The opening quatrain sets the brothel scene. The next five lines evoke the beloved, and the following three lines announce the lover. By the final (unrhyming) couplet, "Schopenhauer is dead," along with his sublimation of desire. Although "the bawd / puts her lute away" at dawn, "the long night phrase" has been seductive.

Coughlan has perceptively paired "Dortmunder" with "Alba," which are placed on facing pages in the collection *Echo's Bones:* both poems evoke Scripture, and both are bathed in music and light. "But unlike the way 'Alba' steers itself successfully towards white counter-revelatory emptiness, 'Dort-

---

A typescript, rejected in 1934 by the Chicago-based *Poetry*, is the earliest extant version of "Dortmunder"—now at ICU. It is the fifth poem in *Echo's Bones*, and Beckett annotated it in the copy at HRC: "Cassel revisited" (*sic*). It was reprinted in *transition* (June 1936) and is found in *Poems*. In the *Beckett Circle* (spring 1998) John Pilling traces the poem's origin to Jean Beck's *La Musique des Troubadours*, rather than to the German beer about which Beckett told Harvey.

munder' ends with the scribe Habbakuk noting the bawd's 'dissolution'"
(195). The scribe has nevertheless recorded the process of that dissolution,
having borrowed and translated exotic phrases from Louis Laloy's *La
Musique chinoise* (Lawlor).

Beckett traveled from Kassel to Paris in February; he remained there
through June, his main occupation being his novel *Dream*. His story *Sedendo
et Quiescendo* appeared in the March 1932 issue of *transition*. That issue
began with a manifesto, "Poetry Is Vertical," to which nine signatures are
affixed—Hans Arp, Samuel Beckett, Carl Einstein, Eugene Jolas, Thomas
McGreevy (*sic*), Georges Pelorson, Theo Rutra, James J. Sweeney, Ronald
Symond. A more accurate title would be "Poetry Is Mantic," and although
Beckett later denied (to me) that he had a hand in the composition of the
manifesto, at least one of its ringing sentences was consonant with his practice: "The final disintegration of the 'I' in the creative act is made possible by
the use of a language which is a mantic instrument, and which does not hesitate to adopt a revolutionary attitude toward word and syntax, going even
so far as to invent a hermetic language, if necessary." Joyce was, of course,
the master inventor of a hermetic language, and he shadowed not only Beckett's early fiction but some of his verse.

"Text"

"Text" is a neutral title that Beckett had already used the previous year for
another poem. In this "prose-poem diapason" (Gross, 83) a woman, like
Joyce's Molly Bloom, is in bed with her cuckolded lover. Although "Text"
names neither its female speaker nor her "cheerfully cornuted Dublin land-
loper," they may be the Smeraldina and Belacqua (as they certainly are when
Beckett revised the prose poem for his novel, *Dream*). The text opens on
erotic invitation: "Come come and cull me." It then rollicks, Joycean fashion, through a lexicon of sexual suggestions—"twingle-twangler, shamehill,
puckfisted coxcomb, doty's potystick, opened its rose and struck with its
thorn, Greek galligaskins."[1] The female persona is imaged as a coalcave, a
cowslip, a lettuce leaf, a rose, a squab, a mare, whereas her partner is relent-
lessly phallic. For all its sexual lexicon, however, the speaker spurns her
suitor, as Pilling notes: "the lover who speaks 'Text' has been obliged by her
'week of redness' to sacrifice, or at least temporarily suspend her lovemak-

---

A typescript of "Text" is found in the Leventhal papers at HRC. First published in
the *New Review* (April 1932), it is reprinted as a "prose fragment" by Harvey and is
available in *CSP*. Gross is the only other scholar beside myself who classifies "Text"
as a prose poem.

ing" (1997, 214). Beckett has written an Anteros piece that reads like an erotic invitation.

More consonant with his temperament was another poem of the same period, which was at first ironically called "Happy Land."

"Sanies II"

The OED defines *sanies* as "thin fetid pus mixed with serum or blood, secreted by a wound or ulcer." Wounds will loom large in Beckett's first decade of writing, and the unsavory fluids will eventuate as words. Like other early poems, "Sanies II" is a dramatic monologue whose persona is delineated with less clarity than his ambience. The forty-one-line poem opens on the "happy land" of the American Bar in Paris, but three repetitions of "there" suggest that that happiness is already distant. More immediate is the pleasure exuded by the poem's persona, after his steam bath and fresh "lash," in his "stinking old trousers," with pockets sewn (against masturbation?). He moves "frescoward" toward a brothel that is adorned, incongruously, with a print of a Puvis de Chavannes fresco of Dante and Beatrice.[2] The persona then cites proper names from fairy tales, which sound curiously comfortable in the brothel setting. A colloquial line leads to pastiche of Shakespeare's Sonnet 116: "they are necking gobble-gobble / suck is not suck that alters." The two lines conflate (and implicitly repudiate) activity in the brothel. "Lo Alighieri has got off au revoir to all that"—precedes a series of macaronics and such outworn words as "hark, ere, thee, thine." A "terrible hush" triggers sexual flagellation, from which the persona asks to be spared. He offers to compensate Becky (the madam whose name begins like that of the author) if she will call off her adders. Old and Latin words eventuate in a prayer, which is twice heard. The first version is truncated: "Lord have mercy upon," and its very incompletion seems to englobe the world as a brothel, where we all suffer a "fessade à la mode." The second prayer and the final, forty-first line of "Sanies II" is set off as a stanza: "Lord have mercy upon us." It is easier to cleanse the body "spotless . . . within the brown rags" than to call off the adders of Becky, Madame de la Motte, and other demons.

Still uncertain of his poetic voice, Beckett composed a long poem, "Spring Song," which he soon jettisoned.

A variant version of "Sanies II" is in the Leventhal papers at HRC. I follow Knowlson and Pilling in rejecting Beckett's own dating of the poem in 1929 (as annotated in his copy of *Echo's Bones* at HRC). The poem's theme and imagery are consonant with the *Dream* material of 1932. "Sanies II" was first published as the seventh poem in *Echo's Bones* (1935) and is available in *Poems*.

"Spring Song"

Of Beckett's erudite verse, this is perhaps the most obscure. It is, however, clear that the 118-line poem, in thirteen uneven stanzas, does not herald a joyful spring. If it was actually written in spring, Beckett had left Kassel for Paris, and yet the German flavor remains. In his correspondence with Mac-Greevy Beckett sometimes designated his sexual tensions as "the German fever," and so it is in this poem. Opening on the line "Styx! Styx!" the poem traces a descent into hell, and the account of the personal inferno divides into two. The first part, larded with German phrases, substitutes a night of hatred for one of love. The second part describes a visit to a brothel, which thrives as a family enterprise. The first-person pronoun is confined to the first part, but both parts express distaste for sexuality. Stylistically, the poem ranges over several idioms: Classical references riddle Negro minstrel dialect; the clown Grock is displaced by the poet Ronsard. Near the end Thanatos appears, along with bloated angels and sperming doves. By its disgust for sex, the "Spring Song" is an Anteros poem, which Beckett was wise to discard—after tinkering with it.

Beckett's frustrations—both erotic and compositional—were less obscurely vented in fiction than in verse. Presumably with the goal of becoming a writer, he initiated a rigorous training program for himself. The so-called *Dream* Notebook at RUL brims with arcane words and quotations, which have been masterfully tracked down by John Pilling (1999a). Knowlson believes it probable that Beckett started *Dream of Fair to Middling Women* during 1931 in Ireland, but he completed it in 1932 in Paris, sending it on to the editor Charles Prentice of Chatto and Windus in London. Existing documents do not reveal when Beckett first decided to weave a novel about his story protagonist, Belacqua. Pilling assumes that *Dream* "became a single entity only as disparate episodes began to accumulate, and as a kind of aesthetic armature . . . was put in place" (1997, 57–58). After completing the novel, Beckett hoped to publish it but could find no takers. Finally turning against his "virgin chronicle," he gave the typescript to Lawrence Harvey, glad to be rid of it. Of Beckett's frequently expressed distaste for his early work, *Dream* is perhaps the prize exhibit. The novel was published only after the author's death.

A typescript of the 118-line "Spring Song" is found in the Leventhal papers at HRC. Knowlson mentions an earlier version sent to Charles Prentice in 1931, and a later version in the possession of Georges Belmont (209, 661 n. 138). It has never been published.

Dream of Fair to Middling Women

The title of *Dream* posits a dreamer; yet no such character appears. Perhaps he is the narrator, as in *Finnegans Wake*. He is not to be confused with the protagonist, Belacqua, who occasionally lapses into a dreamlike state. Two of the three "fair to middling women" indulge briefly in dreams, but the title can scarcely allude to these subsidiary figures. Rather, like so much else in the novel, literary dreams are implied—Tennyson's *Dream of Fair Women* and Chaucer's *Legend of Good Women*. Unlike their literary predecessors, however, the women of Beckett's *Dream* are presented as only "fair to middling." However based on living models, the women are secondary characters in this novel with a male protagonist, who is sometimes designated as "our principal boy," as in English pantomime.

In Paris in spring a young man's fancy might well turn to dreams of love, but twenty-six-year-old Beckett's fancy turned to writing about love—and lust.[3] *Dream of Fair to Middling Women* is a sustained but disjunctive novel. The narrator, a "Mr. Beckett," calls his story a "virgin chronicle" (118), and that chronicle is at once a distanced autobiography, an exhibition of erudition, a parody of coherent narration, a metafictional fiction, and "intricate festoons of words" (226)—a phrase that I borrow from the novel, to epitomize most of Beckett's writing during this period.

Structurally, the book is unbalanced: part "One" occupies less than half a page. Parts "Two" and "Three" occupy some hundred pages each. Addendum "Und" takes up some thirty pages, whereas addendum "And" takes up only three. In parts "Two" and "Three" fiction can break abruptly into metafiction, as the narrator bewails the recalcitrance of his characters. They are equated with notes in a Chinese musical scale, to be manipulated into a melody.[4] However, the protagonist Belacqua is resistant to such composition, and in "Und" he is presented as trine: "Centripetal, centrifugal and . . . not." The narrator, with Dante's help, expands on that "not."[5]

> The third being was the dark gulf when the glare of the will and the hammer strokes of the brain doomed outside to take flight from its quarry were expunged, the Limbo and the wombtomb alive with the unanxious spirits of quiet cerebration, where there was no conflict of flight and flow and Eros was as null as Anteros and Night had no daughters.

The single (undated) typescript of *Dream* is at NhD, and a photocopy is at RUL. An excerpt, "Jem Higgins' Love-Letter to the Alba," appeared in *New Durham* (June 1965), but Beckett resisted requests to publish the complete youthful novel. It was first published in 1992, by the Black Cat Press, Dublin, after his death, with some acrimony between the editor, Eoin O'Brien, and the British and American publisher, John Calder. Page numbers in my text refer to Calder's Riverrun edition, 1993.

> [Belacqua] was bogged in indolence, without identity, impervious alike to its pull and goading. . . . His third being was without axis or contour, its centre everywhere and periphery nowhere, an unsurveyed marsh of sloth. (121)

In spite of his attraction to Belacqua's "third being," Beckett's narrator follows his protagonist through barely distinguishable centrifugal and centripetal adventures, where peripheral characters appear—notably the three fair to middling women: the Smeraldina, the Syra-cusa, the Alba. Belacqua's "calm, blue-eyed, clean, and gentle" Dublin family are occasionally mentioned. The Smeraldina's parents, Mammy and the Mandarin, figure quite prominently in part "Two," and a small society peoples a Dublin Christmas party in part "Three."

Although the novel's title purports to recount Belacqua's amorous adventures among "fair to middling women," the first part is womanless, in its depiction of the child Belacqua on his bicycle (which is indebted to the opening of Joyce's *Portrait*).[6] The second part presents the ambivalent infatuation of Belacqua with the Smeraldina-Rima, who lives in Hesse with her Irish family, and who is mercilessly mocked by Belacqua, and, to a lesser degree, by the narrator.[7] Also in the second part Belacqua in Paris presses a volume of Dante on the reluctant Syra-cusa, but he also patronizes brothels. While visiting the Smeraldina in Vienna, Belacqua receives a letter (in French in the text) from a French friend, and in later conversation with that friend Belacqua expresses admiration of Racine and Malherbe: "They have no style, they write without style, do they not. . . . Perhaps only the French can do it. Perhaps only the French language can give you the thing you want" (48). It is, however, in English that the Smeraldina's father quotes Belacqua to Belacqua: "The reality of the individual, you had the cheek to inform me once, is an incoherent reality and must be expressed incoherently" (101). Yet it is not Belacqua but the narrator who declares that "we" is "concensus, here and hereafter, of me" (5), and, further, "we, extenuate concensus of me" (112), who is in turn a form of incoherent reality.

Although the narrator's metafictional commentary is not confined to "Und," that chapter, where Belacqua sails from the continent back to his native Ireland, is particularly given to "marginalia" about the unsatisfactory nature of his fiction, Belacqua's penchant for "sedendo *et* quiescendo," his ill-fitting shoes, and his desire to write a book. Belacqua himself affirms: "The experience of my reader shall be between the phrases, in the silence, communicated by the intervals, not the terms, of the statement . . . his experience shall be the menace, the miracle, the memory, of an unspeakable trajectory" (138). Belacqua mocks his own intentions, and yet he bases them on

Rembrandt, Horace, Hölderlin, and "Beethofen." He enlarges on the last of these: "I think of his earlier compositions where into the body of the musical statement he incorporates a punctuation of dehiscence, flottements, the coherence gone to pieces, the continuity bitched to hell" (139). As a writer, Belacqua espouses silence and incoherence, so that it is not surprising that he arrives in Ireland "with his palpitations and adhesions and effusions and agenesia and wombtomb and aesthetic of inaudibilities" (141).

By part "Three" Belacqua's romance with the Smeraldina "was all over," and he has become a passive admirer of the Dublin Alba, an independent woman with a taste for brandy and a well-stocked mind that we occasionally penetrate. The narrator teases the reader with his delay in arranging the meeting of Belacqua and the Alba: "Seeing as how we are more or less all set now for Belacqua and the Alba to meet at least" (167). When they do meet, they engage in more spirited banter than was true of the Alba's predecessors. After seeing the Alba on the strand and again at a Christmas party, Belacqua is alone: "(you didn't suppose, it is to be hoped, that we were going to allow him to spend the night there) [at the Alba's home]" (240). Finally, *Dream* loops back to its beginning; in our early view of the adult Belacqua, he is admonished by a wharf watchman, and in our last view of him he obeys an order to move on, again the victim of an authority figure.

Although "Und" is much longer than "And," they are symmetrical in their metafictionality, The second and third parts show more conventional symmetries and oppositions. The narrator early renounces a comparison of the Smeraldina and the Syra-cusa, but there is an implicit contrast between the physical Smeraldina and the more intellectual Alba. The Smeraldina is partial to food, and the Dublin beauty delights in brandy. The Germanified lady writes a comic love letter, and the Dublin lady receives a comic love letter—both quoted in full. Belacqua has a problematic fascination with each young woman, which reaches an unfulfilled climax on successive holidays, when each of them is surrounded by other admirers. Belacqua suffers indignities of illness in the presence of each love, and each one mothers him solicitously. Finally, however, Belacqua is alone, in the snow of Vienna or the rain of Dublin. (Despite Belacqua's surface involvement with fair-to-middling women, the narrator's subtext implies his preference for masturbation.)[8]

Description, dialogue, and a minimal plot—"the virgin chronicle" shows some facility with all three. Beckett's pen flows vividly over drunken parties, such as New Year's Eve in Vienna, more or less in the company of Smerry, and, a year later, Christmas Eve in Dublin, more or less in the company of the Alba. Joyce-like, Beckett displays neologisms and portmanteau words—Smeraldinalgia, coprolalia, impudenda, pianissimissima, triph-

thong, taratantaratartantula, lex stallionis, clitoridian, diademitonically, the-
ologasters. Proust-like, Beckett immerses his tale in the arts—music and
painting, as well as literature. Unlike Proust, however, who does not refer
specifically to his work in progress, Beckett (via his narrator and his protagonist) ruminates about his own process of narration. During the process of
writing, Beckett enfolded that very process into his novel, however he may
have mocked it.

Belacqua echoes the narrator in gnawing at aesthetics, but Beckett also
embeds in this work references to his other works—a practice that will continue through the years. The striking word *sanies* is not yet affixed to a literary genre, but the narrator recollects Beckett's own Anteros poem "cogged"
from Ronsard's "Magic," which is familiar both to Belacqua and the Alba.
Belacqua declares: "There is a long poem . . . waiting to be written about
hens and eggs," and "Whoroscope" was not only written but already published. Resurrected from Beckett's lecture on concentrism is one Jean du
Chas, who, alive and well as Belacqua's French friend in Dublin, replies to a
question about news of the great world—"fair to meedling. The poem
moves, eppure." Chas of *Dream* thus conflates concentrism, the Galileo of
"Whoroscope," and part of the title of *Dream of Fair to Middling Women*.
When Belacqua hears the name of Alba, he undergoes a mystical experience,
which the narrator likens to "assumption upside down," and this experience
is rendered in phrases "cogged" from Beckett's own poem, "Alba."

Dream overlaps with phrases, images, and ideas of Beckett's verse. The
following table is instructive, but not exhaustive:

DREAM PAGE	POEM
33–34, 83–84, 107–8	Sanies II
148, 174, 181–82	Alba
55, 98, 157	Enueg I
28, 105, 113–14, 125, 157	Enueg II
28–29, 111, and passim	Dortmunder
83	Text

Beckett not only mentions "Mr. Beckett" as the author of *Dream;* he
describes meeting Belacqua "outside the enceinte of our romaunt" (186). The
narrator admits to a poem "cogged" from Ronsard, but Beckett ascribes his
own sonnet to Belacqua, and he also informs us that "[Belacqua] did [Rim-
baud] pat into English" (137)—as Beckett himself would translate Rimbaud's
"Le Bateau ivre" into English. In French Belacqua composes a frail couplet,
similar to those that Beckett would later dismiss as *mirlitonnades*. More
ironically, the narrator foists Beckett's own "Calvary by Night" on an
unnamed "homespun poet" at the Dublin Christmas party.

"Calvary by Night"

Harvey links "Calvary" with "Alba" and "Dortmunder" as "a poetic trans-
position of 'mystic' experience made possible through erotic or semierotic
encounter" (276), but to obtain this reading Harvey dredges the eroticism
from other Beckett poems. "Calvary" is above all, as Harvey also realizes,
"the portrait of life as a brief flowering between birth and death" (274), and
the particular life is announced in the title. Beckett relies on the apocryphal
legend of Christ's death by drowning, thereby becoming the prototype of
suffering man, who knows no resurrection but only "re-enwombing" in "the
waste of / the water."

No connection is posited in *Dream* between "Calvary by Night" and
the episodic character of Nemo, who has died by drowning some twenty
pages earlier. Pilling (1997) traces the name to Burton's *Anatomy of Melancholy,* and O'Hara suggests that it derives from Jules Verne's Captain Nemo
in *Twenty Thousand Leagues under the Sea.* Beckett may simply have appro-
priated the Latin word for "no one," since his Nemo functions neither in the
slender plot nor the populous society of *Dream.*[9] Early in the novel he is
described as "the most regrettable simultaneity of notes," "a symphonic, not
a melodic, unit" (11). Virtually disappearing for some hundred pages, Nemo
suddenly reappears: "Now Belacqua is on the bridge with Nemo, they are
curved over the parapet, their bottoms are outlined and not in vain in the
dusk descending" (157).

Not quite the "no one" of Latin, Nemo is an alter ego for Belacqua.
Early in *Dream* the narrator italicizes: "*[Nemo] simply is not that kind of
person*" (10). In the middle of *Dream,* the narrator expresses dissatisfaction
with Belacqua, also in italics: "*[Belacqua] has turned out to be simply not
that kind of person*" (124). At "Homer dusk," an hour usually sacred to
Belacqua, Nemo "is in position" (174). When Belacqua reads in the "horrid
latin" of the Twilight Herald that Nemo died by drowning, he rationalizes
away the verdict of suicide. Suddenly and for the only time in *Dream* the narrator flashes forward to quote Belacqua's description of himself as "a dud
mystic" and "a borderman." The narrator links Nemo's death with Belacqua's moment of self-perception: "Thus through Nemo came Belacqua to a
little knowledge of himself and we (though too late for insertion) to a little
knowledge of Belacqua, and by the end of Nemo were forewarned" (186).
The parenthetical phrase is a blatant untruth, since we are reading that very
insertion. Nemo is a phantom character, who predicts the hovering forms of
Beckett's later fiction—and his fascination with forms of nothingness.

Awarded a paragraph to itself in "Und" is the sentence: "The only unity
in this story is, please God, an involuntary unity" (133). Yet the presence of
Belacqua is the story's main unifying thread, however weak or various. The

narrator usually maintains an ironic distance from his "principal boy," and indeed, from all characters but Nemo. The unity of *Dream* is nevertheless as fragile as the narrator could wish, but the experience of the reader does not lie "between the phrases, in the silence, communicated by the intervals" (138). Rather, the experience of this reader responds to the self-protective varieties of style (including concealed quotation) of a young writer who is wary of lapsing into bald thematic statement, yet who seeks his own way of expressing intense experiences (mainly but not only erotic), which he is reluctant to find either trivial or transcendent. Disdaining the society he renders lubriciously, admiring both the wholeness of Dante and the fragmentation of the troubadour poems, not yet trusting "the ingenuous fibres / that suffer honestly," Beckett poured his temptations, frustrations, and favorite quotations into this first novel, which is as irrational as a dream. Since *Dream* was published only after Beckett's death, the experienced Beckett reader can discern how the twenty-six-year-old writer was feeling his way toward "the inaudibilities" that would be heard in his later prose.[10]

Dream of Fair to Middling Women is often called Joycean, and its lexicon and phrasing do derive from the older writer. However, the novel also departs from the work of Beckett's mentor—the miseries rather than the sensual delights of eroticism, everyday detail without necessary mythic extension, episodic exclusions rather than cosmopolitan inclusiveness, a more pointed humor in passages of dialogue, light-dark contrasts and other images based on painting. Beckett never ceased to admire the older writer, but their relationship became difficult when Lucia Joyce fell in love with Beckett. (Knowlson believes that the Syra-cusa in the novel is based on Lucia.) By spring 1932, Lucia's irrationalism was recognized by everyone but Joyce, and Beckett carefully resumed contact with the Joyce circle. Probably to celebrate Bloomsday on June 16, 1932, Beckett composed a ten-line, two-stanza acrostic poem of homage to James Joyce.

"Home Olga"

In *Dream* the narrator makes several references to a "private joke" shared by Belacqua and the Smeraldina, but he never reveals that joke. The title "Home Olga" relies upon a private joke among a group of young Irishmen in Paris;

First published in *Contempo,* February 15, 1934, "Home Olga" is reprinted in Harvey and in Richard Ellmann's *James Joyce.* Federman and Fletcher correct my errors in *The Comic Gamut.* Ellmann's paraphrase of the poem is mistaken, especially his first sentence: "If Joyce had any hope in his exile that the Irish would renounce Catholicism, the national malady, he, untouched by it, might be able to yield to his comic spirit. His books are full of natural love and silence, in man and woman, and in their portrayer (Joyce), expressed in a *dolce stil nuovo,* and also full of faith and cunning. When he says goodbye he winks because what was shall be again, a point

the phrase was uttered at a party when a bored husband summoned his wife to leave. Subsequently it "became a covert call for relief and regroupment" of the Irish contingent in Paris (Harvey, 296). A call for regroupment may not be entirely flattering to Joyce, and yet Beckett's admiration is evident in the verse that plays on the name of the older writer. Structured in two stanzas, the ten lines of the poem begin with the letters that spell JAMES JOYCE. Gross analyzes the poem in some detail, and yet her summary imposes a symmetry that is absent from the verse: "Where the real subject of the first stanza of 'Home Olga' had been Joyce's accomplishments as a parodist of Yeats, the real subject of the second is Beckett's own accomplishments as a parodist of Joyce" (141). She therefore reads the poem's "real" title as "Homo egal" and "Homo logos"; that is, Beckett is Joyce's equal as a writer.

The actual first stanza virtually buries Yeats under Joyce's genius, and the tone of the second stanza is jocular, rather than parodic. Gross is on firmer ground when she expands on Beckett's skillful arabesques on the Dantean number three. The verse form is Dante's beloved terza rima. The colors of the theological virtues—red, white, and green—shine through the poem's erythrite, opal, and jade. The Dantean virtues of faith, love, and hope are countered by the Joycean virtues of silence, exile, and cunning. Beckett's poem pays tribute to three writers—Dante, Yeats, and Joyce—but the last looms largest by dint of three *J*s in lines 2 and 6 of "Home Olga." Through quoting the triple "adieu" of the ghost in *Hamlet*, Beckett hints at successive poetic generations, and he states this explicitly in both English and Italian: "Yesterday shall be tomorrow" and "Che sarà sarà che fu." Thus, one rapparee writer will succeed another, barring the signature qualification, e.o.o.e.—"errors or omissions excepted"—in this witty encapsulation.

By the time Beckett wrote the poem, his days in Paris were numbered. When President Paul Doumer was assassinated in May, the French police began a roundup of foreigners. Since Beckett lacked the proper documents (as well as money), he left Paris in July. With his fee for translating Rimbaud's "Le Bateau ivre," he headed for London, where he hoped to find a source of income. Although he spent two months there, "in a positive flurry of activity" (Knowlson, 157), trying to publish *Dream* and/or poems, following through on contacts, and even making an appointment at an employment agency, nothing came of his practical steps. He rented a room in Ampton Street, Islington, and as was his habit in any city, he walked in ever-widening circles around his abode. He also read voluminously at the British Museum. Geography and reading were blended in his poem "Serena I."

---

unknown to Homer, but demonstrated by Joyce because he himself is a kind of Christ (another word-man) returned to life: hail and alas!" (714–15).

"Serena I"

The single surviving example of a troubadour serena (by Guiraut Riquier) is a love poem in praise of night, but Beckett's three "Serenas" reject this convention. Beckett ironizes the "serene" resonance of "Serena I" by his choice of *un*serene scenes of cruelty and suffering on his persona's long walk in London. Structured in four unpunctuated free-verse stanzas, "Serena I" is a virtual compendium of unsavory aspects of London. As the persona grows increasingly perturbed at cruelties, he offers a brief prayer and then is momentarily seduced by London place-names that seem to offer promise—Crystal Palace, Blessed Isles, Primrose Hill, Ken Wood, which attract him because (in a sentence that slightly varies from one in *Dream*) "alas I must be that kind of person." Alas, he must be the kind of person who seeks beauty or kindness in a world that flouts them. Increasingly angry at what he sees, the persona repeats the line that offers him the solace of temporary solitude: "but in Ken Wood / who shall find me." In Harvey's view the serena title fits Beckett's poem, since a "daytime existence seems unreal and alien by comparison with the fulfillment of the night" (92). To Beckett's persona, however, both day and dusk display suffering in an alien London that is also an alien world.

Only when Beckett himself was back in his native Foxrock did he complete the poem, in a comparison of his persona with a housefly reveling in its brief existence. Even if the fly is in "the autumn of his life," he is a law unto himself. The poem's final line gives a bitter twist to the biblical injunction against serving God and mammon: "he [the fly] could not serve typhoid and mammon." The implication is that the fly will serve neither, and that the persona too will refuse to serve the blandishments of the modern city.

"Serena II"

Trapped in Dublin by lack of money, Beckett wrote another journey-poem, this time set in Ireland. "Serena II" equates a "clonic earth" with a Kerry Blue terrier's memories of parturition. Beckett's first serena hints at a division between day and restful night, and the second serena contrasts the active day with "damfool twilight," where "it is useless to close the eyes." Admon-

---

In Beckett's list for Con Leventhal at HRC the three "Serena" poems are grouped as "Cri de coeur." "Serena I" was first published as the eighth poem in *Echo's Bones*. In the HRC copy Beckett has annotated: "London/World's End," but he did not use that London location in the actual poem.

"Serena II," included in a November 1932 letter to Thomas MacGreevy, was first published as the ninth poem in *Echo's Bones*. Beckett's copy of *Echo's Bones* in HRC is inscribed "Glencullen/Prince William's seat/Enniskerry," but that background figures only minimally in the poem itself.

ishing an unidentified "you" to say prayers before bedtime, the poetic voice concludes in a near rhyme: "here at these knees of stone / then to bye-bye on the bones." Childhood prayers are twinned with gravestones, and baby talk with skeletal remains. In "Serena I" the persona's rage dissolves into the serenity of an autumn fly. In "Serena II" sun, season, and life all set in the West.

While Beckett, lonely and in poor health, languished at the family home in Cooldrinagh, his friend George Reavey wrote him from Paris about a short story contest under the aegis of Edward Titus, who had praised his translations of surrealist poems. Beckett submitted *Dante and the Lobster*. Although it failed to win the prize, Titus published the story in the December 1932 issue of *This Quarter*. At least Beckett could palliate the Dublin days with Paris publication.

Dante and the Lobster

This story barely fits into my chapter's title phrase—"intricate festoons of words." The theme of Beckett's story—the impossibility of reconciling divine justice and mercy in this world—emerges more clearly than ever before in the work of the twenty-six-year-old writer, and yet it is curtained by the repeated alliterative allusions to the events of the story—*l*uncheon, *l*obster, and Italian *l*esson. Thus we follow Belacqua—for Beckett returns to him post-*Dream*—through his preparation of his lunch, his purchase of a lobster for his aunt, and his near loss of the lobster while he is absorbed in his Italian lesson. Finally, Belacqua learns to his horror that lobsters are boiled alive to be eaten. "Well, it's a quick death," he rationalizes. Abruptly, the narrator demurs: "It is not."[11] The intrusive denial is all the more unexpected because the story has been fairly consistent in its narrative point of view—that of Belacqua. After immersion in Belacqua's desire for solitude, we hear his conversations with tradesmen, with his Italian teacher, with his aunt, but above all we overhear his unspoken thoughts.

Despite a surface acceptance of fictional convention, Beckett marks the story as his own. The Dantean name and the protagonist's dedication to Dante's *Commedia* sound odd in modern Dublin, and it is particularly incongruous that a Dantean character should be reading Dante.[12] The plot lacks exposition, and it displays disjunctions—a paragraph on an unnamed tiller of the field, a digression about the protagonist's sore feet, an excursus into a grocer's thoughts. Although the narrator is subdued, he does intrude to announce the season—and the artifice of fiction: "Let us call it Winter,

---

Dante and the Lobster was first published in *This Quarter* (December 1932). The story was revised—but not "thoroughly," as claimed in Federman and Fletcher—to become the first piece in the collection *More Pricks Than Kicks*.

that dusk may fall now and a moon rise" (20). Unusual in fiction, too, is Beckett's care with sounds—rhyme and alliteration in descriptive passages.

Although the plot is relatively straightforward, the protagonist is not. We do not know Belacqua's age, provenance, or profession. Nor do we know what he looks like, beyond the single phrase "grotesque person." In compensation for this lack, perhaps, we learn a surprising amount about Belacqua's mind, for so short a story. Only a well-educated character would bog down in "the first of [Dante's] great Moon Canti" and would nevertheless persist in deciphering Beatrice's abstruse arguments. Like the protagonist of *Dream*, this Belacqua has a propensity to close his mind until it is "slack and quiet and dim." Yet that mind can turn to action in the external world, such as elaborate preparations for lunch. Narrated like an epic exploit, the lunch may be emblematic: "Sometimes his hunger, more of mind, I need hardly say, than of body . . ." (13). This avatar of Belacqua has a surprising ability to empathize with others; he enters the minds of the tiller of the field (Cain), of a grocer, and even, perhaps, of a lobster who quotes Keats.[13] However, Belacqua does *not* enter the mind of McCabe, the man convicted of six murders, who will hang at dawn. Brooding about justice versus mercy, a theme at least as old as Shakespeare's *Measure for Measure*, Belacqua registers sympathy with the murderer Cain, and not with his victim Abel.

Beckett's title couples a noble poet with an unfortunate crustacean. The story's tripartite structure parodies Dante's trinitarian structure. Despite two time-lapses, Belacqua's adventures are confined to one day, and that day is the last in the life of the condemned McCabe. Although the name is actual, it sonically combines Cain and Abel; McCabe contains both brothers. At noon of that day the chance sight of McCabe's photograph in an old newspaper arrests Belacqua's attention, and although the putative murderer is mentioned only three times thereafter, his imminent execution is suspenseful. Moreover, Belacqua is bogged in the first Moon Canto of Dante's *Paradiso*, but McCabe's sentence leads Beckett's protagonist to gnaw at a line from the *Inferno*, which he reads as a pun—"qui vive la pietà quando è ben morta" [Here piety/pity lives when it is quite dead]. Although Beckett himself had already translated that line in his poem "Text"—"pity is quick with death"—Belacqua is unable to translate it, and his Italian teacher queries: "Do you think . . . it is absolutely necessary to translate it?" (19). Her question is rhetorical in this story of victims—Cain, McCabe, and the lobster— living beings condemned to death.

As God marked Cain with the "stigma of [His] pity," Beckett marks his story with copious religious reference—Beatrice had it from God, Belacqua toasts bread according to his God, and he broods about God's role in Nineveh. Both Belacqua and a nameless grocer invoke God or Christ in their oaths. Belacqua replies in French to Mlle. Glain's account of rescuing the lobster from her cat, but we read in English: "He did not know the French for lobster. Fish would do very well. Fish had been good enough for Jesus Christ, Son of God, Saviour" (19–20). Belacqua sees the lobster "cruciform" upon the table, and when he perceives that it moves, he exclaims in the names of both God and Christ. Belacqua's last words in the story are "God help us all." The prayer is urgent.

In the few months since he wrote *Dream* Beckett has learned to control his tone. Rather than blend narrator and protagonist in a self-protective cynical distance, Beckett ascribes to this Belacqua an acrimonious intensity in his activities, from lunch to lesson. Fleeing from "conversational nuisance" with fellow intellectuals, Belacqua engages the grocer in phrases from a penny dreadful, and his other conversations exhibit the lunge-and-parry of fencing. Belacqua's exclamations to his aunt focus on the lobster-victim, but McCabe too has "about thirty [metaphorical] seconds to live." Instead of insinuating himself into McCabe's mind, Belacqua vents his fury on his lunch—first attacking the bread, then "crowning his exquisite gastronomical experience" with the news that McCabe will not be pardoned. The savagery of that refusal of pardon is parodied in the savagery of that meal. Belacqua is sensitive to a lobster's fate, as he is sensitive to Dante's lack of pity, but he is impenetrable about an execution. Yet it is because of McCabe that Belacqua returns to the pity-piety pun in the *Inferno,* instead of mounting to the *Paradiso* in his Italian lesson. The pity-piety thread fuses the story's events into a coherence new to Beckett.

The execution of the actual McCabe took place on December 9, 1926, when twenty-year-old Beckett was a student at Trinity.[14] A gardener for the McDonnell family, McCabe was blamed for six deaths and arson, but he died protesting his innocence. It is unlikely that Beckett's attention was called to McCabe by an old newspaper. Rather, the cruel sentence, based on questionable evidence, must have made a deep impression on the young man, who then coupled that event with an actual incident involving a lobster (Harvey, 154n). Compassion bleeds through *Dante and the Lobster,* although the narrator avoids poignancy.

1933

The year 1933 was one of personal pain to Beckett. In May he underwent a second operation on his neck. While convalescing, he learned that Peggy Sinclair died unexpectedly on the day of his operation. In June his father died of a heart attack, after an apparent recovery from an earlier attack. Beckett sought refuge in writing. Extant documents do not reveal when he decided to arrange his several Belacqua stories into a book, also salvaging some material from *Dream*. Similarly, it is unclear when Beckett decided to publish his verse as a slender volume, salvaging some material he had already written. What is clear, however, is that Beckett filled this unhappy Dublin year with verse and fiction. His letters to MacGreevy testify to the gradual accumulation of stories, and by September he mentions sending "10 contes" to Chatto and Windus, which is the number eventually published in *More Pricks Than Kicks*.[15]

A Wet Night

The title *A Wet Night* subsumes both the weather and the ebriety of the Christmas season in Dublin. Beckett shapes the *Dream* material into a story that parodically reflects the enveloping snow of Joyce's *The Dead*. The characters of the latter are beholden to the dead, but Beckett's characters are not only buried in social inanities; they are unredeemed by memory of the past. Indeed the protagonist Belacqua is virtually without a past.

The narrator offers images to portray the Alba, and, conversely, his epithets disfigure the party's hostess, Calikan Frica. (*Fricatrice* is an old word for a lewd woman.) The narrator resurrects McCabe in connection with the Frica: "goose, thought Bel, flying barefoot from McCabe" (*MPTK*, 76).[16] Unlikely to be Beckett's oversight, the narrator thus conjoins Belacqua with a victimizing victim, while self-reflexively recalling his own story. The narrator shrinks the already shadowy Nemo of *Dream* to a single opaque reference by an atheistic Polar Bear in the context of suicide. Beckett reduces the lavish metafictional commentary of *Dream,* but he still intrudes digressions into *A Wet Night.* After explicating a French nursery rhyme, the narrator addresses the reader: "Pardon these French expressions, but the creature dreams in French" (82). Belacqua in a pub engages in an imaginary conversation with the real Swiss clown Grock, and when the Alba invites Belacqua to see her home after the Christmas party, the happy swain utters Grock's distinctive phrase "Nisscht moooooooglich." Conceptually, *A Wet Night* retains the focus of "Three" of *Dream* on Belacqua's near-worship of the Alba.

Of the stories perhaps completed by early spring, 1933, two depict an amorous Belacqua—*The Smeraldina's Billet-Doux* and *A Wet Night*—and only one hovers at the edge of metaphysics—*Dante and the Lobster*. Eventually, Beckett retitled the sundry adventures of Belacqua as *More Pricks Than Kicks,* thus signaling that not all the stories can be embraced as

---

Revising sections from *Dream,* Beckett placed *A Wet Night* fourth in *MPTK.* The title coincides with that of a poem by Thomas Hardy, but the phrase is common enough.

Dream[s] of Fair to Middling Women. Despite the biblical resonance of the new title, however (Acts 9:5, "I am Jesus whom thou persecutest; it is hard for thee to kick against the pricks"), the main pricks of Belacqua remain female. As Belacqua would realize on the day of his death: "What a number of women there seemed to be in this place!" (180). Women engage Belacqua erotically in swift succession, eroding his ability to transport his mind to another dimension. *Fingal,* one such story, also plunges the reader into the landscape around Dublin. It is the landscape through which the persona cycles in "Sanies I" (O'Brien, 239), and I intrude the poem into the sequence of stories, as Beckett himself may have done.

"Sanies I"

Even less coherent than "Sanies II," which was written earlier, "Sanies I" also registers temptation by, and mistrust of, erotic experience. In the earlier poem the persona pleads with the bawd to call off her adders; in the later poem the persona himself apparently rejects the "dauntless daughter of desires."[17] On the literal level, the speaker cycles through the Irish countryside, but on the mental level he travels also through his parents' wedding, his own birth, his brief prodigality, and his fear of commitment to a love that entails marriage and children. Gross sees the fusion of such events in the liquidity of the title: "the 'pot-valiant' hero, courageous with drink, 'pants his pleasure,' transforming champagne into semen, and semen into amniotic fluid, amniotic fluid into 'beesting' [animal milk], and 'beestings' into champagne again" (232). Gross assumes that the final lines of the poem are spoken by the "dauntless nautch-girl," but, without any demarcation, the lines seem to me to belong to the persona, who has summoned Anteros to enable him to smile desire away, like the smiling, sated tiger in the limerick.

"Sanies I" resembles *Fingal* both in the landscape and in the lover's rejection of his beloved.

Fingal

Fingal endows Belacqua with a girlfriend, Winnie Coates, to whom he confesses: "I must be getting old and tired . . . when I find the nature outside me

---

In May 1933, Beckett sent an early version of "Sanies I" (entitled "Weg du Einzige") to his friend Thomas MacGreevy (Knowlson, 161). There is no other manuscript before publication as the sixth poem of *Echo's Bones*. The poem in the HRC copy of *Echo's Bones* carries Beckett's enigmatic inscription "Exitus redditus/This evening/Montparnasse/1957," which does not help the dating. A note on p. 173 of *Poems* says: "Both [Sanies poems] are also based on Provençal models." However, there is no Provençal genre of "sanies."

Fingal is the second story of *MPTK*, where it was first published in 1934.

compensating for the nature inside me" (*MPTK,* 31). Nevertheless, Belacqua and Winnie set off together for a long walk through the nature outside him, and at one point he attempts to communicate his enthusiasm for Fingal— "land of sanctuary" (with unmentioned resonances of Macpherson's *Ossian*). When Winnie refuses to share his feeling, Belacqua resolves "not [to] try to communicate Fingal" (27) and indeed barely to communicate with Winnie at all, although he does impart his partiality for the Portrane Lunatic Asylum. Fleeing with a flimsy excuse from Winnie and her doctor friend, Belacqua appropriates a bicycle and is happily in a pub by the time Winnie and her companion set off in search of him.

Beckett's narrator casually draws a metaphor from *Hamlet,* and he introduces a gratuitous old man who tells a tale of Dean Swift's incarceration of his "motte" in a tower. The narrator admits us into Winnie's mind, with its unflattering insights into Belacqua: "You make great play with your short stay abroad" (26). Sporting philosophical terms, the narrator derides his own plot: "Surely it is in such little adjustments that the benevolence of the First Cause appears beyond dispute" (33). It is also the narrator who offers a sentence that is incomprehensible without the recondite knowledge that Swift sometimes signed letters to his Stella "Presto": "Little fat Presto, he would set out early in the morning, fresh and fasting, and walk like camomile" (34). The simile is curious, since plants do not walk. *Fingal* terminates far from Fingal, with Winnie furious at a distant laughing Belacqua, and it is not the last laugh of a more acerbic protagonist than that of *Dream.*

Ding-Dong

In contrast to stories about a more or less enamored Belacqua, Beckett's *Dante and the Lobster* probes Belacqua's mind, and, similarly, *Ding-Dong* is preoccupied with Belacqua's inner life. It also reveals a new tension between Belacqua and his nameless narrator. If Bair is correct that four stories were completed by Easter 1933, *Ding-Dong* is appallingly prescient. The title, drawn from Shakespeare's *Tempest,* is the choral rejoinder of the Spirits, after Ariel sings to Ferdinand: "Full fathom five thy father lies. . . . Sea-nymphs hourly ring his knell."[18] Ferdinand broods: "This ditty does remember my drowned father." Beckett's father did not drown, but within a few weeks he would die of a heart attack. Even before that catastrophe, Beckett was brooding in fiction at the cruelty of human mortality.

The nameless narrator introduces his protagonist, "My sometime friend Belacqua." Except for the epistolary *The Smeraldina's Billet-Doux, Ding-Dong* is the only one of Beckett's early stories to lapse into the first-person pronoun, however briefly. The story might be the prose extension of a jour-

---

Ding-Dong is the third story of *MPTK*, where it was first published in 1934.

ney poem, in its selection of details of misfortune—a blind paralytic beggar, a little girl run over by a bus, a woman's theft of the dead girl's bread. Yet a final figure in this sequence, an old woman beggar in a pub, rises triumphantly above her predecessors, by virtue of a luminous face. Although Belacqua prefers her silence, he also reacts favorably to her "white voice." He never implies that she is drunk or insane; yet she chooses strange wares to sell—seats in heaven—and she offers them at strange prices—four for tenpence or twopence apiece. Early in the story Belacqua notes that the Dublin Bovril sign goes "round and round, like the spheres." Late in the story the nameless shawlie chants: "Heaven goes round. . . . rowan an' rowan an' rowan." When Belacqua renounces his request for change from sixpence, the shawlie blesses him, and he assents: "Amen." Her refulgent countenance lights her way, and Belacqua departs for Railway Street in Dublin's red-light district (O'Brien, 176). The conclusion of *Ding-Dong* is arresting in its flatness after the radiance of Belacqua's response to a beggarwoman.

Of all the stories that were later collected in *More Pricks* the narrator is most telling in *Ding-Dong*. Opening with "My sometime friend Belacqua," he confides: "We were Pylades and Orestes for a period" (37). Belacqua subjects the narrator to "a positive geyser of confidence" about his "moving pauses," but the narrator has already told us: "He was an impossible person in the end. I gave him up in the end because he was not *serious*" (38). The repeated "in the end" underlines and undermines the sentence at a time when British intellectuals, led by F. R. Leavis, were much preoccupied with the seriousness of the fictional tradition. However, Beckett hides *his* seriousness under an ironic mask. In *Dante and the Lobster* the final intrusion of the narrator is abrupt: "It is not." In *Ding-Dong*, where the narrator is omnipresent, he tries to be self effacing through the passive voice (and concealed Dantean reference): "the reader is requested to notice that this *sweet style* is Belacqua's" (45, emphasis added). Also citing Belacqua's "strong weakness for oxymoron," the narrator obligingly coins one. What the reader is not requested to notice is the beggarwoman's failure to include Belacqua in her celestial merchandise, which is far more earthy than Dante's *Paradiso*.

Love and Lethe

Love and Lethe of the pretentious title ridicules conventional short story elements—a love conflict, exposition, climax, and resolution. The love conflict pitches Belacqua not against a rival, but against his reluctance to commit suicide alone. No explanation is offered for his self-destructive urge, but Belac-

---

Love and Lethe is the fifth story of *MPTK*, where it was first published in 1934. Of all the stories of that collection, Beckett in 1938 selected it for translation into French, in the hope of publication in Paris, but the translation seems to be lost.

qua has compacted with Ruby Tough, who is not only past her prime but who also suffers from an unnamed incurable disease and is therefore willing to end it all. Belacqua equips himself with a gun for the occasion, driving Ruby to a deserted spot, and then climbing with her to the crest of a hill, so that the double demise might be enhanced by a splendid view. The couple engage in a "You first" routine, but the gun goes off by accident. Belacqua interprets this as the finger of God, which he promptly translates as "Digitus Dei" but undercuts with "for once." Suicide dissolves into "inevitable nuptial." Given Belacqua's lugubrious predilections, however, this cannot be considered a happy ending.

The narrator is laboriously in evidence in *Love and Lethe*. He offers us an insight into the mind of Ruby's irrelevant mother and two paragraphs on her more irrelevant father. References to painters adorn descriptions of the characters, and as the climax approaches, the narrator informs us: "From now on till the end there is something very *secco* and Punch and Judy about their proceedings" (95). When Belacqua invokes the finger of God, the narrator asks four rhetorical questions about Belacqua's behavior, and he underlines their merely rhetorical quality. Finally the narrator grows benevolent: "May their night be full of music at all events" (100). Before that melodic conclusion, he mentions that when Ruby is dead and Belacqua an old optimist, the latter will realize that on this unique occasion "if never before nor since, [Belacqua] achieved what he set out to do, car [in the words of Ronsard] l'Amour et la Mort-caesura-n'est qu'une mesme chose" (100).

What a Misfortune

The title translates Voltaire's "Che sciagura" from *Candide*, already pressed into Beckett's service for his 1929 dialogue on contraception in Ireland. This misfortune is, however, a wedding—that of Belacqua Shuah (suddenly endowed with an onanistic surname) to Thelma bboggs, a fair-to-middling woman with an excremental surname (since "bog" is Irish slang for a lavatory). Belacqua Shuah's initials reverse those of Samuel Beckett. As lengthy as *A Wet Night*, *What a Misfortune* resembles that Christmas story in its mordant satire on a traditional festivity. Despite the length of the story, however, the plot is sketchy—Lucy dead, Belacqua woos the unimpoverished Thelma, and the bboggs family prepares for the wedding and the ensuing luncheon.

The narrator indulges in caustic similes to describe the putative father of the bride, Otto Olaf, and the actual father of the bride, Walter Draffin (a name that includes *draff*, Beckett's original title for his entire collection of

---

What a Misfortune is the seventh story of *MPTK*, where it was first published in 1934.

stories). Somewhat less elaborately itemized are the bride's mother and sister, the groom's distant handicapped relatives, and the groom's glabrous best man, Hairy Quin, a writer who cannot finish a sentence without pen and paper. *What a Misfortune* mentions not only Belacqua's surname but his occupation—a poet, and therefore deserving of the contempt of Otto Olaf, who has made his fortune in toilet requisites and who spends that fortune on choice furniture, which he refuses to move from 55 North Great George's Street, Dublin, to the prosperous suburb of Foxrock (which may have been Beckett's domicile when he wrote the story). The omniscient narrator predicts that Otto will soon die of a blood clot, but other destinies are left in doubt.

The narrator's malicious mockery pinpoints the two writers at the wedding—huge Hairy Quin and diminutive Walter Draffin. The former misses the point of Belacqua's remarks, and the latter worries about the lack of enjambment on the wedding invitation. Moreover, Walter is working on a book that is "a mere dump for whatever he could not get off his chest in the ordinary way" (133). Its title is *Dream of Fair to Middling Women.*

Rather than the ubiquitous wit of the Christmas party of *A Wet Night,* the fun of the wedding lies largely in its slapstick—the choice of flowers, the rented car, Hairy's damaging drive, a digression on doffing hats at funerals, Belacqua's near arrest, to which are added jokes and toasts. The marriage ceremony is fertile fodder for the narrator's parody: "At length they had consented together beyond all possibility of cavil, the dearly beloved had for ever held their peace and then let their cry come with a rush" (141). At the luncheon Otto Olaf, a devotee of music hall, tells the joke about his weak right lung: "But my left lung," he vociferates, "is as sound as a bell" (143) (like Estragon's in *Godot,* decades later). Walter Draffin's drunken toast enfolds two stale jokes (one in French) and then runs on for many minutes before concluding: "To Hymen's gracious mussy and protection we commit them, now, henceforth and for evermore. Slainte" (148). Belacqua responds in kind, in the "white voice of which he was a master" (learned perhaps from the shawlie of *Ding-Dong*). Only once in this long story does the narrator remember his audience—"whether from coquetry or fatigue we leave it to the reader to determine" (149).

A single footnote graces *What a Misfortune,* referring the reader to *Walking Out* for Belacqua's limited pity. However, the narrator himself sometimes functions like a footnote. Since Alba is a bridesmaid, we are reminded that she "was the nice little girl in 'A Wet Night'" (127), although "little girl" is singularly inappropriate for the woman who invites Walter Draffin (among others) to "see her home." Again acting like a footnote, the narrator reminds us that Belacqua tries to give his guests the slip, as he did to the homespun poet in *A Wet Night.* In this repeat maneuver Belacqua is quite conspicuous, but he nevertheless succeeds in absconding with his bride. As the honeymoon couple speed away in their rented three-wheeled car, the narrator comments, with a sub rosa reminder of Horace: "Lucy was *atra cura* in the dicky" (151). To his new wife Belacqua explains the absence of his veronica from his buttonhole: "Gone west." As in *Dante and the Lobster*, the narrator concludes the story with three cryptic words: "They went further." It is at once a sexual pun on a honeymoon and a metaphysical pun on the misfortune of a worldly fate for one who has longed for time-colored birds. More than any other story of *More Pricks*, *What a Misfortune* insists on its links with earlier stories. Lacking the ostentatious flourish of *Dream*, the new concatenation only occasionally broods about the nature of fiction.

Yellow

In *What a Misfortune* the narrator remarks sardonically: "Say what you will, you can't keep a dead mind down" (140). Belacqua's mind is, however, alive to the last in *Yellow*, the penultimate story of *More Pricks*. In the hospital—we will not know why for several pages—Belacqua is unwontedly preoccupied with his public face, but he has to steel his mind to compose that face. Recognizing that he is "an indolent bourgeois poltroon," Belacqua nevertheless decides to "ginger up his little psyche for the occasion" (161). By chance or by God's will, he recalls a paradox of John Donne: "Now among our wise men, I doubt not that many would be found, who would laugh at Heraclitus weeping, none which would weep at Democritus laughing." Deciding to "do the little soldier," he would act like "Bim and Bom, Grock, Democritus, whatever you are pleased to call it" (163). The proper names juxtapose the laughing Greek philosopher, the Swiss clown of "Nicht möglich," and the Soviet comedians who criticized the regime under the cloak of farce. Belacqua was thinking not only in public terms, but in performance terms.

Belacqua is accordingly sensitive to the setting of his hospital room. Although he offers sprightly conversation to one and all, he is impatient to be done with the scheduled operations on his neck and his toe. Perhaps suggested by the word *theater* for the place of his operations, Belacqua credits an angel of the Lord with reminding him of a theater joke. A parson acting in an amateur production "had to snatch at his heart when the revolver went off, cry 'By God! I'm shot!' and drop dead" (172). The parson agreed, provided he might substitute another word for the deity. However, the revolver actually did go off: " 'Oh' [the parson] cried 'oh . . . ! BY CHRIST! I *am* SHOT!' " Armed with this anecdote, Belacqua descends to the operating theater in the

---

Yellow is the ninth story of *MPTK*, where it was first published in 1934. Knowlson (162) describes the biographical background, since Beckett himself on December 1, 1932, suffered operations on his foot and neck.

company of his favorite nurse, Miranda. Although "he bounced up on to the table like a bridegroom" (174), Belacqua dies from too rich a mixture of the anesthetic. The narrator states the facts: "By Christ! He did die! They had clean forgotten to auscultate him!" Uncharacteristically, Belacqua's last words have expressed concern for the doctor: "Are you right?" But of course he means: Do you have the equipment well under control for me? Well might he ask, given the conclusion.

Beckett himself had undergone this dual operation a few months earlier, and *Yellow* displays Belacqua's consistently brave and comic tone in the face of an operation, which is never minor for the victim. More consistently than in any story since *Ding-Dong*, we follow Belacqua's thoughts, without intrusion from the narrator. Still, Beckett cannot bear to relinquish him entirely. Early in the story, the narrator remarks wryly: "Poor Belacqua, he seems to be having a very dull irksome morning, preparing for the fray in this manner. But he will make up for it later on, there is a good time coming for him later on, when the doctors have given him a new lease of apathy" (162). This narrator is not omniscient about Belacqua's fate, but he can spring into the mind of a theater sister who inveigles her patients to wind bandages. When Belacqua plays with the Scottish brogue of his nurse—"Soon to be syne"—the narrator comments with a Wildean quip: "What his repartee lacked in wit it made up for in style" (170). When Belacqua decides that everything in the hospital relieves suffering, the narrator distances himself from this charitable view: "Observe how he dots his i's now and crucifies his t's to the top of his bent" (173). For all the snide asides of the narrator, however, and although Belacqua's face may be yellow, and his overactive heart may ignite "terrible yellow yerks in his skull" (174), he has behaved bravely on the morning of his death.

Draff

Post-Belacqua fiction, *Draff* begins by concealing the identity of his widow, but in the second paragraph the narrator explains: "Then shortly after [Thelma's death] they suddenly seemed to be all dead, Lucy of course long since, Ruby duly, Winnie to decency, Alba Perdue in the natural course of being seen home. Belacqua looked around and the Smeraldina was the only sail in sight" (175). Not only does the narrator resurrect her from *Dream*, he also "cogs" from that source his page of mordant portraiture, including a parenthetical "thank you Mr Beckett." Married less than a year, the Smeraldina is punctilious about the funeral arrangements for Belacqua, although it

---

Draff is the tenth story of *MPTK*, where it was first published in 1934. Before Beckett fixed on the title *More Pricks Than Kicks*, he thought of entitling the collection of stories *Draff*.

is the maid Mary Ann who admits the undertaker, Mr. Malacoda. Hairy Quin, much improved since his friend Belacqua's death, undertakes to comfort the Smeraldina. Together they view Belacqua's corpse, together they "upholster the grave" with greens, together with the parson they ride to the burial, but on the way home Hairy ejects the parson from the car of Mr. Malacoda. When they learn that the gardener has raped the maid Mary Ann and burned Belacqua's house (in the pattern of McCabe in *Dante and the Lobster*), the Smeraldina accepts Hairy's invitation to live with him and be his love: "Perhaps after all . . . this is what darling Bel would wish" (190).

Draff terminates not on the happy couple but on the groundsman at Belacqua's grave. Surveying the graveyard, he debates with himself as to whether the scene is classical or romantic, and he concludes: "A classico-romantic scene" (191). He remembers the words of one rose to another (as Beckett remembers them from *Dream,* and ultimately from Diderot's "Lettre à d'Alembert"): "No gardener has died, comma, within rosaceous memory." The gardener makes himself comfortable, and the narrator concludes the book: "So it goes in the world." It is a fitting conclusion for a book situated largely in the world that is despised by Belacqua and satirized by Beckett.

With Belacqua dead, and the other characters far from lively, the narrator is ubiquitous in *Draff,* casting a cheerful light on a funereal tale. He coins a rhyme for the Smeraldina's mourning attire: "One insertion in the Press / Makes minus how many to make a black dress?" (178). He utters a distasteful metaphor for the congress of Hairy and Smerry: "They broke away, carrot plucked from tin of grease" (180).[19] The narrator comments on Hairy's efforts to move the corpse's limbs: "Hairy reached out with his *endless arms* and tugged at the *marble members.* Two nouns and two adjectives" (181; emphasis added). He admires Hairy dressing the grave: "What a nerve the man had to be sure" (182). He pretends to curtail his own narration: "Well, to make a long story short . . ." When the Smeraldina desires a moon, the narrator converts it into a prop: "Like a jack-in-the-box the satellite obliged, let down her shining ladder to the shore" (183). In describing the Smeraldina's happy-go-lucky attitude toward the dead Belacqua, the narrator functions as a footnote: "Belacqua had come unstuck like his own favour of veronica in What a Misfortune" (184). Yet the two actual footnotes in this story are singularly unenlightening. The first one compares the Smeraldina's "least clandestine" reaction to Belacqua's death, with the "bella mensogna" of an unnamed poet.[20] The second footnote objects to the Smeraldina's view that she would gratify Belacqua with Hairy, as he had gratified Lucy with her: "A most foully false analogy" (190). When footnotes alone defend the deceased, it is small wonder that Hairy has forgotten the gravestone inscription that Belacqua had endorsed.

Opening on Dante and closing on garbage (draff), *More Pricks Than Kicks* was not designated by Beckett as a novel, but as a group of stories. Nevertheless, the stories concentrate on a single picaresque protagonist whose emotions are screened by a narrator's intricate festoons of words. Less stylistically varied than *Dream,* the stories give the impression of the continuous life of Belacqua, a poet who scorns the world but not its women, who enjoys his own mind most when it is nearly empty, who imbibes alcoholic sustenance in out-of-the-way pubs, and who succumbs with style to death. In spite of three marriages, Beckett's Belacqua shies away from sexual consummation; his family name Shuah links him to biblical onanism; his hobby— not quite the right word—is voyeurism, and he is swiftly replaced by Hairy in the Smeraldina's bed. In Jeri Kroll's succinct phrase: "[Belacqua's is an] approach-avoidance reaction . . . toward sex" (53). Although the imposition of narcissism upon love is explicit in *Dream* and not in *More Pricks,* the implications are nevertheless present. *More Pricks* lacks the inner turmoil of *Dream,* and it evinces a more sustained contempt for how it goes in the world, along with a more sustained immersion in that world. The stories are uneven in quality, with the first the most moving—*Dante and the Lobster.* Since the last story takes place after Belacqua's death, a retrospective atmosphere hints at life's futility.

In early September 1933, Beckett sent ten stories of *More Pricks* to Chatto and Windus, the publishers of his *Proust.* By October, he received a contract for publication. That same month Beckett sent his friend Mac-Greevy an early version of the poem "Serena III."

"Serena III"

In close proximity to the erotic adventures of Belacqua of *More Pricks,* "Serena III" is the only one of the three serenas to treat love, however indirectly. A self-address of the persona, the poem traces an evening itinerary through Dublin and the area southeast of the city, where moon, stars, and structures pulsate erotically. Twenty-seven unpunctuated lines of differing length accumulate into four stanzas. Spurning the first-person singular, the persona registers progress through a series of imperative verbs. Although the phrase "that's the idea" occurs twice in the last sentence, it is hard to pinpoint "the idea" of the poem. Gross's glosses add up to her subtitle, "The Issueless Predicament," but that theme can summarize almost any Beckett poem.

A variant is found with MacGreevy's letters at TCD, but no manuscript is extant for "Serena III," which became the tenth poem of *Echo's Bones.* Beckett's HRC copy is inscribed "James Barry," but no one seems to be able to link that eighteenth-century Irish painter with the poem.

Unlike Dante's Belacqua, the poem's persona admonishes himself to "keep on the move."

"Echo's Bones" (story)

Beckett's narrator of fiction kept on the move by situating Belacqua in an afterworld, haunted by Dantean allusions. As Dante's Belacqua, in fetal position at the foot of Mount Purgatory, relives his life, Beckett's Belacqua, in fetal position on a fence, is afflicted with an afterlife "dose of expiation." Like *Dante and the Lobster,* with its tripartite division into lunch, lesson, and lobster, "Echo's Bones" is presented as a triptych, but the narrator gives unequal attention to the story's three incidents.

The first person to interrupt Belacqua while he is happily smoking on the fence is a seductress called Zaborovna Privet, whom he reluctantly follows to her home, only to be ravished as though he were still the prey of earthly women. After this event Belacqua finds himself back on the fence with another cigar, and he is accosted by a bald giant, Lord Gall of Wormwood. Manhandled and harangued, Belacqua learns that he is to replace the impotent giant in the bed of his wife Moll, in order to beget an heir. This duty eventuates in the birth of a girl, and the narrator repeats a familiar sentence: "So it goes in the world," even though Belacqua is no longer in the world.

The third adventure begins: "To proceed then again more or less as see above, page 7, paragraph 2, Belacqua, at last on the threshold of total extinction as a free corpse, sat on his own headstone, drumming his heels irritably against the R. I. P" (19). That designated paragraph marks the boundary between Belacqua's first and second postmortem erotic adventures, but the third panel of the triptych modulates the key away from sexuality. Belacqua surveys the graveyard, and, like the groundsman of *Draff,* he pronounces the scene classico-romantic; he also intones the groundsman's words (derived from Diderot) about no gardener dying in rosaceous memory. Belacqua catches a glimpse of the Alba in the conning tower of a submarine; she is spearing fish.

Soon Belacqua is joined by the groundsman himself, now christened Mick Doyle. He intends to dig up Belacqua's grave, and, despite the occupant's assurance that nothing of value is there concealed, the two beings set to work. Mick is afflicted with digestive spasms that necessitate his frequent exits, and yet the conversation of the two is rarely interrupted for long. An

---

"Echo's Bones," which Beckett intended as the eleventh story of *MPTK,* exists in typescript at NhD, but a copy is available at RUL. The story "Echo's Bones" has not been published, but C. J. Ackerley prints the opening paragraph in item 99.6 of "Demented Particulars" (1998), his annotations of *Murphy.*

intrepid Belacqua hacks open his coffin and looks inside, while Doyle peers down from ground level. The narrator exclaims at the scene in a run-on sentence:

> Belacqua petrified link-boy, the scattered guts of ground, the ponderous anxiomaniac on the brink in the nude like a fly on the edge of a sore (1), in the grey flaws of tramontane the hundreds of headstones sighing and gleaming like bones, the hamper, mattock, shovel, spade and axe cabal of vipers, most malignant, and the clothes-basket a coffin in its own way, and of course the prescribed hush of great solemnity broken only by the sea convulsed in one of those dreams, ah one of those dreams, the submarine wallowing and hooting on the beach like an absolute fool, and dawn toddling down the mountains. (20)

A footnote adds: "Indeed there was more than a little of the gardener in *Draff* about Doyle." The note does not add that there was more than a little of Beckett's obsessions in this elaborate sentence. Not only does it offer our final view of Belacqua and the bones of the story title "Echo's Bones," but it also reviews familiar images like the comparison of man to a fly, death as a temporary state, life as a dream, landscape as a mirror of the mind, and, in the footnote, a recollection of man's propensity to violence. Although "Echo's Bones" rattles and rambles, the purgatorial triptych repeats the temptations of Belacqua in the world: the choice between a love that leads to domesticity or the substitution in another's domesticity; the role of love as a window into other worlds. With Belacqua returned to the void, the Alba on her submarine sails away: "To hell with him so." The story closes on the narrator's comment about a demented groundsman: "So it goes in the world"— for the third unenlightening time.

Nowhere in the published *Pricks* is the narrator quite so ubiquitous as in the unpublished "Echo's Bones," undercutting his protagonist—"Death does not seem to have improved Belacqua" (16), dedicating two footnotes to Shakespeare, selecting such bizarre elements of landscape as a dying cow or an ostrich named Strauss, adjuring the reader to "bear in mind," and concluding inconclusively with "So it goes in the world."

"Echo's Bones," eschewing the lugubrious for the farcical, does not seek to penetrate into human death. If, as in the other stories, "the early prose seems to be an attempt to exorcize the Beckett that was or might have been Belacqua" (Harvey, 332) the story "Echo's Bones" seems rather to shy away from an experience of death. "Echo's Bones" continues the ironic guard diversely adopted by the narrators of *Dream* and *More Pricks,* and, often, by the floating personae of the poems. For the first time, however, death is rendered as a farcical fiasco, in which the corpse of Belacqua sits on the fence literally, while he is figuratively between two worlds. The purgatorial penance of Dante's Belacqua is transformed by Beckett into pointless repetition of earth-type events, with the added pleasure of choice cigars.

Beckett wished "Echo's Bones" to be published as the last story of the *More Pricks* volume, but the editor of Chatto and Windus rejected it: "'Echo's Bones' would, I am sure, lose [*More Pricks*] a great many readers. People will shudder and be puzzled and confused; and they won't be keen on analysing the shudder" (qtd. in Knowlson, 168). Beckett confided his disappointment to MacGreevy (in a letter of December 6, 1933): "'Echo's Bones' [is] the story into which I put all I knew and plenty that I was better still aware of, [and its rejection] discouraged me profoundly, au point meme de provoquer ce qui suit." What followed was the poem for which he retrieved the title of the story, which would subsequently embrace his collection of thirteen poems. In contrast to many of the opaque, erudite poems of that slim volume, this lyric sings through a festoon of sounds.

"Echo's Bones" (poem)

In the volume at HRC, Beckett has noted: "Echo's Bones were turned to stone. Ovid Metamorphoses." The poem itself consists of five unrhymed lines that can be scanned as rough pentameters. A persona, revealed only by a single first-person pronoun in the opening line, walks all day on an asylum-grave, while living beings revel even as they disintegrate, a prey to maggots. Although the poem's opening word presents death as "asylum," the actual process of flesh decaying is colloquialized as breaking wind and running a gauntlet. Beckett softens these images by a musical interplay of fricative and sibilant consonants.

Evidence is lacking, but it may be this poem that inspired Beckett to collect earlier poems into a single volume, which he titled *Echo's Bones and Other Precipitates*. My dating of the remaining poems is approximate.

"Malacoda"

"Malacoda" and "Da Tagte Es" were provoked by the death of Beckett's father on June 26, 1933.[21] Harvey is ever helpful, but the slender lyric cannot

---

A variant of "Echo's Bones" is included in a December 1933 letter to MacGreevy, and a version is at ICU. "Echo's Bones" was first published as the final poem in the collection *Echo's Bones* and has been frequently republished.

Entitled "The Undertaker's Man" in Beckett's list for Con Leventhal, "Malacoda" is the eleventh poem of *Echo's Bones,* which he kept revising (Knowlson, 209). Beckett annotates the HRC copy with the single word: "Father." The poem was reprinted in *transition* (June 1936) and is found in *Poems.*

be encapsulated in his words, "tributes of a son to his cherished father" (111). The poem itself does not identify the deceased nor a son figure. Instead, grief envelops an unidentified "she."

Beckett borrows not only the infernal undertakers, Malacoda and Scarmilion from Dante's *Inferno* (Cantos XXI and XXII), but he also structures the poem as a verbal triptych, in the manner of Dante. The poem's first word is "Thrice," and the three stanzas are linked through the undertaker's three visits for his three tasks, each one with a verse line of its own—to measure, to coffin, to cover. At these three intrusions, the mourner's grief rises climactically: "hear she may see she need not," "hear she must see she need not," "hear she must see she must." Perhaps it is the infernal Charon who clears the decks for the final voyage, but, as in *Dante and the Lobster*, a terminal voice rebels—"nay." Nay to the nautical half-mast, nay to the several *musts*, nay to the matter-of-fact and insensitive undertaker, impassive in his bowler hat. Nay, by implication, to the obscenity of death.[22]

Although "Malacoda," like earlier Beckett poems, leans on literature and painting, Beckett nevertheless infuses the poem with sufficient feeling to rise above his erudition. A few subversive details may be discerned; Beckett turns Dante's black pitch into lilies; Malacoda's trumpet-rump is muted to a Keatsian sigh through the heavy air; Dante's deceitful Malacoda becomes "incorruptible." In "Malacoda" a bowler hat is a shield of reason against feeling, since funereal ceremony is merely "expert." The traditional funeral wreathe shrinks to a painting, replete with imago or perfect state of an insect, a Beckettian analogue for man. Lacking a persona, the poem "Malacoda," literally "bad end," is acerbic about the appurtenances of death, but sensitive to the grief of the living "she."

"Da Tagte Es"

This poem is subversive of its source, a forty-line poem of the German troubadour Walther von der Vogelweide. The medieval poem is an aubade, with dawn interrupting a dream of an idyllic love; it contains the line "do taget ez und muos ich wachen" [Then dawn broke, and I had to wake]. Beckett in contrast opens on an imperious command to a "you" who is at once a shipborne man waving farewell and a corpse whose breath can no longer mist a glass—incongruously above rather than below his eyes. The implied dawn is death, at once an intrusion and a relief, in this compact quatrain that contains the only rhymes in *Echo's Bones*.

"Da Tagte Es" is the twelfth poem of *Echo's Bones,* where it was first published in 1935. Beckett annotates the HRC copy: "Walther von der Vogelweide," the medieval German poet, whose phrase supplied the title.

"The Vulture"

Goethe in his "Vulture" compares his own song to the bird that hovers over the clouds in search of prey. Beckett's simile is subtler; his vulture devours the living world in order to internalize it. In Harvey's explication the six-line poem traces an art that moves from objective reality to subjective reality, to desubjectification. As the opening poem of *Echo's Bones,* the lines are unusually even, approximating pentameters.

The first two-line stanza opposes and yet blends "*his* hunger" and "*my* skull," as the artistic condition, and the second line—"my skull shell of sky and earth"—presents the skullscape that will loom so large in Beckett's later writing (Ben-Zvi, 1986, 4). The second two-line stanza resonates biblically in the four repetitions of "Take up thy bed and walk." In the Bible the phrase announces a life-enhancing cure, but in Beckett's poem the walk leads to the final two-line stanza in which the living and their abode may serve the artist only after they are reduced to offal. The artist's hunger to create is vulture-like in preying on the living, but Beckett's vulture also preys on his very hunger.[23]

Not until 1934, when various publishers rejected various poems, did Beckett select and arrange thirteen of his poems into a single volume. The connotation of bad luck, based on the thirteen participants of the Last Supper, was already exploited by Beckett in the thirteen lines of "Yoke of Liberty," and in the special significance of line 13 of "Alba," "Dortmunder," and "Sanies I." His thirteen poems, written over a period of five years, were finally grouped as *Echo's Bones,* where the short final poem encapsulates several of the images of the preceding longer poems—the journey, the wind, the fortuitous amalgamation of sense data.

The *Metamorphoses* of Ovid presents an Echo, spurned by Narcissus, who withers away until only her voice and bones remain. The vocability of Beckett's poems is striking, for all their obscurity; they resemble Echo's bones in their song. They are also literal echoes; no poem is without an echo of the European literary tradition—whether of a particular poem or a lyric form. Seven poems resort to troubadour genres; these tend also to echo life-journeys in their ramblings through the geography of Dublin, London, and Paris.[24] Almost all the poems are enigmatic and susceptible of different interpretations.

Beckett's full title for the volume is *Echo's Bones and Other Precipitates.* The word *precipitate* derives from Latin *prae* and *caput,* or "headlong." The implication therefore is that these poems sprang headlong from

---

"The Vulture" is the first poem in *Echo's Bones,* where it was first published in 1935. In the HRC volume Beckett notes: "Not without reference to Goethe's Der Geiergleich."

the unconscious of their author, like the surrealist poems that Beckett translated. Yet Knowlson plumbs the evidence in Beckett's correspondence to show that he revised them carefully. Perhaps this meaning of precipitate was another of Beckett's self-protective gestures, denying the weightiness and the all-too-evident erudition of the poems. A precipitate is also "any substance . . . separated from the liquid in which it was previously dissolved, and deposited in the solid state." In this sense, *precipitate* is a synonym of *bone*, after life's fluids have dried into a voice.

Beckett supplied the title for the thirteen poems, but he refused to have the edition illustrated—an irony in view of subsequent imaged editions of his work (Knowlson, 208). It was Beckett who arranged the poems in the sequence that we read. His first and last poems describe a mordant circle, for the volume opens on an offal-eating vulture, and it closes on the bones left by maggots. After "The Vulture" provides the introduction to art, we trace the "realistic" painful journeys of the two enuegs, which may be viewed as a religious diptych: "Enueg I" subverts the Immaculate Conception, "Enueg II" the Crucifixion. Beckett's personae then seek a temporary solace of sensuality in the brief "Alba" and "Dortmunder." These two aubades serve as a caesura between the "Enueg" journeys and those of the two "Sanies" and the three "Serenas." Two elegies punctuate the sequence of "Sanies" and "Serena" travels. The final lyrical "Echo's Bones" is at once a voyage and an elegy. In the energy of its movement, the collection of poems parallels the movements of the Belacqua of the stories, but most of the stories and poems fail to illustrate the line of "Whoroscope"—"That's not moving, that's *moving*."

Although Beckett spent Christmas 1933 with his family in Foxrock, he had already moved his few belongings to London, with a dual purpose in mind—to begin psychoanalysis (which was illegal in Ireland—Knowlson, 167) and to try to earn a living in journalism. While waiting for the publication of *More Pricks Than Kicks*, he tried to publish poems singly or in groups, but no other poem followed "Alba" into print before the appearance of *Echo's Bones* in October 1935. George Reavey's Europa Press (at 13 rue Bonaparte in Paris) printed a slim but handsome volume, which listed three previous publications "by the same author"—"Whoroscope," *Proust, More Pricks Than Kicks*. By the time *Echo's Bones* appeared, Beckett probably had some form of *Murphy* in mind, and perhaps on paper.

1934–36

These Demented Particulars

1934

While undergoing psychoanalysis with Dr. Wilfred Bion in London, Beckett published very little. I do not imply a plausible concatenation between the two activities, or inactivities, but the analysis—often three sessions weekly—must have been draining, emotionally and financially. Although Beckett hoped to earn money from literary journalism, assignments were meager. During the calendar year 1934 Beckett's prose was confined to seven brief book reviews, a longer review essay, two very short stories, and a piece against Irish censorship. When, years later, I asked Beckett to gather his reviews into a book, he demurred on the plea that they were the miserable results of financial onus or friendly obligation.[1] Since no manuscripts are extant, I comment on them in the order of their publication.

Schwabenstreich (Swabian tricks)

Published in the *Spectator* of March 23, 1934, Beckett's *Schwabenstreich* disparages Edward Moerike's *Mozart on the Way to Prague,* by heaping scorn on that author's other works. Moerike's monograph highlights a single day in the life of Mozart. When en route from Vienna to Prague for a production of *Don Giovanni* in 1787, the composer and his wife were received by the Count and Countess Schinzberg. This event is reported by Moerike in some

---

I loathe notes in the format "I made the following important discovery before I read about it in . . ." However, I indulge myself this once: I titled this chapter "These Demented Particulars" *years* before C. J. Ackerley gave the same title to his annotated *Murphy* (1998). We both stole the phrase from Beckett's Mr. Willoughby Kelly in *Murphy,* 13.

twenty thousand words (Beckett's figure) that arouse the reviewer's dis-
dain—"the cartoon," "pretentious context." What infuriates Beckett is
Moerike's presumption in undertaking "to elucidate the ultimate *Kunsttrieb*
of a musical genius" (*Disjecta*, 62). Having previously called Proust's genius
"inexplicable," Beckett evidently considers musical genius similarly inexplicable.

Proust in Pieces

In the June 23, 1934, issue of the *Spectator* Beckett lacerates Albert Feuillerat
for his *Comment Proust a composé son roman* [How Proust wrote his
novel]. Originally, Beckett explains, Proust had planned a three-volume edition of *A la recherche du temps perdu,* but World War I intervened after the
publication of volume 1. As Beckett had good reason to know, a complete
edition was not published until 1924, two years after Proust's death—in sixteen volumes. Feuillerat, according to an ironic Beckett, "was sensible of
grave dissonances and incompatibilities, clashing styles, internecine psy-
chologies and deplorable solutions of continuity, such chaos in short as
could only be explained by the inharmonious collaboration of the two
Prousts, the pre-War and the post-War" (63). Feuillerat therefore hypothe-
sized the original volumes 2 and 3 of *A la recherche* and then found uncor-
rected galleys of volume 2, which accorded well with his hypothesis. Not,
however, with Beckett's view of a Proust who despises "uniformity, homo-
geneity, cohesion . . . verisimilitude." Beckett thunders that Proust's many
revisions are "an intensification, not a disclaimer of the original conception
and method" (65). Basically, Beckett excoriates Feuillerat for re-creating
Proust in his own neat, dull image.

Poems by Rainer Maria Rilke: Translated from the German by J. B. Leishmann

Presumably Beckett was asked to comment in the July 1934 *Criterion* on J. B.
Leishmann's translation of Rilke's *Poems,* but he spends about three-quar-
ters of the essay on Rilke's poems themselves, and the remainder on the
translation. He approves of neither. He reproaches the German poet for
assuming an "interchangeability of Rilke and God" (67). More personal may
be his view of Rilke's "overstatement of the solitude which he cannot make
his element," as Beckett tried to do (66). These are temperamental
disaffinities, but Beckett is precise in citing particulars of Leishmann's deviation from Rilke's German. It is a craftsman's commentary by one who has
translated comparably difficult material, even though Beckett never considered that German was one of his strong languages.

While living in London, Beckett accepted a review assignment from
Dublin, where he also managed to publish a short poem.

Humanistic Quietism

In contrast to the vitriol of his English reviews, Beckett heaps praise on McGreevy's (*sic*) poems in the July–September 1934 issue of *Dublin Magazine*. His opening paragraph declares that all poetry is prayer, "on any note between and inclusive of the publican's whinge and the pharisee's taratantara" (68). After applying this yardstick to several MacGreevy poems, he concludes that the verse is prayer at neither of these extremes. Twice he uses the word *radiance* about MacGreevy's verse, although the quoted lines scarcely confirm such praise. Jumping to another art, Beckett compares Mac-Greevy's verse with Giorgione's painting. Beckett's final paragraph abandons the poetry-is-prayer metaphor for generalizations: "To know so well what one values is, what one's values is . . . not a common faculty;[2] to retain in the acknowledgment of such enrichment the light, calm and finality that composed it is an extremely rare one. I do not know if the first of these can be acquired; I know that the second cannot" (69). Although the title phrase, *Humanistic Quietism,* does not actually appear in the review, that is what Beckett values in MacGreevy's slim volume.

"Gnome"

The title of the quatrain puns on the diminutive size of the poem and the maxims it contains. The opening verb—"spend"—is a self-command by the persona, which winds through its four lines in a single sentence that lacks punctuation. Unusually for Beckett, the rhyme-syllable *ing* terminates each of the four lines; the first two lines form a pentameter couplet, and the last two a tetrameter couplet. Formally precise, the brief apothegm is atypically unguarded about the fruitlessness of travel and study—activities in which Beckett had engaged. "Learning," repeated in the first and fourth lines, is particularly devalued by this erstwhile academic, who would spend years whittling down his erudition, but traces would inevitably remain.

Perhaps Beckett inveigled Seamus O'Sullivan, the editor of *Dublin Magazine,* to publish the poem "Gnome" because he had commissioned a review. Similarly, perhaps Beckett inveigled the editor of the *Bookman* (London) to publish the short story *A Case in a Thousand* because he had already commissioned a piece on recent Irish poetry. Both the story and the article appeared in the August 1934 issue of the *Bookman,* but the story may have been written earlier, and the review was pseudonymously signed "Andrew Belis," a name Beckett retrieved from his maternal grandfather.

Harvey dates "Gnome" in 1932, but I accept Pilling's later date. The quatrain was first published in *Dublin Magazine* (July–September 1934). It is republished in Harvey and in *Poems*. Federman and Fletcher note that it was inspired by Goethe's *Xenien*.

A Case in a Thousand

This short story is a new departure for Beckett in the simplicity of its diction, the lack of erudite reference, and the prevalence of dialogue. The story may have been triggered by Beckett's watching a boy and his nanny, who are mentioned in a letter of August 4, 1932, to MacGreevy: "I wanted to get off with Nanny."[3] Or it may be based on an actual postmortem vigil, as recounted to Beckett by his friend Dr. Geoffrey Thompson (Knowlson, 175). Perhaps influenced by the ambiguous title of and the astringent loneliness in Joyce's *A Painful Case,* Beckett's story may also reflect his own psycho-analysis. Whatever its source or sources, the story reads like an eruption of the unconscious. Yet Beckett was never a surrealist, who would permit his unconscious to range unreined.

The title *A Case in a Thousand* implies unusual symptoms, but it is not quite clear who shows these symptoms. The story opens on one doctor, Surgeon Bor, but it soon focuses on another, Dr. Nye. Both men display a callous professionalism that the narrator treats ironically. However, it is the hovering presence of Mrs. Bray that solicits compassion. Her nameless son is hospitalized with empyema, and, after one operation of "utmost success," surgeon Bor consults with Dr. Nye as to whether to perform surgery a second time. Dr. Nye is also informed about "the Mother Bray saga." By her unremitting vigil at her son's bedside, Mrs. Bray has irritated both nurses and patients. Her visits were therefore restricted to two hours a day, but she spends the rest of each day "watching the window and waiting for it to be time to come up" (*CSP,* 20). When the nurse points down at Mrs. Bray, Dr. Nye recognizes his childhood nanny. Unable to decide about the advisability of the operation, Dr. Nye lies down alongside young Bray, falling into a "therapeutic trance." Mrs. Bray silently watches them until Dr. Nye "reintegrates his pathological outlook." Impatient with her presence, Dr. Nye wishes he could give her the peppermint creams she craved when he was a child who desired to grow up to marry her.

Dr. Nye recommends surgery, the boy dies, and Mrs. Bray thanks him "for all he had done." When Dr. Nye returns from vacation, he learns that Mrs. Bray keeps a daily vigil outside the hospital. Dr. Nye confronts her: "There's something I've been wanting to ask you," and she counters: "I wonder would that be the same thing I've been wanting to tell you ever since that time you stretched out on his bed" (23–24). That "something" is "a trauma at the root of this attachment," and it is teasingly withheld from the reader as "so trivial and intimate that it need not be enlarged on here." After this mystery, the story concludes inconclusively; Dr. Nye gives Mrs. Bray a box

---

A Case in a Thousand *was first published in the* Bookman *(August 1934), along with the article* Recent Irish Poetry. *The story is republished in* CSP.

of peppermint creams, before departing to perform a Wasserman test (for syphilis) on an old school friend. The short tale is burdened with particulars of the medical ambiance, and perhaps with autobiographical detail.

I cannot pretend to interpret the story. As Rubin Rabinovitz remarks, the slender story frustrates the Oedipal reading with which it flirts: "Those who hunt too eagerly for Oedipus may find themselves being lured into the abode of the sphinx" (1984, 69). A doctor, encountering a woman who attracted him as a boy, gets into bed with her son, and his trance may be a metaphor for ejaculation, since a peeping nurse has "seen what she had seen" (22). As in a dream, Mrs. Bray's son is displaced by Dr. Nye, who reverts to an Oedipal son. With the gift of peppermint creams, he may free himself from her, only to occupy himself with the venereal disease of "healthy" sexuality. What can be salvaged from this teasingly Oedipal jumble is Beckett's (as opposed to the narrator's) distaste for doctors, at a time when he himself was undergoing analysis.

Recent Irish Poetry

Although *Recent Irish Poetry* appeared (pseudonymously) in the same issue of the *Bookman* as *A Case in a Thousand,* it abjures the seeming simplicity of the story for Beckett's more habitual allusiveness, incorporating a modernist and European bias. Beckett divides Irish poets into the antiquarians and the others, with the latter aware of the "rupture of the lines of communication" between subject and object in the arts (*Disjecta,* 70). He then proceeds to fling barbed comments at W. B. Yeats, James Stephens, Austin Clarke, and F. R. Higgins, as well as at younger antiquarians. Beckett situates his friend Mac-Greevy between the two groups and praises him as "an existentialist in verse . . . and probably the most important contribution to post-War Irish poetry" (74). Passing quickly over other names, Beckett designates Denis Devlin and Brian Coffee (both his friends, or at least acquaintances) as "the most interesting of the youngest generation of Irish poets," and he quotes a poem about poetry that he himself might have written, so ir- and antirational is it. In the final paragraph, as though resentful that he was asked to review so many books, Beckett merely mentions four poets without comment.

Christmas Reviews

In the Christmas issue of the *Bookman* Beckett published three reviews. *Papini's Dante* bristles at Giovanni Papini, who presumes in *Dante Vivo* to boast that he can understand Dante because he too is Catholic, Florentine, and a

---

Recent Irish Poetry was published under the pseudonym Andrew Belis in the *Bookman* (August 1934). It is reprinted in *Disjecta.*

Reviews in the Christmas 1934 issue of the *Bookman* are reprinted in *Disjecta.*

versifier. Beckett derides Papini's dictum: "The greatest wrong one can do Dante . . . is to classify his most important work as literature," rather than moral teaching. Beckett resists morality to defend literature. He castigates Papini for presenting the poet as lovable rather than readable, when Dante's own Paolo-Francesca episode testifies "to the incompatibility of the two operations" (81).

Ex Cathezra favors Ezra Pound's *Make It New,* in part because Beckett also enthuses over the range of Pound's interests—the Troubadours, the Elizabethans, nineteenth-century French poetry and fiction, imagism, Cavalcanti. Even when Beckett disagrees with Pound, he withholds his habitual scorn. (Attracted to unanimism, he considers Jules Romains "a poet of importance.") Beckett responds favorably, too, to Pound's combative style—"education by provocation, Spartan maieutics" (79).

At this stage of Beckett's career *The Essential and the Incidental* is his most surprising review. Commenting on the miscellaneous items in Sean O'Casey's aptly named *Windfalls,* Beckett dismisses his compatriot's fiction and verse but salvages two "one-act knockabouts" as "the essential O'Casey," whose talent is evident also in *Juno and the Paycock.* The "chassis" of that play is paralleled by the repeated phrase "expediting matters" in "The End of the Beginning" (itself a Beckettian title). What delights Beckett is "dramatic dehiscence, mind and world come asunder in irreparable dissociation" (82). The review reveals Beckett's own taste for farce, which was to blossom—if that is the word—in *Waiting for Godot.*[4]

As a literary journalist, Beckett's start was unremarkable. Several of the reviews are corrosive, ridiculing a Mozart fancier, an academic Proustian, a celebrated German poet (as well as his translator), a moral interpreter of Dante, and a few contemporary Irish poets. Beckett's rare praise is limited to Pound, O'Casey's farce, and the verse of his Irish friends. At the behest of the *Bookman* Beckett also began an essay on Irish censorship. When that period ical ceased publication in 1935, Beckett updated the piece and sent it to George Reavey in Paris for *transition.* It is uncertain whether *Censorship in the Saorstat* failed to reach its destination, or was refused, but it is quite certain that the essay remained unpublished until 1983, when I included it in *Disjecta.*

Censorship in the Saorstat

The essay is Beckett's withering reaction to the Irish Censorship Act of July 16, 1929. His title links censorship with the Gaelic name for Ireland and the

---

Beckett's letter of May 6, 1936, to MacGreevy mentions that *Censorship* was commissioned two years ago by the *Bookman,* which then ceased publication. Beckett gave the typescript of the essay to Lawrence Harvey, who placed it in NhD. It was first published in *Disjecta* (misdated).

iniquitous biblical land of Tsaor (and perhaps puns on "sour state"). Beckett summarizes the four parts of the recent law. Part 1 "emits" Irish definitions of indecency. Part 2 outlines the methods for choosing the five (rather than twelve) members of the Censorship of Publications Board. Beckett is particularly irate that common sense is to be the main criterion of selection, and that board members need not read the whole of any publication in question. Part 3 extends censorship to judicial documents. Part 4 is most distasteful to Beckett. Under the innocuous phrase "other purposes incidental," the law prohibits any mention of contraception. Beckett fumes: "And should [Erin] be found at any time deficient in Cuchulains, at least it shall never be said that they were contraceived" (87). Anticontraception will lead to a Saorstat where "Sterilization of the mind and apotheosis of the litter suit well together. Paradise peopled with virgins and the earth with decorticated multiparas." Listing some fifty censored authors, Beckett later adds his own registry number—465—but he does not mention the title of his book, *More Pricks Than Kicks,* which was forbidden in Ireland from March 31, 1935, to January 1, 1952 (Bair, 666 n. 11). The Censorship Act was repealed in 1967, but Beckett never wavered in his anticensorship stance.

Beckett's reviews trickled to drought in 1935, when he started or developed a story that would grow into the novel *Murphy.* Earlier he had committed to a notebook skeletal ideas for a novel. What Beckett called the "Whoroscope" Notebook (now at RUL) should more accurately be called the *Murphy* Notebook, since half of its notations eventuated in that novel. Deirdre Bair ignores that notebook but declares: "[Beckett] had begun to write a story during the fall of 1934 in London. It was about a young man, a down-and-out intellectual similar to himself, who lived in the World's End [section of London] with a prostitute he had picked up off the street there" (196). It is possible that she is referring (somewhat inaccurately) to the undated and unpublished "Lightning Calculation."

"Lightning Calculation"

The protagonist of "Lightning Calculation" is named Quigley, and he is writing a book, *The Pathetic Fallacy from Avercamp to Campendonk,* although he himself seems to be free of that fallacy. Beckett's brief story, set in London, follows the protagonist from awakening to teatime, and it itemizes four reasons for his low spirits, in addition to his nameless sweetheart, who is a laundress (and not, as Bair reports, a prostitute). Quigley and his

---

The unpublished typescript of "Lightning Calculation" at RUL is undated, but 1934 is probable. C. J. Ackerley's "demented particular" 96.3 (1998) quotes the paragraph on the protagonist Quigley's choice of biscuits, although he omits the word "*so* to impoverish the nature of an assortment . . ."

sweetheart communicate—or rather do not communicate—through their facing windows. Despite a painful toe, Quigley sets out for the National Gallery but is deflected into a Lyons teahouse. There he asks the waitress for assorted biscuits instead of those "all of a piece." While she is gone, he gulps his tea, and on her return Quigley complains of too much milk in his cup, and asks for more tea. Succeeding with this ruse, Quigley then makes a "lightning calculation" that he can eat the five assorted biscuits in (five factorial) 120 ways. This floods him with happiness, but he realizes that if he insists on eating his favorite ginger last, he is reduced to only 24 ways. The story then concludes: "He made the covenant with himself, never again to allow a paltry infatuation, such as his preference for the Ginger, so to impoverish the nature of an assortment, whether of biscuits or of other material. He finished the Osborne and began the Ginger. It was as though his whole being were renewed." It is Quigley's first step in conquering his will—the enterprise at which Murphy will fail.

The story is undated, but it carries Beckett's address—34 Gertrude Street, London SW 10—between September 1934 and his return to Ireland in December 1935. At some uncertain date Beckett began planning a novel, and those plans are contained in RUL 3000. Some thirty-five notes bear on the novel, and since Ackerley (1998) dates them "late in 1935," I assign them to that year.[5]

1935
⌒

Suitably "expurgated, accelerated, improved, and reduced," Ackerley's description of Beckett's notes follows:

> The *Whoroscope* Notebook identifies (#1) "H'" (the horoscope) and "X" (who became Murphy), in terms of the impetus given by H (a "I/-corpus of motives") to X (who has no motive). The germ of the novel seems to be the horoscope as the director of action, and although Beckett states the "Dynamist ethic of X. Keep moving the only virtue" (#2), the first notes indicate that H, "any old oracle to begin with," gradually acquires a fatality until it is "No longer a guide to be consulted but a force to be obeyed" (#3). The notes are cryptic, and difficult to read, but they testify to a process whereby X and H will be clarified side by side, as "monads in the arcanum of circumstance, each apperceiving the other till no more of the *petites perceptions* that are life" (an echo of Leibnitz's *Monadology*), until they perish together, "fire *oder was*." . . . Recognizable bits of [*Murphy*] begin at #16, with X bound with silk scarves to a chair, the chimes and street cries, *quid pro quo,* "all the colours of the rainbow on floor beyond

curtain," and the telephone ringing: it is his fiancée, with something for him (the horoscope), but he does not want her round yet, so he puts her off with a story about a man paying him a visit *on business*, leaves the receiver hanging, and binds himself up tightly for another spell. Night. Fiancée arrives and finds him trussed up, delivery of H, "coyness of this, she insisting on reading out titbits." They separate (tragic touch), "& this is the prologue. But call it not so." There follow several pages of notes, mostly taken from the *Britannica*, testifying to an early intention of defining the action seriously in astrological terms. This faded. . . . There are other pertinent entries, which indicate the way that *Murphy* began as a patchwork piece, if not a cento. . . . These notes [nos. 20–34] were surely compiled in London before Beckett returned home in late 1935, but thereafter the entries are more random, and undated. (1998, xxiii–xxiv)

At one point, too, Beckett planned to pattern the story on Dante's *Divina Commedia,* but he cautioned himself: "keep whole Dantesque analogy out of sight" (8). In *Murphy* Dante is indeed "out of sight," absorbed by the horoscope, which retains its deterministic power.

While working at these notes, Beckett pursued his psychoanalysis with Dr. Bion, but he discontinued it just before Christmas.[6] He began the first of six notebooks with the title *Sasha Murphy* on August 20, 1935 (Knowlson, 193). On September 8, 1935, after being fascinated by old men flying kites at the Round Pond, Beckett wrote his friend MacGreevy: "My next old man, or old young man, not of the big world but of the little world, must be a kite-flyer." This sentence has sometimes been taken as the springboard of *Murphy,* but the unavailable holograph was begun two weeks earlier. In his letter of September 23 to MacGreevy, before Beckett finished the novel, he reveals its ending: "The book closes with an old man flying his kite, if such occasion ever arise" (qtd. in Knowlson, 197). Knowlson cites kite flying as one of "three main sources of inspiration" for *Murphy.* The other two are Bethlem Royal (Mental) Hospital and the horoscope. (Although horoscopes were evidently favored by Bion and Jung, Beckett had already pondered them in his 1930 "Whoroscope.")

In October Beckett accompanied Dr. Bion to a lecture by Jung at the Institute of Psychological Medicine. In answer to a question, Jung spoke of a ten-year-old child who had a premonitory dream of her own death: "She had never been born entirely" (Bair, 209). It was a sentence that Beckett retained.[7]

In December 1935, *Echo's Bones and Other Precipitates* was published by George Reavey in Paris. Beckett left London for the family home at Cooldrinagh, where he continued to work at *Murphy,* imparting his difficulties in letters to MacGreevy. After about a year of vision, revision, and interruption, Beckett completed the novel *Murphy* in June 1936. It proved more difficult than *More Pricks* to publish, necessitating forty-two submissions before Routledge accepted it in December 1937, when Beckett had already moved his domicile to Paris. For many readers, as occasionally for Beckett himself, the "true" Beckett begins with *Murphy*.[8]

1936

Murphy

Murphy is a common Irish name, but Beckett's Murphy puns on Greek *morph,* meaning form, since both the novel and its protagonist are seeking form. The importance of the character Murphy is highlighted by the fact that the novel bears his name, when neither *Dream* nor *More Pricks* is named for Belacqua. Yet Murphy in his mind-body dualism is the son of Belacqua, as well as of the personae of certain poems of *Echo's Bones.* Murphy is torn between the pleasures of the senses and those of the mind—a conflict externalized in two of the book's characters, the prostitute Celia Kelly (despite her doubly celestial name, from Latin *caelum*) and the schizophrenic Mr. Endon (Greek for "within").

Other proper names in *Murphy* are among the novel's "demented particulars." William Tritt has conveniently grouped the names of sixteen characters of *Murphy,* as well as fifteen names to whom these characters refer (202–3). Almost all the names are decipherable. The grotesque go-between Cooper is predicated on Greek *copros* or dung. Celia's grandfather Mr. Willoughby Kelly flies kites in the sky *(caelum),* and, having excellent French, he diminishes Celia to a mere concessive clause without conclusion—*s'il y a.* Murphy's erstwhile mentor, and that mentor's other student, Neary and Wylie, encompasses space and time (near and while), as well as yearning and wiles. In London's Hyde Park Murphy happens upon a handicapped lady at first called Duck but soon rebaptized Rosie Dew, who

---

The manuscript of *Murphy* is in frustratingly private hands, and scholars are not given access to it. The novel was first published by Routledge on March 7, 1938, and has been reprinted by Grove (1957) in the United States and Calder (1963) in Britain. A formidable work of scholarship, with access to Greek, Latin, French, Gaelic, German, and Italian sources, Ackerley's "Demented Particulars" self-confessedly lacks a sense of proportion because "The commentary celebrates small esoteric details as much as the big ones" (1998, iii). It also contains small esoteric errors, such as indexically listing Beckett's late novel as *Ill Seen Ill Heard,* and misspelling his poem as "Ooftisch." Ackerley's annotated *Murphy* is nevertheless indispensable for any serious examination of that novel. Beckett enlisted his friend Alfred Péron for the translation of *Murphy* into French, which was first published by Bordas in 1947, and then reissued by Minuit in 1953.

is a medium in touch with a fourth-century control named Lena (unlisted by Tritt as either character or mere name), and who is employed by a Lord Gall of Wormwood, now wafted to this side of the grave, from Beckett's unpublished story "Echo's Bones." The names of the Russian comedians Bim and Bom, merely mentioned in *Yellow* of *More Pricks*, are affixed to the Clinch brothers (who have an uncle Bum) on the staff of the Magdalen Mental Mercyseat, often abbreviated as MMM.[9] At that institution two other staff members have comic trochaic surnames of unsavory suggestion—Ticklepenny and Killiecrankie. The names of the three main female characters begin with C—Celia, Miss Counihan, and the foul-smelling London landlady, Miss Carridge, a name punning on miscarriage. Both the frustrated Miss Counihan and the waitress Cathleen na Hennessey phonetically recall and thereby ridicule the symbol of Ireland, Cathleen ni Houlihan. The names of four absent characters pivot on puns—the swami Suk, Neary's wife Cox, her lover Sacha Few, and Ticklepenny's Dr. Fist. A few characters, relieved of the demented particularity of a proper name, are designated by their function— a Dublin Civic Guard, a London chandler and his family, a London charwoman, the coroner of an unnamed county. An anonymous "old boy" is "believed to be a retired butler." Yet all this realistic particularity is skimmed over lightly.

Despite its large cast, the plot of *Murphy* deftly intertwines four strands that may be designated by their principal components—Murphy, Celia, the Irish posse, the Mercyseat population. The four strands are linked through *im*plausible concatenation, where chance is as crucial an agent as it is to John Cage. Murphy and Celia meet by chance. Neary and Wylie meet by chance. Murphy and Ticklepenny meet by chance. Nevertheless, all these characters—even Murphy—attempt to impose their will upon events.

By far the thickest plot strand is that of Murphy. Sometimes viewed as though Beckett's title were *Murphy's Quest*, his protagonist is a questor only to the limited extent that he seeks to retreat into what he calls the little world, that is, his rocking-chair, a mental asylum, or Mr. Endon's company. "I am not of the big world, I am of the little world," he boasts (*Murphy*, 178), but most of Beckett's novel presents Murphy's adventures in the big world, that is, with his lover Celia, who sets him on the job path, with his would-be lover Ticklepenny for whose job he volunteers, with officials and patients of the Magdalen Mental Mercyseat (which proves not to be a little enough world), and finally in the inept hands of the menial Cooper, as ashes after his cremation. The Murphy plot rises to its climax in the Fabian chess game between the protagonist and Mr. Endon. Not only is Murphy outretreated by that "aimiable ga-ga," but in his own final admission of defeat Murphy is vouchsafed a view of Nothing—"the Nothing than which in the guffaw of the Abderite naught is more real" (246). That perception of Nothing translates into Murphy's recognition of his inability to dwell in the little world. "Asylum is precisely what Murphy does not find in the asylum" (Hill, 15). Yet his defeat is enigmatized by the narrator's verse rendition of it:

> the last at last seen of him
> himself unseen by him
> and of himself
>
> (250)

The waltz of pronouns and prepositions intertwines Murphy and Mr. Endon, giving temporary form to interiority. In the "real" world, however, Murphy dutifully terminates his duties at the MMM and prepares to return to Celia. However, he dies in the conflagration in his garret.

Murphy's lover is the Irish-born London prostitute Celia Kelly. At the beginning of the novel the physical woman contrasts with the metaphysical man. Celia embarks on the traditional female quest—for happiness with her lover. Since that happiness is threatened by the practice of her profession, Celia impels Murphy to seek remunerative employment. When that necessitates his absence, Celia, through the unwitting agency of "the old boy," undergoes a conversion to will-lessness. The "rests" in her recital of self-awareness as Murphy's "last exile" (234) are paralleled by the "rests" in Murphy's recognition that "Mr Murphy is a speck in Mr. Endon's unseen" (250). Beckett's *Murphy* closes not upon Murphy, but upon Celia and her kite-flying grandfather. She has evolved from an object of desire for the protagonist to an object of compassion for the reader.

In search of Murphy is the Irish posse numbering four (Murphy's lucky number, according to the often mistaken Suk): Murphy's erstwhile teacher Neary, the Neary ex-pupil Wylie, Miss Counihan of the quasi-carnal relations with all three men, and the ever thirsty Cooper, who is sporadically employed by the other three questors. They move piecemeal from Cork to Dublin to London, with a postnovel return more or less *ad quem*. Their plot spins around Murphy, but its shape is derived from Racine's *Andromaque,* since "the gentle passion" is ignited but not requited. Murphy is desired by Miss Counihan who is desired by Neary who is desired by no one, but is respected for his financial resources. During the course of their quest for Murphy, Neary and Wylie become rivals for Miss Counihan's—er, heart— to imitate her own verbal tic. Like the scheming slave of Roman comedy, the one-eyed, triorchous, acathisiac Cooper bounces from one apex to another of the triangle; as Neary appreciates: "Remember there is no triangle, however obtuse, but the circumference of some circle passes through its wretched vertices. Remember also one thief was saved" (213). Saved or not, Murphy is cremated, and his ashes are finally entrusted to the untrustworthy Cooper.

Wylie and Miss Counihan undergo no catharsis through Murphy's death, unless their coupling be deemed catharsis, but Neary's hair turns white, and Cooper is at last able to sit down and to take off his bowler hat.

As the plots thin out, they are more densely populated. Murphy and Celia dominate their respective strands; four characters track the couple down; but the MMM proliferates with patients and staff members, few of whom figure in the plot. Among the hospital inhabitants, Ticklepenny is said to be "the merest pawn in the game between Murphy and his stars" (85), but he is a key pawn. It is he who recognizes our eponymous hero after their brief encounter in *Romiet and Julio* at the Gate Theatre long ago in Dublin, and it is he who accosts Murphy at his London tea-table and who seizes upon Murphy's offer to replace him at the MMM. A distasteful portrait of a fawning homosexual, the pot poet Ticklepenny not only infiltrates Murphy into the MMM, but he also rigs a makeshift gas contrivance for Murphy's comfort, which will lead to his demise.[10] Comfort and demise may ultimately be synonymous for Murphy.

In the interweaving of these four plots Beckett's narrator shows an affinity for what Celia's grandfather Mr. Kelly calls "demented particulars." Not only are we bludgeoned with the names of even incidental characters like the landlady Miss Carridge, the waitress Vera, the Clinch brothers at the asylum, the medium Miss Rosie Dew, her dog Nelly, her contact Lord Gall, and even the pseudonymous Engels sisters by which Miss Counihan announces the Irish posse, but we are also pummeled with street names in various parts of London, along with the dates of events, and the positions of the sun and the moon, between September 12, when Celia telephones Murphy, and October 26, when, Murphy having been cremated, she wheels her kiteless grandfather uphill out of Kensington Gardens. The unmentioned year is 1935, which Beckett himself spent largely in London.

Like dates, Beckett's particularities of place are more bountiful than ever before (or after) in his writing, but they are also colorless. Malcolm Stuart has shown that the places named are "faithful to external reality," but "action is located, rather than localized" (228). Mays notes that the action of *Murphy* is triangulated upon Cork, Dublin, and London. Except for Shandon's Churchyard, Cork lacks a local dimension. Dublin is limited to Wynn's Hotel, Mooney's Pub, a Dalkey tram, and the statue of Cuchulain before the General Post Office. Murphy's dying wish, however, is to have his ashes flushed down the toilet of the Abbey Theatre on Lr. Abbey Street, Dublin (corrected in the typescript from Hawkins Street). In contrast to Dublin, London locations are abundant, but Murphy's presence is triangulated upon a West Brompton unnamed mews (neologically introduced as a mew), a room in Islington, and the MMM, which is just outside of London.[11] Celia's pitch is specified as the junction of Cremorne Road and Stadium Street in

Chelsea, which was within walking distance of where Beckett himself lived in London (Knowlson, 194–97). Quite far from that area, Celia chooses their room in Miss Carridge's abode on Brewery Road in Islington, equidistant between Caledonian and York Roads (now York Way and still adjacent to Pentonville Prison, near Beckett's first address in London); however, as Ackerley (1998) notes, we are never told the number on Brewery Road. Also unnumbered, but also unnamed, is the address of Celia's grandfather in Tyburnia, but he flies his kite at the Round Pond in Kensington Gardens. When the Irish posse alights in London, Miss Counihan installs herself on Gower Street, Wylie in Earl's Court, and Cooper drinks in faraway Wapping. Although Neary feasts in a Chinese restaurant on Glasshouse Street, he beds down in luxury and nudity at an undesignated hotel, where Miss Counihan and Wylie nevertheless track him down. These and other particular places proliferate in twelve chapters of *Murphy,* but there are occasional errors.[12]

In contrast to these particulars that are unique to *Murphy,* chapter 6 of that novel exists on another plane. Announced three times in chapter 1, the description of Murphy's mind is undertaken before half the novel is over. Like the mind of Belacqua before him, Murphy's mind is trine, but this time the three sectors are clearly designated and separated: (1) the light zone contains forms drawn from the material world, which are entirely subject to Murphy's imaginative manipulation; (2) the half-light zone contains unparalleled forms for Murphy's pure contemplation—in a state called "Belacqua bliss" or "Belacqua fantasy"; (3) the dark zone contains a flux of forms, where Murphy is "not free, but a mote in the dark of absolute freedom" (112). In that dark alone consciousness can apparently dissolve into being.

The self-containment of chapter 6 with its epigraph of distorted Spinoza—"Amor intellectualis quo Murphy se ipsum amat" [the intellectual love with which Murphy loves himself]—is testimony to Beckett's new mastery (and implicit mockery) of conventional novel form. Rounding out the character of Murphy, the chapter also serves to build narrative suspense, since chapter 5 closes: "A shocking thing had happened." Not until chapter 8 do we learn that that shocking thing is the suicide of "the old boy." A character who is seen only with his throat cut, "the old boy" is an unacknowledged alter ego for Murphy; his solitude parallels that to which Murphy aspires, and his violent death predicts that of Murphy; his aura envelops Celia as if he were a substitute Murphy.

Similarly, Celia's grandfather Mr. Kelly is an analogue of Murphy, pulled toward the sky, as Murphy is drawn toward nothingness. Mr. Kelly's Christian name, Willoughby, opposes Murphy's desired will-lessness. Mays summarizes the symmetries between the two characters: "Murphy and Mr Kelly in their chairs, differently at rest and moving, indoors and out, out of the sun and in it, at the same time of day (late afternoon), elaborately clothed and elaborately naked, with and without Celia, their different ideals of joining and severing both doomed to failure" (173). Mr. Kelly's final failure "to determine the point at which seen and unseen met" (280) parallels Murphy's final failure to retreat from the big world into the little world.

Murphy is favored with two analogues (the old boy and Mr. Kelly) and two foils—Mr. Endon and Cooper. As Mr. Endon inhabits the inner world toward which Murphy aspires, Cooper inhabits the big world. Murphy loves to sit in his rocker, whereas Cooper cannot sit. Murphy avoids wearing a hat, but Cooper does not remove his bowler. Murphy never imbibes alcohol, whereas Cooper thrives on it. Murphy speaks eloquently, but Cooper utters only twenty-nine words: "The skill is really extraordinary with which analphabetes, especially those of Irish education, circumvent their dread of verbal commitments" (205). As Murphy in his microcosmopolitanism predicts Beckett's subsequent protagonists, Cooper predicts them in his physical appearance. Noteworthy are Beckett's binary symmetries—Murphy and Mr. Endon, Murphy and the old boy, Murphy and Mr. Kelly, Murphy and Cooper, Neary and Wylie, Celia and Miss Counihan, Bim and Bom Clinch.

The character Celia may have escaped Beckett's control, although not his affections. Weary of the novel, Beckett wrote MacGreevy (on July 7, 1936): "I find the people so hateful myself, *even Celia,* that to have you find them lovable surprises and delights me" (emphasis added). One critic calls Celia "a sympathetic human being" (Kenner, 1973, 66), and another "a moving portrait" (Abbott 1973, 46). One critic compares her to Brecht's Mother Courage (Ben-Zvi, 1986, 51), and another to a Madonna (Bryden, 1993, 36). Or Celia is commended for her "stabilizing and almost noble presence" (Brienza, 98). Aidan Higgins writes: "Celia is Beckett's most sweetly realized female character" (Minihan, 11), and John Pilling concurs in his view of "Celia's simple, straightforward, eminently human sentiments and sentimentality" (1994, 32). Beckett's friend Jean-Jacques Mayoux invokes superlatives: "Celia . . . [est] le personnage le plus humain, le plus digne et le plus simplement émouvant de l'oeuvre de Beckett" (1972, 25) [Celia is the most humane, worthy, and simply moving character in Beckett's works]. Entering the novel as a voice on a telephone, which is soon amplified by a list of her nonvital statistics, Celia grows from a figure arousing sexual passion to one who suffers her own passion. Mistrustful of words, she intuitively senses the fates of "the old boy" and, more slowly, of Murphy. Tempted though she is by will-lessness when bound in Murphy's rocker, she nevertheless rises to worldly occasions, without overestimating the importance of that movement. She initiates her transfer into "the old boy's" room; she recognizes Murphy's corpse by the birthmark on his right buttock; she assists her grandfather to fly his kite, and she gathers him up after the failure of his enterprise. Intermittently, she arranges to practice her profession. In our last view of her she climbs uphill against the wind, pushing her grandfather's wheelchair, whose "levers were the tired heart" (282). Despite Beckett's admiration of Belacquan indolence, he has created an active and sympathetic avatar of the good-hearted whore. Even the narrator, unsparing of barbs against all other characters including Murphy, mellows toward Celia.

Comic characters and adroit plotting notwithstanding, Beckett has not written a conventional novel. Its stylistic diversity has been well summed up by André Topia in "Murphy ou Beckett baroque": "recherche de l'effet et du *conceit,* syntaxe très travaillée, lexique empruntant des termes rares aux langages les plus divers, omniprésence des allusions érudits, jeux sur les multiples facettes des mots, brouillage du texte par des citations, télescopage des registres les plus hétérogènes" (93) [search for effects and conceits, elaborate syntax, a lexicon borrowing rare phrases from several languages, widespread learned allusions, polysemy of words, interruption of the text with quotations, telescoping of heterogeneous registers].

The versatility of the narrator enhances the reader's enjoyment of *Murphy.* No longer intruding as "I," or "Mr. Beckett," the narrator is omnipresent. The heir of the omniscient narrator of premodern fiction, he not only knows all about all the characters, but he also dispenses references to painters, sculptors, philosophers, poets, psychologists, scientists, biblical and mythological characters. (Tritt lists ninety-nine such figures, and Ackerley appends others.) The narrator's vocabulary ranges from the colloquial— *doss*—to the recondite—*spado*—with occasional recourse to neologism— "prosodoturfy," "viridescent," and the "apmonia" that Mays reads as the harmony that eludes both Murphy and Beckett. Like his omniscient predecessors, the narrator addresses the reader directly—"gentle reader," "gentle skimmer," and once he even addresses the printer—"Gentle compositor." Like earlier narrators, too, he intrudes his own judgments on characters, even uttering a sweeping evaluation: "All the *puppets* in this book whinge sooner or later, except Murphy, *who is not a puppet*" (122, emphasis added; "puppet" replaces "character" in Beckett's typescript). He informs us when a character is lying, or when Murphy makes bad chess moves. Like some traditional narrators, he slips unobtrusively into indirect interior monologue; Coatzee counts eleven such slips—seven into Murphy, two into Celia, and one each into Rosie Dew and Miss Counihan (24). Unlike the traditional omniscient narrator, however, the narrator of *Murphy* often poses questions without answering them, and he sometimes animates the inanimate, notably sun, moon, trees, barges, biscuits, and the fatal radiator: "The radiator lit with a sigh and blushed, with as much of its asbestos as had not perished"

(173). Moreover, the verbose narrator occasionally withholds information, such as the location of Murphy's seventh scarf and the crucial identity of whoever flushed Murphy's toilet-radiator.

The narrator's primary stylistic weapon is repetition, and around his repetitions Beckett weaves those of the characters. Rubin Rabinovitz lists over five hundred examples of "reiterated passages," as well as over two hundred examples of "recurring episodes, dual sets of objects, characters with similar traits, and various types of symmetrical configurations" (1984, 71). Repetition runs rife through *Murphy,* but then the narrator subverts his own originality from the first paragraph. Steven Connor believes that "the vacuous repetitiveness of Murphy's life is physically enacted in the text's verbal repetitions" (1988, 18–19). Connor pursues that theme to demonstrate that the novel's repetition becomes a self-consuming metaphor for the ultimate repetitiveness of all language, and for its falsification of what it purports to convey. Although several of the characters repeat their own words— particularly Murphy—it remains overwhelmingly the narrator who repeats himself, and he scarcely falsifies his tale.

A single word can be repeated with a different meaning, such as the *sheet* of paper from which Murphy reads his horoscope, and the bed*sheets* of Mr. Kelly and of Neary (a pun already present in *Echo's Bones*). Several repetitions are quite striking—notably the narrator's confessions of his expurgation, acceleration, improvement, and reduction of accounts by Celia, Neary, and Cooper; his promises of revelations in chapter 6; his taunts to the "filthy censors" and their "synecdoche"; his renditions of the characters' verbal tics—Mr. Kelly's "My rump," Bim's "That is entirely up to you, dear," Miss Counihan's "er," Wylie's "quantum of wantum" in a "closed system," and Celia's shying away from the syllable *whore;* his descriptions of how Mr. Kelly and Murphy, respectively, pinion Celia's wrists, but how Wylie catches those of Miss Counihan. When Neary and Wylie first behold Celia, each of them "staggered reverently to his feet" (231). Celia repeats Murphy's experience in the rocking chair, as rendered in the narrator's similar but not identical phrases.

Most importantly, narrative ends repeat beginnings: Murphy is seen first and last (when alive) bound by scarves to his rocking chair.[13] Celia is seen early and late in the company of her grandfather, who early and late in his bed finds difficulty in summoning his body parts. An objective correlative for such circling is Wylie's handkerchief, which moves from pocket, to mouth, ear, nose, eyes, and back to his pocket (227). In focusing on life's circularity, the coroner hints at the propensity of elements of the novel to circle around to their beginnings: "How beautiful in a way . . . birthmark, deathmark. I mean, rounding off the life, somehow, don't you think, full circle" (267). The birthmark also rounds off the Celia-Murphy union, since it is this same birthmark that Celia notices when she rescues Murphy from his rocking chair, on their first meeting in the book. On the first page of the novel a street-cry sounds like Latin "Quid pro quo." The final words of the novel belong to the cry of the park ranger: "All out." Direct quotation is one of the narrator's artifices, to which he finally comes full circle.

Repetition is the narrator's most obstreperous hallmark, and one of its rhythmic manifestations is a string of words in a series. The novel's opening paragraph plunges us into a series—Murphy's eating, drinking, sleeping, and putting his clothes on and off. A few such series catalogs are pounded at us, for example, Murphy's duties at the MMM: "He would be expected to make beds, carry trays, clean up regular messes, clean up casual messes, read thermometers, write charts, wash the bedridden, give medicine, hound down its effects, warm bedpans, cool fevers, boil gags, sterilize when in doubt, honour and obey the male sister, wait hand, foot and mouth on the doctor when he came, look pleasant" (158). Given the duties, the last phrase is ironically climactic. The narrator again summons a series of phrases to render another climax, when the acathisiac Cooper first sits: "He placed his ancient bowler crown upward on the step, squatted high above it, took careful aim through his crutch, closed his eye, set his teeth, flung his feet forward into space and came down on his buttocks with the force of a pile ram" (273). A little later the narrator is almost filmic in his depiction of Cooper's final disposition of Murphy's ashes; he summons first a series of active verbs but concludes with a series of concrete nouns, for the body, mind, and soul of Murphy are "swept away with the sand, the beer, the butts, the glass, the matches, the spits, the vomit" (275). Noun, verb, or phrase—these series accrete so much detail that they subvert surface realism.

Series and repetitions straddle sense and sound, but the narrator also invests the latter with devices that are favored by poets rather than novelists. Rhyme: a "scarlet harlot" had inhabited Murphy's room, Mr. Kelly lived in "dingy, stingy" repose, but "throttled [sounds] jostled" in his throat. More frequent is the narrator's recourse to alliteration, which blends with assonance in the novel's second paragraph to praise the rocking chair "guaranteed not to crack, warp, shrink, corrode, or creak at night." Miss Carridge's calculated reaction to the suicide of "the old boy" hisses at us: "She slithered to a stop on the steps of the house and screeched for the police" (135). Other fillips of the narrator's sound play beggar categorization: Murphy's uncle is a "well-to-do ne'er'do-well" (17), Mr. Kelly's kite is an "asterisk of sticks" (115, 277), and Miss Counihan addresses Cooper while "stepping out of her step-ins" (204), thus revealing her "hot buttered buttocks" (208).

Murphy never mentions Joyce, but he shares the latter's love of puns, crowned in the barmaid-porter joke. We seem to be in Murphy's mind when he blames the Almighty: "What but an imperfect sense of humour could have made such a mess of chaos. In the beginning was the pun" (65). It is, however, the narrator who puns on "felt" as emotion and cloth, on making good and making no bones, as well as on job and Job. Of the 124 puns indexed by Ackerley, most can be ascribed to the narrator.

The narrator thrusts upon Murphy some of his own erudition, since the protagonist is a onetime theologian and Latinist; a onetime traveler in Paris, Toulon, and Hanover; a onetime owner of books, pictures, postcards, musical scores, and instruments. In the novel's present Murphy is a connoisseur of architecture, painting, and music; an amateur of mathematics, philosophy, and neurology; a devotee of astrology; an accomplished chess player; a discriminating linguist, suiting his vocabulary to his audience, and correctly deriving *cretin* from *Christian, gas* from *chaos.* Sardonically, the narrator encapsulates Murphy's erudition in a phrase that mirrors his own prose: "[Murphy was] one of the elect, who require everything to remind them of something else" (63).

The Bible and Dante are the groundwork of interpretation of Beckett's poems, but the former gave way to the latter in both *Dream* and *More Pricks.* Although Beckett's original notes relied upon Dante, the published *Murphy* restores priority to the Bible, which even serves as a weapon in the hands of Miss Carridge. More telling verbally than physically, however, the Bible is on the lips of several characters—Neary, Wylie, Murphy, Celia quoting Murphy—as well as the narrator. The novel's first sentence plays on Ecclesiastes: "The sun shone, having no alternative, on the nothing new"— "There is no new thing under the sun." The Irish posse exhibit the residue of a Christian education. Neary is to Miss Counihan as Dives to Lazarus; Wylie bequeaths to Neary his view of the horseleach's daughter as a closed system, whose "quantum of wantum" cannot vary; Neary writes of Jezebel Counihan and Judas Wylie, and Cooper has no difficulty in serving two masters. It is Neary who subtends a crucial afterthought to a remark about triangles: "Remember also one thief was saved" (213). Murphy himself quotes Scripture when it suits him; he reassures Celia: "Providence will provide," but the narrator reflects mordantly on its failure to do so. Murphy nevertheless continues to cite the Bible: "The hireling fleeth because he is an hireling." and "What shall a man give in exchange for Celia?" (22). The narrator compares Murphy to Christ; he "turn[s his] other cheek to the dust," and when Murphy falls from the rocking chair, he lies in a crucified position. It is again the narrator who recalls that, as a theological student Murphy used to ponder Christ's Parthian shaft: *It is finished* (72). Murphy, feeling the gulf between the MMM patients and himself, is situated "at the foot of the cross," and he is "stigmatised" in Mr. Endon's eyes. The biblical proliferation is a form of ironic subversion, and yet a sufficiently serious residue remains to tint Murphy as a martyr.

Most remarkable is the narrator's invocation of the Bible when he addresses the reader directly in defense of the sadistic Bom at the MMM: "Oh, monster of humanity and enlightenment, despairing of a world in which the only natural allies are the fools and knaves, a mankind sterile with self-complicity, admire Bom feeling dimly for once what you feel acutely so often, Pilate's hands rustling in his mind" (170). This extraordinary sentence assumes self-blame on the part of the reader, for we are all sinners. By and large, however, the narrator subverts the Bible by parenthetical reference, even while he represents Murphy as an ironic Christ-figure. The narrator is consistently inconsistent toward his protagonist.

The narrator of *Murphy* has access to the minds of the characters. Murphy alone commands an entire chapter, but the narrator penetrates Murphy's mind elsewhere, particularly in his pleasure at the barmaid-porter joke, his Belacqua fantasy, and in his displeasure after his chess defeat. The narrator even mentions what fails to cross the characters' minds, such as an oil stove for Murphy's garret, and the final lyrical kite scene that Celia fails to observe. The narrator also accords attention to the minds of Mr. Kelly, Neary, Cooper, Miss Rosie Dew, Miss Carridge, the nameless coroner, and above all Celia. On first presentation "her brain . . . was not very large" (18), and it concentrates on practicalities, but once in the old boy's room and in Murphy's rocker, she is "In the cell of her mind, teasing the oakum of her history" (149). Without transition, the narrator plunges her into that history; immediately after her tale to the Irish posse: "Her cot had a high rail all the way round" (235). It might be a metaphor for her life.

For the first time in Beckett's fiction, the display of erudition does not impede narration, and for the first time in Beckett's fiction, narration is enlivened by a dazzling variety of dialogue. The novel's first conversational exchange occurs in flashback, upon Murphy's departure from Neary's Grove in Cork; although nominally about love, the "sparkling rally" admits phrases of painting, metaphysics, Victorian fiction; and it serves as exposition. Several later dialogue duets are largely informational—Celia and her bedded grandfather, Neary and Wylie in Dublin, Murphy and Ticklepenny in the restaurant. Sometimes the characters barely hear one another, but at other times conversations position one participant as a figure of authority— the Dublin Civic Guard over Wylie, Murphy over the waitress Vera, Murphy over Ticklepenny, Murphy over Miss Rosie Dew, Bom over Murphy and Ticklepenny, Neary over Wylie and Miss Counihan. The dialogue in Brewery Road is a highly oblique jousting for dominance among several characters, after which Celia remains silent for sixty hours.[14] The final dialogue in the mortuary is an even more populous jousting for authority, which also ends in a draw. Afterward Celia speaks only six more words in the novel.

In their first face-to-face conversation Murphy pleads with Celia: "Oh, do not let us fence, . . . at least let it never be said that we fenced" (35). Yet some of the crisp humor of the book lies in verbal fencing, one aspect of which is jousting for authority. There is, however, one example of a very different kind of dialogue, when Miss Rosie Dew presents herself and her "rutting cur" to Murphy:

> The oui-ja is how I live, I come all the way from Paddington to feed the poor dear sheep and now I dare not let her off, here is my card, Rosie Dew, single woman, by appointment to Lord Gall of Wormwood, perhaps you know him, a charming man, he sends me objects he is in a painful position, spado of long standing tail male special he seeks testamentary pentimenti from the *au-delà*, how she strains to be off and away, the protector is a man of iron and will not bar, plunge the fever of her blood in the Serpentine or the Long Water for that matter, like Shelley's first wife you know, her name was Harriet was it not, not Nelly, Shelley, Nelly, oh Nelly how I ADORE you. (99)

The run-on sentence opens introductorily enough, except for the punning Franco-German affirmative of "oui-ja." Lord Gall, however, explodes the syntax of Miss Dew, his impotence contrasting and intertwining with the sexual heat of her dog. A long standing tail is what Lord Gall cannot muster, whereas Nelly needs the nearby water to cool hers; geography and rhyme conspire to recall the suicide of Harriet Shelley. Although the paragraph rambles without structure, it predicts the associationism of Lucky's more subtly structured monologue in *Waiting for Godot*.

I hope that I have not made Beckett's *Murphy* sound like a grab bag of literary techniques, (as other critics make it sound like a grab bag of Beckett's reading), so I wish to state categorically that it is an enjoyable novel. Although my commentary on *Murphy* is the longest in this book, that does not mean that the novel is Beckett's most important work. Rather, its mastery of "demented particulars" lends itself to particular commentary. *Murphy* is a funny and volatile novel, sparkling in repartee, startling in juxtapositions, shuttling its puppets from pillar to particular, and occasionally risking lyrical passages. It is at the same time a serious novel, as Dylan Thomas realized soon after its 1938 publication: "It is serious because it is, mainly, the study of a complex and oddly tragic character who cannot reconcile the unreality of the seen world with the reality of the unseen, and who, through scorn and neglect of 'normal' society, drifts into the society of the certified abnormal in his search for 'a little world'" (454). Moreover, the seen world is presented with devastating wit, and the unseen in mellifluous but unsentimental prose.

Soon after the completion of *Murphy,* the series of rejections began, making a mockery of the repetitions *in* the novel, but acceptance eventually arrived in December 1937. In the interim Beckett wrote little, but he renewed

Dublin friendships, notably with the painter/writer Jack B. Yeats, whom he first met in 1931, and whose *Amaranthers* he reviewed in an act of homage.

An Imaginative Work!

A blend of admiration and arrogance, Beckett's review opens with a throwback to the Joyce essay of 1929. As that piece pontificates: "Literary criticism is not book-keeping," this piece affirms: "The chartered recountants take the thing to pieces and put it together again" (*Disjecta*, 89). Art, for Beckett, is something incalculable and indivisible. *The Amaranthers* embeds the adventures of James Guilfoyle in the imaginative life of a mountain people. A rambling work in sharp contrast to the carefully plotted *Murphy*, it may have attracted Beckett for that reason. He (unconvincingly) compares Yeats's irony and discontinuity to that of Ariosto. Perhaps retorting to some publishers' rejections of *Murphy*, he declares that Yeats's book is neither allegory, symbol, nor satire. He concludes with a quotation from *The Amaranthers* that praises the work of the imagination. Hence the title of Beckett's review of Yeats's novel, which obliquely epitomizes his own novel as well.

Knowlson summarizes Beckett's frustrations while penury kept him at the family home near Dublin. On the one hand, he resented being forced to live at home, subject to questions about a future career. On the other hand, he apparently tried to lead an active social life, with old and new acquaintances. Mary Manning Howe had been his friend since childhood, and although she had moved to Boston, she spent the summer in Dublin in the company of two young American women. Beckett fell in love with one of them; her failure to reciprocate was the occasion of a new direction in his poetry—more simple and direct than heretofore.

"Cascando"

The title "Cascando" is a musical term that denotes diminishing volume and slowing tempo. Harvey elides meaning into technique: "Beckett works repe-

---

First published in *Dublin Magazine* (July–September 1936), Beckett's *An Imaginative Work!* is reprinted in *Disjecta*.

The dating of "Cascando" is controversial, since Admussen (26) notes that a version rejected by *Dublin Magazine* in 1931 is held at TCD. However, the poem is unmentioned in any document prior to 1936, and stylistically "Cascando" does not contain the obscure erudition of Beckett's 1931 poems. Knowlson and Pilling believe it to date from July 1936, and I accept that date of composition. Variant versions are found in TCD and the Leventhal papers at HRC. Cronin (235) quotes the TCD version. The final typescript is at NhD. Before embarking for Germany, on August 18, 1936, Beckett translated the poem into German, and that version is at RUL. The translation is at once clearer and less wordy than the English. First published (in English) in *Dublin Magazine* (October–December 1936), "Cascando" is republished by Harvey, and is included in *Poems*.

tition into the fabric of his poem, where it suggests more effectively than semantic content the monotony and recurrence that robs reality of its substance" (176). However, I would argue that "Cascando" conveys the recurrence, but not necessarily the monotony of love, which remains an elusive reality. Each recurrence of love, however knowing, is never an exact repetition, and Beckett's verbal repetitions are subtly nuanced. Gross, who does not appreciate this, cites the relevance of Ecclesiastes 3: "To every thing there is a season . . . a time to keep silence, and a time to speak: A time to love." Speaking and loving are problematized in Beckett's poem.

Written in unpunctuated free verse, the eight stanzas of "Cascando" fall into three unequal parts, which Beckett numbers. Part 1 contains three stanzas, part 2 contains four, and part 3 contains a single line. Each of the first two stanzas is an unpunctuated question, which implies a desire to reduce love to an "occasion of/wordshed," that is, stripping language down. The longer, more imaged third stanza evokes the pain of unrequited love, even while trying to achieve some distance from it. In that stanza, too, the erosive effect of time is conveyed through five gerunds and the enumeration, on successive lines, of nine days, nine months, nine lives.

The phrase "saying again," already sounded in part 1, opens part 2, which returns to the frustrations of this particular love, however familiar they may be, and however final they may seem, with six repetitions of *last*. The word *love* threads through all four stanzas of part 2, at once the most personal of experiences and the most hackneyed of words. The second stanza of part 2 fuses emotion with its expression:

> the churn of stale words in the heart again
> love love love thud of the old plunger
> pestling the unalterable
> whey of words

Graphically simple, the old theme dissolves into an awareness that it *is* an old theme. Even as the quatrain laments its staleness, it presents fresh images—the heart as a plunger, the (punning) whey of words; moreover, the heart-thud is onomatopoetic. The third stanza of part 2 returns to the specifics of the lover's ambivalent situation, recapitulating the "pretending" of the first stanza. It is uncertain as to whether that pretense englobes the final two-line stanza of part 2, or whether the persona and all other lovers are an absolute construction in their similar behavior. (Significantly, other lovers are relativized as *that* rather than *who*. In Beckett's German translation, the couplet begins with "So," which links it with what precedes.)

The single line of part 3—"unless they love you"—eliminates the speaker, who is therefore left in a position of pretense, as to loving or being loved.

Pilling quotes the MacGreevy poem, to which "Cascando" responds: "I do not love you as I have loved / The loves I have loved— / As I may love others" (1997, 245). However, Beckett's echoic lines are never that banal and are always more musical. Beckett's lyric poem cannot quite sever intense experience from the need to articulate it. "Cascando" carries the deterioration of love, even as the pain increases; while he suffers, the persona watches himself suffer. Part 1 blends expression and emotion; part 2 fuses emotion into expression; the single line of part 3 is the fragile emotional conclusion. The whole poem announces a new trend in Beckett's verse: personal without being recondite; resonant without being self-conscious; sparely imaged and lexically simple. These qualities will characterize Beckett's French verse of the next few years, but rarely with such control or resonance.

It is not surprising that "Cascando" quickly found its way into print, in contrast to the poems of *Echo's Bones*. Beckett himself may have been unaware of how radically "Cascando" differed from his earlier verse, preoccupied as he was with leaving the family home. Even Knowlson casts no light on how Beckett persuaded his mother to subsidize an extended stay in Germany, and yet he must have had it in mind for some time. Four notebooks at RUL testify to his preoccupation with improving his German (two largely devoted to Goethe's *Faust*). Moreover, why did he choose Germany, where he no longer had relatives? The journal of his six-month sojourn suggests that he might have contemplated a career as an art historian or critic. Whatever his purpose, Beckett left Ireland on September 29, boarding a ship that would carry him to Hamburg, via Le Havre. He visited museums and galleries in Leipzig, Dresden, Berlin, and Munich, and he also took cultural side trips, despite the gathering momentum of Nazism. In the face of the cruel German winter—in politics as well as weather—Beckett pursued his art ruminations doggedly, but if he wrote anything except his diary, it has not come to light. Six months were enough for him. Sick in body and spirit, he decided to fly back to Dublin—the first of his many plane trips. He left Germany on April 1, 1937; the resonance of April Fool's Day cannot have escaped him.

1937–40

∞

No Trifle Too Trifling

1937

∞

Beckett took his German art tour seriously, making copious notes that came to light only after his death. Bair, who had no access to this notebook, stresses Beckett's commitment to art, but Knowlson, who read "the unknown diaries," stresses Beckett's aversion to Nazi personalities and rhetoric. Once back in Dublin, Beckett began his thirty-first year by wriggling out of possible employment. With *Murphy* still under submission, he made halfhearted stabs at journalism and translation. Axel Kaun, whom Beckett had met in Germany, evidently wrote him about translating the poems of Joachim Ringelnatz, the pseudonym of Hans Botticher (1883–1934). Although Beckett refused in a letter that he later dismissed (to me) as "German bilge," he kept a copy of his reply to Kaun, which he later gave to Lawrence Harvey, and which is recognized as a document of critical importance to Beckett studies.

Letter to Axel Kaun

Dated July 9, 1937, and sent from Beckett's own attic in his father's old office at 6 Clare Street, Dublin, the letter begins by disparaging the verse of Ringelnatz. Beckett has read through three volumes, has selected twenty-three possibilities for translation, and has actually translated two poems (translations that he evidently did not keep). Having dispensed with Ringelnatz in about one-quarter of the letter, Beckett moves on to the kind

---

Given to Lawrence Harvey, the typescript of Beckett's letter to Kaun is at NhD, with a photocopy at RUL. It was first published (and translated by Martin Esslin) in *Disjecta.*

of writing that does interest him, and it is a far cry both from Joyce's apotheosis of the word and from Proust's speleology of emotion, as analyzed in his 1931 monograph. By 1937 Beckett has come to feel that his own language is a veil that must be torn asunder: "die Sprache da am besten gebraucht wird, wo sie am tuchtigsten missbraucht wird" (*Disjecta*, 52) [language is best used where it is most efficiently misused]. Instead of lagging behind the other arts, literature should be aware of its own falsity: "Gibt es irgendeinen Grund, warum jene fürchterlich willkürliche Materialität der Wortfläche nicht aufgelöst werden sollte, wie z.B. die von grossen schwarzen Pausen gefressene Tonfläche in der siebten Symphonie von Beethoven, so dass wir sie ganze Seiten durch nicht anders wahrnehmen können als etwa einen schwindelnden unergründliche Schlünde von Stillschweigen verknüpfenden Pfad von Lauten?" (53) [Is there any reason why that frightfully arbitrary materiality of the word surface should not be dissolved, like, for example, the sound surface, devoured by great black pauses, of Beethoven's Seventh Symphony, so that through whole pages we can perceive nothing but a path of sounds suspended in giddy heights, linking unfathomable abysses of silence?] These "abysses of silence" were already predicted in Belacqua's "intervals of silence" in *Dream*, and Beethoven presided over both.

Beckett denies that *Finnegans Wake* approaches the literature he envisions, and although he nods favorably at the "Logographs of Gertrude Stein," he quickly dispraises her for infatuation with her vehicle, that is, words. Beckett's letter then backtracks to espouse mockery of words before grappling with his desire for unwording. He is sufficiently dubious about his German to realize that he must be inadvertently sinning against that language, but he hopes intentionally to do so against his own language, and "Deo juvante," will do so.

It is an astonishing document from someone dedicated to becoming a writer. In a single letter Beckett rejects the particular artisanship of translation and the noble art of literary creation. In less than a decade he had moved from the verbal rapture of his Joyce essay to the desire for a porous language that approaches music. Almost every critic has cited this letter in connection with Beckett's postwar writing. Such "unwording" states a goal that is impossible to achieve—in any language.

While in Germany, Beckett made a number of acquaintances in the art world, many of them Jewish. It is, however, impossible to say whether this fact influenced a poem that he probably wrote back home in Dublin. Provoked by the memory of a sermon he attended with his father, the poem bears a peremptory Yiddish title—"Ooftish," or "[Put your money] on the table."

"Ooftish"

Like "Cascando," this poem eschews the erudite reference of much of the verse of *Echo's Bones*. Unusually harsh even for Beckett, the poem is printed in an unpunctuated rush of its nineteen lines. Although "Ooftish" may have been provoked by a clergyman's sermon, Beckett's own maladies and the malady of Germany must have contributed to the mordant tone. As Harvey reports the sermon, a clergyman addressed his flock: "What gets me down is pain. The only thing I can tell them is that the crucifixion was only the beginning. You must contribute to the kitty" (156). The clergyman is transmuted into the poem's unidentified persona, who implies that suffering is redemptive. Pain is the money that has to be placed "ooftish" [on the table]. Yet Beckett subverts the attitude of his persona by the outrageous varieties of distress he demands for "the kitty." The "we" of the persona generalizes a Christian view of the value of pain, and the "you" of his flock embraces all of humanity. The shift from first-person to second-person pronouns renders the poem widely inclusive.

Although Beckett does not punctuate the poem's nineteen lines, "Ooftish" divides into two nine-line stanzas and a one-line coda. The first stanza, as in earlier "Sanies" poems, encompasses physical maladies, but also an old toga, which hints at a classico-Christian tradition of suffering. This blend terminates in a colloquial refrain line of plosive monosyllables: "we'll put it in the pot with the rest." The second stanza encompasses nonphysical pain—love, time out of joint, aching spirit, pitiable state, and generalized misery; these too dissolve in the same refrain—"we'll put it in the pot with the rest." A proliferation of mainly indefinite or pleonastic *it*s contributes to the universality of misery. The poem's final line englobes all suffering in alliterative plosives that are barely softened by the liquid l's of "it all boils down to blood of lamb."[1]

"Ooftish" sports Beckett's beloved circularity. Although the first line bursts into two imperatives, and the last line is a dogmatic declaration, both lines emphasize the word "down," which summarizes Beckett's view of human movement. Rhythmically, the first stanza accumulates angry imperative verbs, while the second stanza emphasizes pronouns; seven *you*s or *your*s precede three fatuous *we'll*s. Together the two nine-line stanzas build to the final curt tetrameter: "it all boils down to blood of lamb," imparting

---

"Ooftish" was included as "Whiting" in a letter to MacGreevy, but the date of composition is uncertain. Mary Bryden (1998, 148) has traced the early title to Rev. 7:14: "He said to me, These are they which came out of great tribulation, and have washed their robes, and made them *white* in the blood of the Lamb" (emphasis added). The entire verse is apposite. "Ooftish" was first published in *transition* (April–May 1938); it is reprinted in Harvey and in *Poems*.

iambic meter to the verse from Revelation (7:14): "made them white in the blood of the Lamb." Beckett musicalizes the unctuous abruptness of his persona by means of a series of repetitions rich in chiming—"no trifle is too trifling," "love requited and unrequited," "the things taken too late the things taken too soon," "we'll make use of it/we'll make sense of it." Inhabitually plain and plainspoken in Beckett's verse in English, "Ooftish" attempts to expand its persona's sardonic attitude into wide unredemptive resonance. Yet I have chosen one of its phrases as the title of my chapter, for the works of this period are trifling, compared to *Murphy* or the postwar fiction and drama.

At about this time Beckett began or resumed fairly systematic research for a work about that master of the English language, the lexicographer Dr. Samuel Johnson. Beckett's most sustained project of 1937, and perhaps 1938, was that of a play about Dr. Johnson and Mrs. Thrale.[2] It is difficult to ascertain when Beckett was first attracted to Dr. Samuel Johnson. Johnson's Dictionary is mentioned in a letter of September 1934 to MacGreevy, and in 1935 Beckett visited Johnson's birthplace, Lichfield. Beckett probably knew Johnson's Lichfield entry in his dictionary: "the field of the dead, a city in Staffordshire, so named from martyred Christians." Knowlson traces Beckett's intense reading of Johnson to the weeks before his departure for Germany. However, he adds: "Beckett's focused research was conducted in Ireland between April and the early autumn of 1937" (250). As late as December 1957 Beckett wrote to Alan Schneider: "Congratulations on TV Great Cham. Yes, I always had a passion for that crazy old ruffian" (Harmon, 25).

It is probably in 1937 that Beckett filled three notebooks with material about Dr. Johnson and his circle. Beckett believed that the septuagenarian Johnson was impotent and that impotence was a dramatic subject. Although Beckett had resigned from Trinity College in 1931, he retained academic research habits, and he plodded through background materials on the two main characters of his mismatched couple, Dr. Johnson and Mrs. Thrale. The first of his three notebooks is of Munich manufacture, although it is improbable that he began his research in Germany. The second notebook, bought at Browne and Nolan, Dublin, consists largely of quotations from primary sources, and the third, also from Browne and Nolan, contains a scenario of an intended play about the "love affair" between the aging Johnson and Henry Thrale's widow, thirty-one years younger than he. Bair documents Beckett's preoccupation with Dublin theater after his return from Germany, and this may explain the unlikely theatrical turn to his "Johnson fantasy."

Inside the front cover of the first notebook Beckett lists Mrs. Thrale's steps in dissolving her sixteen-year friendship with Dr. Johnson:

Mrs. Thrale meets Piozzi [her children's music tutor] 1780

Thrale dies 1781
Piozzi in Paris July–November 1781
Engagement with P. presumably early 1782
Octo. 1782 [Mrs. Thrale] leaves Streatham & goes to Brighton
    with J.
In Brighton avowal to F. Burney & Thrale daughters
End 1782 Back to London (Argyll St.)
Jan–Feb. 1783 formal engagement & break with P.
April–May 1783 Mrs. T. takes leave of J. & P. who goes to Italy
[Mrs. Thrale] goes to Bath
April 1784 Piozzi Recalled
May " Mrs. T. in London to consult with F. Burney.
After 10 days back in Bath to await P.
July 1984 last exchange of letters with J. Marriage with P. and
    departure to Italy. Does not return to England till 1787.
J. dies Dec. 13th 1784

I have quoted so copiously to show that Beckett still retained the tendency toward the "demented particulars" of *Murphy*. Inside the back cover of the first notebook Beckett offers two alternative possibilities for the shape of the intended play:

Act 1 Mrs Thrale in Bath. April 1784
Act 2 " & J. In London May 1784
Act 3 J. in London July

A line is drawn through the above, and the following is then listed:

1. Streatham. Autumn 1781. [On the facing page Beckett notes an alternative possibility: "or Bolt Court."] Shortly after T.'s death 1781. J. & Barber. J.'s apprehension. Piozzi in Paris. Mrs. T. Bored. Position expounded. J.'s departure (flight) to Ashbourne. Murphy & FB.
2. Streatham. Year later. Mrs. T. makes avowal to Piozzi before Queeney [her daughter]. Confesses to FB. Piozzi to J. impotent salvation, and J. in love misery. Murphy & FB.
3. Argyll St. April 1783. Mrs. T. & J. Mrs. T. & Piozzi. Murphy and FB.
4. Bolt Court. Late summer 1784. Dr. J. & Barber.

Except in the last scene (or act), the writers Arthur Murphy and Fanny Burney were evidently intended as a chorus. Beckett actually dramatized only the alternative possibility of scene 1, but without "J. & Barber."

After some two hundred pages of notes in the three notebooks, the play's structure must have taken shape in Beckett's mind: one act per year for the four years between Thrale's death and Johnson's death. In the center of the third notebook Beckett tried to concentrate on what was relevant to that structure. However, his list of events overflowed any workable scenario. Although his notes succeeded in moving from the circumference of the Johnson circle to Johnson at its center, he did not manage to isolate the Johnson–Mrs. Thrale relationship. Frederik Smith cogently summarizes Beckett's dilemma: "These three notebooks, along with several letters to McGreevy [*sic*], Mary Manning, and others, show that Beckett was drawn in two quite different directions: (1) toward the figure of Dr. Johnson in love with the much younger Mrs. Thrale, including his pet theory on the Great Cham's impotence; and (2) simultaneously toward the image of the physically deteriorating Johnson, that massive intellect in decline."[3]

Apparently, Beckett was unable to write dialogue for the play—for several years. In December 1937 Beckett wrote his friend Mary Manning: "I have not written a word of the Johnson blasphemy. I trust that acts of intellection are going on about it somewhere. Which will enable me eventually to see how it coincides with the *Pricks, Bones* and *Murphy* fundamentally, and fundamentally with all I shall ever write or ever want to write" (qtd. in Knowlson, 250–51). As Knowlson notes, Beckett's prescience is unusual about work that he already viewed as an oeuvre in progress, from which he was reluctant to exclude "the Johnson blasphemy" (I am one of the few critics who do not accept Beckett's holistic view of his oeuvre, which fails to explain the aborted pieces).

More immediately, Beckett also busied himself with "his interpretation of Jack Yeats's painting, his immersion in the philosophy of Schopenhauer, [as well as] his study of the life of Johnson" (Knowlson, 250). However, Beckett's personal life probably took precedence, since his brother Frank was married on August 24. With Frank and his wife Jean away on their honeymoon, tensions were high between Beckett and his mother. Even Knowlson has not ferreted the inflammatory incident that caused Beckett to leave home and Ireland, but it may have been her discovery of some of his writing. In October 1937, Beckett departed for Paris, via London.

Beckett's letters continued to speak of Ireland as "home," even after his move to Paris—with no notion of how he would support himself. He was back in Dublin in November to oblige relatives by marriage, the Sinclairs, with testimony in a libel trial against Oliver St. John Gogarty. It was perhaps during that period that Beckett read in the *Times Literary Supplement* a brief and scathing review of his friend Denis Devlin's *Intercessions,* a volume of poems; I quote the complete review:

> One of Mr. Devlin's poems is entitled "Bacchanal," and all of them are more intoxicated than intelligible. Such lines as the following from a poem entitled "Gradual" are characteristic. [Twelve lines are

quoted.] There are lines here and there which rise above the gulf of tangid [*sic*] incoherence, but not enough of them to form a bridge between the poet and the reader.

Devlin's Intercessions

Provoked to reply, Beckett sent his rebuttal to Paris for the Tenth Anniversary issue of *transition*. Rather than yearning for the unwording of the word, as espoused in his letter to Axel Kaun, Beckett posits an art that formulates a kind of need: "pure interrogation, rhetorical question less the rhetoric." He contrasts that needy artist with "the go-getters, the gerimandlers, Davos and the morbid dread of sphinxes, solution clapped on problem like a snuffer on a candle, the great crossword public" (*Disjecta*, 92).[4] Beckett moves on to (extravagant) praise of Devlin, which he lards with liberal quotation and with passing comparisons to poems of Apollinaire and Hölderlin. He puns in praise of Devlin's musicality—"extraordinary. Extraaudenary." Although Beckett does not quote from the poem "Gradual," he defends it in context, thus directly attacking the respected *Times Literary Supplement*. He denies that his friend's work is overimaged, since imagery arises from "a minimum of rational interference." Withering "the monacodologists" who desire clarity, Beckett closes his review with panache: "Mr Denis Devlin is a mind aware of its luminaries" (94).

Back in Paris in December 1937, Beckett called on old friends, particularly the Joyce family and their circle. He also made new friends among painters, notably Bram and Geer van Velde. Uncharacteristically public, he replied to a questionnaire about the Spanish Civil War: "UPTHEREPUBLIC." In adapting to another war the cry of the Irish Republicans, to whom his family was unsympathetic, Beckett was not aloof from his times. As the year drew to a close, he sent Peggy Guggenheim for her London gallery a translation of Jean Cocteau's introduction to an exhibition of his designs for *Les Chevaliers de la table ronde*, but the English reads decidedly unlike Cocteau and suspiciously like Beckett—with repetitions, sound play, and wordplay. The "translation" opens: "The time has come to do no longer what I do do, the time has come to go on doing what I do do, the time has come never again to do what I have done and undone." And it concludes: "Ladies and Gentlemen, it is a mad thing to exhibit oneself in vain" (Federman and Fletcher, 96). Although English *Murphy* had just been accepted by Routledge, Beckett (under Cocteau's signature) seems to be setting sail for new ports.

Devlin's Intercessions is published, along with "Ooftish," in *transition* (April–May 1938). It is reprinted in *Disjecta*.

Beckett was not ready to undertake the arduous task of another sustained piece of fiction, but he exercised his writerly hand in verse. He returned to the familiar subject of an erotic encounter—at first in English, but thereafter in French. For the most part each poem is titled by its opening phrase.

"They come . . ."

The five-line lyric is built on repetitions of "different/the same," concluding on an equivalence between seeming differences. Harvey contrasts the active "Exeo" of "Enueg I" with the static persona of this poem, toward whom "they come" in a sexual pun. More subtle than the repetition of, and implied equivalence between, difference and identity, is a comparable equivalence between the opening "they" and the three repetitions of "with each"—at once a many and a one. In the original English, as opposed to Beckett's translation into French, sameness has a slight edge over difference, although each is thrice repeated. However, "different" is an adjective, whereas "the same" is not only a noun, but it is particularized by the definite article. Moreover, "the same" slant/rhymes with "come" in the opening line. Eschewing the dramatic monologue of the early English poems, Beckett has shifted to a flat, impersonal statement—a harbinger of the French poems soon to be written.

"Dieppe"

One of Beckett's early French poems, this quatrain was inspired by Hölderlin's lines from *Der Spaziergang*:

Ihr lieblichen Bilder im Tale,
Zum Beispiel Garten und Baum,
Und dann der Steg, der schmale,
Der Bach zu sehen kaum.
        (Federman and Fletcher, 50)

In contrast to the bucolic peace of the German, however, Beckett's "Dieppe" seems strangely prescient of the war that was still in the future. A series of nouns moves from a dead beach to "lights of old." A world is dead, but the world rolls on.

No manuscript of "They come" is extant, for either Beckett's original English version or his French translation. John Fletcher's note in the Minuit *Poèmes* dates "They come" in 1937. Both versions are included in *Poems*.

According to Fletcher's notes in *Collected Poems in English and French*, "Dieppe" was written in 1937. It was first published (along with the following ten poems) in *Les Temps modernes* (November 1946). It was reprinted in *Poèmes* (Minuit, 1969) and in *Poems*.

1938

The new year began badly—nearly fatally. On January 7, while walking with friends on the Avenue d'Orléans on the Left Bank, Beckett was stabbed by a pimp to whom he refused money. All Beckett's friends rallied round, but especially Joyce, who paid for his removal to a private hospital room (Bair, 279–80). While Beckett was in the hospital, he corrected the proofs of *Murphy,* and his friend Alfred Péron suggested that they translate that novel into French (Beer, 1987, 434).

Upon release from the hospital, Beckett searched for a more permanent Paris dwelling than a hotel room, and he found an apartment at 6 rue des Favorites, which he described in a letter: "studio, soupente, bedroom, bathroom, hall, the necessary house and kitchenette. On the 7th floor and well away from Gare Montparnasse," but quite near l'Impasse de l'Enfant Jésus (qtd. in Bair, 286). With the exception of the war years, that was to be his home until 1960. (As late as 1976 Beckett walked there with me and viewed his surroundings with affection.)

Perhaps Beckett's first independent domicile provided the immediate impetus to write in French. Not only did he and Péron embark on the long-term project of translating *Murphy,* but Beckett also translated his *Love and Lethe* from *More Pricks Than Kicks,* and he composed poems in French. Ten of them are dated 1937–39 (in the Minuit *Poèmes*), but it is impossible to ascertain the order of composition. As Pilling (1998) shrewdly observes: "Three more poems *are filed* [at TCD] with the letter to MacGreevy of 31 January 1938: 'Ascension' (with variant readings in the last two lines), 'La mouche' and 'musique de l'indifférence' (with the variant title 'Prière')" (254, note 19). My emphasis underlines Pilling's skepticism as to TCD's inclusion of these poems with the MacGreevy letter. However, since there is no other evidence for dating, I consider these three poems first.

"Ascension"

The title refers to Holy Thursday, when Christ ascended to Heaven. Not until the last of the five brief, uneven stanzas is the subject of Beckett's ascension revealed—an unnamed "elle," who died a bloody death. The "je," "a prodigal in his own way," is an early Beckett protagonist to be incarcerated in a room. The first stanza closes on the radio report of the football World Cup; in contrast, the third stanza describes the chant of the faithful surging through the open window. Between these two stanzas is the single line of the second stanza—"toujours trop jeune." Perhaps the "too young" person pre-

---

"Ascension" was first published in *Les Temps modernes* (November 1946) in a group of twelve poems. It is reprinted in Minuit *Poèmes* and in *Poems.*

dicts the dying "elle" of the fourth stanza—blood all over the sheets, sweet-peas, and "son mec." *Mec* is French slang, corresponding to the English *guy*. Whoever he is, his disgusting fingers close the lids of astonished green eyes. The final couplet, inhabitually rhyming, implicitly contrasts the dead woman with Christ, who ascends to Heaven. "Elle" ascends above the persona's tomb of air, but, a restless spirit, she reaches no destination.

"La Mouche"

This poem reverts to the equation of man and fly, which concluded "Serena I." The title alone names the particular insect. The first of two stanzas situates a window between "la scène" and the persona—empty, except for "elle." The second stanza, composed of past and present participles, closely itemizes the legs, wings, and antennae of the fly, and even the mouth that sucks the void through the windowpane. The persona's thumb is unable to crush the insect, who disturbs the serene sea and sky. Although the man-fly equation of victimization is facile, Beckett shows some skill in the building of that equation.

"Musique de l'indifférence"

This six-line poem is difficult syntactically, and yet the weariness of collapsed loves is unmistakable. I read "couvre" as an imperative addressed to the music of indifference; the lyric is therefore a plea for a lack of emotional response to the silence of the elements and to the voices of broken loves, so that the persona need no longer hear his own lack of voice.

The poems are remarkable only in contrast to most of Beckett's learning-laden English verse; the drive toward a plain and simple style is unmistakable, but one would not guess it from Beckett's critical prose of this period. After visiting his family in Ireland, Beckett and Suzanne Dumesnil, who was to become his lifelong companion, traveled to Brittany to see the Pérons, and there he worked at an essay on aesthetics—in French.

Les Deux Besoins

The short, dense piece is prefaced by an enigmatic epigraph. Beckett excerpted a sentence from Flaubert's *L'Education sentimentale,* which

---

"La Mouche" was first published in *Les Temps modernes* (November 1946) in a group of twelve poems. It is reprinted in Minuit *Poèmes* and in *Poems.*

"Musique de l'indifférence" is the opening phrase of the six-line poem first published in *Les Temps modernes* (November 1946) in a group of twelve poems. It is reprinted in Minuit *Poèmes* and in *Poems.*

Beckett gave the typescript of *Les Deux Besoins* to Lawrence Harvey, who deposited it in NhD. It was first published in *Disjecta.*

occurs some two-thirds of the way through the long book. A drunken pharmacist hums a song about two white oxen, and Sénécal, a minor character, silences him with a hand over his mouth, because he doesn't like disorder. Beckett, in contrast, seems to favor the disorder of irrational song, and the two oxen may represent the two artistic needs of his title, which are stifled by the rational phrasing of an essay. (I am striving desperately to explain the epigraph.)

In his review of Devlin's poems Beckett opposes the needy artist and the greedy "crossword public," and that opposition may lie at the root of *Les Deux Besoins*. However, one of the two needs undergoes a radical transformation. Beckett's artist remains the needy needer, but the second need is complex and difficult to pinpoint. The few commentators on the essay (Harvey, Henning, Locatelli, Pilling) paraphrase its French and impose coherence within their respective lenses for reading Beckett. I perform a similar operation, in an effort to understand this concentrated piece that is at once a retreat from and an advance upon the Kaun letter—as well as a harbinger of the novel *Watt*.

Packed into less than two pages of print (and a diagram), *Les Deux Besoins* is more cryptic than the letter to Axel Kaun. Although Beckett there outlines a difficult desideratum—to subvert literature by means of literature, his purpose is relatively clear. *Les Deux Besoins,* in contrast, resists elucidation of the second need, which is falsified as soon as it is expressed. Art emerges from the tension between the artist's need to need and the need that is needed. Yet Beckett tries to avoid tautology by geometric representation. In the interstices of two superimposed triangles Beckett discerns an awareness of these needs, an awareness that arises from the artist's desire to see (as a visionary sees?) and the act of having seen nothingness. Far from diagrammatic clarification, however, Beckett twists plane logical geometry into his ongoing fascination with the irrational—in composition, mathematics, and cosmology.

Resorting to his habitual repetition, but now idiomatic to the French language, Beckett intertwines the difficulties of the artistic process with his own expression of it: On the first of his two pages Beckett adopts in French the superior tone of his English reviews, to disparage those who are so preoccupied with petty needs that they ignore the major one. In contrast, the artist has two needs: "l'artiste se met à la question, se met en question, se résout en questions, en questions rhétoriques sans fonction oratoire" (*Disjecta*, 56) [the artist attacks the question, places himself in question, turns to questions, to rhetorical questions without rhetorical function (the latter phrase translating one in his Devlin review)]. Spurning scientific and theological explanations, Beckett insists upon the interrogatory nature of art. Mocking his own logical terminology, Beckett concludes that in the logic of art what is lacking are not premises but conclusions. "Until further notice!" In itself this is a lame conclusion to Beckett's complex and concentrated statement of aesthetics, which portrays the artist as a needing being who needs to need. More strongly and perhaps confessionally than ever before, Beckett declares the artist to be "l'être qui *est* besoin et la nécessité où il est de l'être" (56; emphasis added) [the artist who is need, and his necessity to be so]. Beckett neither tried to publish *Les Deux Besoins,* nor did he destroy it.

By the time he wrote this essay, Beckett had probably embarked on serious verse in French, but he may also have composed lighter verses. Knowlson writes that a number of poems in Bram van Velde's papers are annotated "Poèmes à [not *de*] Beckett." Nevertheless, he believes that these poems are by Beckett, notably twenty short poems about Le Petit Sot. "The first poem is actually called 'Le Petit sot,' and the others follow him (always in the first person) in a variety of guises: as horse-rider, traveller, lion, moth, singer, searcher after the moon, and so on. They recreate the games or fantasies of a little boy. They are simpler in vocabulary, syntax and ideas than any of the other poems of Beckett at that time and look at first sight like stylistic exercises" (270). In the Beckett Archive at Reading is a single undated Petit Sot poem, and, far from a little boy, an adult expresses a blend of love and hate.

"Les joues rouges" [Red cheeks]

A twenty-four-line unpunctuated poem, this verse describes a love of hatred, which is not dissimilar to the "love" of some of the French published poems. Syntactically, the poem is something of a tour de force, composed as it is of a single sentence. The first seventeen lines present an "il" who treasures hatred above various beauties and bounties. Not only does "il" cherish his hate, but he nurtures it in the springtime, which is usually associated with love. Almost every line of the poem recapitulates a word of the preceding line, imparting a kind of villanelle music. Only in line 18 is it revealed that "il" is Petit Sot [Little Fool], whose emotional turmoil contrasts with the many-colored crocuses that "sans amour et sans haine / étaient ce qu'ils devaient être." The penultimate line is borrowed from Verlaine's "Il pleure dans mon coeur," but, unlike the French poem's harmony between man and nature, Beckett's line designates the indifference of nature to human emotions.

"Les joues rouges" may be a stylistic exercise, which should be grouped with the twelve French poems that Beckett did publish (only after World War II). As already mentioned, it is impossible to ascertain the order of composition. Pilling writes, "In the event sequence naturally matters less where a new manner clearly matters more" (1998, 156), and he links Beckett's "new manner" to the "wordshed" announced in Beckett's poem "Cascando,"

Unpublished, "Les joues rouges" exists only in typescript at RUL.

which sheds or pares away words. Although the last lyrics of *Echo's Bones* already move in that direction, it is significant that Beckett's shift to French is chronologically close to his two key critical statements, however privately conceived—the Kaun letter and *Les Deux Besoins*. Evidence is lacking, but Pilling deduces "somewhat warily" that "almost all of the 12 French poems 38–39 are actually from 1938" (personal communication). I therefore assign that date to the remaining seven of Beckett's dozen French poems, which he published only after World War II.

Beckett told Harvey that the poems written between 1937 and 1939 reflected "a period of lostness, drifting around, seeing a few friends—a period of apathy and lethargy" (183). Even to Harvey, Beckett did not reveal what he implied in his April 18, 1939, letter to MacGreevy—that he was living with someone he had known for a year or two, Suzanne Deschevaux-Dumesnil. In his letter to MacGreevy Beckett is circumspect about the relationship: "As we both know that it will come to an end there is no knowing how long it may last." In the event "it" lasted over fifty years—or a lifetime.

Harvey reads Beckett's prewar French poems as muted and static continuations of *Echo's Bones*. Unlike that sequence as printed, however, the French group lacks a title to bind them. In spite of occasionally puzzling syntax, the French poems do not convey the impression of someone feeling his way in a foreign language. Far simpler than the English poems, they usually eschew allusive echoes. Only five of the individual poems carry titles, three after places, as opposed to the seven Provençal genre designations of the English poems. With one exception, the French poems resemble the English in being unpunctuated, but they are shorter and less imaged than their English forbears—between four and twenty-three lines. In the order of publication, the first three poems focus on sexual but loveless intercourse, but after that the subjects vary. In four of the poems the word *vide* recurs. Like the English poems, the French verse does not predict the birth of a major writer.

"À elle l'acte calme"

Two unequal stanzas sketch an erotic encounter. Harvey points to the sexual rhythm in such verbal pairs as *les pores–le sexe, l'attente–les regrets, l'absence–la présence, tête-coeur*—in a poem where the persona is at once seduced and bored by the mechanics of the sexual act. The poem has unusual line divisions: in line 3 "pas trop lente" opposes "pas trop long," but one would expect the following word "l'absence" to open the fourth line, oppos-

---

The following seven poems were published in a group of twelve in *Les Temps modernes* (November 1946). They are reprinted in *Poèmes* (Minuit, 1968) and in *Poems*.

ing it to the concluding "présence." Instead "l'absence" at the line's end is the culmination of the initial "l'attente." Comparably, the long fifth line— "les quelques haillons d'azur dans la tête les points enfin morts du coeur" [the few tatters of azure in the head the dead spots of the heart]—falls into a two-part contrast (or resemblance?) between head and heart, which Beckett runs together.

The cryptic second stanza contrasts the partners of the erotic encounter. The opening line of the first stanza, "à elle l'acte calme," is generalized in the opening line of the brief second stanza to "à elle vide." Her emptiness is either contrasted or paralleled by "lui pur / d'amour," which can mean pure in his love or purified of love.[5] Beckett's image compares the sexual act to cessation of rain at twilight. However devoid of love, this sexual encounter has its own late grace.

"Être là sans mâchoires sans dents"

This erotic encounter is inscribed in a single sixteen-line stanza. The narrator is pronounless, but his partner is "elle." A couple prepare for a loveless sex act, whose details are particularized. The lover is jawless, toothless, indifferently losing or winning, humming, playing with his fingers. Awaiting "qu'elle mouille," the passive recipient of sex might be on his deathbed, with his idiotic mouth, formicating hand, and an *eye* listening for the silver scissors of fate. The phrase "qu'elle mouille" (noted from Renard's *Journal* in the *Dream* Notebook) recurs in lines 10 and 15. "Elle's" function is thus reduced to the sexual. The final phrase of far-off silver scissors fuses sex and death—unrhapsodically. It is fitting that "vide" should be repeated in line 7, for this fornication is empty.

"Bois seul"

Given the mechanism of erotic encounters in the preceding poems, it is not surprising that this seven-line poem opens on a series of self-addressed imperatives to function alone. "Seul" is repeated in lines 1 and 2, and line 3 declares that the absent are dead (rather than the contrary), and the present stink. Line 4 continues the opening self-commands, but now the eyes are ordered to depart and look at the reeds. Are they teasing one another or "les ais?" Harvey and Tophoven read the difficult word "ais" as a sloth, but Coughlan argues convincingly for a "brief scene of reeds in a river disturbed by the wind" (202). She is also convincing on the final couplet producing "a powerfully disturbing indeterminacy. . . . An instance of possible transcendence is held suspended, perhaps promised, perhaps not." Beckett himself later came to think that *perhaps* was an important word for him, but the poem is too enigmatic to be summed up in that word.

"Ainsi a-t-on beau"

This poem is a surreptitious sonnet, concealing a traditional division between octave and sestet. Although a few off-rhymes appear—*beaux-eux, ère-père-pire, baisers-penché*—the two parts are more forcefully linked by the near repetition of lines 2 and 13. The octet posits the vanity of all activity, from the first kisses back through glacial periods in which there was already nothing new. The unusual fusion of yesterday and the eons is summed up in the introduction to the sestet: "rêver en générations de chênes et oublier son père" [to dream in generations of oaks and to forget one's father]. Imprisoned in one's own body and in the world's calendar, the human being is devoured by "le temps"—in French both time and weather. Between line 2 and line 13 "le mauvais temps" has grown "pire."

"Rue de Vaugirard"

One of the few French poems with a title, "Rue de Vaugirard" may conceal a joke on Beckett's part, since he entitles a short five-line poem for the longest street in Paris. In the middle of the street the persona (on a bicycle or in an automobile) stops and exposes his license plate to light and shadow, more than ever convinced of "an irresistible negativity." Lights on a number confer no identity.

"Arènes de Lutèce"

This poem is the most active and dramatic, as well as the longest poem of the group. In contrast to "Rue de Vaugirard" and "Dieppe," which are neutral spaces in spite of the titles, "Arènes de Lutèce" is vividly particularized. To present the Roman remains of an amphitheater in Paris (or Lutèce), Beckett revives commas and even periods, which facilitate reading. Four sentences form an unbroken block of twenty-three lines. Like earlier English poems, "Arènes" is a journey poem, but the journey is here confined within the arena location. The persona names the actual entrances to the arena on Rue des Arènes and on Rue Monge; he notices the statue of the paleologist Gabriel de Mortillet (no longer there). He mentions the dark sand and the puddles in the arena, as well as the concrete banister, the surrounding buildings of modern Paris, and the many steps from the ground to the summit of the amphitheater. Above all he notices moving beings—a small green dog, a little girl, a couple of lovers. The persona does not say that he and an unnamed "elle" are lovers, and the bond between them is even more surreal than the green of the dog.

In the opening line of the poem "nous" are seated above the steps of the amphitheater—perhaps in an extraterrestrial realm. The "je" sees us enter, as ugly as unnamed others, but mute. When "elle" stops to watch the dog, "je" climbs the steps. After starting toward the Rue Monge, "elle" follows him, and yet it is "je" whom "je" meets, in the climactic fifteenth line. Thereafter "je" views the scene with other eyes—from the amphitheater to the sky that illuminates us "trop tard." When "je" turns, he is astonished to see her sad face. The division between them is emphasized by repetition and contrast: "Elle se retourne, je suis parti, je gravis seul" opens the second sentence, and "Je me retourne, je suis étonné" opens the final fourth sentence.

In spite of the resolutely prosaic details couched in clear syntax, the poem exudes a visionary quality. The sequence of declarative sentences is dispassionate, and yet a few emotions seep through: "elle hésite," "j'ai un frisson," "je suis étonné." Coughlan's view that the persona "is overcome by self-recognition in mutuality" (200) neglects the persona's final solitude and his companion's "triste visage." Perhaps self-recognition is inevitably solitary.

"Jusque dans la caverne ciel et sol"

The final poem of the sequence takes a very long view indeed of the ravages of time. A single block of twelve uneven lines spurns sentences for a series of phrases connected by "et." Dispensing with a persona, the short poem sweeps from the plains of Etna to the pairing of Proserpine with Atropos. It couples the coming of winter with that of death. With the repetition of "lentement" and "naguère" [slowly and of old], all time seems to drain away. Difficult syntactically, the poem suggests that in mythological time as now, human action and its ghosts will slowly lead to a "vide douteux" and an engulfing shadow. Yet there is peace in that slow extinction. As the final poem of the twelve, it seems to lay to rest some of the frustrations in the other poems.

1939

Beckett was visiting his mother in Ireland when Hitler invaded Poland on September 1, followed by declarations of war on Germany by England and France on September 3. Beckett returned immediately to Paris, traveling through a darkened England, and arguing his way past restraining officials at Newhaven. He had written little since his return from Germany in 1937, and the declaration of war was a further deterrent.

1940

By spring 1940, Hitler's momentum was irresistible, and Paris seemed threatened. In these improbable circumstances, Beckett evidently sought refuge in his "Johnson fantasy." A letter of May 21, 1940, to George Reavey speaks of "half of a first act of Johnson," and we have that half—a scene entitled *Human Wishes.* At some point before spring 1940, Beckett turned away from his notebooks, to use other sources for notes on the Johnson circle. On loose yellow unlined pages, he wrote eighteen pages on Mrs. Williams, eight and a half on Dr. Levett, four and a half on Francis Barber, four on Mrs. Desmoulins, and one on Miss Carmichael. Some of this new material went into his fragmentary scene, although Francis Barber does not appear. For example Mrs. Williams is blind, Welsh, and learned; Miss Carmichael is young and nondescript; Mrs. Desmoulins is the widow of a scribe, and Dr. Levett drinks heavily. The eighteenth-century scholar Fred Lowe makes the cogent point that much of Beckett's material on these loose pages is not found in the notebooks, and that it relies on a different edition of Boswell's *Life.* Lowe thinks that the Johnson-Thrale project died in 1937, and that Beckett in 1940 started on a new work: "[Beckett] makes Mrs. Williams the despotic figure imposing a funereal atmosphere on the company, but the model for her behaviour is none other than Johnson himself. . . . Beckett intended his characters to echo Johnson's speech, and reflect events in his life." Lowe cites Johnson's letter of March 1778 to Mrs. Thrale: "Williams hates everybody. Levett hates Desmoulins and does not love Williams. Desmoulins hates them both. Poll [Carmichael] loves none of them."[6]

Beckett's scene is entitled *Human Wishes,* leaving understood "Vanity of" from Johnson's poem of that title. The first scenic direction is *Silence,* and this will often be repeated. Beckett's pen speeds through his first page, making few changes, but difficulties apparently arose on the second page. Not only are several lines crossed out, but the bottom of the second page blossoms in Beckett's doodles, which are familiar to anyone who has perused his manuscripts. Doodles usurp over half the third page, which have been reproduced and analyzed by Mary Bryden (1992, 55–60): "The sketch consists of three horizontal parts. The top part contains one dog and numerous human figures. . . . The bottom section is made up of four carefully executed lines of music. . . . It is the central panel, however—a crucifixion scene—which attracts the eye" (56). In the crucifixion scene Christ is at the center of the two crucified thieves. Although I agree with Bryden that "the crucifixion metaphor . . . broadens out within Beckett's work to embrace the whole scope of human suffering," she does not relate the doodle to the "Johnson fantasy." Smith does so: "Between the looming and rather bizarre crucifixions of Christ and one of the thieves [the good one] is a sort of cartoon image of what appears to be Dr. Johnson in a bowler and toting a suitcase (labeled with a 'J'), his arm around a more diminutive lady in a wedding gown." Consciously or not, Beckett may have associated Johnson's absurd infatuation with a crucifixion. Or he may have viewed Johnson's whole life as a crucifixion.

Human Wishes

Beckett has disparaged the scene of his *Human Wishes*, but it reveals a budding playwright, with a gift for pattern and tension. The curtain rises on a tableau in Bolt Court in 1781, with Mrs. Williams meditating, Mrs. Desmoulins knitting, Miss Carmichael reading, and Johnson's cat Hodge sleeping, "if possible." The conversation of the human inhabitants is punctured by frequent silences and cemented by frequent repetitions. The dialogue exudes eighteenth-century elegance—the archaic "knotting" for knitting, "relict" for relic, "my dear madam," "pray tell me," "God grant," "I perceive," "upon my soul," "of little consequence," "it is idle to . . ." The "colloquial powers" of Mrs. Williams are succinctly witty.

During the course of the scene, a drunken Dr. Levett in greatcoat and hat appears in the background and wends his way upstairs. He utters no words, but he emits "a single hiccup of such force that he is almost thrown off his feet" (*Disjecta*, 160). The mutual hostility of the three women seeps through their conversation, which alludes to the drama of their time; three dramatists are mentioned by name—Arthur Murphy, Hugh Kelly, and Oliver Goldsmith—Irishmen who wrote successfully for the London stage, two of them dead in 1781, the putative date of Beckett's scene. Brooding on death, blind Mrs. Williams distinguishes between perceiving it by the mind or by the heart. Miss Carmichael reads aloud a beautifully balanced passage about death from Jeremy Taylor's *Rule and Exercises of Holy Dying*. Mrs. Williams, who interrupts the reading with acid comments and questions, guesses (shrewdly) that the author is Sir Thomas Browne, but Miss Carmichael, consulting the book's title page, reveals that it is Taylor, and upon that word Beckett's fragment ends.

With hindsight we can see the future playwright in the dramatic fragment. Visually, the three historical women predict the female trio of Beckett's *Come and Go*, and indeed Mrs. D's "God grant . . ." will later grace the lips of Beckett's Flo. Both the early and later threesome wear long dresses, and visually they recall the three classical Fates or the three witches of *Macbeth*. As later in *Endgame*, the main character of *Human Wishes* is blind, voluble, and decrepit, but acutely aware of his/her surroundings; Mrs. Williams even has a stick that prefigures Hamm's gaff. She enumerates her

---

Both the holograph and the typescript of *Human Wishes* are at RUL. First published in my *Just Play*, the fragmentary scene is reprinted in *Disjecta*, to which my page numbers refer. The scene is not included in *CDW*.

illnesses as proudly as will blind Dan Rooney in *All That Fall*. Miss Carmichael deceives blind Mrs. Williams as Clov will deceive blind Hamm. Other scholars read other predictions into the Johnson scene. Lionel Kelly sees *Human Wishes* at the root of *Krapp's Last Tape:* "The primary impetus for this play seems to me to lie in Beckett's reading of Johnson's *Prayers and Meditations* where Johnson wrote anniversary observances" (36). Frederik Smith believes that the figure of the aged, ailing Johnson is at the root of Beckett's French trilogy of novels, over a decade into the future. Fred Lowe thinks that the change from Dr. Johnson to his household is quite deliberate, with Mrs. Williams displacing Johnson as the fulcrum of the scene.

Human Wishes already evinces Beckett's dramatic techniques: rhythmic and disjunctive dialogue, frequent pauses, reflexive commentary on syntax and dramatic form. Words are counterpointed against gestures, and melancholy is exuded through the comic surface. Beckett's stage trio of women wish for mirth, and yet Mrs. Williams wishes for death, so that the very title *Human Wishes* enfolds Beckett's blend of the tragic and the comic. Ben-Zvi aptly comments: "In one extended section the trio dissect a sentence on the topic of mirth, reordering its parts, ironically [evoking] mirth while presumably extracting all mirth from it, until Mrs. Williams fashions it into a rhymed verse which she demands be copied down. It is not" (1986, 54–55). Analogous to Beckett's metafictional commentary in his fiction of the 1930s is a lone metadramatic remark of *Human Wishes*. When Dr. Levett goes unsteadily upstairs, Mrs. Desmoulins observes: "Now this is where a writer for the stage would have us speak no doubt" (160). Samuel Beckett, the neophyte writer for the stage, does indeed have his characters speak—eloquently, dramatically, and faintly metadramatically. However, the dialogue was not concluded.

Bair quotes Beckett's 1972 explanation for breaking off the play: "It was a question of putting it into the Irish accent as well as the proper language of the period. It would not do to have Johnson speaking proper language, after the manner of Boswell, while all the other characters speak only the impossible jargon I put into their mouths" (255). Knowlson believes that Beckett discontinued the drama because he perceived the similarity between Johnson and himself: "as this decaying, solitary, self-conscious Johnson figure swam more sharply into focus, so Beckett found it increasingly difficult to pursue the original biographical love drama on which he had embarked" (250). I persist in thinking that Beckett could not resolve the conflict between the psychological drama he had painstakingly prepared himself to write and the verbal ballet he actually began to write. Smith adds his own supposition: "I believe that the collapse of *Human Wishes* was caused by Beckett's overwhelming fascination with the rather novelistic figure (at least as he appeared in several of Beckett's sources) of Dr. Johnson himself—the very image of that deteriorating body, slowly declining intellect, and threatening depression of spirit. This enigmatic figure eventually overshadowed his interest in the unlikely relationship between Johnson and Mrs. Thrale." Again, this very probable guess does not preclude the others, all militating against completion of the play. Fred Lowe, who has studied Beckett's scene most thoroughly, offers no explanation of its incompletion, and he writes of it almost as if it were complete.

Beckett's letter to Reavey—"And I wrote half of a first act of Johnson"—is dated May 21, 1940. Perhaps Beckett turned to Johnson in a gesture of escape from a Paris imperiled by advancing Nazi armies, and perhaps he broke off the scene because of the imminent danger of invasion.[7] By June, only a month after his letter to Reavey, Beckett and Suzanne joined the exodus from Paris. In Vichy they saw Joyce—for the last time.[8] Knowlson describes some of the harrowing details of their flight south. Through the generosity of the American Mary Reynolds, they were able to spend the summer in Arcachon. Reynolds was living with Marcel Duchamp, with whom Beckett often played chess. Desultorily, he also worked at the French translation of *Murphy*. When it seemed as though the Nazis would behave decently toward Paris, Beckett and Suzanne returned to the capital, where he concentrated on obtaining documents to legitimize his Paris domicile. The requisite papers were in his possession by November 1940, and this allowed him to queue for the food allowances of Paris residents. In October 1940 the anti-Jewish laws were enacted, and Beckett feared for his Jewish friends. In December 1940, Beckett's friend Alfred Péron joined a newly formed Resistance cell, and less than a year later Beckett followed, although he was a citizen of neutral Ireland.

It would take more than a horoscope to predict Beckett's future writerly achievement. Even Lawrence Harvey, an admirer of Beckett's early literary production, implicitly devalues it: "Between 1931 and 1939 Beckett wrote one novel, a collection of short stories (based on the unpublished 'Dream of Fair to Middling Women'), about ten pages of a play he never completed, a small volume of poetry, and a few scattered reviews, translations, pages of prose, and poems" (206 n. 17). Despite the scant number of pages, however, Beckett's Kaun letter, his Devlin review, and *Les Deux Besoins* are evidence (in three languages) of how seriously and even programmatically he was pondering his commitment to writing, but that did not constitute his only commitment during World War II.

1941–45

Semantic Succour

1941–1945

It is miraculous that Beckett, an Irish national active in the French Resistance, was able to work creatively during World War II. In 1940 Beckett replaced his friend Alfred Péron as the translator of *Murphy* into French, and he told me that he had finished a first version by the time he and Suzanne left Paris in August 1942. The Nazis evidently did not view the French *Murphy* with suspicion, since they did not confiscate it when they ransacked Beckett's Paris apartment, but he took no risks with his next novel, *Watt*. He kept it with him throughout the war, even while sleeping on bare boards as he and Suzanne fled the Nazis on their way to "Free" France.[1] Later Beckett recalled: "I think *Watt* was begun in Paris in 1942, then continued evenings mostly in Roussillon and finished 1945 in Dublin and Paris. It was written as it came, without preestablished plan" (Büttner, x–xi). Without "preestablished plan," *Watt* lacks a notebook analogous to the *Murphy* preparations. Beckett began what gradually became *Watt* on loose white paper, to which he appended a cover sheet: "Begun evening of Tuesday 11/2/41." After filling six unlined pages in which he drew on Aristotle's categories, he shifted to a long, stiff-covered notebook (Pilling 1997, 170). Two notebooks of an ur-*Watt* were penned in Paris in 1941; the third, begun May 5, 1942, in Paris, records the following other places and dates: Vanves, September 4, 1942; Roussillon, November 18 [1942], and March 1 [1943]. The fourth notebook was written in Roussillon and is dated October 4, 1943. The fifth notebook is shared with *Malone meurt*, but the *Watt* section is dated February 18, 1945. The sixth book is undated, but a loose sheet is marked: "Dec. 28, 1944 End." No place is noted for these last two notebooks, but Knowlson believes that *Watt* was completed in Roussillon, and that Beckett merely "tinkered" with it after his postwar return to Paris and to Dublin (303).

Although *Watt* as published was eventually extracted from the six note-books now at HRC, Beckett's original novel is not *Watt*. Part 1 differs most from the manuscript version, with parts 2 to 4 adhering to it more closely. The addenda were indeed added last, and they salvage some of the jettisoned material. Many Beckett scholars agree with Admussen: "The first holograph version of *Watt,* chaotically written and filled with multiple and elaborate doodles and drawings is certainly the most fascinating single Beckett item to be found anywhere" (7).

Ur-*Watt*

The protagonist of the ur-*Watt* is not Watt but James Quin, a sixty-year-old Irishman who is said to spend much of his time reading the nineteenth-century Italian poet Leopardi. The origin of Mr. Knott, Quin is more firmly inscribed in a social milieu. As in the published *Watt,* the ur-Knott's senior servants are named Arsene and Erskine, but Johnny Watt is their junior colleague, who in turn has a more junior colleague named Phelps. Other name changes take place before publication: Mr. Tully to Mr. Gorman, Mr. Gomez (with Spanish *z*) to Mr. Graves, Mrs. Piscoe to Mrs. Gorman (no relation to Mr. Gorman). However, these name changes are insignificant, when compared to the slippery identity of the narrator or narrators. At first he seems to be Quin's servant Johnny Watt, who plans to write a book *A Clean Old Man.* Midway in A4, however, occurs the sentence that opens part 3 of the published novel: "It was about this time that Watt was transferred to another pavilion leaving me behind in the old pavilion." Although the notebook then describes the activities of the two "pavilion" inmates, the name of Sam is absent, as in the published volume at this point. Moreover, the narrator's first-person singular pronoun gives way after A1 to a nameless first-person plural. Quin becomes Knott only in A4, where his name occurs in Watt's inversion "Tonk." Thereafter Beckett revises Quin to Knott, but he is not consistent in his "switch from Quinism to Knottinability." It is also in A4 that the name Sam first appears, replacing a "me" on page 97.[2]

Aside from the identity of the narrator, it is easier to encompass Beck-

---

The *No Symbols* catalog of HRC waxes poetic about the *Watt* manuscript: "It is, at moments, magnificently ornate, a worthy scion of The Book of Kells, with the colors reduced to more somber hues. The doodles, cartoons, caricatures, portraits *en cartouche* include reminiscences of African and Oceanic art, the gargoyles of Notre Dame, heraldry, and more. Beckett's handwriting is at its most deceptively cursive. *Eppur si legge!*" (Lake, 76). That depends on the reader! Often baffled, I rely on spot reading and Beckett's typescript, as well as on Ann Beer's article (1985). I follow Admussen in designating Beckett's *Watt* notebooks as A1 to A6. Since I discuss the ur-*Watt* with frequent reference to *Watt* as published, my comments on the earlier version should perhaps be read after my remarks on the published novel.

ett's name changes than his conceptual changes. Since Beckett began to write on loose sheets of paper, he probably did not at first plan a sustained endeavor. Although he crossed out a list of questions—who, what, where, by what means, why, in what way, when—he reformulated such questions in various lists and sentences, before fixing on the name James Quin.[3] Already in A1 Quin is obsessed with death, waste, and nothingness.

A2 treats Quin's clothes and furnishings, but it also introduces an India Runner duck—whatever that may be. Many pages are crossed out or doodled, but a poem is penned, which became a Beckett favorite. It begins: "who may tell the tale," and it later became the fourth addendum of the published *Watt*.

It is in A3, penned in several places while Beckett eluded the Nazis, that the character Watt moves to the forefront. On the very first page Beckett lists: "1. The Coming; 2. Downstairs; 3. Upstairs. [These are grouped as "The Being."] 4. The Going." In this notebook, too, the narrator becomes a fairly consistent first-person plural. A draft appears of Watt's conversation with Arsene, including the latter's classification of laughs. Many names are listed and crossed out before Beckett creates the millennial Lynch clan. Their dog not only eats Quin's remains; he becomes the fulcrum for a mammoth spectacle of dogs. A more modest example of art is found in Beckett's four different drawings of a circle with a dot at its side, which becomes a painting in the novel; however, it is said to be in much worse condition than in the published *Watt*.

A4 is labeled in Beckett's handwriting "Poor Johnny Watt," and it contains much of part 3 of the published novel: the Frog Chorus, the Louit story (with diagrams of the looks exchanged by committee members), the fishwoman, Watt and Sam at the asylum, Watt's inversions, Knott's movements as described by Watt (and diagrammed by Beckett), and the final page of part 3, virtually as published. On loose sheets attached to the fourth notebook is a first version of the published novel's opening pages, centered on Hunchy Hackett.

A5 opens on the incident with the Galls, after which Beckett evidently wanted to shape his material. He therefore made seven divisions: (1) The painting and the problem of series; (2) Watt's ruminations about Knott's servants; (3) The Frog Chorus; (4) Watt's glimpses of Knott in the garden; (5) Mrs. Piscoe (as the fishwife was still called); (6) The gardener? (7) Conclusion: arrival of Phelps. Beckett then made a note to himself to insert part 3, or what is largely contained in A4. There follow a series of notes to himself, some of which were later incorporated into the addenda of the published novel.

The sixth and shortest notebook contains part 4 in near final form. It begins, as does the published version, with a summary of the perverse order of Watt's narration. It moves on to Watt's departure upon the arrival of Micks (still called Phelps). On the road Watt sees the non receding figure and then arrives at the train station, which is diagrammed by Beckett. A6 ends as the published novel does, except that Mr. Gorman is still Mr. Tully. The manuscript does not contain the addenda as such.

At some point of the manuscript Beckett undertook a typescript, of which 462 pages exist in HRC. It is an ordering, revision, and excision of the material in the notebooks. The general intention is copied from the manuscript: "To endeavour to formulate a modest demand as to of whom it is question. And as to of what. To essay a tentative outline or rough-sketch of mind of same. And of body of same. To hazard a manner of enquiry or search after possible relations with other persons. And with other things. To throw out a cautious feeler with regard to the situation in time. And with respect to the situation in space. To propose with gentlemanly diffidence: the vexed question of the possession; the knotty problem of the act; the well-known teaser of the suffering." The purpose of the novel is, then, inordinately and ironically ambitious.

Beckett begins an outline while Quin is still the protagonist: (1) Naming him; (2) Quin and the piano tuner; (3) Quin and the beggar; (4) The valet Arthur; (5) The birth of Quin (which becomes the account of the birth of Larry Nixon in the published novel); (6) Quin and Hunchy Hackett (including the reference to the ladder); (7) Quin's weakness and tiredness (which are divided into "The Nothingness," "The Sky," and "The Waste). On page 65 of the typescript appear two significant sentences: the first recalls the Jung lecture of 1935: "The plain fact of the matter seems to be that Quin had never been properly born." The second is retained in the published novel: "For all the good that frequent departures out of Ireland had done him, he might as well have stayed there."

Abandoning numerical division long before the end, Beckett typed up material from the notebooks: Arsene and Erskine; Quin's eyes, house, pots, paintings. Hilarious rhymes in an Irish brogue are ostensibly composed by one Matthew David McGilligan, who is not otherwise identified. A letter about music is parodied. After the transcription of the "who may tell the tale" poem, there are sections on "The Box" and "The Casket." The Indian Runner duck makes an appearance, and the narrating "we" meets a watch carrier on Westminster Bridge, as in the published novel.

Arsene grows increasingly important, exchanging trousers with "us." As Arsene dances, his braces burst, and "we" abruptly wonders: "How now to get back to Quin's passage with the duck . . ." Three matches are struck, but a warning is issued: "No symbols where none intended." Ackerley's insight is helpful: "In a context so insistently demanding symbolic interpretation, in the presence of details so often used to translate consciousness into

meaning, the only thing Watt can say is: 'No symbols where none intended'"
(1993c, 186–87). I would add, however, that Beckett deliberately confuses the
consciousness of "we" and Watt, whom Arsene calls Tommy "although our
name was Johnny." Even in the poem it is "*Johnny* will not / Abate one tot"
(emphasis added).

Arsene quizzes Tommy (Watt) about the work he is planning, and only
then does he deliver his disquisition on the three kinds of laughter. "We"
begins a story about a *rabbi* who needs a pair of trousers, but does not complete it. The typescript contains words and music for four voices. Arsene
rambles on about the house-and-parlor maids. On page 237 of the typescript
Quin is crossed out and replaced by *Knott*, whose meals the narrator details.
The necessary dog leads to the millennial Lynch clan, and the canine spectacle is still included in the typescript. On page 298 the nameless narrator
writes about grammar and syntax. After a sudden shift to Erskine and his
bell, Watt admits that he enters Erskine's room "By a ruse," without inversion. The narrator ruminates about servants and service at Knott's house,
and he imagines seeing several images, including Kaspar David Friedrich's
Men and Moon (which would later seed *Godot*).

Rather more insistently than in the notebook, the typescript narrator
broods about the series of dogs and the series of paintings, which lead in turn
to the three different series of frog croaks. Abruptly, the Ernest Louit story
follows, with calculations on cubes and cube roots. Not until page 445 does
the fishwife appear; her name is changed in ink from Mrs. Piscoe to Mrs.
Gorman. After Watt sees Phelps in the kitchen, the narrator voices an incantatory series of questions, whose answer is "Nothing." The typescript breaks
off on page 462: "The strange man was a small fat heavy oily potbellied pot-
bottomed man like Erskine and Arsene. His name was Martin." That name
becomes Micks in the published version.

The notebooks (even inadequately skimmed) and the typescript of the
ur-*Watt* permit the supposition that *Watt* attempted the impossible: at once
to be faithful to interrupted, unpremeditated writing and to impose some
order on that writing. Beckett evidently cherished *Watt*, since he carried the
unwieldy notebooks on his dangerous flight from dangerous Paris. Between
notebooks and typescript, shaping takes place, and further shaping takes
place before publication—for all the seeming *désinvolture* of the finished
novel.

Since Beckett himself selected the material he published as *Watt*, I turn
to that volume. "An exercise" Beckett dismissively labeled *Watt* (to me), but
he nevertheless tried after the war to find a publisher for that exercise. Nearly
a decade passed before he succeeded. Richard Seaver, a young American in
Paris, had read Beckett's French novels, and attended a 1952 radio broadcast
of excerpts from *Godot*. Enthusiastic about his discovery of the unknown

author, he fashioned an intricate arrangement for *Watt*'s publication by the pornography-specializing, Paris-based Olympia Press and an international impecunious group of "Merlin Juveniles," that is, youngsters who started the Merlin Press. Beckett was nevertheless meticulous in his corrections of the galleys, particularly the Frog Chorus, which "cost a significant sum for extra printing charges" (Bair, 434).[4]

Watt

Various editions of *Watt* show minor variations (particularly with respect to the threne of the addenda), but all are faithful to the five-part structure that is not quite chronological: (1) Watt journeys toward and arrives at Mr. Knott's house. (2) Watt serves Mr. Knott on the ground floor of his house. (3) (The first eighteen pages, labeled A by Mood:) After Watt has left Mr. Knott's premises, he and Sam meet and converse in an institution of individual pavilions and gardens. (The last forty-five pages, labeled B by Mood:) Watt serves on the first floor of Mr. Knott's house. (4) Watt journeys from Mr. Knott's establishment. Part 4 opens: "As Watt told the beginning of his story, not first, but second, so not fourth, but third, now he told its end. Two, one, four, three, that was the order in which Watt told his story. Heroic quatrains are not otherwise elaborated." Dismissing this invented genre, the heroic quatrain, the reader is none the wiser about Watt's tale, whose chronological order is I, II, IIIB, IV, IIIA.[5] The addenda are unnumbered, but Watt is mentioned in twelve of the thirty-seven items. Even when Watt goes unmentioned, certain items are relevant to his failed quest at Mr. Knott's establishment.[6] Erratic and macaronic, the addenda serve further to emphasize Watt's vulnerability—and his failure. As published, *Watt* is a difficult text to read; it is the first Beckett text in which the protagonist's hard way is reflected in obstacles to reading, but that does not account for what Ann Beer (1985) calls the "unresolved flaws" of the printed text (54), and which Beckett confessed (to me) were "mistakes, some intentional, some not."

Part I opens at a tram stop, and part IV closes at a railway station. A journey is an old metaphor for life, and Watt's significant life—his exposure to Mr. Knott—is bounded by these terminals. My summary sentence about the novel's structure makes *Watt* sound like a quasi-linear novel about a pro-

---

Beckett extracted the published novel *Watt* from the holograph (six notebooks) via an incomplete typescript also at HRC. Extracts were published in *Envoy* (January 1950), *Irish Writing* (December 1951), *Merlin* (winter 1952–53), *Irish Writing* (March 1953). Merlin and Olympia Press published the whole volume in 1953. The translation into French is by Ludovic and Agnes Janvier in collaboration with the author. Extracts appeared in *L'Ephémère* (summer 1968) and *Les Lettres nouvelles* (September–October 1968) before the 1968 publication by Minuit. My page numbers refer to the Grove Press edition, first published in 1959.

tagonist named Watt, but that is to ignore the way the novel only gradually comes to focus on Watt; it also ignores the many, many digressions from Watt's quest. The reader may be confused by conversations in which Watt does not participate, by seemingly irrelevant monologues, by lists, series, hypotheses, footnotes, permutations and combinations of words, verses, and songs; by dashes, question marks, and parentheses denoting lacunae; and by hilarious passages that may or may not involve Watt. Nevertheless, the faithful reader acquires sympathy for a mild and inoffensive protagonist with a huge red nose, thinning hair, low and rapid speech, funambulistic stagger, taste for milk, wind, and venerable Saxon words, but aversion to sun and moon, sky and earth. (Despite the last dislike, Watt continually falls to the ground.) It is as though the narrator's sporadic affirmations are an effort to compensate for Watt's inability to affirm anything about himself.

The novel slowly presents the physical Watt. His hair is reddish gray, his ears protrude, and his cheeks are fluted. At times he has a vacant look; at other times he resembles the rigid seventeeth-century Judge Jeffreys, and once he reminds Sam, the self-styled narrator, of a Christ-head ascribed to Bosch. Watt rarely closes his eyes, but he sees fairly well when he concentrates. His wounds heal slowly or not at all. On route to and from Mr. Knott's house, he wears a once-yellow bowler hat and a once-green coat with nine buttons; he sports a shoe that is too small for him and a boot that is too large and that is therefore stuffed with two socks, as against none on the other foot. Watt carries two bags, one in each hand; he has an eccentric way of walking and an extraordinary way of smiling. He picks his nose but never uses a handkerchief, although he requests one from Sam, to wipe his bloodied head. His virility is waning, and he smokes cigars. Narrated fragmentarily, Watt's attributes mock realistic character description in fiction.

So, too, his background. Watt's past is imparted to us scantily and piecemeal: his father is dead, he has had at least two romances, he has been close to suicide. An experienced traveler and probably a university man, he is ignorant of painting and physics, but he is "a very fair linguist." However, these incongruous characteristics figure only obliquely in the plot, which hinges on Watt's unconquerable mind, "whatever that might mean" (77).

Watt, first name forgotten, is a middle-aged man who undertakes a gnosiological quest—to use the adjective that Beckett preferred to *epistemological* (Büttner, 97–98). We may immediately associate Watt's name with the question "What?" Yet he never asks that question directly, but seeks "some meaning of what had passed, in the image of how it had passed" (73). A rationalist who hesitantly commits himself to Mr. Knott's irrational establishment, Watt begins with a tendency to seek meaning, which he renders in verbal explanation; he hopes for the "semantic succour" of my chapter title. Yet he sometimes is inhabited by experiences that do not lend themselves to such help. Early in the novel we read about Watt's "opposing impulses, one to still oneself in face of the strangeness of an experience, the other to explain it" (Davies, 14). Late in the novel, Watt cloaks his quietist or poetic impulse in a reversed order of words or sentences. We first witness Watt's mind at work when he is on the train to Mr. Knott's establishment, his back to the engine. He observes a porter wheeling a can from one end of the station platform to the other, and then another can in the opposite direction. "He is sorting cans" is Watt's instant deduction, without reference to the fact that this very porter has just knocked him down. Watt then introduces another possibility for this pointless task: "Or perhaps it is a punishment for disobedience, or some neglect of duty" (26). Still on the train, Watt is subjected to his own inner voices "singing, crying, stating, murmuring, things unintelligible, in his ear," so that he is deaf to Mr. Spiro's discourse (29). Moreover, the narrator assigns these inner voices to a series. Soon afterward, lying in a ditch on the road to Mr. Knott's house, Watt hears a mixed choir and delays leaving his recumbent position until they have completed their song.

On Mr. Knott's premises Watt's mind-machine resumes its reasoning momentum, for he only gradually perceives its inability to encompass experience in that strange realm. On the evening of his arrival Watt parallels the porter in his own back-and-forth movements. Finding the front door locked, he tries the back door; finding the back door locked, he tries the front door again. Finding the front door still locked, Watt tries the back door again and inexplicably finds it open. But the word "inexplicably" is not in Watt's vocabulary, and two possible explanations occur to him. A few minutes later, in Mr. Knott's kitchen, Watt is absorbed in a little game that again parallels the back-and-forthing of the porter, so that he does not notice the entrance of Arsene, Mr. Knott's departing servant. This time Watt ventures no explanation for the strange arrival of the strange man, a strangeness that predicts his subsequent experience at Mr. Knott's establishment:

> But [Watt] found it strange to think, of these little changes of scene, the little gains, the little losses, the thing brought, the thing removed, the light given, the light taken, and all the vain offerings to the house, strange to think of all these little things that cluster round the comings, and the stayings, and the goings, that he would know nothing of them, nothing of what they had been, as long as he lived, nothing of when they came, of how they came, and how it was then, compared with before, nothing of how long they stayed, of how they stayed, and what difference that made, nothing of when they went, of how they went, and how it was then, compared with before, before they came, before they went. (38)

Strange as it is to think of Nothing, that is what ultimately confronts Watt at Mr. Knott's establishment, but not until the end of his stay does Watt learn "to accept that nothing had happened, that a nothing had happened, learned to bear it and even, in a shy way, to like it. But then it was too late" (80). This termination of Watt's quest is revealed after about a third of the novel, but we never learn why it is "too late" (a mundane phrase that had already appeared in Beckett's poems "Enueg II" and "Ooftish").

Early in Watt's service at Mr. Knott's house, his equilibrium is severely shaken by the incident of the Galls, blind father and dutiful son, who arrive to tune the piano, but who finally pronounce it "doomed," along with the piano tuner and the pianist. (These Galls seem unrelated to Lord Gall of "Echo's Bones" and *Murphy*.) Seeking meaning in the incident, Watt finds that it dissolved in his mind "and gradually lost, in the nice processes of its light, its sound, its impacts and its rhythm, all meaning, even the most literal" (72–73). Moreover, the narrator informs us that that incident is the first of a series of events "of great formal brilliance and indeterminable purport" (74). It is the only event to intrude upon the self-sufficiency of Mr. Knott's establishment. To be sure, the gardener Mr. Graves arrives daily from the outer world, the fishwoman Mrs. Gorman calls weekly, and the twin dwarfs Art and Con Lynch nightly lead their hungry dog Kate or Cis to devour Mr. Knott's leftover food. In the main, however, Mr. Knott's premises are sealed off from the external world.

Undeterred by his seclusion, Watt sets his mind to work on the premises. Having pierced through the millennial Lynch clan to its hungry dog, Kate or Cis, he ponders the picture in the room of Erskine, the senior servant. Then he (or Sam the scribe?) gnaws mentally at Mr. Knott's schedule, food, servants, movements, furniture, appearance. Absorbed as Watt is in series, he recalls a chorus of three frogs croaking at intervals, respectively, of seven, five, and three croaks (no thanks to Aristophanes). Watt's romantic interlude with Mrs. Gorman (involving another series of permutations) leads to an account of the domestic (and sexual) troubles of Mr. Graves. When Arthur arrives, Erskine departs, and Watt graduates to the first floor of Mr. Knott's house.

A beautiful summer's day finds Watt, Mr. Knott, Mr. Graves, and Arthur in the garden. Inspired by Mr. Graves's impotence, Arthur launches into a tale of an academic committee's investigation into a Mr. Nackybal's cube-rooting ability, which occupies some thirty pages of the novel but remains unfinished. Although "Watt had little to say on the subject of the second or closing period of his stay in Mr. Knott's house" (199), the narrator says a good deal about the master's clothes, movements, furniture, voice, physical appearance, shoes and boots—which seem to be in perpetual motion. When Micks arrives, Watt finishes his milk and his cigar, puts on his hat and greatcoat, takes his bags, and prepares to depart, not, however, without a last permutation of possibilities of rest, a rest he denies himself. On

Watt's walk to the station he sees an indeterminate figure that arouses his inveterate speculation about its identity, before it disappears without receding into the distance. Arriving late at the train station, Watt spends the night in the waiting room, where, with his mind's ear, he hears "voices whispering their canon" (232), and then the voice of a woman he had known. By the dawn's early light Watt perceives a chair and a picture of a horse. Felled by the opening of the waiting-room door, Watt recalls fragments of a Hölderlin verse (in German) and alliterative English phrases, before he is restored to consciousness by a dousing of dirty water. Up and about again, Watt asks the ticket agent for a ticket, and when that man, a Mr. Nolan, tells him the price—"One and three"—Watt counts aloud: "Three and one." Those are Watt's last words in the book bearing his name. The last reference to him (before the addenda) is that same Mr. Nolan's: "Is it the long wet dream with the hat and bags?" (246). Watt is a paradox and a figure of farce in this gnosiological novel.

In the context of chronology, Watt is last seen in the company of Sam, to whom he ostensibly tells the story we read. The two men first meet on a dilapidated garden bridge when Sam saves Watt from "the subfluent flood" (154) after the latter puts his foot through the bridge floor. Together they repair the bridge, and together in the garden, they delight in destroying birds and offering rats for cannibalization. Interrupted in their pleasures by Watt's transfer to another pavilion, they nevertheless meet again in the wind and sun, through holes in their respective fences. "So we began, after so long a time, to walk together again, and to talk, from time to time. As Watt walked, so now he talked back to front" (164). Although Watt's backward bent has been hinted in his back to the engine en route to Mr. Knott's house, in his explanation of entering Erskine's room "Ruse a by," and in his last words at the station "Three and one," he grows more relentless in his inversions, and Sam reports them to us for seven of the eight stages of his narration of Watt's closing period at Mr. Knott's house.[7]

The addenda lack temporality, but they contribute to our knowledge of Watt—from singular events like Watt's climb to the roof, to rhymed verse about the failure of Watt's quest; from the descant and threne heard by Watt to the "soul—landscape" of his experience of nothing; from Watt's morbid dread of sphinges to his late awareness that "Mr. Knott too was serial, in a vermicular series" (253). The longest addendum concerns Arthur, and it hints that, dissimilar as he is to Watt, he will undergo a comparable initiation; but then the failure of Watt was predicted in Arsene's initial declaration.[8]

With considerable difficulty, I have tried to piece together a sequential account of Watt's disjunctive adventures (written under adverse conditions). The circumstantial evidence of other characters yields information with little illumination. Before Watt arrives at Mr. Knott's establishment, he inspires abuse from the tram conductor and the station porter, surmise from the Nixons and Mr. Hackett, courtesy from the newsagent Mr. Evans, violence from Lady McCann, and a sermon from Mr. Spiro. After Watt leaves Mr. Knott's house, he arouses a glance from an ass or goat, courtesy from Mr. Case, an accidental blow from the door kicked open by Mr. Nolan, a solicitous dousing by Mr. Gorman and Mr. Nolan, and a series of questions from one and all. Watt is not only afflicted with an inquiring mind, but he is the source of inquiry by the episodic others of the book. Not to mention the reader, who seeks to follow the Watt-scenes, enfolded as they are between the disparate but symmetrical monologues of his predecessor and successor at Mr. Knott's house, which are in turn framed by a small chatty society at the tram station and the train station.

Watt is to some extent an example of imitative form (Abbott's phrase, 1973): madden the reader with reason in order to show the madness of reason. By John Mood's calculation, about one-third of the novel consists of lists, sequences, alternations, genealogies, logical possibilities, permutations and combinations. Most of the direct dialogue—whether statement, question, command, or interjection—is prefaced by "He/She *said*" (emphasis added). Phrases of explanation—"One of the reasons for that was (perhaps) this"—precede phrases of illustration—"To mention only" or "Add to this." The conjunctions "because" and "for" are qualified by "but" or contradicted by "not" or "never," and assertions are qualified by "in a way." Many sentences begin with a conversational "Now," which is atemporal, but "never, never" is repeated like a mantra. The very names of protagonist and (perhaps) antagonist, Watt and Knott, become counters in the repetitive play of words. *What* is pounded into *Not* or, more usually, *Knot*.

Ostensibly that pounding is performed by the scribe Sam, who is coy about revealing his own identity. On page 69 we read, incidentally, of "[Watt's] mouthpiece." Some ten pages later, concluding his account of the Galls, the still unnamed narrator offers us this revealing sentence: "For there we have to do with events that resisted all Watt's efforts to saddle them with meaning, and a formula, so that he could neither think of them, nor speak of them, but only suffer them, when they recurred, though it seems probable that they recurred no more, at the period of Watt's revelation, *to me,* but were as though they had never been" (79; emphasis added). Whoever "me" is, he is an external witness of Watt's suffering. Midnovel the narrator makes a sweeping claim that "all I know on the subject of Mr. Knott, and of all that touched Mr. Knott, and on the subject of Watt, and of all that touched Watt, came from Watt, and from Watt alone" (125). At two junctures, Sam mentions his notebook, and yet he impugns Watt's own testimony about Mr. Knott: "what kind of witness was Watt, weak now of eye, hard of hearing, and with even the more intimate senses greatly below par" (203).

Sam too is a problematic witness, for he recounts scenes from which Watt is absent, and he quotes Arsene's monologue verbatim although Watt hears it only "by fits." However, an addendum informs us: "Note that Arsene's declaration gradually came back to Watt" (248). Sam himself points to his difficulty in understanding Watt's several speech inversions, and the scribe also acknowledges that his own hearing gradually fails. Since the Watt-Sam conversations take place in an (unnamed) institution, the reasonable reader may well doubt their accuracy, in spite of the declaration of Mr. Louit in Arthur's tale, as presumably reported by Watt, and then Sam: "So much depends on the accuracy of the record" (186).

But then the narrator—whether Watt, Sam, we, or one unnamed and even unpronounable—makes a series of assaults on the reasonable reader.[9] The narrator asks rhetorical questions, derogates the narration, pockmarks the text with dashes, footnotes, question marks, parentheses. At the level of narration, there are no transitions between many events. Like an omniscient narrator (but how nescient!), the narrator promises information to come or, more rarely, refers to what has already been imparted. Some fifty pages before Mr. Nackybal enters the novel he is mentioned in a comparison; similarly, the dog Kate is mentioned some thirty pages before she figures in the millennial Lynch clan, and the fishwoman is mentioned some seventy pages before she pleases Watt. The narrator digresses into passing minds—Mr. Hackett at age one, Mr. Case the ticket agent, and an ass or goat unseen by Watt. All these devices stress the virtual impossibility of telling a coherent tale.

Sam warns us: "Watt spoke also with scant regard for grammar, for syntax, for pronunciation, for enunciation, and very likely, if the truth were known, for spelling too, as these are generally received" (156). Actually, however, Watt's grammar, unlike that of Arthur in the addenda, is correct, but his syntax is sometimes awkward or confusing—"have still some food got, in the old pot" (96). Faults of pronunciation emanate from Watt—"o'cluck strock," but also from Arthur—"the cute to its roob." Although there are indeed errors of spelling, it is hard to imagine Watt committing them; Tetty Nixon speaks of *dollar* for *dolor, osy* for *osé,* and *wom* for *womb,* which her husband corrects to *woom.* It is unclear whether the spelling errors in examples of Watt's inversions belong to Watt or Sam, but it is clearly the narrator who is aware of the *written* text when he underlines the phrase "because of" six times, only to remark parenthetically: "tired of underlining this cursed preposition" (134). Before a series of semicolons he sighs: "How hideous is the semi-colon" (158). The narrator, rather than Watt, lapses into archaisms in this seemingly contemporary setting—*nay, espied, hasten, unbosom, wont*—and he frequently misplaces modifying phrases. Although the vocabulary is simple, even monosyllabic, some twenty words sent me to the dictionary. Rhyme or alliteration erupt, as it were, without rhyme or reason, as in the following phrase—"cloaca of clonic gratification." The narrator also has a taste for oxymoron—"headlong tardigrade," "implied blatantly," "foundered precipitation," "a bicycle for a Miss Walker." Although most of the repetition—by Watt and others—hinges on permutations and combinations, a sprinkling of the words *little* and *old* helps endear Watt to us.

In this text so rife with devices, Mood and Rabinovitz, respectively, have annotated many errors, and Beckett himself told me that he knew of certain mistakes and knew that there were others of which he was unaware.[10] For that matter, a footnote warns of error: "The figures given here are incorrect. The consequent calculations are therefore doubly erroneous" (104). We can, however, be quite sure (sure!) that cognomen slips are deliberate on Beckett's part:

> Arsene: "with you and Arsene, forgive me, with you and Erskine." (61) [Arsene also calls Watt "Jane" five times.]
>
> Sam: "This refusal by Knott, I beg your pardon, by Watt . . ." (115)

Again and again in the frantic series of series, the text seems to assume its own momentum, with scant propulsion by an author. *Watt* is an exasperating book to read because of what Beckett in *Proust* called "the comedy of exhaustive enumeration" (71). To some extent *Watt* can only be reread, to savor its resonances. Having summarized the incidents in some detail, I now shift to resonances or connections.

The novel opens on Mr. Hackett, who, as we learn twelve pages later, reminds Mr. Nixon of Watt. With reason, for the mind of "Hunchy" Hackett, prefiguring Watt, moves from the evidence of his senses, in logical and comical steps. His last word in the novel is "What?"—the question that Watt never asks. Late in *Watt* the station porter curses Watt, with an inadvertent recollection of Hunchy Hackett: "The devil raise a hump on you" (24). The very first paragraph casts doubt on what Mr. Hackett sees and on how he reasons, for he contradicts himself: "He knew they were not his, but he thought of them as his." After another sentence, the self-contradiction leads to a deduction: "He knew were not his, because they pleased him" (7). The brief second paragraph contains another contradiction, as well as mention of Mr. Hackett's "agitated walk," predicting that of Watt. By the third paragraph Mr. Hackett is in a quandary that again prefigures that of Watt, as to whether to go on or return. An erotically entwined couple inspires Mr. Hackett to draw hilarious conclusions. Then, without so much as a blank space of separation, Mr. Hackett and a policeman confront an empty bench, "still warm, from the loving" (9). Alone on the bench, Hunchy Hackett sits in a quasi-crucified position, foreshadowing Watt's resemblance to a Bosch

Christ. Before Watt enters the novel—"motionless, a solitary figure" (16)—the reader confronts frail logic, disjunction, repetition, contradiction, an authority figure, a religious dimension, as well as a footnote about the "avoidance of the plethoric reflexive pronoun after *say*" (8). The footnote suggests that some of the avalanche of *said*s in the novel may be mental rather than vocal.

On the bench Mr. Hackett is soon flanked by the Nixons, and in the ensuing conversation he lapses into a French word *(primeur)*, reads a bawdy poem, listens to a description of Larry's birth (intertwined with phrases about a game of "slosh," where, resembling copulation, balls are potted). "I am scarcely the outer world" (10), Mr. Hackett assures the Nixons, and Watt will retire from the outer world to serve Mr. Knott. Mr. Hackett recalls his fall from a ladder at age one, and he lyrically imagines the scene, as Watt will often retire into his mind. Once Watt alights from the tram, he *intrigues* Mr. Hackett, as we learn when that verb is sounded four times. When the Nixons depart (after Mr. Hackett has twice mistaken their name), Mr. Hackett looks at the darkening sky, only to disappear from the novel. Before the focus shifts to Watt, the text has subverted names, numbers, and various affirmations. Moreover, if Mr. Hackett reminds Mr. Nixon of Watt, he may remind us of Mr. Beckett, whose name sounds so similar.

It is sometimes suggested that the said Mr. Beckett abandoned exposition and narrative sequence in *Watt* because he wished to immerse us in Watt's experience at Mr. Knott's house. However, the novel begins (and ends) in unknotted (and unidentified) Ireland, whose inhabitants view Watt with small sympathy. Even after Watt's arrival on Mr. Knott's premises, we move in and out of Watt's thoughts, at the caprice of the narrator. We navigate Arsene's stream of consciousness more adroitly than we do that of Watt, and indeed, on rereading, we realize that Arsene predicts Watt's failure; he too has a case of inversion: "with a little fat bottom sticking out in front and a little fat belly sticking out behind" (58). Arsene's "short [and prophetic] statement" is lost on Watt, who, however, is devoted to Sam. Watt and Sam pace together and kill small animals together, but Sam keeps his distance from Watt—a distance of fluctuating penetration into his mind.

Whether or not Sam is the narrator of the book we read, the two companions have considerable stylistic range, between them. The dialogue of parts I and IV is as witty as the social scenes of *Murphy*. Embedded in the exasperating series are nuggets of lyricism. Arsene is quoted on "a being so light and free that it is as the being of nothing" and on the servants' "premonitions of harmony" (39). Although the Galls are deeply disturbing to Watt, the narrator poeticizes meaninglessness: "[The incident] resembled [others] in the vigour with which it developed a purely plastic content, and gradually lost, in the nice processes of its light, its sound, its impacts and its rhythm, all meaning even the most literal" (72–73). Sam describes the land-scape in which he walked with Watt: "In winter there were the thin shadows writhing, under our feet, in the wild withered grass" (154). Later he conveys the quality of Watt's speech: "Of this impetuous murmur much fell in vain on my imperfect hearing and understanding, and much by the rushing wind was carried away, and lost for ever" (156). Lost it may be, but the rhythm recreates it for us. Although neither Sam nor Watt is named in the final sentence of part III, a tragic destiny rises from Sam's verbal rhythm: "And from the hidden pavilions, his and mine, where by this time dinner was preparing, the issuing smokes by the wind were blown, now far apart, but now together, mingled to vanish" (213). It summarizes the significant life of Watt and Sam.

However we react to and interpret the narration of *Watt,* the addenda are impenetrable without access to the ur-*Watt.* As Ackerley (1993c) has shown, thirty of the thirty-seven addenda are comprehensible only through that earlier manuscript. This is a far cry from the notes to "Whoroscope," which refer to ascertainable authority. "Fatigue and disgust" is the narrator's excuse for not incorporating the addenda into *Watt,* but publication *is* a kind of incorporation. Moreover, even without immersion in the ur-*Watt,* we can react emotionally to the addenda, which concentrate references to Watt's effort to enclose nothingness in words, to his awareness that nothing happened, to Watt's rootedness between waste and sky, to his empty heart and empty hands, and to Watt's final weariness—"an old rose now."

The novel must have been important to Beckett, who clung to the manuscript through the most adverse conditions. It is all very well to say that he explored Watt's madness "in order to stay sane" (Knowlson, 303), but the novel itself, like *Murphy* before it, shows sympathy with madness. It is too simple to read Watt's story as that of Beckett himself, in the wake of Büttner, and yet the rendition of Watt's plight does seem deeply felt (and, inhabitually, Beckett helped Dr. Büttner with his research). Not only do we grasp the madness of reason in the face of a fixity of perpetual motion, but through that grasp we achieve the catharsis that eludes Watt. Not permanently or finally, but perhaps we sense the irrational and the ineffable to a degree that Watt rarely does. Through the addenda Beckett (irrationally?) demands that the reader yield to the incomprehensible, however her/his reason may attack other aspects of the novel. As I have tried to do.

Since Beckett once characterized *Watt* as "an exercise," I wonder what he meant. (I didn't dare ask him.) Formal? The novel is a mythic quest—a form that would serve Beckett in French till midcentury. Linguistic? Ann Beer (1985) exhaustively seeks to prove *Watt*'s importance to Beckett's bilingualism, and in spite of seeking she finds unimpeachable evidence of its strategic position in Beckett's oeuvre.[11] Whatever *Watt* meant to Beckett, however, parts of it can be enjoyed by any careful reader. Rather than echo the usually astute Paul Davies ("*Watt* is above all a very funny and enjoyable work" [53]), I would counter: "*Watt* is above all a very painful and demanding work," but it is *also* funny and variably enjoyable. It mocks the contingency of what Mr. Hackett demands for Watt: "Nationality, family, birthplace, confession, occupation, means of existence, distinctive signs" (21). Watt is the first Beckett protagonist to lack all these, for they are irrelevant to his quest. Watt quests through language, but not *for* language. Seeking being with undependable semantic succor, Watt precedes later Beckett protagonists into the unknown; yet language tends to stumble toward the known. For all Watt's stumbling, however, Beckett's stylistic mastery is astonishing, and the mythic hints are resonant. In an incongruous comparison of Watt's colleague Erskine to a fish, the narrator brings himself up short: "But do such fish exist? Yes, such fish exist, now" (120). And yes, such dauntless, daunted heroes as Watt exist, now.[12]

1945

Although American troops arrived in Roussillon in August 1944, Beckett did not manage to leave until April 1945 (Bair, 334). He returned to Dublin via a bomb-damaged London, where English officials viewed him with suspicion, confiscating his passport and the typescript of *Watt*. His Resistance record spoke in his favor. He called on Routledge, the publishers of *Murphy*, but the rejection of *Watt* reached him swiftly in Ireland. Beckett pursued other publishers, and he even engaged the A. P. Watt agency, but the name brought no good fortune (Knowlson, 311).

While in Dublin with his family, Beckett experienced what he himself called "a revelation." Too often, that revelation is eclipsed into that of Krapp's vision in *Krapp's Last Tape*, but Beckett wrote to Richard Ellmann: "All the jetty and howling wind are imaginary. It [the revelation] happened to me, summer 1945, in my mother's little house, named New Place, across the road from Cooldrinagh" (qtd. in Knowlson, 686 n. 55). Knowlson's comment on this revelation seems to me a gem of criticism, and I therefore quote it at some length:

> The image of Beckett undergoing a conversion like a "St. Paul on the road to Damascus" can too easily distort our view of his development as a writer. As critics have shown, some of his late themes are already deeply embedded in the earlier work, particularly his interest in Dem-

ocritus' idea that "nothing is more real than nothing," and the quietistic impulse within his work. But the notion of "THE REVELATION" also hides several earlier and less sudden or dramatic revelations: the certainty that he had to dissociate himself at an early stage from Joyce's influence; the reassessment necessitated by almost two years of psychotherapy; the effect on him of being stabbed and in danger of dying; the freedom to discover himself as a writer . . . living away from Ireland. . . ; the impact of the war years, when his friends were arrested and he was forced to escape and live in hiding. (320)

All these factors contributed to the so-called revelation of 1945, but its fruits were delayed for a few months.

Impeded in his efforts to leave Ireland for France, Beckett joined the Irish Red Cross, which was to set up a hospital unit in war-torn Normandy. Beckett arrived in St.-Lô in August 1945. As driver, interpreter, and storekeeper, Beckett was surrounded by the wounded, the homeless, and the disease-ridden. Although Beckett resigned his post in January 1946, he continued from Paris to aid his Irish colleagues (O'Brien, 339).

"Saint-Lô"

The English quatrain grieves for a French city. Unpunctuated and difficult of syntax, the first two lines contrast with the last two—both sonically and emotionally. The first two lines flow with St. Lô's Vire River and with time's continuum. The river will flow again through sunshine and shadows of a city as yet unbuilt, a new Saint-Lô. A pun on "unborn" condenses the future into the unbearable, and the alliterative *b*s and *r*s may be heard as ripples on the impersonal river. In the last two lines heavy consonants weigh down the mind, which will sink into chaos after it is forsaken by its ghosts. The hard "k" sounds of the short final line contribute to the feeling of sinking. A city may rise again, but the individual mind is embedded in memories.

Even while working in Normandy, Beckett resumed his ties to Paris—preeminently Suzanne. The cultural life of Paris had not ceased during the Occupation, but the August 1945 liberation of the city revitalized it. Separate exhibitions were planned for Beckett's painter friends Geer and Bram van Velde, and the *Cahiers d'art* thereupon commissioned an article from Beckett. Although the exact date of writing is uncertain, there is no doubt that Beckett's first French publication was this piece of art criticism.

Probably written in 1945, while Beckett was with the Irish Red Cross at St. Lô, the poem "Saint-Lô" was first published (with variants) in the *Irish Times*, June 24, 1946, and has been reprinted in collections, including *Poems*.

La Peinture des van Velde ou le monde et le pantalon [The painting of the van Velde brothers, or the world and the pair of trousers][13]

The essay opens with what was to become the climax of Nagg's joke about the tailor and his client in *Endgame*: "But, Sir, look at the world and look at your trousers." Although the article itself makes no further reference to that old joke that denigrates God's creation, its thrust celebrates art above reality. Beckett takes his time, in arriving at his ostensible subject, art, while he ambles in the superior tone of his prewar book reviews—with the significant difference that the sneer is now French.

The first third of Beckett's essay defends nonprofessional art appreciation against the professional criticism that must have irritated him on his return to Paris. Airily, Beckett dismisses particular critics, general aesthetics, pointless anecdotes, catalogues raisonnés, and confused verbiage, of which he cites his own prose as an example. Briefly, Beckett defends individual paintings from discussion and "improvement," of which he gives several examples. These early paragraphs are written with a light touch, not unlike the station scenes of *Watt* in their glib and funny dialogue. Parodying art critics with a sequence of "On lui dit" [He is told], Beckett counters these critics with a series of irate questions. Particularly incensed by the judgment *pompier* [pretentious] as a dismissive term, Beckett rejects comparative evaluation: "Car pertes et profits se valent dans l'économie de l'art, où le tu est la lumière du dit, et toute présence absence" (*Disjecta*, 123) [For profits and losses are equal in the economics of art, where the silenced is the light of the said, and all presence is absence]. Shifting midparagraph to direct address to the spectator, Beckett declares that the only thing that that spectator can know about a painting is whether he likes it, and perhaps why.

When Beckett finally does arrive at the van Velde brothers, he fails to mention a single painting of either painter. Aware that words betray the visual, Beckett cloaks his remarks as personal reactions to the pleasure afforded him by the two brother-painters. He couples the brothers in their representation of change, but he then opposes one to the other; Bram paints

---

Federman and Fletcher quote Beckett that *La Peinture des van Velde ou le monde et le pantalon* was written at the beginning of 1945, shortly after the exhibitions of A. and G. van Velde, respectively, at Galéries Mai and Maeght. However, the dating is problematic, as Knowlson explains: "Beckett himself told his bibliographers that he wrote it early in 1945, but went on to say that this was *after* the Bram and Geer exhibitions, which was a slip of the memory. Certainly it was written before the autumn of 1945" (687). First published in *Cahiers d'Art* (1945–46), it was reprinted in *Disjecta*.

the changed object and Geer the object that changes, the one brother painting extension and the other sequence. Beckett seeks to convey the brothers'
contrasting styles through his contrasting verbal rhythms, but he then
deflates his own verbal flights: "C'est ça, la littérature." Having distinguished between the two forms of painting, Beckett rails against a postwar
term in vogue—"l'humain." When painters themselves ape critics with that
modish word, Beckett wonders about the solitary painting that contains
unheralded humanity. Beckett predicts that much stupid prose will be
penned about these two painters. "J'ouvre la série. C'est un honneur" (132)
[I open the series. It's an honor].

Beckett is facetious about his series of remarks about art, which were
written not long after his series of series in *Watt*. But that was in another language—and almost another world. Without exaggeratedly praising *La Peinture des van Velde*, one can nevertheless take pleasure in the rhetorical vigor
of its series of questions, quotations, and repetitions. Beckett's French is
assured and colloquial, with vulgarities uncustomary in art criticism: "rigolade, iconographie de quatre sous, loufoque, faire son affaire, emmerder,
déconner, foutre le paix, trucs, cochons d'intellectuels." Himself a "cochon
d'intellectuel," Beckett would soon learn to subdue his formidable erudition
to fictions of inchoate feeling.

Arbitrarily, I choose to close this chapter by extending Beckett's "Pantalon" quotation—"J'ouvre la série"—to his French "creative" writing. That
series opens in 1946, extending nonstop to 1950; it is a series encompassing
four novellas, four novels, two plays, a few poems, and miscellaneous art
criticism. However, it is the unparalleled quality of that series that defies criticism.

1946

∞

J'Ouvre la Série

[I open the series]

Beckett spent his first few months in postwar Paris learning the sad fate of friends. Joyce had died in Zurich in 1941, and his faithful amanuensis Paul Léon was murdered by the Nazis in 1942. Alfred Péron, perhaps Beckett's closest French friend, had been tortured in a concentration camp; he died in Switzerland on his way home on May 16, 1945 (Bair, 341). It is impossible to imagine Beckett reveling in Paris scenes of post-Liberation jubilation.

Beckett's most fertile creative period began early in 1946, but light verse in English probably precedes it. An undated, unpublished poem in the Beckett Archive at RUL is marked in Beckett's hand: "1946, after St.-Lô."

1946

∞

"Antipepsis"

A synonym for the title is "indigestion," and the poem's twenty-four lines constitute a witty sally at intellectual indigestion. Unusual in a Beckett poem are the (rough) tetrameter rhyming couplets with occasional enjambment (to which Walter Draffin was sensitive in *Dream*). It is possible that Beckett's poem is an adverse comment on himself, or perhaps on another Trinity graduate in France. Beginning with the cliché about the cart before the horse (changed by Beckett to an ass), the poem soon equates the cart with the mind. Sent to a "foreign part," the mind runs amok, spreading the rumor: "A thought has taken place!" The city reacts with panic, and the poem concludes somewhat mysteriously: "Bring forth your dead! Bring forth your dead!" Is the thought then dead, or is the bassackwards thought wholly inap-

---

The "Antipepsis" typescript, dated 1946, is at RUL. It has been published in *Metre*, December 3, 1997, 5. Phyllis Gaffney persuasively links "Antipepsis" with "The Capital of the Ruins" and Beckett's postwar experience with the Irish Red Cross.

propriate to a "foreign part," which is still shivering from the recent war? Phyllis Gaffney's 1990a summary is apposite: "'Antipepsis' denotes a world upside down, an absurd world where the cart comes before the ass, and where reason has expired" (273).

Beckett thought little of the poem, since he did not even mention it to Harvey. It is nevertheless of some interest that the privations of postwar Paris failed to erode Beckett's sense of humor. In its anti-intellectualism, the poem resembles *Le Monde et le pantalon*.

When the scholar John Fletcher attempted to date Beckett's first sustained French fiction, the author wrote him: "*Mercier et Camier* was first attempt at novel in French and cannot have preceded *Nouvelles*" (Federman and Fletcher, 63). However, the dates on Beckett's manuscripts contradict his memory. The French section of the story *La Fin* was begun in March 1946; the novel *Mercier et Camier* was penned between May and September, the story *L'Expulsé* between October 6 and 14, and the story *Premier Amour* between October 28 and November 12. The story *Le Calmant,* begun on December 23, terminated Beckett's first postwar year, along with that phase of his vision.[1] Although Beckett had lived in France for nearly a decade when he began his matchless series of works in French, his creative language was an invention, as Jean-Jacques Mayoux realized: "Le personnage beckettien semble se confier, se confesser plutôt, interminablement, à un auditeur imaginaire, dans une forme mixte, orale juste assez avec à l'occasion une bonne grossièrté, pour le reste une tenue singulière. Dans l'ensemble, Beckett écrivain français invente un langage" (1972, 34) [The Beckettian character seems interminably to confide in, or rather confess to, an imaginary listener, in a mixed voice, somewhat oral with the occasional vulgarity, but otherwise a singular quality. On the whole, Beckett as a French writer invents a language].

La Fin (*The End*)

La Fin resembles *Watt* in its focus on a skullscape and in its thickets of description into which dialogue occasionally—and hilariously—intrudes; the merciless repetitions of *Watt*'s "he said" translate into the equally relentless "dit-il." Yet *La Fin* is a radical new departure in Beckett's fiction. An anonymous narrator-protagonist says "I," and he tells a story featuring at once excruciating detail and cosmological sweep. Irrational and reason-ridden,

---

La Fin is a Beckett manuscript treasure, now at Burns Library, Boston College. Begun in English, this untitled story shifted to French midway through the narration. In Beckett's bilingual holograph notebook, the English part is frequently dated, whereas the French part is not. The first half of *La Fin,* entitled "Suite," was published in French in *Les Temps modernes* (July 1946) with Beckett expecting that review to print the remainder, which he had not yet completed. This was the occasion of asperities between Beckett and Simone de Beauvoir (Knowlson, 325–26).

timeless and contemporary, particular and universal, the story seems at once a personal adventure and an impersonal myth. Beckett did not, of course, invent the first-person protagonist-narrator, but he endows it with an authenticity that spurns coherence, causality, and concatenation of events.

Until recently, it was thought that Beckett, having posed as a Frenchman during World War II, shifted after the war to creation in French. However, the "Suite" notebook modifies that view of Beckett as a French writer. On February 7, 1946, Beckett began an untitled story in English: "They dressed me and gave me money." In that banal sentence, where "they" is active and "me" passive, the two are implicitly at odds. Beckett continued to trace the oddity of "me," dating each day's pages. On March 13—often a significant number for Beckett—he stopped ten lines down on the twenty-eighth page of his manuscript and drew a horizontal line across the page. In his rushed handwriting, he recapitulated in French a passage he had written about the narrator-protagonist's tutor, who had given him dark glasses and *The Ethics* of Geulincx, and who was found dead on the floor of his water closet (cf. *CSP*, 91). The death of the tutor was the occasion of Beckett's birth as a major French writer. The still untitled story continues as eventually published, except for frequent phrasal variants.

The first word of *La Fin* is not finally the "je" of its first-person narrator-protagonist, but an "ils" without antecedent. The second sentence opens on "je," and for the next five years Beckett's first-person narrators will feel themselves at the (un)mercy of an anonymous "ils." The blend of protagonist-narrator is unstable, predicting the decentered subject of postmodern theory.[2] The "je" of *La Fin* rambles in a vocal prose, although we read the text in long paragraphs of print. Lacking the tensions of Watt-Knott and Watt-Sam, *La Fin* moves arbitrarily, almost surrealistically, through temporary shelters—a bedded room, a basement room, a seaside cave, a dilapidated shed, and a boat, which floats untransitionally into the sea. In each of these shelters the narrator affirms: "J'étais bien dans . . ." [I was comfortable enough in . . .]. Each of these shelters elicits detailed and often incongruous accounts of the objects it contains. Outside these refuges, however, the landscape shifts without warning from an unfamiliar unnamed city with its river, to seaside, mountains, isolated suburbs, and unfathomable sky. The location grows increasingly arbitrary, and the time of action is indeterminate; "un

Beckett's letter to Beauvoir appears in *No Symbols* (Lake, 81–82). The whole of *La Fin* was published only in 1955 in Minuit's *Nouvelles et Textes pour rien*. Translated "by Richard Seaver in collaboration with the author," *The End* was first published in *Merlin* (summer–autumn 1954) and revised in *Evergreen Review* (November–December 1960). It is found in *CSP*, to which my page numbers refer. Gerry Dukes has superbly summarized the publication and translation histories of the four novellas (London: Penguin, 2000).

jour" recurs frequently, and, more rarely: "Je ne sais combien de temps je restai là" (*Nouvelles*, 99) [I don't know how long I stayed there, *CSP*, 88].

In this indefinite time and shifting space, the narrator can be maniacally explicit about certain matters—his clothes (which belonged to a deceased man), his crocus (which never blooms), the way he rides an ass, the way he milks a cow, his carpentry applied to a begging board and to his last refuge in a boat. At times the narrator feels himself part of objects, like the stool of his first room, or the excretion in his shed, or the waves that engulf his boat.

The narrator's close attention to subhuman matter is countered by his lack of involvement with the several human beings who cross his path or his mind. In the narrative the first person to achieve noun status is "le mort," whose clothes the protagonist inherits. He soon meets a M. Weir, who is less weird than his name implies. Later, the "je" encounters a guardian of a cloister, a Greek or Turkish landlady, her successor who expels him, two separate policemen, a priest, his insufferable son, a generous man with an ass and two humble dwellings, a nameless boy who supplies him with milk for a penny (a coin that crops up repeatedly in this French text!), and finally a Marxist fanatic who views the narrator pitilessly as an example of "l'asservissement, l'abêtissement, l'assassinat organisé" (112) [slavery, stultification and organized murder, 94]. The Marxist compares the protagonist to a dog, and indeed his narration abounds in animals—horses, ass, cow, rats, toads, flies, gulls, lice. It is as though the narrator sets out to include in his fiction—"mon mythe"—whatever is usually elided in more conventional stories.

This is glaringly evident in the naturalistic detail that is ignored by such naturalists as Zola and Dreiser. The narrator of *La Fin* is old and feeble when the story opens, and yet he registers mild disappointment that the three women who stuff him into his trousers are uninterested in his private parts. We early hear about the wounds on the protagonist's skull, necessitating a hat, and about the hole in his stool, which accommodates his cyst. In his basement-room the protagonist nourishes a crocus bulb by urination and defecation, but he is expelled from that room in favor of a pig. After sleeping on dung, so that his odor causes his ejection from three buses, the protagonist is welcomed in his friend's seaside cave, where he treats his scalp and his crablice with seaweed. A mountain shed contains disgusting objects that the narrator enumerates. While begging in town, the protagonist scratches himself so satisfyingly that he prefers it to masturbation. During his begging interlude, too, the protagonist's excretions diminish. Yet near his end in the boat, the narrator still manages a feeble fart.

Scatology belongs to the domain of naturalism, but the narrator depicts his excrements with humorous verve, and the entire myth secretes comic incongruities, implying that man's whole physical life is a funny bypath. The unappetizing appearance of the protagonist (inspiring laughter or hostility) is not pathetic but comic, as is his scrupulosity about the decorum of begging, and his resignation to, and even expectation of, mistreatment. The legacy of the narrator's tutor curiously pairs dark glasses with the *Ethics* by Geulincz (*sic*—a work mentioned in *Murphy*). Evicted from the basement-room, the protagonist regrets the instant disappearance of months of calm, whereupon the evictor promptly cautions him: "Du calme, du calme" (95; untranslated). When the protagonist milks a cow clumsily, wasting some milk, he consoles himself: "Cela ne fait rien, c'est gratuit" (103) [No matter, it's free, 90]. In contrast to the abundance of descriptive detail, the story's dialogue is sparse, but it sparkles, from the disobliging M. Weir to the Marxist fanatic and his heckler. When the rats see the protagonist in the boat, he imagines them saying: "Pensez donc, de la chair vivante" (114) [Just think of it, living flesh, 95]. Finally, before unplugging the hole that will gradually admit water into his boat, the narrator is dapper enough to note that a string attaches his hat to his buttonhole.

On first reading, one has the impression that the author recounts anything that comes into his head, but the unconcatenated prose is carefully rhythmed by repetitions and sound play. The narrator may make covert reference to the communicating vessels of the surrealist Breton—"C'est le moment peut-être où les vases cessent de communiquer, vous savez, les vases" (119) [Perhaps it's the moment when the vessels stop communicating, you know, the vessels, 97]—but *La Fin* is patterned writing, for all its oral quality. One can even extract a plot from the narration: expelled from his room, the protagonist seeks a substitute home and eventually finds it in a kind of suicide at sea—an end that gives the story its title. However, imposition of linearity would render most of the story digressive, and it is in these seeming digressions that Beckett magnetizes the attentive reader. As Beckett's art criticism, influenced by Gestalt psychology, scanned the problematic relation of figure and ground, so *La Fin* is his first story to obliterate the distinction between plot and description. "My myth" thrives on its suggestive inclusiveness, musically rendered. Balance and alliteration enhance the rhythm, as in the narrator's account of his own speech: "à force d'assimiler les voyelles et de supprimer les consonnes" (88) [my way of assimilating the vowels and eliminating the consonants, 83]. Yet the prose is rich in vowels and consonants that draw attention to words, and to the mind that combines them.

The narrator's main thread intertwines two themes subsumed by the story's successive titles—"Suite" and "La Fin" (Continuation and End). The continuation oozes through long paragraphs of moribund things, seasons, and incidents in Beckett's most entropic tale to date. The end of the story embraces a mythic heartbeat; it recounts a kind of suicide into fiction.

In 1946 Beckett could not have foreseen his future work, but possibly rooted in his memory emerge the narrator's references to a small boy. In the first of these the boy asks his mother about the sunny sky after a day of rain, and she answers impatiently: "Fous-nous la paix" (83) [Fuck off, 81]. What is curious about this early incident in the "myth" is that the boy is situated neither as a memory nor a fantasy of the narrator. He simply erupts abruptly midparagraph and then vanishes; the narrator's description of a sky triggers a boy's question about the sky. Nearly forty pages later in the French text the narrator recalls himself as a small boy in a high place. The latter image is a variant of the one in the poem "For Future Reference," where a small boy is challenged to dive. Both images about a small boy will gain resonance through later Beckett works, coalescing in *Company*. Almost prophetic of *Godot* is a throwaway line in *La Fin*: "Plus rien, plus rien à faire" (95) [There's nothing more to be done, 87].

Occasionally in *La Fin* we are made aware of the narration as narration: "Tout cela ce sont des mensonges, je le sens" (85) [That's all a pack of lies, I feel, 82]; "Même les mots vous lâchent, c'est tout dire" (118–19) [Even the words desert you, it's as bad as that, 97]; "Assez, assez, les images" (119) [Enough, enough, the next thing I was having visions, 98]; "Mais pour en finir avec ces images" (121) [But to have done with these visions, 99]. The difficulty of telling a tale is demonstrated too in such interjections as "non, faux," (87) [no, that must be wrong, 83] and the rhetorical question "comment dire" (116) [how shall I say, 96].[3]

The last ten pages of *La Fin* constitute an unbroken paragraph, punctuated by several "Je ne sais pas." Beginning with "Je ne travaillais pas tous les jours" (113) [I did not work every day, 95], the text gravitates toward its end, of which we are warned: "Je savais que ce serait bientôt fini, alors je jouais la comédie, n'est-ce pas, celle de—comment dire, je ne sais pas" (116) [I knew it would soon be the end, so I played the part, you know, the part of—how shall I say, I don't know, 96]. The concluding pages of *La Fin* increasingly embrace large natural forces even while meticulously specifying details of carpentry for what will prove to be a coffin. As "the end" was predicted in the story's opening paragraph, so it is heralded in the final long paragraph, which closes imagistically: "La mer, le ciel, la montagne, les îles, vinrent m'écraser dans une systole immense, puis s'écartèrent jusqu'aux limites de l'espace. Je songeai faiblement et sans regret au récit que j'avais failli faire, récit à l'image de ma vie, je veux dire sans le courage de finir ni la force de continuer" (122–23) [The sea, the sky, the mountains and the islands closed in and crushed me in a mighty systole, then scattered to the uttermost confines of space. The memory came faint and cold of the story I might have told, a story in the likeness of my life, I mean without the courage to end or the strength to go on, 99]. Eclipsing continuation into ending, the cosmos into the human heart, a life into an unstable story, these two lyrical sentences close the tale that Beckett *did* tell, and its associational detritus *is* in the likeness of a life, before rationality imposes order upon experience. Fusing mineral, plant, and animal; temporary shelters and expulsion; landscape and skullscape into the process of fabulation, *La Fin* englobes a solitary life and its narration.[4] The combination of a first-person protagonist-narrator and the French language served as a liberating elixir for Beckett.

Mercier et Camier

Beckett shifted sharply from the associative quasi-solipsism of *La Fin* to the dialogue-riddled symmetries of *Mercier et Camier*. Critical attention to *Mercier et Camier* has tended to see it as a precursor to *En attendant Godot,* and it is certainly that, but it is also an achievement on its own, despite Beckett's later dislike of his "first attempt at novel in French." Beckett's original title for this work, begun on May 5, 1946, and completed on September 26, is *Le Voyage de Mercier et Camier autour du Pot dans les Bosquets de Bondy* (Admussen, 67). "Tourner autour du pot" is colloquial French for "to detour," and the voyage of Mercier and Camier proves to be a series of detours from the undesignated destination of the two traveling friends. Further, the title situates these detours in the groves of Bondy, which is colloquial French for "a den of thieves." A single reference to Bondy—*Watt's* evocation of "toute l'agitation du Bondy métropolitain" (197; untranslated into English)—suggests an inferno that, late in the novel, paradoxically calms Mercier and Camier.[5] The long French title therefore implies that the two friends engage in a series of detours within an environment of ill-wishers. The actual title *Mercier et Camier* shifts emphasis from the voyage and environment to the two friends with bisyllabic names, which suggest agency.

More than any previous Beckett fiction, *Mercier et Camier* begins in medias res: "Le voyage de Mercier et Camier, je peux le raconter si je veux, car j'étais avec eux tout le temps" (7) [The journey of Mercier and Camier is one I can tell, if I will, for I was with them all the time, 7]. However, as in *Ding-Dong* a decade earlier, the first-person singular pronoun vanishes, although other telltale signs of the narrator erupt from time to time. *Mercier et Camier* is the account of two old men who undertake a journey together, and the novel ends when they go their separate ways. Early in the novel they are steadfast, if dilatory of purpose, but like their predecessor in *La Fin*, they

---

Under the title *Voyage de Mercier et Camier autour du Pot dans les Bosquets de Bondy*, a holograph in two notebooks is at HRC. A typescript is at NhD. Although completed in 1946, *Mercier et Camier* was not published until 1970, by Minuit, to which my page numbers refer. Six notebooks containing Beckett's translation into English are at RUL, as well as two typescripts. Beckett's English translation was first published in 1974 by Calder and Boyers, and in 1975 by Grove, to which my page numbers refer.

are increasingly reluctant to leave their several shelters—a pagoda in a public garden, an archway, a train, various bars, and especially Helen's place, which is always seductively near. Like their predecessor, too, Mercier and Camier travel mostly on foot, although they own a woman's bicycle. Briefly, they board a train. On their journey Mercier and Camier meet what the narrator calls "une longue série d'êtres malfaisants" (17) [a long line of maleficent beings, 13]. Their conversation notes these beings, as well as other inconveniences, particularly the inclement weather.

Near the end of the book Camier ruminates: "Au fond, . . . on s'est parlé de tout sauf de nous" (206) [Looking back on it, . . . we heard ourselves speaking of everything but ourselves, 119]. Yet much—perhaps most—of their speech pivots on themselves; their conversation is englobed by the narrator in the ubiquitous "Il dit." In their speech Mercier and Camier tell us little about their prevoyage lives—only that Mercier is a family man and Camier a detective. Nor do we ever learn the origin of their friendship, which presumably ends when they separate, unlike their successors, Vladimir and Estragon, who remain together at the end of *En attendant Godot.*

In the original French *Mercier et Camier* has an insistent structure, divided into twelve chapters. Yet the structure mocks itself, for each third chapter consists of a list of events narrated in the previous two chapters—a tersely phrased, occasionally inaccurate, and quixotically selected list.[6] It seems as though the narrator can summarize his narrative only after writing it. Each of the early chapters of narration tends to focus on a particular incident, but transition is lacking between chapters. Four times in the end-of-chapter lists it is noted that "Mercier et Camier confèrent." And their conferences permeate the narrative chapters. Over half the novel is devoted to dialogue, and much of that dialogue is composed of their irrepressible duets. As their travels proceed, however, incidents are recounted, only to dissolve, and sallies are exchanged, only to fizzle.

Although the first word of their quasi-inexhaustible dialogue is Camier's "Rentrons" (13) [Let us go home, 11], the two friends not only persevere in their journey, but they call attention to that perseverence. Mercier early seizes upon the hostility of a ranger: "Serait-ce le coup de fouet dont nous avions besoin, pour nous mettre en route?" (19) [Can it I wonder be the fillip we needed, to get us moving? 15]. With rhetorical flourish calculated to appeal to the ranger, Mercier pleads: "C'est aujourd'hui enfin . . . après des années de tergiversations, que nous partons, vers une destination inconnue, et dont nous ne reviendrons peut-être pas vivants" (24) (in translation, it is Camier who pleads: "The day has dawned at last . . . after years of shilly-shally, when we must go, we know not whither, perhaps never to return . . . alive" [16]). Midvoyage, however, Mercier turns accusingly to Camier: "C'est ça, notre voyage?" (69) [What kind of a trip is this? 45]. The narrator warns us: "A ce moment-là le voyage de Mercier et Camier semblait sérieuse-ment compromis, en effet" (69) [At this point the journey of Mercier and Camier seemed likely indeed to founder, 45]. Increasingly, Mercier and Camier experience difficulty in verbalizing their voyage, but Camier can still issue a call to action: "Que notre devise soit donc lenteur et circonspection, avec des embardées à droite et à gauche et de brusques retours en arriere, selon les dards obscurs de l'intuition" (109) [lente, lente, and circumspection, with deviations to right and left and sudden reversals of course, 69]. When Mercier and Camier wish to toast their enterprise, they are at a loss for words: "Camier ajouta, Et au succès de notre—, Mais ce voeu, il ne put l'achever. Aide-moi, dit il. Je ne connais pas le mot, dit Mercier, ni même la phrase, capable d'exprimer ce que nous croyons être en train de vouloir faire" (140) [Camier added, And to the success of our—, But this was a toast he could not complete. Help me, he said. I can think of no word, said Mercier, nor of any set of words, to express what we imagine we are trying to do, 83]. Finally, Mercier and Camier are better able to speak of parting than of departing.

By means of the dual protagonist—what the narrator of *The Unnam-able* will later call "a pseudocouple"—Beckett submits his quest structure to the vagaries of a relationship. The two hatless old men are visual contrasts: Mercier is tall, gaunt, and gray of eye and beard, while Camier is short, fat, red-faced, and bandy-legged. On their voyage Camier attends to most of the practical details—buying food, making train reservations, finding bars and ordering drinks, worrying about his cyst, breaking their umbrella, fucking Helen, forbidding quotations or accounts of dreams, reviewing the despera-tion of their situation, and suggesting their separation. Mercier is more philosophical; he offers generalizations, and sometimes he sinks into dreams that obliterate his immediate surroundings. Camier charges: "Tu vois des formes qui n'existent pas" (175) [You see shapes that do not exist, 101].

At the beginning of the novel, Mercier and Camier speak of "notre" umbrella, raincoat, sack, and bicycle. They do not speak of "notre" Helen, but she offers to accommodate them both. The narrator early designates Mercier and Camier as "nos deux pigeons" (10) [our heroes, 9]. Their paired-ness is early reflected in the fornicating dogs who cannot separate. Another pairing may be seen in the auxiliary characters of Madden and Conaire. Although they are not twinned in the narrative itself, they are listed in the summary chapter as "hors d'oeuvre" ["interlude" in English]; almost liter-ally, Madden and Conaire are outside of the work, each obliquely reflecting the cruelties of existence. Pairedness also arises in Mercier's confrontation with a *pair* of children, boy and girl. In the course of their travels Mercier and Camier are served by *two* different managers of bars. Early in the novel an authority figure threatens them, and late in the novel they beat an authority figure to presumed death. When a policeman reprimands Mercier and Camier in the company of Watt, the latter testifies to their harmless insanity. In the bar where the manager wishes to eject Watt, Mercier and Camier testify to his temporary insanity, occasioned by the death of his bigeminal— "tout en double sauf le cul" (201) [everything double but the arse, 116]. Implicit is a comment on the binary nature of experience.

These symmetries serve as background for the predominant duologues. Again and again Mercier and Camier address each other in terse and witty duets, where short rhythmic phrases are capped by repetition. Attritively, Mercier and Camier divest themselves of their joint possessions, but not of their words, and they both voice an awareness of words—especially verbs and prepositions. They may walk in different rhythms, they may hear (or imagine) different voices, but they themselves sound similar.[7] The narrator even offers an oblique explanation of their symmetry: "Certes il fallait de la force pour rester avec Camier, comme il en fallait pour rester avec Mercier, mais moins qu'il n'en fallait pour la bataille du soliloque" (131) [Admittedly strength was needed for to stay with Camier, no less than for to stay with Mercier, but less than for the horrors of soliloquy, 78]. The final separation of Mercier and Camier is symmetrically verbalized before it is fulfilled. The novel's initial farce of missed meetings is paralleled by their deliberately missed meetings before they arrive at the fork in the road, from which they go their separate ways. In the last chapter of narration Watt presents them to one another, enjoining them to *retutoyer* one another. However, the resurrection of their intimacy is brief. Mercier and Camier flee together from the bar where Watt curses life, although life's cruelty has been one of their recurrent themes. Mercier and Camier walk a little way together, conversing in a residual duet. However, Mercier fails to arouse Camier's admiration for the skyscape, and after the latter twice approaches the canal, perhaps thinking of suicide, Mercier and Camier take leave of one another. Camier moves on, and we are admitted into Mercier's final thoughts, after the dialogical verve subsides.

The novel's first sentence announces the story's sustained subjects— voyage, Mercier and Camier, time, and especially the narrator himself. Although the narrator then abandons the first-person singular pronoun, his presence is ubiquitous. The first sentence-paragraph is followed by a page of description of the future voyage of Mercier and Camier, which is declared less arduous than that of others who are "poussées par un besoin tantôt clair, tantôt obscur" (8) [driven by a need now clear and now obscure, 7]. It is the narrator who manipulates the farce of the missed meetings of Mercier and Camier, and he is aware of his manipulative hand: "Que cela pue l'artifice" (10) [What stink of artifice, 9]. This is the first of the narrator's several acerbic comments on his own narration. (No other Beckett fiction is so liberally sprinkled with derogatory parentheses.)

Less self-consciously but with sardonic momentum, the narrator sets the scene on Place St.-Ruth with its military legacy of a copper beech; Field Marshal St. Ruth is dead, and the beech is dying. The narrator informs us, before we hear Mercier and Camier, that they speak "par bribes, suivant leur coûtume" (13) [not translated: "in fragments, as is their wont"]. The narrator early warns us: "Certaines choses, nous ne les saurons jamais avec certitude" (12) [Certain things shall never be known for sure, 10]. Early in the novel the narrator retreats during the dialogue sequences, but after Mercier's scatological evocation of the ranger's heroic past, the narrator addresses us directly: "Ne déduisez rien de ces paroles en l'air, Mercier et Camier furent vieux jeunes" (23) [Conclude nothing from those idle words, Mercier and Camier were old young, 16]. The first of numerous injunctions to the reader, this command recalls Beckett's letter to MacGreevy, as he was embarking on *Murphy:* "My next old man, or old young man, not of the big world but of the little world, must be a kite-flyer" (qtd. in Knowlson, 197). The oxymoron "vieux jeunes" subverts human time, and yet it can be explained: old men, Mercier and Camier are young in fiction. The narrator sustains a tendency to belittle both Mercier and Camier, but especially Mercier.

The narrator is scornful of his own prose, but he does not seem aware of his narrative lapses: his protagonists are absent from a long scene in a bar; he describes Helen's carpet and parrot, but never Helen herself. Although Mercier and Camier tell Helen that they were chased by a bull, no one tells us about it; nor is there more than passing mention of a goat that lodges in Camier's memory. Midnovel the narrator enjoins us: "Suivons-les attentivement, Mercier et Camier" (96) (omitted from English translation), but in the second half of the novel the narrator often rambles away from them.

The narrator remarks on his lapses into the present tense, and he also harks back to rhetorical questions, in the manner but not the matter of earlier fiction: "Il recommençait à pleuvoir. Mais la pluie avait-elle jamais cessé?" (36) [The rain was beginning again. But had it ever ceased? 25]. Having established a symmetrical similarity and opposition between Mercier and Camier, the narrator later appears to confuse them: "Laissons-le donc se réveiller, Mercier, Camier, peu importe" (181) [So let him wake, Mercier, Camier, no matter, 103]. No matter because the final loneliness is applicable to Mercier, Camier, the narrator, the reader; the narrative subtly suggests this by its shift to the present tense—self-consciously: "curieux ce soudain temps présent" (182) [not translated: "curious, this sudden present tense"].

Near the end of the novel the narrator penetrates increasingly into Mercier's thoughts. Before a four-page paragraph, in which he describes

Mercier's meeting with a man carrying a folding-board, and with another man accompanied by a donkey, the narrator generalizes: "Mais les Mercier, un rien les arrête, un murmure qui monte, s'enfle, se décompose, une voix qui dit que c'est étrange, l'automne du jour, quelle que soit la saison" (127–28) [But the least little thing halts the Merciers of this world, a murmur coming to its crest and breaking, a voice saying how strange the autumn-tide of the day no matter what the season, 76]. In the second half of the novel the narrator draws our attention to Mercier's ineluctable awareness of being caged in time. A dying fall resonates through the book's leaden skies, frequent rain, fading light, and the relish at cruelties that bear witness to the malevolence of the Almighty. Watt curses life, but Mercier has not only cursed God, he has also declared his temptation to suicide. By the end of the book the narrator lyrically dissolves time into eternity, the living into death. After Camier leaves Mercier alone by the canal, the narrator enters into Mercier's extraterrestrial hearing of human sounds in darkness and rain.

Just before the temporary separation of Mercier and Camier, the narrator exhibits human solitude within a cosmic reach, as he eclipses Mercier into Camier, and both into Dante's Sordello. Returning to his protagonists, the narrator virtually forces a meeting between Mercier and Camier before they take different directions, and he does so by a unique apostrophe to his own fictive character: "A qui le tour, à Camier, alors retourne-toi canaille, et regarde bien. Tu n'en crois pas tes yeux, cela ne fait rien, tu vas les en croire, car c'est bien lui, ton joli coeur barbu, ossu, fourbu, foutu, à jet de pierre, mais ne la jette pas, pense au bon vieux temps, où vous rouliez dans la merde ensemble" (185) [Whose turn now, Camier's, then turn worm and have a good look. You can't believe your eyes, no matter, you will, for it's himself and no error, your boon old weary hairy skeleton of a butty, bet to the world, within stone's throw, but don't throw it, think of the good old days when you wallowed in the swill together, 104]. The apostrophe melodiously approaches the narrator to his character, even while keeping his distance.

The last chapter of narration opens with four pages of rage about the difficulty of sustaining a narrative, before the narrator steels himself for the reentrance of Camier, whom Watt (emerging from nowhere) reunites with a Mercier who is absorbed in a display of hats. The resurrection of Watt may be Beckett's most blatant cross-reference to another of his works (still unpublished at the time of writing *Mercier et Camier*), but it is not the first intratextual reference in the novel. Although Belacqua is absent, the shade of Dante is present. When Camier reminds Mercier that they have agreed to deny themselves quotation, the latter replies, like Dante to Virgil (French version only): "Lo bello stilo che m'ha fatto onore" (100) [the beautiful style that has honored me]. The narrator later describes Mercier or Camier—he fails to distinguish them—seated like a shadow Sordello (French only), and

M. Madden alights from the train at a place where only the damned go. Later, however, Mercier is relieved when Camier informs him that they are walking toward the tower of the damned.[8] Beckettian rather than Dantesque is Mercier's recognition of a man with a folding-board, which irresistibly recalls *La Fin,* as does the man with the donkey who nearly knocks Mercier down. Less complex than Beckett's essay *Les Deux Besoins* is the protagonists' awareness of their two needs—"celui que l'on a, et celui de l'avoir" (117) [the need you have and the need to have it, 72]. The narrator evokes "le vieil enueg" (191, French only), a Provençal word with which Beckett titled two poems of *Echo's Bones.*

It is, however, *Watt* that offers most allusion to *Mercier et Camier.* Before Watt himself arrives on the scene, Camier, like his predecessor, hears a mixed chorus. In a dream Mercier claims to have met the innkeeper as M. Gall, even though his actual name proves to be Gast. M. Gast converses with a patriarchal client named Graves, even as Mr. Knott's gardener. Upon the entrance of Watt, unrecognized by either Camier or Mercier, that erstwhile protagonist claims to know them from the cradle.[9] Grudgingly, Mercier admits: "J'ai connu un nommé Murphy . . . qui vous ressemblait un peu, en beaucoup plus jeune" (194) [I knew a poor man named Murphy . . . who had a look of you, only less battered of course, 111]. In this avatar Watt is not only battered but bitter. He is also resourceful, lying to the gendarme about the sanity of his companions. He makes no mention of the milk that sustained him in his own novel, but he orders whiskey, which perhaps prompts his confession: "Moi aussi, j'ai cherché . . . tout seul, seulement moi je croyais savoir quoi" (198) [I too have sought . . . all on my own, only I thought I knew what, 113–14]. It is a firmer declaration than any made by Mercier or Camier; or even by the narrator. It is followed by Watt's prophecy: "Il naitra, il est né de nous . . . celui qui n'ayant rien ne voudra rien, sinon qu'on lui laisse le rien qu'il a" (198) [One will be born . . . one is born of us, who having nothing will wish for nothing, except to be left the nothing he hath, 114]. Watt's utterance is a paraphrase of the philosopher Geulincx, already evoked in *Murphy.* Watt grows venomous and violent, cursing life; yet he salutes Quin. Only a reader of the ur-*Watt* could know that Quin is the ur-Knott, but Mercier tries to be helpful: "Ça doit être quelqu'un qui n'existe pas" (206) [That must be someone who does not exist, 119]. Indeed he does not. Beckett has jettisoned him—or at least his name.[10]

However Beckett disliked *Mercier et Camier,* it is an accomplished novel. Its descriptions lead to Beckett's trilogy, and its dialogues lead to his drama, particularly *En attendant Godot. Mercier et Camier* is a milestone on Beckett's French path. Having completed in *La Fin* a French story with a first-person narrator, Beckett then attempted the more difficult task of juggling a first-person narrator who focuses on a pseudocouple—"pseudo" because Mercier and Camier may be viewed as the uncomfortable conjunction of mind and body; but also "couple" with individual and increasingly conflicting needs. As in the later *Godot,* anxiety seeps through the humor of the spirited exchanges of the interindependent couple. Beckett controls his humor both in these duets and the narrator's self-scorn. In contrast, lyrical passages convey the traps of time clamping down on the suffering human animal, and these passages sometimes overlap with Mercier's dreams—"ta rhapsodie," says Camier.

Inconspicuously, *Mercier et Camier* follows a self-reflexive byway, that of the authorial vulture. As in the poem of that name, and the unpublished story "Echo's Bones," death is at once desirable and ineluctable. The narrator of *La Fin* inherits the clothes of a corpse, and his own suicide terminates his story. On one level death *is* the story, in that life must cease, in order that narration may occur. In *Mercier et Camier* death hovers over the prose. M. Madden informs the pseudocouple: "toujours dans les cadavres, voilà ma vie" (59) [one corpse on top of another, there's my life for you, 39]. Helen's parrot may be dead, and the waiter Patrick dies while Mercier and Camier sleep. It is, however, in the *outre-tombe* passages of the narrator that Beckett hints at the death-dealing resonances of words, in a last evocation of experience: "Il y a aussi les jolies couleurs, verts et citrons expirants, restons dans le vague, elles palissent encore mais c'est pour mieux vous embrocher, s'éteindront-elles jamais, oui, mais oui, elles s'éteindront" (190) [Then there are the pretty colours, expiring greens and yellows vaguely speaking, they pale to paler still but only the better to pierce you, will they ever die, yes, they will, 109]. By dying into fiction, the narrator lives on.

One might imagine that Beckett's writing momentum during 1946 left him little time for other thoughts. However, for Irish Radio he prepared an address about the work of the Irish Red Cross at St-Lô. Dated June 10, 1946 (while he was composing *Mercier et Camier*), it was apparently never delivered. Even were it broadcast, it would not have been spoken by Beckett, who was back in Paris, immersed in his fiction (O'Brien, 339).

The Capital of the Ruins

Beckett begins by detailing the (sometimes makeshift) physical resources of the Irish hospital in war-torn St.-Lô: "The consequent atmosphere is that of

---

A signed typescript of *Capital of the Ruins* is in the Archives of Radio Telefís Eireann, with a photocopy at RUL. Gaffney (1999a and b) summarizes the problems as to its broadcast, its correct text, and its shifting tones. It was first published in 1986 by Eoin O'Brien in *The Beckett Country* and that same year in *As No Other Dare Fail* (London: Calder). It is republished as appendix 3 of *CSP,* to which my page numbers refer. Gaffney (1999b) relates it to *Mercier and Camier.*

brightness and airiness so comforting to sick people, and to weary staffs" (*CSP*, 276). After presenting these facts, Beckett taunts the xenophobia of the neutral Irish at home in the aftermath of World War II, explaining: "the whole enterprise turned from the beginning on the establishing of a relation in the light of which the therapeutic relation faded to the merest of pretexts. What was important was . . . the occasional glimpse obtained, by us in them and, who knows, by them in us . . . of that smile at the human condition as little to be extinguished by bombs as to be broadened by the elixirs of Burroughes and Welcome, the smile deriding, among other things, the having and the not having, the giving and the taking, sickness and health" (277). It is a surprisingly sweeping claim for someone who was diffident about his own war experiences. Beckett goes on to imply that the exchange of smiles was not always equitable. His final paragraph praises the work of the Irish hospital in war-ravaged St. Lô, and he implies that it will carry its own reward, in the hope "that some of those who were in Saint-Lô will come home realising that they got at least as good as they gave, that they got indeed what they could hardly give, a vision and sense of a time-honoured conception of humanity in ruins, and perhaps even an inkling of the terms in which our condition is to be thought again. These will have been in France" (278). The subtle shift to the first person—"our condition"—links this occasional piece with Beckett's French fiction, also touching on "our [mortal] condition."

Only two weeks later, on June 24, Beckett's poem "Saint-Lô" (possibly written while he was there in 1945) was published in the *Irish Times,* and it may have arisen from the same feeling that the human condition needed rethinking—or refeeling. Even the unpublished poem "Antipepsis" hints at it. His own rethinking or refeeling lay in continuing to work on *Mercier et Camier,* which he completed in September. Almost at once, he then returned to the I-centered ramble in a short story. It deals, in Beckett's description in a letter to George Reavey, with "the same deadbeat as in 'Suite'" (qtd. in Lake, 83).

L'Expulsé (The Expelled)

Beginning with a scene of expulsion from a domicile, *L'Expulsé* seems to recapitulate the opening of *La Fin*. This second story, however, is somewhat

---

The holograph of *L'Expulsé*, dated October 6–14, 1946, is at HRC. First published (with variants) in *Fontaine* (December 1946–January 1947), *L'Expulsé* was republished in 1955 in Minuit's *Nouvelles et Textes pour rien.* Translated by Richard Seaver "in collaboration with the author," it was revised for publication in *Evergreen Review* (January–February 1962) and was reprinted in *Stories and Texts for Nothing* (New York: Grove, 1967) and *No's Knife* (London: Calder and Boyars, 1967). It is found in *CSP*, to which my page numbers refer.

more firmly lodged in the memory of the first-person anonymous narrator-protagonist, who recalls events that occurred long before the putative but undesignated present time. Memory is perhaps the most insistent theme of the meandering tale: "C'est tuant, les souvenirs" (11) [Memories are killing, 46]. Yet memory can fail. On expulsion, the narrator cannot remember how to count the number of stairs down which he is flung, but he is proud to remember that they were few. When the narrator's hat is thrown after him, he remembers the day his father bought it for him, and the mockery of his hatless friends. In the street he looks up at the window of his erstwhile room from which the anonymous "ils" have expelled him, and he reminisces about his skill with geraniums. When two successive policemen (or perhaps the same one returned?) object to the way he walks, the narrator traces the origin of that walk to his schoolboy incontinence. When the protagonist finds himself with money, he recalls that a Maître Nidder bestowed upon him a legacy from a woman whose name he cannot recall. (Nidder is the only proper name in the story, as the authoritative M. Weir is the only name in *La Fin*.)

Past the midpoint of *L'Expulsé*, these random memories cease, and the narrative suddenly takes sequence when, after seeing horse-drawn cabs at a funeral, the protagonist enters one. Despite a certain reluctance on the narrator's part, the cabdriver befriends him. On the driver's initiative, they seek a room for the protagonist, and when all rooms displease him, including that of a hotel, he is invited to the driver's home. Preferring the horse stable, the protagonist passes an uncomfortable night. Since the stable door is locked from the exterior, he leaves through the window, thus expelling himself, in a skew echo of the initial expulsion. The narrator concludes: "Je ne sais pas pourquoi j'ai raconté cette histoire. J'aurais pu tout aussi bien en raconter une autre. Peut-être qu'une autre fois je pourrai en raconter une autre. Ames vives, vous verrez que cela se ressemble" (40) [I don't know why I told this story. I could just as well have told another. Perhaps some other time I'll be able to tell another. Living souls, you will see how alike they are, 60]. It seems probable that the narrator told the story in order to show how alike living souls are, composed of untrustworthy memories.

L'Expulsé conceals its quest: when first expelled, the protagonist lies on the sidewalk and rises only to wander aimlessly. It is the cabdriver who insists that he seek a dwelling; his quest is imposed upon him. When domiciled for the night, the protagonist exercises his ingenuity to depart. *L'Expulsé* is chary of references to the tale as a tale, but we do read such sentences as "Disons les choses comme elles sont" (11) [that's the truth of the matter, 21]; "Ratiocinons sans crainte, le brouillard tiendra bon" (22) [we may reason to our heart's content, the fog won't lift, 51]; "Curieux comme on n'arrive pas à lier certains noms" (28) [strange how one fails to forget certain names, 54]; "cocher, hotel, c'est vraisemblable" (35) [cabman, hotel, it's plausible, 57]. Twice the narrator asks a rhetorical question: "Comment décrire . . ." before proceeding to dwell on his hat and his door. Near the end of his tale, just before descending to the stable, the narrator remarks: "Pas de raison pour que cela finisse ou continue. Alors que cela finisse" (37) [No reason for this to end or go on. Then let it end, 58]. There seems to be a connection between such sentences and the narrator's view of the horse, "comme avec mes yeux de chair" (30) [as with my eyes of flesh, 55], implying that the rest of the narrative is seen with other eyes. (The phrase comes from Job 10:4.)

Reminiscent of *Mercier et Camier* rather than *La Fin* is the underlying sense of a ubiquitous malignancy. A mysterious "ils" expel the protagonist, who is relieved that he is not also beaten. He suspects that his father hatted him out of envy. When the protagonist accidentally knocks down an old woman, he wishes that she may break a femur. Although he narrowly avoids knocking a child down, he would cheerfully lynch young children. The cabdriver not only starves his horse, but he ties the animal's jaws to protect it from offerings of passersby. The protagonist reacts impatiently to the kindnesses of the cabdriver, and he disturbs the latter's wife. Life's cruelties are pronounced in *L'Expulsé*.

On December 15, Beckett wrote his friend George Reavey, "[*L'Expulsé*,] dealing with the same deadbeat as in *Suite*[,] has been taken by *Fontaine*." When the story was republished in 1955 in the book *Nouvelles et textes pour rien*, it was considerably abridged. The book version is shorn of digressive incongruities that render the original narrator-protagonist funnier and more endearing.[11] Perhaps Beckett grew impatient at his own ability to seduce the reader with humor. As finally published, *L'Expulsé* is the shortest of the four stories that Beckett wrote during 1946; it has been stripped down to memory, in which living souls are so alike. Yet the prose is seductive in its sound play and stylistic variety.

As if to underline Beckett's belief that fiction bears only a tangential relation to experience, he no sooner completed *L'Expulsé* than he was *in*cluded in a publisher's list. Pierre Bordas gave him a contract for the French *Murphy* "and a general contract for all future work in French and English (including translations)" (Knowlson, 328). However, Bordas soon broke the general contract, and Beckett was without a publisher for a few years. At the time, however, Beckett must have been sufficiently heartened by his Bordas contract to begin another story. Or perhaps publishers were irrelevant to his narrative, which he withheld from publication until 1970, the post-Nobel year.

Premier Amour (First Love)

Of the four stories of 1946, *Premier Amour* is the most conventional as to plot and character—which is not to say that it is conventional. This anonymous narrator-protagonist is only twenty-five years old at the time of his first (and only) love affair. Events occur in chronological sequence, and some of them display a plausible concatenation. Even the narrator's association of his father's death with his own marriage is an understandable denotation of coming to maturity. *Premier Amour* may thus be read as an abbreviated bildungsroman.

Homeless on a park bench, the protagonist meets Lulu (later called Anne). Sexually (and hilariously) aroused by her, he flees. However, her image is so incisively etched in his mind that he carves her initials in cow-dung, thus recognizing from his reading that he has fallen in love. Returning to the bench, he asks her to sing; he then plays a game with her song, distancing himself till he cannot hear it, and then approaching till it becomes audible again. Unable to tell whether she is beautiful, he recalls the aesthetic quality of his dead father's face. When the narrator-protagonist invites her to speak rather than sing, she informs him that she has two rooms. Unaccustomed as he apparently is to a dwelling, the protagonist soon takes possession of one of her rooms, after frenziedly removing all the furniture but a sofa. That done, he is barely conscious during his night of love. Once he grows accustomed to the room, he is only slightly discommoded by the sounds of his lover's clients in her room. When she reveals that she is pregnant by him, the protagonist urges an abortion. He abandons their home when she goes into labor, but he cannot escape her cries, which haunt him still.

Despite the quasi-coherent plot, however, the manner of telling reveals Beckett. By rhetorical questions, direct address to the reader, and occasional shifts into the present tense, Beckett endows the story with a vocal quality. The narrator also addresses himself, disparaging his prose, but admiring his

---

The holograph of *Premier Amour*, dated October 28–November 12, 1946, is in HRC. A typescript is in the University of California (Santa Barbara). Bair labors the point (192, 358–59, 611) that Beckett did not publish *Premier Amour* with the other stories because it was too personal. However, he may also have felt that it was too explicit and entertaining—like *Mercier et Camier*, which he released only when his publishers pressed him, after the 1969 Nobel Prize. The French edition of *Premier Amour*, like the collected *Nouvelles*, is misdated 1945. Beckett's English translation *First Love* was first published by Calder and Boyars in 1973, and by Grove in 1974, but despite these dates, Beckett corrected the British edition last. It is reprinted with corrections in *CSP*, to which my page numbers refer. *First Love* was the subject of the University of Groningen workshop whose "results" are published in *SBT* 7 (Ayers and van Heusden, 1994).

epitaph couplet, in spite of flawed scansion. Early in the story he cautions himself: "Du calme, du calme" (14) [Softly, softly, 28]. Self-commands tend toward repetition (in French only): "Retardons, retardons" (44) [That's the idea, procrastinate, 41] and "précisons, précisons" (45) [that's the idea, every particular, 41]. Of his night of love, the narrator repeats: "Je n'en dirai pas plus long" (47) [Enough about that, 42]. Single phrases also comment on his tale. A parenthesis encloses: "Je me demande que cela veut dire" (29) [I wonder what that means, 35]. Sardonically, he remarks: "Je ne vois pas de lien entre ces observations" (27) [I see no connexion between these remarks, 34]. The narrator is most skeptical about love: "Je me demande si tout cela n'est pas de l'invention" (22) [I sometimes wonder if that is not all invention, 31]. Describing Lulu's song, he cuts himself short: "Cette phrase a assez duré" (35) [this sentence has gone on long enough, 37]. Attempting to fix the time he returned to Lulu's bench, he hesitates: "comment exprimer cette chose, je ne l'exprimerai pas" (36) [what words are there for that, none I know, period, 38]. When Lulu describes her rooms, he approves: "Enfin un sujet de conversation digne de ce nom" (39) [At last conversation worthy of the name, 39]. When the furniture blocks the doorway of his room, the narrator exclaims: "Un bien grand mot, infranchissable" (42) [translated as "To put it mildly," 40]. Dubious about love, the narrator is drawn to words; while coping with Lulu's furniture, the narrator incongruously hears the word "fibrome" or "fibrone" (42) [in English "fibrome" or "brone," 40]. He loves the words "vase de nuit," which incongruously remind him of Racine or Baudelaire (44, untranslated). Then, belittling his reading, he says sarcastically: "on dirait du Dante" (44, untranslated).

The narrator's story hovers between voice and writing; on the one hand the narrator's colloquial prose sounds vocal; on the other hand, the narrator refers to his writings and his records. Yet it is outside of the context of "mes autres écrits" that the narrator makes oblique intratextual references. For example, the narrator recalls being expelled from his room after the death of his father, even though he pleaded to be allowed to stay, and as in *La Fin*, his father left him some money. Quite explicitly, the narrator recalls having written about his hat, which indeed figures in earlier stories. In *La Fin* the protagonist saw hearts inscribed in cowdung, but in *Premier Amour* he himself does the inscribing. The protagonist of *L'Expulsé* cannot bear furniture in a room, and the protagonist of *Premier Amour* removes the furnishings of his room, "l'un après l'autre . . . des centaines, grands et petits" (42) [piece by piece . . . hundreds of pieces, large and small, 40]. Like the crocus of the protagonist of *La Fin,* a hyacinth attracts this protagonist, and this flower also dies, occasioning the similar refusal of a replacement. The narrator of *Premier Amour* is skeptical about the intellectual love "qui m'a déjà arraché tant de bêtises, à un autre endroit" (30) [which drew from me such drivel, in another place, 35], but he does not specifically name Spinoza or Murphy. Lulu is cross-eyed, like Descartes's "squinty doty" in "Whoroscope." Like Watt, the narrator seeks to clear up perplexities. These reminiscences of earlier Beckett works float up in passing, rather than weighing down the narration; yet they add up to a quality of *déjà entendu* for the experienced Beckett reader, who did not exist at the time of writing.

Although the protagonist of *Premier Amour* is the most plausible character of the four stories of 1946, he is nevertheless estranged from the world at large and from his love in particular. As in the other stories, estrangement is developed through dehiscence, vagueness, and incongruity. More than in the other stories, incongruities tend to be comic: the narrator prefers the odor of cemeteries to those of living beings; while shitting, the protagonist looks at a picture of Jesus; Lulu seduces the protagonist with her song and her muff, and he resents that seduction; the narrator generalizes about women's propensity to undress; a chamber pot inspires the narrator's vision of a grandmother upon it; parsnips are coupled with violets. Humor introduces a passage that links this protagonist to Murphy and Mercier in their affinity for nothingness: "La chose qui m'intéressait moi, roi sans sujets, celle dont la disposition de ma carcasse n'était que le plus lointain et futile des reflets, c'était la supination cérébrale, l'assoupissement de l'idée de moi et de l'idée de ce petit résidu de vétilles empoisonnantes qu'on appelle le non-moi, et même le monde, par paresse" (21) [What mattered to me in my dispeopled kingdom, that in regard to which the disposition of my carcass was the merest and most futile of accidents, was supineness in the mind, the dulling of the self and of that residue of execrable frippery known as the non-self and even the world, for short, 31]. Like Celia before her, Lulu disturbs the protagonist in his desire for immersion in being—or nothingness.

For all the humor of *Premier Amour*, and for all the youth of its protagonist (and whatever its biographical germ), the story sustains Beckett's preoccupation with death. The protagonist of *La Fin* wears the clothes of a dead man; the protagonist of *L'Expulsé* stops to watch a funeral; but the protagonist of *Premier Amour* is a connoisseur of graveyards, preferring one in Prussia to that of his father. He is pleased with his epitaph, which confuses life and death:

> Ci-gît qui y échappa tant
> Qu'il n'en échappe que maintenant.
>
> (10)

> [Hereunder lies the above who up below
> So hourly died that he lived on till now. (26)]

Midstory, in speaking of his hat, the narrator remarks abruptly: "Il m'a suivi dans la mort, d'ailleurs" (30) [I may add that it has followed me to the grave, 35], but we learn no more about his death—or his burial.

Death for Beckett is associated with birth. The protagonist urges his pregnant love to abort, and when she goes into labor, he leaves her. He plays with hearing and silencing the labor cries of his beloved, as he had earlier played with her song. Only when he is on the move can he drown her cries in the noise of his footsteps. No longer believing that her cries will ever cease, the narrator is haunted by the sound that promises new life, and he pities the future pain of that new life. Perhaps the narrator should have taken refuge in other loves. "Mais l'amour, cela ne se commande pas" (56) [But there it is, either you love or you don't, 45] terminates the story. At the beginning and end of *Premier Amour* love is coupled to a father, a new life to someone deceased or absent. "First love" leads ineluctably to suffering and mortality, however comic and vibrant the pathway.

Over a month elapsed between the completion of *Premier Amour* and the beginning of *Le Calmant* on December 23, 1946. Knowlson's biography reveals that this was a time not only of penury for Beckett, but of cold and even hunger in the aftermath of the war. Yet the new story's pain is of another order—a kind of omnipresent lostness.

Le Calmant (*The Calmative*)

Of the four stories of 1946, *Le Calmant* is the most difficult to interpret. Its lack of paragraphing makes it difficult even to read. (After two quasi-introductory paragraphs, the story continues in a single block of some thirty printed pages in French.) In English the title is more arresting than in French—"The Calmative"—(revised from "The Sedative")—but in both languages the title is a neologism. The story itself repeats the word "calm" eight times (six in English). Calm is what the protagonist-narrator seeks, and to that extent *Le Calmant* adheres to the quest structure. Yet the search is not nearly so continuous as that of the protagonists of *La Fin* or *L'Expulsé* for a refuge. Rather, calm seems to entail a surcease of experience, or transmutation of experience into fiction. Thus, the protagonist of *Le Calmant* seeks in his own story a calm analogous to what he obtained as a boy, when his father read to him, evening after evening, from the story of heroic Joe Breem

---

The holograph of *Le Calmant*, dated December 23, 1946 (which is probably the starting date) is in HRC. *Le Calmant* was first published in 1955 in *Nouvelles et Textes pour rien,* to which my page numbers refer. Beckett's translation into English first appeared in *Evergreen Review* (June 1967) and then later in 1967 in *Stories and Texts for Nothing* (Grove) and *No's Knife* (Calder and Boyars). The story is reprinted in *CSP,* to which my page numbers refer.

or Breen, in whose pictures he saw himself. As an adult, the protagonist also hopes for calm from his encounters, but not consistently or emphatically. Although *Le Calmant* does not, like *L'Expulsé*, end with a reference to narration, the impression nevertheless subsists that the story is the calmative.

In *Le Calmant* events are more dreamlike than ever before in Beckett's fiction, and yet dreams are explicitly rejected as jokes, and what is more, significant. Landscapes are vaguer than ever before, and they succeed one another, as the narrator perceives them. Although the protagonist repeatedly strays through deserted streets, he nevertheless meets people. He sees a bald man in a brown suit telling funny stories to appreciative laughter, mainly from women. More touching is his meeting with a boy leading his goat, who offers the protagonist a sticky candy. On the parapet of a cathedral tower the wall-hugging protagonist encounters a man moving in the opposite direction; then he sees a little girl leading a man by the hand. Having entered the unnamed city by the Shepard's Gate (where bats resembled flying crosses), he imagines asking politely for that landmark, and then actually does ask for it when he overtakes someone. However, "J'aurai pu tout aussi bien ne pas exister" (*Nouvelles*, 64) [I might as well not have existed, 71]. Soon falling asleep on a bench, he wakens to hear words addressed to him. They do not calm him, but they lead to his most prolonged communication with another person. Requesting the protagonist to tell the story of his life, the new acquaintance sets an example by telling about his own life, but we hear only about the protagonist's concern for Pauline, the stranger's companion in his story. Then, wishing to sell one of his phials to the protagonist, the man requests a kiss in payment—on the forehead. The protagonist meets no one else.

In *Le Calmant* settings are at once more plentiful and more transitory than in the other stories.[12] The narrator comes upon living beings with surprise: "tiens, des arbres" (44) [oh look, trees! 62]; "voilà les premiers hommes" (56) [there are the first men, 68]. Fear of the light, whose source is unknown, is a recurrent emotion of the narrator. Although the narrator repeats that he never turns back, he seems to pass and repass over the same terrain.

Perhaps the greatest ambiguity of *Le Calmant* lies in its disquieting confusion of life and death. The opening sentence: "Je ne sais plus quand je suis mort" (41) [I don't know when I died, 61] is more shocking than its analogue in Camus's *L'Etranger*: "Aujourd'hui maman est morte" [Mother died today]. Soon the first-person narrator-protagonist reveals murders in his skull and fornications with corpses. During the course of the story he refers several times to his death, but only once to "la vraie mort charnelle" (60) [the rigor of death, the genuine bodily article, 70]. No vulture is mentioned, but that bird seems to hover over this protagonist, estranged from the everyday world, but feeding his fiction on its residue.

More mobile than his predecessors, the narrator of *Le Calmant* is also a subtler storyteller; he glides in and out of his narration. His motion is at once physical and narrational. He calls attention to his difficulties of movement, but, once up and about, he is propelled by a mysterious momentum that seems to be associated with a bright light and deserted vistas. Less colloquial than his predecessors, this narrator is equally attentive to words, which he collects like a connoisseur. Admitting that he resides within a skull, the narrator is the most self-scrutinizing of the French story protagonists. Like his predecessors, he occasionally devalues details of his story, as in his question to the boy with the goat, or his mention of the cap of the man on the parapet. Once he cautions himself: "Assez" (59), and twice he refers to his own myth. He early alerts us to verb tenses: "Car ce que je raconte ce soir se passe ce soir . . . Je menerai néanmoins mon histoire au passé . . . Ah je vous en foutrai des temps, salauds de votre temps" (43–44) [For what I tell this evening is passing this evening . . . I'll tell my story in the past nonetheless (the last phrase is not translated), 62]. The unparagraphed narration begins with the protagonist starting to walk, and journeying becomes the equivalent of narration. Under the duress of fingers around his throat and a caressing voice, the protagonist refers in parentheses to his story in process. Within this story his characters tell stories—the raconteur in a brown suit, his father's reading of Joe Breem or Breen, and the accoster's account of his life with Pauline.

By isolating these tales, I emphasize the storytelling process that is quite subtly enfolded into the actual narrative of *Le Calmant*. On the one hand, the narrator glides into his characters, such as the fictional Joe Breem or Breen; on the other hand, the narrator seems to exult that a character is not he. By the end of *Le Calmant* the brave teenager Breem or Breen is "le pauvre père Breem, ou Breen" (75) [poor old Breem, or Breen, 76]. Even fictions are vulnerable to time. Of the several characters whom the protagonist happens upon, only the boy with the goat and the man with the phials actually address him, and it demands all his resources to reply, so unhabituated is he to speech. Even images escape his control, when he attempts to recall the face of the little girl he thinks he saw on the parapet. Toward the end of the story, he speaks to himself; at least those words present no problem.

The attentive reader of the other stories would recognize their intratextuality in *Le Calmant*. The very title recalls *La Fin*, where the protagonist takes a calmative. Like him, too, this narrator admits: "J'ai tellement changé de refuge" (42) [I have changed refuge so often, 62], and like that peripatetic protagonist, he attaches his hat by a string. Like his predecessors, the protagonist of *Le Calmant* inspires aversion in those he meets, and like them he has a noteworthy walk "chaque pas semblait résoudre un probleme statodynamique sans précédent" (71) [seemed at every step to solve a stato-dynamic problem never posed before, 75]. Both titles of the first story—"Suite" and *La Fin*—are present in a parenthetical self-address of *Le Calmant:* "Comment dire la suite? Mais c'est la fin" (70–71) [How tell what remains? But it's the end, 75]. Several times the narrator of *Le Calmant* yearns for this story to be his last; this desire will be present in future works by Beckett. If *La Fin* is Beckett's breakthrough story into plotless narrative, *Le Calmant* is the most developed and englobing equation of narrative with the process of narration.

I have tried to convey the individuality of Beckett's first French stories, written in the order *La Fin, L'Expulsé, Premier Amour, Le Calmant*. When, a decade later, Beckett published them in book form, he withheld *Premier Amour,* and he reshuffled the other three—*L'Expulsé, Le Calmant, La Fin,* which, he told John Fletcher, might be viewed as Prime, Death, and Limbo (1964, 102). In the *Collected Short Prose, 1945–1980,* first published in 1984, this order is retained, but it is preceded by *First Love,* which becomes the first story of the sequence, and that order is retained in the *Complete Short Prose.* French or English, the new order imposes a chronology upon stories that are profoundly skeptical about chronology. This order also obscures the calculated indeterminacy of the stories; although certain details are vivid, it is difficult to remember which detail attaches to which tale.

Patterns recur. Each story is an anonymous first-person narration largely in the past tense: a man talks about himself, his commentary punctuating selective and disjunctive memories. The protagonists are poor, precise, and utterly unpredictable. They live on the margins of society, whose scorn they accept. The protagonists remember their dead fathers, who are usually associated with hats and with bequests of money. The protagonists are sensitive to animal life, and they are each devoted to a particular plant. The protagonists journey, and their wanderings are juxtaposed against shelters. They roam compulsively—mainly around their nameless native town, which they scarcely recognize. In each story but *Premier Amour* the protagonist is submerged in a crowd, but in all stories he meets someone in an affectional relationship.

More than Beckett's English protagonists, his French protagonists are aware of their own bodies. They have sore scalps, which they hide with their hats, although the hats seem to predate the pustules. In relishing the narration of their physical afflictions, the French protagonists intensify what is lightly rendered for their English ancestors, that is, Belacqua's aching feet still the turmoil of his mind; Murphy's irregular heart is symptomatic of his irregular status in this world; Watt's nonhealing wounds reflect his shattered psyche. So, too, the French protagonists view their bodies as at once an obstacle in their obscure quests, and yet a necessary medium for that quest. Laden with physical and emotional detail, the story's narrator-protagonists accumulate into a generic mature male.

The French stories are a new stylistic departure as well as a new language for Beckett. More than the English fiction, the stories lack exposition, climax, or resolution. They gather force through their alogical immediacy.[13] The French is at once colloquial and rhythmic, simple in vocabulary but phrasally resonant. Since the narrators rarely refer to writing, one has the impression of direct address to the reader. Questions, hesitations, and self-corrections contribute to an oral quality, and yet the sentences are grammatically correct, forming increasingly lengthy paragraphs without topic sentences.

Collectively, the stories testify to the arbitrary nature of narration, so that the overriding point of these stories is that they *are* stories. Nevertheless, they differ in nuance. With his youth, love, and sensitivity to words, the protagonist of *Premier Amour* recalls Murphy, whereas the protagonist of *L'Expulsé*, reasoning and remembering in his prime, resembles Watt. *Le Calmant* and *La Fin* intrude humor into more painful narratives, the one opening on death and the other closing on drowning. All four stories, but especially *Le Calmant,* demand concentration on the part of the reader, and each rereading reveals another verbal treasure, provokes another wave of reflections. Beneath their dynamic surface, the stories yield rich emotional ore.

1947–49

Mais la Réalité, Trop Fatigué
Pour Chercher le Mot Juste

(But reality, too tired to look for the right word)

1947

Perhaps Beckett felt that *Le Calmant* took him as far as he could penetrate toward an avatar of being that was garbed in splenetic namelessness. Whatever the provocation, he veered suddenly from fiction to theater, beginning *Eleutheria* on January 18, and completing that three-act play on February 24. From the unlocalized settings of the French fiction, Beckett turned to a highly localized Paris in his first French play, but neither of these two settings resembles the actual cold, cramped apartment in which he himself was writing.

Eleutheria

Beckett hesitated between *Eleutheria* and *L'Eleutheromane* as the title of his first complete play. The latter translates from Greek as "the lunatic for liberty," and it defines the play's hero, young Victor Krap, although this is not revealed until the last of the three acts—the act that underwent most revision in manuscript. In the first two acts the stage is divided between the furniture-

---

The holograph of *Eleutheria* is in two notebooks at HRC. A typescript is at NhD, with copies at RUL and MoSW. Upon completing the play in 1947, Beckett desired publication and production, but when this did not happen, he came to dislike *Eleutheria* even more than his other works, and he withdrew permission for both. After his death, a translation was proposed by Foxrock in the United States, whereupon Minuit reluctantly published the original French (1995), to which my page numbers refer. The first English translation was published by Foxrock later in 1995, and a new British translation was published by Faber and Faber in 1996. The British translation is superior to the American, but translations in my text were made in 1972 by Beckett, or by me, with his approval for my *Back to Beckett*. Although a "reading" of *Eleutheria* in English took place in New York City, there has been no production of the play.

filled salon of the Krap Paris home and Victor's wretched hotel room, located near l'Impasse de l'Enfant-Jésus—as was Beckett's own apartment. The split stage ostentatiously symbolizes two different ways of life.

Act I satirizes the ailing Krap family, whose heaviest affliction is their son Victor, who left home two years earlier, to live in sordid inertia. After Krap senior dies offstage between acts I and II, Victor opens act II by throwing his shoe at his hotel window and breaking it. A glazier enters immediately (and improbably) to repair it, and he remains present while emissaries from the bourgeois Krap world try to lure or threaten Victor back to the family bosom. As in the well-made play, obstacles vanish in act III. Victor declares his independence: "C'est là la liberté: se voir mort" (149) [Liberty is seeing yourself dead]. At the final curtain, having rejected both suicide and social reintegration, having looked long and hard at the audience, Victor lies down on his folding bed, "le maigre dos tourné à l'humanité" [his thin back turned on humanity].

The act I satire of *Eleutheria* borders on farce. In this French play characters have silly English names like Krap, Piouk, and Skunk. A servant Jacques knocks farcically whenever he enters the Krap salon. M. Krap is unable to urinate. Dr. Piouk espouses birth control and euthanasia to diminish the human race. Farce diminishes in act II, with the arrival of the nameless glazier,[1] whose rhythmic exchanges with his son recall those of Mercier and Camier. The glazier comments critically upon the action in which he sporadically participates. Act III mocks the well-made play when a spectator, a prompter, and the play-text itself appear on stage. Yet the plot rolls mercilessly on toward its resolution, with Victor explaining his stance: "En étant le moins possible. En ne pas bougeant, ne pas pensant, ne pas rêvant, ne pas parlant, ne pas écoutant, ne pas percevant, ne pas sachant, ne pas voulant, ne pas pouvant, et ainsi de suite" (148) [By being as little as possible. By not moving, not thinking, not dreaming, not speaking, not listening, not perceiving, not knowing, not desiring, not being able, and so on]. Although Victor recognizes that his version of liberty is unattainable, he will dedicate his life to its pursuit: "Je ne serai jamais libre. *(Pause.)* Mais je me sentirai sans cesse le devenir. *(Pause.)* Ma vie, je vais vous dire à quoi je l'userai: à frotter mes fers l'un contre l'autre. Du matin au soir et du soir au matin. Ce petit bruit inutile, ce sera ma vie" (162) [I will never be free. *Pause.* But I will ceaselessly feel myself becoming free. *Pause.* I'll tell you how I'll live my life away: rubbing my chains against one another. From morning to night, and from night to morning. That faint vain noise will be my life].

On the one hand, Beckett parodies the well-made play; on the other hand, he departs from that stale form. The usually "heavy" father is quite sympathetic to his wayward son. The usually inconspicuous servants are not only in evidence; they alone are grateful for Victor's "musique." Although the prompter and especially the spectator (who is accompanied by a Chinese torturer) are post-Pirandellian devices, the glazier is a more quixotic anomaly. Not only characters, but incidents subvert the well-made play. In contrast to climactic kisses of that drama, those of *Eleutheria*—one in each act—are decidedly unromantic. Yet, these subversions of the well-made play seem facile diversions for the author of the radical French long stories. As Knowlson recognizes, a major flaw of the play lies in its hero: "Even though the wish for some form of clarification, definition, even explanation of Victor's motives is mocked within the drama itself, it becomes, nonetheless, a very real factor in the failure of the play to hold dramatic interest" (330). Victor is reluctant to speak, but the other characters do so freely—in banal phrases, except for the glazier's rhythmic exchanges with his son.

Despite Beckett's reluctance, after midcentury, to see *Eleutheria* performed or published, the work is recognizably Beckettian: a man's desire to be alone in his bed in a bare room, his search for truth to himself, a bilingual comedy of nomenclature, metatheatrical comment in a piece for theater. These qualities do not, however, constitute a prediction of the creation of *En attendant Godot* less than two years later.[2]

In the meantime daily living was hard in postwar Paris, compelling Beckett to interrupt his creative writing with commissions for translation and art criticism. The latter enabled him to reiterate his admiration for the painter van Velde brothers.

Peintres de l'empêchement [Painters of impediment]

Although Beckett crossed out the title "Le Nouvel objet," that subject was nevertheless on his mind. Beckett opens by referring to his earlier article in *Cahiers d'Art*, to whose ideas he remains faithful. Instead of immediately reiterating his admiration for the painting of the van Velde brothers, however, he is sarcastic about art critics and about artists themselves, who are drawn into the verbal fray about modern art: "la toile et le discours, il n'est pas toujours facile de savoir laquelle est l'oeuf et laquelle la poule" (*Disjecta*, 134) [the canvas and the discourse, it is not always easy to know which is the chicken and which the egg]. Only near the middle of the article does he summon the van Velde brothers in testimony to the vigor of the School of Paris. According to Beckett, both brothers are in mourning for the object, since

A typescript of *Peintres de l'empêchement* (with the title "Le Nouvel Objet" crossed out) is at NhD, dated March 1947. The essay was first printed in *Derrière le Miroir* (June 1948) and is reprinted in *Disjecta*, to which my page numbers refer. It has not been translated into English, except for a passage entitled "The New Object," which may precede the French. Possibly by Beckett, the passage appears in the invitation to the van Velde exhibit at the Koontz Gallery in New York City.

representation is no longer possible for a painter. Geer denies the object because it is what it is, and Bram denies it because he is what he is. Although both are painters of impediment, the one paints the impediment-object, and the other the impediment-eye. For Beckett: "Est peint ce qui empêche de peindre" (136) [What is painted is what impedes painting].

In describing the painting of impediment—especially that of Bram— Beckett gives us a foretaste of his Molloy, who will also be absorbed in unveilings: "Un dévoilement sans fin, voile derrière voile, plan sur plan de transparences imparfaites, un dévoilement vers l'indévoilable" (136) [An endless unveiling, veil behind veil, surface upon surface of imperfect transparencies, an unveiling toward what cannot be unveiled]. As though embarrassed by that poetic flight, Beckett retreats to a sardonic tone, but he closes the essay in flat prose; the modern artist has three choices: (1) to succumb to the outworn subject-object separation; (2) to move beyond representation toward a new relation with the object; (3) to enfold into painting the problematics of the subject-object relationship. There is already a fork in the last way, with the divergent painting of Geer and Bram.[3]

Having camouflaged his art criticism under the persona of a naive amateur, Beckett returned to fiction, beginning Molloy in May 1947 (and completing L'Innommable, the third volume of "the trilogy," in January 1950, after writing Godot). It is possible that between February 1947, when Beckett finished Le Calmant, and May, when he began Molloy, he penned the story F__ to which Suzanne Dumesnil affixed her name, and which Beckett ostensibly translated.[4] The story may, on the other hand, date from 1948, but I prefer to mention it here, to avoid interrupting my commentary on Beckett's three major French novels.

F__

F__ resembles Beckett's four stories of the postwar period in that it is a first-person, alogical narrative exhibiting repetition, fragmentation, interrogation, self-address, and self-correction. It too lacks the exposition, climax, and resolution of conventional short fiction. The characters participate in a problematic relationship that resembles that of A and B early in Molloy, which

---

Neither the original French "F__" nor Beckett's "translation" is extant in manuscript form, and various readers have been suspicious about its authorship. The contributor's note in transition (January 1949) reads: "Suzanne Dumesnil—Forgotten in musical, unknown in literary circles" (151). The future Mme. Beckett may have been "unknown in literary circles" for the good reason that she never wrote anything literary. Of Beckett's biographers, Knowlson does not mention F__ , Cronin believes that such "subterfuge" would not be characteristic of the Becketts (369), and Bair accords the story a full page, in which she guesses shrewdly: "one wonders where the writing ended and the translation began" (387).

may have been written at about the same time. An unnamed "he" bumps into the "I" from behind, with such force that both fall down. In the cold dark windy night—"Those great rifts I saw, filled with black shadow, were the night"—the two characters cannot see one another, but when, after several attempts, they succeed in rising, the man finds that he has lost a "thing," which they seek simultaneously but separately—in vain. They then link arms so as to battle the wind. The narrator is on the way to F__, and the new companion asks whether they are on the road to F__. Although "he" had earlier pleaded that "I" not leave him, he leads the narrator to a roadside ditch, from which he departs with a promise to return. "I" listens to his receding steps and takes pleasure in the thought of his return. However, "the sorry light of dawn" reveals no one on the road, but in the distance the roofs of F__ are visible. The story concludes: "I knew without ever having seen it that it was F__. So. There I was. Or nearly."

One might impose a longer title on the story: "Walking toward F__," or, better, "Struggling toward F__," which would twin the physical and narrative motion. Like Godot, F__ is an indefinite goal that is not reached, but unlike Godot it is not introduced until two-thirds of the way through the work. In the context of Beckett's oeuvre, the journey of F__ is somewhat more goal-oriented than those of the other postwar stories, and it is more arduous than that of the couple, Mercier and Camier. Like Mercier and Camier, however, and unlike their successors Vladimir and Estragon, "he" and "I" finally separate. "I" is left alone, within sight of her/his destination, but only "nearly" there.

The three pages of F__ flow in a single paragraph, punctuated only by periods and rare commas. As in Beckett's French stories, the narrator's difficult progress is reflected in the difficulty of the prose. As in those stories, too, the narrator attempts to impose logic upon chaos. Far from an omniscient narrator, the "I" records the landscape; by 1947 the night, the wind, the distant sea, and the roadside ditch are familiar in Beckett country. Familiar, too, are such stylistic habits as fragmentary sentences, sentences that begin with the conjunction "but" or "and," questions that are unpunctuated by a question mark, the deity used as an expletive, and insistence on the strangeness of events. Less familiar is Beckett's occasional gallicism, for example, "It's of no importance," "the wind bore us a spite," "a heavy labour," "on a so frequented road," "I heard his steps no more." If Beckett did indeed translate the story from the French, it may have been done in haste, replete with gallicisms. Living in poverty, he was translating hurriedly for money, while more sustained work ripened within him.

That was my first lazy guess—before absorbing the illuminating scholarship on Beckett's "leakage" from French in English—Ann Beer on the English *Watt* (1985), Steven Connor on the English translation of *Mercier et Camier*—and I realized that Beckett's gallicisms were consistently deliberate. They were one weapon in Beckett's arsenal for at once subverting and dominating language—any language—because it failed to explore avenues unavailable to the conscious mind. Ann Beer designates these avenues as "the brain's inner life, the worlds before the womb and after the grave, the origins of speech, and what lies beyond the visible stars" (75). Unlike Beckett's French stories, *F__* is bare of minerals, plants, animals, and human society; no stars gleam through these dark rifts. Bold and brief, *F__* is narrated in the past tense, but it startles with the immediacy of its reach toward deep and adversarial realms. It is a story that deserves a double take.

Beckett's six French poems of the late 1940s are usually treated as a group; Harvey, for example, sees in all of them an opposition of the microcosm to the macrocosm. The poems display Beckett's control of French shape and sound. Three of the poems were almost immediately translated into English, for publication in *Transition Forty-Eight*.

"Je voudrais que mon amour meure"

The briefest of the three poems has occasioned most commentary. A response to Yeats's thirteen-line sonnet, "He wishes his beloved were dead," Beckett also seeks solace in that death. Harvey is the first of a number of readers who see Beckett's quatrain as a wish to alleviate the suffering of his mother, afflicted with the Parkinson's disease from which she would die in 1950. However, it seems to me that Beckett banished such explicit autobiography with the war. Rather, the verse enfolds a death wish within a gentle rhythm. Unusual for Beckett in its metrical regularity, the delicate phrasing belies the seeming cruelty of the death wish, as the run-on lines belie (or implicitly contradict?) the desired curtailment of life.

The tender quality of the persona's wish infuses all four octosyllabic lines, which divide into couplets ending in assonance: *meure-tière*, *vais-aimer*. Further sound play is found in the internal assonance and alliteration of *amour-meure* of the first line; an extended alliteration between second and fourth lines occurs in *pleuve* and *pleurant* (as in Verlaine's "Il pleure dans mon coeur / Comme il pleut dans la ville"). Repetitions of the "j" and "v" sounds in "je voudrais" of line 1 and "je vais" of line 3, and the internal rhyme of "ruelles" in line 3 and "celle" in line 4, impart a continuity that contrasts with the implied transience of mortal love.

"Je voudrais que mon amour meure" was first published in English in *Transition Forty-Eight* (June 1948); in the original French in *Gedichte* (Wiesbaden: Lime, 1959). It is included in *Poems*.

"Je suis ce cours de sable qui glisse"

Consisting of two irregular five-line stanzas, the poem contains a familiar Beckettian theme of the circularity of time. The sand, so prevalent in pre-modern hourglasses, is a felicitous image for the transience that is subsumed in the two unpunctuated sentences of the first stanza. The second stanza is one unbroken sentence of direct address to the passing moment. Life is at once built on sand and immanent in sand, blinded by fog and protected by fog, eventuating in a yearning for the solidity of a door that is opened and closed—unaccountably.

"Je suis" opens with a pun, since the French verb can mean "am" or "follow." Unlike the "je voudrais" poem, the admission of the first-person "je" turns on contrast: the present-tense "je suis" in the first stanza changes to a future tense in the second—"je n'aurai plus." In this poem rain of the first stanza, which ends on life's circularity, contrasts with fog in the second stanza, which encloses the persona but also blinds him. Rhyme and alliteration join "pluie" to "poursuit" in the first stanza, and chiming pairs "vivrai" with "ouvre" and "fouler" with "ferme." Both stanzas display the repetitive long "i" keening vowel, eliciting sadness. Harvey suggests that the microcosm and the void grow indistinguishable in this poem, and the flow of sound enhances that feeling of an entropic infinitude.

"Que ferais-je sans ce monde sans visage sans questions"

Again skillful in its quiet enfolding of sound into sense, "Que ferais-je" is a sonnet with nine lines in the octet. In traditional sonnet habit, the octet asks a question that is answered in the sestet, although the entire poem is unpunctuated and unrhymed. Imposed upon the sonnet form is the contrast between the macrocosm of the octet and the microcosm of the sestet—a contrast contained in all three poems of this period. Pervasive in thirteen of the fifteen lines is what Harvey calls the "dark nasal." Although it is somewhat misleading to reduce the different vowels to the singular "nasal," it is nonetheless true that their prevalence bears a resemblance to a voiced sigh. As in the shorter poems, the frequency of sibilants seems to assuage the pain of the persona.

Harvey is particularly acute in describing the alliterative and repetitive

---

"Je suis ce cours de sable qui glisse" was first published in English in *Transition Forty-Eight* (June 1948); in the original French in *Gedichte* (Wiesbaden: Lime, 1959). It is included in *Poems*.

"Que ferais-je sans ce monde sans visage sans questions" was first published in English in *Transition Forty-Eight* (June 1948); in the original French in *Gedichte* (Wiesbaden: Lime, 1959). It is included in *Poems*.

links between synonyms for the macrocosm—"monde," "instant," "onde," "gouffre," and "poussière." In his words: "Rarely . . . does a word that is semantically crucial find itself phonetically isolated" (247). The juxtaposition of "semantically crucial" and "phonetically [un]isolated" admirably limns this sonnet that adds nuance to the macrocosm-microcosm contrast. Here the sestet shows the microcosmic "je" seeking what will become in *Rockaby* "another like herself." I therefore disagree with Harvey, who believes that the thirteenth line is the most important—"dans un espace pantin" [in a convulsive space]. I am struck instead by the need for company, implied in the climactic final rhyming couplet—"sans voix parmi les voix / enfermées avec moi" [Among the voices voiceless / that throng my hiddenness].

If Beckett did indeed write these poems in close proximity to his most celebrated work, *En attendant Godot,* and the inexhaustible novels *Molloy* and *Malone meurt,* it is testimony to his pangeneric range. His six postwar French poems are difficult to date more precisely than 1947–49, the date recorded in the 1959 German *Gedichte.* Since one of the poems is an elegy for his Irish colleague at St. Lô, Dr. Arthur Darley, who died December 30, 1948, it cannot precede that date. Two other poems were not translated for *Transition,* but they are close enough in theme and technique to suggest chronological proximity. Harvey delineates the struggle between macrocosm and microcosm as the burden of all six French poems of the late 1940s, which Beckett may have arranged achronologically for book publication. Although "Mort de A.D." almost certainly dates from 1949, and the remaining two French poems may also postdate the trilogy, I comment here, in order not to intrude on the trilogy, although Beckett may have done so.

"Mort de A.D."

The elegy laments the death of Beckett's friend, Dr. Arthur Darley, whom he met when they were colleagues in the Irish Red Cross in Normandy. A devout Catholic, Darley contracted the tuberculosis he had come to alleviate, and he died in Ireland on December 30, 1948. In Beckett's title for this memorial poem he does not elide the preposition "de" into the vowel initial of his friend, thus offering a bilingually redundant title—Mort dead.

Although the fifteen-line poem lacks typographic stanzas, it falls into three five-line divisions: the first focused on the persona at his desk, the second recalling the life and death of A.D., and the third blending the dead man into his living memorialist. The opening word of the brief elegy is a conjunction—"et," which suggests a continuity of presence. Lines 2 and 5 begin with a past participle ascribed to the persona in the present. Supported by his

---

The elegy "Mort de A.D." was first published in *Cahiers des Saisons* 2 (October 1955) and reprinted in *Gedichte.* It is included in *Poems.*

wooden desk, the persona is filled with contradictions—days and nights indistinguishible, fleeing and fixed, fleeing in fixity in the chiasmus of the fourth line. The second "division" shifts to the unnamed "il," with two past participles and two pluperfect verbs in line 6 signaling what he was and did—phonetically so close in French ("fut" and "fit"). Graphically conjuring a gaunt and bearded face, the elegy presents us with a faith-tormented, sin-burdened man, animated by three present participles—"luisant," "haletant," "dévorant." The third "division" returns us to the persona, who is alive while his friend is dead. Yet both are subject to time's ravages. The old wooden board of line 2 becomes, in line 14 (also opening on a past participle), the old wood that witnesses departures—or a coffin. The final cryptic line, "témoin des retours," implies the presence of absence, the vividly evoked dead man in the mind of the living memorialist.

The elegy is rich in rhyme, and it lingers in the memory through repetitions with shifting resonances. Surrounding the repeated "mort hier" are forms of the verb *être* and the noun *vie*. The black shadow of the persona is paralleled by black sins of the dead friend. The blended days and nights become a saint's day each day, whereas sins are relived at night. The dying time of line 5 becomes the irreversible time of line 13. Since Beckett habitually strips his lines of punctuation, each verse line reflects forward and backward, blurring the distinction between the persona and the dead friend.

"Vive morte ma seule saison"

Harvey points to the antinomies in these five lines—not quite accurately, since *each* line does not unite opposites. Only the first three lines embrace oxymorons: alive/dead in line 1, (Easter) lilies and (Christmas) chrysanthemums in line 2, nests alive and abandoned in line 3. Line 4, however, is entirely dedicated to the mud and leaves of April, which are opposed in line 5 by the beautiful gray frost. Thus the living and dead "only season" of the persona is one of contradiction.

"Bon bon il est un pays"

At first called "Accul" (blind alley), this poem is lighter in tone than the death-drenched poems just examined. Occasioned by the painter Geer van Velde's request for a contribution to his exhibit, it was printed in the catalog of another painter friend, Avigdor Arikha. The poem contains twenty-two lines, divided into three stanzas, which, as Harvey suggests, may be read as a

---

"Vive morte ma seule saison" was first published in *Cahiers des Saisons* 2 (October 1955) and reprinted in *Gedichte*. It is included in *Poems*.

"Bon bon il est un pays" was first published in *Cahiers des Saisons* 2 (October 1955) and reprinted in *Gedichte*. It is included in *Poems*.

sonnet with two sestets. More than the other verse of this period, "Bon bon" (with its explosive opening) demands to be spoken aloud.

The octet describes the microcosm in indefinite, impersonal, sometimes contradictory terms. The first sestet shifts to the first-person pronoun, who clings to the passing instant of the microcosm. The first tercet of the second sestet addresses the irritant directly, denying his world of linearity, exteriority, and even beauty. The second tercet engages the irritant in dialogue, for the repeated "qu'est-ce que c'est" provokes two different responses from the persona: a refusal to answer questions, and a series of nouns upon which synonymity is imposed—"le même." The sequence of nouns in the final line implicitly contradicts Baudelaire's well-known "calme luxe et volupté," for this (desired) "calme" is surrounded by, and perhaps valued above, both love and hatred.

Although these French poems are not without interest, they pale beside the fiction of what has often been called a trilogy.[5] The novel *Molloy* was literally begun while Beckett was in his mother's home (if not her room) in Foxrock, Ireland, where he stayed through May and June 1947. In summer he and Suzanne went to Menton, where a distant relative offered them a dilapidated villa close to the beach. He and Suzanne swam daily, but he worked hard on the novel.

Mercier and Camier engaged in dialogue to avoid "the battle of soliloquy." "He" and "I" of *F__* abridge their dialogue, and the story is finally a soliloquy by "I." That same battle engages the energies of Beckett's subsequent four narrators—Molloy, Moran, Malone, and whoever utters *L'Innommable*. Their soliloquies are battles for words and with words, at once a struggle against a solipsistic "je" and feverish sallies outside of "je." The first three narrators—in two novels—explicitly wage the battle of soliloquy with pen or pencil, although we read their accounts on pages of print.

Molloy

Molloy is named for one of its two protagonists, or, in another reading, for half of its double protagonist. Beckett's novel narrates two quests—that of Molloy for his mother and that of Moran for Molloy. The second quest

---

Written in four notebooks dated May 2–November 1, 1947, the holograph of *Molloy* is at HRC. Knowlson mentions a typescript in Alexis Péron's possession of which a "substantial portion . . . was in the end omitted from the published book" (Knowlson, 688 n. 20). Minuit published the novel in 1951. It was translated into English by Patrick Bowles "in collaboration with the author." However, a fragment of Beckett's own translation is in the MacGowran Notebook at OSU, and a fragmentary typescript is at MoSW. Fragments (with variants) were published in *Transition Fifty* (October 1950), *Merlin* (autumn 1953), *Paris Review* (spring 1954), *New World Writing* (April 1954). The whole translation of *Molloy* was published in 1955 by Olympia

shades the first, and each tale loops back to its beginning. Although Beckett endows his protagonists with proper (Irish) names, neither name—Molloy nor Moran—designates a character, in the fashion of traditional fiction.

Initially anonymous, the protagonist-narrator opens *Molloy* in the first person and the present tense: "Je suis dans la chambre de ma mère . . . Cet homme qui vient chaque semaine . . . Oui, je travaille maintenant. . . . Moi je voudrais maintenant parler des choses qui me restent, faire mes adieux, finir de mourir" (*Molloy*, 7) [I am in my mother's room . . . There's this man who comes every week. . . . Yes, I work now. . . . What I'd like now is to speak of the things that are left, say my goodbyes, finish dying, 7].[6] The opening paragraph of *Molloy* (which Beckett actually wrote last) is a prelude to the unparagraphed narration of some hundred French pages of Molloy's adventures, and it differs from that narration by virtue of shorter sentences, simpler syntax, and closer adherence to immediate detail.[7] Once that introduction is completed, the narrator—we do not yet know that he is Molloy—elides his own expressive difficulties into the beginnings of a story about two men, one small and one tall: "C'est ainsi que je vis A et B aller lentement l'un vers l'autre, sans se rendre compte de ce qu'ils faisaient" (9) [So I saw A and C going slowly towards each other, unconscious of what they were doing, 8].[8] A and B may be unconscious of what they are doing, but the narrator is exquisitely attuned to their problematic movements. Like Dante's Belacqua or Sordello—Molloy forgets which—he seats himself against a rock, but he does so in order to spy upon the two men.

The narrating Molloy tries to embed A and B in an environment, but he is self-conscious about his setting: "J'invente peut-être un peu, j'embellis peut-être, mais dans l'ensemble c'était ainsi" (9) [Perhaps I'm inventing a little, perhaps embellishing, but on the whole that's the way it was, 8]. Inventing or embellishing, Molloy nevertheless fills a few hesitant pages about A and B, before one of them—he forgets which—strolls from town at evening with a cigar and an orange pomeranian. When A recedes into the distance, the narrator pursues him, suddenly on crutches. Molloy re-views B in his hat, armed with a stick or club, only to have him disappear as well. Almost incidentally, Molloy announces his quest: "Mais à propos du désir d'un frère je dirai que m'étant réveillé entre onze heures et midi (j'entendis l'angélus, rappelant l'incarnation, peu de temps après) je résolus d'aller voir ma mère" (19) [But talking of the craving for a fellow let me observe that having waked between eleven o'clock and midday (I heard the angelus, recalling the incarnation, shortly after) I resolved to go and see my mother, 15]. As the angelus

---

Press in Paris and by Grove in the United States. My page numbers refer to the Minuit edition for French quotations and the Grove Weidenfeld *Three Novels* for English quotations.

announces the incarnation, God made flesh, it obliquely announces Molloy's words made flesh, in the person of his mother. Although Molloy will often digress from his purpose, he returns to it every few pages, with a summary statement: "je me rendais chez ma mère, aux crochets de qui j'agonisais" (28) [I was on my way to my mother, whose charity kept me dying, 22]. "Il me revint à la mémoire . . . que j'étais parti aller voir ma mère" (34) [It came back to my mind . . . that I had set out to see my mother, 27]. "Une femme aurait-elle pu m'arrêter dans mon élan vers ma mère?" (75) [Could a woman have stopped me as I swept towards mother? 56]. "Et quoique le souci de ma mère me fut toujours présent à l'esprit" (86) [And though my mind was still taken up with my mother, 64]. "[J]e parle naturellement de ma mère, dont l'image, depuis quelque temps en veilleuse, recommençait maintenant à me travailler" (101) [I mean of course my mother whose image, blunted for some time past, was beginning now to harrow me again, 76]. "J'allais chez maman" (121) [I was on my way to mother, 90]. This repetitive recollection of mother invests her with a mythic dimension.

On his bicycle—"tiens je ne m'attendais pas à ça" (19) [I didn't know I had one, 16]—Molloy sets out upon what he calls an "irréel voyage" (20) [unreal journey, 16] to his mother. After a flashback to his life with mother, when they addressed each other as Ma-g and Da-n, and when Molloy communicated with her by blows on her head, our hero is arrested by a policeman. Not until page 29 of the French text, when he is under interrogation by the police—a hilarious dialogue of questions, echoes, and misunderstandings—do we learn that his name is Molloy. (The name occurs to him as a minor revelation.) Released in spite of his lack of documents, Molloy is an object of curiosity to a shepherd, his dog, and his flock. When Molloy on his bicycle runs over and kills another dog named Teddy, its owner (variously called Sophie, Loy, or Lousse) conscripts Molloy as the dog's replacement in her affections.

About a third of Molloy's narrative is set on Lousse's premises, and she brings to his mind his love affair with an ancient ailing woman whom he recalls variously as Ruth, Edith, or Rose.[9] After Molloy's departure from Lousse, he spends some time at the seaside, where, concentrating on the problem, he manages, despite having only four pockets, to rotate his sixteen stones so that he sucks each in turn, before throwing them away. In a forest Molloy gives bread to a dim man but assaults a respectably dressed charcoal-burner, whom he resembles. Once outside the forest, within sight of his unnamed town, Molloy lies in a ditch and hears a voice: "Ne te bile pas, Molloy, on arrive" (123) [Don't fret, Molloy, we're coming, 91]. Molloy does not fret, but no one comes. His account closes: "Molloy pouvait rester, là où il était" (124) [Molloy could stay, where he happened to be, 91]. Although Molloy is more violent than the protagonists of the four French stories, his narrative nevertheless closes on that calm note. Through events, digressions, and self-disparagement, Molloy stumbles into our affections, in spite of his corrections, distractions, and qualifications.

Beckett's second protagonist, Jacques Moran, arouses distaste from the start. His account begins with a disturbance of his Sunday calm; yet its third sentence maintains, "Je suis calme" (125) [I am calm, 92]. Unlike Molloy's problem-laden revelations about A and B, Moran indulges in proper names and capsule descriptions—of his son, Jacques Moran Jr.; his priest, Father Ambrose; his housekeeper Martha; and even such incidental characters as his dentist, Dr. Py; his attorney, Master Savory; his pharmacist, Mme. Clément; his neighbors the Elsner sisters, their cook Hannah, and their aberdeen terrier Zulu. And especially the thirsty Sunday messenger Gaber, who delivers Youdi's command to seek Molloy. Although we learn of that command on the very first page of Moran's report, some hours pass before Moran himself concentrates on it. At first he is more preoccupied with his religion, his evening meal, his instructions to his son, his son's indigestion, his means of travel, his attire, not to mention his many beloved possessions. Like Molloy's uncertainties, Moran's plethora of certainties undermine the narrative flow.

It is only after attending to what he believes are practical matters that Moran, in the few hours before dinner, climbs into the bed of his darkened room to meditate on Molloy. In a two-page paragraph of subtle sentences that recall the prose of Molloy, Moran envisions an atmosphere of "finalité sans fin" (150) [finality without end, 111], where Molloy is invested with the air of a fabulous being. In that nebulous realm names begin to shed their stability, and Moran's quarry may be Molloy or Mollose—"une première syllabe, Mol, très nette, suivie presque aussitôt d'une seconde des plus cotonneuses, comme mangée par la première, et qui pouvait être oy comme elle pouvait être ose, ou ote, ou même oc" (153) [a first syllable, Mol, very clear, followed almost at once by a second, very thick, as though gobbled by the first, and which might have been oy as it might have been ose, or one, or even oc, 112]. We are back in Molloy's ambiguous country.

Whatever Molloy's true name and nature, Moran is ordered to find him and make a report. Since the Molloy affair disturbs Moran's orderly routine, half of his report is devoted to his deviations from routine, his unacknowledged cruelty to his son, and his preparations for departure. After Moran, accompanied by his son, leaves his well-ordered home and well-appreciated possessions, he begins to shed his respectability. A farmer offers him a ride, which he refuses. Once on his journey, Moran eats canned sardines, which his son purchases in nearby towns. When Moran's increasing disability prompts him to send his son to purchase a bicycle, he behaves atypically. He is tempted by the club of a stranger, to whom he gives bread. When he meets another man, who resembles him, Moran bashes his skull and hides his corpse. Moran has no memory of striking the fatal blow, but he dwells in some detail on his disposal of the body. After his son abandons him, Moran comes increasingly to resemble the Molloy we know—in afflictions and unpredictability. Yet he is still subject to the messenger Gaber, a Virgil who does not guide, but who finds Moran in the thick of the forest and delivers Youdi's order to return home. A shepherd gestures rather than speaking to Moran; a farmer—perhaps the same one who had offered him a ride—is suspicious of Moran. Reduced to rags, Moran crawls along the ground—a virtual reptile, like Molloy at the end of his voyage. At home Moran finds his beloved property in ruins, and he writes his report, in response to a voice: "Elle ne se servait pas des mots qu'on avait appris au petit Moran, que lui à son tour avait appris à son petit" (238) [It did not use the words that Moran had been taught when he was little and that he in turn had taught to his little one, 176]. Moran has learned to convey through words the gap between experience and any account of it.

Early in Moran's quest he recognizes that Molloy is his opposite, but finally there is nothing to distinguish them. This is predicted in their common Irish names (not so common in French); beginning with M, the thirteenth letter of the English alphabet, Molloy and Moran share the same root except for a liquid consonant; *mol* is Latin for soft or malleable. Whether respectable citizen or fabulous being, malleable beyond character, certain men undertake quests, however uncertain of their quarry.

Among its many levels *Molloy* is a kind of detective story. Instead of solving a crime, however, we are teased with clues of twinship between Moran and Molloy. Both receive commands from a thirsty messenger who arrives on the Sabbath, the nominal day of rest. Molloy has a mother, and Moran has a son, whom they treat sadistically. Essential loners, both questors are accompanied during part of their journeys; Molloy suffers the espionage of Lousse, and Moran depends on his son until the latter deserts him. It is on Lousse's property that Molloy loses his bicycle, whereas Moran's son absconds with his bicycle. In their accounts of their travels, both questors often digress from their purpose to which, however, they unfailingly return.[10]

Successors of the "deadbeats" of Beckett's French stories, Molloy and Moran are both afflicted with infirmities, which are described with gusto. Although Moran begins in good health, he soon has a pain in his knee. On his quest for Molloy his knee grows so stiff that he can neither kneel nor sit—Molloy's condition from the start. Both Molloy and Moran have low-hanging testicles and few or no teeth. Both have bad sight but good hearing. Both are inordinately fond of their hats, which Molloy attaches to his buttonhole and Moran ties under his chin; both jam their hats so hard upon their skulls that the hat becomes a virtual body part. Violent at times, both fear violence.

Both Molloy and Moran observe a man with a club. Both Molloy and Moran victimize someone, and both participate in the burial of their victims—Molloy of Lousse's dog Teddy and Moran of the nameless man who resembles him; for both the burials are in some sense their own. Even more than in Beckett's stories, death impinges on experience.

Finally alike in actions and appearance, Molloy and Moran travel through similar environments. Both come from a town situated near the country; Molloy thinks that the town name begins with *B* or *P,* and Moran affirms that it is Bally (which is Gaelic for city—*Baile*). Townsmen though they may be, Molloy and Moran voyage through pastures, seaside, and forests. In this French novel both protagonists measure distances in miles, and they count money in Irish currency. Both Molloy and Moran hear a gong in an unlikely place—ominous to Molloy, practical to Moran. Both Molloy and Moran meet a shepherd with his dog and sheep, and for both protagonists this encounter evokes a reference to the deity, the traditional Good Shepherd: Molloy: "Quel pays rural, mon Dieu" (38) [Good God, what a land of breeders, 29]. Moran: "Quel pays pastoral, mon Dieu" (215) [What a pastoral land, my God, 158]. During times of crisis, both Molloy and Moran record that the weather is fine, but their self-explorations tend to take place in mist or rain.

It is above all in writing that Moran comes to resemble Molloy. Unlike the protagonists of the stories, Molloy and Moran are the proud bearers of names, but the pronoun "je" is their preponderant subject. The malevolent "ils" of the stories virtually disappears from *Molloy,* but there is frequent appeal to a second-person pronoun "vous," whose antecedent is nearly as unstable as "je," but it can designate an implied reader. Almost from the start of his narration Molloy demonstrates the difficulties of narration; that is to say, the simplest descriptive statement elicits rhetorical questions about what is not stated. Both Molloy and Moran inform us that they will not report certain events, cutting themselves off with "Non," "Assez," or "Je ne sais pas." Their pronouns may shift person, and verbs may shift tense; Molloy speaks of the pluperfect and the mythological present, and he worries about a tense for his life, which is at once continuous and over. Moran, imitating Youdi, commands his son in the prophetic present. Both writers are vulnerable to imperatives.

The overriding imperative of *Molloy* is that of writing, which both writers disparage with verve. To different degrees, both accounts zigzag between the immediacy of the process of writing and quests for human prey. Both quests fail; Molloy does not find his mother, and Moran does not find Molloy. However, Molloy in his mother's bed apparently replaces his mother, and Moran in the forest apparently mirrors Molloy. While Moran is alone in the forest, his prose comes to resemble that of Molloy: it spurns paragraphs, interrupts sequence, selects arbitrarily, and imposes repetitive conjunctions that fail to conjoin. Lacking causality, coherence, and continuity, their prose rambles into highly imaged, delicately rhythmed meditations that distinguish *Molloy* from most fiction. Like all fiction, the voyages of Molloy and Moran are imaginary; unlike much fiction, the act of imagining is enfolded into the fiction.[11]

Molloy and Moran have different ways of apprising us as to fictionality, but they do apprise us. Toward the end of his narrative, Molloy predicts that, incapable of moving, he will remain where he is: "Oh je ne me tenais pas ce limpide langage" (118) [Oh I did not say it in such limpid language, 87]. Quoting phrases of that limpid language, which we have already read, Molloy recognizes that "je ne fais que me plier aux exigences d'une convention qui veut qu'on mente ou qu'on se taise" (119) [I am merely complying with the convention that demands you either lie or hold your peace, 88]. Renouncing peace, he writes these lies of fiction, and yet we have an overall impression of veracity.

Molloy's successor Moran proves flatly that words are lies, that reports are fictions. Finally, he admits that he writes in response, not to a command, but to an inner voice. He closes his report: "Alors je rentrai dans la maison et j'écrivis, Il est minuit. La pluie fouette les vitres. Il n'était pas minuit. Il ne pleuvait pas" (239) [Then I went back into the house and wrote, It is midnight. The rain is beating on the windows. It was not midnight. It was not raining, 176]. Fiction is a lie because the writer cannot still the passing moment.

Despite the similarity of Molloy and Moran, it is only the latter who refers by name to earlier Beckett characters. Ruminating about his other assignments from Youdi, Moran states that he never sees his prey again: "Quelle tourbe dans ma tête, quelle galérie de crevés. Murphy, Watt, Yerk, Mercier et tant d'autres" (187) [What a rabble in my head, what a gallery of moribunds. Murphy, Watt, Yerk, Mercier and all the others, 137]. Moran has already mentioned Yerk as a pre-Molloy quarry, but the other three are, of course, Beckett's fictional figures, only one of whom—Murphy—was in print at the time of writing.[12] Today, readers situate Beckett's progeny in relative tranquillity, but in 1947 Moran's brief catalog would have bewildered a reader. His second such catalog is a little longer and more sardonic. It occurs as number 10 of seventeen personal questions, as opposed to sixteen theological questions: "Nous retrouverions-nous tous au ciel un jour, moi, ma mère, mon fils, sa mère, Youdi, Gaber, Molloy, sa mère, Yerk, Murphy, Watt, Camier et les autres?" (228) [Would we all meet again in heaven one day, I, my mother, my son, his mother, Youdi, Gaber, Molloy, his mother,

Yerk, Murphy, Watt, Camier and the rest? 167–68]. Present fiction and past, protagonists and lesser characters, narrative voice and the words it carries—can any realm contain them?

The novel *Molloy* closes on the fictionality of fiction—in a flat contradiction. It is impressive in the stylistic range that probes its genre, and through its genre the human experience reflected through fiction. Beckett himself has disparaged experience as the basis of imaginative writing, and most of his critics (particularly self-styled postmoderns) praise the writing about the process of writing, as opposed to the narrative itself. What I find remarkable, however, is how much lived experience Beckett packs into his sardonic narratives—problematic relationships within family and friendship, physical and mental disintegration of the individual and the civilization, sexual comedy and its proximity to what love may be, cruelty and tenderness, reason and emotion, scatology and eschatology—even while disparaging their bases.

Deeply embedded in *Molloy* are rare moments of lyrical mystery. As early as Molloy's account of A and B, he moves from the landscape to the human core: "Mais ces collines, maintenant, il les connaît mieux, et si jamais cela lui arrive de les contempler à nouveau de loin ce sera je pense avec d'autres yeux, et non seulement cela mais l'intérieur qu'on ne voit jamais, le cerveau et le coeur et les autres cavernes où sentiment et pensée tiennent leur sabbat, tout cela bien autrement disposée" (11) [But now he knows these hills, that is to say he knows them better, and if ever again he sees them from afar it will be I think with other eyes, and not only that but the within, all that inner space one never sees, the brain and heart and other caverns where thought and feeling dance their sabbath, all that too quite differently disposed, 10]. The very humanism that Beckett scorned in his art criticism is couched in a voice that soars above the page into the reader's throat. A master of myriad-toned phrases, Beckett tells a human story, which seems to seize hovering glimpses into our own unconscious.

1948

Malone meurt (*Malone Dies*)

Less than a month after completing *Molloy* on November 1, 1947, Beckett began work on what is usually considered a continuation of that novel. In so

---

Under the title *L'Absent*, the holograph of *Malone meurt* is contained in two notebooks at HRC; the first is begun November 27, 1947 (and also contains *Watt*); the second was completed May 30, 1948. Before publication by Minuit in October

doing, he carried further two strands of fiction—a more relentless parody of that genre and a more incisive probing into the narrative process itself. The title, however, is a new departure. Beckett's earlier novels *Murphy, Watt, Mercier et Camier* are named after his protagonists, who are not the narrators. *Molloy* eclipses the protagonist into the narrator, as does *Malone meurt,* but the presentation of the name Malone does not occur till page 89 of the French text, and it is mentioned only eight times thereafter.[13] In contrast, the advent of death is announced in the very first sentence, and it is regularly recalled thereafter: "La fin d'une vie, ça ravigote" (69) [The end of a life is always vivifying, 212]. The titular verb "meurt" begins Beckett's inconsistent custom of imparting information in a title. Were the title *Malone se meurt,* it would summarize Malone's process of dying, in the closest that French can come to the continuous present tense of English. However, the actual title *Malone meurt* tells us how the novel ends; at the same time, it hints at Beckett's tenuous boundary between life and death, since Malone dies into, rather than in Beckett's fiction. Moreover, Malone's third sentence imparts his expectation of dying "le mois d'avril ou de mai"—in spring when new life comes to the Northern Hemisphere. Later Malone will associate his death with Easter, the day of resurrection of "celui qui le premier ressuscita d'entre les morts" (62) [who was the first to rise from the dead, 208].

It is not difficult to summarize the plot of *Malone meurt,* but it is extremely difficult to summarize the frequent digressions from the plot. Like Molloy and Moran before him, the narrator/protagonist Malone zigzags between his immediate circumstances and the story he is determined to tell, but he does so more self-consciously than his predecessors: "Situation présente, trois histoires, inventaire, voilà" (13) [Present state, three stories, inventory, there, 182]. To begin with, Malone's present state is vividly particularized: hatted but otherwise naked in his bed by a window, he eats from one pot and excretes into another; these pots are delivered and removed daily and anonymously, from a table on wheels, which he can move by means of a stick with a hooked end. Ignorant of how he arrived in this bed in this room, Malone is confident that he will die there, absent from the world. Malone's hearing and sight are dim; his legs are paralyzed, and his arms are nearly powerless. His fingers still serve, however, figuring in his writing and

---

1951, extracts (with variants) appeared in 84 (December 1950) and *Les Temps modernes* (September 1951). A large fragment of Beckett's translation into English—the Saposcat story—is in a notebook at TCD. The entire translation was published by Grove in 1956, and by Calder in 1958, but an excerpt—along with one from *Molloy*—was published under the title "Two Fragments" in *Transition Fifty* (October 1950), and another excerpt appeared in *Irish Writing* (1956). My page numbers refer to the French Minuit *Malone meurt* or the Grove Weidenfeld edition of *Three Novels.*

physically accomplishing that writing, which, it is implied, is what we are reading. Yet what we read has an oral quality, enhanced in the original French by the colloquial *ça*. A little past the midpoint of Malone's account we read: "Ai-je dit que je ne dis qu'une faible partie des choses qui me passent par la tête?" (150) [Did I say I only say a small proportion of the things that come into my head? 253]. Not *écrire* but *dire*—repeated.

Malone's present state entails an active mind in an impotent body, and that mind is irrepressibly articulate. There is no transition between Malone's story and his present state (of mind as well as body):

> Quelque part dans cette confusion la pensée s'acharne, loin du compte elle aussi. Elle aussi me cherche, comme depuis toujours, là où je ne suis pas. Elle non plus ne sait pas se calmer. J'en ai assez. Qu'elle passe sur d'autres sa rage d'agonisante. Pendant ce temps je serai tranquille. Telle semble être ma situation.
>   L'homme s'appelle Saposcat. (21)

> [(Thought) too seeks me, as it always has, where I am not to be found. It too cannot be quiet. On others let it wreak its dying rage, and leave me in peace. Such would seem to be my present state.
>   The man's name is Saposcat. (186)]

Saposcat contains his paradoxical nature in his name, combining soap and dung. He is quickly nicknamed Sapo, a diminutive of Latin *sapiens* and cognate of the colloquial English for a fool—"sap." The eldest son of his bourgeois parents, Sapo is being groomed for a successful career. Although he is carefully crafted not to resemble his creator, Sapo is soon invaded by Malone's fears and desires: "Et pourvu d'un peu moins de force et de courage lui aussi aurait abandonné, renonçant à savoir de quelle façon il était fait et allait pouvoir vivre, et vivant vaincu, aveuglement, dans un monde insensé, parmi des étrangers" (33) [And a little less well endowed with strength and courage (Sapo) too would have abandoned and despaired of ever knowing what manner of being he was, and how he was going to live, and lived vanquished, blindly, in a mad world, in the midst of strangers, 193]. The "aussi" links Sapo to his creator, a shade more forcefully than the English "too." Even in the world of matter, as opposed to thought, Malone's busy pencil is shadowed by the prospective gift of a fountain pen for Sapo.

When Sapo threatens to resemble his creator, he is transferred from his ambitious urban family to the Louis farm (in English the Lambert farm, both recalling Balzac's novel *Louis Lambert*). Resolutely steering clear of Sapo's mind, Malone describes poverty, suffering, and death in this pastoral land. Papa Louis specializes in the slaughter of pigs, and Malone puns mordantly: "Il était réputé bon saigneur" (47) [He was highly thought of as a bleeder and disjointer of pigs, 199] (but in French "saigneur" is pronounced like "seigneur," or the Lord). Other animals meet death on the farm—rabbits, hens, pigeons, goats, mules. Big Louis rescues animals from a quick death to subject them to prolonged suffering: "L'abattoir, dit Louis, voilà où j'achète mes bêtes" (71) [The slaughter-house, said Lambert, that's where I buy my beasts, 213]. Eventually, the beasts die, and Malone dwells at some length on the burial of Big Louis's mistreated mule.

The Saposcat family is laughable in its bourgeois limitations, but the Louis farm plays cruel havoc with the Western pastoral tradition. Despite Malone's determination to remain calm, he invests Big Louis with his own anxiety: "Car il n'ignorait pas la tendance des enterrés à remonter, contre tout attente, vers le jour. En quoi ils ressemblent aux noyés" (71) [For he knew how the dead and buried tend, contrary to what one might expect, to rise to the surface, in which they resemble the drowned, 213]. Big Louis incongruously broods, and Malone's narrative glides into the woes of Mme. Louis, mental and physical. In introducing the troubles of others, Malone is intermittently aware that he speaks of himself: "Je m'entendrai de loin, l'esprit loin, parler des Louis, parler de moi, l'esprit errant, loin d'ici, parmi ses ruines" (77) [I shall hear myself talking, afar off, from my far mind, talking of the Lamberts, talking of myself, my mind wandering, far from here, among its ruins, 216]. Neither in fiction nor self-examination is identity established, but pain is ubiquitous.

Malone shades Mme. Louis with his own uncertainties, but it is to her daughter that Sapo confides that he will return no more. That departure from the Louis farm proves to be Sapo's departure from Malone's story, and death is in the air: "Alors, comme on fait pour les morts même insignifiants, ils rassemblèrent les souvenirs qu'il [Sapo] avait pu leur laisser, s'aidant les uns les autres et s'efforçant de se mettre d'accord. Mais on connait cette petite flamme, ses tremblements dans l'ombre démontée. Et l'accord ne vient que plus tard, avec l'oubli" (79) [Then, as people do when someone even insignificant dies, they summoned up such memories as (Sapo) had left them, helping one another and trying to agree. But we all know that little flame and its flickerings in the wild shadows. And agreement only comes a little later, with the forgetting, 217]. The shadow of memory flickers through the prose, as, a little earlier, Malone's anxieties quiver through the gestures of Mme. Louis and the movements of a shy gray hen. There is more than meets the eye in Malone's present state; or, rather, what meets the reader's eye is an oblique reflection of Malone's painful present state.

After Malone loses his pencil for two days, he conceives the idea of being born into his death. He will do so by making a creature in his own image. In sharp contrast to the fictional Sapo, who was tailored *not* to resemble him, the new creation will reflect him, but not too closely. It takes Malone some time before he finds Sapo again, at an advanced age. Unlike young

Sapo, garmented in realistic detail, old Sapo, soon renamed Macmann, wears a long coat and a hat that is attached by a string to his upper coat-button— by now the typical Beckett costume. Unlike active Sapo, Macmann is motionless on his bench, recalling the Colossus of Memnon. Malone digresses to the horrors of urban life, through which a somber lyricism evokes aspects of man's mortality. With some difficulty, Malone shifts Macmann from thinking to moving; he rolls toward a plain, as Molloy only dreamed of doing. As Sapo sported the gull's eyes of Malone, so Macmann opens his eyes, "à peine plus bleus qu'un blanc d'oeuf" (109) [Bluer scarcely than white of egg, 233]—a harsh description of Beckett's own pale blue eyes.

For all his spirit of method, Malone finds it difficult to weave a narrative about Macmann, and it is achieved only when Beckett returns to his parodic mode. Young Sapo is Beckett/Malone's parody of realistic fiction, and old Sapo/Macmann undergoes three stages of narration, of which only the second is parodic. Although he is seated motionless on a bench when first seen, Macmann soon lies cruciform on the ground in the rain. After the bedded Malone loses his prehensile stick, Macmann is discovered in bed in a room in an asylum. Although Malone calls the Macmann-Moll couple the first phase of his story, it is actually the second—a hilarious parody of romantic fiction. The third phase begins after Moll's death, which is announced to Macmann by his new keeper Lemuel (a name that chimes with Samuel). A new keeper brings Macmann new freedom, and we find him active in the archetypically varied Beckett landscape.

After Malone kills off the aged Moll ("En voilà toujours une de liquidée" [174] [There's one out of the way at least, 266]), he receives a visit that frightens him into revising his plan for disposing of his remaining time: "Visite, diverses remarques, suite Macmann, rappels de l'agonie, suite Macmann, puis mélange Macmann et agonie aussi longtemps que possible" (180) [Visit, various remarks, Macmann continued, agony recalled. Macmann continued, then mixture of Macmann and agony as long as possible, 269]. *Whose* agony is ambiguous, but Malone remains faithful to this revised program. After continuing the story of Macmann in Lemuel's untender care, Malone vows: "Je ne dirai plus je" (208) [I shall say I no more, 283]. As good as his word (with three exceptions), Malone clings to the agonies of the Macmann story for the remainder of his fictional life.

On Easter weekend, which, Malone informs us, was spent by Jesus in hell, Lady Pedal invites six asylum inmates to an island picnic. On their outing the keeper Lemuel kills two sailors with his hatchet, then sets out to sea with his asylum charges, including Macmann. The last broken phrases of *Malone meurt* blend Lemuel's gestures into Malone's dying. Lemuel raises his blood-stained hatchet, but he will not hit anyone any more: "il ne touchera jamais / ni avec son crayon ni avec son bâton ni / . . . / jamais voilà il ne touchera jamais / voilà jamais / voilà voilà / plus rien" (217) [. . . he will never / or with his pencil or with his stick or / . . . / never there he will never / never anything / there/ any more, 288]. Lemuel's hammer and hatchet are assimilated into Malone's stick and pencil; we assume that Malone has died into the end of his story, where the fragmentation of the prose reflects Lemuel's chopping rhythm within Malone's fiction, and the chopping off of life, as in the classical image of the fate Atropos with her shears. Malone's intermittent brooding about death erupts into his final shards of fiction.

Molloy and Moran are the protagonists of their own fiction, but Malone explicitly separates "story" from "present state," and he dwells in and on that sometimes adventurous, sometimes meditative, present. He loses, then finds, the notebook in which he writes; he loses, then finds, the pencil with which he writes (although he never explains how he continues to write, in spite of the loss). He loses, and does not find, his hooked stick that connects him with his possessions. After Malone invents Macmann, who is served by an attendant in the asylum, he ceases to be nourished by his own attendant. Malone observes a couple copulating, and he in turn is observed by a bowler-hatted visitor who strikes him on his head. The copulating couple and the assailant in mourning clothes suggest birth and death, the limits of mortality, and it is his mortality that obsesses the dying Malone. From his opening pages, however, Malone abjures sentiment about his coming death. Like the moribund outside of fiction, this decrepit creature grasps at his possessions—not only the notebook and the pencil, but a hat, a boot, three socks, a pipe-bowl, a packet of letters wrapped in newspaper, a needle between two corks, a photograph of an ass, the top of a crutch, a blood-stained club, the cap of a bicycle bell. Even things are fragmented, in their recollection of earlier Beckett works. When Malone drops his hooked stick, his possessions are henceforth beyond his reach—except for his pencil and notebook, and, perhaps, a French pencil somewhere in his bedding.

Of all Beckett's characters, Malone is the most self-conscious creator of fictions, which he constantly denigrates with such phrases as "je ne peux pas" and "Quel ennui" ["I can't" and "What tedium"]. Nevertheless, he can and does sketch Sapo, Macmann, and their worlds. He does so with exclamations, interruptions, hesitations, digressions, contradictions, self-corrections, and direct address to the reader, absorbing us in his process of writing. So it is almost logical that Malone should carry the freight of Beckett's own fictional past. Malone resembles Murphy in gazing at the stars in London, and in failing by a hair's breadth in communicating with the insane. Malone not only mentions Watt but Mr. Quin of the *Ur-Watt,* and his character l'Anglais (the Saxon in English) claims to dream of Quin. Malone enters the mind of a cabman, who might be the driver in *L'Expulsé.* Like the narrator of *La Fin,* Malone recalls his mother's cutting remark about the sky. Like

Mercier or Camier, the thin colleague of Macmann resembles Dante's Sordello. Like Moran's Gaber, Malone's visitor carries a tightly rolled umbrella, and like Molloy Malone secures his hat with a string. More significant than these circumstantial links is the implication that fiction entails death. It is in the context of his own imminent death that Malone names Beckett's characters: "A ce moment-là c'en sera fait des Murphy, Mercier, Molloy, Moran et autres Malone, à moins que ça ne continue dans l'outre-tombe" (116) [Then it will be all over with the Murphys, Merciers, Molloys, Morans and Malones, unless it goes on beyond the grave, 236]. When Malone asks himself how many he has killed, he specifies that one was struck on the head, and we recall Moran's victim in the forest. Another was burned to death, and this is Murphy. No causes are mentioned for two other deaths, but Beckett's Belacqua succumbed on the operating table, and Mercier and Camier fell a policeman. Malone remembers still another: "Je lui ai tranché la gorge avec son rasoir" (116) [I cut his throat with his razor, 236]. Even the Old Boy in *Murphy* is accorded his passing memento mori. In addition, a footnote in the French text glosses a cemetery.[14] Yet all these deaths cannot be taken literally, as in the realistic novel; they hint at imaginative worlds that lie beyond living experience.

Toward the end of *Malone meurt* Macmann's four picnic companions may be viewed as avatars of Beckett's earlier protagonists: "Donc le jeune, l'Anglais, le maigre et le barbu" (207) [The youth then, the Saxon, the thin one and the giant, 283]. These four distantly resemble Murphy, Watt, Moran, and Malone. Beckett teases us with such piecemeal quasi-equations, but rising above detail is the disintegrating ability of fiction to represent the most fundamental human experience. On the one hand, however, that very inability contributes to the feeling of authenticity of the novel; on the other hand, the Easter outing is a fantastic narrative of suffering without redemption or resurrection.

Molloy is a startling novel, in its stylistic range that mocks, encompasses, and despairs of conveying human experience. *Malone meurt* is at once more parodic, more methodical, more digressive, and more lyrical than *Molloy*. Narrative occupies less than half the novel, and inventory barely anchors the many digressions. Malone is more meditative than his predecessors, and however determined he is to play, his gravity intrudes into his account. He himself is aware: "Et c'est gravement que j'ai essayé de ne plus l'être" (37) [And gravely I struggled to be grave no more, 195]. The struggle is successful in some hilarious passages, but these provide little relief from Malone's obsession with mortality, which he displaces variously: in Mme. Louis's thoughts and gestures, for example, or in the natural world in which Macmann is a mere speck of dust, or in Lemuel's hammer-blows at his own head.

Although Malone in his final narrative fragment dissolves into "Mac-mann, mon dernier," he has already confessed: "Tout est prétexte, Sapo et les oiseaux, Moll, les paysans, ceux qui dans les villes se cherchent et se fuient, mes doutes qui ne m'intéressent pas, ma situation, mes possessions, prétexte pour ne pas venir au fait, à l'abandon, en levant le pouce, en disant pouce et en s'en allant, sans autre forme de procès, quitte à se faire mal voir de ses petits camarades" (195) [All is pretext, Sapo and the birds, Moll, the peasants, those who in the towns seek one another out and fly from one another, my doubts which do not interest me, my situation, my possessions, pretext for not coming to the point, the abandoning, the raising of the arms and going down, without further splash, even though it may annoy the bathers, 276]. Despite the last deflationary phrase, the sentence rhythmically accretes the subterfuges of Malone's fiction, as of Beckett's fiction. Malone comes to realize: "C'est ma vie, ce cahier . . . je veux y mettre une dernière fois ceux que j'ai appelés à mon secours . . . afin qu'ils meurent avec moi" (191) [This exercise-book is my life . . . I want to put down in it, for the last time, those I have called to my help . . . so that they may cease with me, 274]. Malone (me alone) succeeds when Lemuel's weapons melt into Malone's viv-ifying pencil and stick. *Malone meurt* has often been read as a fiction about the fiction-making process, and it is certainly that, but it is deeper than that. It is layered fiction of extraordinary authenticity in which a dying animal articulates his restless mind.

Molloy and Moran differ from the protagonists of Beckett's stories of 1946 in that the named characters refer to their physical circumstances while they write, but it is Malone alone who virtually elides his identity into what he calls his present state. The art of the present state is theater rather than fiction, and Beckett glided on October 9, 1948, into a composition for the-ater—*En attendant Godot.* He later told the scholar Colin Duckworth: "I began to write *Godot* as a relaxation, to get away from the awful prose I was writing at that time" (Duckworth, xlv). However, he did not get completely away, for *Malone* seeps into *Godot.* The very title of each work subsumes the overarching action—dying and waiting, which may be eclipsed into one another. The original title of *Malone meurt* was *L'Absent,* and the very word *Godot* has come to be synonymous with absence. Although the womblike room of Malone contrasts radically with the country road of *Godot,* the moon is visible both to the writer within the novel and to Vladimir and Estragon on the stage. Malone in his room can affirm: "C'est une nuit comme les aimait Kaspar David Friedrich, tempestueuse et claire" (43) [It is such a night as Kaspar David Friedrich loved, tempestuous and bright, 198]. Nearly thirty years after writing that sentence, Beckett told me that the Friedrich painting of two figures looking at the moon was the source of *Godot.*[15] Malone also bequeaths to the two waiting friends a Christian background. Despite Malone's savage parody of Moll with her cross-shaped earrings and tooth, the writer takes heart from one of the thieves crucified with Christ: "il y eut un larron de sauvé, ça fait un joli pourcentage" (153) [one of the thieves was saved, that is a generous percentage, 255]. Vladimir, troubled by the discrepant accounts of the four evangelists, reduces the "pourcentage" to "honnête" [reasonable]. The problematic opposition of the two thieves is more central to *Godot* than to *Malone meurt,* and it is mirrored in the several symmetries of the play (acts, character pairs, tree and stone, hats and shoes, dialogue duets, verbal pairs in Lucky's "think"). Each coupling parallels Luke's version of the Crucifixion, wherein one thief is saved and the other is damned.

Perhaps the most trenchant similarity between the two Beckett works, so close in date of composition, is the problem of living through time.[16] Malone attempts to organize the time at his disposal before his imminent death, and he resolves to abandon gravity for the spirit of play. Malone's stories do not meet that desideratum, but they carry him through the book that we read. Vladimir and Estragon acknowledge that they are bored, but they are ingenious in inventing games to pass the time. In dwelling on time, *Malone meurt* probes to the constituents of fiction, and *En attendant Godot* probes to the constituents of theater—both with lip service to the ludic spirit.

1949

En attendant Godot (Waiting for Godot)

Beckett did not set out to punctuate his fiction with a play. The holograph of his play shows much less revision than do manuscripts of his novels. In a cheap graph paper notebook Beckett's execrable handwriting runs across the recto pages, then doubles back to the book's beginning to continue on the verso pages. Only occasional crossouts and a relatively small quantity of doodles connote impediments to the creative flow. The general impression is

---

The holograph of *En attendant Godot* is contained in a single notebook, dated October 9, 1948, on the first page, and January 29, 1949, on the last. Beckett kept it in his possession (but not in his home) to the time of his death. A photocopy was made available to (selected) scholars by Les Editions de Minuit. Excerpts of *Godot* were taped for *Le Club d'Essai* on February 6, 1952, and broadcast on February 17. The play was originally published by Minuit in October 1952, before the stage premiere on January 5, 1953, and during rehearsals Beckett made minor changes in his prompt copy, now at TCD. Beckett's translation into English was first published by Grove in 1954 and by Faber in 1956. There are so many editions of *Godot* that I forgo page references.

of almost continuous writing, and indeed the play, begun on October 9, 1948, was completed on January 29, 1949. At no point in the manuscript is there a scenic breakdown, as in the aborted *Human Wishes;* nor do we find a cast of characters, as in *Eleutheria.* The improvisatory quality of the play seems to have emanated from Beckett's own quasi-improvisatory composition—at least initially.

The manuscript opens on the bare setting: "Route à la campagne, avec arbre" [A country road, with tree]—themselves horizontal and vertical coordinates on the graph page. There follows a scenic direction about a nameless "vieillard" trying to take off his shoe. Another "vieillard, ressemblant au premier" then enters. The first old man, attacking his shoe again, then speaks what was to become the most celebrated opening line in modern drama: "Rien à faire" [Nothing to be done]. The second old man, moving forward with comic spavined gait, expands "Rien à faire" to the human condition, however he may struggle against its fatalism, "songeant au combat" [musing on the struggle]. Addressing himself as Vladimir, the second old man effectively names himself, and immediately afterwards in the manuscript occurs Beckett's name for the first old man—Lévy—and so he remains throughout the first act of the manuscript. Early in act 2 Beckett suddenly changed Lévy's name to Estragon, but that name enters the dialogue only late in the manuscript, in Vladimir's soliloquy.

When Pozzo and Lucky first enter, they are designated as a large man and a small one; they are seen in comic contrast before they are named. Pozzo announces his name almost at once, but the name Lucky is first attached (by Pozzo) to the rightful recipient of the discarded chicken-bones. The broadly European flavor of the four names—Slavic Vladimir (meaning prince of peace), French Estragon (a bitter herb of Arabic origin), Italian Pozzo (meaning a well), and the ironic English Lucky—emerged during composition, as did the alternate names for the friends—Didi and M. Albert for Vladimir, Gogo, Macgrégor, and Catulle for Estragon. In Beckett's French fiction female names were variable, but *Godot* extends that indeterminacy to the two men who meet each evening to keep their appointment. Although Pozzo's name is stable, it resembles Godot sonically.

The manuscript of *En attendant Godot* differs in many small details from the version published by Les Editions de Minuit in 1952, some three months before the Paris première. However, formal symmetries are present from the start—especially the unparalleled repetition of the first act by the second: at twilight two friends meet by a tree to wait for Godot; a landowner and his knook dally with them and then depart. A boy messenger announces that Godot will not come tonight but surely tomorrow. Upon the boy's exit, night falls swiftly, and the moon rises. Finally one friend suggests that the couple leave, but they do not move.

Because of its very bareness, the plot is fertile ground for a variety of subjects, and the second act echoes the first in such disjunctive topics as food, the tree, bones, the sky, time, place, memory, pain or discomfort, suicide, offstage beating of Estragon, Vladimir's onstage welcome of Estragon, Vladimir's refusal to listen to Estragon's dreams, and the friends' sporadic nostalgia for the past that contrasts with their uncertainty about the future. The variety is camouflaged under the sprinkling of *encores* that underline the repetitiousness of word and deed.

Vaudeville turns erupt from the start. *Godot* opens with a hoary clown number: Estragon struggles to take off a tight shoe, and during the course of the play it is he who is familiarly funny. He begins a bawdy joke, speaks in baby talk or in a foreign accent or with full mouth; he delivers the two-lung number, dangles a phallic carrot, mimics Lucky as a beast of burden, tries to hide behind a frail tree, and finally drops his trousers. Despite Vladimir's superior sophistication, he buttons his fly, laughs painfully, spits disgustedly, pulls miscellaneous objects from his pockets, imitates Lucky, and minces like a mannequin. Together Vladimir and Estragon juggle three hats, take gorilla postures, huddle in exaggerated fright, examine Lucky as an object, pose as scouts on the lookout, "do" the tree, tug at a rope that nearly knocks them down when it breaks. They manipulate their respective props—Vladimir his hat and Estragon his shoe—precisely and identically. Their nicknames Didi and Gogo are comically endearing, and their scenes of cross-talk establish the dominant dialogue rhythm of the play.

In contrast to the vaudeville of Vladimir and Estragon, Pozzo and Lucky are more erratically comic. Pozzo is ridiculous in his self-inflation. Although it is Estragon who mistakes him for Godot, Pozzo twice plays variations on that enigmatic name, but he invokes a genuine deity when he examines his new acquaintances: "De la même espèce que Pozzo! D'origine divine!" [Of the same species as Pozzo! Made in God's image!] A self-conscious performer in act 1, Pozzo sprays his throat ostentatiously, demands undivided attention for his recitation, alternates between lyrical and prosaic tones, and anxiously solicits the reactions of the two friends. Like comics of the vaudeville tradition, Pozzo misplaces his props—pipe, atomizer, and watch. It is when Pozzo boastfully contrasts himself with Lucky that the two remove their bowler hats, and Beckett first notes that all four men wear "chapeau melon" [bowler hats]. We scarcely need Pozzo to point out the contrast between himself and his rarely comic "knook"; yet the object of scrutiny hovers on the comic in the elusive question of why he doesn't put down his bags (and Pozzo's preposterous answer). When Pozzo offers Lucky's performance to the two friends, the knook at first confuses thinking with dancing. Lucky's "think," often performed as a farcical turn, is the bravura piece of the play. Beckett's manuscript reveals little difficulty in its composition, written in a single block on several pages, without the three-part division to which the author later called attention—indifferent deity, dwindling humanity, and stone-cold universe. (In revision, Beckett "vaguened" Lucky's "think" through increased sound play, repetition, and incoherence.) After silence is imposed upon Lucky, the act 1 comedy ebbs toward an end.

In act 2 Vladimir again seeks to fill time, and he is grateful for reinforcements in the return of Pozzo and Lucky. After their reentrance (from the opposite wing, although neither manuscript nor printed versions designates it), the four adult characters take comic pratfalls. That late in the play the characters have already established themselves as performers, physically and verbally—the friends in their duets, but Pozzo and Lucky in their center-stage recitations. Even the day itself has, according to Vladimir, come to the end of its repertoire.

Repertoire it is. Resolutely *ill* made dramatically, *En attendant Godot* seeks to conceal the depth below the farce, but the tragicomic blend has appealed to imaginations throughout "this bitch of an earth." In one way or another, audiences have recognized themselves as waiting, whether in schools, prisons, theaters, or even country roads. So the overarching action of *En attendant Godot* was both new and familiar, or familiar in its novelty. As is the very setting of road and tree, each a metaphor for human life. The bare stage, thin plot, and crepuscular light hint at ghosts of cultural traditions, where each culture has recognized its own.

Although Beckett himself has pleaded that *En attendant Godot* seeks to avoid definition, he has larded it with biblical shards, starting with the neologism God-ot. Elsewhere we stumble on the two thieves, whose iconography on either side of Christ is echoed in act 1 when the friends support Lucky, and in act 2 when they support Pozzo.[17] That slave driver is not only made in God's image, but he answers to both Cain and Abel; as Estragon notes: "C'est toute l'humanité!" [He's all humanity]—both victimizer and victim. Passing phrases of *Godot* whisper about the wind in the reeds and the sheep versus the goats from Matthew, and the unanswered cries for help may reflect mordantly upon the parable of the good Samaritan. Vladimir sententiously assigns every man to his little cross, and Estragon avers that he has always compared himself to Christ. Beckett teases us with fragments of a faith that do not cohere (and they are more numerous in English, the language in which Beckett was taught his Christianity).

Even more insistent than the Bible is the aura of mortality. The many versions of the question about Lucky putting down his bags may be applied to all humanity with its burdens. Linked obliquely to that burden is the shadow of death, however it is dissipated by farce. Early in the play Vladimir expands "Rien à faire" to the suicide that the two friends might have committed in style, jumping from the Eiffel Tower. When suicide shifts to hanging, its gravity is undercut by the anticipation of an erection. Even Estragon's recollection of Vladimir rescuing him from the river (Durance in French, Rhone in English) is squelched by that same Vladimir. At the end of the play the friends' halfhearted attempt at hanging breaks with the fragile cord, but it is vital that Estragon's trousers fall, to sustain the tragi*comic* flavor of suicide.

Suicide is not the only deathly presence in the play. Estragon is confused as to whether the Savior saves the good thief from hell or death. Vladimir warns his friend that, without him, Estragon would be a little heap of bones. We are thus subliminally prepared when Pozzo gnaws at bones, and Estragon gnaws at the gnawed bones. By act 2, we see no bones, but death is present in Vladimir's dog song, which stops each time he reaches the line about burial. When we later hear about bones, they imply the death of civilizations:

> Vladimir: Ce qui est terrible, c'est d'avoir pensé.
> Estragon: Mais cela nous est-il jamais arrivé?
> Vladimir: D'où viennent tous ces cadavres?
> Estragon: Ces ossements.
>
> [Vladimir: What is terrible is to *have* thought.
> Estragon: But did that ever happen to us?
> Vladimir: Where are all these corpses from?
> Estragon: These skeletons.]

A charnel house is the repository of the "more things in heaven and earth . . . than are dreamt of in your philosophy" but are hinted in *Godot*.

On that twilight scene the most frequent scenic directions are "Un temps" (pause) and "Silence," but their invasive force camouflages Beckett's impressive verbal range—colloquial, austere, formal, interrogative, plangent, vituperative, imaged, abstract. The repetitions—particularly the eight refrains of "waiting for Godot"—establish a groundwork of monotony, but from them blossom clichés, puns, synonyms, rhymes, as well as the friends' verbal games of making conversation, questioning each other, contradicting each other, abusing each other. Early in the play a single stressed word highlights language; Vladimir describes his confused feeling: "Soulagé et en même temps . . . *il cherche* . . . épouvanté. *Avec emphase.* E-pou-van-té" [Relieved and at the same time . . . *he searches for the word* . . . appalled. *With emphasis.* Ap-palled].[18] Soon afterward Vladimir seeks the antonym of *sauvé* for the bad thief. Much later he hesitates before declaring that he and his friend are "hommes." Although *En attendant Godot* abounds in pregnant monosyllables like these, it also displays polysyllabic comic catalogs— Pozzo's series of Lucky's dances, Lucky's list of sports, the several synonyms for Pozzo's pipe. In the friends' delicate duets about dead voices Vladimir seeks new sounds, whereas Estragon stalwartly repeats his first metaphor.

Beckett's stage musicality is now a critical cliché, so it is perhaps time to return to the human meaning of the tragicomedy. Beckett himself, in preparing the play for performance, noted the twenty-one cries for help, with fourteen ignored. The first meaningful repetition in the play is "Tu as mal? . . . Mal! Il me demande si j'ai mal!" [It hurts? . . . Hurts! He wants to know if it hurts!]. Before the end of the play, we know that it hurts, and we know that we hurt. Many other phrases have taken on extensible significance, outside of the immediate context of the play, from "Rien à faire" [Nothing to be done] to "Elle ne vaut rien" [Not worth a curse] and including "Pour jeter le doute, à toi le pompon" [Nothing is certain when you're about], "Il y a une chance sur deux. Ou presque" [There's an even chance. Or nearly], "Ce n'est pas folichon" [I've been better entertained], "Ça a fait passer le temps" [That passed the time], "On trouve toujours quelque chose . . . pour nous donner l'impression d'exister" [We always find something . . . to give us the impression we exist], "Je ne veux plus respirer" [I'm tired breathing].

Vladimir's last soliloquy subsumes the dreamlike aspect of the friends' existence, the painful indeterminacy of their situation, their problematic interdependence, their objectification in the gaze of unknown others, and he whimpers: "Je ne peux pas continuer. *(Un temps.)* Qu'est-ce que j'ai dit?" [I can't go on! *(Pause.)* What have I said?]. Is he questioning the immediately previous sentence or the whole speech, with its rewording of Pozzo's memorable image: "A cheval sur une tombe et une naissance difficile. Du fond du trou, rêveusement, le fossoyeur applique ses fers" [Astride of a grave and a difficult birth. Down in the hole, lingeringly, the grave-digger puts on the forceps]? Malone was unable to sustain the spirit of play in his fiction, and Beckett diminishes play as the tragicomedy *En attendant Godot* ebbs to an end—this evening.

Soon after Beckett's return to postwar Paris, he was befriended by Georges Duthuit, who had bought from Eugene Jolas the title of the prewar *transition,* but he changed the "mantic" orientation of the periodical toward art criticism. Duthuit contributed not only to Beckett's social life but also to his precarious material subsistence, commissioning many translations, which Beckett usually chose not to sign. Yet *Three Dialogues* is not a commission, but a distillation of the many art-critical conversations of the two men; Beckett told Federman and Fletcher that the dialogues "merely reflect, very freely, the many conversations we had at that time about painters and painting" (24). To Martin Esslin's query as to whether Beckett wrote down actual discussions with Duthuit, the author replied, "Up," in the humorous tone of the dialogues themselves. Nevertheless, the dialogues were printed in *Transition* as coauthored "by Samuel Beckett and Georges Duthuit," and perhaps Beckett scholars (including myself) have too easily ignored the contribution of Duthuit. I find it surprising that the dialogues have not been professionally performed (so far as I know). Written in English for publication in *Transition, Three Dialogues* shows Beckett's shaping eye (and ironic wit) at work even in art criticism.

Three Dialogues by Samuel Beckett and Georges Duthuit

Three because the initialized discussants B and D focus on three painters— Pierre Tal Coat, André Masson, and Bram van Velde. The dehiscence of the subject-object relation is the thread (and the standard) of B's critique, although "object" is sometimes "occasion" and once "aliment." In the three-scene sketch the two speakers, B and D, articulate their thoughts in the superior, quasi-hermetic phrasing of Beckett's reviews of the 1930s. B opens each of the three scenes; in the face of D's admiration of Tal Coat or Masson, B presents his view of an art of failure, which is an art beyond art. Each scene concludes with B's defeat, but not before he delivers sentences that critics would subsequently apply to Beckett's own work.

In the first dialogue B derides Tal Coat for merely playing variations upon the old traditional relation between the perceiving artist and the perceived object. It is in reaction against "the Franciscan orgies of Tal Coat" that B enunciates his credo of an art of the nonfeasible: "The expression that there is nothing to express, nothing with which to express, nothing from which to express, no power to express, no desire to express, together with the obligation to express" (*Disjecta,* 139). The Wattesque series of negatives are opposed by the (mysterious) obligation to express.

The second dialogue is more problematic to B, since D's Masson (aided by quotations from the painter) recognizes a crisis in the subject-object relationship, and yet he cannot paint the void. D appreciates what Masson *can* paint, causing B to exit, weeping.

By the third dialogue, D is impatient with B, demanding an explanation of his view of van Velde's "art of a new order," which eliminates "occasion,

First published in *Transition Forty-Nine* (December 1949), under the joint authorship of Samuel Beckett and Georges Duthuit, the *Three Dialogues* are annotated confusingly in Federman and Fletcher (24). Beckett translated part of the third dialogue into French, for a Bram van Velde exhibition in 1957. The full text of that dialogue appeared in *Georges Duthuit,* 1976. *Trois Dialogues* was published by Minuit only in 1998, with the first two dialogues translated by Edith Fournier, *Masson* for the first time and *Tal Coat* reprinted from a 1996 catalog in Aix. I inadvertently (but inexcusably) dropped Duthuit's name in the reprinting of the three dialogues in *Disjecta,* to which my page numbers refer.

in every shape and form, ideal as well as material." D then cannily suggests that that very elimination, van Velde's predicament, becomes a new occasion, and he thereby forces B to correct his earlier phrase for Bram van Velde as a painter of predicament (presumably referring to his *Peintres de l'empêchement*). In provoking B to a "connected statement," D admonishes him: "Try and bear in mind that the subject under discussion is not yourself" (144), which suggests to the reader that that is indeed the subject. B's longest speech contains an old Beckett theme: "But if the occasion appears as an unstable term of relation, the artist, who is the other term, is hardly less so." The new rendition of that old theme is, however, more extreme and dogmatic than heretofore; it leads to the inevitable failure of the artist: "to be an artist is to fail, as no other dare fail, that failure is his world and the shrink from it desertion, art and craft, good housekeeping, living" (145). This often quoted espousal of artistic failure must, however, be situated in the context of the anxious relation between subject and object, without converting that relation into a new occasion for art.

Three Dialogues, like Lucky's speech, concludes without conclusion. B seems to elevate van Velde's painting above art. When D requests the second part of B's argument, he, "Remembering, warmly," admits that he is mistaken, but B has been so discursive in his argument that it is impossible to locate the mistake. What is unmistakable is the unstable aesthetic that links B's van Velde with the crisis in Beckett's own fiction, where the occasion, and even the subject, gradually dissolves into the writing process of the protagonists, Molloy, Moran, and Malone.

1950–52

Rien à faire

(Nothing to be done)

In March 1949, some ten months after completing *Malone meurt,* Beckett began a novel as *Mahood,* which he concluded only in January 1950, as *L'Innommable*. Still financially dependent upon translation, he accepted a UNESCO assignment to translate some hundred Mexican poems, about which he later wrote Hugh Kenner: "That lousy Mexican Anthology was undertaken to take the chill of [*sic*] the pot in the lean winter of 1949–50 and with scant Spanish" (qtd. in Cronin, 386). Although Beckett composed from a literal translation by a friend, his Spanish was not "scant," since he had worked at it in the 1930s, when he thought he might go to Spain. As poems in English, the Mexican translations are accomplished lyrics.[1]

L'Innommable continues Beckett's sporadic practice of offering titular guideposts to his readers—although there was no publisher to acquire readers, after Bordas reneged on the contract to publish Beckett's French fiction.[2] Publisher or no, Mahood (manhood) is the fictional avatar of the nameless narrator of the novel, who does not declare himself unnamable. Beckett's change of title implies a change of focus from a fiction of a fiction to a highly charged prose that wavers between fiction, prose poetry, and dramatic monologue, which is spoken by a kaleidoscopic and indeterminate voice. The manuscript of *L'Innommable* testifies to Beckett's difficulties in composition, since it abounds in barred passages and doodles.

1950

L'Innommable (The Unnamable)

It may seem capricious to discuss *L'Innommable* in a different chapter from *Molloy* and *Malone meurt,* when the three novels are often viewed as a tril-

---

The untitled holograph of *L'Innommable* is in two notebooks dated March 29, 1949, to January 1950. They are held at HRC. An extract "Mahood" was printed in *La*

ogy. Beckett himself in a letter of May 26, 1959, to his friend Con Leventhal, mentions a "pseudo trilogy." The third novel of the French sequence not only pulverizes plot, setting, and character, but it preeminently arrives at a new mastery of the rhetoric of in-definition.[3] That mastery creates a verbal uncertainty principle whereby senselessness alone makes sense. *L'Innomma-ble* may be viewed as the beginning of Beckett's late works, which resist read-ing for meaning, even while they do mean. Only the dedicated Beckett reader will travel into these verbal thickets.

The very title of the novel is problematic, lacking the proper name that figures in Beckett's previous novels. In contrast to Moran, Molloy is a fabu-lous being, but the novel *Molloy* subsumes quest fiction only to dissolve it into in-definition; the nameless narrator of *L'Innommable* almost dissolves syntax itself in the search for a language to pinpoint himself, even while yearning for and rejecting a self beyond language.[4] Malone's present situa-tion gains authenticity by contrast with his parodic fictions that are set suc-cessively in city, farm, asylum, and sea. The nameless narrator of *L'Innom-mable* is more briefly but devastatingly parodic, until he submerges parody into denigration of the word-building process in which he is engaged. In the first two Beckett novels the protagonist narrators bear names, but the narra-tor of the third novel is not only nameless but unnamable in language. (Moreover, the French title *L'Innommable* also means "unspeakably vile" or "disgusting.") With each novel, Beckett opens new vistas for fiction, but *L'Innommable* almost abjures fiction in its last comma-hiccupping seven-page sentence. Almost but not quite.

L'Innommable still links up with its predecessors in the seventeen para-graphs of its preamble, and that preamble parallels the preludes to the nar-ratives of Molloy, Moran, and Malone, which situate those fictional writers in time and space. *L'Innommable*, however, opens on subjectless questions, which will not be asked. The fifth sentence, "Dire je," states the book's main theme: how is it possible to say "I?" What can be understood by that pro-noun? Instead of lingering on the problem, the narrator moves on to exam-ine each of his words before arbitrarily letting the pronoun stand. Questions, hypotheses, generalizations, contradictions, and aporia situate this narrator in no time or space. Yet by the fourth French page Malone appears, stripped

---

Nouvelle revue francaise (February 1, 1953) before book publication by Minuit on July 18, 1953. My page references are to this French edition. Extracts (with variants) from Beckett's English translation were published in *Spectrum* (winter 1958), *Texas Quarterly* (spring 1958), and *Chicago Review* (summer 1958) before the first book publication by Grove in 1958. The three novels were first published together by Olympia and by Grove, respectively, in 1959, and by Calder in 1960. My page refer-ences are to the Grove Weidenfeld reprint of 1991. There is no French one-volume edition.

of his "vivacité mortelle" (9) [mortal liveliness, 292]. It is just possible that the constantly moving figure may be Molloy. Even in this specifically designated "préambule," both subject and object, both "je" and his environment, are as indefinite as B finds them to be in the painting of Bram van Velde.

The very first paragraph of *L'Innommable* asks questions, proposes hypotheses, denies affirmations, enunciates resolutions, wavers as to subject matter, breaks off midsentence, and avers that it is impossible to know anything. The opening three adverbial subjectless questions are followed by "Sans me le demander" (7) [Unquestioning, 291]. Disparaging the very questions and hypotheses in which he is immediately embroiled, the first-person narrator resolves: "Je ne me poserai plus de questions" (7; omitted in translation). It is the first and the most egregious of the several resolutions to be broken in the pensum of narration. In that first paragraph, too, the narrator introduces the word "aporia," whose meaning he claims to ignore (although it has already been uttered by Malone). Yet comic irony shades his ignorance, for aporia is immediately followed by a question with another Greek root: "Peut-on être éphectique autrement qu'à son insu?" (8) [Can one be ephectic otherwise than unawares? 291]. The answer is yes, one can knowingly suspend judgment, but the narrator replies with the "Je ne sais pas," which will resound like a mantra through his discourse. The narrator's obligation to speak closes the introductory paragraph: "Je ne me tairai jamais. Jamais" (8) [I shall never be silent. Never, 291]. Never is a long time, and during the course of his discourse, the narrator will often voice a yearning for silence, which sometimes seems to be a synonym of easeful death, or of nonbeing.

Not, however, in the seventeen paragraphs of the preamble, which early describe a collision of two oblong shapes, reminding the narrator of the "pseudocouple Mercier-Camier" (16). Never so designated in their own novel (not yet published, or even contracted, when Beckett wrote that phrase), they nevertheless embody a companionship that is lacking to the solitary revolving Malone, as company is also lacking to a solitary nameless suppliant, and above all to the solitary "je" who speaks or writes. The ninth paragraph of the preamble harks back to the narrator's previous fiction, which inevitably suggests that of Beckett himself: "Pourquoi me suis-je fait représenter parmi les hommes, dans la lumière?" (17) [Why did I have myself represented in the midst of men, the light of day? 297]. Soon calling these fictional representatives his delegates, the narrator disparages whatever they may have taught him. He singles one of them, Basil, as particularly invidious. Gradually, "ils" disperses its fragile identity, and the narrator's "je" occasionally drifts into an "il" or "nous." Whatever the pronoun, the narration deprecates itself. As the preamble ambles on, the narrator dismisses Beckett's previous fictions—"Ces Murphy, Molloy, et autres Malone, je n'en suis pas dupe" (28) [All these Murphys, Molloys and Malones do not fool me, 303]—as well as Basil and his companions, in order to focus, however uncertainly, upon himself.

I have summarized the preamble in the hope of illustrating that its peculiarities and particularities are subject to the microscopic examination of the narrator. This burden is increasingly imposed upon the reader, especially when the narrator abandons paragraphs and, toward the end of his monologue, expresses himself in sentences that run on for pages from which it is difficult to extract excerpts for quotation.[5] Although *L'Innommable* does not fulfill Flaubert's dream of a book about nothing, it hovers at the brink of a pluralistic void, which sometimes seems to be a desired silence, sometimes a possible death/birth, sometimes a core of being, and always a plea for an ineffable depth unavailable to words and yet obligatorily verbal. In reading this dense prose, it is incumbent to absorb every phrase, positioned by ubiquitous commas.

The pronoun "Moi" opens the long postpreamble paragraph—the paragraph containing the bulk of *L'Innommable*. The narrator, ignoring what he has already affirmed and denied, begins again: "Moi, dont je ne sais rien, je sais que j'ai les yeux ouverts, à cause des larmes qui en coulent sans cesse" (29) [I, of whom I know nothing, I know my eyes are open, because of the tears that pour from them unceasingly, 304]. He knows nothing, but he knows something—a rhetorical strategy of contradiction, to which the narrator will often have recourse. Early in the stream of consciousness—but whose consciousness?—the narrator introduces a lying voice, which will increase in importance through an avalanche of words.

Least difficult for the reader is the narrator's patent resort to fiction. Successively, the nameless narrator names his characters Basil, Mahood, Worm, whose resonances subsume human decline: Greek *basileus* or king, Mahood or manhood, and the anti-Mahood Worm, with its grave resonance. In contrast to the picaresque accounts of Molloy/Moran about himself, or to the fictional parodies ostensibly concocted by Malone, the stories of this nameless narrator occupy barely a fifth of his monologue. Basil is renamed Mahood precisely in order to enter a story. As in the earlier two Beckett novels, a maimed body makes the archetypical voyage home, but in this cruel parody of the realistic family novel, Mahood is endowed with a wife (whose name shifts between Ptomaine—Ptoto for short—and Isolde), eight or nine offspring, and aged parents whose observations we hear, as the protagonist staggers toward his dome-home. However, the family vigil is terminated by botulinus poisoning; Mahood returns home, only to face the putrid remains of his family. No one alive can bear witness to his existence.

Within a few pages the narrator embarks on another Mahood fiction. Briefly assigned to an island where he travels in irregular loops from center to coast and back again, he is suddenly mute and limbless in a jar outside a restaurant, near a slaughterhouse. This version of Mahood is tended by a woman alternately called Marguerite and Madeleine. As the story progresses, however, this barely human trunk shrinks, and the ministering woman redoubles her care as she loses credence in his existence. Again Mahood is condemned to lack of witness. Mahood the type-character of manhood has been propelled through two stories that parody Beckett's recent French novels—the inventive voyage of Molloy/Moran and the sustained ego-centered demise of immobile Malone. The new stories are images rather than narratives: one-legged Mahood approaching his rotunda and limbless Mahood in a jar festooned with lanterns. Echoes of the second image erupt sporadically through the digressive account of the nameless narrator, who equates the two tales: "Il m'est ainsi loisible de supposer que l'unijambiste manchot de tout à l'heure et le tronc à tête de poisson où je suis actuellement en panne ne constituent bel et bien que deux aspects d'une seule et même enveloppe charnelle" (73) [I may therefore perhaps legitimately suppose that the one-armed one-legged wayfarer of a moment ago and the wedge-headed trunk in which I am now marooned are simply two phases of the same carnal envelope, 330]. So, too, Molloy and Moran may have been "simply two phases of the same carnal envelope."

Although the Mahood stories fail of the witness that might help define their narrator, although Worm is created about a third of the way through the novel to be the storyless anti-Mahood, two brief fictions nevertheless flicker residually toward the end of *L'Innommable*. The first begins as a task, filling one container and emptying another, as did the station porter in *Watt*, and Moll in the Macmann story of *Malone meurt*. Upon that simple task, this busy narrator begins to build a system of pipes, tanks, and taps, and soon he needs a body to fulfill the project, and a light by which to function. Abruptly, the narrator realizes that he is embarked on another story: "qu'est-ce que c'est que cette histoire, c'est une histoire" (186) [what's this story, it's a story, 398].[6] When the container, now single and shrunk to a thimble, falls to the floor and rolls out of sight, the story is over, whose subject wavered between "je" and "il."

The narrator's final tale disjunctively follows a passage about the night: "Ils s'aiment, se marient, pour mieux s'aimer, plus commodément, il part à la guerre, il meurt à la guerre, elle pleure, d'émotion, de l'avoir aimé, de l'avoir perdu, hop, se remarie, pour aimer encore" (199) [They love each other, marry, in order to love each other better, more conveniently, he goes to the wars, he dies at the wars, she weeps, with emotion, at having loved him, at having lost him, yep, marries again, in order to love again, 406]. The purpose of these events is to evoke emotion—from wife, mother, or mother-in-law. It seems that any female will do, in response to any catastrophe.

Within a few phrases the pronominal protagonist dies on the homeward-bound train, and the second husband hangs himself. Abruptly, the nameless narrator focuses on the door of the fictional dwelling, but he will never know who bolted it, or for what reason, in this shard of a story.

Mahood is the narrator's only fictional character to figure in two of the four stories, but he is also said to be the author of the narrator's narrative. Worm figures in no stories, and he is at times the victim of the Protean "ils" who oppress the narrator. Both proper names disappear by the last of the narrator's stories, drowned in the eddy of phrases. Namelessness is prevalent, but only the title tells us that the narrator is unnamable.

The unnamable narrator's unparagraphed monologue drives on compulsively and self-consciously. He testifies to its accumulation with a few numbers: a thousand words on memory, ten thousand as a pensum, and a blush of shame every thirty- or forty-thousand words, because they do not yield definition. Yet it is through that very in-definition that an impression of authenticity reigns, so that some commentators read *L'Innommable* as a confession of Beckett's own writing obstacles and triumphs. However, the narrator himself disparages his monologue in colorful phrases: "leurs balivernes" (64) [their rubbish, 325], "ce ramassis de conneries" (81) [this torrent of balls, 335], "un vomi de boniments" (82) [the rest of the vomit, 335], "le babil terrifié" (113) [the terror-stricken babble, 354], "la langue de catéchiste" (116) [the catechist's tongue, 356], "cette longue offense au silence" (148) [this long sin against the silence, 376], "la chasse aux mots" (187) [the wordy-gurdy, 399]. On the one hand, the narrator seeks himself in words that he disclaims. On the other hand, he insists that he mouths whatever he hears delivered by anonymous voices, and he is at once hypercritical of what the voices dictate and hyperaware of the techniques of dictation. Thus, he condemns reason even while he reasons with maniacally punctilious logic. He formulates hypotheses and calls attention to them as mere hypotheses. He pours forth a torrent of questions, while repeatedly resolving to ask no questions. He addresses himself, contradicts himself, interrupts himself, and castigates all his utterances as lies. He notes the flowers of rhetoric, specifically summoning metaphors, apostrophes, and an apodosis. He calls repeated attention to grammatical syntax—particularly verbs and pronouns. He speaks of parentheses, although he uses them sparingly. Otherwise his only punctuation marks are (unmentioned) periods and commas run riot—"la virgule viendra où je me noierai pour de bon" (203) [the comma will come where I'll drown for good, 409]. In a tempest of monosyllabic interrogatives and negatives, the occasional polysyllable brings the reader up short—in French or English: *apodosis, aporia, ephectic, exordia, facetiae, naevi, infundibuliform, hippophagist, paraphimotically, succedenae, sargasso.* This recondite vocabulary is imposed upon the sometimes childlike repetitions or exclamations. Turning against words, the narrator resolves to end in laughter, and he gives vent to onomatopoetic nonsense syllables: "je rirai, c'est comme ça que ça finira, par des gloussements, glouglou, aïe, ha, pah, je vais m'exercer, nyam, hou, plof, pss, rien que de l'émotion, pan, paf, les coups, na, toc, quoi encore, aah, ooh, ça c'est l'amour, assez, c'est fatiguant, hi, hi, ça c'est les côtes, de Démocrite, non, de l'autre" (202) [I'll laugh, that's how it will end, in a chuckle, chuck chuck, ow, ha, pa, I'll practise, nyum, hoo, plop, pss, nothing but emotion, bing bang, that's blows, ugh, pooh, what else, ooh, aah, that's love, enough, it's tiring, hee hee, that's the Abderite, no, the other, 408]. (The narrator should not have corrected himself, for Democritus the Abderite was indeed called the laughing philosopher, as Belacqua knew.)

The Mahood stories display maimed bodies familiar from Beckett's earlier work, but the bulk of the monologue is chary of images. An ear, an eye, a mouth are at times obscenely evoked: "l'image d'une grande bouche idiote, rouge, lippue, baveuse, au secret, se vidant inlassablement, avec un bruit de lessive et de gros baisers, des mots qui l'obstruent" (172) [the image of a vast cretinous mouth, red, blubber and slobbering, in solitary confinement, extruding indefatigably, with a noise of wet kisses and washing in a tub, the words that obstruct it, 390]. The narrator pokes fun at imperfect sense organs: "L'oeil se fait tirer l'oreille" (123) [Decidedly this eye is hard of hearing, 361]. A rare simile for thought can startle: "Moi je ne pense, si c'est là cet affolement vertigineux comme d'un guêpier qu'on enfume, que dépassé un certain degré de terreur" (106) [I only think, if that is the name for this vertiginous panic as of hornets smoked out of their nest, once a certain degree of terror has been exceeded, 350].

One repeated image is an unacknowledged borrowing and expansion of Geulincx. The Cartesian philosopher likened free will to walking eastward on a westward sailing ship.[7] In *Molloy* the eponymous narrator-protagonist compares himself to that walker (76); however, demoted to a slave, he crawls eastward on the Dantean black ship of Ulysses (*Inferno*, Canto XXVI). The narrator of *L'Innommable* continues and amplifies this image to a slave who crawls eastward toward the sunrise, praying for a storm (83). A few pages later the sunrise seems glorious to the creeping slave; now wearing a lifebelt, he prays for a shipwreck. Nearly a hundred pages later the narrator claims to be master of the ship—"après les rats." Instead of crawling between the oars, he digresses into the quasi-abstract life he wishes for himself. By the end of the book the Geulincxian residue is imageless: "il s'agit de lui qui ne sait rien, ne veut rien, ne peut rien, si en ne rien voulant on peut ne rien pouvoir" (196) [it's about him who knows nothing, wants nothing, can do nothing, if it's possible you can do nothing when you want nothing, 404]. The old positive negatives of the narrator of *Murphy* are unavailable to the hairsplitting narrator of *L'Innommable*.

Toward the end of the book that narrator inveighs against "ces images où ils m'ont abreuvé, comme un chameau, avant le désert" (207) [these images at which they watered me, like a camel, before the desert, 411]. The book's final image is humble, and it has been prepared in the final story, where pronominal characters disappeared behind a locked door. So, too, the nameless narrator finally voices doubt as to whether words will discover him: "ils m'ont peut-être porté jusqu'au seuil de mon histoire, devant la porte qui s'ouvre sur mon histoire" (213) [perhaps they have carried me to the threshold of my story, before the door that opens on my story, 414].

The narrator of *L'Innommable* is both an heir and an antiheir of Malone. The named narrator created Sapo to escape from himself, but he invested himself in Macmann. However, the nameless narrator of *L'Innommable* seeks himself through "vice-existers" whose words he disclaims, but if they are not his, whose are they? That question becomes a musical and meaningful theme of the book, which increasingly assigns all words to "ils," a pronoun of diverse antecedent. Unable to define himself, the narrator foists perhaps synonymous identities on the "ils" who torment him—"mes délégués" (17) [my delegates, 297], "un consortium de tyrans" (40) [a college of tyrants, 310], "sales types" (19) [low types, 298], "de bien piètres missionnaires . . . au service de l'éphémère rebondissant" (49) [paltry priests of the irrepressible ephemeral, 316], "mes tentateurs" (59) [my tempters, 322], "des ennemis qui m'habitent" (101) |the devils who beset me, 347|, "le même sale individu s'amusant à paraître multiple" (108) [the same foul brute . . . amusing himself pretending to be a many, 351|, "ces fantômes parlants" (146) [these voluble shades, 374], "cher charnier de transfuges" (156) [dear charnel-house of renegades, 380|, "bande de cochons . . . quels rustres" (160) [herd of shites . . . clowns, 383]. His confusion can be confusing: "Ils disent ils, en parlant d'eux, c'est pour que je croie que c'est moi qui parle" (138) [They say they, speaking of them, to make me think it is I who am speaking, 370]. However victimized by "ils," the narrator rarely subdues his sense of irony, and he occasionally pities "ils," attempting to adopt their viewpoint toward his recalcitrant self. Punctuated only by the ubiquitous comma, a colloquy is imagined about himself, each phrase distancing him further from definition, but endearing him further to us, who read his "je":

> Mais, voir plus haut, ne sont-ils pas déjà penchés sur moi, vers moi, à en avoir mal au cou, aux reins, que dis-je, ont-ils jamais fait autre chose, depuis que, pas de précisions temporelles surtout, et, autre question, que viens-je faire dans ces histoires de Mahood et de Worm, ou plutôt que viennent-ils faire dans la mienne, en voilà du pain sur la

planche, qu'il y moisisse. Je sais, je sais, attention, cette fois c'est le grand jeu, tout ça c'est le seul et même boniment, sans bavures, le même que toujours, à savoir, Mais voyons, mon cher, voilà, voilà qui vous êtes, regardez cette photo, et voici la fiche, pas de condemnations, je vous assure, faites un effort, à votre age, être sans identité, c'est une honte. (149–50)

[But, see above, have they not already bent over me till black and blue in the face, nay, have they ever done anything else, during the past— no, no dates for pity's sake, and another question, what am I doing in Mahood's story, and in Worm's, or rather what are they doing in mine, there are some irons in the fire to be going on with, let them melt. Oh I know, I know, attention please, this may mean something, I know, there's nothing new there, it's all part of the same old irresistible boloney, namely, But my dear man, come, be reasonable, look, this is you, look at the photograph, and here's your file, no convictions, I assure you, come now, make an effort, at your age, to have no identity, it's a scandal. (76–77)]

And so on for several pages.

The pacing of the narrator's monologue is so magnetic that most commentators imitate its rhythms. What has perhaps been inadequately appreciated is the technical range of the novel; yes, novel, the English translation of the genre specifically designated on the cover of the French Minuit edition— "roman." Like most novels, *L'Innommable* even has a plot of sorts; a nameless narrator, who is usually subsumed by the pronoun "je," tells of his adventures with and in words, which are often directed in search of his identity, which are often cited as the only means to achieve silence, and which sometimes attain to a dizzying momentum where the syntax, clarified by commas, is nevertheless always decipherable. In spite of the protestations of the narrator—"ne sachant pas parler, ne voulant pas parler" [not knowing how to speak, not wanting to speak]—he speaks with great variety. His images are few but memorable; his rhythms are built on repetition with an occasional chiasmus; interrogatives and negatives abound; continuous self-address is varied by occasional direct address to the reader; syllogisms elide into exhaustive series; maniacal precision can expand into a cosmic sweep; contradictions are laced with oxymorons, and interruptions are retrieved through canny summaries; sound plays arabesques around the syntax. Specifically mentioned and exemplified are ellipses and literalisms, fantastic hypotheses cloaked under reason, metaphors and apostrophes—a cornucopia of rhetorical devices, beneath the self-declared penury of language.[8]

Yet *L'Innommable* is not merely (merely!) a linguistic plenum; like its final story, its words evoke emotion. The in-definition of the narrator accumulates gradually, while his anxiety intensifies in the latter half of the novel.

Nor is it mitigated by the hints that his difficulties are self-created, located in a head. Although the "rien à faire" (163) of *Godot* is occasionally uttered, what is done by the nameless narrator's many words is a series of arabesques on the page, with an aurality unique to written literature. Too often, the final phrases of *L'Innommable* are read as a triumphant triptych, but in context they are a rhythmic and emotional testimony to the continuity of ignorance and impotence: "dans le silence on ne sait pas, il faut continuer, je ne peux pas continuer, je vais continuer" [in the silence you don't know, you must go on, I can't go on, I'll go on]. The conclusion is at once a victory and a defeat, as understood in Daniel Katz's graceful sentence: "The oscillations, repetitions, prolepses, and disavowals create a textual rhythm which the exquisitely balanced and paced phrases are careful to maintain in terms of breath, tongue, and ear" (100). Breath, mouth, and ear are imaged in the text, and we respond with ours.

Beckett completed *L'Innommable* in January 1950, and although he was exhausted, he then produced translations for *Transition*. Incomplete and unpublished among other illegible fragments in the so-called Sam Francis Notebook at RUL are pages of translation of a piece on that American painter, calling him "Animator of Silence." While Beckett stabbed at different genres, Suzanne carried the manuscripts of *Eleutheria* and *En attendant Godot* to the actor/director Roger Blin, who soon informed her that he liked both plays, but he had no funds for production. Nevertheless, Beckett and Blin met in early summer, to their mutual pleasure. Then Beckett left for Dublin, arriving in time to arrange his mother's transfer to a nursing home, since she was severely afflicted with Parkinson's disease. When not at her bedside, he typed up *L'Innommable* and translated into English passages of *Molloy* and *Malone meurt*. May Beckett died on August 25, and Beckett returned to Paris.

Beckett resumed his effort to write another play in French, and his two efforts in RUL ms. 2926 (the Sam Francis Notebook) are separated by his note: "Sept. 15 1950. retour de l'Ireland." The editors of *BatR* list these two fragments under *Endgame*, although they acknowledge that the pieces "cannot be described as an early draft of the play" (34). Predating the final version of *Fin de partie* by some six years, they are limited to an exchange of dialogue between A and B. I follow the *BatR* editors in listing these shards under *Fin de partie*, but I mention them here because they illustrate what will become a habit with Beckett—his preservation of aborted efforts. Midcentury apparently marks the point where Beckett began to discard some of his writings, without literally jettisoning them. Usually, Beckett's handwriting is atrocious in these aborted efforts.

Since it was Suzanne who brought Beckett's manuscripts to publishers, he instructed her that the three novels would have to be accepted en bloc, thus increasing the improbability of publication. Jérôme Lindon of Les Editions de Minuit was enthusiastic about *Molloy,* and after a comedy of missed meetings with the author, he accepted the three novels. Contracts were signed on November 15, 1950, but Beckett was despondent that nearly a year had elapsed without the completion of new work. On Christmas Eve, 1950, however, Beckett started an untitled text in French, which he did complete.[9]

1951
◯

In January 1951 Beckett penned another text, then still another, and so on until they totaled thirteen, Beckett's preferred number. The project occupied him from December 24, 1950, to December 20, 1951, with a one-month hiatus between May 21 and June 25, and a two-month hiatus between September 6 and November 7, 1951. While Beckett worked at the new material, *Molloy* was published in March 1951, and *Malone meurt* in October, to favorable if somewhat bewildered reviews. At about the same time Roger Blin sporadically rehearsed bits of *En attendant Godot,* even though no Paris theater would commit to it. Beckett labored at the *Textes,* notwithstanding the new publications and the doubtful production. When the new work was completed, he exhumed the neutral word he had used before—for poems of the early 1930s. This time, however, Beckett affixed purpose to his texts—*Textes pour rien.*

Textes pour rien (*Texts for Nothing*)

French *pour rien* designates a bar's rest in a musical score, or a momentary silence, but the phrase also puns on worthless, as in English "good for noth-

---

The holograph of *Textes pour rien* in two notebooks (along with unpublished material) is at HRC. The first text was begun Christmas Eve, 1950, and the thirteen were written in the order published, being completed by December 20, 1951, when a subsequently discarded work was begun. *Texte V* was published in *Deucalion* (October 1952). *Textes III, VI,* and *X* were published in *Les Lettres nouvelles* (May 1953); *Texte XI* in *Arts-Spectacles* 418 (July 3–9, 1953); *Textes I* and *XII* in *Monde Nouveau* (May–June 1955)—with variants—before the whole series was published by Minuit in November 1955 in *Nouvelles et Textes pour rien.* Beckett's English translations were first published piecemeal: I in *Evergreen Review* (summer 1959); III in *Great French Short Stories* (Dell, 1960); XII in *The Transatlantic Review* (spring 1967); VI in *London Magazine* (August 1967). Beckett's entire English translation was published by Calder and Boyars in 1967 in *No's Knife;* and by Grove in 1967 in *Stories and Texts for Nothing.* In a letter of September 5, 1980, to the actor-director Joe Chaikin Beckett admits that he only then—in view of a performance—realized the ambiguity of this last title, which should have been *Stories, Followed by Texts for Nothing.* My page numbers refer to the Minuit edition for the French and *CSP* for the English.

ing." Beckett's title subsumes the direction of the texts—toward rest, nothing, nonbeing, or death, which may be but are not necessarily synonymous. Already in the three French novels the word *rien* occurs 658 times, 342 in *L'Innommable* (Fitch 1977, 179). Yet the *rien* seems more intense in these short texts. Individually and globally, the texts cast doubt on the usual parameters of human definition—especially time, place, and memory; yet the irrepressible voice or voices remain humanly resonant, however they may lack individual subjectivity. Moreover, Beckett renounced the narrative drive—the quest—of much of his previous fiction. As Porter Abbott observes, Beckett "exchanged the narrative genre of the quest for the broad nonnarrative genre of the meditative personal essay" (1996, 90).

These essays display both variety and quasi-monotony—a blend that is explicitly mentioned in *Texte IX*. Varying in length from some seven hundred to seventeen hundred words, the *Textes* are not so much monotonous as repetitive, when they raise questions already posed in Beckett's *L'Innommable*: Who am I? Where am I? How did I get here? How do I go on? Whose are the words I mouth? Like *Godot* (completed over two years earlier) the *Textes* are riddled with interrogatives, although Beckett is sparing of question marks as punctuation. Even though the unnamed narrator (or narrators) of the *Textes* poses the same old questions, he does so in a new rhythm composed of breathless short phrases, snatches of dialogue, and brief lyric flights. Gone are the occasional polysyllables and erudite references of *L'Innommable,* to be replaced with a microscopic scrutiny of each monosyllable, especially *moi* and *non.* Self correction becomes less a matter of expression than of directive drive.

Several of the thirteen texts move in a roughly circular pattern, and the whole collection circles back to more or less its beginning in speech. In *Textes pour rien* theme dissolves into technique. Most familiar is the repetition of phrases to denote the repetitive hunt for meaning, identity, or simple (!) silence. The fragmentary phrases reflect the fragmentation of thought, which is ill served by words. Since words are contradictory, negatives and denials proliferate. Each of the texts begins afresh, but they all share a skepticism about the ability of language to affirm anything at all. Yet they keep trying through a shift of context. Thus, one text attempts to sketch landscape, another dredges up memories; a few others weave characters into scenes, whereas a courtroom setting lacks characters. The texts grow increasingly abstract, and certain sentences grow labyrinthine. It is instructive to contrast the explosive first sentence of the sequence with the wayward last sentence. *Texte I* bursts forth, virtually denying the conclusion of *L'Innommable:* "Brusquement, non, à force, à force, je n'en pus plus, je ne pus continuer" [Suddenly, no, at last, long last, I couldn't any more, I couldn't go on]. Sound play (five *us*), negation, and repetition mark the French. That

abrupt opening staccato contrasts with the dying fall of the inconclusive conclusion of the *Textes:* "Et il y aurait un jour ici, où il n'est pas de jours, qui
n'est pas un endroit, issu de l'impossible voix l'infaisable être, et un com-
mencement de jour, que tout serait silencieux et vide et noir, comme maintenant, comme bientôt, que tout sera fini, tout dit, dit-elle, murmure-t-elle"
[And were there one day to be here, where there are no days, which is no
place, born of the impossible voice the unmakable being, and a gleam of
light, still all would be silent and empty and dark, as now, as soon now,
when all will be ended, all said, it says, it murmurs]. Timeless and placeless,
the voice murmurs about time and place. In spite of the "impossible" and the
"infaisable," the words have vivified anxieties.

I will try to comment on each Text individually, as Beckett wrote them,
but the prose is so dense, the repetitions so polyvalent, the rhetoric so sparing of image and figure, that, short of long quotation, I will fail to convey the
magnetism of these lively meditations, which keep announcing their fatigue.

Texte I

Although almost a year elapsed between the completion of *L'Innommable*
and the beginning of this text, Beckett links them by the verb *continuer*. The
novel concludes: "il faut continuer, je ne peux pas continuer, je vais continuer." The text begins, as already quoted: "Brusquement, non, à force, à
force, je n'en pus plus, je ne pus continuer" [Suddenly, no, at last, at long
last, I couldn't any more, I couldn't go on]. Extrapolating on this inability,
the narrative voice does go on to describe a place, which grows into a survey
of topographies familiar from earlier Beckett works. The narrator mentions
a dialogue between his body and his head, but he no longer has the energy
for their conflict. Other beings up above are far. It is not they but anonymous
voices that ask the old metaphysical questions, to which the old weary replies
are given. The narrator tries to confine his words to the present moment and
location, but time and space betray him. Yet he remains susceptible to stories, as when his father read him the story of Joe Breem or Breen night after
night, or when they walked quietly, hand in hand, each plunged in his own
world. (His father's nightly reading of the Joe Breem story abbreviates the
account in *Le Calmant,* written some four years earlier.) That is what
enabled the narrator to go on, and it seems to be working this evening, when
he holds himself in his arms, ready for sleep.

As in *L'Innommable* the frequent *ça* and the reference to voices resonate
aurally. Familiar as are the questions, quotations, and contradictions, the
frenetic rhythm of the novel has slowed to a more leisurely pace. Words associated with fatigue take on a gently rocking rhythm, musicalized by nasals
and alliteration in this tender, backward-looking text.

Texte II

This text goes on by evoking memories—the very word *souvenir* recurs three times. Beginning with the light above of the living, the text circles around to a last memory of a lamp's far-off glow. Between those two lights the narrator summons recollections of living beings who are drawn from several realms—M. Joly, the sexton of *Molloy*, the Graves brothers of whom one might be the gardener in *Watt*, an apparently imaginary garbage-foraging Mme. Calvet with her trident and dog, and Piers, the plowman of Middle English literature in this French piece. Images rather than stories, they contrast with the indefinite present moment. Their memory has permitted the words to go on, however slowly, however seasonally, however changing of mood.

Texte III

After a command to leave all that, this longest of the thirteen texts moves determinedly forward. Almost at once "moi" is denied, no matter who is speaking. A body is necessary, and this one will be an aged child in care of his nursemaid who envelops him in baby talk. When that character fizzles out, the narrator resorts briefly to memories before he creates two ancient ailing veterans, who are among the most mordant of Beckett's comic creations. Situated firmly among their betting companions in Dublin, these military comrades reveal themselves to be escapist memories from the present, where nothing happens and no one passes. The narrator questions why the Dublin scene may not serve as a point of departure, but he is engulfed by the present moment: "Je ne sais pas, je suis ici, c'est tout ce que je sais, et que ce n'est toujours pas moi, c'est avec ça qu'il faut s'arranger" (151) [I don't know, I'm here, that's all I know, and that it's still not me, it's of that the best has to be made, 113]. At intervals the narrator repeats his command to leave all that, and he concludes that the voices have no life in them—after these lively evocations.

Texte IV

This text opens on questions, posed in repetitions: "Où irais-je, si je pouvais aller, que serais-je, si je pouvais être, que dirais-je, si j'avais une voix, qui parle ainsi, se disant moi?" (153) [Where would I go, if I could go, who would I be, if I could be, what would I say, if I had a voice, who says this, saying it's me? 114]. Under the melody lies a Chinese box of voices within voices, ultimately needing the impossible first-person utterer. A confusing conflict ensues, between a third-person and a first-person pronoun, each attempting to devour the other. Gone are the mortals with proper names, Molloy and Malone; the quest now involves the naked first person, but the struggle between nameless persons is fought lyrically to its anticipatory lack of conclusion. The final sentence is an anonymous and indefinite reply to the opening question: "C'est là où j'irais, si je pouvais aller, celui-là que je serais, si je pouvais être" (158) [That's where I'd go, if I could go, that's who I'd be, if I could be, 116].

Texte V

Beckett is sometimes compared to Kafka, and this text dramatizes a trial, in a radically abbreviated version of the Czech author's novel. However, the narrator is not only the victim, but also the court clerk, the judge, an interested party, a witness, and an attorney. No sooner is the courtroom scene set than the narrator is aware of another trial, perhaps in a head. Winding in and out of the trial metaphor, the voice repeats four times "c'est noté," but what is noted is not necessarily clarified or judged, so the narrator cannot believe in his own presence. Soon he tries to dismiss the trial as a game, before dawn disperses everything, with the sounds of the first birds. Nevertheless, the text's last sentences, with phrases of biblical resonance, imply a final judgment: "Mais à chaque jour suffit sa peine, ce sont là d'autres minutes. Oui, on commence à être bien fatigué, bien fatigué de sa peine, bien fatigué de sa plume, elle tombe, c'est noté" (166) [But sufficient unto the day, those are other minutes. Yes, one begins to be very tired, very tired of one's toil, very tired of one's quill, it falls, it's noted, 121]. The trial image has narrowed to the individual soul, after harrowing God's cosmos. Yet the note is paradoxically made *after* the quill falls.

Texte VI

Again we begin with a question: "Entre ces apparitions que se passe-t-il?" (167) [How are the intervals filled between these apparitions? 122]. Sternly, the narrator reins fantasies about "ils" to focus on himself, whom he suddenly finds in central London. Not for long, however, as he re-views nameless characters of earlier Beckett fiction. His varied past yields no clue about the present, which he tries to describe: "Et [sic] bien me voilà, petite poussière dans un petit nid, qu'un souffle soulève, qu'un autre rabat, venus du dehors perdu" (170) [Well look at me, a little dust in a little nook, stirred faintly this way and that by breath straying from the lost without, 123]. Although made of words, he wonders about the material of which he was once made, even to seeing himself at age twelve in a shaving mirror, the one side reflecting and the other magnifying. That mirror carries one of Beckett's most poignant renderings of mortality. At first it reflects his father, and behind him the harbor and the sea; once his father is gone, the same mirror in another house reflects his mother fixing her hair with trembling hands, and behind her is the mountain. These moving portraits lead immediately to a purgatorial chorus: "Je fus, je fus," but at least each member of that chorus was assured of individuality—*je* fus. Turning against the very words of the text, the narrator utters his frustration, recalling the title of Beckett's last novel: "qu'est-ce que c'est, cette innommable chose, que je nomme, nomme, nomme, sans l'user, et j'appelle ça des mots" (173) [what is it, this unnamable thing that I name and name and never wear out, and I call that words, 125]. Yet he hopes one day to combine the words into a story, about living beings coming and going, about day and night coming and going.

Texte VII

However, the very next text begins not with a story but with a question about whether the "je" has exhausted every possibility of finding himself. He summarizes the places he has looked, before denying that he speaks of himself: "Du reste ce n'est pas moi, je ne parle pas de moi, je l'ai dit cent mille fois, inutile de m'en dire confus, confus de parler de moi, alors qu'il y a X, paradigme du genre humain" (177) [It's not me in any case, I'm not talking of me, I've said it a million times, no point in apologizing again, for talking of me, when there's X, that paradigm of human kind, 128]. It is a sly rhetorical strategy, for Beckett's texts are so magnetic in part because, in writing of a "je," he writes of a "paradigm of human kind." Touched on lightly in this text, the paradigm is abandoned for an autobiographical recollection of a specific location—the South-Eastern Railway station (at Beckett's native Foxrock). He digresses a moment from that place but returns to describe it and himself in it, holding a ticket between finger and thumb. The deafening silence makes him wonder whether to abandon the place; perhaps it is already a ruin, where he continues to wait for a train that will never come. Just before the conclusion, he cautions against rushing to a conclusion. In answer to his opening question, the narrator concludes that it would be a waste of time to seek himself elsewhere: "Et personnellement je n'ai plus de temps à perdre, je l'entends dire, et que ce sera tout, pour ce soir, que la nuit arrive et qu'il est temps de s'y mettre" (180) [And personally, I hear it said, personally I have no more time to lose, and that that will be all for this evening, that night is at hand and the time come for me too to begin, 130]. The voice has become impersonal—"je l'entends dire"—in this sentence that stresses the personal creature that has not yet been located, but night is the paradoxical time for beginnings.

Texte VIII

After a month away from the *Textes,* Beckett has his "je" pick up the silence, which is expressed in and broken by words. As in *L'Innommable,* words flow with tears in the old threnody. The narrator asks himself whether it has always been like this, but he can no longer recall the past. He simply goes on talking, in the hope of wearing out his voice and his head. If only he could pierce into "moi, ici," those small, seemingly simple words. He feels himself sundered in two, the one a ventriloquist's dummy, whereas it is the other he seeks: "Mais l'autre qui est moi, aveugle, sourd et muet, cause que je suis ici, cause de ce noir silence, cause que je ne peux plus remuer ni croire cette voix la mienne" (185) [But that other who is me, blind and deaf and mute, because of whom I'm here, in this black silence, helpless to move or accept this voice as mine, 133]. He has a sudden surge of hope that the right combination of words may arrive by chance, but then Aristotle thought there were four million possibilities. Suddenly objects confront him—a white cane and a hearing horn on Paris's Place de la République at Pernod time. They are joined by a bowler hat and worn brown boots, and since these objects move forward together, they must be connected by "le traditionnel excipient humain." He wonders hopefully whether he has a future as a beggar. However, as *Texte V* moved from a courtroom to judgment day, and *Texte VII* from a suburban Irish train station to universal death, so this begging hand expands to seek being or ceasing to be: "Et la main vainement vieille lâcherait l'obole et les vieux pieds reprendraient, vers une mort encore plus vaine que celle de n'importe qui" (188) [And the hand old in vain would drop the mite and the old feet shuffle on, towards an even vainer death than no matter whose, 135].

Texte IX

Increasingly abstract, this text weaves yearning for an exit into oppositions, literalisms, impatience with past strategies. If the "je" could conceive of a way out between "c'est moi" and "ce n'est pas moi," perhaps birth and death would follow, entailing a mother and a tomb. Blows have not borne testimony to the existence of the "je," but perhaps death would confer identity at the gates of the cemetery. Aware that he is confusing past and present, time and space, the "je" tries to return to locating himself, but the phrase of yearning soon recurs: "c'est-à-dire si je pouvais dire, Là il y a une issue" (196) [that is to say if I could say, There's a way out there, 140]. Inhabitually, the "je" allows his yearning to carry him along; if he could utter those liberating words, others would arrive, enabling him to see the skies again, and the stars. The unusually hopeful finale echoes Dante emerging from the Inferno to see the stars again.

Texte X

Unsurprisingly, hope is of short duration, and this text begins with the word "Abandonner" [give up]. Before a "je" appears, we read: "ça parle, quelque part on parle" (197) [there is utterance, somewhere someone is uttering, 141]. Sentences expand on this disbelieving reconstruction of a head, which may eventuate in a past. Perhaps other souls are in the same situation, awaiting a "mise en corps." Then souls, bodies, births, life and death are swept away: "il faut continuer sans rien de tout cela, tout cela est mort de mots" (200) [you've got to go on without any of that junk, that's all dead with words, 142]. Yet the words awaken hope of a voice and silence, a voice of silence. Refusing to be the dupe of words, the "je" prepares for sleep, without accomplishing anything, except going on giving up, without ever managing to be. It is particularly hard to quote selectively from these long sentences of lyrical resignation.

Texte XI

This last text to be written before a two-month break is at once desperate and humorous. The "je" calls for those who knew him, even while realizing that "Nommer, non, rien n'est nommable, dire, non rien n'est dicible" (203) [Name, no, nothing is namable, tell, no, nothing can be told, 145]. The "je" nevertheless seeks a body, a head, and then curses the words that try to make him believe that he has a head and a voice. Calling again on those who knew him, he paints a comic portrait of a studious adolescent, and in the same long sentence he is suddenly old, in the urinal on rue d'Assas. Warming to the body, he amputates limb after limb—a nostalgic recollection of evenings of wandering and questioning. Then the old conflict resurfaces between "je" and "il," running through a litany of distinctions between them, which turn out to be indistinguishable, but he nevertheless mentions them: "je suis en train de le dire, je vais le dire, je vais finir par le dire, puis finir, je pourrai finir, je ne serai plus" (209) [I'm saying it now, I'll say it soon, I'll say it in the end, then end, I'll be free to end, I won't be any more, 147]. The only way for everything to cease is to find a new No that annuls the previous negatives, but "je" knows that that will not happen, and therefore it is time that those who knew him testify to his existence, leading him along a road that is not his, further and further from the other road that is not his. Finally, however, he knows no one and is known by no one; that is all he has to say this evening.

Texte XII

Perhaps it is Beckett's two-month break from the Textes that enabled him to conclude with renewed syntactical energy. This short text opens with a long sentence englobing the "moi-pas moi" conflict and its spatiotemporal tributaries. Dream and memory blend on this winter night. "Il" chants the familiar tune of one who has prevented "je" from living. Voices and ears are everywhere, devouring one another's words. More distinctly than in earlier texts, "je" and "il" are haunted by a third person without number: "Voilà un joli trio, et dire que tout ça ne fait qu'un, et que cet un ne fait que rien, et quel rien, il ne vaut rien" (213) [There's a pretty three in one, and what a one, what a no one, 150]. Rejecting what he is supposed to say, the "je" never-theless says it, realizing that he would need an unwitnessed witness, so it is well that nothing was begun—except for "mots morts" of this exceptionally lively text.

Texte XIII

Although the voice is mentioned in almost every "text for nothing," it is vir-tually ubiquitous in this last text—weak, distant, bodiless, and anonymous. It has not managed to create a life, but that uncreated life is that of "je." Embroiled in concessive clauses of what might have been, pity and hope arise for a moment, only to be firmly banished from the indescribable here-and-now. The "je" twice affixes *derniers* to questions and images, but through those questions and images wind new emotions couched in a labyrinthine syntax, which is occasionally punctuated by brief repetitive sentences. The voice that is said to be weak and distant has the last lovely words, blending illocality and impotence with dawn and an end in silence, darkness, and void—it murmurs. The voice has enunciated for nothing, going on by going nowhere through a lyrical minuet of pronouns and verb tenses.[10]

1952

Textes pour rien was completed on December 20, 1951, and on December 22 Beckett began another work in the same notebook as *Textes pour rien VIII* to *XIII*. Forty-one virtually illegible leaves have baffled scholars. Admussen says of these leaves: "Beckett's handwriting is here at its worst, and this text may well remain impenetrable" (108). However, three typescripts at RUL are apparently revisions of these holographs, which are separated by two legible dates in the manuscript—February 1, 1952, on leaf 12 and February 1952, on leaf 23. Exact dates are problematic during this year, when Beckett tried to go on in fiction and drama. My order of consideration of these unpublished pieces may be wrong, but the abandoned efforts are testimony to Beckett's perseverance.

In the very February during which Beckett worked at the illegible stories in the second *Textes* Notebook, his attention was deflected to his drama. An enterprising young producer, Michel Polac, read a copy of *Godot* in manu-script and chose it to inaugurate a radio series on new drama—*Entrée des auteurs*. He asked Beckett to introduce the program. The latter of course refused, but he did send a letter about his play, which was read on radio on February 17 by Roger Blin, but which was not published until forty-four years later.[11] The letter is light in tone, with Beckett disclaiming all knowledge of his characters, beyond what the play *En attendant Godot* contains. It concludes: "Eux et moi nous sommes quittes." Given the difficulties in finding a theater, Beckett must indeed have felt far removed from the play that had flowed so easily in composition. In the frustrations of 1952, he could hardly predict that the play would render him "damned to fame."

In the meantime he was in the throes of fiction. Four undated typescripts seem to me closer to *Fizzles* than to *Texts for Nothing*, although I would be hard-pressed to differentiate the two subgenres. Hesitantly, I suggest that the *Texts* tremble toward personal essays, whereas the *Fizzles* secrete narratives. Since these stories are untitled, I consider them under the opening phrases of the typescripts, which are misdescribed in *BatR* as "variant drafts of *Textes pour rien*" (182). On the contrary, they are distinctive texts, bordering on nothing in different ways. Varying between nine and sixteen pages, the typescripts return warily to some of the questions raised in the preamble of *L'Innommable,* but the almost determined digressions within each piece announce a different way of approaching nothing.

"Au bout de ces années perdues"

In the opening sentence an "il" addresses himself with three possible procedures: begin again, or retrace the old paths, or, since immobility is impossible, return to the century (or the external world?). He seems to have chosen the second way in the tension between "il" and "nous" (rather than "je"). This narrator will exult in "l'ivresse du monologue retrouvé" [intoxication of monologue rediscovered], or perhaps he will say nothing. Words are there again, even though they are indistinguishable. Unable to find a subject, as when his name was Sapo, "nous" nevertheless is firmly anti-*moi*. "Nous" is equated with the brain, sensitivity, hope, despair, when suddenly a voice is born, preventing a declaration of death. However "ils" differ on the nature of the scene, all parties are agreed that it is in an outer world—except for Milton, who sees a vast waiting room, and "nous" imagines a discussion between Milton and his adversaries. The imaginary dialogue continues about the nature of the place, which soon spills over into time. The name of Milton—poet or fiction?—threads through "nous's" phrases, which crystallize into repetitions of "Je pense." After exhorting himself to fasten on familiar characteristics, "nous" acknowledges: "Comme tout cela est loin" [How all that is far away]. Resigned to admitting that "il" is in a bad way, "nous" concludes that that must be the new point of departure: "écumons à partir de là," he urges, with a verb that can mean anything from "skim" to "seethe." Even though the narrator pronounces "nous" uninteresting, there is the

---

The illegible holograph of "Au bout de ces années perdues" at HRC is dated December 22, 1951. The undated typescript is at RUL.

whole night ahead, and the discourse may not need that long. Sprinkled through the discourse have been references to the necessity of that discourse. Although one cannot be certain, Beckett apparently short-stopped his text, which goes on for a handwritten page beyond the typescript.

"Hourah je me suis repris"

The opening phrase promises an élan that depends upon the return of memory. In the meantime "je" describes his improved condition, especially since he will no longer pose the old questions about his voice and identity. Inclined to believe that the narrating "je" is already dead, he is forced to lend credence to his convalescence. "Je" hopes to go on, by sticking to the surface of the withered grass. "Je" doesn't know how long he has lived "cette vie nomade dans un petit espace" [this nomadic life in a small space]. Perhaps always. Desiring not to talk about himself, he will focus on a "semblable" [semblance]. Making several references to that "semblable," "je" keeps finding details in his memory. "Je" would even use the third-person pronoun, were he not afraid of confusion between "les deux gaillards, celui qui cherche et celui qui manque" [the two fellows, he who seeks and he who needs]. Suddenly, "je" finds that he has a dozen assistants. Spurning images, "je" keeps telling himself how much remains to be done, but he does not actually start the doing; instead he repeats that he is waiting for his memory to return. Near the end of the text, "je" summarizes its few highpoints: "Bon, j'énumère, semblable à dénicher, douze disciples ou assistants, revenu de loin, niveau de la mer, rond d'herbe flétrie, nomadisme restreint" [Good, I enumerate: to seek a semblance, twelve disciples or assistants, returned from afar, sea-level, a circle of withered grass, limited nomadism]. Beckett then abandons the text midsentence. Although some of its repetitions recall those of the preamble of *L'Innommable,* the suspicion of a "semblable" is new and newly phrased; the text adheres more closely to an essay than a narrative mode.

"On le tortura bien"

This text plumps for narrative in its account of how the story was told. As Ann Beer (1987) reads the holograph, three characters live together by the sea, sleeping in the same bed, with rules as to who should occupy the middle

---

The illegible holograph of "Hourah je me suis repris" at HRC is dated 1.2.52. The undated typescript is at RUL.

The illegible holograph of "On le tortura bien" at HRC is dated February 1952. The undated typescript is at RUL. It is this text that Ann Beer (1987) tried valiantly to read as "Emmanuel, Popel, etc.," but the typescript shows that she is often mistaken.

position for a month. Popol cooks and knits; Matt is a writer; Emmanuel is the first-person narrator, born on Good Friday (like Beckett himself, and like his fictional Jean du Chas, of 1930). However, these proper names appear late in the manuscript, and they change even later to Pat, Mat, and Nat. As though Beckett's handwriting were not sufficient obstacle, the versos of several leaves show floor plans that might relate to the story, but are, I believe, sketches for the Ussy house built with the money left him by his mother. (However, he sometimes referred to his Ussy cottage as "the house built by Godot.")

RUL typescript 1656/3 opens: "On le tortura bien, jusqu'à ce qu'il parlât" [He was thoroughly tortured, until he spoke]. The victim is called "le narrateur" by the actual narrator of Beckett's story, and the situation prefigures that of *As the Story Was Told,* where someone is tortured to tell a story. As in the later tale, the torture takes place in a tent. Reluctant to witness cruelty, *our* narrator waits outside the tent after instructing Pat in the application of torture, while Nat records the utterances of the victim. "Je's" account then shifts away from that victim to the relationship between the three colleagues, for whom the nameless narrator's death (mentioned almost incidentally) is a liberation. The three colleagues sleep together and have sex together—an activity from which the victim demurs. Always together, the three colleagues change their identical costumes for each fresh victim, and some three pages are devoted to their ridiculous clothes.

Although their tastes are quite different, the three are compelled to subdue them in their life together, including nights in the same bed, each hooked up to a bottle. The text introduces a five-year monthly table, indicating the volume of liquid—presumably urine—each contributes to the bottle. "Je" begins to tell a tale of his fall, but virtually every sentence brings a new digression—all of which Nat is noting, so that the narrator Mat once addresses us, "Cher lecteur." Mat talks continually "sans solution de continuité." He imagines someone sticking a fork in his rectum, thus forcing him to connect his utterances: "Et que, qui plus est et puisse être exigé, à n'importe quel moment, que je le tire au clair, le rapport en question, et le légitime, au cas où il paraîtrait, aux yeux de qui de droit, entaché d'obscurité, ou de fatuité, ou de vacuité, pour ne pas dire inexistant" [And what is more what might be required at a given moment that I clarify the relationship in question, and legitimize it, in case it might appear to whomever it may concern, shadowed in obscurity, or fatuity, or vacuity, or even failing to exist]. Thus the initial torturer has, at least mentally, replaced the silenced victim. Beckett probably did not intend the final sentence of the typescript as a conclusion, since the holograph continues for an illegible leaf. Nevertheless the skepticism about the discourse is retrospectively climactic. The whole piece demonstrates Beckett's return to narrative, after his essayistic venture in the *Textes pour rien*. Moreover, the metanarrative resonance is newly cruel, graphic, and mordantly comic.

"Ici, personne ne vient jamais"

The piece is the most colloquial of the four stories, and it seems most resistant to interpretation. The pronounless speaker in a lifeless place imagines a discoverer of that place and various possibilities for him or them to abandon it. After some five pages, he arrives back at his opening statement: "ici nulle créature ne vient jamais." Like earlier Beckett places, this one abounds in darkness and silence, and like earlier Beckett narrators, this one recognizes that he is in a skull. Close at hand are Beckett's characters, both recent and less recent: "Mat et Nat et Pat, vieux maniaques d'un instant, avec leurs culottes bouffantes, chapeaux cloche et lit à trois places, et Quin et Watt" [Mat and Nat and Pat, old momentary maniacs, with their ballooning trousers, bowler hats, and bed for three, and Quin and Watt]. Words keep pouring out in huge numbers that will occupy twenty pages. Yet the French pronoun *on* enables the text to remain impersonal. Momentarily, "On est l'endroit" [One equals the place]. Momentarily, there is a return to the possibility that someone once came to this deserted place. However, the evanescent moment precludes certainty: "On n'est plus là où le mot est tombé" [One is no longer there where the word fell]. Beckett imagines the narrator seated in France scribbling in a child's graph paper notebook (like the one that contains his holograph), but he prefers to equate the person and the place: "ici c'est moi, maintenant c'est moi." The narrator will start again from a new basis. Pursuing a self, the text grows more labyrinthine in the last half-page sentence "pour faire une présence" [to announce a presence]. Although that sentence begins "Heureusement," with relief that all the old narrative subterfuges are no longer necessary, the sentence ends "et ce serait dommage" [and that would be too bad]. Finally the place is the place of narration, conclusively abandoned.

The four typescripts may have been intended for publication together—like the four stories several years earlier. Rather than a continuous-discontinuous "je," however, these stories vary in their narrative emphasis: the first is resolutely third-person, whereas the second is as resolutely first-person. The third story, with its three colleagues, demonstrates the difficulties of telling a story, which is its ostensible subject. The fourth story shifts from figures to the world into which they are thrust. Composed for the most part in short phrases, all the stories build on associative digressions from a ratio-

---

The first sentence of the typescript at RUL corresponds to the opening of a (largely) illegible holograph in the MacGowran Notebook at OSU, which is dated March 15, 1952, and which begins: "Ici, personne ne vient jamais."

nal continuity of thought. All the stories derive comedy from the imperturbable doggedness of their narrators, and from the imaginary dialogues that they insert. Collectively, they affirm that narrative is no longer possible. In-definition is the new order.

As so often, Beckett was harsh toward his work, since the four unpublished pieces are at once very funny and very painful. They should be published, if only as "Faux départs," although I do not think them "faux." (I find it disturbing that the strongest narrative of the four should use the imagery of torture, which was still being discovered after World War II. It would not be Beckett's last indulgence in such imagery.)

Blocked in fiction, Beckett also made a stab at a play, which *BatR* describes as "an untitled, unpublished dramatic fragment in French . . . existing in one manuscript and one typescript" (25). The manuscript is dated June 18, 1952, but the typescript is undated. The six handwritten leaves are largely illegible to me, but *BatR* gives a comprehensive summary.

"Coups de gong" [Strokes of the gong]

Before dialogue opens, l'Englouti [the Buried One] is buried to the rhythm of gong-strokes, which are counted aloud by l'Anonyme [the Anonymous One]. Camier (evidently retrieved from his novel) can no longer speak articulately; instead he erupts in nonverbal sounds and murmurs. Ropes are attached to the necks of l'Englouti and l'Anonyme, which apparently pull them into two holes, but l'Anonyme frees himself in time to avoid burial. He then moves his arms mechanically and repeats: "C'est justice." L'Envoyé [the Messenger] descends on a rope from the flies. He and l'Anonyme narrowly escape falling into the holes. After inspecting the medals of Camier and l'Anonyme, l'Envoyé leaves. L'Anonyme delivers a page-long monologue, punctuated by his movements around the stage. He bewails his suffering and losses. Beating himself on the head and the chest, he intones: "Quelle paix." The fragment aborts when l'Anonyme says "Quel" as he strikes his heart, and "Vide" as he strikes his head. The strokes of the gong have translated into blows on the heart and head, but the holes in the ground will have to wait a decade before *Happy Days*.

Midcentury found Beckett varying the ways in which *rien* could be nuanced and subdued in writing, but by 1952 his several efforts at drama and fiction came to nothing. In 1952, too, Beckett was asked to contribute to a projected book that would be composed of reproductions of "paintings by well-known artists and texts by important writers" (Bair, 416). Since the book was to include some work of Beckett's painter friend Henri Hayden,

Untitled, the three leaves of the typescript at RUL open on the three words, "Coups de gong."

with whom he had shared refugeedom in Roussillon, Beckett wrote a tribute, but the collection never came to fruition.

Henri Hayden, homme-peintre [Henri Hayden, man-painter]

Less than two pages in length, the homage returns to the superior tone of Beckett's earlier art criticism, and yet Hayden's paintings would seem problematic to Beckett, since they are not abstract. True to habit, Beckett does not comment on individual paintings, and he attaches these landscapes and still lifes to the subject-object crisis. His opening sentence notes the paradox of using words about an art that refuses them. He then cites Gautama as the authority for the declaration that it is equally mistaken to affirm that the "moi" exists as it is to affirm that it does not—a view that corresponds with that of his recent fiction. Beckett finds a similar attitude toward "moi" in Hayden's paintings, with their faint shadow of the doer and of what is done.

A paragraph is devoted to what Hayden does not paint—various blatant avatars of subject and object; instead there is a quiet acceptance of the small and the insubstantial. From the fragility of representation arises an ironic humor, to which Beckett attests with his beloved chiasmus: "Tout est reconnaissable, mais à s'y méconnaître. Etrange ordre des choses, fait d'ordre en mal de choses, de choses en mal d'ordre" (*Disjecta*, 147) [Everything is recognizable, but in order to ignore it. Strange order of objects, made of an order lacking objects, of objects lacking order]. Beckett declares that our time is haunted by an opposition from which we shrink, which becomes a facile springboard for all-or-nothing. It is then all the more astonishing to find a painter, who is quietly hopeless in all that din, and who tolerates the self as it is, and nature in all its unseizable aspects. Despite Beckett's friendship for Hayden, the critique is laborious in trying to assimilate the painter's landscapes into the subject-object crisis.

The second half of the twentieth century found Beckett at a creative impasse of which he was often to complain. At least his play *En attendant Godot* went into rehearsal late in 1952, with Beckett only occasionally present. It would open with the new year.

Beckett's *Henri Hayden, homme-peintre* was first published in *Cahiers d'Art–Documents,* November 22, 1955, and is reprinted in *Disjecta*. It has not been translated into English.

1953–58

Then These Flashes, or Gushes

1953

On January 5, 1953, *En attendant Godot* opened at the Théâtre de Babylone in Paris, but Beckett sought refuge in Ussy. Although the production was not the incendiary explosion of which legends are made, it did bring Beckett some modest public attention. Since he was already at a creative impasse, buffeted between "je" and "il" in fiction, the staging of *Godot* offered him no palliative. On the contrary. When Suzanne reported to him that Estragon's trousers failed to drop at the end of the first performance, Beckett wrote Blin indignantly. The undropped trousers proved a harbinger of other irritations during 1953. In February an excerpt from *L'Innommable* ("Mahood") was published in the prestigious *Nouvelle nouvelle revue française,* and he was annoyed by misprints. In August *Watt* was published in Paris by an improbable partnership of young foreign editors of *Merlin* (a short-lived periodical) and a seasoned editor of pornographic books; it too sported misprints, in spite of Beckett's painstaking correction of the galleys. After years of translation for small sums, Beckett felt compelled by requests from theaters in England and Germany to consider translating *Godot.* Even pleasures were tainted by his failure to write anything new: Meeting Joyce's biographer, Richard Ellmann, Beckett was reminded of the older writer's unflagging creativity, in contrast to his own flagging efforts. Reacting companionably to his new American publisher, Barney Rosset, Beckett had nothing new to offer him.

1954

The new year threatened to be comparably unproductive. A notebook at TCD contains six leaves of a jettisoned story, which is dated January 1954, but I am unable to decipher it. Beckett did manage in February to pen a short appreciation of his friend, the eighty-three-year-old painter Jack Yeats, for an exhibition at the Paris Galérie des Beaux Arts—the Irish artist's first continental exposure. Beckett was dissatisfied with the essay, but it is a prose poem of criticism.

Hommage à Jack B. Yeats [Homage to Jack B. Yeats]

The homage consists of nine paragraph-versets on a single page. Beckett rephrases his view of nine years earlier, that nationality and affiliation are irrelevant to the artist. Beckett praises Yeats's "uniquely self-pervaded" art, which is at one with its "wellhead." He evokes these "images of . . . breathless immediacy," "beyonds of vision," "mastery which submits in trembling to the unmasterable." Were Beckett to have enfolded the *Hommage* into a collection of his poems, it would not be out of place.

Undated manuscripts suggest that Beckett, blocked in fiction, turned to drama. For all the many scenic directions of *Godot,* however, and for all Beckett's skepticism about language, it does not seem to me predictable that he would turn to mime. The *Mime du rêveur A* was jettisoned before completion, and although it is undated, it may have preceded the several abortive steps toward *Fin de partie.*

Mime du rêveur A [Mime of Dreamer A]

The mime play's setting is a dimly lit room with two high, round, curtained windows. The only furnishings are small benches under the windows and a central rocking chair. The single character, A, wears a bathrobe, scarf, cap, socks, and mittens; a noise of wind suggests the cold. When A moves, one leg is seen to be shorter than the other, so that he sometimes loses his balance, but he steadies himself by holding on to the "rocking chair" (an English phrase in the French typescript).

Although there is no scenic division, the action is tripartite, pivoting on three unwritten mime scenes within the main mime. Action starts when A

The appreciation of Jack Yeats was first published in *Les Lettres nouvelles,* April 1954. I was ignorant of Beckett's superb translation of this homage in 1971, when I had the temerity to translate it for Roger McHugh's *Jack B. Yeats: A Centenary Gathering* (Dublin: Dolman Press). Beckett's version appeared that year in *Jack B. Yeats (1871–1957): A Centenary Exhibition.* Beckett's French and English texts are published in *Disjecta.*

Beckett gave a four-leaf typescript of *Mime du rêveur A* to Lawrence Harvey, who deposited it in NhD. It has been published in (a barely readable) facsimile by Stanley Gontarski as appendix B of his *Intent of Undoing.*

first loses his equilibrium. Like Dr. Levett in Beckett's early scene *Human Wishes,* A hiccups with such force that he is thrown off balance. Once steadied, he looks at the audience, then removes spectacles from his bathrobe pocket and looks through them at the audience. He replaces the spectacles in his pocket, whence he removes a photograph. Unable to see it in the dim light, he takes from his pocket a magnifying glass and a box of matches. Three objects and two hands make for such awkward manipulation that he burns himself. After replacing the objects in his pocket, he climbs up to each of the windows in turn; however, after pulling back one curtain to look out, he renounces before pulling the second curtain aside. Back at the rocking chair, A takes a syringe from his resourceful pocket, sterilizes the needle with a match, and, turning his back to the audience, pulls his bathrobe aside to inject himself in the buttock. After dragging the chair to stage right, he falls asleep, and for thirty seconds he dreams the unwritten mime B—before waking.

After a blackout, the original dim lighting is restored, and A removes a notebook from his pocket. Holding it close to his eyes to read the desired passage, he takes a pencil from his pocket and crosses something out. When he inserts earplugs into his ears, the wind stops. He pulls a larger syringe from his pocket, wipes the needle on his bathrobe, and injects himself as before. After dragging the rocking chair to stage left, he falls asleep and has a one-minute dream—mime B again—before waking to the sound of the wind. After another blackout, A and the rocking chair are back at stage center. From his pocket A removes a mirror and the box of matches. Lighting a match to see himself in the mirror, he burns himself; brooding, he burns himself again. He removes a third, even larger syringe from his pocket and injects himself by sitting on the needle, whereupon he falls to his side. He rises, silences the wind by putting his fingers in his ears, moves unsteadily toward the rocking chair, and collapses at its foot. He falls asleep a third time. Now, however, the mime within the mime plays through without interruption, but the duration is unspecified. Finally, A's breathing continues for about ten seconds before darkness and silence envelop the stage.

A few details will be recycled by Beckett: the set and the window business in *Fin de partie,* the rocking chair and photograph in *Film,* the spectacles and magnifying glass in *Happy Days.* More telling than details, however, is a repetition of genre in the mime within the mime of *Nacht und Träume* of 1982. The very genre of mime suggests Beckett's frustration with language at this time—a frustration that he tried to convert to a wordless farce. The increased size of each of A's syringes is funny, as are the injections themselves, but the connection is tenuous between the injections and the B dreams, which Beckett failed to write. What we cannot know is why Beckett abandoned a promising mime.

In 1954 and/or 1955 Beckett made several stabs at a play with French dialogue, which did not eventuate as *Fin de partie* until June 1956. It is probable that Beckett erupted in flashes or gushes of drama *and* fiction, mainly French but also English. A manuscript notebook at OSU contains what is probably the first one-act version of *Fin de partie* as its final entry, and this cannot predate February 16, 1956, the date on act 2 in TCD. By its position in the notebook, an untitled *foirade* is seen to predate the one-act *Fin de partie*—perhaps 1953 or 1954. Later occupying different positions in the several collections of *Foirades* or *Fizzles,* the prose piece is usually titled by its opening words.

Il est tête nue . . .

Bareheaded and barefoot, ill-clothed and occasionally bleeding, the pronominal protagonist zigzags stubbornly through a walled path in a threatening landscape. Memory does not enable him to situate his journey, but an impersonal narrator recounts it in excruciating detail. Since the dark is impenetrable, the protagonist keeps his eyes closed, although he speaks yearningly of what he might see if there were light. When he declares: "ça marche" (*Pour finir,* 18), it can mean "it's OK," and Beckett's translation reads: "no complaints." Literally, however, "ça marche" is "it walks," objectifying the protagonist "il." The narrator affirms that the protagonist's legs, like those of Murphy, are in good condition. (Mention of the earlier voyager contrasts with the unreal quality of *this* one.) After tracing zigzags, ascents, and descents of "il," the narrator poses the question: "Où donc l'attend-elle, la vie, par rapport à son point de départ, au point plutôt où il eut soudain conscience d'être parti, en haut ou en bas?" (19) [Where is it then that life awaits him, in relation to his starting-point, to the point rather at which he suddenly realized he was started, above or below? 226]. There is no reply, but the very question establishes a connection between movement and the awareness of it.

Paola Zaccaria has attempted a chronology of the *Foirades,* and I quote her on the difficulties: "The five [*Foirades*], written between 1950 and 1960, were published in the French magazine *Minuit* in 1973; in 1976 four editions of [them] were published: *Pour finir encore et Autres Foirades* [*sic*], *For to end yet again and Other Fizzles* (London, Calder), and two American editions by Grove Press and Petersburg Press respectively. Each of the four editions arranged the stories in a different order" (105). The artist Jasper Johns apparently arranged the five stories of the Petersburg edition, but the other different orderings were probably deliberate on the part of Beckett, who also dated them differently at different times. To minimize confusion, I designate the individual *foirades* by opening words, rather than number. I choose the order of publication in the periodical *Minuit,* although my page numbers refer to the books, *Pour finir* and *CSP.*

In the protagonist's compulsive progress he sometimes licks the walls. Breaking the silence are noises of things falling and the sounds of his body moving, minutely particularized. He acquires a few memories, but they are precarious, and, periodically vanishing, they return to inform him that he is old and close to death. The air is foul, but were he to breathe any other, it might be fatal, unless the transition be ever so gradual; it is only in the context of that transition that the pronoun "il" gives way—once only—to the noun "l'homme." Slowly his *histoire* (story and history) is shaped, with its several superlatives—"Bref tous les sommets" (24) [In a word all the summits, 228]. The story's final complex sentence denies the very story that has been told, and yet the narrator promises a sequel: "Quoi qu'il en soit son histoire va ainsi se constituant, et même se modifiant, dans la mesure où de nouveaux hauts et de nouveaux bas viennent pousser dans l'ombre et vers l'oubli ceux temporairement à l'honneur et où d'autres éléments et motifs, tels ces os dont il sera bientôt traité, et à fond, à cause de leur importance, viennent l'enrichir" (25) [So with one thing and another little by little his history takes shape, and even changes shape, as new maxima and minima tend to cast into the shade, and toward oblivion, those momentarily glorified, and as fresh elements and motifs, such as these bones of which more very shortly, and at length, in view of their importance, contribute to enrich it, 228]. The serpentine syntax contributes to the narrator's dour view of composition. Moreover, bones are hardly an example of a *fresh* element and motif. Yet the *foirade* presents a new fusion of motion and environment, of life and consciousness, of memory and history, via a zigzag and sometimes injurious path.

Ambulation as verbal exploration is by now a familiar Beckett motif, but this brief, goalless journey is energized by its own momentum. Rigorously impersonal, the narrator nevertheless implies a subtextual pain in the memory of light, in wounds and sounds of falling, inability to distinguish the journey from the protagonist's consciousness of it. For the reasonable reader, it is an impossible journey: why should "il" strike the right wall when he turns left, and vice versa? And how can "il" squeeze past walls that almost meet? More than in the *Textes pour rien* or the abandoned typescripts, this undated *foirade* is confusingly candid about the impossibility and implacability of a mental journey.

The story may be painful, but it is not solemn. Flitters of humor are evident in the protagonist's stance as he waits for his own decision about ambulation, in the affirmation that a ray of light confers gaiety, in references to his weak head, and in the sequence of summits and near-summits. Twice, the narrator corrects his account with an abrupt "non." Several times the narrator utters a summary "voilà." Finally, the protagonist's history is unstable.

Not only are Beckett's prose and his characters' journeys mutually reflective, but this untitled *foirade* resonates to *all* individual histories, with their wavering maxima and minima, and their shady memories.

1955

From an Abandoned Work

In his introduction to *The Complete Short Prose* Gontarski implies that Beckett shifted from French to English, at the suggestion of his American publisher, Barney Rosset, in a letter of February 5, 1954. If this is so, it would be an early example of what became not infrequent in later years—Beckett's creation sparked by a specific request. Moreover, since the request came in English, so did the response. On a fair copy of *From an Abandoned Work* Beckett wrote: "This text was written 1954 or 1955. It was the first text written directly in English since *Watt* (1945)" (Admussen, 54). Beckett has told me and others that *From an Abandoned Work* was the residue of some "old shipwreck," but the OSU holograph does not quite bear this out, since the published story salvages about two-thirds of the "abandoned work." The

---

The undated holograph of *From an Abandoned Work* was excerpted from a somewhat longer, untitled story in the MacGowran notebook at OSU. It was first published (with considerable editorial revisions) in *Trinity News*, June 7, 1956, whereupon Beckett wrote H. O. White of Trinity (July 2, 1956): "Trinity News made a great hames [*sic*] of my text with their unspeakable paragraphs and varsity punctuation." The story was printed correctly in *Evergreen Review* 1, no. 3 in 1957, and separately by Faber in 1958. The BBC broadcast it on December 14, 1957, as "The Meditation." Translated into French by Ludovic and Agnès Janvier "in collaboration with the author," it was published by Minuit in *Têtes-Mortes* in 1967, where it is misdated 1957. *From an Abandoned Work* is included in CSP.

In a letter of January 13, 1965, to Shivaun O'Casey, Beckett suggested a possible staging for his story:

> Moonlight, Ashcan a little left of centre. Enter man left, limping, with stick. . . . Advances to can, raises lid, pushes about inside with crook of stick, inspects and rejects (puts back in can) an unidentifiable refuse, fishes out finally tattered ms. Or copy of FAAW. Reads aloud standing "Up bright and early that day, I was young then, feeling awful, and out—" and a little further in silence, lowers text, stands motionless, finally closes ashcan, sits down on it, hooks stick round neck, and reads text through from beginning, ie. Including what he had read standing. Finishes, sits a moment motionless, gets up, replaces text in ashcan and limps off right. Breathes with maximum authenticity, only effect to be sought in slight hesitation now and then in places where most effective, due to strangeness of text and imperfect light and state of ms. (Qtd. in Bair, 578)

main omissions concern the protagonist's "murder" of his mother, and perhaps his father.

Without documentary support, I am inclined to date the story in 1955, after Beckett's 1954 departure for Ireland, when he learned that his brother was suffering with lung cancer. He remained at Frank's side from April till his death on September 13. Afterward Beckett attended to practical matters for Frank's family, whom he always cherished. When Beckett returned to France, he fled to Ussy, where he may have toiled simultaneously at several works. Perhaps he began the new year with a new story. First published in *Trinity News,* that story marks the earliest example of Beckett's generosity to his university, and he was ill repaid. It was undoubtedly he who told Federman and Fletcher that the story was published with "variants" introduced by the student editors, who "treated the contribution from him with little regard for accuracy of punctuation" (27). The phrasal variants may result from Beckett's revision of the original publication, but punctuational variants result from student editorial enterprise. Beckett's single mammoth paragraph is hacked into "normal" divisions. Beckett's commas are relieved by semicolons and question marks. Although the story's narrator twice refers disparagingly to Beckett's native language—"nice word, for an English speaker," "awful English this"—Beckett wanted *his* English printed exactly as it was written, down to every comma and disindentation.

Beckett's title suggests that the story is a residue of a jettisoned work, but it may also pun on another meaning of "abandoned" as "unrestrained" or even "shameless." The frenzied energy of the English contrasts with the relative calm of the French stories of the 1940s. The English narrator is pressed to finish the arbitrary story he has to tell, and his narrative is shorter than its French predecessors. Susan Brienza writes that only 30 of 113 sentences are syntactically complete, with elision quite frequent. Within the fragmented sentences of the shortened story are a plethora of short words, all of which contribute to the hurried effect. Although the narrator tells his story in the first person, he frequently omits the pronoun *I,* as one does in correspondence. Beckett leaves it ambiguous as to whether the story is spoken or written; on the one hand, the narrator complains of his sore throat, and the voice that isn't his; on the other hand, the narrator requests: "please read again my descriptions" (*CSP,* 161). Told mainly in the past tense, the story slips now and then into the present. Perhaps this can be explained by an almost incidental phrase "bygone they can be told" (162). Memory feeds narrative.

Although the story is Beckettianly unconcatenated, and although it is printed as one gigantic paragraph, the narrator insists several times on the structure that he has imposed—three randomly chosen days in his life. (He does not mention Easter, but he too engages in resurrection—of memories.)

The three days are not allotted equal time in the narration. Over half the story is devoted to the first day, which is summarized: "this day with the white horse and white mother in the window" (160–61). The second day's event barely mentions the color white, but it is there nonetheless, in the stoats who attack the narrator, so that he might have been bled white, like a rabbit. The third and briefest day is colorless, with the narrator observed by the roadman Balfe, who terrified him as a child, but whom he now resembles. Upon that tripartite division the narrator overlays a pattern familiar from Beckett's French work—out from a dwelling in the morning and back to it in the evening. Despite insistence upon "day after day, out, on, round, back, in" (163), the narrator does not end quite where he began. Instead, he concludes: "just went on, my body doing its best without me" (164). For all the vivacity of the narrative, the "I" is finally sundered from his busy body.

The English narrative is more active and physical than its French predecessors, but some incongruous details are familiar: the alternation of sun and rain, the rapidly changing landscape, the protagonist's awkward locomotion and his falls to the ground, his costume including a stick but discarding his greatcoat, his age and weakness, flora and fauna (including white imaginary animals), life and death, mother and father, desire to end. As in the French stories, experience bristles with contradiction and negation; many sentences begin with *But;* other sentences invert subject and predicate. Specifically, the narrator characterizes his mind as "always on the alert against itself" (157). The narrator's rage and violence, also familiar from earlier work, are declared to be unrelated, but the reader tends to relate them, linking them to the narrator's thrice mentioned curses on this subliminal Easter.

Not only subject matter but verbal devices are familiar from Beckett's French fiction: the adroit repetition of key words, frequent alliteration, chiming, and even occasional rhyme. Self-correction is less ostentatious, but the word *no,* set off by commas, occurs sixteen times in a kind of counterpoint to the progress of the text. Other words reflect hesitancy about the account— "perhaps," "I do not know," "I suppose." For all his uncertainty, however, the narrator declares that words are his only love, and verbal "flashes, or gushes" animate the text (and form my chapter title).[1] Occasionally, the syntax is difficult, for example, "With so much life gone from knowledge how know when all began, all the variants of the one [fall?] that one by one their venom staling follow upon one another, all life long, till you succumb" (162). Or "No, back to that far day, any far day, and from the dim granted ground to its things and sky the eyes raised and back again, raised again and back again again, and the feet going nowhere only somehow home, in the morning out from home and in the evening back home again, and the sound of my voice all day long muttering the same old things I don't listen to, not even mine it was at the end of the day, like a marmoset sitting on my shoulder with its bushy tail, keeping me company" (158–59). After a distinctively English segmentation of syntax, the final image of the exotic marmoset is startling. As in this story's French predecessors, the theme is reflected in techniques of repetition, fragmentation, and verbal play, but the energy of the English creates a new desperation about an endless, pointless quest. The repeated rhyme "Vent the pent" gives imperative force to verbal abandon,[2] and yet a semblance of coherence is imposed by repeated adverbs of time—now, then, always—in this timeless tale of three days. Even the simplest repetitions are fraught with ambiguity, as in the word "over," which embraces both repetition and finality. In the original draft of the story, the narrator walked in time to "over," one syllable for each step—o-ver—which led to the anagrammatic play on "over" and "vero." The implication emerges that truth comes only with death, or at least with some form of unwitnessable finality.

Although the narrator early affirms his attraction to the color white, he views it invariably in moving beings—his mother, a distant horse, a tribe of stoats, a bled rabbit, and dream animals, which betoken his active imagination. White, the absence of color, is ascribed to motion outside the narrating self. Yet the word "white" anchors the colorful narrative, despite its storm of commas, and its cadenced slippage of "day" and "way." Even more than its French predecessors, the abandoned work is a construction; life in motion is an arbitrary fiction—especially for one who loves "all things still and rooted" (155).

Having condemned myself to chronology, I have to select the order in which I mention Beckett's undated, unpublished pieces of the early 1950s. It is, however, known that in 1955 Beckett completed a mime play. As would happen not infrequently, it was Beckett's generosity that extricated him from a writing impasse; he composed *Acte sans paroles I* for the dancer-mime Deryk Mendel. Playing in cabaret skits, Mendel requested new material from a number of Paris-based authors—Ionesco, Schéhadé, Audiberti, Adamov, and Beckett. The last of these was the only one to respond—after Suzanne reported favorably on Mendel's performances. Within a few weeks Beckett sent Mendel the mime play, and he suggested a musical accompaniment, to be composed by his cousin, John Beckett. The latter is quoted by Knowlson: "I did a little prelude—it [the mime play] only lasted about twenty minutes in all—just a kind of rumpus going on, and then the music which was all based on this kind of kaleidoscopic variation of a small number of [piano] ideas, with the ring of the xylophone and the harsher side drum. It was all very brittle sounds" (378). Knowlson traces Beckett's taste for mime to his love of silent films, and yet mime is a logical, if unpredictable, genre for the author of *Textes pour rien*, with their mistrust of language.

Acte sans paroles I (Act Without Words I)

Acte sans paroles I is at once Beckett's busiest and most approachable play. In theme it is a Beckettian version of the Tantalus myth. Having displeased the gods, Tantalus was condemned to be "tantalized" eternally by a spring from which he could not slake his thirst, and by a tree whose fruit was always beyond his reach. The spring metamorphoses into Beckett's carafe of water, and Beckett's tree offers not fruit but shade from the "éclairage éblouissant" [dazzling light]. Beckett's Tantalus-figure is unaware of his sentence, and as an actor he is unaware that he is condemned to center stage, for menace lurks in the wings and the flies. Beckett's play is an un-Brechtian learning play; in the lineage of Murphy and Victor Krap, who both strove for will-lessness, the mime-clown learns to achieve it. From the moment he is flung on to the stage, the single character reflects. Later, he suffers the clown's frustration with intractable objects. Reflection finally teaches the clown that "wisdom . . . consists not in the satisfaction but in the ablation of desire" (*Proust*, 7).

The anonymous mime is flung backward onstage from the right wing—the first of his comic pratfalls. Cued by a whistle, he exits right and is flung to the stage again. Then symmetrically on the left. However, after the second whistle from the left, he balks at exiting, and the sudden movement produces another pratfall. After a small tree and a large scissors descend separately from the flies, he sits in the shade and trims his nails. The shading branches fold down against the tree trunk, and a carafe of water descends from the flies, which he tries in vain to reach. Successively, three different-sized cubes are lowered from the flies, and after pratfalls as he attempts to reach the water by maneuvering the cubes, he desists. Cued by a whistle again, a knotted rope descends from the flies, which he climbs to reach the water, but he is dropped to the ground—without water. He takes up the scissors to cut the rope and just manages to do so, as he is raised perilously off the ground. He tries to lasso the carafe, but it disappears into the flies. With cubes and lasso, he tries to capture a bough of the tree, whether to trap the shade or to hang

---

Although completed earlier, the mime *Acte sans paroles I* was first performed and published with *Fin de partie* in 1957. *Acte sans paroles I* was at first called *Soif*. The mime play was viewed by Beckett as "in some obscure way, a codicil to *End-Game*, and as such requires that this last extremity of human meat—or bones—be there, thinking and stumbling and sweating, under our noses, like Clov about Hamm, but gone from refuge" (letter to Barney Rosset, August 27, 1957, qtd. by Zilliacus 1976 as epigraph). Beckett's English translation was published with *Endgame*, by Grove and Faber, respectively, in 1958. It is found in *CDW*, to which my page numbers refer.

himself. However, the branch collapses elusively against the tree trunk. He carries the cubes to their original position and coils the lasso on the smallest cube, having interspersed each of his actions with reflection.

Once more the whistle blows from the right wing, and once more he succumbs, only to be immediately flung back. When the whistle blows from the left wing, he does not move. Once more he takes up the scissors ostensibly to trim his nails, but after reflection he feels his neck and then places the scissors on the lasso on the small cube. He opens his collar and feels his neck, but the small cube, with scissors and lasso, disappears into the flies. He sits down on the large cube, which is pulled up from under him, occasioning his final pratfall. On the ground: "Il reste allongé sur le flanc, face à la salle, le regard fixe" (123) [He remains lying on his side, his face towards auditorium, staring before him, 206]. Each in turn, the carafe and the shade tree are dangled before him, but he does not move. After four repetitions of "Il ne bouge pas," the play ends when "Il regarde ses mains" [He looks at his hands]. He has learned *not* to use his hands, in defiance of whistled temptations.

Technically, Beckett's title is inaccurate, since the mime play is speechless but not wordless. The carafe is labeled "Eau" [water], homonym of "Oh," which can be a cry of surprise or distress, as Beckett would demonstrate a decade later in *Come and Go*. Two of Beckett's wordless props are comic by disproportion—a *small* tree and *large* scissors. The knotted rope makes for awkwardly comic climbing, and a lasso lends itself awkwardly to the capture of a branch of a tree, however small. (A handkerchief in the French text disappears from Beckett's English translation.) The cuing whistles from the theater flies and wings are faintly comic. The sequence of actions demands an agile performer, but even a reader can appreciate the pratfalls and the frustration after reflection. Nor need the reader be familiar with Tantalus to recognize the allegory. The mime's wishes and flashes accrete into a farce-punctuated education—toward immobility.

Acte sans paroles I is Beckett's only work that can confidently be assigned to 1955, the year that *Godot* played to acclaim in London. With the designated New York director Alan Schneider, Beckett went to London to see the production of the young Peter Hall. He disapproved of it. That same year Beckett may have tried his hand at another French play. An undated fragment at RUL (1227/7/16/2) has been linked with *Fin de partie,* notably by Admussen, who believes that the parallels are "even closer here than in the . . . 'Mime du rêveur A'" (111). Since I see little resemblance between *Fin de partie* and both those aborted works, I comment separately upon them. Naming the fragment after its main characters, I note that there are virtually no scenic directions.

"Ernest et Alice"

Ernest is fastened to a cross, which is raised by day and lowered by night. His face is hidden by a handkerchief, and a champagne bucket hangs around his neck. His wife Alice climbs a ladder to answer a number of Ernest's requests before they prepare for the visit of his mother, Anita. Alice washes her husband's feet but desists because he is ticklish. When the doorbell rings, Ernest's mother enters, and both women cooperate on the feet washing. As Ernest's mother prepares to wash his face, the bell rings again, and the fragment ends. Admussen draws parallels with *Fin de partie:* "Ernest's immobility, the handkerchief covering his face, the ladder, the fact that they are running out of various provisions, the childlike conversation, and most of all the master/slave relationship [between Ernest and Alice]" (111). However, I would argue that the relationship between Ernest and Alice cannot be summarized as master/slave, and that their conversation is inaccurately designated as childlike. I prefer to consider this piece as an odd fragment, unrelated to *Fin de partie.*

1956

The stemma of *Fin de partie* is the most problematic in Beckett studies. Of the stages admirably deduced by Gontarski, only one is dated, but we do know that Beckett considered the play complete in June 1956. Although Gontarski discusses *Mime du rêveur A* and "Ernest et Alice," he does not include them in his list (1985, 44–45). He was probably unaware of the fragments in the Sam Francis Notebook at RUL. I believe that Restivo exaggerates the "ending" quality of those fragments, but I accept them as the origin of the stemma because of traces of the B-A master-servant relationship.[3] Indebted to the pioneering work of Gontarski and Restivo, I submit the following stemma:

> 1. Two A-B exchanges in the Sam Francis Notebook at RUL (ms. 2926)—five leaves and ten leaves, respectively. The second fragment is dated September 15, 1950, and annotated "retour de l'Irlande" (where Beckett had buried his mother). Restivo sees the two fragments as a " 'double try' . . . experimenting different attitudes" (*SBT* 3, 93).

The unpublished fragment "Ernest et Alice" is a nine-leaf typescript at RUL. Bryden (1998) discusses it briefly in her summary of the role of crosses in Beckett's oeuvre (142–43).

2. Four-leaf holograph fragment in TCD, involving a master-servant pair X and F (ms. 4662).

3. In Sam Francis Notebook twenty-three-leaf X-F dialogue related to, but much more developed than the above.

4. Twenty-one-page typescript at RUL, labeled by Beckett "Avant *Fin de partie*." The fragment consists of a dialogue between the self-questioning X and his factotum F; it carries step 3 two typed pages beyond the holograph (ms. 1227/7/16/7).

5. Fifty-nine-leaf, two-act typescript at RUL; development of above into a complete play, with characters again labeled A and B (ms. 1600). This is the version mentioned in Beckett's March 13, 1955, letter to Pamela Mitchell (Knowlson, 366).

6. Twenty three leaf holograph at OSU, containing act 1 of an untitled play, which is closer than above to *Fin de partie*.

7. Miscellaneous leaves at OSU, with the first mention of Pépé and Mémé.

8. Nineteen-leaf holograph at TCD, containing act 2 of item 6, dated February 16, 1956.

9. Sixty-five-leaf typescript of two-act version of *Fin de partie* at OSU.

10. First one-act version in MacGowran notebook at OSU. Probably May or early June 1956. Although begun with "I" in the middle of the line, there is no "II."

11. Thirty-five-leaf, one-act typescript at OSU. The names Hamm, Nagg, Nell, and Clov are added in ink in the margin of the first page, and Hamm for the first time summons Clov with a whistle, instead of a drum.

12. Thirty-eight-leaf, one-act typescript at OSU. Although labeled "Final draft," it lacks Nagg's joke about the tailor and Clov's "Quelques mots . . . de ton coeur."

13. Notebook labeled "Eté 56" at RUL containing ten leaves of "Fin Scraps," most notably Nagg's tailor joke.

The final draft, a posited typescript of the newly titled *Fin de partie*, contains the tailor joke and Clov's last monologue.[4]

I will confine my commentary to the initial impetus (step 1), the first complete play (step 5), and the two-act version (step 9), to suggest how Beckett gnawed at the recalcitrant play. (The drafts are untitled, but I list them under their principal characters.)

"A et B" (step 1)

Restivo teases themes of *Fin de partie* from these early fragments, but *BatR* is more accurate about the first fragment: "A and B . . . discuss the uncertain, possibly divine, presence of a third, whom they cannot see. . . . Another [main] preoccupation is with their own presence/absence" (34). Most telling is Beckett's early effort to enfold an actual stage situation into the dialogue, for example, "A: Vous vóilà donc le héros, et moi le valet. Nous commençons à nous dessiner" [There you are the hero and I the servant. We are beginning to identify each other].

The second, longer fragment (rather fancifully described in *BatR*) opens on an intimidating stage direction: "Chacun à part A et B, debout, se faisant face, à 3 metres l'un de l'autre, parlent en même temps, à voix basse. Paroles inintelligibles sauf par bribes, lorsque l'un d'eux se taît ou que la voix, s'enflant, domine celle de l'autre" [Separately, A and B standing opposite each other at a distance of three meters, speak simultaneously in low voices. Unintelligible words except in snatches, when one of them is silent, or when one voice rises to dominate the other]. However, certain intelligible words repeat compulsively, e.g., "pitié," "peur," "ce n'est pas le mot," "il n'y a rien à faire." The problem of presence is more acute than in the first fragment, and this one breaks off in the pair's unintelligible murmur.

"X et F" (step 5)

Although a global scenic description is lacking, the stage room contains two high windows and an exit to F's kitchen. X is center stage in a wheelchair. Again and again he summons F by beating on a drum that is fastened to his chair. In their dialogue X addresses F as "tu," but the servant addresses X as "vous." The play opens on a monologue by X, in which he announces that he is blind and paralyzed—unless he is lying. Later X ruminates that F sometimes lies, but he cannot know when. Both X and F accept their master-slave relationship, so that F wants to address X as "Votre honneur," and to bring him his porridge. Several times X orders his chair to be placed in the exact center, or to be wheeled round the room. X demands his Bible and orders F to read from the Psalms and from Jeremiah, but he impatiently interrupts the readings. X calls for his syringe that is filled with F's "mélange," which they pun as "eau de ville" (instead of "eau de vie"). As their activities run down, X asks for a dog. X orders F to describe their location, which is revealed as Picardy after World War I. In F's absence, X tries in vain to move his wheelchair. X orders F to take his temperature, but since it is 88.6 Fahrenheit, neither of them can convert it to Centigrade. X calls first for his wife, then for his mother. In F's absence, X narrates an account of his mother's accident and her long convalescence. F then enters disguised as the mother, and they speak as though X were a small child. X grows impatient with this game and orders F to get rid of his mother. In F's absence, X ruminates about how badly he plays. When F is again summoned, X mentions the Bom affair, and F corrects him to Bim, who was apparently an old woman who died of thirst. X attempts to exonerate them from responsibility for her death, even hinting that she might not be dead, but F insists: "Si, si, elle est morte," whereupon Beckett's fragment stops.[5]

For all the details of *Fin de partie*, this fragment rambles as it repeats phrases and movements. Although the X-F relationship is fraught, the repetitions do not build tension. Above all, the fragment lacks memorable images, although X cherishes his visible possessions—drum and stick, Bible, syringe, baptismal spoon. Beckett's French flows colloquially, but it rarely falls into rhythmic patterns.

This draft died stillborn, but Beckett salvaged much of the material for steps 6 and 7, which Gontarski discusses in detail. It is impossible to determine how much time elapsed between that draft and the first version of a play involving four characters.

"A et B" (step 9)

With this draft of what became *Fin de partie*, Beckett began to think in performance terms, since he inks before act 1 "75 minutes," and before act 2 "55 minutes." The four characters are not listed, and when they appear, they are designated by initials: A and B for master and servant, P and M for the old people in ashbins. Detailed scenic directions describe the set, costumes, and opening mime of the two-act play. Noteworthy are A's red robe, nightcap, blanket, and handkerchief. A, B, and P have red faces, whereas M is white of face. When the play begins, the ashbins are covered by a sheet, as is the wheelchair of A. Action starts when B looks through each window in turn, then removes the sheets. Dialogue starts with B's monologue describing A, but each verb is followed by "ou fait semblant de. . . ," thus emphasizing the actor's pretense. In B's first monologue, too, he poses the question as to whether he will leave or stay until one of the two dies. When B retires to his kitchen, slamming the door, A wakens, and he too speaks in monologue, affirming that everything should end, but he hesitates to end. A then summons B by tapping on the drum attached to his chair; in dialogue they "tutoient" each other. Their conversation is rhythmic, even in the crossed-out enumeration of B's duties. A feels feverish, and B fetches a large thermometer from the offstage kitchen. B recites an unwritten sonnet while A waits to learn his fate; his temperature is 88.6, which B declares is normal. P rears his head to demand his "bouillie," but there is no more pap, and he is solaced with a "gressin." By page 10 (of sixty-seven) A declares: "C'est une fin de journée comme les autres" [It's the end of the day like any other day].

P, who pops up often in this version, summons M by tapping on her bin-lid. They converse rhythmically about their failing sight and hearing, and they recall the accident in which they lost their legs. M declares: "Rien n'est plus drôle que le malheur" [Nothing is funnier than unhappiness]. She advises B to desert, before he pushes her back into the bin—on A's command. After B wheels A part way around the room, and then back to the center, he looks through the window and intones the zeroes, but expands to: "Tout est foutu" [Everything is corpsed]. B finds a flea in his trousers, and A curses B. After B brings A the unsatisfactory toy dog, he returns to his kitchen. P and A converse about M's possible egress from her ashbin, and P curses A. When alone, A tries to move his wheelchair with the gaff. On A's command, B reads to him from the Bible—first about the flood, and then about the generations of the long-lived patriarchs. This inspires A to call for a woman, so he too can engender: "Mère, femme, soeur, fille, putain, ça m'est égal. Une femme. Deux mamelles et une vulve. Va me chercher ça" [Mother, wife, sister, daughter, whore, it's all the same to me. A woman. Two tits and a hole. Go bring me that]. B leaves and reenters in wig, false breasts, and skirt over his trousers. In the ensuing scene he shifts intermittently from a woman's voice to his own, as each man tries to foist "her" on the other, before "she" leaves with B. Unable to convince P to listen to his story, A nevertheless narrates the scene of the man begging bread for his son. Unable to continue, A strikes the drum by accident, and B enters. Although there is no scenic direction for P's entrance, he complains that M doesn't respond to his knock on her binlid. Refusing to return to his bin, P informs B that he wants to hold M's hand. B peers into M's bin, and there is a "long silence" before he stands up and takes off his yellow beret. When P asks: "Alors?" B lifts the old man's cap as a sign that M is dead. A yawns, as before, and closes the act with the nonsense syllables: "Oh là là."

In act 2 M's bin is gone, but the setting otherwise remains the same. The three men wear black headgear, and their faces are white. The first words are A's "Finie la rigolade" [Our revels are ended]. Even more than before, this act is propelled by A's commands. Cruelly, he orders B to fasten a cang around P's neck, to force his company upon him. Cruelly, A beats P on the head to elicit the story of his life. Once P is free of the cang, he asks for his cap, whereas A orders B to wheel him back to stage center. B is torn between the rival commands: "A moins d'un fait nouveau nous sommes figés pour l'éternité" [Without a new event, we are fixed for eternity]. The "fait nouveau" occurs when A and P each accede to the other's wish. P's cap restored to him, he examines himself in a small mirror: "J'ai vieilli" [I've aged]. Learning that B has not yet made the sawdust he has promised, P remarks: "Ce n'est pas la peine" [It's not worthwhile]. B muses that these may be P's last words, and indeed they are his last words in this two-act version of what was not yet entitled *Fin de partie*. Dribbling toward its end, the act includes scenes with the alarm clock, A's recollection of the madman, the lack of "calmants," a turn about the room, mention of the death from darkness of a nameless *Mère*, B's hitting A with the dog. Ordered to look out the window yet again,

B reports the sight of a small boy. After A's guilty monologue, B enters, disguised as the boy he described. A promises him chocolate, but "the boy" is hungry and leaves A mid-monologue. When A is alone onstage, he buries his face in his hands.

Although this two-act play contains most of the themes, many of the scenic directions, and much of the dialogue of *Fin de partie*, it is less relentless.[6] Props include a Bible and lectern, a rolling pin mistaken for a telescope, a thermometer, a cang, as well as the yellow berets and black hats of the three men. B's two disguises are not only digressive, but they are overly vigorous for an entropic action. So, too, is the physical torment of P. In Beckett's fiction blows on the head struck Molloy's mother, Malone himself, and his fictional Lemuel, but it is less painful to read about than to see violence onstage. For all the nuanced repetitions and suffocating atmosphere of this two-act play, its action is more dispersed and realistic than the final revised version.

Linearity is imposed by my account of Beckett's drafts of *Fin de partie*. He may have interspersed these drafts with some flashes and gushes of fiction, which were later gathered into *Foirades,* and still later translated as *Fizzles*. It is certain, however, that on January 11, 1956, Beckett wrote Alan Schneider: "I am writing an even worse affair [than *Godot*] and have got down the gist of the first act (of two)." His letter of April 12 compares the play-in-progress to a three-legged giraffe. By June 21 the acts were condensed to one: "Have at last written another, one act, longish, hour and a quarter I fancy." (He was short by five minutes for his 1967 German version.) Beckett hoped that *Fin de partie,* along with *Acte sans paroles,* would premiere at the Marseilles Festival of the Avant-Garde in early August, but contracts did not arrive, and the plays were withdrawn (Knowlson, 384).

Fin de partie (*Endgame*)

Given the kaleidoscope of fragmentary scenes during Beckett's process of composition, the taut concentration of *Fin de partie* is a triumph of final authorial control. Compared to the difficulty of composition, the difficulties of performance of *Fin de partie* pale. Nevertheless, in spite of the success of *Godot,* no Paris theater welcomed the new Beckett play, which therefore had its French premiere at the Royal Court Theatre in London—on April 1, 1957, preceded in February by publication.

See the preceding pages for the manuscript stages of *Fin de partie.* It was first published by Minuit in 1957. The holograph notebook of Beckett's English translation is at HRC; it is dated May 7–June 5, 1957. *Endgame* was published in 1958 by Grove and Faber, respectively. My page numbers refer to the Minuit text for the French, and *CDW* for the English.

Fin de partie retrieves from earlier drafts a sparsely furnished indoor set-ting. The action takes place in a family living (and dying) room, which may also be viewed as the inside of a skull. On the one hand, we witness an ordi-nary day in the lives of the four family members: "C'est une fin de journée comme les autres" (28) [It's the end of the day like any other day, *CDW*, 98]. At the same time, both the day and the family members are not only extra-ordinary, but unique. These human beings are the last of their species, and this day ebbs in a playlong "gray light."

No cross is seen on stage, but a crucifixion is implicit in the names of the four characters—a hammer and three nails (Hamm a truncated hammer, French *clou* or Clov, German *Nagel* abridged to Nagg, and Nell punning on English nail). The three nails are familiar from iconography of the Crucifixion, but Beckett drives them with his Hamm-er. Rather than a pre-lude to resurrection, this crucifixion underlines the finality of the play's title. Yet the end of the play resembles the beginning: Nagg and Nell invisible in their respective ashbins, and Hamm front and center in his wheelchair, his face curtained by his handkerchief. Although Clov no longer stands next to Hamm, he adopts his earlier hunched stance, despite his odd assortment of accoutrements. To the eye, Clov alone differentiates the end from the unveiled beginning of *Fin de partie*.

As the cross disappears from Beckett's stage, so does the physical Bible, but the biblical echoes abound. The names of Nagg and Hamm transliterate Noah and Ham of Genesis; as biblical Ham was cursed by Noah for seeing him naked, Beckett's Hamm is cursed by Nagg for refusing him the promised sugar plum. Hamm's face is first and last covered with a veronica, although Beckett subsequently omitted the facial imprint. In the original French Hamm addresses his handkerchief as "Vieux linge," suggesting the linen in which Christ's body was wrapped. Hamm mocks Clov with the Aramaic "Mene, mene," from the Book of Daniel, which trails the entire prophecy: "God hath numbered thy kingdom, and finished it." Much of the play's spare imagery echoes the Book of Revelation: earth and sea, light and dark, beginning and end. Clov declares the sound of the alarm is "Digne du juge-ment dernier!" (67) (changed in English to "Fit to wake the dead," 115). Hamm's chronicle takes place on Christmas Eve, but rather than a time of joyous birth, Hamm's protagonist may "celebrate" by refusing food to a dying child. In his anger at the supplicant, Hamm as protagonist invokes the miraculous manna of the Israelites: "Mais enfin quel est votre espoir? . . . Qu'il y ait encore de la manne au ciel pour des imbéciles comme vous?" (73–74) [But what in God's name do you imagine? . . . That there's manna in heaven still for imbeciles like you? 118]. When Clov reports seeing a boy from the window, Hamm imagines the risen Christ: "La pierre levée," and he guesses that the boy views the refuge "avec les yeux de Moïse mourant" (104) (untranslated). As the play winds down, Hamm distorts scriptural phrases: "Léchez-vous les uns les autres!" and "Paix à nos . . . fesses" [Lick your neighbour as yourself! [125]; the second phrase is not translated]. Twice Hamm calls his father, as Christ called his God. However, the redemptive promise of Scripture is subverted in the residual world of Hamm and Clov.

In a play whose title contains the word *fin* and whose dialogue boldly opens with the word of the dying Christ—"Fini"—moribundity is ubiquitous. The French title *Fin de partie* is vaguer of reference than its English translation; "partie" is any part, not only a game. The key word is *fin*, which is echoed in the repetitions of Clov's opening sentence. Hamm's first monologue reiterates his desire and yet his hesitation to end. "Assez, il est temps que cela finisse, dans le refuge aussi. (*Un temps.*) Et cependant j'hésite à . . . à finir. Oui, c'est bien ça, il est temps que cela finisse et cependant j'hésite encore à—(*baillements*)—à finir" (17) [Enough, it's time it ended, in the refuge too. (*Pause.*) And yet I hesitate, I hesitate to . . . to end. Yes, there it is, it's time it ended and yet I hesitate to—(*he yawns*)—to end, 93]. Forms of the verb *finir* thread through the play, mainly in Hamm's speech. It is, however, Clov who announces the depletion of an odd assortment of items; there are "no more" bicycle wheels, pap, nature, sugar-plums, tide, navigators, rugs, pain-killer, coffins, in the order of announced disappearance. When Hamm learns that there are no more coffins, he hesitates no longer: "Alors que ça finisse! . . . Et que ça saute!" (102) [Then let it end! . . . With a bang! 130]. Hamm's only exact repetition of the title occurs when he believes Clov has deserted him—"Vieille fin de partie perdue, finir de perdre" (110) [Old endgame lost of old, play and lose and have done with losing, 132]. In an ending world, generation is an ever-present danger; the human race may evolve from the flea in Clov's crotch; a rat or a boy may germinate life. Plant life seems to be more acceptable, since Hamm and Clov hope forlornly for seeds to sprout. In sum, we hear about a moribund world outside the refuge, but Hamm, as opposed to the protagonist of his chronicle, is at first ambivalent about its actual death.

Clov in contrast begins in indifference: "Alors nous mourrons. . . . Alors nous ne mourrons pas" (20) [Then we'll die. . . . Then we shan't die, 94–95]. However, he progresses to a longing for order under the final dust: "Un monde où tout serait silencieux et immobile et chaque chose à sa place dernière, sous la dernière poussière" (78) [A world where all would be silent and still and each thing in its last place, under the last dust, 120]. It is Clov who announces that "on dirait" that Nell is dead in her ashbin, and it is he who declares that he will not bury Hamm. Dispassionately, he summons the alarm clock *not* to ring if he dies in his kitchen. Despite the playlong asperities between Hamm and Clov, they cooperate in verbalizing the play's anticreation theme.

More cruelly than in earlier drafts, the afflictions of the four characters contribute to the suffocating atmosphere. Instead of an ark filled with animals "the male and his female," Hamm's visible animal kingdom has shrunk to a sexless three-legged toy dog. The four names pun on the animality of their bearers: Hamm and Clov as spiced meat, Nagg and Nell of equine resonance. All family members call attention to their maladies; Clov cannot sit, and he has such pains in his legs that he can hardly think. Hamm cannot stand, and he claims to be blind; he speaks of a heart, a vein, an artery in his head, and in his breast is a living sore. Nagg has lost his tooth, so he can only suck his dog biscuit; he and Nell laugh about the accident in which they lost their legs. Clov later announces that Nell has no pulse. Although there are "no more" coffins, death hovers in the air.

The male characters nevertheless play while they live. The red faces of Hamm and Clov opposed by the white faces of Nagg and Nell suggest chess or checkers. (Beckett eliminated these colors in his own production.) The whistle around Hamm's neck recalls referees or umpires in sports. Hamm's three repetitions of "A moi. De jouer" [Me—To play] demonstrate his awareness of his stage life as a game. When Hamm prepares for the end with the word "Jeter" [Discard], a game of cards comes to mind. Earlier, Hamm summons the lexicon of formal drama, which is a form of play—*replique, aparté, soliloque* (rare in French)—and Clov contributes "gagner la sortie" [to exit]. The name Hamm abridges Hamlet, the most celebrated character of drama, and, like that dramatic hero, Hamm is also a ham actor. Hamm even dramatizes an imaginary being who can make sense—as he cannot—of the activities onstage: "Ah, bon, je vois ce que c'est, oui, je vois ce qu'ils font!" (49) [Ah, good, now I see what it is, yes, now I understand what they're at! 108]. In preparation for the end, Hamm quotes a line of (Baudelaire's) poetry, and recitation is another form of play. Nagg's joke of the Englishman and the tailor is *his* contribution to play, as is Clov's feigned interest in Hamm's chronicle (as well as a song that Beckett deleted). It is that chronicle that constitutes Hamm's main form of play. In French Hamm designates it as a "roman," and it sports both the past definite verbs of French written fiction and the formulaic repetitions of oral epic—not to mention a paradoxical description: "Un long silence se fit entendre" (71) (omitted from the English translation). Beckett's scenic directions instruct Hamm to shift from "Ton normal" to "Ton de narrateur," but Hamm is also a critic of his composition, even while it is in progress: "Joli ça." "Ça va aller." "Ça, c'est du français!" "Un peu faible ça" (for the howling wild wind) (72–74). Hamm's self-evaluations subsume style rather than content, and yet fictionalizing seems to be an instrument of cognition for him. When Hamm requests a few last words from Clov's heart, he frames Clov's rhetoric in fiction—"sans que je lui demande rien, il m'a parlé" (107) [without my having asked him, he spoke to me, 131].

Part of the playlong conflict between Hamm and Clov lies in the former's gamesmanship, which is opposed by the latter's earnestness. Although Nagg's curse provokes Hamm to announce the end of playing: "Finie la rigolade" (78) [Our revels now are ended, 120], Clov later implores him: "Cessons de jouer!" [Let's stop playing!]. Hamm retorts: "Jamais!" (102) [Never! 130]. Since Clov shortly afterward announces his sighting of a small boy, he may finally be playing. We will never know, but what we can know is Clov's innocence about the language that Hamm and Nagg can manipulate playfully. Early in the play Clov mistakes Nell's advice to desert, as a reference to the desert. He sees nothing incongruous in applying the colloquial "La vache!" [literally, "the cow"] to his flea. Or reporting legless Nagg's consent to listen to Hamm's story: "Il marche" [He's walking]. Or designating the sound of the shrill alarm clock as "inouïe" [unheard]. Clov has to be taught the difference between coïte and coïte [laying, lying]. When Hamm feigns modesty about the progress of his story, Clov literalizes his cliché: "Mieux que rien! Ça alors tu m'épates" (81) [Better than nothing! Is it possible? 121]. Although Clov is able to utter a Latinism—"Mortibus"—he is withering about the language that Hamm has taught him: "J'emploie les mots que tu m'as appris. S'ils ne veulent plus rien dire apprends-m'en d'autres. Ou laisse-moi me taire" (62) [I use the words you taught me. If they don't mean anything any more, teach me others. Or let me be silent, 113]. In the final moments of the play he does indeed remain silent.

The playlong dying subverted by playing was present in some of the earlier drafts of Fin de partie, but what distinguishes the final version is the sheer quantity of repetition, which frequently lends itself to extensible significance; that is to say, its meaning extends beyond its specific reference, for example, Nagg's "C'est dur! Je ne peux pas!" (24) [It's hard! I can't! 97]. Or Nell's "C'était profond, profond" (36) [It was deep, deep, 102]. Or Hamm's "La chose est impossible" (22) [The thing is impossible, 96]. Or Clov's "Mieux que rien! Ça alors tu m'épates" (81) [Better than nothing! Is it possible? 121].

Beckett introduces a device into Fin de partie—what I call cruel logic—that enters the dialogue by a seemingly neutral conjunction "alors" [then]. For example, early in the play both Hamm and Clov declare that they have had "assez" [enough], whereupon Hamm announces gloomily: "Alors il n'y a pas de raison que ça change" (19) [Then there's no reason for it to change, 94]. Or in Beckett's favorite exchange (Haerdter, 54) Hamm asks what Nagg is doing after Nell's death:

Clov: Il pleure.
Hamm: Donc il vit. (84)

[Clov: He's crying.
Hamm: Then he's living. (123)]

In an often quoted sentence from a German rehearsal, Beckett under-lined the obvious: "Es gibt keine Zufalle im *Endspiel*, alles ist auf Analogien und Wiederholungen aufgebaut" (Haerdter, 54) [There are no accidents in *Endgame*. Everything is based on analogies and repetitions]. Clov's opening mime displays symmetrical gestures toward the two windows. Once the re-ciprocal action between Hamm and Clov begins, there is repetitive strain in Clov's desire to retreat to his kitchen, countered by Hamm's commands, which keep him on stage. Hamm at the beginning and end holds his "vieux linge" at arm's length. When Nagg and Nell emerge from their respective ashbins, their fingers are visible before their heads appear. With the same gesture, Nagg raps on Nell's binlid, and Hamm raps on the back wall. Clov imitates the posture of the toy dog before Hamm. Clov twice pushes Hamm's wheelchair in a semicircle round the asylum. The three generations of men take the same pose to pray—and to break off prayer. Near the beginning and near the end of the play Hamm sniffs to detect Clov's presence—and fails. At the beginning and end of Hamm's presence, he folds and unfolds his hand-kerchief with mirrored gestures.

It is, however, verbal repetition that is unprecedented in *Fin de partie*. Clov's "Je te quitte" [I'll leave you] is the most frequently repeated phrase in the play. Nine times we hear: "il n'y a plus" [There are no more]. Hamm asks seven times for his *calmant* [painkiller]. Between them Clov and Hamm enunciate six and a half *zeros*. Hamm and Clov volley five repetitions of *gris* [gray]. Both in Hamm's chronicle and in his own person, Hamm exclaims: "Mais réfléchissez, réfléchissez, vous êtes sur terre, c'est sans remède!" (73, 91) [Use your head, can't you, use your head, you're on earth, there's no cure for that! 118, 125]. Twice Hamm begs Clov's pardon—to no avail. Both Nell and Clov ask: "Pourquoi cette comédie, tous les jours?" (29, 49) [Why this farce, day after day? 99, 107]. Both Nagg's lower back and the bricks at the back wall are "creux" [hollow]. Nell is twice nostalgic about "hier" [yester-day], but the same word triggers Clov's outburst against Hamm. Both Mother Pegg and the earth are "éteinte" [extinguished].

Even when the phrasal repetition is not exact, rhythmic structures repeat. The "Alors" or "Donc" of cruel logic is recurrent. Early in the play Hamm charges Nagg: "Maudit progéniteur" and "Maudit fornicateur" (23–24) [Accursed progenitor! Accursed fornicator! 96]. As Hamm curses Clov, Nagg curses Hamm. Nell tends to answer all Nagg's questions by "Non," before she has grasped their import. Twice Hamm calls for his dog. Twice Hamm commands Clov to use "la lunette" [the glass]. Thrice Hamm and Clov agree that they could not laugh today. Several times Hamm and Clov indulge in stichomythic exchanges, sometimes in quatrains:

Hamm: Pourquoi restes-tu avec moi?
Clov: Pourquoi me gardes-tu?
Hamm: Il n'y a personne d'autre.
Clov: Il n'y a pas d'autre place. (20)

[Hamm: Why do you stay with me?
Clov: Why do you keep me?
Hamm: There's no one else.
Clov: There's nowhere else. (95)]

Or Nagg and Nell speak in a rhymed quatrain in the original French:

Nagg: Tu me vois?
Nell: Mal. Et toi?
Nagg: Quoi?
Nell: Tu me vois? (30)

[Nagg: Can you see me?
Nell: Hardly. And you?
Nagg: What?
Nell: Can you see me? (99)]

The most telling rhythm joins the end to the beginning of the play: Clov's opening monologue affirms: "Les grains s'ajoutent aux grains, un à un" (15–16) [Grain upon grain, one by one, 93]. By the end it is Hamm who intones: "Instants sur instants, plouff, plouff, comme les grains de mil de . . . *(il cherche)* . . . ce vieux Grec" (93) [Moment upon moment, pattering down, like the millet grains of . . . [*he hesitates*] . . . that old Greek, 126]. Thus, grains and moments inexplicably accumulate into a life, but also into a performance of *Fin de partie.*

The play stings with pain, but it is never solemn. As Nell early affirms: "Rien n'est plus drôle que le malheur" (33) [Nothing is funnier than unhappiness, 101]. (For Beckett, this was the most important sentence in the play [Haerdter, 50]). Nagg counters Nell's nostalgia with his joke about the tailor. When Hamm remarks: "C'est d'un triste" [This is deadly], Clov enters to retort: "Ça redevient gai" (45) [Things are livening up, 106]. The reflective observer imagined by Hamm is subverted by the flea in Clov's trousers. The silent prayer is punctuated by derogatory exclamations. Hamm's eloquent prophecy for Clov is deflated by the latter's inability to sit. Even Hamm's last mordant monologue is undercut by Clov's incongruous costume.

Although *Fin de partie* contains only one ambulatory character, it sports a surprising variety of motions—staggering, climbing, entering, making an exit, unveiling, folding and unfolding, shaking, knocking, reaching, carrying, dropping, posing, pushing, tapping, striking, wiping, tearing, throwing, covering. The play displays comparable verbal variety, which embraces Scripture, mythology, biology, games, jokes, puns, poetry, nostalgia, prophecy, horseback and telephone, tragedy and comedy, and the habits of daily living. *Fin de partie* is sparely inclusive. Unlike *Godot,* which is theatrically indestructible today, *Fin de partie* has to play in tautened medleys that demand concentration from actors and audience.

Godot magnetized admirers among British intellectuals, notably at the BBC, which acquired the broadcasting rights to Peter Hall's 1955 production but never acted upon it.[7] By 1956, however, with rumors of a new play in the air, Beckett was more actively wooed by the BBC, and he was evidently seduced by radio, a genre that was new to him. In a letter of July 5 to Nancy Cunard, he wrote: "Never thought about Radio play technique, but in the dead of t'other night got a nice gruesome idea full of cartwheels and dragging feet and puffing and panting which may nor may not lead to something" (qtd. in Knowlson, 385). In fact, the sounds Beckett heard in his mind's ear led eventually to *All That Fall,* which he sent to the BBC on September 27. *All That Fall* was first broadcast on January 13, 1957, and Beckett had no part in its transmission. Only later, through the director Donald McWhinnie, did he meet Pat Magee, who played Mr. Slocum, and Jack MacGowran, who played Tommy in this all-Irish cast.[8]

All That Fall

Although a play was not *commissioned* by the BBC, Beckett was prompted by their interest to return to the English language. Ignoring the jettisoned and untitled *From an Abandoned Work,* he mistakenly thought that the radio play was his first return to English after a decade of French writing.[9] Beckett's early draft of the radio play contains the cartwheels, dragging feet, puffing, and panting that he mentions in his letter to Nancy Cunard, but it lacks the stylized humor of the completed *All That Fall.* Notable revisions

---

Random notes for *All That Fall* are contained in the so-called Eté '56 Notebook at RUL. A very early version of *All That Fall* lodges in a notebook dated September 1956, which is at HRC, as is the original typescript. Zilliacus (1976) compares the early draft with the final version, and Pountney summarizes the differences. *All That Fall* was first broadcast by the BBC on January 13, 1957. It was published in 1957 by Grove and Faber, respectively. Exceptionally, the translation into French was undertaken by Robert Pinget, who consulted with Beckett, and also exceptionally, it was telecast in French on January 25, 1963, and staged at the Berlin Schiller Theater in January 1966. Pountney's appendix 1 tabulates the manuscript holdings of Beckett's plays written between 1956 and 1976. The list begins with *All That Fall.* The radio play appears in *CDW,* to which my page numbers refer.

are the addition of rural sounds, physical afflictions, and the characters' punning names. The title itself is changed from "Lovely Day for the Races" to the biblical *All That Fall,* and the name of the protagonist changes from Emma Kennedy to Maddy Dunne Rooney (mad done ruin). The radio play is unusual among Beckett's plays in being firmly rooted in Ireland of the 1930s, but its title signals that it is not a realistic play. The single and singular viewpoint is that of its protagonist, Maddy Dunne Rooney.

From a pastoral spring background, Maddy Rooney sets out to meet her blind husband Dan at the Boghill railway station near the race course. On the way she is overtaken by fellow townsmen (with punning names) in vehicles of increasing speed, which Katharine Worth sees as "a whole history of human transport" (1999, 30): Christy walking beside his cartload of dung, Mr. Tyler riding on his bicycle, Mr. Slocum driving his automobile with new balloon tires. Although Maddy arrives late at the station, her husband's train is even later, delayed fifteen minutes on its half-hour journey from an unnamed city. United with her husband on his birthday, Maddy leads him toward home. Dan Rooney evades his wife's query as to what delayed his train, but from a boy who runs after them Maddy learns of the fall of a child onto the track and under the train wheels.

Lasting a little over an hour in performance, *All That Fall* is structured in three unequal parts; the longest contains Maddy's stationward journey; next comes her arrival at the station itself; and last is the homeward journey, upon which the play ends (but without the arrival home). Since Maddy takes the same route to and from the station, motifs repeat in inverse order: Schubert's *Death and the Maiden,* a golden laburnum tree, a preacher named Hardy. The rural sounds that open the play—sheep, bird, cow, cock—are briefly evoked to note their absence on the homeward journey. The bright day has clouded over.

On the blind medium of radio, two-hundred-pound, voluble Maddy Dunne Rooney is accompanied by her blind husband Dan. Near the middle of the play Maddy summarizes the setting: "The entire scene, the hills, the plain, the racecourse with its miles and miles of white rails and three red stands, the pretty little wayside station, even you yourselves" (*CDW,* 185). By midplay, however, this is mere background, for voices and noises have animated the scene, from the opening rural cries and dragging feet to the toil up the station steps at this juncture. Not only does each animal have its own voice, but each vehicle has its distinguishing sound. Briefly though we hear Maddy's neighbors, their speech is individualized—Christy's "Ma'am"-studded servility, Mr. Tyler's lascivious suggestiveness, Mr. Slocum's elaborate courtesies, Mr. Barrell's snappish impatience, Miss Fitt's rhetorical spirituality. Tommy and Jerry chime in with their few words at the station, and the latter's four-word finale is devastating: "Under the wheels, ma'am."[10]

The title (which occurred to Beckett late in the process of composition) comes from Psalm 145, verse 14, which Maddy quotes to Dan: "The Lord upholdeth all that fall and raiseth up all those that be bowed down." This occasions "wild laughter" from the aged, ailing couple. Radio obscures the upholding and raising of anyone by anyone, but the play's dialogue is sown with words that lead up to the biblical text. Greeted by the bright day, Maddy wonders whether it will "hold up," and Mr. Slocum, remarking that Maddy is "bent all double," holds her up to get her into his automobile. Miss Fitt describes Maddy as "bowed and bent," and Maddy tells Dan that he is "bowed down over the ditch." Maddy fears that "the rain will begin to fall and go on falling," and that "the first great drops will fall." Although the old couple sit briefly, they never fall, but at the shocking end of the play we learn that a child has fallen to her death.[11]

That death has been prepared by many details of the play. In Zilliacus's felicitous summary: "The incidents written into the play serve as staves for a threnody on the theme of decay and meaningless death" (1999, 32). Maddy repeats the adjective *poor* some dozen times. She hears Schubert's *Death and the Maiden* from a "*ruinous* old house" on the outward and homeward journeys, and on both trips she notes the laburnum tree (labor-numb). Christy's wife and daughter are ill, Mr. Tyler's daughter has had a hysterectomy, Mr. Slocum's mother is sick, a hen is run over, Maddy thinks of her dead daughter Minnie, Mr. Barrell's father didn't live long enough to enjoy his retirement, Miss Fitt is "a bag of bones," hymns are linked to the maritime disasters of the *Titanic* and the *Lusitania,* Jerry's father has been taken away, Dan Rooney masochistically takes delight in his own afflictions, and Maddy recalls the dying girl mentioned by the mind doctor. Summarized baldly in this way, illness and death may sound solemn, but the Boghill-dwellers announce these contretemps lightly. Mishaps to human beings are comically interspersed with recalcitrance of means of locomotion: Christy's hinny refuses to move; Mr. Tyler's bicycle tire loses air; Mr. Slocum's automobile does not start; the train has been halted by an accident. It is all part and parcel of a deflationary pattern, in Zilliacus's phrase "a droll dirge."

The lexicon of death and disintegration is so unusual as to shade into the comic. Mr. Barrell reacts to Mr. Slocum's "crucifying his gearbox." Mr. Tyler recalls the "bawdy hour of nine," when Christ was crucified. Dan Rooney accuses his wife: "You stop dead," but he describes himself as "buried alive" in his basement office. Strikingly (and suspiciously) he confesses to the desire to "Nip some young *doom* in the bud" (emphasis added).[12] Although Dan accuses Maddy of "struggling with a dead language," her words are vividly alive with intimations of mortality. Maddy describes herself as "destroyed." She declares it "suicide to be abroad," but staying home is "a lingering dissolution." Since she seethes in her skin, she longs to "be in atoms." Her day is clouding and shrouding.

At the same time Maddy challenges ubiquitous depopulation. She links her journey to the "up mail," with its connotation of virility. She claims that all she ever wanted was to be loved twice daily, instead of perfunctorily kissed. She rejects the tepid advances of Mr. Tyler (whom she twice calls Mr. Rooney), and yet she woos him to unlace her corset behind the hedge. She resents the insinuation that she is as stiff as Mr. Slocum, whose name puns upon his potency, and her entrance to his car is ecstatic with sexual suggestion. While climbing the station steps on Miss Fitt's arm, Maddy taunts the spinster with talk of honeymoon couples on the Matterhorn. Maddy shocks Dan by asking for a kiss in public. On her homeward walk, Maddy wonders whether hinnies can procreate. In this radio play, where the bowed and fallen are mainly women, Beckett creates his first female protagonist, a spirited descendant of the Wife of Bath.

Early in *All That Fall* Maddy characterizes her words as "bizarre," which derives from Spanish *bizarro,* meaning brave or gallant, and, for all her picturesque complaints, that's what Maddy is. Dan Rooney is the heir of Hamm of *Fin de partie* in his anticreationism, but Maddy is irrepressibly alive, and she lives through her language, which she nevertheless denigrates: "A few simple words . . . from my heart . . . and I am all alone . . . once more" (182). Her words are framed in nature—the rural sounds that precede language, and the wind and rain that succeed it. Although these sounds are heard on radio, it is with voluble animals that human speech contrasts; the doves' billing and cooing arouse Maddy's carnality, and she appreciates that the lamb's language has not changed since Arcady—unlike the slippery puns, precisions, synonyms, and catalogs that strew her own speech.

Like *Godot* and *Fin de partie, All That Fall* enfolds the Bible. Beckett told Colin Duckworth: "Christianity is a mythology with which I am perfectly familiar, so I naturally use it" (1972, 18). *Godot* was structured on its two symmetrical thieves; *Fin de partie* was set in a refuge from a residual flood; the very title of *All That Fall* is excerpted from Psalm 145. Maddy early encounters Christy, who has no head for heights; he walks beside his hinny, whereas Christ entered Jerusalem high on his steed. Mr. Tyler declares it a "divine day" for a race meeting. Tommy receives no thanks for a Christian act. Hetty Fitt offers Maddy a reluctant helping hand, and she worries about her mother's "fresh sole," rather than her immortal soul. Dan Rooney compares himself and Maddy to Dante's damned. Maddy is more concerned with biblical mistranslations than with moral lessons: not an ass's colt but a hinny, and not sparrows "than many of which we are of more value." Climactically, Maddy and Dan "join in wild laughter" at the biblical verse emphasized in the play's title.

Beckett, however, evokes reflective laughter at the verbal diapason of *All That Fall.* It is as though he set out to prove the contention of Nell of *Fin de partie:* "Rien n'est plus drôle que le malheur." His radio threnody plays melodiously and Irishly through a comic soundscape.

Not until 1957 would Beckett actually hear *All That Fall,* and in the meantime—December 1956—he began and soon jettisoned a play in English—"The Gloaming."

"The Gloaming" (revised as *Rough for Theatre I*)

Originally entitled "The Beggar and the Cripple" (which I prefer), the play resurrects an old topos of a blind man and a lame man, who together function as a whole man. (In Beckett's manuscript B may designate the blind man, and C the cripple.)[13] At twilight in a town square blind B on a folding stool plays his fiddle and begs for alms. One-legged C enters on a wheelchair, which he propels by means of a pole. C endows B with his son Billy's name, suggesting that they join forces. Their dialogue delineates their respective situations, bereft as they are of the women who succored them in the past. When B gropes his way to C and pushes the chair, the latter strikes him with his pole. At C's request, B sinks to his knees to adjust the blanket around C's foot. B rests his head on C's knee but is pushed so roughly that he falls. B then recalls the harsh words of his woman: "You'd do better crawling on all fours, with your father's medals pinned to your arse and a money box round your neck. You and your harp!" Standing, B listens to sounds he cannot identify, and C claims to see "it." He threatens to make off with B's belongings, and he predicts that another old man might emerge to find him playing a harmonica or singing. Taunting B, C pokes him with the pole, which B wrenches from C's grasp. C queries: "How shall we finish this now, Billy?" He throws the pole to C, who catches it, and poles himself backward toward the right wing. C watches while B gropes his way toward his stool in order to resume his opening position. C wonders how he can help B: "Is there

---

The fragmentary "Gloaming" has a curious history, unique in Beckett annals. Begun in December 1956, it was apparently jettisoned, but the holograph is found at RUL. Although the title has been crossed out and is difficult to read, it is probably "The Beggar and the Cripple," and not, as stated in *BatR* (46), "The Beggar and the Fiddle," despite the attractive pun. At some point in the 1960s it was exhumed by Beckett, reworked in French, and published in *Minuit* (March 1974) under the title *Fragment de Théâtre.* Book publication was delayed until 1978, in *Pas suivi de quatre esquisses,* but in 1975 Beckett translated the French text into English, publishing it in 1976 as *Theatre I* in *Ends and Odds,* and subsequently retitling it as *Rough for Theatre I.* He rarely granted permission for performance.

nothing I can do for you, Billy?" B replies with a yearning to be back with his father, fishing for mackerel. "To the time when it was still time."

"The Gloaming" is not only wordier than *Fragment de théâtre I* (its revised translation into French); it is also more sentimental. In revision, Beckett terminates the fragment while the blind man still has the lame man's pole in his possession. In the revised script, too, C grows progressively more antagonistic to B. The blind man and the lame man could join forces to their mutual advantage, but the play breaks off after the former renders the latter helpless. Not only destiny but human perversity contributes to their wretched state. When they first meet, each exclaims at the other's affliction: "Poor wretch!" When the play concludes, the poor wretches are more wretched. Even in its primitive version, however, "The Gloaming" is distinctive and dramatic in the twilight quality of a dialogue that is anchored in the concrete situation of the characters, and yet reaches beyond them to dreams, music, and memories. Beckett was right to salvage the fragment—and shape it with excisions and echoes.

1957

The January 13 BBC broadcast of *All That Fall* was imperfectly heard by Beckett in Paris, but he was sufficiently impressed to promise to try to write another play for its director, Donald McWhinnie. More immediately, he submerged himself in self-translation, and his letters are testimony to his frustration. After resisting for a time, he began the Herculean task of Englishing *L'Innommable*. He then laid that aside for a while to tackle *Fin de partie*, for he had promised an English version to George Devine, the artistic director of the Royal Court Theatre in London. This was his main occupation between May and August; he titled the play *Endgame*, with its chess resonance. He wrote MacGreevy: "I find it dreadful in English, all the sharpness gone, and the rhythms. If I were not bound by contract to the Royal Court Theatre I wouldn't allow it in English at all" (qtd. in Knowlson, 393–94). While gnawing away at *L'Innommable*, he also revised some of Elmar Tophoven's translations into German—at the translator's request.[14] Among Beckett's many visitors toward the end of the year, Alan Schneider came to consult on the American premiere of *Endgame*. Donald McWhinnie came from London to consult on Pat Magee's BBC reading from *Molloy* and *From an Abandoned Work*. Beckett wrote Rosset: "If I felt less shaky I'd go over, the 3rd [the BBC Third Programme] being untakable here" (qtd. in Knowlson, 394). In the event, the broadcast was "takable" enough for Beckett to be haunted by Magee's whispered rasp of a voice.

1958

With *Endgame* announced for the Royal Court season, Beckett rejected Devine's several suggestions for an accompaniment, since the play was considered too short for a full evening in the theater. Beckett hoped to come up with "something else from my own muckheap more acceptable than the mime" (qtd. in Knowlson, 398). While in the final throes of translation of *L'Innommable*—on February 20, to be specific—Beckett began the "Magee Monologue," with the Irish actor's whispering voice in his mind. He made rapid progress, and within three weeks *Krapp's Last Tape* was completed. Despite the relatively swift composition, the "Magee Monologue" went through seven stages before it became *Krapp's Last Tape,* as published. Gontarski analyzes these stages in some detail, but present throughout is the basic conception of an old man listening to tapes recorded on his birthdays.[15]

Krapp's Last Tape

Krapp's Last Tape is Beckett's most approachable stage play, and in performance it can be reductively sentimental: an old man looks back regretfully upon a life in which he sacrificed love to artistic ambition. Krapp's name, appearance, and initial gestures move him toward farce, but in most performances, pathos outweighs farce. Moreover, Beckett later so radically reduced the clown elements that directors would be well advised to consult his revised text. Remaining, however, are Krapp's unshaven face, his shortsightedness, his worn black-and-white costume, the large silver pocketwatch that he sees with difficulty, and the phallic resonance of the slippery banana. Sharp contrast is maintained between Krapp's circle of light and the

---

Indebted to Gontarski's stemma, I list the main steps of *Krapp's Last Tape:*

1. Holograph in RUL's Eté '56 Notebook. An old man A searches for a tape before settling down to listen to it.
2. In same notebook, the reminiscence of the love scene. A is lubricious, desiring "Intercourse."
3. Ts 1 at HRC includes the above versions, and revises A's desires to *less* sex and alcohol. The opposition is sharpened between light and darkness, white and black.
4. Holograph in RUL's Eté '56 Notebook. The opening mime is revised.
5. Ts 2 at HRC further modifies the opening mime, revising the business with keys and banana. A, now named Crapp, makes notes on envelopes, looks up "viduity."

surrounding stage dark, and Beckett's successive versions underline the opposition of noise and silence, motion and immobility. In a letter of January 4, 1960, to Alan Schneider, Beckett emphasized the contrasts: "Black and white (both dirty), the whole piece being built up in one sense on this simple antithesis of which you will find echoes throughout the text (black ball, white nurse, black pram, Bianca, Kedar—anagram of 'dark'—Street, black storm, light of understanding, etc.). Black dictionary if you can and ledger. Similarly black and white set" (Harmon, 60). In Beckett's final version, Krapp begins with a bare table, but he goes backstage three times—for a large dusty ledger, for tin boxes of tapes, and for the tape recorder, which in performance is almost always operated by an offstage technician. The voice of thirty-nine-year-old Krapp is actually taped, and the live actor has to react each evening to his own taped voice.

Krapp's Last Tape opens on a tableau, with an old unkempt man sitting motionless at his bare table. Interrupting his opening gestures, he bursts into fragmentary phrases. When sixty-nine-year-old Krapp first seeks box three, spool five in the ledger, its contents are unknown to us. Once that tape is in place, old Krapp reads aloud from the ledger, offering piquant glimpses into his autobiography. Old Krapp looks back and to his left before beginning his main stage activity—listening. He reacts to his voice at age thirty-nine with grunts, brooding, and laughter. He can laugh at an earlier Krapp, but not at himself in the present. After young Krapp's evocation of the girl in the shabby green coat, old Krapp shuffles to his cubbyhole for a drink. The passage on his mother's death prompts another exit for a dictionary, from which he reads Beckett's specially composed definition of "viduity." After listening to an extended passage on his mother's death, Krapp broods on disparate "moments," but he thumps the table impatiently at the mention of his "memorable night." Fast forwarding without escaping that night, Krapp curses, winds forward again, curses again, and winds forward to the middle of the "Farewell to love." When that segment nears its end, he winds back

---

6. Ts 3 at HRC emphasizes sexuality with respect to the banana and the dark nurse. Elements of pathos counter this aspect.

7. Ts 4 at HRC sharpens Krapp's solitude. The black ball is given to the white dog.

Beckett notes to himself that he still needs instructions about a tape-recorder. He is still mulling the title of *Krapp's Last Reel*.
First published in *Evergreen Review* (summer 1958), *Krapp's Last Tape* was published by Faber in 1959. It was first performed by Patrick Magee (who also played Hamm) on a double bill with *Endgame* at the Royal Court on October 28, 1958. Translated into French by Pierre Leyris and the author, it was first published as *La Derniere bande* in *Les Lettres nouvelles* (March 4, 1959) and revised for the book with *Cendres* (Minuit, 1960).

and listens, his arms in a virtual embrace of the tape recorder. He broods, switches off, and goes backstage for a second drink. He returns somewhat unsteadily, armed with a microphone, and he manipulates reels in preparation for recording. At first reading from an envelope, Krapp starts to record his past year, but brooding interrupts. In contrast to the younger Krapp's actual experiences with women, old Krapp confines his conquests to Effi, a character in a novel, and the aptly named Fanny, "Bony old ghost of a whore." Krapp recalls going to Vespers, as when he was a boy. However, the memory of love overwhelms him, and his last live words repeat a phrase from box three, spool five: "Lie down across her." He tears the new tape off, to replay the old one. With another look back left into darkness, he resumes his opening position, but this time he plays through and past the end of "Farewell to love," where he tries to rationalize his choice of thirty years ago. The play ends in silence and immobility, as all lights fade, except the "eye" of the recorder.

Trying first to dominate the sensual by the spiritual, and then to enfold the sensual within the spiritual, Krapp is punished by both emotional and literary failure. Beckett's remark to Pierre Chabert is sometimes quoted: "I thought of writing a play on the opposite situation, with Mrs. Krapp, the girl in the punt, nagging away behind him, in which case his failure and his solitude would be exactly the same" (qtd. in Gontarski 1985, 61). I do not think that Beckett meant this seriously.

Krapp is a self-centered individual, who is incapable of seeing the *pattern* of his life—a series of failed resolutions. However sardonic old Krapp is about his life, he has committed it to tape, upon whose wealth he draws. He seeks to hear "the Farewell to Love," but he inadvertently bestows on us the passages about mother a-dying, and about the equinox, which Beckett renders indeed memorable. An early review praised "a form which combines the immobile mask and the mobile face, mime and speech, monologue and dialogue, and offers all their various resources to one performer" (qtd. in Fletcher and Fletcher, 119). In addition, the play blends farce and fantasy. The pathos aroused by the visible old man is undercut by phrasal ironies that have turned to rust in old Krapp's vest and trousers. Actors and readers should be aware of the range of moods of a moribund Krapp.

Beckett, eager to see *Krapp* onstage, was beset with the irritations of censorship. When the archbishop of Dublin required changes in readings of Joyce and O'Casey at the Dublin Festival, Beckett withdrew his own work—an interdiction that remained in effect until 1960. In England the Lord Chamberlain had the power of theater censorship, and he objected not only to the prayer in *Endgame* but to a passage of the punt scene in *Krapp's Last Tape.* The press was quick to seize on the illogicality of censoring

Endgame, when there had been no objection to *Fin de partie* in London, but logic was not the Lord Chamberlain's strong suit. The license to perform was finally granted only three weeks before the double bill opened, and Beckett attended all the rehearsals, to the delight of the director Donald McWhinnie and the actor Patrick Magee. Beckett continued to sharpen and simplify the play in other productions—in German, French, and English, for he directed or advised *Krapp's Last Tape* more often than any other of his plays. Knowlson associates Beckett's affection for the play with Ethna Mac-Carthy, his old love at Trinity College, and perhaps the prototype of the girl in the punt. His June 2, 1958, letter to her seems to bear this out: "I've written in English a stage monologue for Pat Magee which I think you will like if no one else" (TCD).

The enforced delay in the 1958 Royal Court double bill left Beckett with time on his hands, which he was unable to fill with new writing. Krapp (a name resurrected from *Eleutheria*) did not prove a fertilizer. In May Beckett went to Zurich for an exhibition of the paintings of Bram van Velde, toward whose appreciation he had been instrumental. In June he reread Dante's *Divina Commedia.* In July he and Suzanne invited friends to spend his unexportable dinars in Yugoslavia. At last in August he dabbled with a play in French, which, like "The Gloaming," he broke off and jettisoned, only to exhume it over a decade later. I am guessing that a related fragment in English preceded the French play, *Fragment de théâtre II.*

"Last Soliloquy"

The fragment is a dialogue about a last soliloquy before a suicide. The speakers of the dialogue are named P and A (Protagonist and Antagonist?). A is trying to compose his last soliloquy before suicide, while P supplies comment and criticism. *BatR* notes that "it is unclear whether the suicide is 'real' or part of rehearsals for a play" (64). The latter seems more probable, if one heeds A's line, "Fuck the author. Fuck all authors." Or P's instructions to A: "Take it from what." The dialogue stops with P's "What not if not what not?" (recalling *Watt*). Yet there follow scenic directions for a curtain and ovation. Rather than a sibling of *Endgame* by way of the phrase "Last Soliloquy," the fragment seems a prediction of *Catastrophe* by way of *Fragment de théâtre II.*

An undated, unpublished fragment at RUL bears the title "Last Soliloquy" for ms. 2937/1–3. In spite of its title, *BatR* correctly describes the three-leaf holograph as a *dialogue* between P and A.

Fragment de théâtre II

Although Beckett was unable to complete this fragment either, he carried it further. On the one hand, the fragment is unique in revealing Beckett's predilection for detective stories; on the other hand, it is an unusual detective story, since the crime is unmentioned, and the culprit is also the victim. Moreover, the punishment—an enforced suicide—is repeatedly mentioned, but not carried out.

A and B, who call each other Bertrand and Morvan, are a blend of detective and judge, who are entrusted with sifting through documents that will determine whether the third character C lives or dies. At opposite ends of the stage A and B are seated at identical tables with identical table lamps. Yet B is the driving force in this investigation, and although he early orders, "Qu'il saute" [Let him jump], B conscientiously reads aloud from the documents at his disposal. They add up to a highly satiric, unsympathetic portrait of C, who stands mutely at the upstage center window, his back to the audience. More reluctantly, B reads from C's unposted letter to an "admiratrice anonyme" (54), but he skips many phrases to arrive at the main verb. It is a routine matter to the two officials, which they wish to dispatch speedily. However, B's lamp unexpectedly goes dark at intervals, and he moves to A's desk. At one point A leans out of the window to examine C's face—"Il n'est pas beau" [Not at his best]. For different reasons, A and B arrive at the same verdict; B bases his sentence on the documentary evidence, and A on psychology, but, only momentarily interrupted by the cry of a cat, B repeats his opening decree, "Qu'il saute, qu'il saute" [Let him jump], and A acquiesces. Realizing that they have time before their train, A regales B with the recollection of another case, when a bird interrupts them with its song. It proves to be a thrush who sings, undeterred by the presence of its dead mate in the cage. B notes that there is neither seed nor water in the cage, but A sees an old cuttlebone. After a long pause, A goes again to C. Trying vainly to alert B to what he sees on C's face, A raises his handkerchief "timidement" to it. It is the last gesture of a play in which human beings pronounce a death sentence on another human being, who is not at home in an apartment where a cat is unfed, and where a bird, nourished on a fishbone, sings although his mate is dead. Cruelty or callousness is ubiquitous.

The rather heavy-handed satire against insentient officials recalls the

---

A thirty-three-leaf holograph of *Fragment de théâtre II* is at TCD, marked in Beckett's hand "abandoned" (Pountney goes into detail on the "four separate attempts" at the play, but she forgets that Beckett finally published the play as *a fragment*). Two typescripts are at RUL. The play appears in the original French in *Pas, suivi de quatre esquisses* (Minuit, 1978). It was first published in Beckett's English translation *Rough for Theatre II* in *Ends and Odds* (Grove, 1976; Faber, 1977). It is included in *CDW*.

prewar Beckett. For all the wit and slapstick, the play takes a long time to make its point. However, it does show Beckett reaching in a new direction, somewhat reminiscent of Kafka. A's final gesture of raising a handkerchief to C's face is suitably ambiguous. What occasions the tears of the silent victim C? Will A's concern mitigate the sentence imposed on C, or is this a superfluous refinement toward one who is condemned to jump to his death?

Fragment de théâtre II was the only piece that Beckett managed to write for the remainder of 1958. He spent three weeks in October at Royal Court rehearsals of *Krapp* and *Endgame.* In November he flew to Dublin to see his old friend who was dying of cancer—Ethna MacCarthy Leventhal. Back at Ussy by year's end, he took up again the scraps of a radio play he had put aside when he embarked on *Krapp's Last Tape.*

1959–61

Fresh Elements and Motifs

1959

Beckett continued to think that he was at a creative impasse, but he also continued to experiment with new forms of drama and fiction. I draw the title of my chapter from Beckett's translation of the *foirade,* "Il est tête nue," but the phrase is applicable to other works as well. At the end of 1958 Beckett started a story, which he labeled "Pim," and that fiction became his major preoccupation during 1959. However, lesser works also exhibit fresh elements—the radio play *Embers* and the mime play *Acte sans paroles II.* In the periodical *Minuit,* where five of his eight *foirades* were first published, four of them are dated "années 50," but when they appeared in the volume *Pour finir encore et autres foirades,* the date changed to "années 60." Beckett wrote John Pilling that the *foirades* "dated from after *How It Is*" (Knowlson and Pilling, 132), and that novel (which began as "Pim") was completed in French in July 1960. Of the French *foirades,* the only manuscript extant is "Il est tête nue," but it is undated. Because of its position in the MacGowran notebook at OSU. I assigned it to 1955, and I suspect that three of the four early *foirades* were written between that year and 1959. Since there is no datable evidence, however, I am arbitrarily commenting under 1959. The last year of the 1950s would then contain and predict "fresh elements and motifs" in both prose and drama. I begin the chapter with a work that we can date approximately.

Embers
The BBC production of *All That Fall* pleased Beckett well enough to continue in the radio genre. Beckett's early drafts of *Embers* have disappeared,

---

Two undated typescripts of *Embers* exist; the (probably) earlier one is at TCD, the later one at HRC. *Embers* was sent to the BBC in February 1959, and it was broad-but the script entitled *Ebb* was sent to the BBC in February 1959 (Pountney, 107). Of two undated typescripts, one differs from the final version in presenting voices in flashback. The protagonist resembles Krapp in having two voices—an older and a younger one. The music and riding lessons of the protagonist's daughter Addie are added to the typescript, as afterthoughts. The apparently later typescript contains proper names added in ink, and it is otherwise close to the final version.

Beckett's restlessness within a single genre is evident if we contrast *All That Fall* with *Embers*. Both plays view their respective worlds through a single consciousness—Maddy in the one, Henry in the other. However, Maddy's mind is exuberantly inclusive, whereas that of Henry is obsessive and enigmatic. Maddy's resonant voice responds to a diapason of nonverbal sounds, whereas Henry's brooding voice is counterpointed mainly against the sound of the sea, which is heard during the play's 228 pauses (Zilliacus's count, 1976, 91). *All That Fall* opens on lively animal-sounds, whereas *Embers* opens on an unidentifiable slurring sound, followed by footsteps on gravel. Maddy laughs at a verse from Scripture, but Henry calls upon Christ and evokes him subtly. Maddy recalls the past sporadically, but her voice on radio animates the present. Henry conflates past and present, fact and fiction. He enlivens ghosts, he punctures memories with older memories, and he struggles with a composition.

Critics of *Embers* sometimes quote Beckett's remark to Paul-Louis Mignon: "*Cendres* repose sur une ambiguïté: le personnage a-t-il une hallucination ou est-il en présence de la réalité?"[1] [*Embers* depends on an ambiguity: is the character hallucinating or faced with reality?]. However, Beckett uttered this sentence in the context of his refusal to permit the transfer of the radio play to the stage. The ambiguities of *Embers* are multiple, and hallucinations or imagination may be the reality of the protagonist Henry, whose name we learn only when it is spoken by the second character to be heard—Ada.

Despite the pyric residue of the title *Embers,* the play opens and closes with the sound of the sea, and to some extent the play pits the fire of life against the sea of death. All sounds—*bruitage* and voices—are conjured by Henry to shut out the sea, which we hear before we can identify it. Henry's abrupt opening words are at first puzzling, as they plunge us in medias res; a masculine voice repeats three monosyllabic commands: "On," "Stop," "Down." Gradually, however, Henry's words build a dramatic structure. In John Pilling's summary: "Henry utters two long speeches which frame two

cast on June 24, 1959. It was first published in *Evergreen Review* (November–December 1959) and is included in *CDW*. Translated into French by Robert Pinget and the author, it was published by Minuit in 1959, with *La Dernière bande*.

central incidents" (1976, 99). However, Henry's two long monologues are varied, and the two incidents overlap. An outline may clarify the structure cited by Pilling:

Henry's first monologue
>   Mental meeting with his mute, blind, drowned father
>   Amplified hooves
>   1. Story: Bolton admits Holloway and pleads with him before the embers.
>   Amplified drip
>   2. Story continues briefly: Holloway complains to Bolton, who repeats: "Please!"
>   Memory of father calling Henry a "washout" triggers
>   Memory of daughter Addie and her wail
>   Memory of trivial conversation with Addie's mother Ada
>   Memory of Addie's walks with Henry, who talks obsessively

Scene 1
>   Meeting with Ada, whose voice is low and remote. Her mention of Addie triggers

Scenes 2A and 2B
>   Addie's music lesson and riding lesson, in which the child's wails are "amplified to paroxysm"

Scene 1 continued
>   Ada's present *Don't*s elide into that same word, at first amplified and then cut off in the flashback love scene near the "suddenly rough" sea.
>   Ada and Henry disagree about the sea, and she advises him (twice) to see Holloway because "there must be something wrong with your brain" (*CDW*, 260).
>   Ada prophesies that Henry will eventually be alone with his voice.
>   Ada, urged by Henry to talk on, recalls a violent scene at Henry's home; his father departed, as did Ada soon afterward.
>   Ada describes Henry's father on a rock before the sea—"just the great stillness of the whole body" (263).
>   Ada leaves.

Henry's concluding monologue
>   Hooves and Ada do not respond to his call.
>   Henry weaves a story about Ada returning to look again at his father.
>   3. Bolton-Holloway story. Holloway offers Bolton an injection, but the latter can only plead monosyllabically while looking his companion in the eye. Holloway covers his face,
>   At the sea, Henry refers to a little book.
>   After a series of *Nothing*s, perhaps read from the book, perhaps in response to it, Henry concludes, "Not a sound."
>   The final sound of the sea gives him the lie.[2]

Beckett's scenic direction after the Henry-Ada love scene flashback is "End of evocation" (260), but the play itself is endlessly evocative. My break-down of the structure relies on words that blend memory and imagination, time and eternity. However, much of the poetic quality of *Embers*—what I might call the embral quality—lies in the vivid repetitions and the sound play of the Bolton-Holloway story, the direct address of Henry to his father, the seascape duologue of Henry and Ada, and the wail-inducing strictures of Addie's childhood. Woven around the evocative words is a range of sounds. The hiss of the sea is counterpointed against the grating of Henry's boots on the shingle, against the hard sounds he conjures, against the sharp ruler and sharp hoof-trots, as well as against the bars of Chopin. Moreover, Beckett exploits the technical feats of radio, since wails and pleas are amplified to the point of paroxysm, before being cut off abruptly.

The diverse sounds, the declarative sentences, and the dialogue exchanges of Henry's "life" scenes contrast markedly with the staccato phrases, self-corrections, parallelisms, and repetitions of Henry's fiction about Bolton and Holloway. In life and fiction, however, phrases are simple but vivid: "Listen to the light," "everything always went on forever," "an old man in great trouble," "the spire white to the vane," "chilled to the medulla," "it's a lovely peaceful gentle soothing sound," "every syllable is a second gained," and the (Shakespearean) "naughty world." Even out of context, these phrases are resonant, and *Embers* also resonates through pause and repetition, through expressions of pain and occasional vulgarity, through mono-logue, imitation, and dialogue, which expand the radio genre meaningfully.

Two illuminating commentaries on this radio play are sensitive to its evocative quality.[3] Hersh Zeifman (1975) reads *Embers* as a quest for salva-tion, with Christ the Savior embodied in or linked to Henry's father, as well as to Ada and Addie (both punning on *Dad*). Zeifman argues convincingly, and yet he ignores much of the text, and he does not mention Christian Ember days, connoting penitence. Paul Lawley seeks to enfold Zeifman's reading into his view of the play: "Presenting as it does the tenacious but futile struggle of a consciousness for survival and towards identity amidst both outer and inner flux, *Embers* embodies the central Beckettian preoccu-pation" (1980, 36). Lawley therefore cites images of moribundity: the sea of oblivion along with Ada's words about it, the bright constellation Vega look-ing green, hooves no longer galloping, a fire dying to embers in the story, and the ninth-hour panhysterectomy equated with an an-aesthetic. I am too swiftly summarizing a subtle and sensitive reading, although I am wary of the phrase "*the* central Beckettian preoccupation" (emphasis added). Law-ley's most acute sentence describes the central dynamic of the play as "the struggle between Henry's constant desire for a 'hard' differentiation of iden-

tity and the insidious but seductive pull (or sucking) of 'oceanic' dedifferen-
tiation which finds its low remote voice in Ada" (31).[4]

Death and depopulation are comically presented in *All That Fall*, but a
waning world (or nonbeing, or the void) is poetically rendered in *Embers*.
Like Hamm in *Endgame*, Henry desires and fears the end; he keeps the sea of
oblivion in sight, but he tries to drown its sound. The voices conjured by
Henry are redolent of the stillness he both desires and delays: his father is
mute, his surrogate Bolton (bolt-on) is limited to the word "Please," Ada's
voice is low and remote, Addie's paroxysmic wails are "suddenly cut off,"
and the plumb-er accomplishes "Nothing." Reinforcing moribundity, drowning is both image and event in the play, and Beckett has earlier cited the legend of a drowned Christ. Henry's Bolton-Holloway story corrects "shutters"
and "curtains" to "hangings"—a word that is often repeated—and Christian
iconography equates a gallows with a cross. The ambiguities of the play lie
not in hallucinations, nor in literal life and death, but in the hints of time
within eternity, in mysterious plea and counterplea, in teasing antimonies and
implied parallelisms, for example, Henry-Bolton-victim-Christ versus Father-
Holloway-savior-Christ. Finally, *Embers* is an ironic title for a seascape. Like
Henry's father, a radio audience is dumb and blind, but an act of attention
will enable us to "listen to the light" of these verbal embers.

While Beckett continued trying to write fiction, he told his composer
friend Marcel Mihalovici that he could not manage a libretto for an opera,
but he offered any existing text. Mihalovici chose *La Dernière bande*, Beckett's translation into French of *Krapp's Last Tape*. That spring Beckett
worked closely, if sporadically, with the composer and Blin: "Beckett [went]
through it line by line while Roger Blin acted it and Mihalovici took careful
notes on the cadence of the text" (Bair, 505). Beckett's short play eventually
graced a musical score of 146 pages, performed in under two hours.[5]

On May 25 Beckett's old friend Ethna MacCarthy Leventhal died of
cancer. During May, too, Suzanne's tenacious flu worried him, and he himself had flu in June. The couple agreed that they needed a larger, airier apartment. They purchased one still under construction, where they were to live
to the end of Suzanne's life, and nearly to the end of Beckett's. Some time
before summer Beckett wrote his second mime play.

Acte sans paroles II (*Act Without Words II*)

Despite Beckett's impression that his two mime plays were completed "at
about the same time," they are separated by four years. In both mime plays
an irresistible destiny—a whistle in the first play and a goad in the second—

The two mime plays were first published separately—*Acte sans paroles I* with *Fin de
partie* in 1957, and *Acte sans paroles II* in an early version in *Phantomas* (January

cues characters into stage presence. However, the *Acte I* character learns to subdue his desires, whereas nothing is apparently learned by the two characters of the second play, who may be unaware of each other's existence.

Near the right wing are two sacks and a neat pile of clothes, topped by the hat and boots celebrated in *Godot*. After two thrusts of a long horizontal goad, A crawls out of his sack, "s'immobilise, rêvasse, joint les mains, prie, rêvasse, se lève, rêvasse" (106) [halts, broods, prays, broods, gets to his feet, broods, *CDW*, 203]. He swallows a pill before a series of slow actions—dressing, eating disgustedly, carrying both sacks to the left, undressing carelessly, swallowing another pill, praying, and crawling back into his sack; all his activities are interspersed with brooding. In contrast, a single thrust of the goad (now on a wheel) animates B, who consults his watch before exercising, brushing his teeth, combing his hair, putting on and brushing his clothes, brushing his hair (with the same brush, and, in English translation only, looking into a pocket mirror), savoring a carrot, consulting a map with a compass, carrying both sacks toward the left wing, undressing neatly, exercising, completing his routine, winding his watch, and crawling back into his sack. B's activities are interspersed with consultation of his watch. Beckett stipulates that their respective stage days are to have "à peu près la même durée" (105) [approximately the same duration, 209]. The mime play ends when the goad—now on two wheels—repeats its double dart before A emerges from his sack to pray. Thrust into the light of life, conditioned to the clothes of a culture, the individual may move to his own rhythm, but whatever the tempo, the repetitive cycle is relentless—and lugubriously funny, if it is precisely timed.

On July 2, 1959, Beckett flew to Dublin to be awarded an honorary degree by Trinity College, his alma mater. It was perhaps at that time that a play for Trinity was requested of him. By October 24, deep in the intricacies of "Pim," he declared himself incapable of writing the play. On March 29, 1960, he assigned to Trinity all performance royalties for *Krapp*, requesting no publicity. Returning to 1959, I am arbitrarily assigning four of his eight *foirades* to that year.[6] The French verb *foirer* has several meanings, but two are pertinent for Beckett: to fail, and to have diarrhea. Thus, the unusual noun *foirade* means at once a failure, and a diarrheal excretion. In one form or another, Beckett has affixed both meanings to his writing, so it is not surprising that he uses that French noun for eight brief stories, dating from 1955 to 1975. Subsequently, and with many misgivings, he translated the seven that were written in French, grouping the English eight under the title *Fizzles*.

1959), and in English translation in the periodical *New Departures* (summer 1959). In French they are available in the Minuit volume *Comedie et actes divers* (1972). In Beckett's English translation they are available in Faber's *CDW*.

Au loin un oiseau (*Afar a Bird*)

The title phrase occurs once in the story, in the context of an active "il," who wars with the narrating "je," as in *L'Innommable* a decade earlier. As in the closing pages of that novel, too, breathless phrases are separated by commas. *Au loin*'s three-plus pages of French text constitute a single sentence fragment, lacking a final period. The "je" speaks that fragment, constantly aware of "il." Yet they are both on earth, where birds are far. The story opens: "Terre couverte de ruines" (37) [Ruinstrewn land, 232], and we read that phrase four times in the narrative, so there can be no doubt as to the setting of "il's" quest, which "je" has renounced. "Il" lives a surrogate life and death, with "je" inside him. "Il" looks like earlier Beckett characters: feet splayed, bent over his staff, in long stiff coat; and he seeks to give voice to "je," who banishes him: "mais plus rien sur lui, cette image" (38) [but no more of him, that image, 233]. Even if "il" kills himself because of "je," the latter will subsist in his bones and the sand. In order to bar "je" from "il," the first-person narrator will fill "je's" head with "souvenirs et regrets confus, confusion d'êtres aimés et impossible jeunesse . . . des visages. . . , des noms, des lieux" (39–40) [confusion of memory and lament, of loved ones and impossible youth, . . . faces . . . names, places, 233]. In short, fiction. Shadowing Beckett's own fiction, "il" will confuse his mother and whores, his father and the old tramp Balfe. "Je" will give "il" a mangy old dog to love and lose on this ruinstrewn land, dotted with "petit pas affolés" (40) [little panic steps, 233] by "il." From the subject-object conflict, images and emotions have emerged.

J'ai renoncé avant de naître (*I gave up before birth*)

First published in *Minuit* 2 (January 1973), this *foirade* seems to me to crystallize the inseparability and opposition of "je" and "il," without residue of the ruinstrewn earth. Although the *foirade* begins with a capital letter, it repeats and continues the breathless phrases of *Au loin un oiseau*, this time to a final period. As in *Au loin*, the "je" gave up before birth because "il,"

Whenever this *foirade* was written, *Au loin un oiseau* was first published in 1973 in a deluxe edition illustrated by Beckett's friend Avigdor Arikha (New York: Double Elephant Press; Paris, Fequet & Baudier). The Victoria and Albert Museum catalog to Arikha's 1976 Beckett exhibition describes the edition: "An hitherto unpublished text from the fifties with 5 aquatints [Coat, Ruin, Stick, Stones, Grass]." Otherwise unpublished, it became the sixth *foirade* in the 1976 *Pour finir* volume. Ending without a final period, it seems to be followed by *J'ai renoncé avant de naître*, which is the third *foirade* in the volume.

the other, is born already containing "je." This "il" is not imaged, but the "je" still figures in an inner life. However, this is far from formulaic in the sequence of juxtapositions within their relationship: birth, thought, speech, death, bones, dust, burial—often in the very phrases of the other *foirade*. "Il" alone, not "je," had a life, and he will take his own life, because of "je." Although we read: "il ne dira plus jamais je" (29) [he'll never say I any more, 235], only two dozen words pass before "je" is back in an "il," who will neither speak nor think. Because of "je," "il" will sleep badly, walk badly, be unable to stand still. Finally, as in the other text, but this time unparticularized: "il n'y a plus rien dans sa tête, j'y mettrai le nécessaire" (29) [there's nothing left in his head, I'll feed it all it needs, 235]. At two junctures we read "ici un long silence" [here long silence], as though someone stopped to think in this narrative where speech and thought are coupled; or perhaps, if *Au loin un oiseau* is earlier, several of its contextual phrases have given way to silence. Yet words have fizzled through again.

Horn venait la nuit (Horn came always at night)

Also published in *Minuit* 2, this *foirade* contrasts markedly with its companion. The first word is a proper name, which is virtually unpronounceable in French. Horn, a conveyor of sound in English, is also the subject of the brief opening sentence. Yet it is not Horn but "je" who is the subject of the narrative. Unable to bear being seen, "je" suffered Horn to come at night and remain only five or six minutes. Horn consulted his notes by flashlight, but he spoke in darkness, where, aided by mirrors, "je" inspected his own face. Horn disliked interruptions, but "je" interrupted him with a request to turn his light on his face, then a request to be silent. Once, when "je" asked for light on Horn's face, it remained there for the entire five or six minutes of his visit, and "je" cites several proofs that this took place in outer space. Although "je" thought his traveling days were over, he begins to doubt it. Therefore he gets out of bed and takes a few steps in his room, while holding on to his bed. "Je" has been ruined by a surfeit of athletics in his youth, wearing out the machine (his body?) before its time. When he was over forty, "je" was still throwing the javelin.

It is possible to interpret self-inspection, inspection of the tellingly named Horn, and athletics as forms of mental exercise "afin qu'il me serve de leçon" (34) [that it may be a lesson to me, 230]. The varied length and syntax of the sentences are themselves a form of verbal athletics. Yet this throwback to simple gestures and sentences and to a messenger who clouds the personal issue is couched in prose with a dying fall, whose narrator gleaned nothing from past exertions.

Vieille terre, assez menti (Old earth, no more lies)

Published in *Minuit* 4 as *Foirade IV,* this is the most difficult of the brief, concentrated stories, and it was perhaps written later. Notably, the relationship between the narrator and the narration is radically destabilized. In the very first sentence, we read not only of the familiar "je" and another, but the apostrophized earth is both me and on me.[7] Flat contradiction tends to replace the earlier oppositions, and verb tenses belie their apparent repetition, twisting the speaker into different forms of an object: ". . . quel refus, comme elle me refuse, la tant refusée" (35) [. . . what refusal, how you refuse me, you so refused, 238].

Although this fizzle, like the others, is published in a single paragraph, it falls into three parts. The first apostrophizes the earth. The second introduces the image of the cockchafer (*hanneton* in French, which also implies stupidity). This insect's larvae grow for three years in the earth; then mobile creatures emerge to devour any vegetation in their path, particularly oak leaves. With a whirring sound, they fly at night, perhaps to the river.[8] The third section suddenly shifts to a man in a room, looking out of windows at the sky that gives way to "visages, agonies, les différentes amours, bonheurs aussi" (36) [faces, agonies, loves, the different loves, happiness too, 238]. Pain and faces, love and death, love in death, the narrator longs for calm at his window, but this is denied him: "non, hoquets et spasmes, mer d'une enfance, d'autres ciels, un autre corps" (36) [no, gasps and spasms, a childhood sea, other skies, another body, 239]. This unstable "je," like the cockchafer, battens on the earth, but "je" yearns for the sky during an indeterminate life that is (thrice repeated) *trop tard* (too late).

Unlike the longer *Textes pour rien,* and the abandoned untitled texts, these early *foirades* achieve what is virtually impossible (a word that recurs in *J'ai renoncé* and *Au loin*)—narratives about elusive or unstable subjects, which shift from text to text. As Rubin Rabinovitz showed in some detail, these early *foirades* recapitulate in truncated form the quest fiction that Beckett wrote before midcentury. However, such narration could not be sustained, and in the same issue of *Minuit* as *Vieille terre,* Beckett published a different kind of narrative with a large number of beings in a lunar landscape, which was probably written in the 1960s.[9]

Despite the residual journeys of these early *foirades,* Beckett's major occupation during 1959 was what became *Comment c'est.* The first of five revision-gnarled notebooks was begun on December 17, 1958, and the fifth is dated January 6, 1960, but revision was not completed until July of the latter year. Before the end of 1959, however, Beckett published two excerpts in ephemeral avant-garde periodicals: In November *L'Image* appeared in French in a new English periodical *X* (which lasted three years), and in

December "Découverte de Pim" appeared in the French *L'VII*. They are still cast in punctuated sentences. It was in revision of the whole that Beckett conceived the verset format.

L'Image [The Image]

L'Image is a solid block of words, like much of Beckett's post-*L'Innommable* short fiction. *L'Image* opens on a noun—the tongue, which takes up a mouthful of mud and hesitates about whether to swallow it or spit it out. Without deciding, the narrator shifts from tongue to hands. The right hand grasps a sack, but the left hand has a quasi-independent existence. The narrative then briefly situates legs and eyes. The first-person possessive pronouns for these body parts lack self-consciousness: "je dis me comme je dis je comme je dirais il parce que ça m'amuse" (11) [I say me as I say I as I would say he because it amuses me]. Without transition, the "je" sees himself at age sixteen on a beautiful day of April or May. He holds the hand of his girlfriend, whose other hand holds a leash attached to a gray terrier. The meadow is full of lambs and their mothers. Briefly, the narrator marvels at his descriptions of flowers and animals, but then accepts them, in what seems to be developing into a love scene of a couple who climb a mountain to have a picnic. The couple is at first motionless, but soon they shift the holding hands. A strange digression occurs: "j'ai l'absurde impression que nous me regardons je rentre la langue ferme la bouche et souris" (14) [I have the absurd impression that we are looking at me I pull back my tongue close my mouth and smile].

Abruptly the lovers are deromanticized: the girl is ugly, the protagonist is odd of dress and stance. They move, and when the dog moves with them, the occasionalist Malebranche is invoked: "il a eu le même idée au même instant" (15) [it had the same idea at the same instant]. Before the couple's three-hour climb up the mountain the narrator ruptures the idyllic scene: "j'ai envie de crier plaque-la là et cours t'ouvrir les veines" (15–16) [I want to shout leave her there and rush to slit your vein]. When the couple picnic in a lovely landscape, the narrator undercuts their endearments with the rhythm of their mastication. After a brief fog, the couple recede into the distance; the dog vanishes, and the sheep are as still as granite, but an immobile horse is newly visible: "les bêtes savent" (17). We do not learn what animals know,

---

Drawn from the second of the five "Pim" notebooks, (i.e., *Comment c'est*), *L'Image* also exists in a separate typescript, both held at HRC. First published in *X* (November 1959), it was republished in its own volume by Minuit in 1988, presumably with Beckett's permission. In 1990, after Beckett's death, it was anonymously translated and published by John Calder in *As the Story Was Told,* which occasioned a flurry of disapproving letters. It is included in *CSP* in a translation by Edith Fournier. For my purposes, I have translated phrases myself.

but the contrast is clear with the self-conscious narrator who observes his own hand in the mud. He is still smiling, although "ce n'est plus la peine" (18) [it's no longer worth the effort]. The tongue reaches into the mud, but it is not thirsty. It draws back into the mouth, which closes, probably in a straight line. The narrator has made the image.

For all the unpunctuated, unconcatenated phrases, that image is incisively etched. Each object, each gesture is precisely limned, even to the number of degrees in the angle of the young lover's splayed feet. From the tongue reaching down into the mud to its reentrance into the straight-line mouth, each detail is isolated. Framed by the mud-dipping tongue, the vivid scene— an image in slow motion—is at once specific and resonant in its detail; disrupted and continuous in its action; touching and hilarious in its account of young love. In a 1939 poem, "Arènes de Lutèce," Beckett had already introduced a narrator who watches himself, but in *L'Image* the narrator has the absurd impression that the image reflects back on its creator. No longer wrestling with the subject-object conundrum, Beckett will weave the image deftly into the novel-long narrator/narrated of *Comment c'est*.[10]

1960

Comment c'est (How It Is)

This novel, at first titled "Pim," was insuperably difficult for Beckett. Five manuscript notebooks are fraught with revision, and not until the fifth note-

---

HRC holds the five "Pim" notebooks, begun December 17, 1958, and completed January 6, 1960, which became *Comment c'est*. "There are extensive revisions, deletions, and additions throughout" (Lake, 119). A sixth notebook, containing further revisions, was completed on June 7, 1960. The first four notebooks and the first typescript show (relatively) conventional punctuation. Versets erupt in the fifth notebook. The excerpt "Découverte de Pim," published in the French review *L'VII* in December 1959, sports paragraph-long sentences, punctuated by commas. At some point after the first typescript Beckett thought of a block format, running phrases together, unalleviated by any punctuation. *L'Image*, published in *X*, dates from this phase of his composition. The second typescript displays the versets of the final version, which was published by Minuit in 1961. Before that, *Evergreen Review* (September–October 1960) published Beckett's English translation of the first eight pages (in versets, but with variants) under the title "From an Unabandoned Work." Prior to the 1964 Grove publication of *How It Is*, excerpts (in versets, but with variants) were published in July 1962 in *Arna: University of Sidney Review*; in summer–fall 1962 in *Paris Review*. The conclusion was published in summer 1963 in *Transatlantic Review*. Beckett's difficulties with this recalcitrant text and its translation are thus traceable in manuscripts and publication of excerpts.

book did Beckett conceive of unpunctuated versets of varying length, themselves usually composed of short noun phrases. Not only was the material itself intractable, but Beckett translated certain passages while still revising the French text. His two versions differ markedly, for French tonic rhythm contrasts with English accentual rhythm, and this is especially noticeable in small word groups.[11] Puns sometimes defeated Beckett, beginning with the title. *Comment c'est*, pronounced exactly like *commencer* [to begin], is rendered in English by the more stolid *How It Is*. In French and English, however, the three-word, three-syllable title opens interrogatively, and ends in a minimal statement.

Before plunging into substance and form of what the French book cover labels "roman," I want to dwell a moment on its visual aspect in print. Given Beckett's love-hate relationship with words, and his protagonists' yearning for silence, the spatial analogue would be a blank page. *Comment c'est* seizes on that analogue. Often repeated in the text is the fact that words come only when the panting stops. During the fictional panting in the mud the actual page space is blank, and that facilitates reading the unpunctuated prose—a facilitation that is noted in the text: "les blancs sont les trous sinon ça coule" (104) [the gaps are the holes otherwise it flows, 84]. When the fictional panting stops, the narrator can hear words that were once outside him, but are now within. Those words seek to convey this latest version of the narrator's life. Sustaining that novel-long tension of words versus silence, the versets vary from one word (rare) to over a hundred. Within each verset, however, we read in short phrases. One of the many problems of commentary resides in the richness of each verset—the repetitions, nuances, and singularities; the stripped grammar and global reach, the occasional Latinate polysyllable among the monosyllables, the erudition within the melody.[12]

None of these complexities enters Beckett's summary to Donald McWhinnie:

> A "man" is lying panting in the mud and dark murmuring his "life" as he hears it obscurely uttered by a voice inside him. . . . The work is in three parts, the first a solitary journey in the dark and mud terminating with discovery of a similar creature known as Pim, the second life with Pim both motionless in the dark and mud terminating with departure of Pim, the third solitude motionless in the dark and mud. It is in the third part that occur the so-called voice "quaqua," its interiorisation and murmuring forth when the panting stops. (Qtd. in Knowlson, 413)

After the explicitly designated invocation, paragraph or verset 3 concludes: "les murmures dans la boue," and that mud has been traced to the fifth circle of Dante's *Inferno*, where the Wrathful, naked in the mud, maul each other cruelly. However, Dante's mud is swiftly negotiated by the visitors, whereas Beckett's mud is eternal and ubiquitous. He had already quoted Leopardi in his monograph on Proust—"E fango è il mondo" [and mud is the world]—and he now creates that world. Mud is an inspired metaphor for consciousness—warm and traversable. Above the novel's mud is life in the light, with its dreams, memories, and fantasies, but the mud itself is a performative medium: curtains can open within it, as in the theater; images and scenes can vanish through cinematic blackouts. For all the theatricality of the scenes, we are continually reimmersed in a muddy darkness and silence.

Mud is not Beckett's only debt to Dante. The number three is emphasized—sacred to the Florentine, but arbitrarily chosen by the French-writing Irishman.[13] Like *La Divina Commedia*, *Comment c'est* has a tripartite structure, and like that epic each part ends climactically: Beckett's part 1 closes when the narrator feels Pim's buttock, and part 2 closes when Pim abandons the narrator: "moi seul dans le noir la boue" [alone in the mud yes the dark]. The whole terminates in a resolution of sorts: Dante's pilgrim finds redemption in heavenly love, and Beckett's narrator experiences a kind of relief in his forthcoming death: "JE VAIS CREVER hurlements bon" [I SHALL DIE screams good]. Although Beckett's narrator lacks a Virgil in his Inferno, he creates guidance by inventing creatures to feel his pain.

The very first verset of *Comment c'est* announces the narrative as a quotation: "je cite . . . je le dis comme je l'entends." Almost immediately, however, a seeming contradiction arises: "voix d'abord dehors . . . puis en moi" (9). The voice is both an utterance and a quotation, first outside and then within. Unpunctuated with quotation marks, the words of the voice are only occasionally the subject of inquiry as to their source, as was the case in earlier Beckett fiction. The voice early promises "songes, souvenirs, bribes," but dreams and memories, redolent of "ma vie dernière état," elongate the "bribes" into coherent if unpunctuated declarative sentences. Soon the voice reaches for a listener and a writer: "un qui écoute un autre qui note ou le même" (10) [someone listening another noting or the same, 7]. In the central event of the novel, the meeting of the narrator and Pim—or rather the narrator's education of Pim—we read the roman capital letters inscribed on Pim's back, but his responses are quoted. Thus, language—oral and written—literally enters the narrative, and for many critics it *is* the narrative. However, this is to ignore the intricate plot, the ephemeral characters, the striking setting, and the indefinition through accretions, contradictions, and qualifications.[14]

In print the novel's title is followed by the arabic numeral 1, resplendent on a page of its own. On the first page of text we see versets of approximately equal length. Number and verset announce a radically new form. Not only will the arabic 1 eventually be followed after some fifty pages by 2, and after some sixty pages by 3, but the tripartite structure of the work will often call attention to itself. The three parts are named in the very first verset—"avant Pim avec Pim après Pim"; or, by the middle of part 1, "le voyage le couple l'abandon" (24). In part 3, however, this becomes "avant moi avec moi après moi" (127). Structurally, the narrative thus announces a rigor, even a rigidity, that seems the antithesis of earlier Beckett fragmentation. One does not have to read very far, however, to realize that there is spillage; meeting with Pim and abandon by Pim are already and repetitively prophesied in part 1. Beckett described the situation: "the 'I' is from the outset in the third part and the first and second, though stated as heard in the present, already over" (qtd. in Knowlson, 413). Even Beckett's explication implies the novel's erosion of time, which suffuses the text: "ces mots encore ces jours nuits années saisons cette famille" (21) [these words here again days nights years seasons that family, 17].

The triune plot is repetitively asserted, and repetitively interrupted. Lest we lose the thread, however, we are hammered with the insistent phrase: "on parle de . . ." before subjects as various as a sack, a hand, memory, a can opener, the species, fingernails, a foot, holes, a life, a voice, breath, the track, and diverse pronouns. Irregularly, a verset of summary reviews events up to that point—"récapitulons." Not only do events break out of their respective boundaries, but so do images. Part 1 presents several images, not always designated by that word—a memory of scissoring a butterfly's wings, a child praying at his mother's knees, a hand pulling a crocus on a string, a dream of Christ in an alb, and the extended scene of adolescent love, which is announced as the last image, but which is nevertheless followed by others—an Eastern sage whose nails grow through his palms, Pim's watch ticking timelessly, the sexuality and hospitalization of Pam Prim, and especially the narrator's instruction of Pim. The very word *image* seems restricted to the narrator's memories or dreams, whereas Pim enters into scenes. In part 3 images thin out, and yet they are recalled nostalgically: "quelques vieilles images toujours les mêmes plus de bleu fini le bleu jamais été le sac les bras le corps la boue le noir cheveux et ongles qui vivent tout ça" (129) [a few old images always the same no more blue the blue is done never was the sack the arms the body the mud the dark living hair and nails all that, 109]. Remarkably condensed, the medley turns away from the blue of imagination to focus on the materiality of living tissue. As there was structural spillage, so there is image spillage from the englobing mud gifted with sacks, to the tales that take life therein.

It is often said that there are no characters in *Comment c'est,* and yet Beckett began the novel with the proper name Pim, which puns in French on *pain* or bread, the so-called staff of life. Other proper names rhyme (or slant-rhyme) with Pim—the alternative partner Bom (which puns on *bon* or good), the wife Pam Prim, the observer Kram and the note-taker Krim (punning on German *Krimkram* or junk), and even a dog Skom Skum (with an unsavory flavor in English)—"m à la fin et une syllabe le reste égal" (75) [m at the end and one syllable the rest indifferent, 60]. The terminal *m* has replaced the initial *M* of earlier Beckett names. Not mentioned in the text is Beckett's own name, Sam, which may occur to readers. It is true that none of the novel's monosyllabic names develops into characters, and yet their imagistic import grows through incremental repetition.

Pim and Bom have a history in earlier Beckett works. In the story *Yellow* of *More Pricks Than Kicks* Bim and Bom are unidentified, but they are grouped with Grock, the Swiss clown whose humor derived from human impotence, and with Democritus, the Greek philosopher who laughed at metaphysics. In Beckett's novel *Murphy* Bim and Bom Clinch are the sadistic attendants of the Magdalen Mental Mercyseat. In the first published version of *En attendant Godot,* in a passage later deleted, Estragon compares Pozzo and Lucky to Bim and Bom "les comiques staliniens" (56). Bim and Bom were Russian clowns who wrapped criticism of the Soviet regime in a cloak of laughter. In a draft of what became *Fin de partie* the predecessor of Mère Pegg is called Bim or Bom. It would appear that Beckett found the monosyllables Bim and Bom to be imbued with a blend of the cruel and the comic. In *Comment c'est* Pim and Bom do not form a couple, as in prior works, and yet they are joined through the first-person narrator, who recounts his instruction of Pim, and who pointedly refrains from an account of his own victimization by Bom, which would be redundant.

Pim's instruction makes painful reading, and yet the narrator is also able to put himself in Pim's mind, even though he later affirms: "jamais eu de Pim jamais eu de voix" (91) [never any Pim never any voice, 74]. Je, Pim, and Bom may coalesce, but indelibly etched is a tiny figure in the mud, trying to escape torture by reciting the story of his life, whether "LA-HAUT DANS LA LUMIERE" or "ICI AVANT MOI" (88, 90) [ABOVE . . . IN THE LIGHT or HERE BEFORE ME 72, 73].

No character can vie with Pim in importance, but Pam Prim takes on a certain contour. With love grown cold, she jumps or falls from a window and breaks her spine; in the hospital she cannot turn her head to see the flowers, but on her deathbed she forgives everyone. Flagrant in her woes, Pam Prim figures in a pietà. Yet more narrative attention is accorded to Kram and Krim. First named toward the end of part 2, Kram soon elides into Krim, but then they are reseparated, and Kram is traced to the thirteenth generation, before he and Krim exchange roles. Toward the end of part 3 they are reintroduced: "Kram qui écoute Krim qui note ou Kram seul" (161) [Kram who listens Krim who notes or Kram alone, 133]. However nonrealistic the scene, one part of the mind observes it, and the other finds words for it, to be delivered in "cette voix anonyme," in which we all constitute ourselves by the memory of our lives.

Rhyming names, tripartite plot, ubiquitous mud, and a tin-filled sack that sustains a figure moving through indefinite but vast tracts of time—these are the nominal ingredients of *Comment c'est,* but digression is as frequent as repetition. The narrator himself mentions his considerable education—anatomy, arithmetic, astronomy, geography, geometry, humanities, mathematics, natural history, and physics. Not only does the narrator sprinkle his monosyllables with polysyllables, but he also carelessly calls up rather obscure proper names—Belacqua, Malebranche, and Heraclitus, who are familiar Beckett references; and, newly relevant, Erebus, Haeckel, Klopstock, Thalia. Such proper names stand out from the oral quality of the versets, laced as they are with colloquialisms, but the narrator also refers to marks of writing—commas and parentheses, which are absent from the text we read.

It is the text we read that is a veritable tour de force. The grammar may be "midget," but it is inviolate. The word *bribes* [scraps] is repeated some fifty times, and each verset is built of sentence scraps. In spite of a paucity of copulative verbs, the meaning is rarely in question. However, a word may resonate in two successive phrases, or a word will end one verset and be immediately salvaged to begin the following one, shifting the emphasis. This narrator, like earlier Beckett storytellers, plays with third- and first-person pronouns, but his main grammatical concern is verbs in this timeless tale, where words like *jour* and *année* are suspect. Past, present, future, and conditional tenses are mentioned in the text, and subjunctives are suggested by the repeated interrogatives. One has to be very sure of French grammar to read this "grammaire d'oiseau" (94) [midget grammar, 76].

Skillfully as Beckett juggles phrases, *Comment c'est* is emotionally enthralling in its resolutely unsentimental intensities, nuanced by humor. Muddy setting, shifting and skeletal plot, rhyming monosyllabic names, minimal objects set in odd contexts—"quelque chose là qui ne va pas" [something wrong there]—are themselves faintly comic. Quite farcical are the ungainly teenager and his ugly girlfriend, accompanied by her genital-absorbed dog. Horrific as Pim's torture is, it can have a comic edge as well: "suite de dressage pas la peine sautons" (85) [training continued no point skip, 69]. Skip though we may, the scene bleeds with the narrator's pain, as well as that of Pim, who is once called "pauvre." Nevertheless, comic kernels are discernible: a sack of cans that jangle like castenets; the possibility that Pim's language may be Italian, which is unknown to the narrator (although not to Beckett); the fixing on the name Pim because it is "moins anonyme" (74); the expletive "foutre" excused by "je cite" (159). One verset opens "tant de mots tant de perdus" (116) [so many words so many lost, 95] when the losses caused by elision are ubiquitous in the text. A brief verset plays on "Dieu" as agonizing absence and thoughtless blasphemy: "Dieu sur Dieu désespoir de cause confusion complète s'il y croyait il y croyait puis pas plus moyen ses raisons dans les deux cas mon Dieu" (91) [God on God desperation utter confusion did he believe he believed then not couldn't any more his reasons both cases my God, 74].

My quotation of even an entire verset loses resonance because the fabric of *Comment c'est* is so tightly woven, and the novelistic build of the work is unquotable. Difficult as the text is to read, Beckett immerses us gradually. The early versets are short and compassable, but soon they lengthen and climax in part 1 on *L'Image*. It is illuminating to contrast a verset with an excerpt from the block-original in *L'Image*:

> la tête rejetée en arrière nous regardons j'imagine droit devant nous immobilité de statue à part les bras aux mains entrelacées qui se balancent (12)

> [heads thrown back we gaze I imagine before us still as statues save only the swinging arms with hands clasped (66)]

> la tête haute nous regardons j'imagine nous avons j'imagine les yeux ouverts et regardons droit devant nous immobilité de statue de part et d'autre à part les bras qui se balancent ceux aux mains entrelacées quoi encore (35)

> [Heads high we gaze I imagine we have I imagine our eyes open and gaze before us still as statues save only the swinging arms those with hands clasped what else (29)]

The verset is musicalized by increased repetition, and the French introduces the shades of different meaning in the word *part*. The double "j'imagine" underlines the scene as a composition, and this is emphasized by the final question *quoi encore*.

Toward the end of part 2, the versets grow in length and abstraction; like Pim, we suffer instruction. Part 3, with its abstractions and arithmetic, is the most difficult to read, and that part is sprinkled with recurrent references to "notre justice," affirmed by the refrain "c'est juste," which can mean both "It is just" and "It is accurate." The narrator tries to salvage "notre justice une seule vie partout mal dite mal entendue" (162) [our justice one life everywhere ill-told ill-heard, 134]. Abbott links this with Beckett's subversion of the epic tradition: "Bringing to ruin the epic of containment and radiant design, Beckett concentrated attention on the wonders of origination" (1994, 120).

As the end of the novel approaches, the narrator looks longingly toward that end: "pour en finir avec cette voix autant dire cette vie" (174) [to have done with this voice namely this life, 144]. Yet the form of the actual end is carefully prepared: "sous la forme familière de questions que je me poserais moi et de réponses que je me ferais moi aussi invraisemblable que cela puisse paraître" (174) [in the familiar form of questions I am said to ask myself and answers I am said to give myself however unlikely that may appear, 144]. By the end of *Comment c'est*, however, that final inner turmoil is not at all "unlikely."

Betraying Beckett's subliminal intention to eschew lyricism, I end my commentary on *Comment c'est* by quoting two versets, whose beauty seems to me self-evident:

> je vois toutes grandeurs nature comprise si c'est la mienne ça s'allume dans la boue la prière la tête sur la table le crocus le vieux en larmes les larmes derrière les mains des ciels toutes sortes différentes sortes sur terre sur mer du bleu soudain or et vert de la terre soudain dans la boue (26)

> [I see all sizes life included if that's mine the light goes on in the mud the prayer the head on the table the crocus the old man in tears the tears behind the hands skies all sorts different sorts on land and sea blue of a sudden gold and green of the earth of a sudden in the mud (21)]

Compressed into some fifty words are not only echoes of Beckett's previous soulscapes, but, more globally, we pierce the glories and the sorrows of the world, as perceived by human beings. Perhaps the genus is clonable; certainly it is interplanetable. The quoted passage seems to me to foresee the comico-pathetic nature of the species.

In contrast, my last quotation is virtually self-sufficient:

> sur le bas-ventre boueux j'ai vu un jour faste pace Héraclite l'Obscur au plus haut de l'azur entre les grandes ailes noires étendues immo-biles vu suspendu le corps de neige de je ne sais quel oiseau voilier l'al-batros hurleur des mers australes l'histoire que j'avais mon Dieu la naturelle les bons moments que j'avais (42)

> [on the muddy belly I saw one blessed day saving the grace of Hera-clitus the Obscure at the pitch of heaven's azure towering between its great black still spread wings the snowy body of I know not what frigate-bird the screaming albatross of the southern seas the history I knew my God the natural the good moments I had (34)]

And *we* have good moments in visualizing this extraordinary white bird with black wings, even if Heraclitus (no more obscure than the narrator) denies that we can step into the same mud twice. This unnatural natural history is blessed with oppositions and contradictions, in which perhaps lies our hope.

It required the seclusion of Ussy to enable Beckett to complete *Comment c'est*. Back in Paris, demands on his time accelerated. With increasing fame, he resolutely refused interviews, but he was generous to scholars who studied his work. As his papers and books accumulated, his small apartment near rue de Vaugirard seemed daily smaller. In spite of delays in construction of the new apartment, Beckett occasionally tried to write there, even before it was habitable. However, it was at Ussy that he began a work that proved sustainable—a play in English that would grow into *Happy Days*. From Paris he wrote Alan Schneider on September 23, 1960: "I don't see the play at all clearly, but a little more so. The figure is a woman as far as I can see. Bright light, flowers and a large handbag containing all vital necessities from revolver to lipstick. Would like to try it in English but fear it will have to be in French again" (Harmon, 74). As we know, he managed it in English.

1961

Happy Days

After the difficult prose poetry of *Comment c'est,* Beckett may have sought relief in a change of language and genre. What began as a "Female solo" shifted rather abruptly to a middle-class marriage, then evolved back toward its original genre, so dominant is his final Winnie. Beckett's male-figure disappears offstage between his first and second holographs, which are separated by a mere two days. In contrast to *Fin de partie*, where Beckett in manuscript eclipsed two acts into one, he doubled the initial act of what was not yet called *Happy Days*. Of the nine steps of composition (a fortuitous birth-figure), step 6 has fascinated Beckett scholars because of the author's nota-

---

Admussen, Gontarski 1977, and Pountney describe the manuscripts of *Happy Days,* and I draw upon their work, although I have fingered the manuscripts at RUL and OSU.

Step 1 is found in the Eté '56 Notebook at RUL. It consists of an incomplete holograph and general notes; begun October 8, 1960, it lacks a final date.

Step 2 (H-1) at OSU. First full holograph version, in one act; begun October 8, 1960, and completed January 14, 1961.

Step 3 (TS-1) at OSU. First typescript in one act is undated.

Step 4 (H-2) at OSU. Second holograph version, acts 1 and 2; act 1, January 16–20, 1961; act 2, February 2–7, 1961.

Step 5 (TS-1) at OSU. First typescript, act 2 only; no date.

Step 6 (TS-2) at OSU. Second typescript, acts 1 and 2; act 2 probably typed before act 1; no date.

tion to himself: "Vaguen"—a despecifying process that would become habitual in the composition of his drama.

Beckett not only changed language and genre, but also gender and ambience in this new example of "fresh elements and motifs." Ubiquitous dark mud is replaced by a desiccated earth under a never-setting sun, and the naked male horizontal figure is supplanted by an upright, if buried, woman. The new gender also entails a feminine, object-laden world. A can opener was incongruous in the primeval slime of *Comment c'est,* but, as Winnie intones repetitively, everything is "strange" in the changeless heat of *Happy Days.* The concealed variety of the novel precipitates into the cruel invariant etching of Winnie in her grave, and yet death is withheld.

Despite these obvious contrasts between these closely spaced works, Beckett nevertheless infused *Happy Days* with scraps of *Comment c'est.* The image is more brightly lit, but it too contains a life-sustaining sack/bag and an ineffectual prayer. In both works the solitary protagonist describes a couple who are holding hands, and in both works a life story is narrated. In both works timebound words are viewed skeptically—"cette famille" in the novel, "old style" in the play. Most strikingly similar is the shape of habitual utterance—fragmented into phrases where negation, interrogation, and repetition proliferate. (In *Happy Days* repetition is more evident to the reader than the spectator; time and again Beckett writes "do" in his scenic directions, a conventional abbreviation of *ditto,* but also an injunction to do or perform.) These resemblances underscore the specific theme of imposing pattern on chaos, and the global theme of irresistible entropy. Beckett's sequential compositions deftly blend the strange and the familiar as specks in eternity.

Winnie says that objects have a life of their own, but it is she who endows them with life, through word and gesture, which are rarely simultaneous. Her early prayer closes, "World without end," and her world is liter-

---

Step 7 (H-3) at OSU. Third holograph, act 1, March 29–May 12, 1961; act 2, May 13–14, 1961.

Step 8 (TS-3) at OSU. Third typescript, acts 1 and 2, no date (close to final version).

Step 9 (TS-4) at OSU. Fourth typescript, acts 1 and 2, no date, with indications of the sources of Winnie's quotations, which, however, are gradually introduced from H-1 on. Gontarski's table shows where each quotation was introduced.

Both Gontarski (1977) and Pountney trace the evolution of the play from a somewhat realistic middle-aged marriage to the cosmic resonance of the final *Happy Days.* The play was published by Grove (1961) and by Calder (1962). Beckett's French translation *Oh les beaux jours* was published by Minuit (1963) and by *l'Avant-Scène* (June 15, 1964). James Knowlson has edited a useful bilingual edition (Faber, 1978), as well as a production notebook (Faber, 1985) and (Grove, 1986).

ally without end. Winnie is that human fragment within eternity who realizes, by act 2, that time itself is "old style." Over a decade earlier, Pozzo of *Godot* cautioned Vladimir not to believe that time had stopped. Winnie is faced with the same dramatic infinitude.

It is by a rasping bell that Winnie is forced into consciousness—after a few seconds in act 1, "at once" in act 2. In act 1 she begins her bell-bound day with prayer, but soon deity becomes a mere expletive as she marshals her resources for conquering the time of each day: objects and her husband Willie, composition of a story in act 2. As Beckett noted in a letter to Alan Schneider: "Times when she can't speak, times when she can't move" (Harmon, 95). She is bolstered by the unexpected—memories and two events; most of the former are erotically tinged, and the minimal latter range low and high—a crawling emmet and an exploding parasol. Determinedly, Winnie endures each happy day by following a routine; she carefully deploys objects, husband, prayer, and, in act 2, her story. In both acts she survives by talking her way through each day—"old style." Although her quotations from English verse have given happy days to Beckett scholars, they are not part of her strategic arsenal, but are triggered by emotional association. To judge by quantity, Shakespeare is her favorite author, since she draws upon *Hamlet, Romeo and Juliet, Cymbeline,* and *Twelfth Night.* Milton's *Paradise Lost* is all but lost in her double evocation of its "holy light." In act 1 she quotes (and sometimes misquotes) from the Khayyam-Fitzgerald *Rubaiyat,* Gray's "Ode on a Distant Prospect of Eton College," and Browning's *Paracelsus.* Like Winnie's own speech, her quotations are more spare in act 2—Keats's "Ode to a Nightingale," Yeats's *At the Hawk's Well,* Herrick's "To the Virgins to Make Much of Time." She praises the maudlin line of Charles Wolfe as "exquisite," and she has forgotten other "unforgettable" and "immortal" lines. Her truncated and sometimes erroneous quotations are at once the residue of a "nice" literary education and a wink from Beckett to us, over Winnie's head. If we know the poems, we recognize an ironic context—pain, death, madness, dereliction, and desolation—that belies Winnie's repeated declarations of her happy day.

Climatically, that day at first seems heavenly, with its golden sun, but we soon share Winnie's discomfort under its relentless glare. The colloquial phrase for decrepitude—one foot in the grave—is extrapolated by Beckett to become one of the indelible images of modern drama. A female upper torso bakes in a blaze of hellish sun. Yet Winnie "keeps herself nice" in this inferno—brushing her teeth, rouging her lips, filing her nails, uncrumpling the feather on her hat, addressing commands to herself, engaging her husband in verbal intercourse. For the most part, her activities are dependably routine in this incongruous context, but Willie is unpredictable.

In the Beckett tradition of contrasting members of a pair, Winnie and

Willie are opposites, in spite of their nearly identical names. (Moreover, their initial *W* turns Beckett's beloved *M* upside down.) Female versus male, refined versus coarse, loquacious versus taciturn, Winnie and Willie were compared by their creator to a bird and a turtle. Certainly Winnie's pecking and singing are birdlike, and the adverb *up* chirps through her monologue— "bobs up," "bubbles up," "drift up," "floats up," "putting up," "holding up," "stuck up," "well up," "bring up," "ran up," and "sucked up." If Willie is a turtle, however, he is quite accommodating under his carapace. His very first gesture is to return Winnie's dropped parasol. He lends her his cherished pornographic postcard; he solves her grammatical problem about hair; he responds five times with *Yes* to her questions, and for her he repeats: "Fear no more." He identifies the burden and the motion of the emmet, and he joins Winnie in laughter. Although he occasionally expresses irritation, he never reproaches Winnie for the injuries he suffers. His name is British slang for a penis, and he puzzles suggestively over her phrase "*Sucked* up?" He shows more fingers than Winnie requests, and he hums to her music-box melody. In his most extended speech, he defines "hog" self-reflexively. In act 2 we learn that he has given Winnie her bag and parasol, as well as his revolver—the only objects in Winnie's reduced world. Willie may be taciturn, but he is companionable, climaxing in his act 2 appearance "dressed to kill." His single uttered monosyllable of act 2 puns on Winnie's name—and gives no clue as to his intention.

For all Willie's husbandry, *Happy Days* is Winnie's play, and actresses have viewed its challenge as a Hamletic summit. In a moribund stage world an actress, having memorized a killing part, has to enact a moribund woman, who is denied the mercy of death. As *Comment c'est* resorts to images, numbers, and capital letters to engulf us in our own situation, *Happy Days* does so more simply. The residual lyricism of quotation is bent by Winnie toward resolute cheer, but chinks riddle her stance, such as the dubious efficacy of divine help: "prayers perhaps not for naught" (140). Wavering between Pandora and Cassandra, she utters an awareness that many of us have known: "To have been always what I am—and so changed from what I was" (161). Although she calls Willie's attention to her verbal "heights" (154), she is also intermittently aware that "even words fail, at times" (147). Although words do not fail *her* for the duration of the stage happy days, Beckett conveys a feeling of their failure through her frequent pauses, self-interruptions, and constant qualifiers—"hardly any," "so far," "after all," "not quite," "not yet," "not all," "for the moment." Sometimes her words hide prophecies. In act 1 she predicts that the earth may cover her breasts, and she wishes that Willie would come to her side of the mound. These events happen in act 2. Toward the end of act 1 she says once what will become habitual in act 2, when she corrects: " I used to . . ." to "I say I used to . . ." Even memory precipitates to the momentary immediacy of her words. In the middle of act 1 Winnie asks Willie: "Was I lovable once, Willie? Was I ever lovable?" (150). Beckett's achievement—and it is hard to state this unsentimentally—has been to create a lovable woman in an impossible situation, which is also an image of the mortal condition.

Winnie begins her day with a childishly endearing self-command—a prelude to her many self-addresses. Soon she animates the inanimate: she nicknames and speaks to the revolver, she endows both the revolver and her fingernail with gender (him), and she mentions an emmet's arms. Long before she narrates her story she exhibits a winning talent for imitation—of Willie, of Mr. Shower/Cooker and his wife or fiancée. Winnie is ashamed when sorrow intrudes, lowering her head when her voice breaks. The more painfully we are immersed in Winnie's situation, the more we can appreciate her courageous enumeration of "great," "tender," "many," or "abounding mercies" (Beckett's manuscripts reveal that he considered the titles *Great Mercies, Tender Mercies, Many Mercies*).

Winnie's lovability is enhanced in the contrast between acts 1 and 2. Pre-eminent is the burial of her entire torso. The act 1 delay in her response to the bell shrinks to an immediate alertness in act 2. When she summons the energy to speak, it is no longer a prayer but a residual (Miltonic) acknowledgment of the tradition of light as life: "Hail, holy light"—even though the sunlight has treated her cruelly. Tacitly, she acknowledges our attention—still looking at her, still caring for her. We may not realize that she has forgotten her "unforgettable line," but we are probably aware of the depletion of her quotations over the course of act 2. Although she can no longer forage in her bag, she is cheered by its visible presence. Lacking facility with objects, she converts her face into a prop that may sustain her. In act 1 Winnie can stretch the inscription on her toothbrush to a persistent preoccupation, but there is no print to offer her solace in act 2. In compensation, her memories augment; in addition to kisses and Charlie Hunter, she recalls Willie's admiring words, gifts, proposal, and wedding. Although she continues to address an absent Willie, her endearments diminish. Eroticism threads in and out of Winnie's memories, but it is explicit in the pornographic postcard of act 1, and in her story of act 2. However, she conceals her prurience toward the card, and she displaces sexual fear to fictional Millie's screams at a mouse running up her thigh. Although Winnie phrases the departure of the Shower/Cooker couple identically in the two acts—"Last human kind to stray this way"—she adds an improbable qualifier in act 2: "Up to date." If Winnie is occasionally irritated—but more often grateful—with Willie in act 1, she is alternately scornful and encouraging to his visible presence in act 2. Her meaningful music-box melody—*merry* widow—is merely hummed in act 1, but in act 2 she sings the banal lying words. Although both acts carry her present-tense declarations of happiness, they are ironically subverted by her final future-perfect tense: "this will have been another happy day!" (159).

The finale of *Happy Days* (over which Beckett labored in composition) undermines a recurrent expressive pattern. Some dozen times in act 1 Winnie utters a few monosyllables; then she smiles, after which she utters two syllables ("old style" or "no no"), before she stops smiling. By act 2 this pattern usually changes to syllables, smile, syllables, broader smile, syllables "old style" or "no no," smile off. With less to smile at, Winnie's smile broadens. At the last, however, it is not her own fragmentary speech but the *Merry Widow* lyrics that prompt her smile to Willie. This time she utters no syllables before "smile off."

Before Beckett stopped revising *Happy Days*, he and Suzanne traveled in February to Bielefeld, Germany, for the premiere of the Mihalovici opera of *Krapp*. Although Beckett made no public statement about the work, he was evidently caught off guard in a bookstore, and his remarks were later quoted in German theater programs:

> For me, the theatre is not a moral institution in Schiller's sense. I want neither to instruct nor to improve nor to keep people from getting bored. I want to bring poetry into drama, a poetry which has been through the void and makes a new start in a new room-space. (Qtd. in Knowlson, 427)[15]

Although the Becketts socialized affably with the musicians, the milieu soon palled. With his German translator, Elmar Tophoven, Beckett drove off to Amsterdam to recover in museums. Back in Paris in March, he and Suzanne decided to be married, without fuss or festivity. For testamentary reasons an English registry was necessary, and Beckett's British publisher John Calder arranged for a Folkstone civil ceremony, predicated on Beckett establishing two weeks' residence there. No sooner was Beckett back in Paris than he was interrupted in his revision of the Winnie-Willie marriage by a revival of *Godot*—with a tree by Giacometti replacing the coat hangers of the premiere nearly a decade ago. Far more than then, he made his presence felt at rehearsals.

Once *Happy Days* was in the mail to his publishers, Beckett flew to London in June to discuss a Royal Court production—and to see McWhinnie's television *Godot*. He was disappointed: "My play was written for small men locked in a big space. Here you're all too big for the place" (qtd. in Knowlson, 436). He was also disappointed by a dull cricket game at Lord's. Back at Ussy, he discovered that his cottage had been burgled and trashed, but his papers and books were merely scattered, rather than missing. For someone as orderly as Beckett, this was an irritation, but at least it did not occur while he was in the throes of new work.

Early in 1961 he had accepted a commission from the BBC to compose a radio play, to be accompanied by the music of his cousin, John Beckett— "a text-music tandem" (Zilliacus 1976, 99). In March John had an automobile accident, which delayed his work, but Beckett produced a script by November, for which John wrote the music independently. Both Beckett cousins eventually found the music unsatisfactory.

Words and Music

The neutral title conceals the difficulty of a text, which accommodates Music as a character in its own right. Although the title was at first only provisional, Beckett may have kept it because it sports the initial *M* and its obverse *W*. The play's first director, Michael Bakewell, wrote a plot summary: "Croak, an aged tyrant, has two servants—Words and Music. He shouts out at them themes—'love,' 'age' etc., which they attempt to portray and which sharpen his memories of a woman once loved whose memory he cannot escape" (qtd. in Zilliacus 1976, 100). Although the résumé is accurate as far as it goes, it fails to disclose that the play is a composition about composition, into which are enfolded two of Beckett's loveliest lyric poems—poems that he was able to recite many years later, without music.

Plot and reflexivity are easily discernible in this enigmatic radio play, but Zilliacus (1976) was the first to call attention to its medieval atmosphere, with Croak as a chatelain, fitfully in command of his feudal servants, Words and Music. Tension rises between them, as they separately respond to Croak's commands, in ways designated by Beckett's scenic directions; Words is pedantic, whereas Music is overemotional. Ultimately, however, they join in two lyrics and a scene. Yet the final victory belongs to Music, after the departure of Croak. I will argue that the play needs to be read, as well as heard, however seductive Music may be.

Croak is on easy terms with his servants, whom he addresses by the decidedly unfeudal names of Joe and Bob. However, his own name is never heard, and the obvious pun has to be read. He is never said to croak his words, but his name suggests that he is a dying man. Croak's club is problematic, since its function is not designated. He thumps with it when

A holograph of *Words and Music*, dated November 20–22, 1961, is at MoSW, which also possesses an undated typescript with ink revisions. The play was first published in *Evergreen Review* (November–December 1962), and it is included in *CDW*. Beckett's French translation is included in *Comédie et actes divers* (Paris: Minuit, 1972). A useful bilingual edition appears in Mayoux (1972). The play was included in (but not written for) the BBC fortieth anniversary season in 1962; it was broadcast on November 13. It has since been broadcast with the music of other composers, notably Humphrey Searle and Morton Feldman. Brater, Worth, and Zilliacus (1976) discuss broadcasts in some detail.

aroused, but why a club, which has led a commentator to say that he beats his servants with it? Obviously, Beckett wanted to punctuate words and music with a hard sound, but why not a cane or crutch? I have no answer, but "club" needs reading.

Although the plot is clear, the situation is somewhat obscure. Words and Music, Joe and Bob, are evidently summoned at Croak's whim to "play" together. Both of them "tune up" while waiting for Croak, who is delayed by a (Yeatsian) face on the stair of the tower. Bob conducts his orchestra, but Joe recites by rote a Cartesian disquisition on Sloth (the sin of Dante's Belacqua). Initially, Joe's prose is hard to follow, and it is also nonsense, since sloth by definition cannot possess the urgency claimed for it. When Croak arrives, announcing the theme of "Love," Joe barely varies his Latinate phrases, while Bob plays melodically. Croak reacts painfully to Joe, who in turn reacts painfully to Bob, but on the radio, it is impossible to identify which one is moaning and groaning. In print, there is no problem.

The expression of the music and the rhetoric of the words seem to me comic, as are Croak's repetitions of "My balms," after their groans. Joe's questioning of the meaning of *love* and *soul* also strikes me as funny, and that passage contains Beckett's only abbreviation of *ditto* as "Do" in the scenic directions. Is this a misprint, or is it significant? In either case, laughter is evidently not desired, since Beckett's scenic direction specifies that Joe speaks: "With sudden gravity" (omitted from his French translation). I do not understand why the emotional turmoil provoked by "Love" should lead Croak to set the new theme, "Age"; or why Joe falters on that theme; or why it is Age and not Love that prompts Croak to order Words and Music—more and more violently—to join forces. On radio the faltering composition, led by Music, is hard enough to follow, but the scenic direction for Music— "Suggestion for following"—is impossible. How is a listener to know that Music triggers the words that follow? Admittedly, the fourteen-line song is verbally melodic. The song is Beckettian in its evocation of an impossible love with a cosmic effulgence.

It is, however, uncertain whether the song prompts Croak's final theme of "The face," or whether the face in the ashes wrings from Croak a verbal reminder of the face that originally delayed him. Words and Music assume that "The Face" is another set theme, and their opposition exhibits full strength, with Joe "cold" and Bob "warm." Zilliacus was the first to realize that Joe's prose describes a postcoital woman, but he fails to note that a man—probably her partner—is observing her. Joe must have some insight into Croak's past, since it would be hard for anyone to recognize "Lily" from his vivid yet unparticularized portrait. When Music plays on over Joe's protests to "Triumph and conclusion," why is Joe "Gently expostulatory" to Croak, who is reduced to a "Faint thump of club?" Be that as it may, the text-music tandem becomes conciliatory, as Words follows Music's lead. The sequence is meaningful: Words begins the prose postcoital scene in Latinate sentences, but the portrait gradually grows more concrete. It is over the protests of Words that Music drives in "Triumph" to a conclusion. When Words resumes, the phrase "Then down a little way" triggers his low poetic tone for the verbal music of the wellhead—in Zilliacus's telling phrase, "visible from the heart of their darkness" (1976, 110). I am puzzled that Joe is "shocked" at Croak, but his post-Croak plea to Music for music is understandable. Finally, Words implicitly rebels against his departed master; rather than the commanded "together"-ness, a sigh by Words may acknowledge emotion beyond the power of words. Perhaps Music is the new master.[16]

When critics consider the radio plays at all, *Words and Music* and *Cascando* are usually paired. So they should be—each written for a musician friend, each featuring a threesome with Music as one member, each intended for radio, and each almost devoid of referential content. Zilliacus, however, emphasizes that *Esquisse radiophonique* was composed between the two plays—chronologically and thematically.

Esquisse radiophonique (*Rough for Radio I*)

The text-music tandem continues in this *esquisse,* but its ambiance is quite fresh. As opposed to the medieval frame of *Words and Music,* we have modernity with its telephones and busy surgeries. The new language entails a new view of the words-music partnership: in *Words and Music* they loathe one another, but they are obliged by their master to cooperate, and by so doing they apparently escape his control. Although the plot is skeletal, it builds toward its conclusion. The "esquisse" falls into two distinct scenes involving a single protagonist, who is so severely afflicted with words and music that he seeks medical attention. In the first (expository) scene an unnamed woman calls upon the protagonist, to listen to the unheard words and music, first separately and then together, although they are said to be unaware of each other. The nameless woman, an uninvited creditor, represents the audience, who also turn knobs in order to listen, and who presum-

---

A holograph of *Esquisse radiophonique* at McMaster University, Ontario, Canada, is dated November 29, 1961, just two days before the first holograph of *Cascando.* The "Rough" was not published until September 1973 in *Minuit 5.* It is included in Minuit's *Pas, suivi de quatre esquisses* (1978). Beckett's translation into English was first published in *Evergreen Review* (May–June 1963). Since Beckett refused permission for radio broadcast, he was disingenuous in informing Fletcher and Zilliacus (1976) that there were no plans for radio production. Brater (46) mentions that Edward Beckett learned of an unauthorized French broadcast in 1962. Beckett's English translation is included in *CDW.*

ably fail to understand that hearing the two different sound-threads has become a need of the composer.

No sooner does the woman take her leave, with an odd question about the carpeting, than the protagonist telephones a doctor, pleading the urgency of his call, and revealing his comic name Macgillycuddy. (Not only does the name begin with Beckett's signature *M*, but it blends gills and cud to suggest a monstrous animal.) Although Macgillycuddy has told the woman that he needs the sound-threads (left blank by Beckett), he suffers from them. Again he calls the doctor, with increased urgency. It is presumably the doctor who returns his call, while Voice and Music play together: "C'est pareil!" [Like one!]. It is not clear from Macgillycuddy's words whether he suffers most when they play or when they stop; when they are separate or together. What is clear is his suffering, and he understandably takes small comfort when he quotes his doctor, whom he addresses with the *tu* form: "qu'est-ce qui se ressemble? . . . les râles?" [What are all alike? . . . last what? . . . gasps? 271]. After pleading with his respondent not to hang up, the protagonist is again at the mercy of the "faiblissant" sound-threads. This time the telephone rings, and the doctor's assistant informs him that the medical man is detained by two deliveries—one a breech birth—and his visit is therefore delayed till the next day at noon. As Voice and Music play together into silence, Macgillycuddy whispers: "Demain . . . midi." The *esquisse* ends thus abruptly.

Chockful of a world that is irrelevant to the pain of the protagonist, the sketch deserves Beckett's disinclination to have it performed. Unlike the love-hate ambivalence toward the sea, expressed by Henry of *Embers,* this protagonist's pain exceeds its (unwritten) cause, and that pain is diminished by the comic ambiance of the visiting woman and the (unheard) voices on the telephone. What the sketch does accomplish is Beckett's shift to French before composing *Cascando,* which "vaguens" and rounds out this abortive effort.

Cascando

This radio play recycles an old Beckett title, and a recent suffering protagonist afflicted by words and music, but there are "fresh elements and motifs."

As Zilliacus writes of *Cascando,* "The making of the text is more accessible to reconstruction than that of any other radio work of Beckett's" (1976, 118). Zilliacus performs a scrupulous reconstruction, but for my purpose it is sufficient to quote Beckett's letter accompanying his gift to the Theatre Collection of Harvard College Library: "Herewith mss of *Cascando.* It tells its own shaky story. I Original ms. [dated December 1–13, 1961] II Typescript of Voix 1 (Ouvreur). III Typescript of Voix 2 (élément soi). IV Typescript of Voix 2 (élément histoire). V Typescript of completed piece. VI Typescript of my English translation. VII Typescript of preced-

The subtitle stipulates "pièce radiophonique pour musique et voix," and in French *voix* can be single or plural. Like *Words and Music, Cascando* contains two voices but three characters. (Mihalovici's letters to Zilliacus make it clear that he considered his music to be a character, but it actually functions like background music.) Unlike the master-servant relationship of Croak and Joe, however, Opener and Voice interact at once more directly and more obliquely. Voice and Music are usually heard in response to Opener's description of what he does, but Beckett himself is chary of scenic description. Moreover, he denies himself the nonverbal sounds that fill his other radio plays.

The Voice opened by Opener is rhythmically different from his own, with panted phrases as opposed to his own brief declarative sentences, even when quoting hearsay. In the long days of May (while Beckett wrote in December), Opener opens in turn Voice and Music, and then opens their blend. Opener at first says that he opens them at will, but by the end it becomes an involuntary compulsion—"je dois ouvrir." Earlier, he confesses: "C'est ma vie, je vis de ça" (52) [It's my life, I live on that, 299]. Opener is sensitive to outside commentary on his life and occupation, and he ruminates on the critique that has assailed him in the past. Twice he appeals to us: "Ecoutez." He denies any resemblance between his own voice and the one he opens, and soon he denies replying to his critics, who by this time have left him alone. He fears opening, but he has to open, so he opens. Although response to his opening is not always instantaneous, and although we occasionally hear Voice and/or Music without his command, the pattern of Opener-Sound is nevertheless established. When Opener used to ask himself or wonder (the same verb in French) what "it" is, he replied: "Une image, comme une autre" (59) [An image, like any other, 303]. By the end Opener fervently approves of the Voice-Music blend: "C'est bien!" (60) [Good! 304].

What he approves is the final duet about Maunu ["naked miseries"; Woburn in English]. As Beckett indicated in his letter (quoted in my note 10, this chapter), Voice has two strands—self and story. Both motifs are familiar

---

ing revised. . . . It is an unimportant work, but the best I have to offer. It does I suppose show in a way what passes for my mind and what passes for its work" (qtd. in Zilliacus 118). The original French manuscript of this "unimportant work" required five stages of composition. First broadcast with Mihalovici's music on French radio on October 13, 1963, the tape was accidentally erased. This is especially unfortunate, since Beckett took an active part in rehearsals. The French text was first printed in *L'VII* (April 1963) and then in *Dramatische Dichtungen*, vol. 1 (Frankfurt am Main: Suhrkamp, 1963); it was reprinted in *Comédie et actes divers* (Paris: Minuit, 1966). Brater is excellent on the comedies of errors on publications in English—as well as on the several broadcasts.

to readers of Beckett's fiction: the self seeks the right story, which will enable him to rest at last; the story narrates the restless adventures of Maunu—the quest as soulscape. Voice may burst forth in either strand, but when Music accompanies Voice, it is always with the self strand. Through Voice's alternation of self and story threads a yearning for oblivion—the self through the right story, and the story through the death of its protagonist (in crucifixion position). Again and again, the story-Voice is on the point of reaching rest, when Maunu lifts his face from mud, sand, stones, or bilge; he rises to his knees and then to his feet; he is on his way again. Although the play closes on harmony between Voice and Music, the former's self-phrases repeat what has already been voiced in the very first aria.

Voice occasionally echoes Opener. Both cheer Maunu on: "Allons, allons" [Come on, come on]. In Voice's first speech, where the "self" thread gives way to the "story," he announces: "fait que ça . . . ça ma vie" (49) [all I ever did . . . in my life . . . with my life, 297]. Similarly, Opener announces: "C'est ma vie, je vis de ça" (52) [It's my life, I live on that, 299]. Voice sometimes probes into Maunu's head, and Opener quotes those who think they can probe into *his* head. It is hardly surprising, then, that Opener approves the harmony between Voice and Music. All friction spent, *Cascando* modulates more subtly than *Words and Music*.

Unlike Croak, who suffers from the Music-Words duet, Opener marvels at their union: "D'un astre à l'autre, on dirait qu'ils tombent d'accord" (55) [From one world to another, it's as though they drew together, 301]. It is an introduction to the play's most striking image, uttered not by Voice but by Opener. He is, however, wrong, when he claims that that image is "comme une autre" [like any other]. Having situated Voice and Music in different worlds, Opener proceeds to shrink them to two outings and a single return. (In French, "deux promenades, puis le retour" [59]). Redolent of pleasure, the image is then humanized by the Opener: "On dirait qu'ils se donnent le bras" (59) [As though they had linked their arms, 303]. Opener introduces this image cluster after he has been overwhelmed—by what? "Bon Dieu!" he exclaims while Music plays unbidden. When Music falls silent, Opener repeats: "Bon Dieu bon Dieu." Brater reads this as the play's climax, in which Music establishes his superiority, but that seems to me to ignore the end, with Opener's fervent approval of the text-music tandem, however it recycles old phrases. Rest is both attained and not attained by the three characters of *Cascando*. It is not attained because Maunu still clings on, in the linked arms of Voice and Music. It is attained because Opener approves the joint repetition of phrases without closure. And it is attained because this radio play comes to an end. With scarcely an unusual phrase, Beckett has created an unusual text-music tandem that can be viewed as a play-making process, a sifting through conscious and unconscious creativity, and a movement through externals toward being.

Although *cascando* might be translated as waning, there is no waning of Beckett's radiophonic control in the seemingly wayward *Cascando*. Zilliacus charts Beckett's progress toward that pinnacle: "*All That Fall* tells a story; *Embers* portrays a storyteller; *Words and Music* and *Esquisse* still have remnants of character and milieu; these are discarded in *Cascando* which, instead of focussing on a story, focusses on the storytelling condition" (1976, 143). However, it is not the focus but the dramatic tensions and the verbal harmonies that distinguish these radio plays. For *Words and Music* and *Cascando*, as well as *Rough for Radio I*, Beckett was at the mercy of a composer to bring his work to performance. It is possible that he reacted against this constraint to create *Rough for Radio II*, where Music is not a character, and where we are presented with still another perspective on the process of creation. Although Beckett considered that both *Roughs for Radio* were unfinished, he told me that he found a dramatic quality in that very incompletion. However, he did not permit the broadcast of *Rough for Radio I*, whereas he did agree to the performance of *II*—albeit long after its probable date of composition.

Pochade radiophonique (*Rough for Radio II*)

Still exploring his medium, Beckett introduces the sounds of Dick's whip (in French "nerf de boeuf," in English the more brutal "bull's pizzle"), of the Animator's cylindrical (!) ruler, and even of the Stenographer's pencil, as well as the sighs and sniffles of Animator and the nonverbal cries of the victimized Fox. Moreover, on this blind medium, Dick of the whip is mute. Although the torture of the victim can be gleaned from these sounds, words are at the core of *Rough*'s action. Animator, Stenographer, and Dick have been delegated to provoke Fox (or vox) to the utterance that will liberate them all. As his name implies, Animator animates the action; he decides

---

The date of *Pochade radiophonique* is problematic. When originally published in the periodical *Minuit* 16 (November 1975) it was dated "années 50," but when gathered into the slim volume *Pas suivi de quatre esquisses* as *Pochade radiophonique,* this was changed to "années 60?" It is not mentioned by Admussen or Federman and Fletcher, but *BatR* says of an undated typescript: "An early but not the earliest version of this piece for radio" (86). Zilliacus in his 1976 book did not mention it because he did not know of its existence (personal communication). It was first produced in Beckett's English translation, for his seventieth birthday. Martin Esslin, who directed it at the BBC, did not know when it was originally written (personal communication). The few critics who mention the play apparently agree with the description in *CDW*: "Written in French in the early 1960s." Beckett's English translation is included in *CDW*.

when Dick is to ply the whip, and he reviews the words of Fox, as recorded by Stenographer. The torture of Fox recalls the torture of a narrator in the unpublished "On le tortura bien," as well as the "education" of Pim in *Comment c'est,* and it predicts comparable cruelties of such later Beckett plays as *Catastrophe* and *What Where.*

As Martin Esslin (who directed the play for the BBC) pointed out, the basic situation explodes the creative process into four figures: the plunge into the unconscious of Fox, its painful drive by Dick, the verbalization as noted by Stenographer, and the critical control by Animator. The play also offers some sexual byplay between the aged Animator and the attractive Stenographer. Seemingly digressive, her attractions prove functional. Animator rejects Fox's three fragments of a soulscape that parodies Beckett's own fiction, and he urges the introduction of characters—especially since Fox has mentioned a twin brother within him and a Maud who offers to suckle that twin. After Animator orders Stenographer to kiss Fox "au sang" (82) [till it bleeds, 282], the former inserts his own phrase into the prose of Fox—"entre deux baisers" (84) [between two kisses, 284]—over the protests of Stenographer. The play breaks off—or ends—on Animator's weary hope: "Demain, qui sait, nous serons libres" (85) [Tomorrow, who knows, we may be free, 284].

Rough for Radio II is one of Beckett's quartet of radio plays about the pangs of composition—sounds and voices emerging from the dark. Yet this short play contains astonishing verbal variety: the Latinate sentences of disapproval by unnamed superiors; the erotic banter of Animator, his gratuitous literary references, his alternation of hesitation and self-inflation; the subservience of Stenographer, her deft parrying of Animator's eroticism, her timid suggestions for pity toward Fox. The latter's prose, for all its parody of Beckett, is also riven with pain. Paul Lawley has appreciated how the medium of radio has served Beckett so that "the energies of his perennial preoccupations—imperfect being, utterance and the process of creation—are simultaneously contained and released" (1988, 10).

In 1961, Beckett completed the translation of *Comment c'est* (which went through eight drafts), three or four radio plays, and the stage play *Happy Days.* One might call it a creatively happy year, and the decade was only beginning.

1962–69

A Little Rush, Then Another

As was becoming habitual, Beckett jabbed fitfully at creating texts in each of his two languages, but he found it difficult to complete even brief compositions. For example, although a sexual triangle might seem like the quintessential French subject, he began such a play in English in 1961; he gnawed at it sporadically during 1962, and, dissatisfied with the result, he nevertheless gave it to the Tophovens to translate for a German premiere in Ulm. After that June 1963 production (directed by Deryk Mendel, on the same program as both *Acts without Words),* Beckett revised his English and French versions of *Play* for premieres in 1964. Although my chapter title is drawn from *Play,* and although it encapsulates the phrasal rhythm within that play, it is not applicable to Beckett's actual process of creation. However, the phrase is somewhat better suited to the mime play that he conceived for the Irish actor Jack MacGowran, which he aborted before completion.

1963

"J. M. Mime"

Although Beckett abandoned his mime play for Jack MacGowran, his effort has interested Gontarski and Pountney. "Beckett outlined a maze of possible correct paths and errors for two players, either a son and father or a son and mother [one carrying the other, and both naked under their greatcoats], to describe all the permutations of possible paths along a square bisected at first

---

The holograph of "J. M. Mime" is in TCD (MS no. 4664, an undated notebook that also contains a brief aborted dialogue, the "Kilcool" fragments, and a translation into French of the radio play, *Words and Music).* The mime has been published in photocopy by S. E. Gontarski (1985, appendix C).

from corners to corners. Beckett's first major revision was to 'complicate if necessary' by adding two more bisecting lines, doubling the number of possible paths" (Gontarski 1985, 159). Beckett also introduces a dialogue between the two characters, one leaf of which seems to concern their pattern of locomotion. The rest of the holograph consists of a monologue by the son (presumably J. M.), but no one has remarked on the contents, which I cannot decipher.

Some time afterward he began another mime play, which he jettisoned—"Mongrel Mime."

"Mongrel Mime"

Beckett's title "Mongrel Mime" is puzzling, but since the word *mongrel* means "mixed," perhaps he is referring to the inclusion of a voice in a mime. In the revised version of the play, the stage is divided into three oblong boxlike compartments, each five feet deep and five and a half feet high, but with gradually decreasing width. These boxes are colored a gradually deepening gray. All the side walls, except for the one on the extreme right, have white doors that can open in both directions. Each door sports a black knob, a black bolt, and a lattice in a black frame.

A small man, M, in his shabby black coat and hat has to stoop under the low ceiling. A voice commands M, and it does so monosyllabically: "Shut. Lock. Bolt." M follows instructions, but he discards the key in the lattice. After "Rest. On," M advances to the exit door and enters the next cubicle. "Same procedure." The sounds of shutting, locking, bolting, and falling key are unrealistic and identical; they change from sharp to barely audible, and the pauses grow longer between each command and M's obedient action. Since the rightmost wall has no door, M can make no final egress. M has been instructed to his own destruction. Yet one can imagine a tense, funny enactment of "Mongrel Mime."

Beckett also ventured into silent film. His American publisher, Barney Rosset, requested a short film script from three of "his" playwrights—Beckett, Ionesco, and Pinter—and Beckett's scenario was the only one to be filmed. In contrast to the slow evolution of *Play*, or to the abandoned mimes, *Film* moved swiftly to a conclusion. Rosset made his request of Beckett in February 1963, and in four April days at Ussy Beckett wrote the script. In May he showed it to Alan Schneider, the designated director of the film. Beckett sent the typescript to Rosset, before his June departure for Ulm and the German premiere of *Play*. A year later, in the summer of 1964, Beckett came to New

---

"Mongrel Mime" is Beckett's title for an unpublished mime play. A holograph and a typescript are in the Lake collection at HRC. M. Lindon refused me permission to publish it in facsimile.

York for the filming of *Film*, whose shooting closely followed the indications of the script (except for whittling down the opening street scene).

Film

Beckett's governing idea is present from the first: "For one striving to see one striving not to be seen." In practice, this means that the protagonist is split into O and E, or the object and the eye. By the mechanics of the film medium, both halves of the protagonist are subject to the camera's eye, and indeed *The Eye* was the film's first title. In the published version of *Film* Beckett early states his conception and his conclusion:

> *Esse est percipi* [To be is to be perceived—Berkeley].
> All extraneous perception suppressed, animal, human, divine, self-perception maintains in being.

If to be is to be perceived, not to be perceived is not to be. Beckett's dense English sentence therefore implies his protagonist's desire for nonbeing through suppressing perception of him by humans, by animals, and by an image of the divine. (The quoted sentence takes no account, as the actual film does, of *imagined* perceiving eyes in a window, a mirror, and diverse objects.) Eyes prove to be ubiquitous, and the film protagonist, played by Buster Keaton, therefore approaches no closer to nonbeing than do Beckett's fictional protagonists.

In Beckett's three-part script, perception is perceived in a somewhat different sequence from the graduated "animal, human, divine" of his summary. His script is divided into (1) the street, (2) stairs, (3) the room. The first two locations are seen through E's eyes, and the third through O's eyes. Yet since E and O represent two aspects of a single protagonist, the convention is early established that E cannot see O when he is within his "angle of immunity." That angle is breached briefly and inadvertently in parts 1 and 2, but O is seen full-face only in the "investment" of part 3, where Beckett calls for a "flagrant dissimilarity" between the perceptions of O and E. He also calls for a "comic and unreal" climate throughout, which he encourages by such details as the protagonist's winter clothes on a summer day, his "comic

---

Two holograph versions of *Film* are at RUL, and Gontarski's excellent analysis is found first in Beja, Gontarski, and Astier 1983 and then in chapter 7 of his *Intent of Undoing* (1985). In the latter volume appendix A is an edited version of Beckett's remarks at a preproduction conference. Seven tapes of that conference are at the George Arents Research Library at Syracuse University. HRC has mimeographed copies of three Grove film scripts, one by Beckett. *Film* was published by Grove in 1968 in *Cascando and Other Short Dramatic Pieces*. It was republished in 1969 with an essay by Schneider, and production shots. My page references refer to this edition. *Film* was translated by Beckett and published with *Souffle* in 1972, by Minuit.

foundered precipitancy," his visible paranoia, and several of his actions in his mother's room. Beckett's script shows his awareness of the dynamics of film.[1]

In the street the protagonist (like his predecessors in Beckett's fiction) wears a long coat and a hat on this warm June day, and he moves in the opposite direction from other human beings, avoiding their gaze. E perceives a shabby genteel couple, the lady accoutred with a lorgnon and the gentleman with a pince-nez, and each of these aids to perception figures in comic play before and after the couple's "agony of perceivedness." However, the lady's pet monkey is innocent of perceivedness. (The monkey does not appear in the actual film.) At the stairs of part 2, the protagonist flees perception by the descending flower-seller, and her "agony of perceivedness" is so acute that she falls to the floor, scattering her flowers. Her age and frailty diminish the comedy of her pratfall, but the oblivious protagonist speeds past her, and up the two flights of stairs to his mother's room.

Comedy is most skillfully sustained in the film's third part, The Room, which is itself divided into three parts: *(a)* preparation and occlusions, *(b)* rocking-chair examination of photographs, *(c)* investment. It is animal perception that offers most of the comic turns in *Film:* the large cat and the small dog who stare at the protagonist and who stubbornly reenter the room after ejection; the unblinking eyes of the parrot and the goldfish, which the protagonist finally covers with his overcoat. In Schneider's words: "By the time we got to the sequence with the animals [Keaton] was in his element. This was straight slapstick, a running gag, the little man versus a mutely mocking animal world" (Schneider 1969, 81). A print of God the Father is torn down by the protagonist. (In the actual film of this third part, the protagonist imagines eyes in the back of the rocking chair, in the mirror, in the window, and even in the envelope containing his photographs.) Settled in his rocking chair, his back to its back, the protagonist gazes at seven ages of his life, captured in photographs. All but the seventh show acts of perception. (Although the script does not mention this, Beckett notes it in his letter of June 29, 1964, to Schneider: "we actually see him being observed . . . Thus the photos and their destruction parallel triple perception [human, animal, divine] from which he seeks to escape and his efforts to obliterate it" [Harmon, 159].) In the seventh photograph, he is seen full-face, and he wears a patch over one eye. If the photographic biography "invites laughter," the last snapshot nevertheless implies a crisis that causes the protagonist at age thirty to look "over forty." It is with that photograph that the protagonist begins almost ritually to tear each one in turn.[2] Whatever mood Beckett intended for the end of part 3, "the investment," it remains a puzzling sequence, eye to eye, and patch to patch. Only in 1969, five years after completion of the script and four years after filming, did Beckett consent to the publication of *Film.*

Probably after completing *Film*, Beckett began a "female solo," which he titled "Kilcool." Perhaps working simultaneously on *Play*, Beckett closed the year in incompletion. However, he did advise Blin on the French production of *Oh les beaux jours*, in which Madeleine Renaud was to play Winnie for the next quarter-century.

"Kilcool"

Beckett attempted four outlines for a possible play, which he entitled "Kilcool," and Gontarski found it difficult to impose sequence upon the fragments: "the episodes change so frequently . . . that grouping the attempts under a single title is somewhat misleading" (1985, 135). "Kilcool" is an apt title only for the first brief monologue of a recently orphaned girl, who has traveled from Dublin to her aunt's home in Kilcool. The girl is unhappy that she cannot join her mother in the dark silence, and she resists the aunt's efforts to convince her to accept her lot.

In his second attempt Beckett confines the monologist to a kind of coffin, unable to move but nevertheless able to speak. After listing eight themes for development, Beckett begins his third attempt at a monologue. The body is still confined, but the eyes can move, as well as the lips. As Gontarski notes, this attempt seems more promising in that (1) the monologist can see light and hear a voice within, and (2) Beckett has clarified his stage image: "Old woman's face, 4 ft. above stage level. Slightly off centre, lit by strong steady light. Body not visible. Stage in darkness. Nothing visible but face. Gray hair drawn slightly back from forehead. Shrill . . . voice, bad enunciation" (139). Pauses allow the relief of silence to the monologist, and Beckett calculates how much silence results from various combinations of three-second pauses.

A new theme is introduced of a creature within the monologist, seeking to escape. Beckett fills two further manuscript leaves, but it is impossible (for me) to tell whether they belong to this aborted play or another. The image of a spotlit head will languish in Beckett's unconscious until the 1970s, and the inner being may have been transferred to Fox in *Pochade radiophonique*, whose date is uncertain. Even aborted, "Kilcool" proved pregnant for Beckett.

However, Beckett's major dramatic effort was *Play*. After working on English, French, and German versions of *Play*—sometimes simultaneously—Beckett by the end of 1963 felt he had taken the text as far as he could. Suzanne Beckett saw Deryk Mendel's second German production of 1963,

---

Of the twenty-three holograph leaves in Trinity ms. 4664, some seven appear to be outlines or dialogues of "Kilcool," which is a town (spelled Kilcoole) south of Dublin. Gontarski analyzes the holograph in detail.

and the playwright wrote Schneider: "The problems still are: 1. Urns. 2. Lighting. 3. Faces. 4. Voices. 5. *Da capo*" (Harmon, 144). Despite Beckett's attention to detail in his scenic directions, the productions of *Play* were strewn with difficulties. Alan Schneider directed the English-language premiere in January 1964, in New York City—without the "Repeat." George Devine directed an embattled London premiere in April 1964, at the National Theatre. In Paris in spring, Beckett virtually replaced the often absent Jean-Marie Serreau as the director of *Comédie*—in a stageless, underequipped rehearsal room. Although Beckett received no credit in the theater program, Paris rehearsals of *Play* marked the beginning of his career as a director.

Play

Rather than list the various versions of *Play,* I will try to summarize Beckett's revisions of what I view as a key dramatic text. Like its predecessor *Happy Days, Play* began in a somewhat realistic situation—rival lovers Syke and Conk vie for the affections of redheaded Nickie. However, for Beckett "somewhat realistic" is far from realistic, since the three characters are encased in white boxes, with faces spotlit. In early revision, the lovers' triangle changes to a man and two nameless women, who are designated by Beckett's favorite letters—M, W1, and W2. Piecemeal the three characters narrate their sexual twists and turns, with the dialogue circling back to its beginning. By the fourth typescript, white urns replace the oblong boxes, and M's hiccups hint obliquely at contrition on his part. That typescript also separates the characters' memories of their past relationship from their recognition of their present situation, and this becomes more explicit in the next version. The sixth typescript contains the three elements of Chorus, Narration, Meditation (although they are not so labeled), and each speech is elicited by a

---

The early English versions of *Play* are at MoW, and the French are at RUL. Gontarski (1985) has studied the English-language manuscripts, and Blackman summarizes the English and the French manuscripts. Both correct Admussen's errors, but, since Blackman does not avail himself of Gontarski's designations for the many manuscripts, I have not been able to collate their analyses. Gontarski 1999 gives a coherent account of *Play* on page and stage. *Play* was first published in the Tophovens' German translation in *Theater Heute* (July 1963), and I am grateful to Julian Garforth for photocopying it. After the German performances, Beckett revised the shape and color of the urns, the appearance of the actors' faces, and the provocation of speech by the spotlight (immediate, rather than the two-second delay of the German version). The English text in *CDW* omits the words italicized:

> W2: When he came again we had it out. I felt like death. He went on *and on* about why he had to tell her. (310)
> W1: Or you will weary of me. *Get off me.* (312)

Beckett's French translation appears in Minuit's *Comédie et actes divers.*

spotlight. Although the speech is not yet quickened, the entire play is repeated. Only after seeing the world premiere in Ulm, Germany (June 14, 1963), did Beckett change the shape and shade of the urns, as well as the portraits of their inhabitants: "Faces so lost to age and aspect as to seem almost part of urns" (CDW, 307). As Beckett wrote to Schneider: "They are all in the same dinghy at last and should be as little differentiated as possible. Three grey disks. . . . Voices grey and abstract as the faces, grey as cinders" (Harmon, 145).

Play is divided into three unequal parts, which Beckett termed Chorus, Narration, and Meditation, although he did not designate these divisions in the published text. The Meditation is over twice as long as the Narration and Chorus combined. The play's dialogue opens and all but closes on the simultaneous speeches of the choral trio, which are incomprehensible. Even at the "rapid tempo" finally desired by Beckett, the Narration introduces the audience to the familiar topos of an erotic triangle. The lower voices and dimmer light in the Meditation enhance the eerie quality of the triangle, which is fictionally eternal. Although the basic erotic situation is evident on first hearing, details are savored only in the "Repeat." Pervasive is a tale of passion told by toneless voices elicited from impassive faces. (The only two expressive directions—"vehement" and "hopefully"—are found in the Meditation.)

For all the brilliance of performers who have to subdue their theatricality, only readers can appreciate Beckett's dramatic skill in *Play*. Nearly forty years earlier he had written of Joyce's *Work in Progress:* "it is not only to be read. It is to be looked at and listened to" (*Disjecta*, 27). Conversely, *Play* is not only to be looked at and listened to, but it is also to be read. The Chorus is incomprehensible, since the three mouths speak simultaneously, but the precisely cadenced phrasing hints at a shared fate, which is also implied by the common opening word "Yes." Yes, the trio are in this semidarkness together; yes, they are provoked into speech by a spotlight on their faces; yes, they are virtually indistinguishable from one another; yes, their urns touch, but they cannot. Yet the immediate divergence of their words ironizes the affirmation of their opening "Yes."

The Narration sports clichés of the well-made play, but some twenty such phrases are delivered as quotations, with the neutral verb *said* masking the emotional content. Each of the opening speeches of the Narration quotes the imperative *Give:*

W1: I said to him, Give her up.
W2: . . . Give him up, she screamed, he's mine.
M: . . . Give up that whore, she said, or I'll cut my throat—*(hiccup)* pardon—so help me God. (308)

Never has melodrama been so succinct, although not until M's sixth speech will he be heard as an amoral *raisonneur*: "Adulterers, take warning, never admit" (310). From the beginning, however, individual agency is subverted when sound, sense, or image is shared by the members of the trio. In the lines quoted, for example, *giving* is not the generous verb so often cited in the King James Bible. In *Play* giving is what one or another demands—each person designated by a pronoun, instead of a name. Despite their common and ungiving situation, M's sentence is distinctive in its juxtaposition of "whore," suicide threat, oath, contrition (via a hiccup); the very density of clichés serves to subvert them.

One could comb the entire Narration for similar strands of verbal telepathy—odors, animals, oaths, confessions, money, morning, and especially human physicality that reaches a pinnacle in W1's portrait of W2: "Pudding face, puffy, spots, blubber mouth, jowls, no neck, dugs you could . . ." (310). Although the characters' bodies are invisible in their urns, their speech bristles with body parts. Although they are immobile in their urns, their speech speeds through arrivals and departures. Although their voices are toneless, their words chime in rhyme and alliteration. The only proper name in *Play* belongs to the valet Erskine, who is said to come and go on the earth, like Satan in the Book of Job, but in the Narration, it is the three principals who are said to come and go incessantly. Each of them is also given to quotation, which climaxes in M's contrast between speech and thought:

> I ran into your ex-doxy, she said one night, on the pillow, you're well
> out of that. Rather uncalled for, I thought. I am indeed, sweetheart, I
> said, I am indeed. God what vermin women. Thanks to you, angel, I
> said. (311)

The euphony of *ex-dox, pillow-well-uncalled, vermin-women,* and the pulsing dental consonants clothe M's hypocrisy with a musical charm. Moreover, the rhythm of the hand lawn mower (to which M and W2 refer) reflects the overall rhythm of the phrases of the Narration—"A little rush, then another."

The rhythm of the Meditation is more erratic and more repetitive. However, the (unprinted) title is not quite accurate, since some of the trio's speeches are still redolent of earthly passion, as each of them imagines a pairing of the other two. Their verbal telepathy diminishes to snatches about gratitude to God, expressions of pity, a speculative "perhaps," and the "you" of direct address to the spotlight. Each of the principals repeats her or his *own* words, but especially M, whom the spotlight sometimes interrupts midphrase, and he seems compelled to repeat in order to continue. Not only is the spotlight itself more hesitant, but the concreteness of the Narration's lawn mower gives way to the Meditation's "great roller," whose momentum involves strain. Yet the phrases are briefer than before.

Thematically and lexically, the three parts of *Play* differ, but they all reflect on the predicament of the characters. The unintelligibility of the Chorus echoes the senselessness of the human situation. The restlessness of past passion is reflected in the Narration of walking and talking on earth. The inscrutability of human destiny is suggested in the broken phrases and hesitancies of the Meditation, with the very spotlight wavering in its demands. Finally, the dynamics of living and loving are ephemeral play—a word of myriad meanings in English.

Consummate precision is mandatory for the performance of *Play,* but perhaps the reader alone can appreciate why it took so long for Beckett to refine the play. Not only is the spotlight as personal a character as Music in Beckett's recent radio plays, but the dialogue is more intricately interwoven than can be seized by listening. Yet *Play* is very much a stage play, in which the eerie visual scene is counterpointed against the clichés of melodrama and the uncertainties of ontology. *Play* is a template for Beckett's stage plays to come—visually striking, verbally brief and strictly rhythmed, technologically demanding, situationally static, temporally floating, and humanly revealing.[3] It is rigorous in enclosing each figure in her/his own consciousness, in spite of a quasi-continuous narrative elicited by the spotlight and absorbed by the audience. Beckett's subtitle for *Play* is "a play in one act," and that act is steeped in mortality, which will become Beckett's most dramatic theme. Yet how variously he will stage it.

1964

For a writer, Beckett was deeply involved in performance. To quote Knowlson: "His diary was full of promises already made: to help [Michael Blake] in London with [a Magee-MacGowran] *Endgame;* to oversee a French revival of *Fin de partie,* before it set off on tour; . . . to assist with two productions of *Play,* one in France and one in England; finally . . . to fly to the United States to help with the shooting of *Film*" (455). Not only did Beckett fulfill these commitments, but he spent Christmas in London advising the British director Anthony Page on still another *Godot,* with Nicol Williamson. Yet his hope was to write fiction. After his return from New York, he aborted four short pieces and one longer one. He grouped the four brief pieces as *Faux départs* [Wrong starts] and, in spite of the title, he published them the following year—in a German periodical. However, he withheld the longer piece for nearly a decade, finally permitting its publication as *All Strange Away.*

Faux départs

Of the four "wrong starts," the first three in French stop short of a hundred words each, whereas the fourth in English is double that length, and much of it is later recapitulated at the beginning of *All Strange Away*. *Faux départ 1* introduces a problematic narrator, who has fitted up a container in which he can sit, stand, or kneel. Should he introduce himself? "Bah." *Faux départ 2* repeats phrases of *1*, but gives the dimensions of the container as one meter by three; the narrator and his corner of the earth are spinning toward winter, and he wishes he could be under the earth, or in that other void—silence and darkness. *Faux départ 3* offers each sentence its own paragraph. "Je" is back, along with commas and a period. "Il" speaks of himself in the same phrases previously uttered by "je." After recapitulating a statement about steps, "il" can drop his white cane and lie down.

Faux départ 4 resembles *Faux départ 3* in that each of its nineteen sentences is awarded its own paragraph, but now in English. The text begins peremptorily: "Imagination dead imagine" (272). Wearily, the imagination creates a place with someone it, but without entrance or egress. As in the first two French paragraphs, positions are described, as well as apparent grammars of Jolly, Draeger Praeger Draeger. The narrator commands himself to imagine light, but it is sourceless. After a lifetime of walking crouched, the narrator comes to a halt in a summary sentence: "When it [the light] goes out no matter, start again, another place, someone in it, keep glaring, never see, never find, no end, no matter" (273). The prose is so elliptical that I am tempted to read it as Beckett's self-commands, anxious to follow his imagination into uncharted ways. The English language freed him to do so, for before the end of the year he completed *All Strange Away*.

After *Comment c'est*, where the narrator/narrated suffered a conflict between life in the light and in the mud, between spoken and written words, Beckett tried to strip his fiction down to bare basics. In Judith Dearlove's formulation: "The works written prior to *How It Is* are concerned with the problems of a mind-body dualism. . . . The pieces written after *How It Is*, on the other hand, turn from an emphasis upon the mind's limitations to consideration of its imaginative constructions" (150, 152). Beckett's new narrators would try to imagine simplified figures in an enclosed space. Of these "closed space stories," *All Strange Away* is perhaps the strangest.

Faux départs were first published in June 1965 in the German review *Kursbuch*—in their originary languages, three French and one English. They are reprinted as appendix 2 of *CSP*.

All Strange Away

Since this fiction opens, "Imagination dead imagine," *All Strange Away* is sometimes compared with that later text. Lake's *No Symbols* cites the similarities: "(a) both take place inside a tomblike enclosure, with rotunda; (b) both deal with dead bodies, but living imaginations [not so]. . . ; (c) silence, whiteness, light, and heat are significant elements in both texts" (135). However, the syntax of the single twelve-page paragraph of *All Strange Away* is so elliptical that the slender narrative is hard to follow, and its references to points on an imaginary geometric figure are confusing rather than "all that most clear." Some two-thirds of the way through the text, the word "Diagram" is centered, but no actual diagram appears, of a body inscribed in a hemicycle. (The synonym of hemicycle, semicircle, lacks the resonances of enclosure—hem—and of repetition—cycle.) The several descriptions of the geometric deployment of parts of the human body make for difficult and tedious reading, which is, however, clarified if the reader actually draws a diagram.

In this new fictional form Beckett's narrative tone is uncertain, with such recurrent verbs as *try, say,* and such faltering phrases as "for example," "for instance," "for the moment," "yet to be imagined," "if this maintained," and a sprinkling of vague *now*s and equally vague *later*s. Imperative verbs, which have occasionally enlivened Beckett's French fiction, run rife in self-address, as the narrator shifts and corrects his focus, or delays his account: "leave it for the moment," "look at that later," "details later," "imagine later." Quotations of the constrained figures are announced only by a comma and a capital letter. The quotations are almost always preceded or followed by the phrase "no sound." Since the figures speak (soundlessly) of themselves in the third person, the quotations sometimes elide confusingly into narration. Proper names do offer a point of purchase, but they yield precedence to the shimmering descriptions of place, or to the complex play of light and dark. Six times the narrator masters his narrative sufficiently to write: "aha," and yet the entire piece is bathed in an air of weariness: "that again" or "not that again." Even the experienced Beckett reader may stumble in the irregular alternation of light and dark, of silence and unheard

---

A jacket blurb on the Calder 1979 edition of *All Strange Away* lists the date of composition as 1963, but Knowlson dates it in 1964. The piece was titled over a decade later, when Beckett submitted to its publication—in a deluxe edition to benefit the family of the recently deceased actor, Jack MacGowran. A photocopy of a typescript is at HRC. Gontarski 1998 cites errors in the various printings, before inclusion in *CSP*. Beckett did not translate it into French. An extended analysis is that of Peter Murphy, which first appeared in *JOBS* 5, and then in his book. James Hansford's dissertation is illuminating.

speech that is nevertheless quoted, and in folds of a human figure cramped into a tight container. Repeated imperatives buffet the reader toward what seems to be a "prying" into a zero degree of being. "Imagine what needed, no more, any given moment, needed no more, gone, never was" (*CSP*, 170). The workings of imagination are (usually) those of the narrator, whereas the figures seek hope in Fancy (capitalized in the text). Demanding a concentrated act of attention on the reader's part, *All Strange Away* is rewarding in its graphic but timorous reach toward basic being, beneath a narrative aura.

The piece opens on an explosive, contradictory imperative: "Imagination dead imagine" (169). This may be read as "Imagination is dead, but imagine anyway" or "Imagination is dead; imagine that," and it is immediately followed by "A place," and then "someone in it." As in almost all Beckett's previous fiction we read: "that again." The epic voyage "like after the war" is at once rejected, to be replaced by a container, "no way in, none out, try for him there." At first "he" is sought in a cube six feet high and five feet square, but when that proves inadequate, "another place, someone in it." Although "he" is not found, the narrator's problematic search continues, sometimes through glaring eyes. "He" is stripped, shrouded in black, repositioned, and he utters a soundless phrase: "Fancy is his only hope" (170). Briefly described, "he" is nevertheless absent: "No way in, none out, he's not here." The structure is tightened as "he" soundlessly murmurs phrases already used by the narrator. Faces appear on the walls, and soon they resolve into Emma, "lovely beyond words." Her very name feminizes the letter *M,* and soon "he" crouches to see all of her body, murmuring of his sexual possession of her. However, the narrator forbids imagining a life with Emma. For the second time "his" limbs are inscribed in the hermetic structure: "but of him nothing and perhaps never save disjointed segments variously disposed" (172). Eyes nevertheless occasionally "rive their unseeingness," and imagination is ordered to lodge a dying fly, before it too is banished: "No, no image, no fly here, no life or dying here but his, a speck of dirt. Or hers since sex not seen so far, say Emma."

The narrator shifts focus from "him" to Emma. Like "him" before her, she gyrates through various positions, murmuring soundlessly of Emmo possessing her. She is the passive counterpart of active Emmo. However, as James Hansford observes: "[Emma] *fancies* herself the passive partner in sexual activity whereas Emmo *imagined* himself its active instigator" (1983, 53, Hansford's emphasis). She also lends herself more readily to the narrator's portraiture, with her long black hair and eyelashes. Cramped in a three-foot cube, she too murmurs soundlessly: "Fancy is her only hope, or, She's not here, or, Fancy dead" (174). Having "great need of words," the narrator commands himself to "Imagine other murmurs, Mother mother, Mother in heaven, Mother of God, God in heaven, combinations with Christ and Jesus" (175), and yet the narrative continues about "her." After her hair and lashes disappear, her dwelling shrinks from a cube to a rotunda, two feet high and two in diameter. There being no alternative, her limbs are now redeployed geometrically "in one half of the available room leaving the other empty, aha" (177). It is after this spin of Emma's body parts, which are assigned small letters, that the word "Diagram" appears in large letters.

She, no longer named, shares the narrative with the object she holds— "no true image [but] small gray punctured rubber ball," which emits a faint hiss when squeezed and a pop when released (178). "So little by little all strange away," declares the narrator, as the text grows ever stranger. However familiar the repeated phrases, they are punctured by new suffering, as we read "past her best" and "other meat." The irregular alternation of light and dark summons sleep, trailing its nightmares. A curious memory intervenes of the body trying to writhe to its right side—and failing. Life in the rotunda is as frail as a hothouse leaf on earth. The "unstillable turmoil" is broken by repeated phrases of earlier quotations, this time unmurmured. The constrained body is last seen mysteriously on her right side, still clutching the gray ball or bulb that hisses when squeezed and pops when released.

At two intervals there are probes into Emma's memory "of a lying side by side." The long final sentence of *All Strange Away* sounds and subsumes many of the phrases that have constructed this strange piece:

> Within apart from Fancy dead and with faint sorrow faint memory of a lying side by side and in sleep demons not yet imagined all dark unappeasable turmoil no sound and so exhaled only for the moment with faint sound, Fancy dead, to which now add for old mind's sake sorrow vented in simple sighing sound black vowel a and further so that henceforth here no other sounds than these say gone now and never were sprayer bulb or punctured rubber ball and nothing ever in the hand lightly closed on nothing any length till for no reason yet imagined fingers tighten then relax no sound and to the same end slip of left hand down slope of right upper arm no sound and same purpose none of breath to the end that here henceforth no other sounds than these and never were that is than sop to mind faint sighing sound for tremor of sorrow at faint memory of a lying side by side and fancy murmured dead. (181)

In spite of the three repetitions of "No sound," the sentence makes sense only when read aloud, at least mentally. "Within" is where Fancy and memory dwell, the capital letter perhaps designating the relative importance of the respective mental faculties. However, if nightmare demons are not yet imagined, neither are reasons for the tightening and relaxing of the now empty hands. For the first time the often repeated "Fancy dead" is actually sounded, however faintly, and the words are accompanied by a faint sigh. In previous sentences the uncapitalized letter *a* anchored Emma's head, but in this final sentence "a" becomes a Rimbaudian black vowel, sounding like the makeshift musical instrument once in her right hand. Soundless and purposeless, the whole figure embodies denial, and yet, "sop to mind," breath sighs, however faintly, and it circles us back to the "memory of a lying side by side," a position that is never seen in *All Strange Away*. After scrupulously articulating all that is "gone now and never were," a human figment remains. At the last, fancy is unquotedly and uncapitalizedly murmured dead, and the long final sentence is its strange sighing requiem.

Considering each Beckett creation in chronological order, I have tried to limit reference to works "not yet imagined." However, I except *Play* and *All Strange Away*. As *Play*, also finalized in 1964, is the template for the relentless concentration of Beckett's later plays, so *All Strange Away* predicts much of his late difficult fiction (and my commentary often consists of an attempt to trace the narrative). Most similar are the brief "closed space" pieces, such as *Imagination morte imaginez, Bing,* and *Sans*. The dry tone and the geometry of *All Strange Away* lead to *Le Dépeupleur;* the hesitant variants of "try" will be read again in the *Still* trilogy; the imperatives infuse *Company;* the mythic female figure trembles toward *Mal vu mal dit;* the elliptical sentences are simplified and musicalized in *Worstward Ho*. The sensitivity to sound—rhyme, assonance, alliteration—looks both backward and forward in Beckett's work.

Prophetic as it now seems, *All Strange Away* is a considerable achievement in and of itself: at once weary of seeking minimal being and imagining it tentatively anew; at once denying images and compelling the reader to imagine them; at once soundless and grounded in quotation; at once evocative of bodily tortures and setting the suffering body to rest. Created in solitude, the figures elicit words that are nostalgic for an intimacy that may be achieved only in fancy. Although the narrator and the created figure both "glare" on occasion, they never see eye to eye.

While working at the pains or pasts of his highly stylized characters, Beckett himself was in poor health. Plagued by dental and vision problems, he underwent surgery of the palate in November, only to be informed that further surgery would be necessary. Nevertheless, at the request of George Devine of the Royal Court Theatre, he flew to London to advise the director Anthony Page on a revival of *Waiting for Godot*. There the publisher John Calder informed him of his plan to start a new theater in Soho, to which he hoped Beckett would contribute a play. Although the theater failed to materialize, Beckett dedicated the play *Come and Go* to Calder.

1965

Come and Go

Unlike Beckett's other dramatic pieces in English, *Come and Go* did not start in comparative realism. From the very first version of this "dramaticule," Beckett evidently conceived of patterned movement and dialogue, revolving around a mystery. Nevertheless, the play drafts grew progressively more stylized. Beckett's first title was "Good Heavens," for that was the response of, successively, A, B, and C, to the unheard secret whispered to each in turn. By the first typescript, the three women are named Viola, Poppy, and Rose, and they engage in lubricious dialogue. By the second typescript, however, they bear their monosyllabic names; they follow the strict sequence of exit, reentrance, and dialogue, each exclaiming "Oh" to the unheard news of catastrophe. As Beckett would note for his German production: "Opener [of dialogue] always one to go."

Like their predecessors in *Play,* the trio of *Come and Go* offer a minimum of flesh to the spectator, for they wear long coats and broad-brimmed hats that shade their faces. Although their "ages [are] indeterminable," their costumes situate them in another era, and their low-voiced, genteel speech confirms their distance. When first viewed on their nearly invisible seat, they seem to float on air. As each woman in turn glides noiselessly into darkness, the equilibrium is delicately unbalanced. One member of the remaining pair whispers into the ear of the other, who, "appalled," exclaims: "Oh." The recipient of the secret asks whether the absent one is aware of her fate, and the imparter of the secret invokes God in a pious hope for ignorance. After each of the three women has departed, reentered, and uttered her lines, they resume their seats, joining hands in a geometric pattern. First and last, Vi is in the center, but Ru and Flo have exchanged positions.

Repetition and difference structure the brief piece. The opening tableau is shadowed by female trios in art and legend—the three graces, the three fates, the three sisters of folktales and Chekhov. In Beckett's final text the dialogue opens with the utterance of two of the three monosyllabic names—

A holograph and typescripts of *Come and Go* are at MoSW, with photocopies at RUL. Written in English in January 1965, the play was first published in Beckett's French translation *Va et vient* (in *Comédie et actes divers,* 1966). The first production, in January 1966, was in the Tophovens' German translation, and Beckett directed his French version in February. First published in English by Calder and Boyars in 1967, that version was later revised by Beckett, as was the version in *CDW.* His final revision is published only in volume 4 of *The Theatrical Notebooks of Samuel Beckett,* ed. S. E. Gontarski (London: Faber, 1999). Breon Mitchell (1976) traces the manuscript stages of the "dramaticule."

"Ru" and "Flo"—and this immediately sets the climate of rue and the tempo of flow. The first full line of dialogue—Vi's "When did we three last meet?"—echoes the witches of *Macbeth,* but displaces the question from the future to the past. Flo's imperative rejoinder—"Let us not speak"—is the first of several negatives and is itself negated, since the three women continue to speak. After each woman in turn departs into darkness, the remaining two follow a strict verbal pattern:

> The speaker utters the listener's name, and the latter responds: "Yes."
> The speaker asks the listener's assessment of the absent one, and the latter replies neutrally.
> The speaker whispers a secret, and the listener, appalled, exclaims: "Oh."
> As the speaker "puts her finger to her lips," the listener asks whether the absent one is aware of her fate, and the speaker prays for ignorance, with the word "not" figuring in both question and prayer. Interrogatives and negatives dance together.
> When the three women reclaim their invisible bench, they speak about their past, especially in the central Ru-Vi duet.

> Ru: Holding hands . . . that way.
> Vi: Dreaming of . . . love.

Flo, holding the left hands of her companions, utters the concluding words: "I can feel the rings."

Not only does Beckett stipulate that "No rings [are] apparent" on the women's highly visible hands, but his revised text punctuates that absence gracefully: "Hands taken in air at top of gesture sink gently plumb together." Breaking their colorless vocal expression only in compassion, the three condemned women of indeterminable age can continue to dream of love and its symbols. To paraphrase Beckett's scenic direction, verbal pattern and stylized gesture sink gently plumb together, as mortality sounds its plangent note. The rings may not be apparent on fingers, but they are a metaphor for the wringing mystery at the heart of mortality.

I have argued that *Play* requires reading to savor its subtleties, and I now argue the opposite for *Come and Go.* Only in the theater can one appreciate the terpsichorean play of movement and stillness, going and coming, question and answer, gesture and melody of *Come and Go.* Beckett visualized it precisely, as he wrote to Alan Schneider: "I see *Come & Go* very formal. Strictly identical attitudes & movements. . . . Same toneless voices save for 'Oh!'s" (Harmon, 417). He did not burden the director with what Hersh Zeifman perceived: "a five-act Shakespearean tragedy played in three minutes by three ghosts playing with three [Shakespearean] echoes" (1983, 143).

Mortality may have been on Beckett's mind as he approached his six-tieth birthday. He was advised to pay more attention to his health, partic-ularly to refrain from smoking and drinking. Instead, he flew to Berlin to help Deryk Mendel with his production of *Warten auf Godot* at the Schiller Theater, from which he absented himself for a London weekend during which he advised Jack MacGowran on his one-man Beckett show, "Beginning to End." No sooner was Beckett back in Paris at the end of February when he learned of an Italian actress on a hunger strike because another actress had the rights to perform *Giorni felici*. Although the mat-ter was eventually resolved, the atmosphere was scarcely conducive to his own writing. Nevertheless, during March in his Ussy refuge he managed to complete a French text with which he had struggled sporadically for some months.

Imagination morte imaginez (*Imagination Dead Imagine*)

As in *All Strange Away*, but in about a thousand words, or one-fifth its length, and in French, Beckett's unstable, impersonal narrator attempts to build an edifice—what his English translation calls "a little fabric." In the earlier work, resistance was immediately encountered; so also here. Brater has summarized the startling start of the short text: "Beginning with two sen-tences mediated by sixteen high-voltage stops [one period in a whirl of com-mas], *Imagination Dead Imagine* initiates a riot of caesuras that allows a voice to interrupt itself at almost every turn, modifying and modulating each beat in the unfolding action" (1994, 85). Yet through that flurry an architec-ture is discernible. Of the seven pages as printed in *Têtes-Mortes* the first two and the last one bristle with commands that end on the same French open vowel-sound: *taisez, entrez, mesurez, sortez, rentrez, frappez, ressortez, reculez, survolez, descendez, attendez*. The narrator is apparently addressing himself, but we too are included in those formal imperatives that surround the still, central scene with actions.

Early introduced, a white rotunda contains two inscribed figures. Within that small rotunda (eighty centimeters high) light and temperature fluctuate unceasingly—and erratically. Although one tends to associate the color white with freezing, it is hot in this edifice, and, conversely, black is

---

Six drafts of *Imagination morte imaginez* are at RUL. First published individually by Minuit in 1965, *Imagination morte imaginez* was later included as the third of *Têtes-Mortes* (first in the 1967, then in the 1972 edition). Translated by Beckett soon after it was written, it appears in *CSP*, to which my page numbers refer.

cold. Rather than a pendulum-type oscillation between light/heat and dark/cold, however, the variations are swift and unpredictable. Only the bodies are immobile, each folded in three, more or less in fetal configuration. Each within its own semicircle, the two figures are back to back, and head to arse. They are distinguishable sexually only by the long hair "d'une blancheur incertaine" [vaguely white] of the woman. Although the figures are motionless, their breath nevertheless mists a mirror, and their left eyes open irregularly "bleu pâle aigu" [piercing pale blue]. Only once are their eyes simultaneously open. The figures are neither dead nor asleep, and the bodies' stillness within the surrounding light/temperature storm is striking for those who can recall the opposite (i.e., bodies rushing about in a relatively stable climate).

Fluttering both within and outside the edifice, the narrative voice delivers an imperative that does not terminate in the *ez* sound: "Faites seulement ah à peine" (57) [Only murmur ah, no more, 185], and a faint shudder, instantly repressed, is evident to the abruptly introduced eye of prey. That eye is itself the prey of the imagination, even while it preys upon the circumscribed bodies at the very limit of life/death. The white rotunda is lost during the course of the narrative, then "Retrouvé par miracle" (55) [Rediscovered miraculously, 184]. By the finale, the narrative voice abandons imperatives for negatives and interrogatives, but it remains curious about human beings: "sinon ce qu'ils font" (57) [if not what they are doing, 185]. Caught between cold black and hot white, seeking purchase both outside and within a little fabric, the imagination irrepressibly wonders about residual human life. Condemned to a deathlike immobility in fetal position, both figures are vividly seen by our reading eyes of prey.

Beckett on his fifty-ninth birthday began a television play for the actor Jack MacGowran. By May 1, the first draft was completed, although he refined it through seven further versions in English. Knowlson assures us that Beckett had MacGowran's "doleful, haunted eyes and expressive face in mind" (475), for his first, unsolicited, uncontracted venture into a new medium, which was not yet ubiquitous in 1965. With characteristic modesty, Beckett did not assume that MacGowran would necessarily want to perform the television play. Or, if he did, that anyone would broadcast it. Süddeutscher Rundfunk proved more hospitable than the British Broadcasting Corporation, and Beckett himself directed the Tophovens' German translation, with Deryk Mendel as Joe and Nancy Illig (who was W1 in *Spiel*) as the Voice. Broadcast in Germany on Beckett's sixtieth birthday, *Eh Joe* marks the first time Beckett was actually credited with direction. He continued his relation with Süddeutscher Rundfunk into the 1980s.

Eh Joe

From the first, Beckett envisaged the basic dramatic situation: A Christian womanizer imagines an accusing female voice. The single holograph presents her accusation in a torrential block of words, but on the verso Beckett lists a few verses from the Bible. In the first typescript, each sentence of the woman's monologue receives a line of type; the man's name is Jack until midway through the monologue, where the rhyming phrase "Joe's woe" provokes the change to Joe. The next stage of revision focuses on Joe's opening movements, which Beckett diagrams. Beckett's subsequent versions match his text to the camera moves, with scrupulous attention to timing. Finally the woman's voice speaks in ten paragraphs, punctuated by nine camera moves.

It is possible to view Eh Joe as a banal melodrama: because of unrequited love, a woman commits suicide, and her lover feels remorse. However, this bald summary neglects Beckett's unusual television devices—rigorous separation of camera and voice, limitation of the versatility of the camera, invisibility of the owner of the voice, inaudibility of words toward the end, photogenicity of an intensely listening face. Although Zilliacus (1976) mentions that the photographed man is religious, I think that the text is witness to a crisis of faith. Beckett has been quoted on Eh Joe: "It is his passion to kill the voices which he cannot kill" (qtd. in Knowlson, 474). The pun on passion is probably deliberate. However, the voices of Joe's past— only his parents are mentioned—are moral voices, but in the present intensity of listening the voice is sarcastic about a residual Christian morality, and it is crucial to remember that the voice exists only in Joe's mind. The words that Joe hears in a woman's voice are his own, and he smiles triumphantly when he finally achieves silence.

Zilliacus summarizes the similarities between Eh Joe and Film: the camera investigation of a room, a perceived person versus a perceiving device. However, Joe's unrelenting image is more stark than that of the Keaton-character, and the emotional climate is at once more sardonic and more painful. I summarize the substance of the voice in Joe's mind, adhering to Beckett's paragraphs:

1. Although the woman's voice may be low and rhythmic, the words immediately taunt Joe.
2. Speaking of herself, she sketches Joe as a womanizer.

The holograph and eight typescripts of Eh Joe are at MoSW, with photocopies at RUL. Eh Joe was first published in Beckett's French translation in Arts (January 5–11, 1966). Even in book publication, French preceded English: the first in Comédie et actes divers (Paris: Minuit, 1966), and the second in Eh Joe and Other Writings (London: Faber and Faber, 1967). The play is included in CDW, to which my page numbers refer.

3. She situates herself (and us) in Joe's mind—a mind that is habitually accused by voices. In this paragraph she introduces the striking phrase "mental thuggee" as Joe's way to suffocate these voices.

4. Shifting between second- and third-person pronouns, her voice implies Joe's fascination with the voices; they are a passion in both senses of the word.

5. The voice rounds out her own portrait as a character, but then she shifts to a portrait of the voice, which is cruelest when Joe has to strain to hear "the odd word."

6. Although guilt has been suggested earlier, this paragraph is specifically Christian. It opens: "How's your Lord these days?" It mocks "The passion of our Joe" (CDW, 364). Drawing upon Luke 12:16, the voice threatens divine punishment, but it does so tauntingly.

7. Only now does the voice introduce Joe's victim, in strangely impersonal phrases: "The green one. . . . The narrow one. . . . Spirit made light" (365). Disturbing is the juxtaposition of the last phrase with the final coarse comment: "No more old lip from her."

8. Divine agency and human event are first blended in this paragraph. The cliché of a death announcement is quoted: "On Mary's beads we plead her needs and in the Holy Mass" (365).

9. The narration of the suicide comprises about a quarter of the play's speech. The detail of the three attempts is excruciating, and Beckett rarely allows taunting interruptions of this account of a failed drowning, a failed wrist-slitting, and the drawn out swallowing of tablets. It is Joe who imagines the minutiae he strains to hear: the dying woman calls his name, and she lays her face on stones. Finally her love seems greater than that of God. Although Joe may not hear: "Compared to Him," we read it (367).

Eh Joe makes enormous demands on its one visible actor. Yet he and the television audience may be confused by the opening mime. Like the protagonist of *Film* (and especially for those familiar with *Film*), this protagonist paranoiacally ascertains that he is alone. Only in retrospect does the question arise as to whether Joe's way of insuring self-enclosure is as suitable to voices as to eyes. In his scenic directions, Beckett uses the abbreviation "do," and we who read it associate it with a verb of action—when Joe will be motionless for most of the film. It is only when the voice utters its words that Joe is at once transfixed and defenseless. The television listener, unlike Joe, does not want to kill, throttle, squeeze, silence, choke, or commit mental thuggee on the words, but, listening intently, we watch Joe listening—and finally we too strain to hear about the suicide that accuses Joe.

We can usually ascertain the correct dates for Beckett's dramatic pieces, but the fiction is more problematic. As Deirdre Bair writes: "Beckett himself is not exactly sure of the order in which he wrote [the prose pieces of the late 1960s]. What is definitely known of this period is that he was determined to break away from theater, and worked diligently at prose with results that he usually found unsatisfactory" (585).

Assez (Enough)

Assez is a throwback to Beckett's first-person, walking narrator whose prose comes to us in sentences and paragraphs.[4] Although the story's first sentence is an imperative of erasure—"Tout ce qui précède oublier" [All that goes before forget]—the rest of the paragraph introduces a pen with a will of its own and an emergent voice—those essentials of "l'art et la manière" of narrative. Moreover, the narrative consists of what is *not* forgotten, as it shuttles between the present tense and a past companionship—not a memory of lying side by side, but of walking hand in hand, or of lying down enfolded in another, as well as four accounts of a parting. The word "assez" occurs four times in the text, and it englobes the entire tale in its final appearance as the first word of the last sentence. The narrator has had "enough" of the narrative, whose fictionality is explicitly "enough," rather than "too much."

The narrating "je" tells an achronological tale of being taken in hand at age six, by an older man. Although the pair have spent many years circumnavigating the globe, the "je" limits the account to the last decade, between two dates: the old man's reference to his (unparticularized) infirmity and the old man's command to leave him—whether momentarily or permanently. The "je" gradually particularizes their life together: the landscapes through which they walked, the virtually horizontal upright posture of the old man, his resort to a mirror to see the sky, the minimal speech of the old man, his cubing ternary numbers and fumbling for words. The world is thus reduced to simple, combinatory elements, repetitively or perhaps accretively viewed. Although the "je" utters three denials of ever asking a question, two questions are answered as if they were asked. Although the pair acquire the force of natural phenomena (with the incongruous detail of gloves on their clasped hands), they calculate distances with the aid of a pedometer, and Brater has shown that the calculations are untrustworthy (1994, 64–65). The pair walk on stemless flowers, and midway through the account, the "je" acknowledges: "Je vois les fleurs à mes pieds et ce sont les autres que je vois. Celles

---

Nine drafts of *Assez* are at MoW, with photocopies at RUL. First published individually in 1966, *Assez* was republished as the second of *Têtes-Mortes* (first in the 1967, then in the 1972 edition). Beckett's English translation *Enough* first appeared in *Books and Bookmen* (April, 1967) and then in *No's Knife* (Calder and Boyars, 1967) and is included in *CSP*, to which my page numbers refer.

que nous foulions en cadence. Ce sont d'ailleurs les mêmes" (39) [I see the flowers at my feet and it's the others I see. Those we trod down with equal step. It is true they are the same, *CSP*, 189]. It is also true that this may be the most lyrical paragraph in the pared down prose, enfolding past experience into present fiction. Even repetition is spare, and sound play is virtually absent. In contrast to most of Beckett's fiction, which emphasizes its devices of expression, this narrative's lean prose teases us with the subliminal sexuality between the two figures, and their compulsive companionship in motion and at rest. The narrator's words echo those of her/his mentor—few in number, clear in syntax, determinedly narrative. Unusually for Beckett, calm reigns over the couple and in the account.[5] Yet Hansford has discerned beneath the calm a shift of authority from the old man to his narrating protégé. Woven through the four accounts of the couple's separation is a metafictional commentary about rendering those accounts.

The last paragraph opens: "Nous vivions de fleurs" and it closes: "Assez mes vieux seins sentent sa vieille main" (47) [We lived on flowers. . . . Enough my old breasts feel his old hand, 192]. Paradoxically, this tale that is almost bare of flowers of rhetoric implies that traditional image. Existing in a residual solitude, where the verbal cadence echoes the rhythmic circumterrestrial tread, the androgynous "je" recreates a past decade when words could evoke images and people; when they could combine to render a relationship. Carefully concealing the gender of the narrator, Beckett in *Assez* resorts for almost the last time in his fiction to the first-person singular, the conventional designation for a self, which Beckett finds forever elusive.[6] Yet, paradoxically, this first-person text nostalgically embraces a couple. Strikingly, the couple is at once human and mythic, a voice and a pen, experience and its narration, a text-in-progress and its own fictionality. Beckett pared down his French so that it could be all the more polyvalent.

1966

In January of the new year, Beckett complained in a letter to me that there loomed ahead of him "14 weeks nonstop theatre, cinema, tv." Although this was something of an exaggeration, it may reflect his frustration with his recalcitrant fiction. He co-directed *Eh Joe* for the BBC in London after taking sole charge for Süddeutscher Rundfunk in Stuttgart. In Paris he advised on Robert Pinget's *L'Hypothèse* and directed *Va et Vient*, his first independent stage directing credit. His many visitors usurped writing time, but among them the designer Jocelyn Herbert was able to convince him to see an oculist about his weakening eyes. The diagnosis was double cataracts, and he was placed on medication before an operation was advisable. Mortality was surely on his mind, when he penned his briefest play, *Breath*.

Breath

Called by Beckett "a farce in five acts," the thirty-five second sketch is its author's most extremely reduced view of human destiny. On a stage "littered with miscellaneous rubbish," a faint cry is heard, and faint light is held for five seconds. Breath and light increase over a period of ten seconds; they remain at maximum for five seconds. Light and breath decrease over a period of ten seconds, and the same cry is heard again. Silence and dimness remain for five seconds, and the playlet is over. If *Come and Go* is a "dramaticule," *Breath* might be called a "technicule," dependent as it is on technology. Beckett's scenic directions stipulate that the two recorded cries be identical and that the light and (amplified) breath be "strictly synchronized" (*CDW*, 371). The elemental symmetries of life on earth rely upon sophisticated theater electronics.

Worried about the coming operations on his eyes, Beckett canceled the second operation on his palate, and in May he fled to Ussy to work on *Le Dépeupleur*, which he had begun in 1965. Immersed in a whole population, the text proved unmanageable, but he continued to fret over it when he and Suzanne went to Italy. Only on his return to Paris in July did he put it aside— he thought, definitively. Beckett has linked the unwieldy French text with a shorter one, which he managed to complete by August. At first called *Blanc*, it was soon retitled *Bing*. Almost triumphantly, he wrote to a friend: "Seem to have got something suitably brief and outrageous all whiteness and silence and finishedness. Hardly publishable which matters not at all" (qtd. in Knowlson, 481).

Bing (Ping)

From the earliest of his ten drafts of *Bing* Beckett envisioned a lone still figure in a white box, whose displacements occur abruptly and onomatopoeti-

---

Although a fair copy of *Breath* has been widely reproduced, no holograph is extant. In summer 1966, Beckett recited *Breath* to me, in response to my question about what he had written. Sent to Kenneth Tynan in 1969 for his revue *Oh Calcutta*, the staging became the most notorious deviation from Beckett's text. First published as the "Prologue" to *Oh! Calcutta!* (New York: Grove, 1969), it was printed correctly in the second impression (1970) and then by Calder in *Gambit* in 1970. It is found in *CDW*, and in Beckett's French in *Comédie et actes divers* (1972).

Various early versions of *Bing* are at MoW, with photocopies at RUL. First published individually in 1966, *Bing* was republished as the fourth of *Têtes-Mortes* (first in the 1967, then in the 1972 edition). Federman and Fletcher publish Beckett's ten

cally—in early drafts through the sound "paf," in the final French version "hop," and only in English translation "ping" (after "pfft" was discarded). From the first draft, the narrative is couched in brief verbless phrases, and it is read (with difficulty) from a single block paragraph, in which periods are the only punctuation. In these phrase-sentences, as in the versets of *Comment c'est,* single words can float meaning or emphasis. Phrases are musicalized by rhyme, assonance, and alliteration.

Demanding as *Bing* is to read, the overall architecture is fairly clear. The narrative begins with the phrase "Tout su," and proceeds to subvert the "all" that is "known," by means of minute modifications of repeated phrases. Some hundred words are permuted and combined into a thousand about the still white figure that is barely visible in its still white surround. In this rain of repetitions corporeal words mentioned only once are arresting— the fallen "ongles" and the fallen "cheveux," which precede the sentence containing "chairs" and "cicatrices." Seven times we read of the pale blue eyes of the figure, and toward the end of *Bing,* we twice encounter a foreign, imploring eye—the second time immediately before the arrival of silence and completion, if not quite the "finishedness" mentioned in Beckett's letter.

In *Bing* a sentence may be defined as a phrase beginning with a capital letter and ending with a period, but with only minimal recourse to grammar, since verbs are absent as well as articles, pronouns, prepositions, and conjunctions. *Bing* contains seventy of these telegraphic sentences, all but the first harboring some degree of repetition, which can subtly shade the meaning, or offer outright contradiction. The energizing sound "hop" occurs ten times, and in all but the tenth it accompanies a sudden displacement of the nude white body, one meter tall. The sound "bing" (how pronounced? Nasal French or plosive English?) occurs twenty times, and, although it is five times followed by "silence," it elsewhere hints of life—"murmurs, perhaps a nature, an issue, an image, a meaning, not alone." The final "bing silence" punctuates these human residua, and in French it is "hop" that finally announces that the piece is completed—French "achevé" or English "over," the word cherished by the raging, violent, moving protagonist of Beckett's *From an Abandoned Work,* a decade earlier.

Bing, also haunted by the color white, lacks the abandon of the earlier story. The third-person, literally omniscient narrator (Tout su—all known) strives to localize the white body in its white container. For the reader the

---

versions of *Bing* in an appendix to their bibliography, and I describe these in *Back to Beckett* (254–56). Beckett's English translation eclipses "hop" into "ping," and he adds "toes joined like sewn." *Ping* first appeared in *Encounter* (February 1967), and it is included in *CSP,* to which my page numbers refer.

white body is at first barely distinguishable from his white box. Legs and mouth are reduced to seams; with heels at right angles and hands hanging palms front, the feeling is one of martyrdom, which is later confirmed by "invisibles cicatrices" [scars invisible]. Even though the narrator begins with objective description, he soon resorts to memory—"ça de mémoire" [that much memory]. Although murmurs begin by being "tous sus," they soon hint at an issue, a nature, another being. In the white container against a background of almost white traces, the few colors are noteworthy. The body's pale blue eyes are thrice designated as "seule couleur," but several times the color blue appears elsewhere, as in "bleu et blanc au vent" [blue and white in the wind]—the French rhyme emphasizing the poetic association. However, blue is *not* the "seule couleur," for we are also "donné" rose with its floral or fleshly resonance, as well as black traces, crumbling quickly to gray. The lack of color reinforces the stillness of the moribund scene. So, too, repetition here seems to still motion. Sound-echoes hover over the upright coffin: "nu-su-tu-vu-cousu-issue; face-trace"; "bleu-yeux-creux"; the assonant "lumière-chaleur" and the many nasals that form rhymes and off-rhymes with the ubiquitous "blanc." Elizabeth Segrè has analyzed the parallel threads of polysemy, oscillatory rhythms, long-term dissolution, and phonetic patterning, which complicate this brief text.

Toward the end of *Bing* the repetitions of "inachevé" change to "achevé," and the adjective "dernier" precedes "couleur" and "ailleurs." A foreign eye makes its entrance in two sentences of some phonemic variety: "Bing peut-être pas seul une seconde avec image même temps un peu moins oeil noir et blanc mi-clos longs cils suppliant ça de mémoire presque jamais" (65) [Ping perhaps not alone one second with image same time a little less dim eye black and white half closed long lashes imploring that much memory almost never, 195]. By the end of the incantation the heart has twice evoked a soundless breath, and, with the once-blue eyes now white holes in the body's head, the final sentence opens on that head. The last (sourceless) murmur repeats the phrase "peut-être pas seul" before directly (not memorially) evoking the half-closed, unlustrous black-and-white eye that manages to implore, before the final silence and completion. The investigative eye is finally investigated.

In spite of the climactic conclusion, *Bing* is recognizably a Beckett text in that the grammatical ellipsis mirrors the narrative ellipsis. As the little body is barely human, the prose is barely comprehensible. Yet the foreign eye implores the text for continuity, in a work that exceeds *Imagination morte imaginez* in the relentlessness of a white body lost in a crumbling gray world. *Bing* is a bare narrative, in which neither the narrator nor its creation is quite obscured.

In the same month that Beckett completed *Bing* (August) he rushed to

Ireland when his sister-in-law Jean succumbed to cancer. Returning to Paris in September, he advised on a new production of *Comédie*. After seeking some sun in Greece, he returned to translations and obligations in the Paris winter. Two scholar-acquaintances made an unusual request, in spite of Beckett's frequent refusal to comment on or explicate his work (even though he sometimes did). Raymond Federman and John Fletcher wished to compile a bibliography of and about Beckett's work—in English and French. Whatever prompted Beckett's consent, it is not difficult to imagine the appeal of the project both to his sense of order and to his feeling for the primacy of his writing, as opposed to performance. Re-viewing old materials, dating them to the best of his recollection (sometimes inaccurately), he may well have been heartened at the quality and quantity of his creative work, but there is no syllable of evidence to this effect. Instead, he was moved to write a paragraph for his painter-friend Avigdor Arikha, which managed to encapsulate their shared aesthetic concerns.

Pour Avigdor Arikha

James Hansford paraphrases this lyric of criticism, which was written by Beckett for his friend, a painter and engraver. "The object (the 'unself') is 'impregnable' because the 'eye and hand' of the artist 'unceasingly changes' its constitution and disposition; and the artist in his turn is 'unceasingly changed' by the attempt at representation" (1985, 77). Almost wholly abstract, Beckett's paragraph nevertheless captures the efforts of eye and hand to render the "unself." In spite of the impossibility of the task, the image appears during a truce of this war of the internal and the external, the subject and the object.

1967

Escaping to Ussy early in the year, Beckett began a play for Madeleine Renaud, at which he worked fitfully for over a year, before abandoning it. In spite of his cataracts, he still drove his car in Ussy; because of his cataracts, he fell into the pit of a garage, which he did not see. His friends the Haydens

---

Written "pour Avigdor Arikha," who had a 1967 exhibit at the Galérie Claude Bernard, the manuscript is doubtless in the possession of the artist. It is published (along with Beckett's English translation) in the catalog to Arikha's Beckett Exhibition at the Victoria and Albert Museum, February–May 1976. The English version is reprinted in James Hansford's article on *La Falaise* (1985), and it is printed in both French and English in *Disjecta*.

nursed him through two cracked ribs and many painful bruises. Back in Paris in March he learned of the death of one of his oldest friends, Thomas Mac-Greevy. The latter's heirs, two nieces, wrote to ask Beckett for instructions about the disposal of his many letters, which MacGreevy had saved. Beckett's wish was that the letters be destroyed, and for a time he thought that his wish had been honored.[7] These physical and emotional burdens may account for the dearth of writing—except for tinkering with a recalcitrant play.

"Medical Monologue"

I am unable to read the unpublished, jettisoned holograph. Of the four typed leaves of my arbitrarily titled fragments, the last two seem to be a revision of the other two, since each consists of a woman's monologue about medications. In the first monologue she reports her conversation with a doctor about the unpredictable effects of drugs. Shifting to the present tense, she examines two liquids for self-injection. The second version of this monologue is restricted to an examination of the two liquids onstage, labeled A and B. This second monologue is drier, with calculations about dosages and effects. The piece breaks off when she asks herself why she continues, and she answers herself: "On est fait aussi pour aller, tant qu'il y a quelque part, ou je me reponds, C'est l'appel de la pointe [?], ou il faut bien se fixer, sous peine de rebrousser chemin" [One is also created to go on, as long as there is somewhere, or I answer myself, It's the call of the pinnacle, or one has to stop somewhere, or risk beginning again].

Unable to complete new work, Beckett turned to what had become a compulsion to translate what was already written in one of his languages. Since young French admirers, Agnès and Ludovic Janvier, were summering near Ussy, he enlisted their aid in the translation of *Watt*, which he could not face alone.[8] On August 18 he flew to Berlin, where he was committed to direct *Endspiel* at the Schiller-Theater Werkstatt. While there, he signed an appeal for the release of the Spanish playwright Arrabal from Franco's prison. In Berlin Beckett had a recurrent nightmare that he attributed to smoking strong French cigarettes (Gauloises), and he replaced them with the cigarillos to which he was addicted for the last two decades of his life. After the opening of *Endspiel*, Beckett flew to Berne to consult an eye specialist, who confirmed the double cataract diagnosis, and who cheered him with a

---

Listed in *BatR* as "Petit Odéon Fragments," the aborted medical monologue is found on seventeen leaves of a notebook (MS 2927) and four pages of a typescript that probably revises that holograph (MS 1227/7/16/3). The beginning of the notebook is dated February 1967, and the last written leaf is dated April 1968, but I am assuming that most of the notes were composed in 1967, which is the year they are twice mentioned in letters to Alan Schneider. On March 28, 1967, Beckett wrote me: "Little Odéon play down the drain," but he evidently continued to tinker with it.

prognosis of successful operations and improved vision in the near future (Knowlson, 492).

1968

The year is celebrated in the West as one of activism and rebellion. For Beckett it was a year that began with an idea for another television play for Mac-Gowran, continued with his final trip to Ireland—for the funeral of his aunt Peggy, John Beckett's mother—and climaxed with a lung abscess that kept him housebound for a half-year. So ill was Beckett that he could see no one; nor even speak on the telephone. As he wrote Richard Seaver on June 21: "I get up, dress and sit around, drinkless and tobaccoless. It seems a long time since I answered the phone or saw anyone" (qtd. in Knowlson, 723 n. 63). Yet he worked fitfully—during March, April, and September—at a text that eventually became the *foirade Se voir*. Only in summer did he begin to heal. By December, Beckett had to escape the Paris winter, so he and Suzanne flew to Portugal. In three months there Beckett slowly regained his health—such as it was.

1969

Although the *foirade Se voir* is undated, 1969 seems a probable year for its completion. The piece was begun in March 1968, and, according to *BatR*, it went through five drafts before being broken off in September 1968. The manuscript of continuation has not been found.

Se Voir (Closed Place)

An arena is surrounded by a ditch. Between the two is a track just wide enough to admit the passage of a single person. In the arena may be millions of bodies: "Sans jamais se voir ni s'entendre. Sans jamais se toucher" (*Pour*

Five separate beginnings of *Se Voir* are contained in RUL 2928, a slim notebook titled by Beckett "Fragments Prose début 68," although it actually contains a draft, dated September (as well as an aborted teleplay of 1972). There is no full holograph version, but RUL holds two corrected typescripts of *Se Voir*. It was first published as *Foirade V* in *Minuit* (May 1973), and although it is the last *foirade* in the volume *Pour finir encore et autres foirades* (Paris: Minuit, 1976), it is Fizzle 5 in Beckett's English translation (Grove, 1976). *CSP* corrects the title of the British Calder edition—from "Closed Space" to "Closed Place." My page references are to *CSP*.

finir, 51) [Never seeing never hearing one another. Never touching, *CSP,* 236]. The narrator shifts attention from the arena to the deep ditch, with its several lots of brilliance and many more of darkness, each lot with just enough room for an average body in diagonal. The arena and the ditch are separated by the narrow track on which lie dead leaves. In spite of its French title, which means "to see oneself," no self is visible; the English title is more clearly referential—"closed place." Yet the concentric circles of ditch and track also mirror the human eye, which thus "se voit."

As in other pieces of the 1960s, *Se voir* is written in short sentences punctuated only by periods. The narrator tries in vain to introduce sequence through such connectives as "puis" and "donc" [then and therefore], but time has apparently abandoned this small, densely populated world. As in *Imagination . . .* and *Bing,* the narrator seems to create his world as he describes it: "A part ce qui est dit il n'y a rien" (51) [There is nothing but what is said, 236]. However, the sayer and the saying vanish after the thirteenth brief sentence, and the narrator assumes a tone as dry as the leaves on the track. Yet there rustles a human residue in the dead-leafed track, where "Jamais deux ne s'y croisent" (53) [On it no two ever meet, 237]. *Se voir* may be Beckett's bleakest vision. At least it is mercifully brief.

Committed to direct *Das Letzte Band* at the Schiller-Theater Werkstatt in late spring, Beckett sought renewed energy in the play about a wearish old man. In February he sent Alan Schneider a sketch for a television *Krapp,* in which the American director would guide the Irish actor Jack MacGowran. The television suggestions have been published by Zilliacus (1976) in a book that should be republished. I quote the important concept of two cameras, which Schneider recognized as a separation of outer from inner probing:

> Two Cameras A and B. Cut from one to other as required.
> A mere eye [cf. *Play*] . . . frontal, covering general situation and exits to "darkness" backstage and back to table. It is free to vary its images, i.e. to move forward and back and to left and right of general axis, provided no element of the total situation be at any moment lost in the process.
> B investigates, from all angles and often from above, detail of table situation, hands, face, machine, ledger, boxes and tapes. This camera listens and its activity is affected by words spoken. It can thus be used, not only as "savage eye," but as a means to distinguish in this recorded past those moments which matter little or nothing to Krapp from those which matter much or extremely. It arrives at this by a corresponding reduction or cessation of activity expressive of Krapp's changing levels of attention. . . .
> Camera B:
> Krapp though hard of hearing hears acutely, but sees little or nothing (in the present). This camera is Krapp's hearing plus acute eye.

Latter function inhibited at moments of most avid listening and fully active at those of least. Its accurate use depends therefore on assessment of Krapp's levels of intentness, or listening values. (204–5)

Zilliacus comments, "The cameras are made to reinforce particles or segments of action which have already been emphasized in performance" (205), and such segments are reflected in Beckett's own German production of *Das Letzte Band*.

Back in Paris Beckett liquidated his obligations, so that he could retreat to Ussy in order to write. The result was another short French piece that rushes at one, through its repetitions. After his debilitating illness, Beckett achieved a new approach to a narrative about a residual being.

Sans (*Lessness*)

According to Knowlson, Beckett wrote part of the blurb on the book cover of his English translation of *Sans—Lessness*. He summarized the concern of the new work with "the collapse of some such refuge as that last attempted in *Ping* and with the ensuing situation of the refugee" (500). Although *Sans* returns to the paragraphs disdained in *Bing*, periods remain the only mark of punctuation of the 120 separate sentences, grouped in twenty-four paragraphs.[9] The text keeps doubling back on itself, with some hundred phrases often repeated. At its center is a small, still, naked body, with beating heart and pale blue eyes. That "refugee" figures only slenderly in the remainder of Beckett's blurb: "Ruin, exposure, wilderness, mindlessness, past and future denied and affirmed, are the categories, formally distinguishable, through which the writing winds, first in one disorder, then in another." The binary oppositions of "disorder" are past and future, denial and affirmation. Narratives are read sequentially, but reflection alone can enable one to discern the temporal resonances of the quantities in Beckett's *Sans*: 2 x 60 sentences, the number of seconds in a minute, or minutes in an hour; 24 paragraphs, the number of hours in a day; the limiting number of seven sentences to a paragraph, the number of days in a week. The 52 repetitions of the word *sans* in the French text may hint at 52 weeks in a year, and the number factors into 4 x 13, the latter a longtime favorite of Beckett. However Beckett played with numbers in *Sans*—and he did—it is the words that relate a baffling, sometimes contradictory story.

Beckett's bookjacket blurb implies that the truest refuge is the collapse of refuge. All is ashen gray—toppled walls, earth, sky, and even little body.

Sans's original six "families" of ten sentences each are in Yale University Library. Pountney's appendix 2 prints a useful montage of the families in *Lessness*, Beckett's ingenious translation of his French title. First published alone in 1969, and then as the fifth and last of the 1972 edition of *Têtes-Mortes*, *Sans* was translated by Beckett, and its first English publication was in the *New Statesman*, May 1, 1970. It is included in *CSP*, to which my page numbers refer.

The very memory of them is denied, and yet memories intrude into the paragraphs that lack topic sentences. "Aucun souvenir" is the only key-word always to occupy the terminal position in its sentence, thus condemning what precedes it to oblivion. In six out of ten of these memoryless sentences, we read of an "oeil calme," perhaps the heir of the foreign eye of *Bing*. In contrast to the end-sentence "aucun souvenir," the "jamais" that signals denial of a past, occurs most usually (in eight of the ten sentences) at the beginning of its sentence; yet, paradoxically, "never" evokes the very events that are denied. Toward the end of *Sans* we read of figments, dreams, or imagination of life in time: "Jamais que silence tel qu'en imagination ces rires de folle ces cris. Jamais qu' imaginé le bleu dit en poésie céleste qu'en imagination folle." [Never but silence such that in imagination this wild laughter these cries. Never but imagined the blue in a wild imagining the blue celeste of poesy, *CSP*, 201]. The French text harbors echoes of a well-known sentence of Malebranche: "L'imagination c'est la folle du logis." The antique resonance of "celeste" indicates some distance from such works of the crazed imagination. It is in sentences affirming past and future, or passing time, that Beckett is most ingenious: the "il" will curse God in a blessed time, rain will fall on him in another blessed time; unhappiness will reign in still another blessed time. When "il" moves, so will sky, air, and sand; even on his back "il" will take an epic step; as "il" relives day and night, his heart will beat again. It is at once an escape from fixity and a condemnation to repeat the past—if only in imagination.

For all the ashen gray surround, it is on "petit corps" and "il" that the narrative concentrates. Although "petit corps" is only one of Beckett's six language-groups that constitute *Sans,* the body also enters three sentences of the outer-world group, and we attach to that body the future-tense verbs that promise an improbable life. It is almost (but not quite) beyond belief that Beckett's last paragraph of *Sans* arrived by chance. Three of its four sentences begin "Petit corps," fixing the body in our minds, and the paragraph climaxes on the disclaimer of the final sentence, which cannot be subjugated into a family: "Chimère l'aurore qui dissipe les chimères et l'autre dit brune" [Figment dawn dispeller of figments and the other called dusk, 199]. The sentence is provocatively pluralistic: Is it a figment that dawn is a dispeller of figments? Does a figment dawn dispel dusk, along with other figments? Is dusk another dispeller, or another figment? The whole paragraph may be a figment, but it is a figment without "sans."

Sans, constructed as it was by "an ingenious interaction of chance and choice" (Brater, 94), is perhaps Beckett's most difficult piece to read *as narrative*. Although the ellipsis is less enigmatic than that of *Bing*, the presence of verbs entails new problems; it is impossible to make logical sense of passing time—"Faces blanches sans trace tête par l'oeil calme toute sa raison aucun souvenir" (76) [Blank planes sheer white calm eye light of reason all gone from mind, 198]—which is one way of dismissing life. Yet through Beckett's combined and recombined sentence-segments threads a celebration of the imagination that defies the ravages of graying time. Rather than representing a progression toward the dimming of the self—*sans*, lessness—*Sans* regenerates conflict: refuge versus ruins, past versus future, affirmation versus denial, blessing in misfortune. The final sentence of *Sans* reads suspiciously like a residual catharsis.[10]

Before *Sans* was written, Beckett grouped his three chronologically close stories as *Têtes-Mortes*, a neologism redolent at once of skulls and stilled minds.[11] Preceded by his translation into French of *From an Abandoned Work*, these three tales, each hovering over a kind of burial, end on a little rush of life: the androgynous narrator of *Assez* feels an old hand on her/his old breasts; the voice of *Imagination morte imaginez* wonders about an eye-flicking pair; the chanting narrator of *Bing* murmurs about an imploring black eye in a still white scene. The three works present different hermetic worlds, but the human inevitably intrudes: *Assez* traces a timeless liaison nourished by the flowers of rhetoric; *Imagination morte imaginez* rescues barely living human bodies from a tempest of uncertainties; *Bing* permutes its way toward a white body in a white container, which is finally subjected to an imploring human eye. After *Sans* was completed, with its tension between what is given and what is imagined, Beckett retained the title *Têtes-Mortes* for the five pieces in French (but he withheld *Se Voir* for the *Foirades*). Read sequentially, a narrative progresses from a first-person account of three arbitrarily chosen days to a first-person evocation of a couple, to three formally different reductions to residual, minimal human being. These five tales, turning on repetition, display variations of Beckett's "art and craft," and if, singly or collectively, they do not crest in a victory of the self, life is at least discernible—in its subtlest signs.

On October 23, 1969, Beckett's publisher-friend Jérôme Lindon sent a cable to Tunis, where the Becketts were seeking sunshine: "Chers Sam et Suzanne. Malgré tout ils t'ont donné le Prix Nobel—Je vous conseille de vous cacher. Je vous embrasse" (quoted in Knowlson, 505) [Dear Sam and Suzanne. In spite of everything, they have given you the Nobel Prize—I advise you to go into hiding. With affection]. The good advice proved impossible to follow, although it was a fortunate accident that Beckett was relatively inaccessible in Tunis. The notion of the Nobel Prize was abroad for some time, but the fait accompli was an irritation to the Becketts. Not only did Lindon represent Beckett in Stockholm in December, but the writer remained far from Paris till the end of January 1970. For a year after that Beckett blamed the prize for the paucity of his new work.

1970–76

Soudain ou Peu à Peu
(All at once or by degrees)

1970

By the time Beckett received the Nobel Prize, four of his publishers had become his friends—Lindon, Calder, Rosset, and Unseld—and it was to avoid disappointing these friends that he exhumed unpublished works—*Premier Amour, Mercier et Camier,* fragmentary plays, short pieces that he gathered as *foirades.* He agreed to a commercial printing of *More Pricks Than Kicks,* which had been restricted to scholars. While struggling with translations in Paris, he also undertook to direct Jean Martin, the original Lucky, in *La Dernière bande,* his translation of *Krapp's Last Tape.*

Most importantly, the prize impelled Beckett to look again at fiction he had discarded in 1966, after months of concentrated work. In jettisoning "Chacun son dépeupleur," he thought he had salvaged *Bing.* On the holograph of the abandoned text he had written: "Though very different formally, these 2 mss. belong together. *Bing* may be regarded as the result or miniaturisation of *Le Dépeupleur* abandoned because of its intractable complexities." Beckett paired these two texts, but they are indeed "very different formally." At the most obvious level, *Bing* is much shorter than *Le Dépeupleur,* and its individual sentences are also much shorter. A cylinder-imprisoned population precipitates to a single small white body in its cubical container. In both works, however, Beckett moulds a patterned world of the imagination, with only minimal narrative thrust.

Le Dépeupleur (The Lost Ones)

Beckett's French title is a neologism derived from a line in Lamartine's poem, "L'Isolement"—"Un seul être vous manque, et tout est dépeuplé!" [You lack

---

Eight drafts of *Le Dépeupleur* are at MoW, with photocopies at RUL. *Le Dépeupleur* was first published by Minuit in 1970, with incorrect dates (1968–70). Excerpts

308

a single being, and the world is depopulated]. Lamartine, a Romantic poet who felt lonely after the death of his beloved Mme. Charles, emotionalized about his indifference to the beauties of a sunset. In the cylinder that houses the two-hundred-odd inhabitants of Beckett's piece, however, emotion is spare, and only in the final, fifteenth paragraph is "tout . . . dépeuplé." Lamartine's depopulator is death, or at least the mourned dead one. In Beckett's world death occurs only in his 1970 termination of the piece that he labored over in 1965 and 1966.

All drafts of *Le Dépeupleur* wield numbers and descriptions, in a way that is reminiscent, not of *Bing*, but of *All Strange Away*, which was completed the year before *Le Dépeupleur* was begun. In that narrative the phrase "if this is maintained" occurs twice, and "if maintained" occurs once, and we find echoes in the five repetitions of "si cette notion est maintenue" of *Le Dépeupleur*. In both works we read about a last person who is subjected to a sourceless fluctuating light, and in both works we are confronted with naked figures at the mercy of a hostile environment. The sometimes convoluted syntax of the earlier piece cedes in *Le Dépeupleur* to impersonal declarative sentences, where a sentence must again be defined (as in *Bing* and *Sans*) as whatever begins with a capital letter and ends with a period (the only punctuation in *Le Dépeupleur*, aside from four question marks). These sentences are grouped in fifteen paragraphs, which vary in length between some 150 and 1,500 words.

To some extent Samuel Beckett is present in each of his narrators, although author and tale-teller should never be simply equated. The narrator of *Le Dépeupleur* shares its author's taste for numbers and logic, but he is a rare example of one who is innocent of irony (although Beckett can be ironic through him). Cold and determinedly clinical, the narrator presents us with a population inhabiting a rubberlike cylinder. What other Beckett narrator could make such naive statements as "Ces rares et brèves relâches sont d'un effet dramatique inexprimable pour en dire le moins" (32) [The effect of those brief and rare respites is remarkably dramatic to put it mildly, *CSP*, 213]; "Tout est donc pour le mieux" (37) [So all is for the best, 216]; "Exemple entre mille de l'harmonie qui règne dans le cylindre entre ordre et laisser-

---

were published earlier: the penultimate paragraph as "Dans le cylindre" in *Livres de France* (January 1967); the second paragraph as "La Notion" in *L'Ephémère* (spring 1970); paragraphs 3 and 4 as *L'Issue* (Paris: Georges Visat, 1968); the first paragraph as *Séjour* (Paris: Georges Richar, 1970). Under the title *The Lost Ones* (which shifts the emphasis from an abstraction to people), Beckett's translation was published by Calder and Boyars in 1972, and that same year by Grove. My page numbers refer to the Minuit edition for the French and *CSP* for the translation. The English translation sports a wider lexical register than the French, and this has been astutely scrutinized by Connor (1988, 104–11).

aller" (39) [One example among a thousand of the harmony that reigns in the cylinder between order and licence, 216]; "Qu'il n'existe aucun règlement visant à prévenir une telle injustice montre clairement qu'elle ne risque pas de se perpétuer" (44–45) [That there exists no regulation tending to forestall such injustice shows clearly it can never be more than temporary, 219]? In such sentences Beckett regales the attentive reader with the limitations of his narrator.

The narrator imperturbably itemizes the excruciating conditions that govern the behavior of the cylinder's inhabitants, as well as the behavior itself. In the accretion of detail, the narrator naively affirms: "Car seul le cylindre offre des certitudes et au-dehors rien que mystère" (38) [For in the cylinder alone are certitudes to be found and without nothing but mystery, 216]. By the time the narrator makes this statement, however, it is evident that cylinder certitudes are *not* to be found. A work of the imagination has its own seeming will.

Beckett's own incertitudes are evident in his manuscripts. At one point in his composition, he thought of assigning each subject to a given paragraph, as indicated in the following list: "2. Population et notion. 3. Séjour. 4. Issue. 5. Zénith. 6. Echelles code. 7. Echelles transport. 8. Sédentaires piste et vaincus. Piste arène. Population notion 2. 9. Eclairage-température avec conséquences." However, he did not adhere to this plan, and later drafts testify to Beckett's increasing difficulty with a text that gripped him in its vise. The last paragraph of the manuscript begins: "Autant le cylindre admet la fatigue autant il inclut le repos" [As the cylinder admits fatigue, it also includes repose]. But Beckett himself found no repose. The verso of his last manuscript leaf lists sixteen problems with, or self-commands about, the text. Uniquely, five years elapsed before he could conclude this work.

As published, *Le Dépeupleur* opens with a verbless sentence, which contains the single appearance of the title: "Séjour où des corps vont cherchant chacun son dépeupleur" [Abode where lost bodies roam each searching for its lost one, 202]. The narrator then describes the cylinderscape and its occupants. His dry, academic style dominates the long first paragraph, which introduces us to fluctuations of light and temperature, naked bodies searching in an enclosed cylinder, desiccation of inhabitants' skin and its effects on their behavior, their desire for ladders that can be climbed to niches or tunnels in the upper half of the cylinder wall. In that first paragraph alone subjects are announced: "Lumière. . . . Température. . . . Echelles. . . . Niches ou alvéoles" (7–12) [The light. . . . The temperature. . . . The ladders. . . . The niches or alcoves, 202–3]. Almost parenthetically, we learn that the inhabitants' search will be vain; that moments of fixity look like a finale. Nothing is revealed about the inhabitants' feelings, but we read about their inability to copulate, the indescribable sound of their kisses, their blows against the body and even the head, their acrobatic climb up the ladders, their inadvertent meetings from opposite ends of a tunnel. (We never learn how many of the twenty alcoves are actually tunnels.)

Although the very first sentence announces that each of the cylinder-dwellers is seeking her/his *dépeupleur* ("lost one" in English), the search soon shifts to a possible exit from the cylinder, and then that search dissolves into the elaborate rules by which searching is conducted. Above an imaginary circumference halfway up the cylinder are twenty recesses or alcoves, which are arranged in irregular quincunxes—harmoniously arranged, if anyone could achieve sufficient perspective to observe them. Propped inharmoniously against the cylinder wall are fifteen ladders of different length, each missing various rungs, and these rungs serve as weapons. On each ladder a single climber is permitted to mount to an upper recess, which is much coveted because the cylinder-floor offers less than one square meter to each inhabitant. The narrator classifies the cylinder occupants according to their conduct in the search: (1) the climbers who constantly move; (2) the watchers who move and stop; (3) the sedentary who are immobile, except for their violence when stepped on; (4) the vanquished whose heads are lowered in their immobility. Not only do these designations ignore any goal of the search, but the categories continually shift. However, at the time of narration the proportions are harmonious:

5 vanquished × 4 = 20 sedentary × 3 = 60 watchers × 2 = 120 climbers,

or 205 in all, 200 in round numbers. Among them a few vanquished are particularized: paragraph 10 presents a young white-haired woman with a baby in her lap. Not until paragraph 14 are we offered a portrait of a vanquished woman seated gracefully against the wall, with long red hair that curtains her face and body; she is the north, the only point of orientation in the cylinder.

The inhabitants seem to dwell eternally in this inferno, since the narrator generalizes their behavior, eschewing specific incidents. Although he tries to be scrupulous in reporting the complicated movements and stillnesses of the population within the cylinderscape, he has to battle with rules and subrules. In paragraph 12 the syntax grows as complicated as the laws it describes. Each of the fifteen ladders may hold only one climber at a time, with descent having priority over ascent. On the cylinder floor the ladders must be carried in one direction only, and the prospective climbers must line up before each ladder unidirectionally along the cylinder wall, which also supports the sedentary and the vanquished. Searchers not yet queuing for a ladder must circle countercarrierwise in an inner circumference, and still other searchers may gather pell-mell in the central arena. Our eyes of flesh read that an "oeil de chair" [eye of flesh] cannot differentiate the three areas;

nor can it distinguish between the climbers, the watchers, the sedentary, and the vanquished, who slip in and out of these categories. As readers, we are in a hell of a Dante-nourished imagination, where this horrific notion is temporarily maintained, and yet the narrator's logical illogical legalisms recall our real world.

Although the narrator never enters the mind of any cylinder-dweller— "Nul ne regarde en soi où il ne peut y avoir personne" (27) [None looks within himself where none can be, 211]—we sense an intensity of suffering. With parchment-dry skin, the cylinder-dwellers are tortured by touch, and yet the lack of floor space forces constant contact. The cylinder's rubberlike wall retains no mark of foot, fist, or head that strikes it; thus the cylinder is impervious to human pain. Yet human action is widespread: Ladder climbers can be assaulted, sedentary ones react violently when stepped on, coition is frenzied, and infringement of rules incites mob action.

As the account acquires complexity, pain is registered mainly by the eyes—"données bleus de préférence en tant que plus périssables" (34) [blue for preference as being the most perishable, 214]. In the very first paragraph we learn that the flickering light afflicts the eyes. Paragraphs 10 and 11 are largely devoted to eyes: the watchers devour the climbers with their eyes, and with their eyes the sedentary gape at every passerby. The vanquished usually close their eyes, and yet ocular fever may sear them again. Were it possible to focus on an eye over a period of time, one would observe the pupil gradually overwhelming the whole organ. Husband and wife may exchange a glance before going their separate ways: "Quoi qu'ils cherchent ce n'est pas ça" (32) [Whatever it is they are searching for it is not that, 213]. For the word "vaincu" trailing its pathos, an intelligent observer might mistakenly substitute the word *aveugle*. Although the narrator several times describes moments of rigid fixity in the flux of the cylinder, only in paragraph 13 does he inform us that inhabitants' eyes are then turned on the void, and only in paragraph 14 do we learn that the vanquished are forbidden to deny any part of themselves to the scrutiny of other eyes. The various searches seem finally to precipitate to the organ of sight.

Fourteen paragraphs of increasingly convoluted observation precede the final paragraph, which alone progresses narratively. As late as paragraph 6 the narrator mentions "un *premier* aperçu" (emphasis added), and he begins the finale hesitantly: "Ainsi de suite à ce que vers l'impensable fin si cette notion est maintenue seul un dernier cherche encore par faibles à-coups" (53) [So on infinitely until toward the unthinkable end if this notion is maintained a last body of all by feeble fits and starts is searching still, 222]. At the "unthinkable [but readable] end" the last body is surrounded by those that are baked or frozen rigid. "Si c'est un homme" [if a man] he rises and opens his burning eyes. He carves his way to the north, kneels before her, and parts her heavy hair. Lifting her face and wielding his thumbs, he forces open her eyes and gazes into "ces calmes déserts" (54) [those calm wastes, 223] until his own eyes close. Her head falls forward again, and he retreats to his own final position, whereupon the temperature drops to zero, the light to darkness, and the insectlike hum to silence—as has been earlier predicted in the second paragraph: "Dans le noir froid de la chair immobile" (14) [In cold darkness motionless flesh, 205]. Finally it comes to pass.

The narrator retains sufficient omniscience of the narrative tradition to prophesy the end of the cylinder-dwellers, which they themselves cannot imagine. In other respects, however, the narrator lacks the certitude that he ascribes to the abode. He hedges his descriptions with such disclaiming adverbs as "environ," "plus ou moins," "peut-être," "presque," "chiffre rond," "sans doute," "inexprimable." As he accumulates details, he begins to contradict himself: Having predicted that the myth of an exit would be the last to disappear, he does not mention it in the finale. After affirming that the presence of a ceiling exit cannot be ascertained, he suggests a possible manipulation of the ladders to enable reach of that height. After stating that copulation is impossible, he mentions "the work of love." It seems at first that the worst violence in the cylinder is exercised by the sedentary when they are stepped on, but by paragraph 14 the violence exercised by climbers subject to search "dépasse . . . tout ce que dans le genre le cylindre peut offrir" (52) [none approaches this, 222]. In paragraph 11 all is announced for the best, but by paragraph 15 the final freeze does not read as though it were for the best.

During the course of narration the narrator grows increasingly uncertain. In the first paragraph the dimensions of the cylinder are inexplicably harmonious, but by paragraph 11 numbers run wild. After the rules and sub-rules are delineated, we learn that the inhabitants are ignorant of the large picture, and they search by intuition. In paragraph 12 the narrator asks questions that he doesn't answer, although he states that the answers are clear and easy to give, if one dares. He compares incomparables like the skin and the soul, in their response to the merciless climate. By paragraph 12 he acknowledges: "Tout n'a pas été dit et ne le sera jamais" (45) [All has not been told and never shall be, 219]. Nevertheless, what *has* been told is a cruelly gripping account of a social system that is at once self-enclosed and parallel to those we know; of a mythology that sustains a series of laws that obscure the myth; of an unknowable beginning and an unthinkable end that are nevertheless narrated; and of inconstancy of purpose during an existence of life as excrescence. Although the last figure—if a man—is also inexplicably the first to bow his head, the gesture is hardly triumphant, as is the acquisition of will-lessness in *Act without Words I*, written over a decade earlier. Yet, the cylinderscape itself is a complex and complicated creation, whose dynamic theatricality is in tension with the dry narrative tone. Particularly telling is the human emotion of the little people, to which the narrator is virtually insensitive. In a performance adaptation of this fiction the actor David Warrilow captured the radically divergent movements of narrator *and* cylinder-dweller.[1]

Wearied of the post-Nobel fuss in Paris, and disappointed that his eyes were not yet "ripe" enough for cataract surgery, Beckett sought respite in Sardinia, where he received news of the death of his old friend, the painter Henri Hayden, whom he had met in Roussillon, where they were both refugees. Back in his Ussy cottage, Beckett may have dabbled at what he later released as *foirades*. Certainly he gave a paragraph for illustration to the painter Geneviève Asse. Published with her engravings as *Abandonné*, it was revised for the opening of the *foirade Pour finir encore*, which was not completed until 1975.

Abandonné

It seems inevitable that Beckett should offer a text to a visual artist. The eye and hand were at the center of the paragraph he wrote for his artist friend Avigdor Arikha in 1966; so this paragraph focuses on the skull and the hand. In Beckett's later piece both members are detached from a body; the skull rests on a board, and the hand, bound by a silver thread, is cut off at the wrist. The skull is surrounded by a black void that is only occasionally pierced by slow flashes of faint light, and the hand appears in one of those flashes. In the last sentence of the paragraph the skull begins to prepare to end. The title is therefore ironic, in that the work of the skull is not abandoned, even if it is beginning to end. (Indeed Beckett did not abandon the image of the skull on a board in the void, which figures in *Pour finir encore*.)

At long last on October 14, 1970, Beckett's left eye was operated upon, gradually opening new detail to his physical vision. Although the eye healed well, he at first needed help in navigation. His painter-friend Avigdor Arikha guided him through a Bram van Velde retrospective at the Musée National d'Art Moderne, and he was delighted with his new appreciation of the latter's paintings (Knowlson, 514).

1971

Beckett translated *Film* into French before the operation on his right eye on February 17. Again the result was successful, although synchronization of

The paragraph *Abandonné* first appears in the illustrated edition published by Georges Visat in 1971; it is reprinted in *Beckettiana* (February, 1997). Knowlson explains the source of the title (512–13).

both eyes seemed slow to him. Flu drove him to Italy in spring, but he was back in Paris by July, to prepare the German text of *Happy Days,* which he had promised to direct at the Schiller Theater in Berlin. As always in that city, he interspersed rehearsals with social affability. After the premiere he stayed on a few days to rehearse Jack MacGowran in his one-man Beckett show. Returning wearily to Paris, he needed rest, and Suzanne arranged for a month in Malta. There at the cathedral in Valletta he admired Caravaggio's painting *The Beheading of St. John the Baptist.* He later wrote Knowlson: "Image of *Not I* in part suggested by Caravaggio's *Decollation of St. John the Baptist*" (521). The "in part" is Beckettianly ambiguous. A severed head was already present in Beckett's "Kilcool" fragment of 1963. Knowlson links the Auditor of *Not I* with a horrified spectator in Caravaggio's painting, and he also suggests that the Auditor's gesture is found in a Mattia Pregi painting hanging near the Caravaggio in Valletta (729 n. 88). Perhaps what Beckett borrowed from Caravaggio is his celebrated chiaroscuro. Just as later painters were influenced by Caravaggio's contrast of brilliant light and deep shadow, so Beckett staged a spotlit mouth and a faintly lit Auditor.[2]

1972

Before committing *Not I* to paper, however, Beckett tried to fulfill a December promise to Luigi Majno of Milan, who wished to publish a deluxe edition of a text by Beckett with etchings by his friend, Stanley William Hayter of Atelier 17 in Paris. On January 19 Beckett wrote eight heavily revised sentences of what would become *Sounds,* but which he temporarily abandoned (RUL 1396/4/45). Perhaps those sentences sensitized Beckett to stillness, so that he was impressed during February in Morocco, by a still figure in a djellaba, who seemed to be listening intently. Knowlson guesses that "the image of the djellaba-clad figure coalesced with [Beckett's] sharp memories of the Caravaggio painting" (521). Yet in 1971, while walking after a Berlin *Happy Days* rehearsal, Beckett asked me: "Can you stage a mouth? Just a moving mouth with the rest of the stage in darkness?" I didn't realize it at that time, but he must have been mulling over *Not I,* even though the earliest manuscript is dated March 1972. Whatever figures or paintings may have catalyzed the process, Beckett's verbal blockage at last dissolved—with fluidity. Between March 20 and April 1 he penned a draft of *Not I,* adding addenda on April 21.

Not I

"I hear [Mouth] breathless, urgent, feverish, rhythmic, panting along, without undue concern with intelligibility. Addressed less to the understanding than to the nerves of the audience which should in a sense *share her bewilderment*," Beckett wrote to Alan Schneider, the play's first director (Harmon, 283). Audiences do indeed "share her bewilderment," but nerves do not necessarily war with understanding, *pace* Beckett. It is to the understanding that the title is addressed, over Mouth's head, as it were, since her ruthlessly third-person monologue avoids the pronoun "I." The Auditor's gestures respond to Mouth's four insistent denials; at her vehement fifth refusal, he is immobile, defeated. Beckett's French translation freights the Auditor's gesture with blame as well as compassion: "le geste consiste en une sorte de haussement des bras dans un mouvement fait de blâme et de pitié impuissante" (24). In Beckett's second French production (1978) the Auditor finally covered his ears with his hands, as though unable to bear the persistent fiction. I do not wish to argue against the presence of this visually striking opposition—the illuminated Mouth versus the shadowy Auditor, which embodies the conflict between a self-denying narrative and her confessor, accuser, or alter ego. However, I find that opposition (corresponding to the I-he opposition in Beckett's fiction) less intense than the inclusion of the theater experience within Mouth's monologue.

For some fifteen tense minutes an audience focuses on a spotlit hovering mouth while listening to the verbal stream it emits. Within that verbal stream are recurrent references to a buzz "so-called" and a beam, which are analogous to the verbiage and the spotlight that assail us in the theater. For some fifteen tense minutes we strain to hear and follow the narrative, and that narrative tells of words involuntarily heard and deciphered. Phrases like "not catching the half of it," "no idea what she was saying," "hanging on its words," "straining to hear," "piece it together," "trying to make sense of it,"

Gontarski cites two holographs of *Not I,* "at least eight typed versions, two synopses, a corrected proof, an acting script, and an outline of dramatic pauses [all at RUL]" (142). He reconstructs the probable chronology of composition. Pountney's appendix IV photocopies Beckett's handwritten analysis of *Not I.* Her appendix V prints Beckett's synopsis of the play. Her appendix VII charts different aspects of the two holographs and the six typescripts. Since Gontarski and Pountney have studied earlier versions of *Not I* (including the "Kilcool" manuscript of 1963), I glance at them only briefly. *Not I* was first performed in Alan Schneider's September 1972 production, with Jessica Tandy as Mouth. Later in 1972 Beckett assisted Anthony Page at the Royal Court production in London, with Billie Whitelaw as Mouth. *Not I* was first published separately by Faber in 1973, and then included in *Ends and Odds,* Faber and Grove, respectively. Beckett's French translation *Pas moi* was first published in *Minuit* 12, and subsequently in book format by Minuit in 1975. A penetrating study is Tubridy.

"no one could follow" are pertinent to She in Mouth's story, but also to us in the theater.

Mouth's staccato phrases impose an overwhelming feeling of fragmentation, and yet the story is surprisingly coherent—at least in reading. However one may miss details, a tale unfolds of a baby girl abandoned by her parents and brought up in a religious orphanage. Although the woman is speechless for most of her seventy years, she is suddenly afflicted with speech while she is in a meadow on an April morning. In Mouth's speech She alternates consternation *at* her speech with memories from her past, and those memories can be arranged into a rough biography of the nameless protagonist: silent shopping in a market, silent awareness of tears on her hand in Croker's Acres, silent defense in a courtroom, and, once or twice a year during winter, a sudden rush of shameful speech. The three silent events are framed by the spring and winter speech-eruptions. All the events are framed by a premature birth and She's surprising arrival at three score and ten years, or the biblical span of a life.

Thus to linearize the life narrated by Mouth is to betray it, for the tempo, the repetitions, and the interruptions of the verbal onslaught are designed for piecemeal understanding. Like *Play* nearly a decade earlier, *Not I* begins and ends unintelligibly, but readers or listeners will focus on what is intelligible *to them.* Nevertheless, the pervasive opposition of Mouth and Auditor is punctuated by the interrogative mode of Mouth's words. She is interrupted by twenty-two inaudible questions, to which she invariably reacts with "What?" Most of these questions lead to revisions of her narrative, but she is adamant about her retention of the third-person pronoun, She. Almost at the midpoint of Mouth's monologue, we hear: "whole body like gone . . . just the mouth," and in the theater we cannot escape from that mouth of a figure that is literally "gone" from our sight.

Most of Mouth's narrative is told in the past tense, when it resorts to verbs at all, but the April scene takes place in the present, each evocation adding a detail. On first mention She is seeking cowslips when darkness falls; the second evocation brings an awareness of words; the third mentions purgation and larks; the fourth suggests penance; the final phrases, uttered as the curtain descends, have all been heard before. In spite of their poetic resonance, they imply an eternal inferno. More subtly than the da capo of *Play,* *Not I* denies an end to its victim; for Beckett punishment is purgatorial without purgation (cf. Zeifman 1976).

The tale of Mouth, unlike the erotic triangle of *Play,* opens in pathos. No sooner has the infant been abandoned, however, than Mouth declares it "so typical affair" for this atypical event. The play's progression resembles that of *Play* in its accumulation of specific verbal detail in the context of an eerie stage picture. The monologue's vocabulary is simple, but it offers some variety. Biblical or hymnic echoes—"tender mercies"—are juxtaposed against clichés—"godforsaken hole, sweet silent as the grave." When studied, the clichés themselves reveal a literal and deepened meaning. Not only is Mouth prompted by her own "What?" questions to revise or repeat aspects of her story, but she herself ruminates occasionally: "who feels them [eyelids]?" "where was it?" And, twice: "could that be it?" As in Beckett's fiction, the indeterminacy of "it" broadens the scope of the text; "it" could be voice, brain, or life.

As unobtrusive as Mouth's lexicon is the musicality of the monologue. Beyond her control are the twenty-two unheard questions, but she introduces variety in the two screams, the two emphasized words (italicized in print), and the two different pairs of laughs. Her interjections are apparently involuntary, but they too add variety to her furious rhythm: two instances of "Good God!" five of "ha!" nine of "imagine!"—plus other exclamations that are not repeated. The monologue is further musicalized by subtle sound play: alliteration—"steady stream . . . straining to hear"; off-rhyme—"quicker and quicker . . . flickering away." Many of the text's noun phrases are often repeated, and sometimes permuted, as in Beckett's late short fiction. Many present participles energize the text, as do the rhythmic breaks. Artaud espoused a theater where metaphysics would be absorbed through the skin, and *Not I* almost achieves it.

It is impossible to address *Not I* as a mere (mere!) text, without according attention to its literally stunning effect in the theater. Yet it is probable that the play has had more readers than spectators, and for all their musicality, *words mean.* The unintelligible words that frame the monologue suggest an unremitting, repetitive fate, and this is corroborated by certain words that are intelligible. Early and late in the monologue, we hear: "no love . . . spared that." Love is undesirable, something "vented," like anger. Although She thrice couples "God is love" with mercy, she also breaks into laughter at the idea of a merciful God. She finds the return of words so fearful because they may trail a rebirth of feeling. Although Mouth does not explicitly affirm the realization of this fear, She is forced to acknowledge the voice as her own, in part because she is so aware of how words form in the mouth, with almost no direction from the brain. In contrast to the past-tense narration of She's memories, Mouth's brain in the present prays for words to stop. In vain. Finally, the sudden darkness in April proves to be both a crucifixion and a resurrection—a crucifixion because speech is a martyrdom, and a resurrection because the awareness of speech has restored feeling.

Not I is an exceedingly rich text. It is Beckett's most economical text to date to embrace its own performance; a disjunctive biography is fused into a sustained theatrical experience. Under its surface fragmentation lies the tale of a mythic figure. Bare of striking phrases, the text can shade meaning through the position of its repetitions: "drifting" can refer to She or a ray of light; "oh long after . . . sudden flash" is temporally disorienting; when "in control" is followed by "under control," the reasoning brain is undermined; "staring into space" occurs in meadow, market, and courtroom; "lived on and on . . . guilty or not" reverts to Beckett's familiar depiction of life as a sentence; "flickering away like mad" might be mind or mouth; "no matter" late in the play subsumes indifference toward the astonishing lack of physical matter on this stage. While Mouth and Auditor are all but immobile, the text is active with human movement—the positions of the invisible body, the possible flow of feeling into it, the word-formation of the visible mouth, the blinking of an eye, the company of larks and grass in an April meadow (Lawley 1983). Words come to and through She only in the dark, and in a darkened theater the spotlit mouth offers us an unparalleled experience.

Written relatively quickly, *Not I* is perhaps the most demanding of all Beckett's plays for its actor. Even though Winnie presents a more sustained challenge, Mouth requires more vocal dexterity, and more sheer concentration. As intrepid actresses have realized, they enact a reaction to a verbal onslaught that mirrors their own consternation at the onslaught that they nightly have to enact. To some extent, their controlled paroxysm reacts to absences—no body, no face, no colleague to cue her, no possibility of responding to audience reaction. It is common knowledge today that Jessica Tandy, the first Mouth, depended upon a teleprompter, but other actresses just "pick it up" and go on. Knowlson writes: "A discussion of *Not I* should begin with the scalding intensity and overpowering nature of the play as a theatrical experience" (Knowlson and Pilling 1979, 195). It is astounding that Beckett was able to predict that experience in his text.

With *Not I* completed, Beckett in June set about creating a text for Bill Hayter to illustrate. It took him some six weeks to evolve the thirty sentences of *Still*. In contrast to the writing rooms of Molloy, Moran, and Malone, the room of *Still* has windows that face in three directions. In contrast to the strict architectonics of Beckett's late French pieces, the natural world is a distant setting for the unnamed subject of *Still*.

Still

The title is a pun, at once motionless and continuous. Beckett's deceptively simple text conveys an impression of both stillness and continuity. Sentences

---

The twelve-leaf holograph of *Still* at RUL is inscribed "Paris, 17 June 1972" on fol. 1, and "Paris, 26 July 1972" on fol. 12. *BatR* discerns four complete stages of this work, which were followed by various revisions in typescripts. Majno's deluxe edition (where it was first published in 1974) contains not only three etchings by Hayter, but also photocopies of preliminary drafts of both artist and writer. Hayter's etchings are so filled with small designs that figures are barely discernible; a wicker chair

appear in an unbroken paragraph, and, newly subjectless, they are distinguishable only by the opening capital letters and the terminal periods. Neither question mark nor exclamation point—so profuse in the recent *Not I*—disturbs the declarative prose, with its accretion of noun or adverbial phrases. The word *still* occurs twenty-four times, "here an adverb, here an adjective, here a noun" (Brater 1994, 71). Occasionally, the word *quiet* is a synonym for *still,* but the word *calm* of earlier Beckett pieces is absent (although it occurs in Beckett's French translation). The lexicon of *Still* is quite plain, but an old-fashioned "ope" contrasts with the brisk "ditto" and "etc." Phrasal repetition is frequent in *Still,* but it lacks urgency. Elision is frequent, as though it is not worth the time to utter prepositions, or articles.[3] Alliteration, rhyme, and off-rhyme occur sparingly. Yet the word *still* is sonically enhanced by rhymes and assonance: "till," "fall," "all," "whole," "skull," and such chiming words as "detail," "valley," "follow," "deasil," "normally," "finally," "casually," "possible."

Knowlson cites autobiographical elements of a text intended for a visual artist: the windows of Beckett's Ussy cottage, his valley view often painted by Henri Hayden, a wicker chair in which Beckett often sat, the head-in-hand pose that Beckett often took, and that his friend Avigdor Arikha sometimes drew. Yet, writing in Paris, Beckett must have visualized himself at a distance, at an unstable distance. In Knowlson's words: "the viewpoint [in *Still*] constantly shifts and readjusts itself" (525). At different times the text's figure faces three cardinal directions, but never the north.

After the fluctuating light of the recent French texts, *Still* moves toward the desired dark—asymptotically. Beginning with the word "Bright," and ending with the word "sounds," *Still* also aspires to synesthesia. As phrase follows quasi-independent phrase, stillness somehow supervenes over the trembling, twanging, and slow motion within the text. The protagonist figure, lacking pronominal designation, is sometimes standing, but more often seated. That figure does not even appear in the first of the thirty sentences, which limns instead the setting sun. In spite of changes in position, and the opening and closing of eyes, the figure appears "quite still" until we

---

appears in all three prints: the first views a seated figure from the back, the second views the figure standing, and the third views a gigantic head head-on. Breon Mitchell describes the effect: "The colors and lines are carefully calculated to create a sense of depth within the room, and the surface undulates like brightly colored shifting waters, flowing along the concave and convex surfaces of the sinuous lines" (1999, 183). After publication in the deluxe Majno edition, *Still* appeared in *The Malahat Review* (January, 1975). In Beckett's French translation, *Immobile* is first published separately in 1976, and then included in *Pour finir encore et autres foirades* (Minuit, 1976); it is Fizzle 7 in *Fizzles* (New York: Grove, 1976). My page numbers refer to *CSP.*

are startled by the first quiet climax: "close inspection not still at all but trembling all over" (*CSP,* 240). Nevertheless, the impression of stillness continues to envelop the figure who is seated with legs and arms at right angles "as in that old statue some old god twanged at sunrise and again at sunset" (241). In Greek legend, however, the Colossus of Memnon was "twanged" only at dawn.[4] Beckett's introduction of sunset and the repeated "old" hint that we are moving toward the stillness of death. Instead of reviewing a life, however, this figure looks toward natural scenes until they fade in the fading light. Usually, the narrator describes motions in a temporal sequence, but twice he breaks it: "to anticipate" and "back a little way." Although the seated figure was found to be trembling beneath his apparent stillness, a slower motion proves more climactic: "this movement impossible to follow let alone describe." Yet the movement *is* described, when the hand almost hungers to support the head, and the position of the fingers obliterates vision. In spite of faint stirrings during the night, stillness still reigns. The final sentence, with its liquid *l*s and susurrant *s*es, glides onomatopoetically toward stillness, and yet it introduces the only commands of the thirty sentences: "Leave it so all quite still or try listening to the sounds all quite still head in hand listening for a sound" (242). Although a sound is denied by the piece's title, the listening still lives.

Between visitors, travels, translations, and dental problems, Beckett completed no new work during the remainder of 1972. He did, however, start in French a film or television script, which is found in RUL, in the same notebook as drafts of the *foirade Se voir.*

"F1 et F2"

The setting is a room containing a window, a door, two chairs, and a television set in the center. After preparing her cassette, F2 inserts it into the recorder. She is dressed for winter, whereas F1 on the screen is dressed for summer. F2 stops the video at a close-up of F1. Beckett notes confrontations between F1 and F2, once even suggesting that F1 can stare back at F2. Near the end of his notes Beckett introduces F3, but her role is not clear. As stated in *BatR:* "The notes . . . reveal that reflections of the observer-camera image are always 'mobile' and thus may be seen, while the observed-camera image reflection is always blocked. Effectively, this means that the observed parties cannot see their reflections" (132). However, Beckett aborted these reflections.

"F1 et F2": RUL 2928 is a slim green notebook labeled by Beckett: "Fragments Prose début 68," but the notebook also contains four leaves dated November 1972, and titled "Film Video-Cassette projet." Hard to read, Beckett's notes are well described in *BatR* (132), except that I found two—and not three—diagrams.

In this year, too, Beckett began a double translation, which would be published only in 1977 as *Long after Chamfort*. Double because he translated Chamfort's French into English, and Chamfort's epigrammatic prose into his own taut verse. I delay comment to 1976, the date of completion of the versification.

1973

Preoccupied with translations and the London premiere of *Not I*, Beckett did not return to the subjectless prose of *Still* until June. Even in my comments on that story, it has been difficult to avoid a subject pronoun, and Beckett was unable to sustain that absence in his next text.

Sounds

This second text of what will be a minitrilogy shares the stillness of the first, in spite of its title. *Sounds* is briefer than *Still*—twelve sentences as opposed to thirty, and the sentences themselves seem to be shorter, although with less elision. The sentences are usually subjectless, but three *he*s wander through (as well as two *his*es, and a *himself*). "He" is continuous with the earlier unnamed subject, as evidenced by the phrase "as shown," and by variants of the final phrases of *Still*. The earlier figure looked out in three directions, but this figure actually leaves the room at times. Torch (American flashlight) in hand, he makes his silent way to a tree that he embraces "as if a human." The earlier figure gradually eliminated the visible, but this one slowly dispenses with the audible. Somewhat nostalgically, the narrator carries us through a diapason of absent sounds—nightbirds, leaf, tree, faint creak of wicker chair, ghosts or motes in the sun, the wind, and breath. When sound is all but gone, in the penultimate sentence, a mother bends over the crib "to feel pulse or heart"; unstated is the implication that these sounds register life. The last sentence, subsuming euphonies and familiar phrases, parallels the earlier finale in its imperative force against one of the senses: "Leave it so then this stillest night till now of all quite still head in hand as shown listening trying listening for a sound or dreamt away try dreamt away where no

---

After abandoning the early draft of *Sounds* (dated January 1972) Beckett penned four leaves at Ussy between May 5 and 20, 1973 (RUL 1396/4/46). In June he wrote and revised a manuscript of twenty-seven sentences. Three undated typescripts contain further revisions. There are thus six drafts of *Sounds*, which was first published in *Essays in Criticism* (April 1978), thanks to John Pilling's request to Beckett. It is reprinted in appendix 1 of *CSP*.

such thing no more than ghosts make nothing to listen for no such thing as a sound" (*CSP*, 268).

Sounds is another still story of asymptotic life. It is less visual than *Still*, but more—one might almost say metaphysical. The double "dreamt away" of the last sentence is first read in the second sentence (along with the rare pronoun "he"): "he having been dreamt away let himself be dreamt away" into a world of negatives, almost indistinguishable from basic being. The figure may have acquired a pronoun, but he still possesses only enough identity to dwell in a dream. Or he is wafted away from the waves and particles of sound, into a ghost realm of pure imagination. That is why we twice read: "worse than none the self's." If death and void were final, silence would reign; but the residual self is "worse than none" because it breathes uninterpretably.

Almost immediately after completing *Sounds*, Beckett began work on *Still 3*. The last (but not final) manuscript of the former is dated June 1973, and the latter (also not final) is dated June 29, 1973. Along with the title on the first leaf is a circled 17, and I wonder whether it was intended for Hayter and his Atelier 17 to illustrate. If so, it is a more formidable challenge to a visual artist than the original *Still*.

Still 3

When Beckett began *Molloy* in 1947, he did not expect it to grow into a trilogy. Comparably, when Beckett agreed to write a text for his friend Bill Hayter to illustrate, he probably did not expect it to grow into a trilogy. However, his realization is evident in the title *Still 3*. The manuscripts offer no evidence of a *Still 2*. Nevertheless the third title might be a witty reminder of the continuity of the trinitarian tradition—both religious and literary. The short piece is indisputably a continuation of the earlier texts, with its figure seated in a wicker chair, head in hand—"as shown" again. However, this figure, once again lacking a pronoun, actually sits still in a text whose sentences are more brief and abrasive than in the earlier two pieces.

Still 3 opens on an interrogative—"Whence"—and three of its first seven sentences bristle with (unpunctuated) questions. "Perhaps [it is] mere fancy" that the right valley wind will carry the sound of the incarnation bell—as it did for Molloy a quarter century earlier. In the next sentence a figure *is* incarnated—Mother Calvet, whom we last read about in *Texte pour rien II*. She has retained her go-cart, if not her dog, and her activity at dawn

---

Three much revised leaves of *Still 3* constitute RUL 1396/4/51. It contains twenty sentences, as opposed to the thirteen finally published in *Essays in Criticism* (April 1978): 156–57. It is not, as Gontarski claims in *CSP*, a "variant on 'Still'" (291), but the final story of the *Still* trilogy, which is reprinted in appendix 1 of *CSP*.

and dusk recalls the colossal statue of *Still,* which was "twanged" at dawn and dusk. Mythic figures both, the one was seated in repose, whereas the other was busy scavenging through refuse. The third *Still* text does not contain stillness.

Midway through this text we are plunged into a nightmare of faces. They appear "one by one never more at a time," and yet the feeling is that of an entire population—as in *Le Dépeupleur.* Ageless, bodiless, colorless, and genderless, the faces are almost geometric entities. As the narrator tries to focus on a single face, he urges himself: "try dreamt away saying dreamt away." In the antepenultimate sentence the narrator seeks to start again from the pondering head so as to visualize a single face. But the penultimate sentence records the failure to isolate a face, reduced to "it." Yet the very last sentence presents a life-size face, "marble still so long then out." A work of art, as opposed to a human face, can be "marble still," and that perhaps is the precipitate deposited by the dream—the dream that came to one seated with head in hand, senses closed to the material world, and sentences cunningly syntaxed. Only the artifact attains stillness and soundlessness.[5]

The *Still* trilogy originated in Beckett's desire to supply a text for illustration by his friend Bill Hayter, who lived near him in Paris. Another request was made in unhappy circumstances: the German poet Günther Eich committed suicide at age sixty-six, and Beckett was asked by his German publisher to contribute to a memorial volume. Beckett responded to the request with *As the Story Was Told.*

As the Story Was Told

After the *Still* trilogy, with its wavering subjects and elliptical sentences, *As the Story Was Told* is astonishing in its surface simplicity. *Our* story is told by a first-person narrator, who is a self-effacing protagonist. Moreover, he tells the story in complete sentences, replete with subjects, verbs, commas, and even dashes. The first five words of the story become its title, announcing the subject of telling a story. Yet the sentence continues, with insistence on the first person: "As the story was told me I never went near the place during sessions" (*CSP,* 255). Inquiring first about the place, and only secondly about the mysterious sessions, the narrator does not reveal the accounts he is given. The events in the tent (where the sessions take place) are so harrowing

---

The holograph of *As the Story Was Told,* a typescript, and a photocopy of another typescript are at RUL. The holograph is dated August 3 and 4, 1973, and the complete revision was sent to Suhrkamp on August 8. Published in English (with a German translation by Wolfgang Hildesheimer), it was reprinted in Calder's volume of short prose, and is found in *CSP.* Beckett did not translate it into French—or German.

that the narrator raises his hand—presumably to cut the report short. He next wants to know where he was "while all this was going forward," and he is located in a hut in a grove. That hut reminds the narrator of a summer-house in which he used to sit as a child. Within it is "a small upright wicker chair with armrests" (256). Without transition, virtually conflating memory and present action, a hand in the doorway holds out a sheet of writing, which the narrator reads and tears in four, before returning the paper to the waiting hand. "A little later the whole scene disappeared." We are not told which scene, but we read that "the man succumbed . . . though quite old enough at the time to die naturally of old age." In the two sentences following this subdued climax, dashes enclose two seemingly unrelated matters: that the narrator was always still and had grown increasingly so with the years; that the narrator cannot give the man's name. Having asked no questions since the beginning of the story, the narrator now asks what the man was required to say. The story's final sentence is "No, was the answer, after some little hesitation no, I did not know what the poor man was required to say, in order to be pardoned, but would have recognized it at once, yes, at a glance, if I had seen it" (256). At the Kafkaesque last, it is difficult to disentangle the final "I's" from the narrator, or the sense of hearing from that of sight. The unnamed victim (named Fox in an earlier draft) is "required to say," and yet the speaker would have *seen* it in a glance. Earlier, the narrator *read* from "a sheet of writing," in an act of *seeing*. Even earlier, the inaudibility in the hut of cries from the tent is "not so strange as at first *sight* it *sounded*." Heard or read, a story can only circle round the pain at its core.

James Hansford offers an extensive commentary, from which I excerpt his basic interpretation: "I am suggesting that the 'hearer' of the story (who is also the narrator of the text we are reading) is actually the man in the tent [who finally succumbs], but that because of the divisive nature of creative activity . . . they are not identified with each other" (1982b, 78). I accept this dualism, but I would emphasize that the narrator gradually woos our sympathy for the victim, whose demise is so cruelly accomplished. *As the Story Was Told* recapitulates the tent, torture, and dual storyteller of the jettisoned "On le tortura bien," but it focuses more pointedly on the cruelty of creation.

Beckett's story was a contribution to a memorial volume. It is possible that Eich's creations caused him to take his own life, and it is certain that he and Beckett were only a year apart in age. I would nevertheless argue that Beckett's latent return to "I" is meant to represent every-I, recoiling from evident, but deliberately generalized, cruelties. Teller and hearer, tent and hut, story and vision, are intertwined in the inability to escape the suffering of being. As *this* story is told, Beckett expresses that pain in crystalline sentences, which accumulate into a cloud of unknowing.

1974

For all his revision of the short texts of 1972–73, Beckett placed little value on them. Believing he could no longer sustain a narrative, he began late in 1973 and continued in 1974 to versify some of the pithy maxims of the eighteenth-century French writer Sébastian Chamfort (who committed suicide during the Reign of Terror). Beckett wrote these on the spur of the moment, jotting the jingles down on whatever piece of paper was at hand. On October 23, 1973, for example, he wrote me that he "did a couple more Chamfort and one Pensée Pascal." I delay comment to 1976, the publication date.

Beckett also wrote graver verse. "Hors crâne" and "Something there" are versions of the same poem. Related in mood to *Still*, they both testify to something outside the head, "not life necessarily." However, the rhythms of testimony differ in the two languages.

"Hors crâne"

Consisting of twelve brief lines, which are grouped in four stanzas of three lines each, the poem is chary of images. The skull dominates the first six lines, and although it is the last shelter, from the outside it resembles Bocca frozen in the ice (in the ninth circle of Dante's *Inferno*). It is not clear whether the alarmed eye belongs to the skull or to an observer, when it opens and closes, finding nothing. The final tercet "vaguens" phrases of the opening tercet—"sometimes, as if something, but not necessarily life." For all its brevity, and despite its opening two words—outside skull—the lyric reaches out cosmically from within the skull.

"Something there"

This version of the lyric consists of three irregular stanzas—the first two in nine brief lines, and the third in eight. The first stanza presents a head (rather than a skull), outside of which there may be something. The second stanza banishes the head with "the faint sound," but the eye opens and "shutters." Life is implied in the *nine* lines of each of these stanzas, but the third stanza,

---

First published in the periodical *Minuit* 21 (1976), "hors crâne" is republished in *Poems* with the date 1974, although the 1978 edition of the French poems dates it in 1976. Mentioned in letters of March 1, 1974, to Kay Boyle, and March 7, 1974, to George Reavey, it undoubtedly precedes "something there." I thank Mary Bryden and John Pilling for this information.

Because Beckett's translation, "something there," is rhythmically so different from "hors crâne," I break my own rule about not commenting on translations. First published in the English periodical *New Departures* (1975), "something there" is republished in *Poems* with the date 1974.

curtailed to eight lines, concludes: "something / not life / necessarily." Being is not quite life, and yet it is, as hinted by the inversion of normal English "not necessarily life." The images of skull and eye are more striking in the original French, but Beckett may have intended to increase instability in his translation. "Something there" is a rarity in Beckett's self-translation, in that it *increases,* rather than shrinks, the number of words.

"Dread nay"

The poem consists of eight stanzas, each of which groups eight brief, unpunctuated, uncapitalized lines. As in the previous two poems of 1974, head and eye are imaged. However, the relationship between them is almost narrative. The head is "as dead," until the eye opens and shuts. Surrounding the "asylum head" is "snow white / sheeting all"—which may be hair, or the cosmos. The fourth stanza offers horrific details of the head frozen in Dante's ninth circle. Whatever it was that shocked the eye open, stirring it with dread, that opening is a form of "nay to nought." The last three stanzas repeat that eye opening, that "rent" in a head that was "as dead." The eighth stanza's opening line, "so ere," with its antiquated word that off-rhymes with "so stir" in the fifth line, endows the eye's reaction with a momentary nay to dread, before all is infernally frozen.

Read in sequence (not as they are printed in *Poems*), the three poems form a frail lyric trilogy about the impact of an outer world upon the head and eye. To that extent these poems may be read as Beckett's reaction against his recent fiction, which sought to seize on thought from both within and outside the head. Toward midyear he turned to another genre—drama—in which the head is at once a setting and a character, while its thoughts are voiced (but not spoken) in three separate strands. Although Beckett sent me a typescript of *That Time* (as he almost never did, of works in progress), he did not yet send the play either to Alan Schneider or the Royal Court.

Approaching his seventieth year, Beckett had few spare moments. In October he went to London to attend rehearsals of Peter Hall's production of *Happy Days.* Back in Paris he spent November and December reviewing and memorizing the German text of *Warten auf Godot,* for his directing project at the Schiller Theater. On December 26, he and his designer Mathias flew from Paris to Berlin.

The holograph of "Dread nay" is in Burns Library, Boston College. "Dread nay" first appears in *Collected Poems in English and French,* dated 1974, and bare of notes. In the second line of the fourth stanza the words "hell" and "ice" are run together—surely a typo. The last four stanzas appear in *Frank* No. 14 (1992), erroneously entitled "Rondelay."

1975
∞

While struggling with rehearsals of the German *Godot,* Beckett wrote a short piece to be included in a book of homage to his old friend, the painter Bram van Velde.

La Falaise

The eighty-year-old Bram van Velde, who signed his paintings "AvV," had been painting abstractly for thirty years, and yet *La Falaise* [The cliff] might be a verbal analogue of one of his images. Beckett's paragraph opens on a window somewhere between earth and sky. The window frames a cliff, whose top and bottom elude the eye, wherever it alights, but whose sides are bordered by two panels of white sky. The narrator poses three questions, seemingly uncertain of what is seen. Wherever it alights, the eye cannot find "une face," which can mean either face or surface. Midway through the paragraph we read: "Il [l'oeil] se désiste et la folle s'y met" (55). "La folle" that takes over when the eye gives up is the imagination, as portrayed in an often quoted sentence of Malebranche: "L'imagination c'est la folle du logis" [Imagination is the madwoman of the dwelling].[6] The shadow of a ledge emerges, and the narrator addresses himself or us: "Patience elle s'animera de restes mortels" [Patience it will be animated by mortal remains]. These remains are at once mortal and deadly, and they crystallize into a skull, whose eye sockets summon a memory of looking. When the cliff occasionally disappears, the eye flies toward far-off whites or blanks. Or it turns away from a direct view.

Over the course of the paragraph the narrator glides from a cliffscape to an imaginary image, analogously to the way van Velde might paint. The eye guides the narrative (as it guides the painter). Introduced as unable to see the top or bottom of the cliff, it soon seeks restlessly but fails to find "une face." Finally, at moments when the cliff disappears from view, the eye looks toward far-off whites, or turns away from any image (seen or unseen). Sight has given way to second sight, or imagination, before the visual vanishes. Van Velde's suspicion of painting parallels Beckett's suspicion of language. Yet van Velde is admired as a colorist, while Beckett strips the verbal palette to white and colorless. Van Velde's abstractions invite the viewer to read an

---

A (much revised) holograph and six typescripts of *La Falaise* are at RUL. First published in *Celui qui ne peut se servir de mots* (Montpellier: Fata Morgana, 1975), *La Falaise* is reprinted in the 1991 edition of *Pour finir encore et autres foirades* (after Beckett's death). Edith Fournier's English version, *The Cliff,* draws phrases from Beckett's other works; her version is included in *CSP.* I am indebted to James Hansford's searching analysis of *La Falaise* (1985).

image into his disturbing amalgam of forms and colors, as the skull with its residual optic caverns suggests images.

Hansford proposes another image: "For the reader, the single solid paragraph—a block of language—is itself a cliff-like surface upon the page. . . . In reading and reconstructing visual and imaginative experience, the reader's eye moves 'vers les blancs lointains' upon which Beckett has inscribed the record of a perpetual struggle" (86). Yet Beckett's final sentence presents another option for the eye—to turn away from what it faces.

Beckett himself, however, was hoping his eye would sustain a longer text. During 1974, at the request of the painter Jasper Johns, he translated five *foirades* for the latter to accompany with etchings. It may be during that period that Beckett again tried to end a piece that had preoccupied him intermittently since 1969. During 1975 he cast it in final form, and by December of that year he translated *Pour finir encore* into *For to end yet again*. I am guessing that his finalization of the French text took place during early summer, after he returned from directing the Berlin *Godot*, followed without interval by directing the French *La Derniere Bande*, and *Pas moi*. Or perhaps he returned to the story in July, after six weeks in Tangiers. Whatever its exact date, *Pour finir encore* became the first and the title *foirade* of the French collection published by Minuit in 1976—*Pour finir encore et autres foirades*.

Pour finir encore (*For to end yet again*)

This is one of Beckett's most difficult texts to interpret. As published by Minuit, the sixty-three sentences, each beginning with a capital letter and ending with a period, are printed in a block of seven-plus pages. Repetition and elision are so frequent that it is hard to follow a narrative. As Porter Abbott remarks in a sensitive appreciation of the piece, "there is the faint stirring of narrative here on the cusp of story" (1999, 17). Although this mode is not new in Beckett's fiction, three individual images are newly arresting—a giant skull, a small body, and twin dwarfs. More graphic than the verbs "finir" and "commencer" in the first sentence (often linked for Beckett) is a skull on a board, surrounded by a black void. That skull's contents are particularized in the next few sentences. The eleventh sentence presents "l'expulsé" [the expelled], but although the noun recalls the story of 1947, the

---

The much revised holograph of *Pour finir encore* is in the Burns Library at Boston College. Dated 1963 at the beginning of his notebook, the earliest draft may have preceded the paragraph *Abandonné* that Beckett offered to Geneviève Asse in 1970. An undated photocopy and an undated carbon (in my possession) are versions along the way. The *foirade* or fizzle occupies different positions in the French, English, and American collections of the eight *foirades*-fizzles. First published by Minuit in 1976, it became the title *foirade* of the volume. Translated by Beckett, it was published that same year by Calder and by Grove, respectively. It is found in *CSP*.

small, gray, rigid body resembles that of the more recent *Ping* or *Sans*.[7] By the twenty-first sentence two white dwarfs are sighted, carrying a sheeted stretcher through the ubiquitous gray dust. For the rest of the text, the narrator slips without transition, and with considerable elision, from the spasmodically moving dwarfs to the motionless expelled one. The former are perfectly synchronized, whether trudging through the dust or setting their burden down. The latter experiences more climactic movement, for he (pronounless in the text) falls like a statue through a quadrant, face to the dust, but still breathing, and with blue eyes still open. Finally, the gray figure and the white dwarfs are both compared to marble.

After the first twenty sentences, the skull is rarely mentioned, but the gray world may be in its unstable mind, and the most striking neologism in the text is attached to that mind: "Comble de la voûte cyclopéenne jaillie du front en surplomb bombe blanche vers le ciel gris la bosse d'*habitativi*té ou amour de foyer" (12; emphasis added) [Atop the cyclopean dome rising sheer from jut of brow yearns white to the grey sky the bump of habitativity or love of home, *CSP*, 245]. As in *La Falaise,* white seems to be the color of the imagination, enveloping the white dwarfs and their stretcher (a litter in Beckett's English), but the quoted enigmatic sentence may suggest that the mind yearns to take the white of imagination to the far-off sky, there to dwell.

As in *La Falaise,* the eye provides a semblance of continuity to the narrative. We are not told whose eye first registers the small standing body, then the moving dwarfs joined by the stretcher, then, on closer inspection, their oval featureless faces. I place the ownerless eye in the skull, which can observe other eyes—the blue ones in the little gray body, and those of the dwarfs who occasionally survey their path. We are told what the eye cannot see—the fallen gray body among the ruins that have crumbled to gray dust under a sky that is deserted by its vultures. For vultures Beckett uses the rare word "charognards" (which he translates as "scavengers"). The desertion of the artist-figure from the sky may have moved it into a skull. Perhaps the narrator quotes the skull when his rare imperative addresses the small fallen figure: "venu d'une lie de vie au terme du long sur pied tombe tombe sans crainte tu ne pourras plus te relever" (13) [murmur from some dreg of life after the lifelong stand fall fall never fear no fear of your rising again, 246]. As in earlier Beckett works, the intimation is that death or an end brings relief. After this command the narrator returns to the skull, with a kind of summary of the whole story: "Crâne funéraire tout va-t-il s'y figer tel pour toujours civière et nains ruines et petit corps ciel gris sans nuages poussière n'en pouvant plus lointains sans fin air d'enfer" (13–14)[8] [Sepulchral skull is this then its last state all set for always litter and dwarfs ruins and little body grey cloudless sky glutted dust verge upon verge hell air not a breath? 246]. The narrator answers his own question in the negative. This work of the imagination is temporary; the black void returns, this time in an ashen color. What was leaden is now ashen, "d'une fin dernière si jamais il devait y en avoir une s'il le fallait absolument" (14) [a last end if ever there had to be another absolutely had to be, 246]. Although the word *dernière* threads through the narrative, the last concessive clause riddles it.

Focusing on narrative and images, I have skimmed over Beckett's musical repetitions, resonant elisions, appository ambiguities, and human residue of a gray Limbese world through which whiteness glimmers, whether gradually or by degrees.[9] Compassion pervades the text like its gray dust, to which the ruins have crumbled. Significantly, the text's first sentence closes on the verb "commencer" [to begin], but it does not end with "une fin dernière," for a last end is only temporary. The French title puns on *encore,* which can mean "still" or "again." As long as consciousness lasts, the mind thinks still and again, creating resistant worlds. Worlds can be quite literally suggested by the image of white dwarfs, which is the astronomical term for dying binary stars. Dying but still active.

The graphic images with their dying fall resisted Beckett's control during a period of composition that may have lasted as long as a decade. In 1971 he sent me a 261-sentence draft, which tells essentially the same story. Virtually every sentence of the final text is already present in the longer version, but the position and resonance wring changes. At an intermediary stage the stretcher dominated a radically abbreviated version of the story, and Beckett wrote me in 1972: "I'm struggling to extract a *caput mortuum* from the Dwarfs" (*sic*). However, the skullscape he extracted is neither dead, nor deadly, in this hermetic text to be finished—encore.

Beckett's dedication to skullscapes at this time (or that time?) eventuated in uncannily different works—the enigmatic French *Pour finir encore* and the approachable English *That Time.* Even if the former developed by degrees, and the latter emerged virtually all at once, they were completed in close temporal proximity, and both works distort rational chronology.

That Time

After the hesitancies of *Pour finir encore, That Time* shows a sure hand. Despite Beckett's shift in originary language, the drama salvages several

A holograph and nine typescripts of *That Time* are at RUL. Begun in Paris on June 8, 1974, *That Time* was not completed until August 1975. However, the fifth typescript, dated July 10, 1974, is quite close to the play as published—individually by Faber in 1976, then in *Ends and Odds,* by Faber and Grove, respectively. It was first performed at the Royal Court Theatre in 1976, for Beckett's seventieth birthday season. It appears in *CDW,* to which page numbers refer, but there is an error on page 390, three lines from the bottom: "altogether" should be "together." Beckett's French translation *Cette fois* was published alone in 1978, and then in 1982 in *Castastrophe et autres dramaticules.*

items from the *foirade*. First and foremost is the skull or head, to serve as both character and setting. In both works, too, dust plays a crucial role: in the story it devours monuments, and in the play the dust envelops a library. Despite the change in language, one syllable is common to the two works— *ah*. "Sable fin comme poussière ah mais poussière en effet profonde à engloutir les plus fiers monuments qu'elle fut d'ailleurs par-ci par-là" (8) [Sand pale as dust ah but dust indeed deep to engulf the haughtiest monuments which too it once was here and there, 243]. This *ah* serves as an intensifier of the omnivorous depth of the dust. In the play the "ah" (twice heard) is an interjection of impatience: "was your mother ah for God's sake all gone long ago" (*CDW*, 389).

If I open my commentary on these echoes, it is because most critics have cited echoes of other Beckett works in *That Time*, like the familiar white hair, long green coat, compulsive walking, and awareness of stones and stories. Amateurs of Beckett may take pleasure in a character who looked "like something out of Beckett," as he phrased it in an early draft of the play.[10] Yet the writer bent his considerable talents to rendering aspects of memory that might be familiar to anyone. An old man perhaps on his deathbed absorbs memories, for the most part passively, but with an occasional "no" of self-correction. The nameless protagonist, addressed as "you" ("tu" in Beckett's French translation) is an everyman, and like the medieval Everyman at the point of death, he re-views his life.

Ten feet high on stage is a lone head, whose white hair surrounds him like a halo. The head's memories are heard by him and us through three spaced loudspeakers. When words reach him, his eyes close; they open twice during the course of the play, and, finally, when he smiles. Each loudspeaker delivers its own story. The A speaker tells of an old man who makes a vain search for his childhood refuge. The B speaker tells of the exchange of vows of love. The C speaker tells of an old derelict seeking shelter from winter rain in public buildings. Almost any theatergoer would recognize that all the words carry memories of the man whose head is visible, and almost any theatergoer would recognize that memories surge up unbidden. The theatergoer would recognize this because Beckett's text is carefully constructed of seemingly associational phrases. Recalling past moments, the phrases are enlivened by many present participles. Ostensibly memories, the phrases address "you," who is at once the visible head and the semivisible audience members in the theater.

Although the A, B, and C voices span childhood, maturity, and old age, they are all three refracted through memory, so that phrases acquire shading and resonance through repetition and juxtaposition. Each voice repeats certain phrases, and other phrases are shared by two of the three voices.[11] However fragmented the life story, readers and especially theatergoers supply a "solution of continuity" for a recollected or reconstructed life, when memories dissolve into fictions, and vice versa.

Antoni Libera has analyzed the prevalence of triadic forms, images, and events in *That Time*. The A, B, and C voices are never heard in that order, but in dominant patterns for each of the three parts: ACB for youth, CBA for maturity, BAC for old age. Each voice remembers three places, each with its concomitant posture of the protagonist. In Libera's suggestive summary: "Looking at the play allegorically, we might see it in the following terms: childhood is the period of ignorance when man can naively and almost successfully deceive himself concerning his isolation. . . ; early youth is the period of love, during which one creates the illusion of being in communication with someone else. . . ; old age is the period of faith, in which one treats fictitious beings as if they were real" (88). Looking at *That Time* in more theaterwise fashion, we might see it as Beckett's twist of the three-act well-made play. The thirty-six paragraphs are grouped in three sets of twelve, each one introduced by a brief silence, after which the head's eyes open, but the eyes close again when the words flow again. The first silence punctuates the B-voice's doubts about the love vows: "just another of those old tales to keep the void from pouring in on top of you the shroud" (390). The second silence climaxes in skepticism about the protagonist's past; unable to reach his childhood haunt among the giant nettles of Foley's Folly, he sits on a step: "not knowing where you were or when you were or what for place might have been uninhabited for all you knew like that time on the stone the child on the stone where none ever came" (392). In the third "act," traditionally the resolution of the well-made play, the A-voice renounces his search for the childhood site, but he is "talking to himself being together that way," even as the child once did. The B-voice remembers the scenes of lovers' vows exchanged, but now he is alone by the window "when you tried and tried and couldn't any more no words to keep [the shroud] out" (394). There is thus a kind of negative progress within the A and B narratives, but the finale belongs to the C-voice who hears words in the dust: "come and gone no one come and gone in no time gone in no time" (395). The title's "that time," twenty-two times repeated, and often varied with "that" and "time" in other phrases, is finally subverted to "no time," whose colloquial sense is "very quick," and whose literal sense is "timeless." Behind them both is God's sentence upon Adam: "From dust thou art; unto dust shalt thou return" (Gen. 3:19).

Using simple words and a few graphic images, Beckett has produced a haunting text about human solitude. The A-voice conveys the vulnerability of the child among "giant nettles." The B-voice renders a solitude in love "always parallel like on an axle-tree." Most memorable are birth and death in the C-voice, from "curled up worm in slime when they lugged you out and wiped you off and straightened you up" (390) to "a great shroud billowing in all over you on top of you" (394). "That time" is the brief interval between those events, however it may be shaded in memory.

Early in 1975, Beckett was preoccupied with directing *Godot* at the Schiller Theater, and with thinking through the beginnings of *Footfalls*. He nevertheless wrote to Alan Schneider on March 23: "Having trouble in the odd spare moment with *That Time*. Text & idea more or less okay but not yet the image" (Harmon, 324). By August 8, he wrote again: "The delay in parting with [*That Time*] is due to misgivings over disproportion between image (listening face) and speech and much time lost in trying to devise ways of amplifying former. I have now come to accept its remoteness & stillness—apart from certain precise eye movements, breath just audible in silences and final smile—as essential to the piece & dramatically of value" (328). "Essential to the piece" the quasi-still head may be, but, having seen several productions including Beckett's own, I remain unconvinced that it is of *dramatic* value. A fine actor like Pat Magee or David Warrilow can imbue one of Beckett's most resonant texts with haunting rhythms, but even the chiseled features of their faces can do no more than offer a context—replete with the smile that lends itself to interpretations as divergent as relief, acceptance, liberation, self-recognition, or response to a change in rhythm.

1975
∾

During the rehearsal period of the Berlin *Godot,* I almost daily walked with Beckett to or from the Schiller Theater, but it is only now in retrospect that I marvel at how variously he may have written, while concentrating on theater immediacies. He precipated *La Falaise* from an homage to Bram van Velde; he may have pored over the story *Pour finir encore;* he may have "tinkered" with the stage play *That Time;* he may have conceived of the television play *Ghost Trio.* Although the last of these was not actually written until 1976, I once saw the Beethoven score on his Berlin work table. I also strolled through a museum with him, where he surprised me by stopping to draw my attention to the sound of the visitors' footsteps. Although I didn't realize it at that time, he must have been meditating on his play for the actress Billie Whitelaw.

Footfalls
Performed in half an hour, *Footfalls* divides into four scenes, marked off by successively fainter chimes and successively dimmer lights. In the first three

The holograph and five typescripts of *Footfalls* are at RUL. The holograph contains three dates—March 2, October 1, and October 25—on which Beckett wrote drafts of,

scenes a woman in "worn grey wrap" paces the length of a lighted strip of board—nine steps and turn, nine steps and turn. From scene to scene, the light dims, and the pacing slows. After the three scenes of fading, the fourth and final scene comes very close to zero, with its bare board and vertical light: "No trace of May." Gray of face and garment, May's skeletal hands shrivel her shoulders in a stoop. The dialogue, which gave Beckett trouble during composition, is rhythmic and resonant.

The earliest title of the play is *Footfalls/It All,* and that rejected title hints at an equivalence between the anxious steps and ubiquitous pain, as though suffering had to be audible. On a page of ends and odds at the end of Beckett's holograph, he titles his four scenes: "Dying mother, Mother back, Epilogue [changed to appendix], Empty strip." Although repetitions within each voice appear as early as Beckett's first draft, it is only in his final revision that he introduces echoing rhythms within the mother-daughter exchanges of scenes 2 and 3, each spoken by a single voice.

"Dying mother"—she is invisible, but her voice from darkness reaches her daughter, who may be remembering her progenitor's last illness. Early questions touch on sleep; the mother's sleep is deep, but she is worried by the daughter's sleepless pacing. The ministrations offered by the daughter to her invalid mother glide gradually from the modern to those of biblical reso nance. The mother responds in puzzling fashion; she accepts the proffered care, but "it is too soon" (400). Evidently, suffering must run its course. The dialogue then shifts to the respective ages of mother and daughter; each knows the age of the other, but not her own. The mother asks the daughter's forgiveness, presumably for having brought her into the world. Through their respective reactions, both women equate living in time with suffering. The formality of the mother's last question hints at the daughter's breadth of compassion: "Will you never have done," rather than the modern, "When will you stop . . . revolving it all?" As in earlier Beckett works, "it" is an englobing uninnocent pronoun. By the end of the first scene we have seen the daughter "revolving it all," and heard about it.

"Mother back"—Beckett's second scene resists realistic explanation. In drafts right up to the first production, Beckett situated the mother's voice in

---

respectively, part 1, part 3, and part 2 of *Footfalls.* Probably later than any of these is an inserted leaf of additions to part 1. Gontarski (1985), Pountney, and *BatR* describe the successive stages of composition, with the last of these the least confusing. Pountney notes the variants in the Grove 1976 and Faber 1977 editions of *Ends and Odds. CDW* contains a number of omissions and errors. The only correct English text is published in volume IV of *The Theatrical Notebooks of Samuel Beckett,* ed. S. E. Gontarski (London: Faber, 1999). Beckett's translation into French was first published separately in 1977, then in 1978 by Minuit in *Pas suivi de quatre esquisses.* It contains Beckett's changed scenic directions.

M's mind, but he then decided that V's voice is inaudible to M. The mother comes back from the grave, to address this theater audience on this evening: "See how still she stands," "But let us watch her move" (401). However explained, or unexplained, the mother's monologue encloses a mother-daughter duologue between two passages of description. The first passage situates her daughter's pacing in their home, where she and it began; the implication is that awareness of suffering was transmitted to M's feet. In the mother-daughter duologue the name May is repeated, linking the mother's biographical account to the actualities of the first scene. As scene 1 arouses sympathy for the dying mother, scene 2 arouses sympathy for the obsessively pacing daughter, both scenes ending on the double "It all." Before those two pregnant syllables, the mother prepares us for the daughter's forthcoming monologue, since she "Tries to tell how it was."

With Beckettian irony, the appendix is the longest and most climactic scene of the play. However, he retitled it to "Sequel," which puns on "Seek well." Scene 3, spoken by the visible daughter, divides into three unequal parts: sequel, semblance, and (untitled) story. The sequel, spoken on audience right, obliquely continues the account of the figure, who, "as though she had never been, it never been," walks "up and down, up and down" in the transept of a locked church (402). The mother's "your poor mind" of scene 1 is here balanced by the daughter's "His poor arm" of Christ, whose cross gives shape to churches. Although the gray woman seen resembles the ghostly woman heard about, this distanced "she" makes "No sound. None at least to be heard." The brief "semblance" reviews what is visible—"A faint tangle of pale grey tatters."[12] The ghost is then rendered more ghostly by a rare simile: "like moon through passing rack." The longest section of scene 3 is M's creation of still another mother-daughter duologue, and, inhabitually, the actress stands on audience left for this narration. This time both fictional women have names: the mother is Mrs. Winter, who is soon abbreviated to Mrs. W., and the daughter is Amy, an anagram of May. Although M appeals to "the reader," no book is visible. M tells of a mother and her daughter at their Sunday evening meal. Mrs. W. asks her daughter's corroboration of an unspecified strange event at evensong. Amy denies that she was there at all, and, puzzled, Mrs. W. (Double You) affirms that she heard her daughter's "Amen" in response to the verse from Cor. 2:13, about the *fellowship* of the Holy Ghost: "I heard you distinctly" (403). Unable to go on, M takes a few steps and then pauses. When she returns to audience right, there is another "Long pause." Omitting the names of the speakers, she then continues her story to the end—in an exact repetition of the last speeches of the actual mother-daughter exchange of scene 1, but now the daughter alone speaks both parts. These scene-to-scene repetitions and changes make for tension in the theater.

Beckett's scenes both progress and repeat in *Footfalls.* On the one hand, we move from an actual dialogue about suffering, to a mother's monologue in a biographical flashback, to a daughter's monologue that is explicitly called "Sequel" and that makes three obliquely sequenced efforts to fictionalize "how it was." On the other hand, all three scenes repeat how it is when mothers and daughters are interlocked in suffering. Mothers give birth to daughters who give birth to daughters, who give birth to human beings who begin to die as soon as they are born. In scenes 2 and 3 the mother asks the daughter, echoically: "What do you mean, May/Amy . . . what can you possibly mean?" Beckett leaves the possible meaning in mystery, but he etches that mystery in a memorable phrase—"frozen by some shudder of the mind," and he casts the mystery's rhythm in two different echoic voices. The play's power lies in the tattered gray tangle, where places, times, and words are fused in a stage presence that revolves around absence. This pacing figure is aware of her own abrasive steps, and upon her is foisted an "Amen" even when she is absent from vespers—because at that time she is listening to her footfalls in a locked church. Beckett's three moving scenes choreograph "revolving it all." They culminate in a human "Amen" to a prayer without evidence of divine presence. Finally, human presence vanishes.

Beckett thought it ungracious not to participate in planned celebrations of his seventieth birthday. The Royal Court Theatre planned a Beckett Season for the occasion, with two world premières—*That Time* and *Footfalls.* The BBC also wished to mark the event with a special program. *Not I* had been filmed in February, and Beckett pondered on what might accompany it. He may have begun *Ghost Trio* while rehearsing *Godot* in Berlin, but his holograph is clearly dated 1976.

1976

The Bible mentions three score and ten years as a terminus, but for Beckett his seventieth year marked new beginnings—heightened abstraction in television writing and his first piece for concert performance.

Ghost Trio
Although Beckett's late work is haunted by ghosts, the television piece alone admits them to the title. *Tryst* was Beckett's working title, and since the pro-

---

The holograph and two typescripts of *Ghost Trio* are at RUL. *Ghost Trio* was first published in the Grove Press *Ends and Odds* (1976), but without Beckett's revisions that were incorporated into the Faber *Ends and Odds* (1977). Beckett advised on the

ducer was *Tristr*am Powell, one person was unhappy at the change, but he did not communicate this to Beckett. The playwright's adoption of the unofficial title of Beethoven's Piano Trio no. 5 in D Minor calls attention to *his* three instruments—Beethoven's Largo, a woman's voice, and a camera eye. "Trio" may also embrace the play's three characters, its three movements, or its three camera positions.

Beckett's teleplay is divided into three parts—Pre-action, Action, and Re-action, which are hard to read, although practically useful to the television director. In the Pre-action a woman's voice presents to the television viewer her own voice and "the familiar chamber"—wall, floor, door, window, and pallet in spartan surroundings. However, the chamber is not familiar in itself, but a composite of the almost bare chambers in Beckett's several works. (The repeated "No shadow" was omitted because this proved impossible to obtain in production, and the "Dust" is invisible.) At the voice's bidding, the camera closes in on rectangle-specimens of the elements mentioned, and this enables Beckett to reduce the room's contents to a kind of cubism. As Linda Ben-Zvi notes: "Each rectangular shape is seen against a still larger rectangle: the window against the wall, the door against the wall, the pallet against the floor, even the [cassette] against the stool" (1985, 35). After reviewing this quintet of the room's components, the voice announces: "Sole sign of life a seated figure" (409). However, the sole sign of life is not the motionless figure but the "faint music" emanating from what is not yet seen to be a cassette. Except for the invisible "Dust" invoked by the voice, there has been perfect concord between voice and camera in the Pre-action.

The Action begins climactically: "He will now think he hears her" (410). After twice lifting his head toward the door, the figure glides to the door, opens it in stylized fashion, and looks down the corridor. He then goes to the window and looks out, then to the pallet and looks at it. On the wall above the pallet is a mirror, in which he sees his reflection, surprising the voice: "Ah!" (411). It may be the figure's cue for rebellion, for when the voice utters: "Now to door," he returns to his stool and cassette. He bends to the music until the voice announces: "He will now again think he hears her." He raises his head and goes to the door as before, but his movement is "irresolute." To the music heard for the first time from a distance, and growing louder without being instructed, the voice orders "Stop" and is obeyed. She

---

BBC production of *Shades (Not I, Ghost Trio,* and *. . . but the clouds . . .),* broadcast on April 17, 1977—over a year after Beckett's seventieth birthday. Beckett directed the German version, and in description I follow that version. Aside from *Eh Joe,* none of Beckett's television pieces was translated into French by him. Edith Fournier's renditions are found in Minuit's *Quad et autres pièces pour la télévision* (1992). Detailed discussions of *Ghost Trio* are Knowlson 1986 and Herren. I am indebted to both of them, although I do not share their admiration of the piece.

then commands "Repeat," and she is so flagrantly ignored that she is heard no more. In the Pre-action the camera is mobile, and the man immobile. In the Action the camera is virtually immobile, but the man moves around the room.

The hyphenated Re-action means both repetition and opposition, in disobedience to the voice's last order. Now figure and camera move both in familiar and in new configurations. The woman's voice is no longer to be heard, but *bruitage* is audible. When door and window open and close, they creak. The open window discloses the sound and sight of rain outside. There is no cry of surprise when the figure (and we) see his face in the mirror, but when he cocks an ear to the door, the sound of steps is followed by two knocks on the door. The "No one" of the Action gives way to a boy "in black oilskin with hood glistening with rain" (413). Moreover, "Boy shakes head faintly," before he departs, with "receding steps." The figure returns to his stool. With head bent over the invisible cassette, the figure listens to the end of the Largo, after which he raises his face to the camera (in a faint, unnoted smile) before the final fadeout.

I have recounted the plot in detail (1) to stress Beckett's aural and mainly visual patterns; (2) to suggest how Beckett has abstracted his approach to television in the decade since *Eh Joe;* (3) to raise the question of rendering ghosts without memorable phrases. Since I hope that 1 and 2 are self-evident, I pause at 3. In broadcasting Beckett's three *Shades,* the BBC enlisted the aid of Martin Esslin (critic, director, and Beckett enthusiast) to guide prospective televiewers, and his message was basically: "Surrender to the images." Yes, but I at least need to find some meaning in the images. For all Ronald Pickup's skill (I am less appreciative of the German actor Klaus Herm, a favorite of Beckett), what is he conveying? A monastic figure yearns for "her" to keep a tryst. As in *Godot,* the boy messenger announces a nonarrival, but this time there is no promise of tomorrow. The purity of the Action seems to be sullied by the realities of the more closely observed Re-action, and the figure retreats into music.

Beethoven's Largo is all very well, but I miss Beckett's verbal largo in *Ghost Trio.* I never expressed my disappointment to Beckett, but he volunteered the information that Beethoven was not the origin of the teleplay. He told me: "I wanted a calm scene which revealed an inner storm as the camera approached, but the figure resisted me, so I resorted to rectangles." I have mulled over that "so," and I think it means that the rectanglism of the Pre-Action is subverted by the *bruitage* of the Re-action. Pure form is assailed by an outer world. Knowlson praises the "intriguing ambiguity" (199) of the play, and Ben-Zvi its "powerful visualizations of the agony of waiting and the pain of solitude" (1985, 257). Most provocatively, Herren reads the teleplay as the triumph of image over word: "The stubborn persistence of music and mise en scene to continue communicating meaning even in the absence of language is the surest indicator of [the figure's] victory over [the Voice] . . . the meaning one derives from *Ghost Trio* is not namable, but it is palpable" (90, 92). For me, however, *Ghost Trio* contains too little ghostly substance: "the motion alone is not enough, I must hear the [words], however faint they fall."

Beckett was seventy years old on April 13, 1976, and three days later he flew to London for rehearsals of the Royal Court Beckett season. Affable and unusually sociable, he advised McWhinnie on *That Time* and *Play*, but he independently directed *Footfalls*, with Billie Whitelaw. Back in Paris, he learned of deaths of loved ones—Dr. Geoffrey Thompson in July, whose residency in a psychiatric hospital had served as a setting for *Murphy;* George Reavey in August, who had published *Echo's Bones* and tried in vain to find publishers for *Murphy* and *Watt*. For the second time burglars broke into Beckett's cottage at Ussy, stealing a chess set given him by his father. At the end of August he flew to Berlin to direct *Damals* and *Tritte*, with somewhat less pleasure than in London. In mid-September the American composer Morton Feldman came to Berlin to see him, with a request for a new piece to be accompanied by his music. Within a few days Beckett mailed *neither* to Feldman.

Neither

Generic definitions break down for Beckett's late works. The stage plays *That Time* and *Footfalls* lean toward short fiction, and *neither* is often considered a poem. In editing *CSP,* Gontarski quotes Beckett's British publisher, John Calder, as to why he did not include it in *Collected Poems:* "We did not do so, because Beckett at the last moment said that it was not a poem and should not be there" (284). Gontarski then concludes: "since the piece is a work of prose, there is no question of retaining the line endings of [prior publications]" (285). But he does, since each line is its own paragraph. Eight translators of the piece (into six languages) referred again and again to the poem, *pace* Beckett.

This does not mean that the brief piece lacks narrative thrust. The subjectless piece is Kafkaesque, in the doors that close when approached, and that open when distanced. Rhythmically, the words are gently binary—to

A photocopy of a typescript of *neither* is at RUL. The piece was first performed with Feldman's music in Rome on June 12, 1977. First published in *High Fidelity and Musical America* (February, 1977), and then (with errors) in *JOBS* 4, it is reprinted in *CSP*. Although Beckett did not translate it, eight intrepid members of different countries tried to do so, and the instructive account of their difficulties appears in Van der Weel and Hisgen *SBT* 2. For illumination of both Beckett's text and Feldman's music, see Laws.

and from, inner to outer, self to unself, back and forth—so that "neither" leaves one in a limbo. At last, however, sounds cease, and the light is "unfading on that unheeded neither." The final "unspeakable home," perhaps in apposition to "that unheeded neither," conveys a deathly peace, or perhaps a peaceful death.

The Polish critic Antoni Libera, one of the translators of *neither*, subsumes it thus: "Nothing can be said about what exists when there is no motion, except that it is the opposite of what existed when there was motion. Since what existed when there was motion had the characteristics of exile and wandering. . . , what exists when there is no motion could be described as the characteristics of a home" (Van der Weel and Hisgen, 356). Catherine Laws summarizes the short piece with lucidity: "Beckett's 'Neither' [*sic*] is free from the specifics of name, place, or event, evoking nothing more substantial than oscillatory motion. The sense is of a dislocated 'between-ness,' a ghostly movement coming and going between different gradations of shadow, between self and unself equally impenetrable, achieving stasis only through the abandonment of such distinctions and even then located by the negative, inexpressible terms of 'unspeakable home'" (59–60). In his seventieth year, the old master had not lost his gift for creating resonant images, even though the words languish unheard in Feldman's "opera."

Beckett flew directly from Berlin to London for the filming of *Ghost Trio*. While there, he viewed the BBC film of the Royal Court *Play*, which was intended to complete his BBC "birthday" program, but he was so dissatisfied with it that he offered to try to write another short television piece. As in the case of the almost simultaneous work on *Pour finir encore* and *That Time*, he was able to work simultaneously on two extremely different pieces—"Long Observation of the Ray" being abandoned on November 19, and . . . *but the clouds* . . . being sent to the BBC on November 25.

"Long Observation of the Ray"

Although Beckett did not title the piece, it proves to be a good description of a prose piece that preoccupied him at (at least) two junctures, toward the end of 1975, and then again in November 1976. The first page of the holograph announces eight subjects, to be examined in an intricate pattern of sentences, where a sentence must again be defined unsyntactically, as a phrase opening with a capital letter and closing with a period. The first subject is "Observa-

---

A four-leaf holograph of "Long Observation of the Ray" is dated October 27, 1975, and three undated typescripts revise this material. A two-leaf holograph is dated November 19, 1976, and an undated typescript follows that version. All are at RUL. In that archive's *The Ideal Core of the Onion* (1992) Steven Connor writes about the manuscript, a discussion to which I am indebted.

tion," and it is the only one of the eight that Beckett expanded, before abandoning his intractable pattern.

As in other late pieces, Beckett moulds a hermetic unit for observation—first a cube, which he changes to a sphere. In 1975 he is concerned with the ray of light that probes that sphere, and his revisions reveal the reductive and impersonal way the narrator examines his structure. By 1976, he isolates what he calls "eye-mind" to focus on their cooperation and opposition, as in the old Cartesian body/mind heyday. As Connor rightly observes: "the disposition of elements in the text, chamber, ray, source of light, eye and mind can never in fact be concentrated into simultaneous co-presence, can never be grasped all at once" (1992, 88). Or, in Beckett's sentence: "Or most arduous of all with where they are the straining eye the struggling mind and how communicate." This text, devoid of human agency ("so far," as Winnie might say), breaks off after a table of calculations.

Connor conveys the intractability of the task Beckett set himself: "in *Long Observation of the Ray* we not only see the observing ray in the act of observing, we see the observing mind observing itself in the role of the observing ray" (90). Moreover, these observations failed to elicit memorable phrases from Beckett, whose narrator is even drier and more literal than that of *Le Dépeupleur*. Finally, the author abandoned the project and turned to a different kind of long observation.

. . . but the clouds . . .

As in the case of *Ghost Trio*, Beckett was quite sure of his conception from the start, and like the earlier teleplay this one makes difficult reading. In spite of his cast list of five entities, this work is also a "ghost trio," which now consist of a man, a woman's face, and phrases from Yeats's "The Tower," that masterly poem of rage against old age, which closes on a quiet acceptance. As in "Long Observation of the Ray," Beckett seeks to trace the working of a mind, and he enfolds that process into the work itself: "Let us now make sure we have got it right" (*CDW*, 219). Since television is a visual medium, Beckett conjures images accordingly.

The view of M is invariant—in robe and skullcap, seated at an invisible table. It is he who narrates the M1 scenes—an exterior and an interior view. The former, dressed in dark hat and greatcoat, wandered west (offstage) dur-

---

Two holographs, four typescripts, and a photocopy of corrected page proofs of *. . . but the clouds . . .* are at RUL. The first untitled holograph is dated "Le Touquet, 21 October 1976," and the second "Le T, 25, 10." Presumably, Beckett secluded himself for a few days to compose *. . . but the clouds . . .*, which was sent from Paris to the BBC on November 18. It was first broadcast on April 17, 1977, and first published in *Ends and Odds* (Faber, 1977). With the exception of *Eh Joe*, none of Beckett's teleplays was translated by him into French.

ing daytime, and the latter, dressed in light robe and skullcap, retreated into his sanctum (offstage) at night. There, crouching and seen by none, he begged "her" to appear. His muse seems to be a distillation of a loved one, now dead. M outlines her three forms of appearance, to which her face accedes: gone in a breath, or lingering, or, undescribed, silently mouthing Yeats's phrases. After vainly pleading that she look at him, or speak to him, M acknowledges "case nought," when he begged in vain, then turned to "more . . . rewarding" activities," like cube roots or "nothing, that MINE" (421). With M1 gone west, W appears unbidden to M, and his voice alone intones the Yeats phrases, as we view her immobile face. The fadeout is on M at his invisible table, having reviewed his work of inspiration.

Although the same BBC team produced . . . but the clouds . . . and Ghost Trio, and Beckett was present at both tapings, the former seems to me marred by overreverence. Whereas Beethoven's music dictated the slow movements of the human agents in the earlier piece, the Yeats lines are at once peaceful and inspirational, in contrast with M1's activities. His invariant routine and costume changes seem to me an unintentional Bergsonian comedy. The whole teleplay is conceived as a narrative of past events; it virtually opens with revisions, then travels to repetitions of routine gestures, until the routine itself masters the gesture. The narrative encompasses both yearning and derision—"begged in vain" and "nothing that MINE." A telecast has yet to capture that blend.

Before Christmas Beckett flew to London for the recording of . . . but the clouds. . . . For all his active participation in performance during his seventieth year, his writing energy did not flag. In addition to the works mentioned in this chapter, he wrote two short poems, a quatrain "after" Chamfort, a couplet "after" Pascal, and at least the first verses of "gloomy doggerel," which he later called Mirlitonnades. Slightly more substantial poems are "roundelay" and "thither." Their brevity and elision were prepared by the "translations" from Chamfort, begun in 1972. Although Poems groups these small poems as "translations," I place quotation marks around the word because Beckett makes free with Chamfort both in sense and rhythm.

Long after Chamfort

Beckett's poems are literally long after Chamfort (1740–94), whose Pensées, maxims, et anecdotes were published only after his death. However, the

---

The "translations" from Chamfort were penned between 1972 and 1976. "Hope is a knave" first appeared in Hermathena (summer 1973) and five others in Blue Guitar (December 1975); the last two (one based on Pascal) first appear in Collected Poems in English and French (London: Calder, 1977). An extended analysis of these eight poems is made by Genetti (1994).

"long" is a funny title for these very short versifications of Chamfort. Celebrated before the Revolution for his pithy witty epigrams, Chamfort probably appealed to Beckett for his cynicism and brevity. Of his hundreds of apothegms, only seven were rhymed by Beckett—five into couplets, and two into quatrains (as well as one couplet based on Pascal). Occasionally, Beckett's strain toward rhyme contributes its own wit—shocking/galloping, feet/lot, mine/in, death/healeth. A global summary of the contents might be: Life is not worth living, nor thinking about.

Beckett's first six poems are crystal clear despite their brevity, but the last Chamfort quatrain introduces the ambiguity that becomes almost a matter of principle in *Mirlitonnades*. Either a space or a comma should separate its two couplets: "sleep till death / healeth /come ease / this life disease." "Come" may be a subjunctive verb whose subject is "Death," or it may be an imperative implicitly addressed to death. Unlike the Chamfort verses, the Englished Pascal conceals its rhyme: "how hollow heart and full / of filth thou art." The verse recalls Hamm's pronouncement over two decades earlier: "the bigger a man is the fuller he is . . . And the emptier." It is a sobering, if not quite sober, thought for a man of three score and ten years.

In November Beckett also wrote an eight-line versicule, which is a virtual résumé of . . . *but the clouds . . .* :

> rentrer
> à la nuit
> au logis
> allumer
>
> éteindre voir
> la nuit voir
> collé à la vitre
> le visage
>
> [back
> to night
> place to sleep
> light on
>
> light off see
> night see
> stuck to the pane
> the face][13]

The "rhymerie" became the first of a group of French small poems, which he later called *Mirlitonnades*.

1977–89

Comment Dire
(What is the word)

1977

It is likely that the biblical life-span of three score and ten years struck Beckett's mind during his seventieth year, but he remained active. He flew twice to Germany: in May to Stuttgart to direct his recent two teleplays, and in September to Berlin to direct Rick Cluchey in *Krapp's Last Tape*. There and elsewhere he scribbled brief poems, mainly in French, on whatever bit of paper came to hand—appointment pages, backs of letters, cigarillo wrappings. Dated between 1976 and 1981, most of the verse was written during 1977. However impromptu in origin, these odd scraps of paper were saved by Beckett and subsequently copied into a small notebook now at RUL.

Mirlitonnades
Two substantial articles help explicate the verse. David Wheatley publishes draft versions of some poems and comments briefly on all of them (but he is insensitive to French rhyme and rhythm). Matthijs Engelberts selects the more amusing examples to savor as "light verse" (and he corrects some of

---

As described in *BatR*, ms. 2460 at RUL "contains thirty-six irregularly shaped scraps of paper which feature manuscript drafts" of the brief poems, *Mirlitonnades*. However, the catalog's explanation of the title *Mirlitonnades* misses its point; a *mirliton* is a kazoo or makeshift musical instrument consisting of two thin membranes through which the breath or voice passes; it is often wrapped in colored papers. *Vers de mirliton* is therefore doggerel, but in inventing the word *mirlitonnade*, Beckett endows it with connotations of fragility and brightness, while not quite succumbing to the pejorative *vers de mirliton*. Beckett copied these scattered poems into the so-called Sottisier Notebook in preparation for publication. The poems are published in the 1978 Minuit *Poèmes* and in the 1984 Calder *Collected Poems, 1930–1978*. Kevin Perryman has skillfully translated six of them into English (*Babel* 6 [1990]). The most detailed analysis is that of Cerrato.

Wheatley's errors). Beckett's small poems seem to me to be sprightly rhymes about dark moods. Tossed off in lieu of sustained work, the verse is Beckett's way of teasing himself about his own obsessive themes—death, nothingness, fragility of the body, inadequacy of language. As published, the rhyming epigrams move from skepticism about words to desire for the peace of death. Rhymes contrast light and dark, sound and silence. Or individual body parts are imaged—eye, head, foot, heart, even fingers. Engelberts has pinpointed what these poems share—rhymes, puns, brevity, unusual word order, and a light tone for lugubrious subjects.

Mirlitonnades may be an acquired taste for Beckett readers, and even though I have acquired it, I don't ascribe much importance to this light verse, which reflected his passing thoughts and travels, and my comments are therefore cursory. On the verso page of his first poem of 1977 Beckett calculated seventy years in days, hours, and minutes, and then rounded out the results—twenty-six thousand days, six hundred thousand hours, three and one-half million minutes. Setting these aside, he chose for his poem an obsolete measurement "milliasse," as strange to the francophone as the anglophone reader. "somme toute / tout compte fait / un quart de milliasse / de quarts d'heure / sans compter / les temps morts." I dare not translate this, but even without French, the reader can savor the repetitions and the feeling of relentless arithmetic, which climaxes in dead time.

Another *mirlitonnade* reflects Beckett's mood. An April 10 letter to Alan Schneider announces that he had tried in vain to write something new, and he added jocularly: "Wish I could do an Atropos all in black—with her scissors" (Harmon, 355). On April 21 in Tangiers he did indeed "do an Atropos," without naming the Greek fate who cut life off:

> noire soeur
> qui es aux enfers
> à tort tranchant
> et à travers
> qu'est-ce que tu attends
>
> [dark sister
> who art in hell
> wrongly slicing
> and cross-cutting
> why dost thou delay]

It is improbable, however, that Beckett would call such amusement *writing*. In addition to *Mirlitonnades,* Beckett penned the short lyric "One Dead of Night," but letters to various friends testify to his efforts to sustain narrative prose at this time. In January 1978 he began a piece on which he was unable to make headway.

1978
∞

Verbatim

Although some of the phrases of this fragment were salvaged for *Company*, completed in 1979, *Verbatim* is at once more chaotic and more reason-ridden. The word *verbatim* does not appear in the text, where a voice is usually pronominalized to "it." The fragment opens: "Speaking of itself in the third person singular it began by saying it would not cease till hearing cease" (189). Questions are then raised about whose hearing is involved, and after replies are delayed till later, words are ascribed to "now the voice—now the mind of which in some way it was the utterance." Leaf 2 (of seven) opens with a sentence that might be cherished by postmodernists: "As though perhaps one does not so much say what one thinks as think what one says" (190). The dry narrative continues with the "harping" of the voice. By way of "romance" and travels, a character appears—"wayfarer out since dawn plodding forward through the gloaming." Leaf 3 follows the wayfarer as he listens, calculates, and senses his father's shade at his elbow. Without a break, Beckett's prose elides into the voice and its flat tone, despite interrogations, affirmations, negations, interjections, optations, imperations, with examples of each.

Leaf 4 harps on the voice's harping. Questions are asked and shelved. The voice is unfixed in direction, and the mind is perhaps "not well." However, the voice "reverts in haste to the long disuse that so impoverished its wordhoard and weakened its grasp of reality" (192). The word "silent" provokes tears and the possibility of a return of feeling, and even of a face to accommodate the tears. Surmise is rife in questions about seductive silence and similarly seductive dark. The problematics of hearing return. At the end of leaf 5 reason is named for the first time, although it has been functioning throughout. "Here to its surprise reappearance of figure adumbrated." Leaf 6 paints a figure on Ballyogan Road, "in the interests of verisimilitude" (193). His garments are detailed, along with his father's shadow. However,

---

The seven-leaf holograph of *Verbatim* is at RUL. This has been usefully published as "The Voice VERBATIM" in Charles Krance's *Samuel Beckett's Company/Compagnie and A Piece of Monologue/Solo: A Bilingual Variorum Edition* (New York: Garland, 1993).

this elides into a supine hearer "stretched out one hearing only on and off his own spent breath." The last leaf describes the great coat on the supine figure; is it listening? Further questions are again delayed: "And back to now." The "now" consists of recollections of what the voice said about itself: "It. Mind. Voice. Old. Toneless. Breathless. Faint. Faltering," and finally "Indefinable." The fragment breaks off: "Of one whose mother tongue as foreign as the others. Tonic stress very weak." In English, as opposed to French, there is no tonic stress. In the "Sottisier" Notebook, Beckett evidently envisaged a conflict between voice and mind, and yet he notes that "either . . . or" is abolished. He also outlines speech by three voices that are "one and the same."

It is easy to siphon off the phrases and concepts of "Verbatim" that would later nourish *Company*. What is not easy is to reconstruct the rush of words after "long disuse," which Beckett may have taken down "verbatim" from his mind, without stopping to shape them, although he did reread and comment on them on verso pages of his holograph. The title "Voice/Verbatim" does not seem applicable to the fragment, and my wholly intuitive guess is that the idea of some such dictation enabled Beckett to write on—after a delay of some months.

Although Beckett tried to escape from involvement in performance, March found him directing Roger Blin's friend Delphine Seyrig in *Pas,* his translation of *Footfalls*. In August an actor friend, David Warrilow, wrote him to request a play with "an image of a man standing on stage lit from above. He's standing there in a sort of cone of light. You couldn't see his face and he's talking about death." The subject was irresistible to Beckett, and in October he began a manuscript entitled "Gone," but it lay fallow for over a year, before being completed as *A Piece of Monologue*. When play and fiction proved recalcitrant, Beckett continued with short rhymes, but he also worked fitfully during 1978 at the longer pieces. In spite of his good resolutions, he continued to direct; September found him again in Berlin's Schiller Theater, this time with *Spiel,* and at the same time he guided Rick Cluchey's group in *Endgame*.

1979

The new year brought a continuation of performance, since Beckett went to Stuttgart in January for another telecast of *Eh Joe*. Later in the year he might have been heartened by the completion of pieces of fiction and drama—*Company* in July and *A Piece of Monologue* in December, as well as occasional verse.

Company

Rarely did Beckett display his shaping hand with more grace or versatility than in the transition from "Verbatim" to *Company*. The solid prose block of the former is molded into fifty-nine paragraphs of the latter, just short of sixty, a number ineluctably associated with passing time. "All at once over and in train and to come" (38). At once timed and timeless, the narrative is, inhabitually for Beckett, appealing in its seeming simplicity. Katharine Worth has summarized the situation: "the man alone in the dark, listening to a voice he can't control and which he both dreads and longs to hear" (176). Involved are "the mental struggles, the anxieties as well as the ecstasies of the imagination at work, the ingenuities of the wit" (177).

The text opens: "A voice comes to one in the dark. Imagine." The ensuing account obeys that behest, which is particularized in paragraph 2: "That then is the proposition. To one on his back in the dark a voice tells of a past." Yet the voice's memories are almost always couched in the present tense. Three figures take form—a hearer who would say "I" if he could speak, a voice, and a protean other. Paragraph 3 introduces the latter two: "Use of the second person marks the voice. That of the third that cankerous other." No sooner are they enunciated, however, than the pronouns disobey the rule. Not until paragraph 7 does the second-person pronoun lapse into memory, and he does so without transition. Memory sometimes wars with reason; Enoch Brater notes that "the rhythm of reason [is] constantly backtracking on itself to amend a phrase, repeat it with minor variation, or take up yet another possible cause in a mad search for the irresistible *mot juste,* [while, in contrast,] the rhythm of memory, even when fabricated by a suspect voice in the dark, is swift, incisive, and direct" (1994, 118). Beckett himself is quoted by Gontarski about a French staging of the novel: the third-person voice was "erecting a series of hypotheses, each of which is false," whereas the second-person voice "was trying to create a history, a past for the third-person" (1987, 196). Nevertheless there is occasional seepage from one rhythm to the other, and both indulge in lyric intervals.

The *Company* Notebook, RUL ms. 1822 contains the holographs of both Beckett's original English and his translation into French. Burns Library at Boston College contains two typescripts. Before the 1980 Calder and Grove publications, paragraph 39 of *Company* was published as *Heard in the Dark 1* in *New Writing and Writers* 17 (London, 1979); and paragraph 40 as *Heard in the Dark 2* in *JOBS* 5 (autumn 1979). Except for minor revisions, these are excerpts from the novel, and should not have been included in *CSP*. Beckett's translation *Compagnie* was published by Minuit in 1980. Charles Krance has usefully edited *Company/Compagnie*. Although Beckett did not retain the paragraph numbers of his manuscripts, I nevertheless refer to the text of *Company* by these paragraph numbers. Peter Murphy's chapter 10 draws provocative parallels between *Company* and *As You Like It*.

What readers tend to retain are the second-person memory-scenes of the voice, in the immediacy of their present tense. Of the fifteen such scenes, seven focus on childhood, two on adulthood, four on old age; one lacks age designation, and one takes place on the birth day of "you."[1] Most eventful are the evocations of childhood—the boy reprimanded by his mother, the boy blessed by a beggarwoman, the boy urged by his father to dive, the boy's jump from a tall tree, the boy's sight of a far-off mountain, the boy's rescue of a hedgehog, the boy's imitation of his father's chuckle. Scenes tend to merge of an old man in a long green coat and a worn block hat, tramping through the fields, with or without his father's shade. The two scenes of adulthood involve relationships with women. Extrabiographical are a scene near the beginning and one near the end of *Company:* paragraph 9 accompanies "you's" father on the day of his birth, and the achronological "you" of paragraph 58 follows a second hand and its shadow around a timepiece. These fifteen scenes compose only about a third of *Company.*

It is in the other two-thirds that we absorb some fifty repetitions of the words "company" and "companionable." Kateryna Arthur has admirably phrased how these affect the reader: "the writing constructs and simultaneously deconstructs the concept of company, developing it as a reassuring possibility with all its human connotations of community, communication and friendship, while also parodying it by presenting it as merely an aspect of narrative, a textual device or a conjuring trick invented by the writer-deviser who is himself 'devised'" (141).[2] Moreover, company is linked with a spectrum of incongruous effects, from possible improvements to the voice or hearer, to a choice of postures, to a dead rat or a fly, to an unscratchable itch. At times, too, synonyms are offered for "companionable," which hint at a pleasurable fable—"entertaining" (41), "diverting" (49), "endearing"(54), "alacrious" (58). Despite the yearning for company, however, the text ends and almost begins in solitude: paragraph 2 prophesies: "You will end as you now are," and paragraph 58 affirms: "And you as you always were." Paragraph 59 consists of the single word "Alone." Yet many avatars of company have been devised in the interim.

In an early review John Pilling wrote: "*Company* succeeds in de-familiarizing the familiar and making the strange even stranger" (1982, 131). At the same time, the text is somehow reassuring in its familiarity to Beckett readers, and it is unforbidding in its strangeness (unlike, for example, the ironically titled *All Strange Away* of 1964). Pilling himself devotes most of his review to companionable echoes in *Company* of a score of other Beckett works, as well as allusions to Shakespeare, Milton, and the Bible. Many of these echoes must be deliberate on Beckett's part, although the manuscripts disclose no evidence of a list gathered from rereading (as they do disclose lists for the memory scenes). Nor is it clear from the manuscripts when Beckett adopted an echo principle for *Company,* and yet it is pervasive. Pilling is an excellent excavator of erudite ore, and Enoch Brater follows in his wake (to mix metaphors). Literary allusions (including auto-allusion) are one kind of echo, but I refrain from adding to their respective compendia. I am also uneasy with an implication (of which I too have been guilty) that echoes of earlier work validate *this* work.

Examining *Company* itself, we notice the repetition of phrases: "vice versa," "for the moment," "up to a point," " to and of whom," "leave it at that," "and so on," "from nought anew," "quick leave him," and "upturned face." Except for the last, these are unusually neutral phrases. Calling attention to themselves are the phrases or sentences that are uttered by the unnamed narrator and then immediately repeated as quotations. Although repetition-in-quotation occurs elsewhere in Beckett's work, it is relentless in *Company.* The first quotation from the voice is "You are on your back in the dark," and that sentence repeats what has already been narrated, redolent of the ambiguity between "the dark" as lack of light and as a metaphor for consciousness. The phrase will be repeated, with variations, countless times. (At least I wearied of counting.) These quotational echoes are all the more insidious in that quotation marks are absent from the text. It is not unusual in European printing to mark a quotation only by setting it off with a comma and a capital letter, but all the commas of *Company* perform that single function. They therefore disappear from the last few paragraphs, where the crawling creator is too preoccupied to quote the voice, if indeed it is still there.

Not only does *Company* contain these textlong echoes, but it also abounds in what might be called spot echoes. Two paragraphs in particular (which were individually published as *Heard in the Dark* 1 and 2) contain spot echoes in double focus. Paragraph 39 tells of an old man on his feet in a snowlit scene, as viewed by one on his back in the dark. Paragraph 40 is even more complex, for "On your back in the dark you remember"—two overlapping scenes in a summerhouse. In the first memory a boy imitates his father's chuckle, an echo within the double focus, but since the adult awaits his lover, there is a triple time-exposure—the one on his back eliding the childhood scene into adulthood and then back again. The other adult love scene in paragraph 48 contains a single sentence that doubles the focus: "In your dark you look in [her eyes] again." A lyrical childhood scene also contains double focus; paragraph 29 describes the child's distant view in the past, and twice the present intrudes: "You lie in the dark and are back in that light." Involuntary memory was for Proust a source of epiphany, but for Beckett's voice it is echoic, shifty, and evanescent. Yet it contributes to the wealth of paragraph 58, where time and theme and image blend the two rhythms of *Company,* just before the fable comes to an end.

Paragraph 56 presents a virtual image of doubling, as the watch's second hand is always accompanied by its shadow, however that shadow may change form and position. In that paragraph, too, "you" are "numb with the woes of your kind," so that you escape into the study of the movements on the face of the dial (as elsewhere in Beckett mathematics provides escape from emotion). Finally, however, and despite what else might be said about "the subject of this second hand and its shadow," you "return to the woes of your kind." Nor is it fortuitous that the *second* hand receives such close scrutiny in an echoic text, where dawn and sunlight create your shadow "And those of other objects also." Time's echoic shadow hangs over both animate creatures and inanimate objects in Beckett's imagined world.

Aspects of *Company* even smaller than paragraphs also display echoes. In the very first memory, the boy rephrases his question to his mother, and that is what the voice does again and again in its ratiocinative sentences. In that early memory, too, the boy's reprimand is the more poignant because the mother "shook off your *little* hand" (emphasis added), and several paragraphs later the hearer wonders endearingly about his "little void." But hands are not always little; in paragraph 21 an imagined hand fills the whole field, and in paragraph 56 the revolving watch hand usurps the available space. Persona and object are both subject to shadowing, but the eye of *Company* remains human, even when "hooded." It can fill a whole field in paragraph 22, but by paragraph 48 lovers' "eyes [are] in each other's eyes." A nose is mentioned only once in *Company,* but the sense of smell secretes an echo. In paragraph 33 the fate of the hedgehog is encapsulated by "The stench." Yet by paragraph 51 an odor is desirable: "How much more companionable could his creator but smell. Could he but smell his creator." More seriously, the phrase "never forgot" links his mother's cutting remark with the hedgehog's putrid remains.

The echo of a single word may sound after a long interval: the boy's "uneasiness" about the hedgehog is echoed in Haitch's "uneasiness" about his status. Both the midwife and the father sport gray moustaches. The old man's quarter-boot is echoed in Dante's quarter-smile. The "beeline" to a gap in a hedge in paragraph 39 shifts to a beeline crawl in paragraph 50. The unusual word "withershins" appears in paragraphs 39 and 50. Perhaps the most arresting example of echoing (as well as other devices) occurs at the beginning and end of paragraph 52: "Can the crawling creator crawling in the same create dark as his creature create while crawling? . . . no he could not. Could not conceivably create while crawling in the same create dark as his creature." The recumbent posture, the excess of alliteration, the position of the word "create" and the ambiguity as to whether it is a verb or a past participle, the verbal proximity of conception and creation—all these conjoin to deromanticize the act of creation, even while it is being performed.[3]

Less obstreperously verbal are other echoes—particularly in the memory scenes. Consistently, the old-man memories present him with head sunk or bowed, and this contrasts with the upturned face of one on his back in the dark. (Yet the graying father of "you" presents an upturned face to his son.) More varied is the position of the boy's head. In the first memory scene he looks up, both to his mother and the sky. In the diving scene he looks down at his father, and in the tree scene he actually dives after looking down. In the lyrical scene of paragraph 29 he looks into the distance. As an adult his eyes are level with those of his lover, but this occasions his mental calculations, and, imagined from above, an isolated leg occasions further calculation. In the final love scene of paragraph 48 the lovers gaze into each other's eyes, he on his back looking up at her behind a tent of black hair. In contrast to these textlong head positions, echoes are more sparing for the rendition of suffering. In paragraph 11 we hear: "You first saw the light of day at Easter and now." A few sentences later: "You first saw the light of day the day Christ died and now" (The "and now's" couple Christ's suffering with everyman's). By paragraph 38 pain enters quietly: "You were born on an Easter Friday after long labour." Pain is more voluble by paragraph 54: "You first saw the light and cried at the close of the day when in darkness Christ at the ninth hour cried and died." Both "you" and Christ cry, and the long *i* sounds like crying. Such various and repetitive echoing is multiply meaningful—as the contrast of comic and conceptual, as evidence of the musicality of words, as testimony to the inadequacy of language to experience, as fabled by a voice that remembers while flouting chronology.

The web of echoes is subtle and intricately woven, but it does not impede the narrative. Paradoxically, the narrative accrues not to the memories, which are achronological and discrete, for example, a brave boy for the father is a naughty boy for the mother. The last paragraphs (50 and above) trace a continuous fable of the crawling creator, creating a fable for company. In this narrative, sound play is often muted, and puns are few, but they are nevertheless worth noting: "lying" is a posture and a narrative device; "no truck" on a road suggests the vehicle; "fast" usually means still, but it is shadowed by its pace. In the summerhouse scene (40) occurs this curious sentence: "Or for affair as now." The scene treats obliquely of a sexual affair, but the context is closer to the French generalization of business. A last example is memorable, in its image of memory: "As best to erode the drop must strike unwavering. Upon the place beneath" (38). The raindrop echoes Portia's speech about mercy in *The Merchant of Venice,* but a larger drop erodes the place where identity is configured by memory, which is perhaps itself a form of fiction.

Throughout the text, the language is slightly archaic—"whence," "thither," "sere," "cleave," "whereof," "hitherto," "bootless," "bourne," and the prefix *a-* is such words as "ado," "akin," "anew," "afar," "afrolic." Occasionally, one is brought up short by an unusual use of a word. Uncertainty is "kindled" in the mind, and a good deed can "kindle" a glow. A boy cherishing a memory "hoards it in your heart." In paragraph 49 we come upon "the repent amble," which means creeping but also puns on penitence. In paragraph 26 we read: "Till the eye closes and freed from pore the mind inquires." Converting a poring eye to a noun renders it more fleshly, to contrast it with the mind; at the same time the lack of punctuation permits "freed from pore" to modify the mind, which thereby acts more freely. In that same paragraph, nothingness is unattainable, and the text continues: "No. Unhappily no. Pangs of faint light and stirrings still." Light as a pang is perhaps more arresting than the final phrase, which will become the title of a later Beckett work.

Almost every sentence of *Company* functions multiply. If light is pangful, however, the poring mind can be comic. Lying on your back is verified by "hind parts." Deflationary devices lighten the text: "your mind never active," "with what reason remains he reasons," "with what judgment remained," "with what feeling remains." Yet this impoverished creature is capable of uttering commandments: "Let there be a fly" (32); "Then let him move. . . . Let him crawl" (44); "let be faintest light" (51). For readers familiar with "something out of Beckett," the long green coat and buff block hat of the old man of memory are reassuringly grotesque, as is his penchant for mathematics. Comically, Beckett even teases the French language with a temporary character named Haitch "Aspirate." French grammar distinguishes between the aspirate and inaspirate *H,* neither of which is pronounced, so Beckett aspirates in English. As Beckett mocks grammar, so too ratiocination: "He speaks of himself as of another. He says speaking of himself, He speaks of himself as of another" (30). Perhaps the wryest humor focuses on the crawl, so much less painful than those of Molloy or Pim: "Crawling in the dark in the way described was too serious a matter and too all-engrossing to permit of any other business were it only the conjuring of something out of nothing" (52). The word "serious" leavens the funny sentence, and the "only" is the coup de grace of disproportion.

With such comic thrusts (often invented in revision), Beckett keeps tragedy at bay. *Company* is spared the anguish of much of Beckett's earlier fiction. Even in the aporias of the third-person pronoun, the old oppositions are no longer wrenching—subject-object, light-dark, language-silence, exterior-interior. Somehow, in the constant play of shades and light, all vantage-points can be accommodated, even if they cannot be located, and even if answers to questions are delayed. A new gentleness suffuses *Company,* not unlike Shakespeare's late romances after the tragedies.

As mentioned earlier, the actor David Warrilow in August 1977 asked

Beckett for a play in which a man is "talking about death." In his reply Beckett sent Warrilow a single sentence: "My birth was my death," but declared himself incapable of continuing "on that old chestnut" (Knowlson, 572). Nevertheless, he did continue on October 2 and 28, without informing Warrilow. By November, however, he found himself "becalmed in deep water and likely to founder" (qtd. in Knowlson, 573). The piece remained "becalmed" for over a year, until Martin Esslin asked Beckett for a contribution to the resurrected *Kenyon Review*. It was not unusual by this time for a Beckett piece to respond to the request of a friend, but *A Piece of Monologue* is the only example of one that was prodded by two requests—that of David Warrilow in August 1977 and that of Martin Esslin in January 1979. It is worth noting, however, that Beckett tried to incorporate a fragment of *Monologue* into *Company*. On May 17, 1978, in the course of revising the novel, Beckett wrote a paragraph that he later deleted; it begins: "Birth was the death of you." It continues with a hand holding a lighted spill, while another hand lifts off an oil lamp's globe, and then its chimney. The action concludes: "Spill to wick. Chimney back on." This sequence is developed and repeated in *A Piece of Monologue*. Onstage, however, stands an electric lamp, perhaps suggested by paragraph 56 of *Company*. A short sequence occurs in both works: "Light dying. Soon none left to die. No. No such thing as no light. Died on to dawn and never died." Nevertheless, *A Piece of Monologue* sheds its own dim effulgence.

A Piece of Monologue

Not until April 28, 1979, did Beckett give the play its final title, after working on it as "Gone." That title may harbor a pun that bears on the mood of the piece—"a peace of monologue." As in the contemporary *Company*, the anxiety of earlier binaries is "gone," and we feel an acceptance not only of a monologue about death, but of being the only one left to utter that monologue. The piece is at once a lament for the brevity of human life, a threnody for a primeval family, and a lyric about lyricizing. Opening on the word "Birth," and closing on the word "gone," the monologue is a piece in the sense that all life is fragmentary—until it ends. Simple in its appeal to the eye, *A Piece of Monologue* is dizzyingly complex in conception, glinting through

---

Krance usefully lists the manuscript versions of *A Piece of Monologue*, which are at RUL: ms. 2068, entitled "Gone" and dated October 2, 1977, with revision of the first thirty lines; ms. 2072, still entitled "Gone" and dated October 28, 1977. Typescripts 2069 and 2070 are still entitled "Gone." The piece was first published as *A Piece of Monologue* in the *Kenyon Review* (summer 1979) and appears in *CDW*, to which my page numbers refer. Translation into French proved so difficult that Beckett published *Solo* as "adapté" rather than "traduit de l'anglais." It appears in Minuit's 1982 volumes *Solo, suivi de Catastrophe* and *Catastrophe et autres dramaticules*.

several meanings of piece—fragment, length, entity, example, weapon, coin, play, game counter.

Although Beckett added the stage directions only in 1979, they are crucial to performance. A white-clad speaker is at "same level, same height" as a standard lamp with "skull-sized white globe." These two uprights—visual approximations of one another—are separated by two meters, or about the space that would be occupied by either of them toppled. However, they do not topple, and they do not move—except for the figure's lips in narration. The lips tell of his mirror image—white hair, gown, and socks—engaging in a nightly routine. Looking first out of a window, then groping his way to light an oil lamp, he faces a blank wall to which pictures of loved ones were once pinned. Gradually, this routine gives birth to the word "Birth" and to a few details of a birth. When "dark slowly parts again," he visualizes a funeral scene in the rain. Porter Abbott (1996) tries valiantly to "normalize" (his word) the narrative sequence into three loops, each one containing This Night, The Birth Night, and The Funeral. However, he has to juggle the text to do so, and, more importantly, he thereby normalizes the incantatory quality of repetitions of the nightly routine and its unpredictable interruptions. Anna McMullan comments: "Just as the extremities of birth and death merge or metamorphose through the earlier repetition of phrases, the relationship between [the window and wall] poles of the nightly ritual becomes increasingly ambiguous through the pattern of repetition" (67). The verbal rounds of a routine that is far from routine are in dynamic tension with the two visible uprights, each topped by a skull-sized globe, only one of which enfolds consciousness.

The stage of *A Piece of Monologue* is bare, except for its two verticals and a piece of a horizontal pallet-foot, but the narrated persona moves between birth and death, between white and black, between a walled, windowed room and a rain-soaked gravescape, between ghosts of loved ones. Almost every critic who comments on *A Piece of Monologue* succumbs to the word *ritual,* and although it is a word I shy away from, it does seem apt. Yet the ritual gravity weighs slowly. The beginning still sports shreds of the comic; even the repeated "Birth was the death of him" recalls an Irish cliché of casual conversation: "[So-and-so] will be the death of me." Humor-tinged, too, are "*ghastly* grinning," "suck first fiasco," "mammy . . . nanny . . . bandied," all with their sound play. Even the mention of funerals cannot mitigate the "few"-ness of long life. Ben-Zvi (1986) has translated two and a half billion seconds to seventy-nine years, and thirty thousand nights to eighty-two years (which Beckett calculated in his manuscript). With the first of seven repetitions of "he all but said . . . loved," we enter a graver domain. Even there, however, a match struck on a *buttock* is still residually comic. Moreover, in realistic terms there is no reason for the unnamed "he" to strike a match before he bares the wick of the oil lamp. After the ripping off the wall of pictures of loved ones, however, the dirge is unrelieved. Moreover, the ripping of pictures is said to take place "Over the years." The ripping off the wall prepares us for the unusual phrase "rip word."

The first repetition of lighting the lamp is quick, with the figure white against the "black vast." Man and lamp, if not quite sacramental, have become artifacts: "Gown and socks white *to take faint light*" (427; emphasis added). Only then is the word "Birth" uttered. A birth occurs as the light dies in a cosmological context: "Dies on to dawn and never dies." This time a spill performs the gestures that light the wick of the oil lamp. Although a spill is "a thin strip of wood, spiral tube etc of paper for lighting candles" (Fletcher and Fletcher, 244), Beckett exploits the spillover effect of the word in his gestural ballet. A flame is secreted by the ceremonial lifting of globe and chimney, and by the lowering of the wick. In keeping with the dirge, they are "Again and again gone."

When the dark parts to admit a gray light, we envision the rain-soaked funeral scene with its empty grave. We hear a puzzling: "Thirty seconds." The wait for a word now becomes part of the nightly routine. As Kristin Morrison comments: "birth . . . like a foetus gathers itself in his mouth and then like an infant emerging from the womb parts the darkness and thrusts itself forward" (11). Birth, however, soon opens out to the entire scene: "Slowly the window. That first night. The room. The spill. The hands. The lamp. The gleam of brass" (428). After the funeral scene the account briefly mentions "other matters," but returns to what we see and hear—"Lip lipping lip." The very feel of the word in the mouth seems to validate experience, even while the several *fades* make us aware of the theater artifact. As before, "Thirty seconds" unaccountably add to the two and a half million previously mentioned. The half-minute is uttered for a third time when the coffin is lowered into the grave. After sacramental echoes of the whole narrative, "No such thing as whole," the "he" becomes a ghost or a ghost-ridden memory: "Thirty thousand nights of ghosts beyond. Beyond that black beyond. Ghost light. Ghost nights. Ghost rooms. Ghost graves. Ghost . . . he all but said ghost loved ones. Waiting on the rip word."

The rip word has been glossed as birth, gone, begone, but Beckett deliberately did not particularize it, even while it ineluctably abbreviates "Requiescat in pace." For that matter, the text's few puns may be read as rip words: wrench, pane, globe. On analogy with rip tide, Morrison glosses: "The rip word is that disturbance in the flow of language which reveals what is hidden, the unpleasant or discreditable truth which may be disguised or submerged but never completely evaded" (104). The text is accompanied for its last thirty seconds by the "lamplight begin[ning] to fail." The last words of *A Piece of Monologue* are "The globe alone. Alone gone," but in fact we see in the dim light the two globes that retain to the end their echoic image. With the simplest vocabulary—a profusion of monosyllables—and understated rhyme, assonance, and alliteration, Beckett has cadenced a human threnody that is at once a lamentation and a secular benediction on parting the dark.

On his seventy-third birthday Beckett sent *A Piece of Monologue* to both David Warrilow for performance and Martin Esslin for publication. In May he flew to London to direct Billie Whitelaw in *Happy Days,* selecting Leonard Fenton to play Willie because the actor could sing Schubert's *Winterreise*—in German. However, rehearsals were less pleasurable than usual. (Knowlson's pp. 579–80 are tactful, but Billie Whitelaw is more candid in her autobiography.) Beckett blamed his text, which had evidently lost what attraction it may have had for him. It was the last time he worked with Whitelaw in the theater.

Beckett was never able to predict whether the voice that came to him in the dark would speak English or French. The manuscript of *Un soir* is undated, but it was at first intended as the opening paragraph of *Mal vu mal dit,* whose earliest date is October 24, 1979. The shorter text may have been shadowed by the death on October 3 of one of Beckett's oldest friends, Con Leventhal. Ten years older than Beckett, he had replaced the writer as an instructor at Trinity College. He had married Beckett's Alba, Ethna MacCarthy, and shortly after her death in 1959 he had moved to Paris, living not far from Beckett, who wrote of him: "A friendship of over 50 years through thick and thin. Now ashes in urn No 21501 in the basement of Père Lachaise Columbariesca" (qtd. in Knowlson, 568).

Un soir

This long paragraph opens with a corpse on the ground. To call *Un soir* a short story is to highlight its slight narrative content. An old woman, in search of yellow flowers to adorn her dead husband's grave, stumbles upon a body. My summary sentence, however, normalizes Beckett's chronology. In the order of telling, the discovery of the body is followed by a portrait of the finder. Since the body lies face down in its long green coat, its irregular buttons are hidden from view. If he were upright, the coat would sweep the ground. Then, as in the stories of the 1940s, the narrator comments on his narration: "Cela a l'air de se tenir" [That seems to hang together, *CSP,* 253]. Moving back to the old woman, the narrator warns himself: "Attention"

The undated, four-leaf holograph of *Un Soir* is RUL 2204. Krance guesses that these leaves were torn from RUL 2203, which contains a draft of *Mal vu mal dit. Un Soir* was first published in *Minuit* 37 (January 1980). Beckett's translation into English (RUL 2466) was first published in *JOBS* 6 (autumn 1980) and is included in *CSP.* Original and translation are published in Krance's bilingual variorum edition of *Mal vu mal dit* (New York: Garland, 1996).

[Not too fast]. After about a quarter of the brief story, the narrator focuses more firmly on the old woman—her long black garment, her long black shadow, her surprise that there are no lambs in this lambing season. If a third party surveyed the scene, only the two bodies would be visible, both "immobile." Again the narrator congratulates himself: "Cela a l'air de se tenir" [That seems to hang together]. After another few sentences he warns himself again: "Attention" [Not too fast]. At about the midpoint of the paragraph he instructs himself: "Au présent pour finir" [In the present to conclude]. Then sentence by present-tense sentence, the narrator builds the old woman's portrait. Her shadow irks her, as well as the familiar sound of her dress on the grass. She sneaks up on the rare flowers. One sentence is startling: "Elle avance les yeux mi-clos comme aspirée par l'incendie" [She moves with half-closed eyes as if drawn on into the glare. Literally, however, as if breathed by the flame]. Almost in a void, annoyed by shadow and noise, she happens on the body. The narrator repeats the opening words about that discovery, and then he joins the two figures—black and green garments, yellow flowers and white hair, dying and dead: "Petit tableau vivant comme on dit" [Tableau vivant if you will. In its way]. The last few sentences re-view the scene, and the piece concludes: "Tout cela a l'air de se tenir. Mais ne pas en dire davantage" [All that seems to hang together. But no more about it, 254].

Finally, Beckett himself wrote "no more" about this delicate effort to merge the dying and the dead, where yellow flowers and spring lambs (with their resonances) are rare or absent. The sun sets at last, giving way to the starless moonless night that has always appealed to Beckett's imagination.

Although manuscripts of *Mal vu mal dit* are only sporadically dated, Beckett probably began the first holograph notebook in 1979, but he found it exceedingly difficult to continue, and he did not manage to complete it till late 1980.

1980

Beckett would be seventy-five in 1981, and several academics undertook celebrations. Stan Gontarski, then at the Ohio State University, planned a conference and hoped that Beckett could contribute a new play. Dan Labeille, at the State University of New York, had a grant to film a rehearsal of a Beckett play, and he too requested a new one for the occasion. Beckett himself in May interrupted work on his fiction in order to spend some two weeks in London, again directing Rick Cluchey's group in *Endgame*. Affable to many visitors, he did not appear to be under strain to return to France. Perhaps drama gave him a respite from his difficulties with the French fiction.

Although Beckett was dubious about new work for Gontarski and Labeille, he did not offer *Mal vu mal dit* as an excuse. Nevertheless, *Rockaby* was completed in August, and *Mal vu mal dit* in September. The two works share an old woman in black who is at home in neither an outer nor an inner world. Different as they are in scale, genre, and language, they are comparably and incomparably lovely.

Rockaby

A "prematurely old" woman in a sequin-studded black evening gown and a skew headdress listens to her recorded voice as she slowly rocks back and forth, her feet on a footrest. The image is incongruous: the grandmotherly rocker and the defiantly elaborate costume. A spotlight is constant on the huge-eyed, expressionless face, but the rocking motion produces a pointillist glitter from sequins and trimmings. The arms of the rocker "suggest embrace," and the gradually softening recorded voice suggests a verbal embrace. The synchrony of the rocking motion and the dimeter verse lines— one back-and-forth rock per line—plays against the recorded narrative that has been aptly summarized by Hersh Zeifman: "The story V narrates is a lullaby turned threnody, its movement a contraction and descent—a journey from the outside (a "going to and fro" in search of another) to the inside (a retreat into the room and a more passive variation of that search) to a still deeper inside (the abandonment of the search through a descent into the . . . [maternal] rocking chair" (1987, 144). Journey and search, lullaby and threnody are rendered in a soft voice, and yet the recorded monologue erupts into hard words: "rock her off / stop her eyes / fuck life / stop her eyes / rock her off / rock her off" (*CDW*, 442). The hard consonants are palpable in the advent of an enacted death, as "head slowly sinks, comes to rest."

This simple little play is fiendishly difficult to achieve precisely, and it does not lend itself to company on the same program. Whatever hurdles this creates for producers, two able Beckett critics have regarded *Rockaby* talismanically. Enoch Brater concludes his *Beyond Minimalism* on that "perfor-

---

A series of holographs, typescripts, and translations into French of *Rockaby* are at RUL, and younger eyes than mine should attempt a stemma. It is a common error among critics to say that *Rockaby* was written for Billie Whitelaw. In fact, it was I who suggested Whitelaw to Labeille, when the previously contracted actress withdrew. Schneider's letter of February 15, 1981, mentions Whitelaw, whom he had not yet met, and he certainly set the wheels in motion, but the idea was mine. *Rockaby* was first published by Grove in 1981 in *Rockaby and Other Short Pieces*. It is included in *CDW*, with two lines omitted. Beckett's French translation *Berceuse* was first published by Minuit in 1982, first in *Berceuse, Impromptu d'Ohio* and then in *Catastrophe et autres dramaticules*. The Pennebaker-Hegedus film of the making of *Rockaby* is available commercially. ·

mance poem," and Jonathan Kalb opens his *Beckett in Performance* on Billie Whitelaw's "inadvertent interpretation." They are so discerning in their
commentaries that I can contribute only a few afterthoughts. Moreover, the
Pennebaker-Hegedus film of rehearsals of *Rockaby* has virtually conferred
ownership of that play on Billie Whitelaw. Yet Beckett did not write it with
his favorite actress in mind. Rather, the initial conception virtually sprang
forth fully formed, in spite of his doubt about being able to write a play for
Labeille's project. From his very first undated, five-leaf holograph, Beckett
evidently visualized the figure in a rocking chair. Her monologue (for taping)
was originally scribbled in prose punctuated by dashes and dots, and
although her tale wavered between a first-person and third-person pronoun,
Beckett already underlined the lines that were to be accompanied by her live
voice. By the first typescript, Beckett broke the recorded monologue into
unpunctuated rough dimeters, and Brater's description is apt: "*Rockaby* is
Beckett's first play in which the language is not merely poetic, but a poem
complete in itself" (170).

The final poem lasts some fifteen minutes in performance, and yet it
encompasses four movements, each of which is introduced by a single word
of the live actress: "More," and each movement but the last is punctuated by
a "faint fade" of light. Typically Beckettian, an end is contained in the beginning verse line of each of the four movements: "till in the end" for one and
three, "so in the end" for two and four. To the asymptotes of fainter fade
and softer voice we might add the number of blended lines in "Time she
stopped." The two voices join three times in the first movement, two each in
the second and third, but not at all in the longest final movement. The actual
stoppage replaces the live voice.

Who is the "she" who is finally stopped? The ninth line of the final movement is "mother rocker," a designation that is heard only once. Is the phrase
ellipsis for mother in the rocker, or is it an appositive for the chair itself? In
either case it prepares the narration that "mother rocked . . . till her end
came." As the live actress's eyes close, the verse lines involve eyes closing.
"Time she stopped" is heard only on tape, a few lines before "was her own
other" (the word "another" is the only trisyllable in the play). When the
recorded voice reaches the familiar line, "saying to herself," it self-corrects:
"no / done with that . . . / saying to the rocker." I have already quoted what it
says to the rocker—hard words in a soft voice. Finally, it seems to me, the lady
in black is Everywoman, her own mother and her own other. From cradle to
grave, we seek another, and sometimes, for a while, the blinds are up, but like
Everyman in the medieval morality play, we die alone, when the bough breaks.

Beckett was averse to playing *Rockaby* and *Footfalls* on the same program (Harmon, 391), and *Not I* is equally intransigent. The reader, however,
can savor the variety of stage images in Beckett's three brief woman-plays,

and the diversity of the finales. For all the April background, *Not I* presents an inferno in the onslaught of speech speed, which continues after the curtain. *Footfalls* paces about pain, but finally the cosmos is bare of the human excipient of suffering. *Rockaby* is the most merciful of the three "woman" dramaticules, for death comes to soothe the searching spirit.

In November Beckett wrote Gontarski that he was "struggling to finish . . . current prose," but would try again to produce a play for the Ohio symposium. He made several "faux départs" before sending *Ohio Impromptu* mid-December. Scholars have seized gleefully on a crossed-out but legible page of the holograph, which is not realistic but real; that is to say, it does not present a fictional situation, but a predicament of one who has to address "The students . . . and the professors." Beckett pokes fun at his difficulties with selfhood: "Myself? I said. What are you insinuating?" Doubly crossed out is the concluding exchange of that page:

> Yourself before, they said.
> *Pause.*
> And after.
> *Pause.*
> Not during? I said.
> (Qtd. in Beja et al., 191, 192)

Then putting aside his self-mockery, Beckett shifted to a serious ambience, and a sad tale within a play: "Little remains to be told." Although he revised the piece until the end of the year, his second "départ" already contains the two figures, the book, the knocks, and the essential story. Only in the final typescript was the hair of the look-alikes changed from gray to white.

Ohio Impromptu

Beckett's title follows French dramatic tradition in designating a specific locale for a metadramatic play that is completely scripted, despite the everyday meaning of *impromptu* as improvised. He sails in the wake of Molière, Giraudoux, and Ionesco. However, Beckett deviates from the tradition in that (1) he writes in English; (2) he stages not a play about a play, but a play about a "sad tale," ostensibly read in a book. That tale begins outside on the Isle of Swans (with its swansong resonance); it continues in a room, and it progresses to a deeper interior. In *Rockaby* the tape self-corrects: "saying to

A three-leaf holograph and two typescripts of *Ohio Impromptu* are at the Ohio State University Library, and these are published in facsimile and transcription in Beja, Gontarski, and Astier. The revised script was first published by Grove in *Rockaby and Other Short Pieces* and is included in *CDW*. Beckett's French translation, *Impromptu d'Ohio*, was first published by Minuit in 1982 with *Berceuse* and then in *Catastrophe et autres dramaticules*. Illuminating is Astier.

herself / no / done with that." So, too, in *Ohio Impromptu:* "Thoughts, no, not thoughts. Profounds of mind." Like *Rockaby,* too, *Ohio Impromptu* closes on a still tableau. However, not until the last scene of *Rockaby* does "she" become her own other/mother, whereas "he" of *Ohio Impromptu* is more insistently "othered."

Twinned by black coats and white wigs, two figures are set off by a white deal table and chairs. For all the stark black-and-white scene, however, the relationship between the verbal and visual is grayly ambiguous, like the two zeros that enclose the "high" of Ohio. In the third paragraph we hear about the costume of the figure in the tale—"long black coat . . . and old world Latin Quarter hat." Not until the sixth paragraph do we hear that his nightly visitor also wears a "long black coat." By that time we have absorbed four sets of Listener knocks: the first knock stops the Reader, and the second signals him to continue from the beginning of the interrupted sentence. Thus, the visual doubles have their verbal analogue at the knock-level.

More subtle doubles occur within the sad tale. Twice we are told: "Little is left to tell"—separated by nearly ten minutes. Although we see the double figures, the tale's room and window are "single." Both stream-arms and relief "flow." An isle and an emotion are caught at their "extremity." Both the tale's protagonist and his visitor see "the dear face" and hear "unspoken words." The protagonist of the tale opposes "alone together" with "alone," and in the tale itself "mind" is paralleled by "mindlessness." The singular "Yes" affirms terror after a long lapse, with "redoubled force." Within the tale the two men "grew to be as one," but after the tale is told, they "sat on as though turned to stone." Finally nothing *is* left to tell because the last (repeated) knock elicits no continuation. The two visible figures look at each other as though *they* are turned to stone. It is indeed a sad tale, in which nothing brings relief from the vestigial grief for a "dear one."

The intensity of *Ohio Impromptu* is impressive, and even surprising, when Beckett's main efforts, as his letters testify, concentrated on his "French prose," provisionally entitled *Traces,* and corrected only in galleys to *Mal vu mal dit.* The fiction was completed before the play, but I preferred to comment sequentially on the two dramas.

Mal vu mal dit (*Ill Seen Ill Said*)

At this writing, I am inclined to value *Mal vu mal dit* (or perhaps *Ill Seen Ill Said*) as The Beckett Masterwork. The short piece of Beckett's late fiction demands a full volume of commentary, but that must be a different book.

A series of holographs, typescripts, and translations into English of *Mal vu mal dit* are at RUL. Charles Krance estimates that fifteen months elapsed between the original opening (which subsequently became *Un Soir*) and the final corrections of page

The title is both true and false. The piece's protagonist, her abode, and her environs are seen and described with fine precision, so the title is false; on the other hand, these elements hover so ephemerally between an outer and an inner world, between reality and its opposite, that the title is true. The title is thrice repeated within the text, but the context fails to lend it conviction. In paragraph 41 the protagonist's dwelling is said to be ill seen and ill said. In paragraph 49 the ill seen ill said is scrapped, for the eye is a stranger to it all. The agent of seeing is a frequently summoned eye, but the agent of telling is anonymous and perspectiveless. *Mal vu mal dit* is told in sixty-one paragraphs, thus flirting with the time-associated number, sixty. Like paragraph 58 of *Company,* paragraph 44 of *Mal vu mal dit* is dedicated to the face of a dial, around which a single hand revolves. As in the earlier work, too, at stake is human life. However, the later text is unsparing in its equivocation about life: the protagonist is both alive and dead, and she herself "en veut . . . au principe de toute vie" (1) [rails at the source of all life]. In no other work is Beckett's narrator so obsessed with a single figure—"cette vieille si mourante" (15) [This old so dying woman]. Many of the sixty-one paragraphs make some mention of "elle," although in the original French that pronoun is diluted by other figures. Thus, "elle" is not only the black-clad, white-haired protagonist, but also Venus, the moon, a stone, grass, flesh, a door, a clock, a hand, and a partition. One has to read carefully to ascertain the identity of "elle," but then her identity is elusive to the narrator, who apparently possesses Job's "eye of flesh." An imaginary stranger finds no one in her dwelling. Her black garments are untarnished by falling snow. She curtains her windows with men's greatcoats, and she lies on her pallet bed under another greatcoat. She is at once domestic and mythic.

Like much of Beckett's late prose, the sixty-one paragraphs of *Mal vu mal dit* are composed of short sentences, which are punctuated only by periods, question marks, dashes, or the rare exclamation mark (and three commas that introduce brief quotations). The paragraphs vary between four and twenty-seven lines in Krance's bilingual edition. As in much of Beckett's late prose, phrases are repeated, and yet one has no sense of the echo principle of *Company.* Rather, repetitions acquire accretions, so that we only gradually come to savor the many details that constitute "elle," even though the first

---

proof—from October 24, 1979, to January 21, 1981, but the main holograph notebook covers a year. Minuit first published *Mal vu mal dit* in 1981, and it was soon followed by Beckett's English translation in the *New Yorker,* October 5, 1981. (I recall Beckett's surprise when he received page proofs of this printing—proofs he gave to me.) Grove published *Ill Seen Ill Said* in 1981, and Calder published it in 1982, later including it in collections of Beckettiana. Charles Krance's bilingual edition (Garland, 1996) is invaluable. Again I cite paragraph rather than page numbers.

paragraph already announces a narrator, adjured to tell "on." Dressed from neck to boots in black, "elle" is bluish white of face and hands, but her eyelashes are black, in a residue of the brunette she must once have been. Seldom seen in motion, she can be captured in different postures: "Debout ou assise. Allongée ou à genoux" (16) [Standing or sitting. Lying or on her knees]. Now she is visible, now she vanishes—to the eye that has no need of light, that is, the eye of consciousness.

Introduced in the context of the sky and its planets, "elle" is born in a mythic dimension, which is enhanced through scattered references. Encircled by a mysterious twelve figures, she resonates through Christ's apostles and the signs of the zodiac. Followed by a lamb, endowed with a pisciform buttonhook, she is further associated with Christ. Her rigid pose when seated is that of the Colossus of Memnon. Drawn to a gravestone as rough-hewn as Michelangelo's Brutus, she presents its mirror image when she kneels, and she is several times associated with the immobility of stone. Critics have compared her to the Virgin Mary, Mary Magdalene, Demeter, and forms of a *mater dolorosa*. However, the text never designates her as a mother, and only obliquely as a widow in her black weeds.

Subverting "elle's" mythic dimension is a domestic aspect that is new in Beckett's late fiction. "Elle" sits in a spindle-backed wooden chair, or she lies on a pallet bed without a pillow. She alternates between her two windows, and when she lies down, she can see the rafters by the dim light of two skylights. When she eats, graceful gestures bring her head to a bowl of slop and the bowl to her mouth, although she has a spoon. A bit of pulp is caught at the corner of her mouth, as is not infrequent among the aged. Although most of her body is hidden by her long black garment, the narrator notes the absence of her ring finger. When first presented, "elle" is within her cabin, but as early as paragraph 2 she is outside, negotiating a path through a circular zone of stones that encroaches on the grass, and the stones are surrounded by pasture, which contains the tombstone. Inside or out, in crocus time or snowfall, she erupts suddenly and cannot be summoned at the narrator's will. In the main, she looms large when outside her cabin, and when within she watches the far-off skies. In contrast with these vasts are domestic objects. The eyes in her head are paralleled by the cabin's two windows and its two skylights in the roof; in French the "jours" admit a light of "demi-jour." The curtains over her windows are made of a man's greatcoat hung on a rod—as in the dwellings of the poor. So, too, the cover on her pallet bed is another greatcoat. The most striking object in her room, however, is a buttonhook, unserviceable because its hook is out of shape. Pisciform and silvered, it hangs on a nail. As an object, the buttonhook is redolent of a bygone time; as a symbol, it recalls Christ crucified at Golgotha (made explicit in paragraph 57 of the text). Some two-thirds of the way through

Mal vu mal dit the last domestic objects appear—a coffer and a trapdoor. The coffer yields a sheet of paper, which will be knifed to particles in paragraph 54. The trapdoor is never entered.

Unique to *Mal vu mal dit* is the domestic authenticity of the poor old woman, who makes do with her familiar objects in a familiar environment, which is also eerily strange. Twinned with the gravestone before which she kneels, she is distinguishable by her trembling: "D'un frisson infime venu de son profond" (26) [With faintest shiver from its innermost]. "Elle" has been likened to Beckett's own mother, but she is not unlike my mother and your mother and every lonely old so dying woman—a phrase that wrenches normal word order in French or English. At once real and imaginary, remembered and fictional, domestic and mythic, cosmic and common, failing and dignified, springlike and wintry, she looks down when out of doors, but when indoors she looks up at the skies. Linked to a crocus, a lamb, and a useless buttonhook, she wears mourning for the human species, which is slowly being devoured by stones, "S'amoncelant . . . [et] gagnera les cieux. La lune. Venus" (23) [Ever heaping . . . (and) will gain the skies. The moon. Venus].

"Elle" is an unparalleled achievement, but she is not the only character of *Mal vu mal dit*. (I say character for lack of a better word to designate the protagonist and the narrator.) The "ill" seer-sayer takes the form of an eye in this narrative, but the eye has a distinctive voice. "Elle" never had much converse with herself, but the eye resorts to frequent self-address. In the very first paragraph the narrator utters "Encore" three times, to urge the narration on (or in French, to say it again), and by the end of that paragraph it calls for the present tense: "Comme si elle avait le malheur d'être encore en vie" [and this in the present as had she the misfortune to be still of this world]. It is a minimally useful admonition, since the paragraph has been couched in the present tense. As the narrative gathers momentum, the narrator cautions himself with such phrases as "Attention," "Du calme," "Assez," "Laisser," "La suite" [careful, gently, enough, leave it, on]. Twelve times (thirteen in Beckett's translation) the narrator interrupts himself with a dash, only to continue with a contradiction, amplification, or intensification. Before the narrative eye identifies itself, "elle's" cabin is subjected to the scrutiny of an "imaginaire profane" (6) [Imaginary stranger]. In some of the last paragraphs, however, it is hard to know whether the events involve "elle" or the observing eye, but powerfully graphic is a pupil that virtually devours the iris against a shrunken white background.

Among the remarkable achievements of this remarkable narrative is a simultaneous dying of a character and a story. As early as paragraph 10 we read: "C'est la vie qui finit. La sienne à elle. La sienne à l'autre. Mais si différemment" (10) [What but life ending. Hers. The other's. But so otherwise]. Much of the narrative will recount the "otherwise." From the first paragraph "elle" rails against the source of life, but only gradually does the outside eye take comfort in the invasion by the stones. Dead and alive, fact or fiction, "elle" hovers between the two, as the narrator builds on a well-known phrase of Malebranche: "L'imagination c'est la folle du logis"—"La folle du logis s'en donne à coeur chagrin" (12) [Imagination at wit's end spreads its sad wings]. The narrator couples "Choses et chimères" (15) [Things and imaginings], which prove to be indistinguishable. More confused than ever before, imaginative discovery seeps into invention. Negations and contradictions oppose narrative, and yet the narrator summarizes the story close to its midpoint (paragraph 27): "Le fermer tout de bon et la voir à mort. Au cabanon. Par la caillasse. Dans les champs. Dans la brume. Devant la tombe" [Close it for good and all and see her to death. Unremittent. In the shack. Over the stones. In the pastures. The haze. At the tomb].

The eye on leave from (Dante's) frozen inferno can cry again, and it is not always clear whether the tears belong to the narrator's or narrated eye. Yearning for an end, like earlier Beckett narrators, the eye tries to close its lid on the account, shutting out all but the void. Panic past, however, the eye reexamines the scene in the difficult paragraph 29. In an imbroglio of several "elle's," hands wring to a heart rhythm, then rise in a palms-up gesture, before the introduction of the only first-person pronoun of the narrative: "Voilà *nos* creux" [Behold our hollows; emphasis added]. Although the hollows are difficult to envisage, much less to share, an implication follows that "elle's" missing finger was torn off with the keeper ring on a panic-filled day. The observing eye's panic at the beginning of the paragraph melts into the panic of "elle's" ring-finger. And blame is ubiquitous. "A tout la faute. Tout" [All to blame. All].

Gradually, the narrating eye absorbs the death wish of its protagonist. Having described itself unflatteringly, it finds "elle" indulging in what may be a smile. In paragraph 49 the eye hopes for closure: "Bazardé tout le mal vu mal dit. L'oeil a changé. Et son pisse-légende" (49) [Scrapped all the ill seen ill said. The eye has changed. And its driveling scribe]. The bit of paper in the coffer is by paragraph 54 hacked to shreds and thrown away. Yet the next white page remains to be blackened (as Beckett indeed wrote on for seven pages). Returning for a last look within the cabin, the eye notes that the rods and the nail are empty of their objects—coat-curtains and buttonhook. The latter, however, is mordantly "Bon pour le resservice . . . Au lieu-dit du crâne" (57) [All set to serve again. . . . At the place of the skull]. Several times "elle's" body has been compared to stone, but this last look focuses on her face and then her eye, which is almost engulfed by the pupil. The watching eye finds it difficult to tear itself away from these last ocular traces: "Vite des fois que soudain oui adieu à tout hasard. Au visage tout au moins. D'elle tenace trace" (60) [Quick say it suddenly can and farewell say

say farewell. If only to the face. For her tenacious trace]. The last moments of that last trace burst forth colloquially: "Ciel terre et tout le bataclan. Plus miette de charogne nulle part. Lechées babines baste. Non. Encore une seconde. Rien qu'une. Le temps d'aspirer ce vide. Connaître le bonheur" [Sky earth the whole kit and boodle. Not another crumb of carrion left. Lick chops and basta. No. One moment more. One last. Grace to breathe that void. Know happiness]. This so dying and yet so lively narrative closes on the shock of carrion leading to a void of happiness. "Elle" and the narrative eye may trace a death drive, and yet the whole story seethes with outrage against human mortality.

Manuscripts testify to Beckett's pains with *Mal vu mal dit*. He pared away figures and objects to achieve the monumental simplicity of the final fiction. Although he engaged in his customary sound play between morphemes—alliteration, assonance, even rhyme—the sonorities are muted.[4] The vocabulary, too, is simple and unpretentious, with the single exception of the word "strangurie," which means a painful, drop-by-drop emission of urine. The word occurs in paragraph 50, where attention is called to another word: "Moindre. Ah le beau seul mot. Moindre. Elle est moindre. La même mais moindre. . . . Elle finira par ne plus être" [Less. Ah the sweet one word. Less. It is less. The same but less. . . . It will end by being no more]. Less thus constitutes a giant step en route toward the final void. (In English translation the word "collapsion" is arresting.)

In the subtle, circular road that approaches that void, the phrases usually treat the specifics of the imagery. Occasionally, however, a sentence rises to quotable generality, and I close my commentary with a few verbal lodestones. In his English translation Beckett confers trembling on figure and object alike: "elle's" hand trembles, as does her body, and only the trembling distinguishes her from a tombstone. At the door of her dwelling she holds a trembling key, and within her cabin the buttonhook trembles on its nail, as do the curtain-coats on their rods. In paragraph 58 "elle's" face can be distinguished from true plaster only by an "imperceptible tremor" (In French the verbs are less repetitive—*trembler, frémir, vaciller, balancer*). Grass and "elle's" hair both shiver. In this piece that seeks to pierce to the root of the imagination, a last object is viewed ironically—a trapdoor. Black in the ebony floor, it is barely visible: "Prometteur ce flagrant souci de camouflage" (39) [Promising this flagrant concern with camouflage]. Gutterals underline the oxymoronic flagrant camouflage. More penetrating is a metaphor for the impassive face of "elle": "Silence à l'oeil du hurlement" (25) [Silence at the eye of the scream]. The most repetitive sentence explicates the title, as well as the mood of other late Beckett works: "La tête trahit les traîtres yeux et le traître mot leurs trahisons" (46) [The mind betrays the treacherous eyes and the treacherous word their treacheries]. As the main verb, "betrays" may mean both conceals and reveals. The eyes are treacherous, unable to distinguish memory from imagination, and the reflective words are therefore treacherous in their translation. Yet the mind acts upon the ocular and linguistic treacheries, trailing its own betrayals in this fiction that is so faithful to Beckett's vision.

Not only was *Mal vu mal dit* a difficult year in composition, but the translation too occasioned Beckett's discouragement. He may have undertaken it even before he finally revised the original. His holograph translation notebook at RUL is begun in December 1980 and completed in January 1981—one of his most brilliant self-translations.

1981

⊗

After his sustained verbal invention of *Mal vu mal dit,* Beckett seems to have experienced a reaction against verbal expression, which took three different forms. *The Way* is informed by numerical symbols in its two brief paragraphs; the television play *Quad* eschews words completely; and *Ceiling* seeks to strip words to strict perception. (However, he did indulge in a few brief poems—perhaps for eventual inclusion in the *Mirlitonnades* they resemble.)

The Way

The two brief paragraphs occupied Beckett during much of the month of May. Although the piece contrasts an 8-shaped path with an ∞-shaped path, a manuscript states explicitly what the whole implies: "The two ways were one way." It is a way that already attracted the attention of the young author of *Dream* (227), but the later narrative progresses from "8" to "∞," as the narrator takes the path traced by each title figure. Halfway through the first paragraph the journey becomes a "plod." If the journey's seconds had been numbered, other numbers might come to light. Then, as though backing off from the path, the narrator mentions obstacle-thorns, mist, half-light, and sand so loose that it covers any possible remains: "No one ever before so . . ."

The second paragraph suits its perspective to its title-symbol "∞." Although the word "same" is repeated thrice, the viewpoint has shifted to the near-infinite: "Were the eye to look unending void." The loose sand of

---

Seven consecutive holographs and typescripts of *The Way* are at HRC, with photocopies at RUL. First published as "Crisscross to Infinity" (a title foisted on Beckett) in *College Literature* 8, no. 3 (1981), the two paragraphs are omitted from *CSP*. *The Way* has not been translated into French.

the first paragraph is replaced by "bedrock underfoot," which is equally impervious to human remains. "No one ever before so—" A bleak picture of numbers in a Möbius strip, *The Way* offers no way to consciousness, however conscientious the plod. The annotation of the HRC catalog makes a large claim that *The Way* "is the distillation of all the journeys made by all of Beckett's eternal wanderers" (174). However he labored over the short piece, I prefer the undistilled ways.

Late in 1979 or early in 1980, Beckett had written to the head of Süddeutscher Rundfunk in Stuttgart about a "crazy invention for TV." However, the "crazy invention" was radically revised in production during June 1981, which must therefore be considered its completion date.

Quad

Quad as published incorporates several stages of Beckett's manuscript. This is at variance with Beckett's usual habits, so perhaps Beckett did not read proof for *CDW* (which also contains errors). Beckett's diagram on page 453 is more helpful than the three pages of scenic description.

Before a fixed camera, four gowned and cowled players enter a square, one by one, until the four walk simultaneously. Each of the figures walks four times through a side and a diagonal of the square, always avoiding the square's center by an abrupt leftward movement. As the players enter the square separately, so they leave it one by one, until all is still. The four players wear differently colored garments, and their walk is accompanied by different invisible percussion instruments. Timing is crucial, for no two players must meet, and each must swerve leftward to avoid the mysterious center. The entire series of courses is performed four times.

This much is present in Beckett's conception for *Quad*, but, while directing it in Stuttgart, he was told that a rough print in black and white had been impressive, and, agreeing, he added a second act to the teleplay, omitting colors and percussion. The players perform their square rounds only once, with ineffable weariness. The second act thus contrasts with the colorful frenzy of the first.

Tired by the intense concentration of directing *Quad*, Beckett found refuge on the beaches of Courmayeur. While there, he began a short piece that *No Symbols Where None Intended* says was "written for the painter Avigdor Arikha and concerned with the nature of perception" (169). If so, it

---

The holographs and typescripts of *Quad* at RUL are undated, but the final two-part conception emerged only during filming in Stuttgart. Written in English, the play was first published in *CDW* in 1984. Edith Fournier's French translation appears in Minuit's 1992 *Quad et autres pièces pour la télévision*. It was first broadcast by Süddeutscher Rundfunk in 1982, and at the end of that year by the BBC.

is perception of being, rather than an intake of the senses. Before completing that piece, Beckett on April 9, 1981, wrote what might be considered an antiperception *mirlitonnade:* "Ceiling / lid eye bid / bye bye." The three lines are barely intelligible, but they do fix the eye on the ceiling, as it departs from the unconsciousness of sleep.

Ceiling

Ceiling attempts to render verbally the preverbal moments of wakening to consciousness. Through five drafts the details are stripped down and rendered more abstract. By the final holograph version, the phrase "A patch of ceiling" is omitted, leaving the title alone to relate whiteness to consciousness. The piece's spareness continues the antiverbal thrust of the other two works of this year.

In its final version *Ceiling* is structured in five prose paragraphs, which are separated by the monosyllable "On." Each successive paragraph is shorter than its predecessor, and each repeats phrases of its predecessor. On awakening, eye and mind are englobed in whiteness, and the phrase "dull white" dulls the lexicon of repeated phrases.

The first paragraph presents a lazy awakening, with four repetitions of the sentence "When in the end they open [bidden or unbidden] they are met by this dull white." The second paragraph denies knowledge of a past, "Save dimly of having come to." Consciousness entails "dread of being again." The second paragraph concludes like the first: "Further one cannot." And yet, "further" is implied by "On." The third paragraph resumes the coming to consciousness of the mind, but this is now followed by an awareness of the dull white body. The refrain phrase is now curtailed to "Further one—." The fourth paragraph recapitulates the several phases of coming to consciousness, and the refrain phrase shrinks to "Further—." The final abbreviated paragraph for the first time introduces breath: "Endless ending breath." While one is conscious, the breath of life is endless, however life may be ending. This time the paragraph is followed neither by "On" nor "Further." It ends enigmatically and yet climactically: "Dread darling sight." Is this conclusion a distant apposition of the earlier "dread of being again?" Or is "dread" a near synonym of awesome, acknowledging the appeal of being wakened to full perception?

When Beckett returned from Courmayeur to Paris in July, he became aware of plans to celebrate his seventy-fifth birthday by performances and discussions at the annual Festival d'Automne. The seventieth birthday events

---

Six holographs and three typescripts of *Ceiling* are at HRC. *Ceiling* is published in French and English, respectively, in *Arikha* (Paris: Hermann; London: Thames and Hudson, both 1985) but not in *CSP.*

in London's Royal Court Theatre were small-scale, but Beckett could not face the larger event, and he absconded to Tangiers, after writing the organizer to thank him for "the great honour being paid to my work" (Knowlson, 591). While away, Beckett wrote several English sentences of what, after seven months, became *Worstward Ho*. At some point during the year Beckett also wrote a poem beginning "the downs," which should be published. Inconsistent as I am about commenting on each Beckett poem, I wish I could replace commentary by quotation.

"The Downs"

The untitled, unpunctuated poem consists of seven eight-line stanzas, except that the first stanza contains seven lines. The movement of the poem is from a summer walk of a loving couple to a winter scene whose human residue is reduced to lamplight. Repetitions and assonance musicalize the short lines. Repeated in the first and second stanza are the lines "hand in hand / one loving / one loved," which are not mutually idyllic. By the time the couple gaze down at the foam below (third stanza), love is not mentioned. The fourth stanza opens "no speech," and further parallels "speechless on" with "speechless back," but the couple still return to the hut at night. The fifth stanza eliminates humans as winter arrives, and the final line is the longest of the poem: "black flood foaming on." The sixth stanza denies thought to "meaningless flood," and this winter stanza ends with "no meaning." The seventh and final stanza retrieves a faint light on the foam and the snow. As in some of Beckett's late prose, this poem finally enfolds an interior into an exterior scene.

Beckett spent much of the rest of the year translating his recent "dramaticules" into French, but in February 1982, he composed a new play in French.

1982

Catastrophe

Beckett wrote *Catastrophe* for an Avignon program to honor the imprisoned Czech playwright Václav Havel, and the earliest drafts envisage staging a dis-

---

Found only in RUL 2911/1, the untitled poem I am calling "The Downs" exists in typescript. RUL 2911/2 is a photocopy of a page of the holograph, dated Paris 1981. *BatR* deduces from this page: "The poem is much less precise metrically at this initial stage, with undifferentiated stanzas and lines of unequal length" (4).

Three holographs and two typescripts of *Catastrophe* are at RUL. The play was first published in *Solo suivi de Catastrophe*, Paris: Minuit, 1982, and then the same year

aster. In its original Greek meaning *catastrophe* is a turning point, but French and English concur on its modern meaning of disaster. Beckett sets his *Catastrophe* in an unnamed theater, and the three main characters are designated only by initials (P for protagonist, M for *metteur-en-scene*, A for his assistant), but the offstage lighting technician is playfully named Luke. Props are few: a plinth for the protagonist, a chair and a cigar for the director, a pad and pencil for the assistant. Costumes are more elaborate: the fur coat and toque of the director, the white overalls of his assistant, and above all the black robe over the ash gray night attire of the protagonist. Lighting changes are couched "en termes techniques" [in technical terms].

The scenic directions state: "Répétition. On met la dernière main au dernier tableau" (71) [Rehearsal. Final touches to the last scene, *CDW*, 457]. In performance the "final touches" emerge only gradually, as the dictatorial director issues orders to his assistant: the protagonist's clawlike hands must be removed from his pockets and unclenched; his hat and robe must be removed so that he shivers; his cranium, hands, and legs must be whitened. Ungraciously, the director accepts the assistant's suggestion that the protagonist's hands be joined, but he reacts fiercely against her suggestion of a gag: "Quelle idée! Cette manie d'explicitation!" (77) [For God's sake! This craze for explicitation! 459]. Under the director's impatient instructions, his assistant manipulates the protagonist as if he were a prop, rather than a human being. Departed to the stalls to view his handiwork, the director rejects his assistant's final suggestion that the protagonist raise his head to show his face. Pleased with his protagonist's misery, the director admires his product: "Formidable! Il va faire un malheur. J'entends ça d'ici" (80) [Terrific! He'll have them on their feet. I can hear it from here, 461]. These final words of the play are then subverted by the scenic directions: "P relève la tête, fixe la salle. Les applaudissements faiblissent, s'arrêtent (81) [P raises his head, fixes the audience. The applause falters, dies, 461].

The protagonist's defiant gesture is always interpreted as a *triumphant* turning point, and that gesture emerged only in Beckett's final revision. It is the very gesture that was previously suggested by the assistant, who is a somewhat ambiguous figure—subservient to the director, but wiping his traces from the chair. The director is unambiguously unpleasant, and Beckett ascribes to him some of his own characteristics. The director's cruelty to his actor parallels that of Beckett himself in the theater, and his continual

---

in *Catastrophe et autres dramaticules*, to which my page numbers refer. The play was first performed (with the protagonist bound from shoulders to knees) in Avignon on July 20, 1982. Beckett's English translation was first published in *Hiroshima* (Quisberg, 1982) and then in the *New Yorker*, January 10, 1983; it was reprinted by Faber and Grove, respectively, in 1984. It is found in *CDW*.

smoking mirrors Beckett's habit, although I never heard him ask for a light. He too might reject "explicitation."

The final applause is problematic. Since the fictional setting is a rehearsal, there is presumably no audience, and what we hear is what the director imagines. Yet it is late in the play to enter the limited imagination of a satirized character. The recorded applause is therefore puzzling, but in the theater it almost always triggers actual applause. Like the director, Beckett has staged a catastrophe, which forges a link between tyranny and theater.

Despite constant complaints in his letters, Beckett apparently enjoyed some of his theater work—especially when Billie Whitelaw was involved. Perhaps he renounced theater directing when even she could not bring him pleasure at the 1979 production of *Happy Days*. In the early 1980s, however, he did look back nostalgically to the precision of his televisual work with Süddeutscher Rundfunk in Stuttgart. Although he felt that "there is not much invention left in me, crazy or otherwise" (qtd. in Knowlson, 599), he finally responded to the virtually blanket invitation to Stuttgart of Dr. Müller-Freienfels.

Nacht und Träume

Beckett's last two original television pieces (probably unconsciously) resurrected early aborted efforts. As *Quad* successfully negotiated the geometries of the abandoned "J. M. Mime" of 1962, so *Nacht und Träume* successfully enfolds the dream of the abandoned *Mime du rêveur* of 1954. The title comes from the words of a Schubert song, the last seven bars of which are heard in the otherwise silent teleplay.

In the dim light of a stripped-down room, A hums the song as he rests his head on his hands on a table. This pose in right profile is faintly visible throughout. Superimposed on it is his dream—B on a podium in the same pose, but with left profile to audience, "faintly lit by kinder light than A's" (*CDW*, 465). An unattached left hand comes to rest briefly on B's head. An unattached right hand offers a cup to B's lips, before withdrawing; then the right hand wipes B's brow before withdrawing. B looks up, raises his right hand, and the unbodied right hand rests on B's palm, whereupon B lays his left hand on both hands. All three hands "sink to table and on them B's

---

An unpublished poem of 1977 in the Sottisier Notebook predicts the teleplay, *Nacht und Träume*: "one dead of night / in the dead still / he looked up from his book / from that dark / to pore on another dark / till afar / taper faint / the eyes in the dead still / still afar / his book as by / a hand not his / faintly closed / for good or ill / for good and ill." The (probable) production typescript is at RUL, which also contains a letter from Beckett to Jack Garfein, giving permission for a stage production, which he "cannot imagine." Broadcast in June 1983, *Nacht und Träume* was first published in *CDW*. Beckett did not translate it into French, but Edith Fournier did.

head" (466). The disembodied left hand once more rests gently on B's head. When the dream fades out, A raises his head and hums the Schubert bars. After fadeout, the dream is repeated, but "in close-up and slower motion." After a return to the opening view of A, the dream fades out, and so does A.

Even in my dry summary, which follows Beckett's "action" scenario, the movements are not only comforting but rhythmic. Knowlson's description of *Nacht und Träume* is appreciatively lyrical, but in actual performance the lighting is so dim that this viewer's reaction was eclipsed by the strain to see what was happening. Knowlson closes his account: "it attracted an audience of two million viewers" (600). I hope they could see better than I.

The high point of Beckett's year was the completion of *Worstward Ho,* which he found impossible to translate.

Worstward Ho

Beckett's inspiration for *Worstward Ho* lies in Edgar's speech of *King Lear:* "The worst is not so long as one can say, / This is the worst." Beckett himself referred to the piece in progress as "Better worse," and much of the final text plays arpeggios upon that oxymoron. Structurally, this third work of still another trilogy is built in paragraphs, but they are briefer, more numerous, and more peremptory than heretofore. Well over half the sentences in the ninety-six paragraphs constitute the narrator's self-commands toward worsening, from the first word "On" to the last, again "On." (The reader reads such self-commands also as imperatives to her-/himself.) The title (conceived late in composition) indicates the mood and the direction; it might be extrapolated to: in this imaginative uncertainty let us sally forth by negation and subtraction, in the hope of reaching an end. Over the course of the narrative, worsening comes to be equated with lessening.

As often before in Beckett's late fiction, the narrator attempts to summon a body in a place; an "it" in a dim light whose source is unfathomable. Soon an eye-clenching head comes into view, resting on crippled hands. Through phrasal qualifications, shadowy figures accrete, and paragraph 36 attempts to limn them in order: "From now one for the kneeling one. As from now two for the twain. The as one plodding twain. As from now three for the head. The head as first said missaid." The kneeling one is later desig-

---

The holograph and two typescripts of *Worstward Ho* are at RUL. The manuscripts are less drastically revised than the other two pieces of this late trilogy. The last page of the holograph contains two English *mirlitonnades*. The Sottisier Notebook contains Edgar's quotations on "the worst," as well as other lines of Shakespeare. *Worstward Ho* was first published by Calder and Grove, respectively, in 1983. Edith Fournier's French translation *Cap au pire* was first published by Minuit in 1991. The Limited Editions Club in 1989, Calder in 1992, and Grove in 1996 all published the late trilogy with Beckett's title *Nohow On.* I quote by paragraph number.

nated as a woman, the plodding pair wear long coats, and the head's clenched eyes stare; the figures are unstable. To move worstward, images have to go or to be unsaid—as the narrator juxtaposes active and passive verbs. One and two are banished from the skull, and briefly preying eyes are resurrected, but white and pupil dissolve into their prey.

In paragraph 39 the narrator wishes to subtract the imagined world, and he/it tentatively experiments with what can be said to be gone. The vasts of void seem almost gone, but the dim cannot go. In the last third of the piece words are acknowledged as mindless: "No knowing what it is the words it secretes say. No saying. No saying what it all is they somehow say" (58). Almost predictably, the narrator is gnawed by the desire for absence: "Longing that all go. Dim go. Void go. Longing go. Vain longing that vain longing go" (72). With double negatives and pejorative superlatives, the indomitable narrator sets about failing better. The many avatars of the head or skull in Beckett's writing now crystallize: "One dim black hole mid-foreskull. Into the hell of all. Out from the hell of all. So better than nothing worse say stare from now" (88). Yet finally the figures or shades remain, "All gnawing to be naught. Never to be naught" (93). In a surge of diminishing negatives, the narrator concludes with energy:

> Enough. . . . Three pins. One pinhole. In dimmost dim. Vasts apart. At bounds of boundless void. Whence no farther. Best worse no farther. Nohow less. Nohow worse. Nohow naught. Nohow on.
>   Said nohow on.

At the limit of intelligibility, which nevertheless puns on "know how," consciousness and its diminished words have driven the fiction "on" through a thicket of neologisms, which are comprehensible.

Verbally, *Worstward Ho* is a tour de force, constituted mainly of monosyllables in rhyme and off-rhyme: *go/no, on/gone, soft/left/rift, know how/nohow*. The quasi-palindrome "gnaw-on" summarizes both the global plot and the individual events, but the goal of this "on" is for all to be "gone." The alliterative *worse/words* is Beckett's most reductive insult to the language about which he is ever skeptical. In this dry lexicon, provision is briefly made for suffering: "Say remains of mind where none to permit of pain. Pain of bones till no choice but up and stand" (6). Yet there is little pain cited thereafter. On the contrary, verve is born of contradictions and neologisms: "meremost minimum, thenceless thitherless there, whosesoever whencesoever say, unlessenable least, best worse, ununsaid when worse said." Perhaps the climax resides in "Unmoreable unlessable unworseable evermost almost void" (86). The "almost" is important, for finally the shades penetrate the void, as the narrative seeps through Beckett's joyful verbiage: "his many coined words, the stripping away of syntax, the grammatically perfect but unconventional affixations show delight in the language he had once abandoned" (Beer 1994, 219).

The figures are mere shades; yet they retain their humanity—"Never to be naught" (93)—in this spirited finale of Beckett's late trilogy. The author told Enoch Brater, who asked him if *Company, Ill Seen Ill Said,* and *Worstward Ho* constituted a trilogy: "I hadn't thought of it as such, but I suppose so—more so than the other works called the Trilogy" (12). The three narratives are continuous in their discontinuous web of paragraphs harmonically woven around a family of shades in the dim sourceless light of the unquenchable imagination.

1983

Quoi où (What Where)

Of all Beckett's plays *Quoi où* seems to me unique in trying to translate to the stage the problems of his recent fiction. The imagining self seeks distance from his work, and yet he tries to pierce to the whatness and whereness of that work. That process is dramatized through the passing seasons, as figures are stripped of individuality, down to the bones of their articulations. *Quoi où* is also the last of Beckett's "torture" pieces in which a victim is coerced to speak.

V, the voice of Bam, is represented by "un petit porte-voix à hauteur d'homme" (85) [a small megaphone at head level, 469]. Like Opener in the radio play *Cascando,* V controls the action, and that action involves four characters whose names differ only by a vowel—Bam, Bem, Bim, Bom. With long gray hair and in long gray gowns, the four are "aussi semblables que possible" [as alike as possible]. They are apparently avatars of the same figure, whom V calls into being. V's opening words are "Nous ne sommes plus que cinq" [We are the last five]. Only *four* figures are visible, but V-megaphone completes the quintet. Bam's voice seeks perspective on his fictional creations, and Bam resorts to (offstage) torture to penetrate their most secret being.

V directs the figures, "D'abord muet" (86) [First without words, 470]. He corrects his first glance at the stage, switching the light off, then on again. With Bam on stage, his head high, V claims to be alone in spring. Then Bom

Composed in February–March 1983, *Quoi où* was translated almost immediately into English, in which language the premiere took place on June 15, 1983, under Alan Schneider's direction in New York City. The original French text appears in Minuit's *Catastrophe et autres dramaticules* in 1982. *What Where* is included in *CDW*. Beckett's revision for television is at RUL and is published only in volume IV of *The Theatrical Notebooks of Samuel Beckett,* ed. S. E. Gontarski (London: Faber, 1999).

appears, "Reparait" [Reappears]. His head is bowed, but when Bim enters, his head is high. Bim exits, followed by Bom. These movements are repeated by Bem and Bim, then Bam and Bem. After words are introduced, the same movements are performed in slower motion. To each gray figure in turn Bam (not V) poses insidious questions: "Alors? . . . Il n'a rien dit? . . . Tu l'as bien travaillé? . . . Et il n'a rien dit? . . . Il a pleuré? . . . Crié? . . . Imploré grâce? . . . Mais n'a rien dit?" (89–90) [Well? . . . He didn't say anything? . . . You gave him the works? . . . And he didn't say anything? . . . He wept? . . . Screamed? . . . Begged for mercy? . . . But didn't say anything? 472]. The physical placidity of the figures we see contrasts with the cruel interrogation that we hear about. Bam accuses each of his mirror images of lying, as each in turn fails to elicit an offstage confession from his victim. The interrogation proceeds through summer, and V makes critical comments, like a narrator in Beckett's fiction. Upon hearing "Ce n'est pas bon," Bam changes the confessional question from "Quoi" to "Où"—both encompassed in the title. V recognizes the repetitive nature of the interrogations: "Ainsi de suite" (96) [So on, 496]. Finally, with Bam again on stage, but head now bowed, V declares that he is alone in winter: "Le temps passe. / C'est tout. / Comprenne qui pourra. / J'éteins" (97) [Time passes. / That is all. / Make sense who may. / I switch off, 476].

Like the narrators of Beckett's recent fiction, V tries to set a scene—albeit offstage. As the seasons come and go, so do the creatures of V's imagination, but, however "given the works" on Bam's command, they are unable to articulate either their own identity or their abode. It is hard to "make sense" of a pastime or a lifetime spent in such activity. It is even harder to render such creative obsession stageworthily, and I do not think that Beckett succeeded in doing so. More importantly, Beckett did not think he succeeded, and in 1985 he reconceived the piece for television, to be with the Stuttgart team a last time.

1985

Was Wo (What Where)

Prior to arrival in Stuttgart, Beckett cut about a quarter of the German text of Was Wo, as translated by Elmar and Jonas Tophoven. Visually, he substi-

---

Beckett's production notes for the television version of Was Wo are found at RUL, and they are described in BatR (104). That version has been published, as pointed out in an earlier footnote. Pierre Chabert and S. E. Gontarski have respectively adapted the shortened television version to the stage.

tuted masklike faces for the full-length gray figures. For exits and entrances of Bam, Bem, Bim, and Bom, he substituted fadeouts and fadeups. Voice and Bam were immediately linked through V's new opening line: "I am Bam." The play's title was recalled more explicitly by changing "it" to "what" in the phrase "He didn't say it?" The two nonconfessions thus bear more pointedly on "What" and "Where." Beckett tautened the relationships among V and B\2m\m by omitting the three passages in which V declares the sequence is "Not good" and therefore "start[s] again." Thus, the repetitive accounts of the fruitless interrogation are more closely timed, and the seasonal changes undergo acceleration. Although the dialogue of the revised stage version is an exact translation of the television German, the effect is radically different between the masklike faces and the residual full-length stage figures.

Perhaps nothing was committed to paper, but on Christmas Day Beckett wrote Rick Cluchey: "I have tried again in vain to write a short piece for you."

1987

In poor health—emphysema was diagnosed in 1987—Beckett nevertheless tried to write, as if he could not imagine living without it. Except for the revision of the play *Was Wo,* however, he confined his efforts to fiction and verse—as when he began to write, nearly sixty years earlier. Not only were the physical demands of theater rehearsal too great for his frail body, but in 1984 he lost two director friends who had been so instrumental to the production of his drama. Roger Blin died in January, and the cremation at Père Lachaise was so brutal an event that Beckett broke into sobs (Knowlson, 611). Alan Schneider's death in May was differently traumatic; the American director, in London for rehearsals, was on his way to mail a letter to Beckett when he was felled by a motorcycle. His head hit the curb, and Schneider never regained consciousness. For some of us, it was the end of an era of fidelity to Beckett.

To Rick Cluchey he wrote on May 25: "Try on & mostly off to finish a short tailpiece for Rosset & Co. Nothing doing so far." But something eventuated.

Stirrings Still

Beckett's final work of fiction must have been envisaged as a finale, but its creation took Beckett some three years of sporadic work. He made several

---

Many holographs and typescripts of *Stirrings Still* are at RUL. As noted in *BatR:* "The order of composition is complex, and not easy to establish" (175). I cannot

"faux départs" in both English and French. Variants of the first sentence occurred to him as early as 1983. Although the "he" of the narrative is seen to rise and go, it was the going that challenged Beckett at an age when he believed he was failing. Only by the end of 1984 did he substantially complete what he still called "Fragment," which became the first part of *Stirrings Still*. In 1986, he completed substantially what became the second part. When he sent me a copy, I was dazzled—not least by what seemed to me a subdued phrasal recollection of his previous work. I wrote him in enthusiasm about a new trilogy under way, and I suspect that I was not the only one to suggest this, but Beckett did not complete the third part till late 1987.

From Beckett's long revisionary period emerges a text of startling simplicity and mortal resonance. On the one hand, *Stirrings Still* subsumes such avatars of Beckett's previous fiction as the questor in hat and long coat, the meditator seated at his desk, the observer and the observed. On the other hand, the text can stir readers unfamiliar with Beckett's earlier work. Separating and yet fusing the outer world and the inner one, residual life and its neighborly nothing, observation and imagination, the piece articulates a narrative progression, often in familiar Beckett phrases. In the seven-paragraph part 1 the protagonist watches himself in hope and fear. In the one-paragraph part 2 questions arise, but the wish to end advances. In the one-paragraph part 3 an unheard inner word heralds the end, which nevertheless harks back to the beginning. Even in Beckett's last piece of fiction, completed when Beckett was over eighty, ends lead to beginnings.

As usual in Beckett's late prose, sentences are designated by capital letters and periods—the latter the only mark of punctuation, except for one question mark and one set of parentheses. Moreover, these paragraphs lack self-consciousness; gone are references to pen or voice, first- or third-person pronoun, present or past tense. Even proper nouns are contextualized: "Darly for example died and left him." Walther, with its German spelling, took thought while sitting on a stone and crossing his legs. The narrative is stripped to motion and emotion, reality and imagination, mind and mortality, affirmation and contradiction.

Part 1 opens on "him" at his table, watching himself rise and go. He

---

establish it, and I know of no one who has done so—yet. The account of *Stirrings Still* in *BatR* is unusually detailed. In RUL 2934 occurs the poem "Brief Dream," which is not related to the fiction. There is also a brief dialogue between M and W, about a white land, but that too seems unrelated to the fiction. *Stirrings Still* was first published in 1988 by John Calder and Barney Rosset in a deluxe edition with illustrations by Louis le Brocquy. Although dedicated to Barney Rosset, who had been summarily dismissed from Grove Press, which he founded, the narrative did not answer a request. The fiction appears in *CSP*, and Beckett translated it into French as *Soubresauts*, which was published by Minuit in 1989, the year Beckett died.

recalls that he used to stand on a stool, when his own light went out, to peer out the clouded window at the cloudless sky, without ever looking at the ground below. This first of seven paragraphs in part 1 is almost monosyllabic, and it still harbors active verbs and repetitive rhymes of *light/night/out*. In the second paragraph, "he" watches himself rise with the difficulties of an old man. He disappears and reappears, perceptible only by the change of place, as the narrative moves forward through gerunds—"hoping," "fearing," "wondering," "waiting." It is in this paragraph that Darly and "others . . . too . . . leave him till he too in his turn." The third paragraph startles with a polysyllabic neologism "whithersover," without direction. Although earlier there was light, now he wanders the back roads in the dark, seeking "A way out." The fourth paragraph introduces sounds: a clock strikes the hours and half hours, and cries are heard afar; both are "now faint now clear." Back with his head on his hands on the table, he half hopes and half fears that he hears the last of striking and crying. Again we read the sequence of gerunds—"hoping," "fearing," "wondering," "waiting." In the brief fifth paragraph he recalls lifting his head from his hands, before returning them to rest. Verbs vanish from the sixth paragraph, where outside and inside grow indistinguishable. A series of double negatives equates movement with stillness; old places with new. Only the strokes and cries are "The same as ever." In the last paragraph a series of *perhaps*es suggests that strokes and cries will end, unless they are merely lulled, after which all will continue. The abrupt final sentence introduces new nouns for what has been otherwise specified: "And patience till the one true end to time and grief and self and second self his own." The clock-strokes of time, the cries of grief, the he-self at his table, and the second self created by the imagination—all arrive eventually at "the one true end."

Part 2 shifts the tone to self-deflating irony—"right mind, remains of reason, more or less reasonable being." Sentences grow longer and more convoluted, as they reflect "his" bewilderment. Clock strokes, at first reassuring, turn to alarm, and cries are an "enlivener of his solitude." He seeks help in faulting his memory, but then ceases to do so. He finds himself in a field of gray grass, "verging here and there on white." Again moving "from bad to worse," he tries to think, but then resigns himself to not knowing where or how, whence or how. "So on unknowing and no end in sight." Although he previously declared himself without wishes, he finally wished the strokes and cries to cease "now faint now clear." What began almost humorously ends in sorrow.

Part 3 focuses on the inner man. The first sentence introduces "a word he could not catch," but it also predicts a possible end. He asks himself whether he is not already there where he cannot get "out of it." Twice he wonders whether to press on or "stir no more." The "hubbub in his mind so-called" is such that no further words emerge from deep within, but only the desire to end. Harkening back to the final sentence of part 1, part 3 closes: "Time and grief and self so-called. Oh all to end." The second self of the imagination has dissolved into the so-called self. Poignant without solemnity, graphic without fear of abstraction, intimate and impersonal, *Stirrings Still* does still stir the reader, with prose edging on stillness.

While struggling with his last recalcitrant text, Beckett had to breathe with an oxygenator. For a while he continued to smoke his cigarillos but after a while found that they lost their taste. Nevertheless, he managed to write a quatrain "Là" for Jim Knowlson, and a six-line poem, "Brief Dream." Death hovers over both.[5]

1988

In July a dizzy Beckett fell in his kitchen, where he was discovered unconscious by Suzanne. Hospitalized for tests, he was thought to have had a stroke. He watched himself slowly regain speech and mobility, and by September he committed the process to a poem in French—"Comment dire." That question was already posed in his earliest French fiction, and although Beckett never felt that he discovered an answer, he cast the question as his final burden. "Comment dire" was started in the hospital, and it was completed in the rest home where Beckett spent the last year of his life. At first he took walks around his abode, but soon he grew too frail for this pleasure. In his final year he compiled carefully penned instructions for the Leiceister Haymarket Theatre, where Antoni Libera directed David Warrilow in *Krapp's Last Tape* and *Catastrophe*.[6] Separated in their abodes, Beckett and Suzanne communicated by telephone. Suzanne died at home on July 18, 1989, and Beckett in the hospital on December 22, 1989.

"Comment dire" (What is the word)

The first phrase of the first draft (of seven) of "Comment dire" is "mal dire" [to say badly], and I may be projecting, but the subsequent broken phrases

---

Holographs and typescripts of "Comment dire" are at RUL, where the former are described in *BatR*: "Thus there are, in all, seven drafts of the poem from its inception to its completion, placed chronologically by Beckett in this exercise book" (11). When I visited Beckett in 1988, he gave me the exercise book to bring to Reading. After reading the poem (and its drafts), I thought of the actor Joe Chaikin, who suffered aphasia after his third open-heart operation. Since Joe knows no French, I asked Beckett to translate the poem, but he could not recall having written it. After I sent him a copy, he dedicated his translation to Joe. It was Beckett's last creation.

seem to me to echo Beckett's actual aphasia—curt, abrupt, and repetitive. In that draft the search for a word is rendered as "quel est le mot." With the third draft and the introduction of the word "folie," Beckett begins to exercise control over his material. Finally, each of the poem's fifty-three lines ends in a dash, and an occasional line still sounds aphasic: "tout ce ceci-ci—." Yet the last revision is a musical structure retaining only the recollection of aphasia. Beckett has cast a cold eye on his own experience. The poem is not divided into stanzas, but the repetitions of "comment dire" punctuate different thoughts, which I venture to summarize in English: (1) Folly of what is the word (2) in view of seeing what is given, what is the word (3) in view of seeing what is given here, what is the word (4) see fading to seem to need to glimpse, what is the word (5) and where, what is the word (6) there "afaint afar away over there," what is the word (7) in view of all this folly of wishing to believe having glimpsed what far away what, what is the word (8) what is the word. My clumsy paraphrase displays my habitual search for meaning, but Beckett's last poem accretes its phrases rhythmically, to render the particularity of overcoming verbal paralysis, and the generality of articulating the mortal situation, which many have recognized as their own.

"Comment dire" was first published in 1989 in limited and trade editions, copyrighted by Minuit. Beckett's English translation first appeared after Beckett's death in *Irish Times*, December 25–27, 1989, in *Beckett Circle* (spring 1990), and in *As the Story Was Told* (New York: Calder, 1990).

Appendix 1: Beckett and Performance

Facts siphoned from Knowlson and generously edited by Gontarski.

1952 Attended a few rehearsals of Blin's *En attendant Godot* in Paris
1957 Attended rehearsals of Blin's *Fin de partie* in Paris and London
1958 Attended all rehearsals of McWhinnie's *Krapp's Last Tape* and many of Devine's *Endgame* on a double bill at the Royal Court Theatre, London
1961 Helped Serreau with a revival of *Godot* in Paris
1962 Helped Devine with *Happy Days* at the Royal Court, but was "kicked out"
1963 Helped Blin with *Oh les beaux jours* in Paris and was welcomed
1964 Helped Michael Blake in London with Magee-MacGowran *Endgame* for Paris
Helped Serreau with *Comédie* and Devine with *Play,* commuting between Paris and London
Helped McWhinnie in London with Magee-MacGowran *Endgame* for the Royal Shakespeare Company (RSC)
Helped Schneider film *Film* in New York City
Helped Page with *Godot* revival at Royal Court
1965 Helped Mendel with *Godot* at Schiller Theater, Berlin
1966 Directed Pinget's *L'Hypothèse* as well as his own *Va et vient* in Paris
Codirected with Alan Gibson *Eh Joe* for BBC in London
Directed *Eh Joe* for Süddeutscher Rundfunk in Stuttgart
1967 Directed *Endspiel* at Schiller-Theater Werkstatt
1969 Directed *Das letzte Band* at Schiller-Theater Werkstatt
1970 Directed *La dernière bande* at Récamier in Paris
1971 Directed *Glückliche Tage* at Schiller-Theater Werkstatt
1972 Helped Page with *Not I* at Royal Court

1974   Helped Peter Hall with *Happy Days* at National Theatre, London

1975   Directed *Godot* at Schiller Theater

Directed double bill at Petite Salle of the Théâtre d'Orsay, Paris, of *Pas moi* with Renaud and *La dernière bande* with Chabert

1976   Directed *Footfalls* with Billie Whitelaw at Royal Court

Helped McWhinnie with *That Time* and *Play* at Royal Court

Directed *Damals* and *Tritte* at Schiller-Theater Werkstatt

Helped McWhinnie with teleplays *Ghost Trio* and . . . *but the clouds* . . . at BBC

1977   Directed *Geistertrio* and . . . *Nur noch Gewolk* . . . at Stuttgart

Directed *Krapp's Last Tape* with Cluchey in Berlin

1978   Directed *Spiel* at Schiller-Theater Werkstatt and at same time Cluchey *Endgame*

Directed Seyrig in *Pas* and Renaud in *Pas moi* at Théâtre d'Orsay, Paris

1979   Directed *Hé Joe* in Stuttgart

Directed Billie Whitelaw in *Happy Days* at Royal Court

1980   Directed Cluchey in *Endgame* at Riverside Studio, London

1981   Advised by telephone on Schneider's *Rockaby*

Directed *Quad* at Stuttgart

1982   Directed *Nacht und Träume* at Stuttgart

1984   Directed Cluchey's *Godot* in London

Advised Chabert on triple bill in Paris: *Berceuse, Impromptu d'Ohio, Catastrophe*

1985   Directed revised *Was Wo* in Stuttgart

1986   Advised Chabert on *Quoi où*, television *Was Wo* adapted to the stage, Théâtre du Rond-Point, Paris

1989   By mail, advised Libera on double bill of *Krapp's Last Tape* and *Catastrophe* (starring David Warrilow) at Leicester Haymarket

Appendix 2: Beckett's Self-Translations

The entries are alphabetized by originary language.

Acte sans paroles I	Act without Words I
Acte sans paroles II	Act without Words II
Assez	Enough
Bing	Ping
Bram van Velde	Bram van Velde (Dialogue III with Georges Duthuit)
Breath	Souffle
Le Calmant	The Calmative
Cascando	Cascando
Catastrophe	Catastrophe
Come and Go	Va et vient
Comment c'est	How It Is
Company	Compagnie
Le Dépeupleur	The Lost Ones
Eh Joe	Hé Joe
Embers	Cendres (with Robert Pinget)
En attendant Godot	Waiting for Godot
Esquisse radiophonique	Rough for Radio I
L'Expulsé	The Expelled (with Richard Seaver)
Film	Film
La Fin	The End (with Richard Seaver)
Fin de partie	Endgame
Foirades	Fizzles
Footfalls	Pas
Fragments de théâtre I et II	Roughs for Theatre I and II
From an Abandoned Work	D'un ouvrage abandonné (with Ludovic and Agnès Janvier)

Happy Days	Oh les beaux jours
Imagination morte imaginez	Imagination Dead Imagine
L'Innommable	The Unnamable
Krapp's Last Tape	La Dernière bande (at first with Pierre Leyris)
Malone meurt	Malone Dies
Mal vu mal dit	Ill Seen Ill Said
Molloy	Molloy (with Patrick Bowles)
Murphy	Murphy
Not I	Pas moi
Ohio Impromptu	L'Impromptu d'Ohio
A Piece of Monologue	Solo (adaptation)
Play	Comédie
Pochade radiophonique	Rough for Radio II
Premier amour	First Love
Quoi où	What Where
Rockaby	Berceuse
Sans	Lessness
Still	Immobile
Stirrings Still	Soubresauts
Textes pour rien	Texts for Nothing
That Time	Cette fois
Watt	Watt (with Ludovic and Agnès Janvier)
Words and Music	Paroles et musique

Poems

Comment dire	What Is the Word
Dieppe	Dieppe
elles viennent	They come
Hors crâne	Something there (adaptation)
je suis ce cours de sable qui glisse	my way is in the sand flowing
je voudrais que mon amour meure	I would like my love to die
que ferais-je sans ce monde	what would I do without this world

Notes

1929–31: Rather Too Self-Conscious

1. Fittingly, my first endnote pays tribute to the erudition of John Pilling. He is perhaps not responsible for the jacket blurb that praises his 1997 book as "for the first time [in Beckett studies] a coherent critical narrative." However, I think almost every book on Beckett reads like "a coherent critical narrative," and that is precisely what I hope to avoid. This is not to deny that I learned a great deal from some of these narratives, especially Pilling's.

2. The source of the quotation is a note attached to the dissertation of Terence McQueeny, "Beckett as a Critic of Proust and Joyce," RUL. McQueeny is informative about Beckett's dependence upon Croce and Michelet for Vico; upon McIntyre for Bruno; upon Dandieu and Schopenhauer for Proust. He characterizes Beckett's essay as "a brilliant mosaic of secondary sources done by a rushed apprentice." P. J. Murphy, "Portraits of the Artist as a Young Critic" (*JOBS* 9/1), discusses the essay (provocatively) in connection with the story *Assumption*.

Publication of a book on Beckett and Dante would help scholarship. Cf. Murphy et al.: "Monograph studies of Beckett and Dante, Beckett and the Bible, Beckett and Shakespeare—to name only the instances of greatest need—would be valuable contributions to Beckett criticism" (63). In the meantime the following comment usefully on Dante in Beckett: Harvey, especially chap. 2; Rabinovitz 1994, chap. 6; Robinson; Levy's chapter on *Mercier and Camier*; Pilling 1997. Daniela Caselli's 1999 dissertation at the University of Reading and Francesca De Moro's 1996 dissertation at the University of Pisa should be published.

3. Some sixty years later Beckett told Knowlson that he had actually written on Jouve *before* his arrival at the Ecole Normale, but if the essay ever existed, it has not been found (Knowlson, 86). See Pilling 1997 and Murphy 1999 for the argument that Beckett intended a writerly career even as early as the Joyce essay.

4. Verdicchio has commented astutely on Beckett's quixotic slant on Vico, transmuting him into Joyce's ancestor.

5. Contrary to some assumptions, Beckett did not study Dante at Trinity College. His card of May 18, 1983, to Roger Little states: "No, he [Professor Rudmose-Brown] had no part in the Dante revelation. This I seem to have managed on my own, with the help of my Italian teacher, Bianca Esposito" (Little, 40). I am grateful to Daniela Caselli for bringing Little's article to my attention.

6. Gross reads the final word "moon" as a sexual pun on a woman's bottom; "And so the sexual and religious materials in Beckett's poem on Tiresias would seem to be unified after all." The poem does not seem unified to me, but it nevertheless bears testimony to Beckett's outrage at the lack of divine compassion.

7. In a long, learned article in *The Art of Rhetoric* Edouard Morot-Sir ignores the "legendary tale of origin" of "Whoroscope" to argue, "All Beckettian characters or impersonations come from Descartes" (98). A sensitive reading of "Whoroscope" is at the base of Morot-Sir's argument, but I cannot agree with his view of Beckett's systematic and overall Cartesian coherence.

8. W. J. McCormack has commented perceptively on Beckett's nineteen translations for Nancy Cunard's *Negro Anthology*.

9. Cauliflowers have no heart, nor onions a core—real or ideal—as Beckett implies when he labels the images "nox vomica."

10. Bruce Arnold reports or imagines Beckett's paper entitled "le convergisme": "In *le convergisme* Beckett created among Parisian café society a group of *convergistes* whose leader, a poet, had a distinctive saluation [*sic*]: 'Pose culotte et baise' he would say in preference to 'Asseyez-vous et soyez à votre aise.' The rest of this work has been lost." One might add: "Well lost," since it is so misrecalled (15).

11. Knowlson writes: "According to Georges Pelorson, the idea of the play was his alone and the cutting up of Corneille's text . . . was also done almost entirely by himself, with very little help and advice from Beckett" (125). However, Beckett spoke to me of the burlesque as though it was a joint project, but he doubted whether the text of *Le Kid* was ever written down.

12. Pilling reads a passage of *Dream* biographically, in order to date some of these poems. He also cites an August 1931 letter from Beckett to the editor Charles Prentice as evidence that a form of "Walking Out" and "TWO" of *Dream* were written by that date. Knowlson dwells on Ethna MacCarthy, Beckett's fellow student at Trinity, as the impetus behind "Yoke of Liberty" and "Alba."

13. The images derive from Louis Laloy's *La Musique chinoise* (Paris, 1910), as Sean Lawlor has shown (Pilling 1999a, no. 498), but the musicality is Beckett's.

14. Harvey believes that Beckett also draws on the melancholy Provençal *planh*, but "Enueg I" seems to me sufficiently sardonic to be classified as an enueg, and even the more lyrical "Enueg II" introduces jarring colloquialisms. The editors of Beckett's letters inform me that "Serena I" was once entitled "Enueg II," so that he may have considered "enueg" with its resonance of ennui a catchall title for his verse of this period. Ann Lecercle offers a detailed analysis of "Enueg I," upon which I draw.

15. The source of Beckett's Belacqua is such common knowledge in Beckett scholarship that it is difficult to trace its first appearance in print—perhaps Walter A. Strauss's "Dante's Belacqua and Beckett's Tramps." Not until 1998, however, did C. J. Ackerley (19) suggest a purgatorial source (Canto XXXI, ll. 116–17) for the name of the Smeraldina: "li smeraldi / ond'Amor già ti trasse le sue armi" [The emeralds from which Love once shot his darts at you].

1932–33: Intricate Festoons of Words

1. Pilling has traced a number of Beckett's words to five plays of the Jacobean dramatist John Ford (1999b, 9).

2. Knowlson (139) summarizes the biographical detail; Beckett was ejected

from a Dublin brothel when he reacted with hilarity to a picture of Dante and Beatrice. However, in his poem the Dublin brothel, with Becky Cooper in attendance, is transported to a Paris setting.

3. Both Pilling's annotations of the *Dream* Notebook (1999a) and Bryden's *Samuel Beckett and the Idea of God* illuminate how Beckett draws upon Augustine's *Confessions*. Knowlson goes into convincing detail on the biographical roots of *Dream*.

4. Sean Lawlor shows that Beckett purloined phrases from Louis Laloy, *La Musique chinoise* (Paris, 1910), to sustain this conceit. Lawlor expanded on this in a brilliant seminar paper at the University of Reading on May 22, 1999.

5. Caselli 1999, chap. 2, renders a sophisticated account of the function of Dante in Beckett's *Dream*.

6. Admussen quotes Federman: "A first chapter was projected, covering Belacqua's boyhood, but was never written" (102). Pilling, however, argues that the purpose of the brief opening chapter is to flout time (1997, 60).

7. The Smeraldina is anatomized physically and ridiculed linguistically. Deirdre Bair, citing Mary Manning Howe as her source, affirms that the Smeraldina's letter in *Dream* is a "verbatim" quotation from a letter to Beckett by Peggy Sinclair, "who wrote English phonetically as she spoke it with her heavy German accent" (146). I find this difficult to credit, especially since (1) the letter contains sly puns—"whitch, maid me cry, evedintly, bees summing"; and (2) Bair's summary of *Dream* is riddled with errors. Farrow's analysis of the linguistic quality of the Belacqua-Smeraldina love affair evades any credence in Bair's statement. Knowlson quotes Beckett, that the epistolary story is "a mixture of fact and fiction" (146).

8. Yoshiki Tajiri demonstrated this on pp. 4–5 of *Dream*, in a paper presented at the University of Reading on May 22, 1999.

9. O'Hara reads Nemo as "a consciousness powerless to accept the roles it must play" (36). Pilling writes: "Nemo is a nutshell illustration of Beckett's ability to re-write previous literature and make it mean something quite other than its originators intended" (1999a, 67). He goes on to summarize Beckett's "re-writing" of Joyce's "The Dead" and Proust's "Guermantes party." Gross's entire thesis rests on this "ability," as does Ackerley's sophisticated annotation of *Murphy* (1998). Tracing the sources of Beckett's "ability" enhances one's pleasure in this first novel, but it does not confer value on that novel, as scholars imply.

10. Among those prophetic inaudibilities is toying with the figure eight—"The bumless eight of the drink figure. You did not end up where you started, but coming down you met yourself going up" (226). Half a century later Beckett would incorporate that figure into a short prose piece, *The Way*.

11. Decades later, Beckett joked (to me) that he briefly considered amending the end to "Like Hell it is," but he preferred three words to four.

12. Chapter 3 of Caselli's dissertation discusses this.

13. On original publication of *Dante and the Lobster*, quotation marks punctuate "Take into the air my quiet breath" from Keats's "Ode to a Nightingale," but Beckett omitted them in *MPTK*. A scrupulous scrutiny of the differences between the magazine and book versions of *Dante and the Lobster* has been made by Kay Gilliland Stevenson. Anthony Farrow is illuminating on Dantean detail and counterpoint, not only in this story, but also in the other *Pricks*.

14. For the material on McCabe I am indebted to Kroll. In *The Beckett Country* Eoin O'Brien was "unable to find a newspaper photograph of McCabe" (361 n.

9). Beckett retained the devastatingly ironic name of McCabe's actual prison—Mountjoy—but he changed the name of the hangman from Pierpont to Ellis.

15. Pilling (1997, 96) reviews the paucity of evidence for the dating of the stories. *Sedendo et Quiescendo* and some form of *Walking Out* were completed in 1931, but the others are probably later, and I follow Pilling's guesses.

16. Beckett's note 864 in the *Dream* Notebook is "as much pity due to a woman weeping as to a goose going barefoot." Pilling (1999a) has traced the odd simile to Burton's *Anatomy of Melancholy* III, 126.

17. Gross reads "Sanies I" as "a masturbatory fantasy of a return to the womb the whole drama of which takes place only in the speaker's psyche" (226). Although she may be right about the penile imagery of the bicycle—"The ritter (German: 'rider') *is* the 'Ritter' (German brandname for a bike)" (239), the "masturbatory fantasy" seems to me unproved.

18. James Acheson (1997, 27) argues that the title derives from the "Cyclops" episode of Joyce's *Ulysses*.

19. Item 219 in the *Dream* Notebook notes this image, which Pilling has traced to Renard's *Journal*. Somewhat later, in the *Murphy* Notebook Beckett writes: "Le chien se retire de la chienne comme une carotte rouge d'un pot de graisse."

20. Daniela Caselli (1999) has located the phrase in Dante's *Convivio* (II, i, 1), "veritade ascosa sotto bella mensogna" [truth hidden by a beautiful lie].

21. Harvey dates six poems of *Echo's Bones* after the death of William Beckett in 1933, but he does not indicate which poems (155).

22. C. J. Ackerley (1983) cites the relevance of Beethoven's last quartet to "Malacoda."

23. Lecercle reads "The Vulture" as a poem of sutures. For her the first key couplet blends inner and outer worlds by chiastic sound play; the third couplet blends the part and the whole. The entire poem announces the theme—suture—and the technique—chiasmus—of the whole collection. Although suggestive, Lecercle imposes too tight a structure on a collection of often revised poems. Peter Murphy (1990) makes large claims for "The Vulture": "Beckett has made 'The Vulture' a major work in his canon by continually 'rewriting' it in his prose works" (18).

24. In her analysis of the collection as an ensemble, Lecercle reads *Echo's Bones* through chiasmus, numerology, and geometry, sometimes ignoring the literal meaning of the lines. Against the title's bones she pits the image of a rotten egg. In that symbol she believes that Beckett sutures birth to death; moreover, the poems circle through the seasons (beginning and ending with winter) and through the twenty-four hours of a day, although the light is always crepuscular. Her argument embraces phonemes, words, line lengths, and stanzaic patterns. Although I am indebted to her readings, I am somewhat skeptical of her two main metaphors—suture and the rotten egg. Certainly the thrust of the poems conveys an existence that is sullied, even doomed, from birth or from conception, and yet *enueg* does not seem to me to pun on "in you(r) egg." More importantly, a suture implicitly eradicates the pain of irresolvable contradictions that, *pace* Bruno, do not always constitute identities for Beckett.

1934–36: These Demented Particulars

1. I believe that Beckett eventually consented to the publication of his criticism in *Disjecta* because he was embarrassed at having slept through an appointment with me on December 18, 1982.

2. Although I copied the article from *Dublin Magazine* and checked it with Beckett, I believe there are misprints that I did not point out to him: there is a superfluous "is," and the word "doubled" is more intelligibly read as "doubted."

3. I am grateful to John Pilling for calling this letter to my attention.

4. Parenthetically (or endnotely), I note that O'Casey's other one-acter, *A Pound on Demand*, features a drunken Irish laborer named Sammy, whose friend tries to make him sign a form for a post office pound on demand. Their ineffectual antics lead to their humiliation by a policeman, as happens to Belacqua of Beckett's own fiction. Yet Beckett's review ignores this bright sketch.

5. I am indebted to Daniela Caselli's (1999) transcription of the notes, where Beckett's handwriting was undecipherable to me.

6. Two articles (Anzieu and Bennet) see Beckett and his analyst Bion as brothers under the skin. Both articles contain errors about Beckett, so I am skeptical about the fraternity.

7. Bair performs her own psychoanalysis on Beckett: "[He] seized upon this remark as the keystone of his entire analysis. . . . He was able to furnish detailed examples of his own womb fixation, arguing forcefully that all his behavior, from the simple inclination to stay in bed to his deep-seated need to pay frequent visits to his mother, were all aspects of an improper birth" (209). More significant for Beckett's readers is Jung's reinforcement of the writer's own womb-tomb fantasy with which he had burdened Belacqua, and which would emerge sporadically in more sophisticated forms.

8. Two monographs, Harrison and Kennedy, are entirely devoted to *Murphy*. Virtually a monograph is the rich article of Bernard Brugière. I am also indebted to Mays 1982. Knowlson is discerning about the biographical background of *Murphy*, including Beckett's reading. Begam provides a comprehensive and comprehensible Derridean reading of the novel. Ackerley's 1998 annotated *Murphy* is indispensable for further research.

9. Ackerley (1998, 156.5) usefully traces the names Bim and Bom in Beckett's later work.

10. Mays (1982) convincingly establishes Ticklepenny's source in the Irish writer Austin Clarke. Beckett's slanderous portrait parallels his earlier caricature of Peggy Sinclair as the Smeraldina. Ackerley (1998) designates Ticklepenny as, rationally, the only possible igniter of Murphy's gas radiator, hence as Murphy's murderer. However, Ackerley appreciates that the novel cannot be appreciated rationally. Moreover, Beckett in his typescript inks in "trap" for "door," and it is possible that this is a trap for any reader seeking the remorseless logic of detective fiction.

11. Its springboard is the Bethlem Royal Hospital in Beckenham, on the border of Kent and Surrey, where Beckett's friend Dr. Geoffrey Thompson was serving a psychiatric residency (Bair, 205).

12. Rubin Rabinovitz (1984) has traced a number of errors in the novel's particulars, but Ackerley (1998) corrects Rabinovitz. Several commentators demur at a horoscope based on the unrevealed date of Murphy's birth, and J. C. Eade has demonstrated the astrological impossibility of Suk's horoscope. Ackerley's index lists fifty-two items under "unreliable narrative."

13. The narrator stipulates that there are seven scarves, but he accounts only for six. Bair quotes Beckett's admission that this was his mistake (670), but I am skeptical. Many intentional and unintentional mistakes will be built into *Watt*, and

I think that they begin in *Murphy*. Cf. Begam on Murphy's scarves (62) and Ackerley 1998, 2.2.

14. Harold Pinter, who early read Beckett's novels, has built much of his
drama on this fulcrum of domination.

1937–40: No Trifle Too Trifling

1. Harvey prints the final line as "it all boils down to the blood of the lamb."
Only in 1977 did Beckett permit "Ooftish" to be reprinted, without the definite articles in the last line, somewhat diminishing the sacramental association.

2. This may be the place to correct Deirdre Bair's statement, which is end-
noted by one of her multiple attributions: "The American scholar Ruby Cohn asked
Beckett for the manuscript in the late 1960s, and he gave it to her, saying he was glad
to be rid of it" (257). I often asked Beckett whether I might read his manuscripts, but
I never asked, would never ask, for a gift. I did not even know of the existence of the
three Johnson notebooks and the abortive scene, *Human Wishes*, when I found them
(personally delivered by Beckett) at my Paris hotel. After surveying the contents, I
told Beckett by telephone that the material should be in a library. (The Reading University Beckett Archive was not yet founded.) He replied that he didn't want it in a
library and didn't want it discussed. I did not discuss it, but when I was working on
Back to Beckett in 1972, I asked him whether I might not mention the existence of
the scene, and he replied: "Yes, why not?" Emboldened by this relaxation of his vig-
ilance, I asked him in 1979 whether I might describe the material and publish the
scene in my *Just Play*; he graciously consented, and (again with his permission) I
reprinted the scene in *Disjecta*.

3. Frederik Smith has examined the Johnson-Beckett relationship, and he
kindly made his material available to me before publication. Smith quotes from
Beckett's August 4, 1937, letter to MacGreevy: "[Mrs. Thrale] had none of that need
to suffer or necessity of suffering that [Dr. Johnson] had . . . he, in a sense was spir-
itually self-conscious, was a tragic figure, i.e., worth putting down as part of the
whole of which oneself is part, and that she, being never physically self-conscious is
less interesting to me personally. The groom didn't have what she wanted either,
Piozzi being a poor performer." The context casts a mordant light on the human
wishes of both Beckett's principals. Fred Lowe, an eighteenth-century scholar who
was also generous with his findings, has commented perceptively on Beckett's Johnson in *SBT* 8 (not yet published as I write).

4. The Davos reference is to *The Woman of Andros* by the Roman playwright
Terence: "I am Davos [the slave] not Oedipus." Beckett implies that the gerryman-
dler, unlike Oedipus, fears sphinxian riddles.

5. Tophoven's German translation (probably with Beckett's approval) is
based on the contrast: "für sie die Liebesleere / er der Liebesreine."

6. Lowe's is the most thorough commentary on the Johnson material, which
he graciously sent to me before publication.

7. Knowlson reports on an interview with the English actor Peter
Woodthorpe, who played Estragon in the London premiere of *Godot*, and who was
told by Beckett in 1955 "that he would like to see him playing Dr. Johnson in a play
that he dreamed of writing. It would, he said, be a monologue with Dr. Johnson and
his cat, Hodge, as the only characters; other cats might enter, he added, but no other

human being! . . . When Woodthorpe wrote to him later reminding him of his proposal, Beckett replied that he had given up the idea." Knowlson comments that the play "had still not been entirely abandoned" (699 n. 166).

8. Joyce fled to Zurich in neutral Switzerland, where he died in 1941. In 1958 Beckett met the doctor present at Joyce's death. Beckett in 1955 was best man at the wedding of Stephen Joyce, the grandson of James.

1941–45: Semantic Succour

1. Marjorie Perloff (in chapter 4 of *Wittgenstein's Ladder*) reads *Watt* through Beckett's Resistance activities, as well as through Wittgenstein's *Investigations*. Rejecting the usual quest-novel view of *Watt*, she adheres to Beckett's sequence of the four parts as published. Watt's asylum sojourn is therefore not the end; instead Watt is left in limbo, since no one boards the train for which he buys a ticket. As I understand Perloff's last paragraph, Watt (and by extension, Beckett) is finally freed to dissociate language from any given "use-context."

2. The quotation comes from David Hayman in an email of February 17, 1997. I am grateful to that scholar for the information about the name Sam. Ann Beer ascribes importance to "we" as narrator: "the underlying narrator is a plural self, made up of all the speakers in the novel" (1985, 56). However, "we" seems to me more evanescent than Beer indicates.

3. Ackerley traces these questions to Geulincx's *Ethica*, VI, I. 1 (1998, 28).

4. Moreover, different editions of *Watt* play musical scales with the music: In Ackerley's summary: "some editions (Olympia, Grove and Italian) presenting the complete sentence of introduction with the music; others (Calder, Swedish and Spanish) retaining the sentence but omitting the music; yet others (Minuit and German) omitting both" (1993c, 186) Cf. Lees 1983.

5. Beckett's letter of April 12, 1978, to Dr. Büttner states: "Only one part [of *Watt*] is in the asylum (though all told there), the other 3 in Knott's house" (159). Beckett's memory is here as inaccurate as some of the statements in the novel itself.

6. Ackerley has published an indispensable article about "Beckett's deliberate use of the addenda to evoke echoes of *Watt*'s past and the stages of its composition" (1993c, 175). Ann Beer's dissertation is also enlightening about the addenda. Caselli (1999) reads the addenda as a *mise en abyme*.

7. Sam counts eight stages, but he slips on "the fifth, no, the sixth stage" (166). In the manuscript, we are provided with examples of all eight stages. Ann Beer notes the special strangeness of words created by the inversion of letters in the word, in Watt's sixth stage (1987, 70).

8. Büttner assumes that Watt's quest reflects that of Beckett himself, and for that reason perhaps he believes that the quest was successful, ignoring the evidence of the novel itself, where Watt is broken in speech and spirit. Beer, too, relates Watt's quest to that of Beckett: "Watt's heart-rending vulnerability and stoicism as he buys his train-ticket and vanishes from the narrative become the emotional correlative of his creator's act of self-exile from 'home,' the decision to explore an alien realm of the imagination in an adopted tongue" (1987, 66). I prefer to read *Watt* as fiction, however "Mme. Bovary" may be "moi."

9. Cf. Brater 1981. Brater assumes that each of the four parts posits a different narrator, but none of the parts is stylistically homogeneous. However, I agree with

Brater that the narrator is deliberately indeterminate. Ann Beer quotes John Chalker approvingly: "There is no base within the work from which the action or events can be viewed" (1987, 73 n. 72). This is deliberate in-definition on Beckett's part.

10. Mood has compiled a table of thirty-seven lists, series, permutations, and combinations, in which he finds twelve mistakes "not counting those where awareness of the mistake or incompleteness is acknowledged" (262). He guesses shrewdly what Beckett affirmed to me: "Beckett is not just competently expressing incompetence but . . . he has also done it incompetently, i.e., by including mistakes of which he was not aware, at least at that time" (263).

11. I quote her view of seminal themes in *Watt:* "The sense of self and otherness is developed through the juggling with personae and pronouns; the idea of life as a disease or a slow dying appears; and several long passages explore the idea of the human eye (I) and its spiritual and material functions" (74).

12. *Watt* has a special resonance for faithful Beckett readers. As the addenda incorporate the history of the growth of *Watt,* the published novel incorporates flitters of Beckett's past work and predictions of its future. Past: The obverse of *Che Sciagura* figures in Arthur's recommendation of Bando for Mr. Graves's plight. Dr. Johnson is saluted in "The Vanity of Human Wishes." Mr. Knott's two needs differ from those of *Les Deux Besoins,* but they remain binary. The unpublished story "Echo's Bones" and *Murphy* are reflected in a "bitter stout porter." Turning from "the dark shingle . . . to the lights of the little town" recapitulates the movements in the poem "Dieppe."

Almost uncanny is the prediction of works to come, as studied by Beer (1987, 74–75). Sometimes this is done by a suggestive word or phrase:

Erskine, *passim*	W2's butler in *Play*
Mr. Ash's half-hunter, 44	*Godot*
the standard oil-lamp, 45	*A Piece of Monologue*
ill-told, ill heard, 71	*Ill Seen Ill Said*
to the buff, 99	*All That Fall*
Erskine's bell, 118ff.	The bell of *Happy Days*
with only shades to keep you company, 62	*Company*
together again after so long, 161	*Ohio Impromptu*
box or urn, 80	*Play, Bing, Lessness*
ten or fifteen times,	*How It Is*
	paces, acres, minutes

More extensive forecasts follow:

Watt departs wearily "at the end of a day that was like the other days"; similarly, Hamm will ask Clov: "It's the end of the day like any other day, isn't it, Clov?"

After the leap-year threne the narrator comments: "Bun is such a sad word, is it not? And man is not much better, is it?" The implied equation of man and object is paralleled by the more inclusive "one syllable and m at the end" of *How It Is.*

Watt's juggling of hypotheses will be a feature of *The Lost Ones.*

Watt's nightmare about "dives from dreadful heights into rocky waters, before a numerous public" (222) recapitulates Beckett's own nightmare, already used in

"For Future Reference" and to be recycled in the future *Eleutheria, Godot,* and *Company.*

Watt's sensitivity to footfalls will emerge in the title of Beckett's late play, which also recycles "to put it mildly" (76–7) and "as though they had never been" (79).

Arsene is aware that "when you cease to seek you start to find" (44), but Didi and Gogo still seek:

> Vladimir: When you seek you hear.
> Estragon: You do.
> Vladimir: That prevents you from finding. (59)

Both works reflect mordantly upon the biblical "seek, and ye shall find" (Matt. 7:7).

This series would seem to suggest that Beckett formulated certain phrases and themes, only to play fugal variations upon them. To some extent this is true, but only to some extent, and, for all its repetition and reduplication, *Watt* is a key text beyond that extent.

13. Federman and Fletcher quote Beckett to the effect that the article was written at the beginning of 1945, shortly after the exhibitions of A and G van Velde, respectively, at Galeries Mai and Maeght. However, the dating is problematic, as Knowlson explains: "Beckett himself told his bibliographers that he wrote it early in 1945, but went on to say that this was *after* the Bram and Geer exhibitions, which was a slip of the memory. Certainly it was written before the autumn of 1945" (687 n. 4).

1946: J'Ouvre la Série [I open the series]

1. Admussen reads Beckett's note to Federman and Fletcher as an implication that these are not the earliest dates for *L'Expulsé* and *Le Calmant,* but, having examined the manuscripts at HRC, I believe they are the original versions.

2. The most thorough examination of this subject is Katz.

3. Several of these "writerly" phrases were added later than the "Suite" notebook.

4. *Les Temps modernes* did not publish the second part of *La Fin.* About three-fifths of the story was published in the periodical, ending: "Mais le jour vint où, regardant autour de moi, je me trouvai dans les faubourgs, et de là aux vieilles erres ce n'était pas loin, au-delà du stupide espoir de repos ou de moindre peine" (105) [But the day came when, looking round me, I was in the suburbs, and from there to the old haunts it was not far, beyond the stupid hope of rest or less pain, 91]. Beckett's post–*Temps modernes* revisions increase the story's flatness and its repetition, which builds a subdued chant.

5. Eric Levy finds more resonances of Dante. Caselli (1999, chap. 6) examines the novel as a (Dantean) palimpsest.

6. Beckett's English translation does not number the summary outlines as separate chapters, and it therefore contains only eight chapters. Cogent comparisons between the French and English versions are Connor 1989, Praeger 1992, and Gaffney 1999b. Crombie translates and publishes Beckett's excisions, with innovative typography.

7. Mercier and Camier speak similarly even in the mixed register of the English translation, which Connor 1989 analyzes admirably.

8. I choose only the highlights of Levy's cornucopia of Dante. Caselli (1999) views the Dantean references as part of Beckett's intratextual palimpsest, or self-reference, or autography.

9. Acheson, 92, summarizes the differences between identically named characters in *Watt* and *Mercier et Camier*.

10. Quin's name will reappear mysteriously in *Malone meurt,* 146.

11. Cf. Stefano Genetti: "Au cours de sa révision, l'auteur . . . accentue un humour basé sur la respiration haletante de la prose et sur le pullulement des allitérations, sur la distorsion de la logique syntaxique, la manipulation des règles de l'association sémantique et l'exploitation des ambiguités lexicales, un humour qui cultive l'ellipse, le jeu de mots, l'alternance discordante des niveaux stylistiques, le retournement du lieu commun, l'hyperbole, la litote et la rétraction paradoxales" (1998, 30). I nevertheless find the final version less prodigal of humor than is the *Fontaine* version.

12. Eoin O'Brien finds less local reference for *The Calmative* than for the other stories.

13. The immediacy is stronger in the original French because the often repeated "Je dis" and "Il dit" can be either present or past tense, whereas the English translation tends toward the past.

1947–49: Mais la Réalité, Trop Fatigué Pour Chercher le Mot Juste [But reality, too tired to look for the right word]

1. The glazier in Baudelaire's "Mauvais Vitrier" has been viewed as a symbol for the poetic imagination. Although Beckett must have known that poem, as well as the glazier in Strindberg's *Dream Play,* he conceives a more sardonic craftsman.

2. See McMillan and Fehsenfeld for a view of *Eleutheria* as a "Discourse on Dramatic Method."

3. Like the preceding essay on the van Velde paintings, *Peintres de l'empêchement* has often been read as a comment on Beckett's own work, and the piece was probably commissioned because of his affinity with the painting of the Dutch brothers. I am not, however, inclined to see in it a discourse on artistic method, as does Pascale Casanova.

4. The translation is unsigned in *transition,* but Federman and Fletcher, who consulted with Beckett for their bibliography, note that Beckett's work for *transition* is sometimes unsigned. "Mr. Beckett is certain, however, of having translated [F__]." (493). They also believe that he wrote the contributor's note about Suzanne. Lake, ed., describes F__: "A short story by Beckett's wife, written at the time Beckett was writing *En attendant Godot*" (74). Beckett may be the source of that statement, but I am nonetheless skeptical about its factuality.

5. In Gontarski's introduction to the Grove Press *Nohow On,* he decries the use of the word *trilogy,* but his substitution of "3 in 1" (Beckett's term) does not seem to me an improvement.

6. Page numbers for the translations of the trilogy into English are problematic, depending on the edition. I have chosen the Grove Weidenfeld, single-volume edition of the three novels, which is both convenient and relatively accurate. For different editions of *The Unnamable,* see Wagner.

7. Bruno Clément has written brilliantly about Beckett's preambles, 125–33.

8. In the original French the two men are A and B, but Beckett changes them to A and C, in English, perhaps to suggest Abel and Cain.

9. As in *Premier Amour* the narrator is uncertain of the name of his love, but also of the name of his protectress. Women in Beckett's French fiction seem to be less stable of identity than men, who are themselves unstable.

10. Cf. Katz, 72: "both stories tell of long bicycle trips. . .; both narrators suffer from progressive physical incapacitation. . .; both spend protracted stays in a forest, in which each commits a brutal murder; and both finally arrive at the destination where we find them at their stories' beginnings, and where accounts of their experiences are demanded by vaguely defined 'others.'"

11. In an illuminating monograph Dina Sherzer distinguishes the narratives of the trilogy from their several metanarrative strands. Although I am indebted to her work, I engage in a more "naive" reading.

12. *Murphy* was published by Bordas in French while Beckett was writing *Molloy*. Katz weaves subtle arguments about Beckett's predilection for M- and W-names, but he does not mention Yerk.

13. According to the count of Barale and Rabinovitz.

14. Glasnevin in Macmann's poem is footnoted as "Nom d'un cimetière local très estimé," as indeed it is—in Ireland.

15. Knowlson believes that Beckett was confusing the Berlin Friedrich painting with a similar one that he had seen in Dresden in 1937: "In any case, the Berlin painting is so similar in its composition to the Dresden picture that what he said could apply equally well to either" (342). The moon looms large in both, and Malone not only mentions Friedrich, but uses the moon as a fulcrum for one of his most lyrical passages (171).

16. The similarities between *Mercier et Camier* and *En attendant Godot* have been explored by Colin Duckworth.

17. Beckett traced the arbitrary salvation-damnation of the thieves to a passage in Augustine, which he quoted to Harold Hobson, the English critic: "Do not despair, one of the thieves was saved. Do not presume, one of the thieves was damned." However, no one has been able to find that sentence in the works of Augustine. C. J. Ackerley convincingly argues that Beckett drew it from Robert Greene's "The Repentance of Robert Greene," which ends: "To this doth that golden sentence of S. Augustine allude, which hee speaketh of the theefe, hanging on the Crosse. *There was* (saith hee) *one theef saved and no more, therefore presume not; and there was one saved, and therefore despaire not*" (1998, 213.2).

18. The French *pou*, or louse, causes Vladimir to reexamine his hat for a foreign body. This pun is lost in English translation, but the new pun on "pall" enhances the death imagery. Much later, when they speak of being bound—*lié* in French—Vladimir does not "fait la liaison" phonetically between *pas* and *encore;* this subtle soundplay is lost in translation.

1950–52: Rien à faire (Nothing to be done)

1. RUL ms. 2926, Beckett's so-called Sam Francis Notebook, contains a Spanish vocabulary, miscellaneous notes, and drafts of two translations of Mexican poems.

2. *L'Innommable* is unmentioned in Connor's classification of Beckett titles as naming, quoting, and generic; it would seem to belong to the "exceptional" few, which "stand firmly outside their texts and comment bitterly on them" (1988, 42).

3. Clément links that rhetoric, which he examines in all Beckett's works, to the five parts of classical rhetoric. To do that, he seems to me to stretch the classical forms considerably. He also implies that Beckett is imbued with a spirit of system, which the narrator of *L'Innommable* explicitly rejects. I nevertheless enjoyed Clément's work, and I draw upon it, probably more than I realize. I have also learned from Hill's *Beckett's Fiction in Different Words*. A danger of critical commentary on *L'Innommable* is falling into its seductive rhythms.

4. Early criticism, including my own, wrote of the Unnamable as the narrator. More recent criticism balks at the very word *narrator,* substituting *voice* or *scribe.* I continue to use the word narrator, without the implication of a coherent narrative or definable subjectivity; he/she/it narrates words, or, better, words are narrated.

5. I use the third-person singular masculine pronoun for the genderless narrator, in order to avoid the clumsiness of a constant *her/him,* or *her/his.*

6. The French is more polyvalent, since the question is a colloquial exclamation, meaning something like: "What are you talking about?"

7. Rupert Wood translates the relevant passage: "If a voyager is in a ship which carries him briskly westwards, there is nothing to stop him from walking eastwards on board the ship" (43).

8. Recent criticism reads all three novels as writing about writing. Although Katz claims not to limit Beckett in this way, his dense prose sometimes seems to focus on writing about writing.

9. The manuscripts of *Textes pour rien* show continual work. Bair is mistaken in her view of the texts as "the short prose pieces he turned to during the next two years whenever he had spare time or when pressures in his life grew so intense that he needed a release and a respite" (408). The texts exhibit their own intense pressures.

Peter Murphy views the *Textes pour rien* as a "first step towards a confirmation of the Orphic vision of an engagement of the imagination with the world" (52).

10. Brienza goes into illuminating detail on Beckett's tense shifts, but she herself shifts confusingly between the French and English texts.

11. Beckett's letter was printed in *Le Nouvel observateur* (October 24–30, 1996, 52), along with reminiscences of Michel Polac. Edith Fournier's English translation of Beckett's letter was published in the *New Yorker,* June 24, 1996. Angela Moorjani has published the fullest account of the radio broadcast, as well as her translation of Beckett's letter (1998).

1953–58: Then These Flashes, or Gushes

1. The love of words is not present in the *Trinity News* version of the story.

2. Remarkably, Beckett keeps the rhyme in his French translation: "hors le for." He introduces other rhymes in French, particularly the repeated "vite la suite."

3. Knowlson and Pilling are dubious about the dating of those fragments, because it is so unlike Beckett to allow five years to elapse between versions of a play

(personal communication). I find little of *Fin de partie* in these fragments, but I assign them to the stemma as a matter of convenient collation with *BatR*. Restivo (1994) is most insistent on the seed of *Fin de partie* in the 1950 scene.

4. Also at OSU is a forty-two-page typescript of Beckett's translation of *Fin de partie* into *Endgame*, with ink corrections of "sedative" to "pain-killer," and ink additions of "and engraver" and "Our revels now are ended."

5. Actually, the RUL fragment ends with the first mention of Bom and Bim, but the TCD holograph continues the incident, as described.

6. Even the tailor joke is skeletally present. In act 2, B, bent over P's ashbin, is told an unheard joke at which both laugh. Rising while still laughing, B repeats the punchline: "Regardez le monde!" [Look at the world!]. My translations in the text are patterned on Beckett's own eventual translations into *Endgame*.

7. This account is a brief summary of what Martin Esslin (1986) and Clas Zilliacus (1976) have described in greater detail.

8. The play's director, Donald McWhinnie, writes in *The Art of Radio* a fascinating account of the BBC broadcast of *All That Fall*.

9. Beckett wrote Jean-Jacques Mayoux: "C'est la première fois, depuis 45, que j'écris directement en anglais" (Mayoux 1957, 350n). This sentence is quoted by Zilliacus, who points out Beckett's error, and who also cites his "explanation" of the original shift to French (1976, 29).

10. Clas Zilliacus examines the several forms of language closely (1999), but his view depends on reading, as well as listening.

11. Critics of *All That Fall* are divided on the question as to whether Dan Rooney pushed the child, but of course Beckett meant to leave it a question. Or, as Zilliacus states it: "The final fall is not that of little child or ball-like object but of rain, a veritable Flood" (1999, 308).

12. In the holograph this is more realistically motivated, since the Coates twins had pelted the Rooneys with mud; and it is more realistically stated: "I should like to kill a child before I die. A little girl."

13. Gontarski (1985, 56) notes the analogy with Florian's 1792 *L'Aveugle et le paralytique* and with W. B. Yeats's 1926 play, *The Cat and the Moon*.

14. After 1957 Tophoven and his wife Erika shared the labor of translation into German. In her words: "pour moi les pièces de théâtre et pièces radiophoniques écrites en anglais, pour Elmar les textes français. Une fois la première version terminée, chacun lisait, annotait, corrigeait le travail de l'autre" (*Trans Litterature* 8 [1985]: 36).

15. Gontarski writes: "Through seven preliminary versions Beckett exploited the technical and dramatic potential of the tapes, amplified and universalized Krapp's conflict, developed the black/white Manichean or Gnostic imagery that dominates the play, and orchestrated the tone from the singular pathos of stage 1 to the final patho-comedic ensemble" (1985, 58). Beckett accomplished these changes by quite small steps. I do not agree that the Manichaean imagery "dominates the play." Although the autobiographical references seem to me quite subdued, Knowlson notes them with his customary tact. He also corrects the widespread belief that the playwright had never seen a tape-recorder when he wrote the play, since Beckett saw one at the Paris office of the BBC, where he went in January 1957, to hear a tape of Pat Magee reading extracts of his work. That may even be the seed of the "Magee Monologue," whose first scribbles are dated February 20.

1959–61: Fresh Elements and Motifs

1. First published in an interview with Mignon in *L'Avant-Scène* no. 313.

2. In *CDW* the crucial final scenic direction—"Sea"—is omitted.

3. Enoch Brater opens *The Drama in the Text* with an evocation of Beckett's radio voices, but I think he underestimates the difficulty of listening to them "off book." For example, "*Embers* relies on such a disarming exactitude in its synchronization of sound and silence that the piece can come to life only in performance" (29). It seems to me that the play must be read, as well as listened to, if one is to savor it.

4. Lawley shifts his ground somewhat in "Samuel Beckett's Relations" (1997). Ranging over several works, Lawley parallels relational scenes involving mother and father figures with relation as narration. His is a subtle argument, but I think in *Embers* he focuses too monolithically on Henry's father. A close stylistic analysis of the Bolton-Holloway story is offered by Avila.

5. The opera, published with the text in three languages, is dated May 25–December 30, 1959.

6. Paola Zaccaria has summarized the difficulties of dating and ordering the *Foirades:* The five *Fizzles,* written between 1950 and 1960, were published in the French magazine *Minuit* in 1973; in 1976 four editions of the *Fizzles* were published: *Pour finir encore et autres foirades* (Paris: Minuit), *For to End Yet Again and Other Fizzles* (London: Calder), and two American editions by Grove and Petersburg, respectively. Each of the four editions arranged the stories differently (Butler and Davis, 105).

7. We also read the word "grifane," which is absent from French dictionaries. Beckett probably borrowed it from Dante's "occhi grifagni" in line 123 of *Inferno* IV. He translates it as "ravening."

8. In connection with these insects, Beckett's narrator quotes a line from Canto VII of the *Inferno,* which is omitted from the English translation: "Tristi fummo ne l'aere dolce" (45) [We were sad in the sweet air].

9. *Se voir,* the seventh *foirade* in *Pour finir encore,* is fragmentarily started in RUL ms. 2928, which Beckett labeled "FRAGMENTS PROSE DEBUT 68."

10. In a letter of August 13, 1961, to Hugh Kenner, Beckett so described the narrator of *Comment c'est,* and several critics have accepted the term. I waver, a posture that the novel encourages.

11. Hugh Kenner was perhaps the first to note, "*How It Is* [is] so completely rethought in English that 'translated' seems an inapplicable word" (1968, 207). Useful in this connection is Yves Thomas.

12. In correcting the proofs for the English (Calder) edition of *How It Is,* Beckett tried to insure that the end of a verset never coincided with the end of a page, thus emphasizing the continuity or flow.

13. Caselli's longest analysis (1999, chap. 8) is concerned with *How It Is/Comment c'est.*

14. Porter Abbott (1996) subtly analyzes the triune reading response to *Comment c'est;* almost simultaneously occur (1) the impulse to normalize the prose; (2) the floating quality of phrases rendering them resistant to normalization; (3) the almost hypnotic effect of the sound play.

15. There are three further sentences quoted, but I have never believed Beckett

spoke them, so arrogant are they. This is not hero-worship, but sensitivity to a tone, which is utterly foreign to the man.

16. Cf. Beckett's comment to Katharine Worth: "Music always wins" (1999, 16).

1962–69: A Little Rush, Then Another

1. Brater (1987) reads a history of silent film into *Film*.

2. Photograph 2 is an actual photograph of the child Beckett—already described in *Comment c'est*.

3. Cf. Knowlson: "the fascination of watching his 'talking heads' at close quarters, pouring out their torrents of sound, was probably a key factor in inspiring later plays like *Not I, That Time, Footfalls* and *Catastrophe* in which the theatrical spotlight plays such a crucial role" (461).

4. I am no longer certain that the word "throwback" was actually used in my conversation with Beckett, but he told me that *Assez* had to be put in its correct position before *Imagination morte imaginez* in *Têtes-Mortes*. My interpretation of the story is indebted to James Hansford's dissertation.

5. Cf. Lawley 1983b, which examines wordplay in the English translation, and which argues for the fictionality of the narrative.

6. Critics (including me) have played guessing games about the gender of the narrator, and this was probably what Beckett intended. In the first draft both men suck each other's penises, and although the narrator's penis disappears from the second draft, Beckett told Linda Ben-Zvi: "They are both men" (1990, xii). He told me: "Men don't have breasts." Up through the last typescript, plural hands feel the narrator's breasts. Brater, who regards *Enough* as a key text in *The Drama in the Text*, is discerning about the androgyny of the narrator.

7. Beckett himself is my source of information about the MacGreevy letters. However, the librarian of Trinity College wrote me on September 8, 1998: "The Beckett/MacGreevy correspondence (TCD ms. 10402) was bequeathed by Thomas MacGreevy to the College with the proviso that it did not become available to readers until after Dr. Beckett's death." I can only suppose that the nieces did not know of this bequest when they wrote Beckett. The letters were presented to the college "in 1976 and 1978."

8. Janvier describes their work in terms worthy of Watt himself: "Dans ce jeu auquel nous l'invitions, mieux, auquel il s'invitait à travers nous et qu'il a joué avec obstination pendant de longs mois, nous avons beaucoup proposé, parfois disposé, il a parfois proposé, le plus souvent disposé" (64) [In this game to which we invited him, or, better, to which he invited himself through us, and which he played stubbornly for long months, we proposed much, sometimes disposed, sometimes he proposed, and most often disposed].

9. Critics (including myself) have tended to discuss Beckett's method of composition, rather than the narrative thrust of this lyric of fiction, but I here consign that method to this endnote. Beckett penned sixty sentences, ten in each of six groups. Each of the six groups is "signed" by elements common to the ten sentences composing it:

Group A Collapse of refuge Sign "vrai refuge"
Group B Outer world Sign "terre," "ciel," juxtaposed or apart
Group C Body exposed Sign "petit corps"
Group D Refuge forgotten Sign "aucun souvenir"
Group E Past and future denied Sign "jamais," except in one sentence
Group F Past and future affirmed Sign the future tense

Having composed the sentences, Beckett left the paragraphs to chance. On separate pieces of paper he wrote the numbers 3, 5, and 7 twice, and the numbers 4 and 6 thrice. He then drew each number randomly from a container, to designate the number of sentences for each paragraph. Then he repeated the entire process, weaving a narrative of 120 sentences. The number of sentences in successive paragraphs has been noted by Brater (1994, 95):

$$4 + 5 + 3 + 5 + 3 + 6 + 7 + 6 + 7 + 4 + 4 + 6 = 60$$
$$3 + 4 + 4 + 6 + 7 + 6 + 5 + 7 + 3 + 6 + 5 + 4 = 60$$

10. For an almost antithetical reading, see Solomon.

11. *Tête-de-mort* is French for skull and cross-bones, and Beckett's neologism blends this association into the dead mind.

1970–76: Soudain Ou Peu à Peu (All at once or by degrees)

1. Fortunate audiences of the Mabou Mines production of *The Lost Ones* now constitute a group of privileged readers. Even though Beckett did not see that production, he retained affection for the group, and especially for the actor, the late David Warrilow.

2. The printed scenic direction indicates Mouth "faintly lit from close-up and below," but every production I have seen, including two directed by Beckett, spotlights the mouth.

3. Some time in the 1960s Beckett expressed admiration (to me) of Céline's title *D'un château l'autre*, rather than *D'un château à l'autre*. The omission of the preposition seemed to him brilliant.

4. In *Malone meurt* Macmann is once compared to the Colossus of Memnon (98).

5. Beckett once told me that he had hoped in *Still* to look out, to look in, and to dream, but that the dream resisted him. Perhaps he meant the *Still* trilogy.

6. I thank Michèle Praeger for this information, and for help with the enigmatic French of *La Falaise*.

7. Both Brienza and Rabinovitz (1992) list parallel passages in *Sans* and *Pour finir encore*—in English.

8. There is no question mark in the original French, which is more musical than the English; the shades of Beckett's translation are fascinating.

9. Abbott (1999, 19) offers a brilliant guide to the musicality of the text in English.

10. The phrase was present in typescript no. 5, which he sent to me in 1974, and I implored him to remove it, as too coyly self-referential. He never commented on my plea, but the offensive phrase is absent from the final text.

11. Connor (1988) lists examples on p. 136.

12. Inexcusably omitted from *CDW*.

13. Translated by Kevin Perryman, *Babel* 6 (1990).

1977–89: Comment Dire (What is the word)

1. Ben-Zvi (1986) describes the memory-scenes in detail, and Moorjani summarizes them. Abbott (1996) unaccountably totals them at sixteen. On the cover of RUL ms. 1822 Beckett lists and numbers fifteen scenes, but he omits the birth scene, and he includes one he did not develop: "Black thread . . . white hair." No one has enumerated the paragraphs of the "you" scenes, which I hereby do: 7, 9, 10, 13, 16, 24, 27, 29, 33, 39, 40, 48, 53, 56, 58. I agree with Ben-Zvi that paragraph 47, the parents bending over the cradle, is not a memory scene; moreover, the occupant of the cradle is a voice—"No trace of love."

2. Katharine Worth has described performances of *Company*, which she views "as a source and nourishment of company" (1999, 175).

3. Krance, reinforced by Beckett's French version, believes that "create" is an error for "created" (101). He thus misses the bold comedy of the sentences.

4. Pilling (1986) analyzes a passage sonically.

5. The poems "Là" and "Brief Dream" are published in *JOBS* 2/1 (spring 1992), with notes by Gontarski.

6. The double bill opened on October 5, 1989, playing for three weeks, and later transferring to London's Riverside Studio, and to Parma, Italy. Beckett did not see the production.

Works Cited

Abbott, H. Porter. 1973. *The Fiction of Samuel Beckett: Form and Effect*. Berkeley and Los Angeles: University of California Press.

———. 1994. "Beginning Again: The Post-Narrative Art of *Texts for Nothing* and *How It is.*" In Pilling, ed.

———. 1996. *Beckett Writing Beckett: The Author in the Autograph*. Ithaca, N.Y.: Cornell University Press.

———. 1999. "Samuel Beckett and the Arts of Time: Painting, Music, Narrative." In Oppenheim, ed.

Acheson, James. 1997. *Samuel Beckett's Artistic Theory and Practice*. Basingstoke: Macmillan.

Acheson, James, and Kateryna Arthur, eds. 1987. *Beckett's Later Fiction and Drama*. London: Macmillan.

Ackerley, C. J. 1993a. "The Unnamable's First Voice." *JOBS* 3/2 (spring).

———. 1993b. "Beckett's 'Malacoda': Or, Dante's Devil Plays Beethoven." *JOBS* 3/1 (autumn).

———. 1993c. "Fatigue and Disgust: The Addenda to *Watt.*" *SBT* 2.

———. 1998. "Demented Particulars." *JOBS* 7.

Admussen, Richard L. 1979. *The Samuel Beckett Manuscripts: A Study*. Boston: G. K. Hall.

Anzieu, Didier. 1989. "Beckett and Bion." *International Review of Psychoanalysis* 16:163–69.

Arnold, Bruce. 1964. "Samuel Beckett." *Dubliner* 3, no. 2: 15.

Arthur, Kateryna. 1987. "Texts for *Company.*" In Acheson and Arthur, eds.

Astier, Pierre. 1986. "Beckett's *Ohio Impromptu*: A View from the Isle of Swans." In Gontarski, ed.

Avila, Wanda. 1983. "The Poem within the Play in Beckett's *Embers.*" *Language and Style* 17, no. 3.

Ayers, Caroline, and Barend van Heusden. 1998. "An Introduction to the Groningen Workshop on Beckett's 'First Love.'" *SBT* 7.

Bair, Deirdre. 1978. *Samuel Beckett*. New York: Harcourt Brace.

Barale, Michèle Aina, and Rubin Rabinovitz. 1988. *A Kwic Concordance to Samuel Beckett's Trilogy*. New York and London: Garland.

Beach, Sylvia, ed. 1929. *Our Exagmination round His Factification for Incamination of Work in Progress*. Paris: Shakespeare and Co.

Beer, Ann. 1985. "'Watt,' Knott, and Beckett's Bilingualism." *JOBS* 10.

———. 1987. "The Use of Two Languages in Samuel Beckett's Art." Ph.D. diss., Oxford University.

———. 1994. "Beckett's Bilingualism." In Pilling, ed.

Begam, Richard. 1996. *Samuel Beckett and the End of Modernity*. Stanford, Calif.: Stanford University Press.

Beja, Morris, S. E. Gontarski, and Pierre Astier, eds. 1983. *Samuel Beckett: Humanistic Perspectives*. Columbus: Ohio State University Press.

Ben-Zvi, Linda. 1985. "Samuel Beckett's Media Plays." *Modern Drama* (March).

———. 1986. *Samuel Beckett*. Boston: Twayne.

———, ed. 1990. *Women in Beckett: Performance and Critical Perspectives*. Urbana: University of Illinois Press.

Bernard, Michel. 1996. *Samuel Beckett et son sujet: Une apparition evanouissante*. Paris: L'Harmattan.

Bishop, Tom, and Raymond Federman. 1976. *Samuel Beckett*. Paris: L'Herne.

Blackman, Maurice. 1985. "The Shaping of a Beckett Text: *Play*." *JOBS* 10.

Brater, Enoch. 1981. "Privilege, Perspective, and Point of View in *Watt*." *College Literature* (fall).

———. 1987. *Beyond Minimalism: Beckett's Late Style in the Theatre*. New York: Oxford University Press.

———. 1994. *The Drama in the Text: Beckett's Late Fiction*. New York: Oxford University Press.

———, ed. 1986. *Beckett at Eighty/Beckett in Context*. New York: Oxford University Press.

Brienza, Susan. 1987. *Samuel Beckett's New Worlds*. Norman: University of Oklahoma Press.

Brugière, Bernard. 1982. "*Murphy* de Samuel Beckett: Ironie et parodie dans un récit de quête." *Etudes Anglaises* (January–March).

Bryden, Mary. 1992. "Figures of Golgotha: Beckett's pinioned people." In Pilling and Bryden, eds.

———. 1993. *Women in Samuel Beckett's Prose and Drama*. Lanham, Md.: Barnes and Noble.

———. 1998a. *Samuel Beckett and the Idea of God*. New York: St. Martin's Press.

———, ed. 1998b. *Samuel Beckett and Music*. Oxford: Clarendon Press.

Butler, Lance St. John, and Robin J. Davis, eds. 1990. *Rethinking Beckett*. New York: St. Martin's Press.

Büttner, Gottfried. 1984. *Samuel Beckett's Novel "Watt."* Trans. Joseph P. Dolan. Philadelphia: University of Pennsylvania Press.

Casanova, Pascale. 1997. *Beckett l'abstracteur: Anatomie d'une révolution littéraire*. Paris: Seuil.

Caselli, Daniela. 1996. "Looking It Up In My Big Dante: A Note on 'Sedendo et Quiesc[i]endo.'" *JOBS* 6/1 (autumn).

———. 1999. "Dante and Beckett: Authority Constructing Authority." Ph.D. diss., University of Reading.

Cerrato, Laura. 1999. *Génesis de la poética de Samuel Beckett*. Buenos Aires: Fondo de Cultura Economica.

Chabert, Pierre, ed. 1986. *Revue d'esthétique*. Toulouse: Privat.

Clément, Bruno. 1994. *L'Oeuvre sans qualités: Rhétorique de Samuel Beckett*. Paris: Seuil.

Coatzee, John Maxwell. 1969. "The English Fiction of Samuel Beckett: An Essay in Stylistic Analysis." Ph.D. diss., University of Texas.

Cochran, Robert. 1991. *Samuel Beckett: A Study of the Short Fiction.* New York: Twayne.

Cohn, Ruby. 1973. *Back to Beckett.* Princeton, N.J.: Princeton University Press.

———, ed. 1975. *Samuel Beckett.* New York: McGraw-Hill.

Connor, Steven. 1988. *Samuel Beckett: Repetition, Theory, and Text.* Oxford: Blackwell.

———. 1989. *"'Traduttore, traditore'*: Samuel Beckett's Translation of *Mercier et Camier." JOBS* 11.

———. 1992. "Between Theatre and Theory: *Long Observation of the Ray.*" In Pilling and Bryden, eds.

Coughlan, Patricia. 1995. "'The Poetry Is Another Pair of Sleeves': Beckett, Ireland and Modernist Lyric Poetry." In Coughlan and Davis, eds.

Coughlan, Patricia, and Alex Davis, eds. 1995. *Modernism and Ireland: The Poetry of the 1930s.* Cork: Cork University Press.

Crombie, John. 1987. *Mac.* Paris: Kickshaws.

Cronin, Anthony. 1996. *Samuel Beckett: The Last Modernist.* London: Harper Collins.

Cunard, Nancy. 1969. *These Were the Hours.* Carbondale: Southern Illinois University Press.

Dante Alighieri. 1954. *The Inferno, The Purgatorio, The Paradiso.* Bilingual ed. London: J. M. Dent.

Davies, Paul. 1994. *The Ideal Real: Beckett's Fiction and Imagination.* Rutherford, N.J.: Dickinson University Press.

Davis, Robin J., and Lance St. John Butler. 1988. *"Make Sense Who May."* Gerrards Cross: Colin Smyth.

Dearlove, Judith. 1982. *Accommodating the Chaos.* Durham, N.C.: Duke University Press.

De Moro, Francesca. 1996. "The Divine Florentine." Ph.D. diss., University of Pisa.

Doherty, Francis. 1992. "Mahaffy's *Whoroscope." JOBS* 1/2.

Duckworth, Colin, ed. 1966. *En attendant Godot.* London: Harrap.

Duffy, Brian. 1996. *"Malone meurt:* The Comfort of Narrative." *JOBS* 6/1.

Dukes, Gerry, ed. 2000. *First Love and Other Novellas.* London: Penguin.

Eade, J. C. 1982. "The Seventh Scarf: A Note on *Murphy." JOBS* 7 (spring).

Ellmann, Richard. 1959. *James Joyce.* New York: Oxford University Press.

Engelberts, Matthijs. 1998. "Beckett et le light verse." *SBT* 7.

Esslin, Martin. 1986. "Samuel Beckett and the Art of Radio." In Gontarski, ed.

Farrow, Anthony. 1991. *Early Beckett: Art and Allusion in "More Pricks Than Kicks" and "Murphy."* Troy, N.Y.: Whitson.

Federman, Raymond. 1965. *Journey to Chaos: Samuel Beckett's Early Fiction.* Berkeley and Los Angeles: University of California Press.

Federman, Raymond, and John Fletcher. 1970. *Samuel Beckett: His Works and His Critics.* Berkeley and Los Angeles: University of California Press.

Fehsenfeld, Martha. 1986. "'Everything Out but the Faces': Beckett's Reshaping of *What Where* for Television." *Modern Drama* (June).

Fitch, Brian. 1977. *Dimensions, structures, et textualité dans la trilogie romanesque de Beckett.* Paris: Minard.

———. 1987. "The Relationship between *Compagnie* and *Company*." In Friedman, Rossman, and Sherzer, eds.

Fletcher, Beryl, and John Fletcher. 1985. *A Student's Guide to the Plays of Samuel Beckett*. London: Faber.

Fletcher, John. 1964. *The Novels of Samuel Beckett*. London: Chatto and Windus.

———. 1967. *Samuel's Beckett's Art*. London: Chatto and Windus.

Fournier, Edith. 1990. "Preface" to her French translation of *Proust*. Paris: Les Editions de Minuit.

Friedman, Alan, Charles Rossman, and Dina Sherzer, eds. 1987. *Beckett Translating/Translating Beckett*. University Park: Pennsylvania State University Press.

Gaffney, Phyllis. 1999a. "Dante, Manzoni, de Valera: Beckett . . . ? Circumlocutions of a Storekeeper: Beckett and Saint-Lô." *Irish University Review* (autumn/winter).

———. 1999b. "Neither Here Nor There: Ireland, Saint-Lô, and Beckett's First Novel in French." *JOBS* 9/1.

Genetti, Stefano. 1994. "Molto Dopo Chamfort, Beckett." *Quaderni di Lingue e Letterature* 19.

———. 1998. "La Plaine dans la Tête j'allais à la Lande." *SBT* 7.

Gontarski, S. E. 1977. *Beckett's "Happy Days": A Manuscript Study*. Columbus: Ohio State University Press.

———. 1985. *The Intent of Undoing in Samuel Beckett's Dramatic Texts*. Bloomington: Indiana University Press.

———. 1987. "Company for *Company*." In Acheson and Arthur, eds.

———. 1998. "A Copy-Text for *All Strange Away*." *JOBS* 8/1.

———. 1999. "Beckett's *Play in extenso*." *Modern Drama* (autumn).

———, ed. 1986. *On Beckett: Essays and Criticism*. New York: Grove.

Gross, Katherine Travers. 1970. "In Other Words: Samuel Beckett's Art of Poetry." Ph.D. diss., Columbia University.

Grossman, Evelyne, and Régis Salado, eds. 1998. *Samuel Beckett: L'écriture et la scène*. Saint-Just: Sedes.

Gussow, Mel. 1996. *Conversations with (and about) Beckett*. London: Nick Hern Books.

Haerdter, Michael. 1968. "Samuel Beckett inszeniert das *Endspiel*." In *Materialien zu Becketts "Endspiel."* Frankfurt am Main: Suhrkamp.

Hansford, James. 1982a. "*Imagination Dead Imagine*: The Imagination and Its Context." *JOBS* 7.

———. 1982b. "Seeing and Saying in *As the Story Was Told*." *JOBS* 8.

———. 1983. "Skullscapes: Imaginative Strategies in the Later Prose of Samuel Beckett." Ph.D. diss., University of Reading.

———. 1985. "Imaginative Transactions in *La Falaise*." *JOBS* 10.

Harmon, Maurice, ed. 1998. *No Author Better Served: The Correspondence of Samuel Beckett and Alan Schneider*. Cambridge: Harvard University Press.

Harrington, John, ed. 1993. *The Irish Beckett*. Syracuse, N.Y.: Syracuse University Press.

Harrison, Robert. 1968. *Samuel Beckett's "Murphy": A Critical Excursion*. Athens: University of Georgia Press.

Harvey, Lawrence. 1970. *Samuel Beckett: Poet and Critic*. Princeton: Princeton University Press.

Hedberg, Johannes. 1972. *Samuel Beckett's "Whoroscope."* Stockholm: Moderna Sprak.

Herren, Graley. 1998. "Unfamiliar Chambers: Power and Pattern in Samuel Beckett's *Ghost Trio*." *JOBS* 8/1.

Hill, Leslie. 1990. *Beckett's Fiction in Different Words.* Cambridge: Cambridge University Press.

Janvier, Ludovic. 1986. "Traduire *Watt* avec Beckett." In Chabert, ed.

Jeffers, Jennifer, ed. 1998. *Samuel Beckett: A Casebook.* New York: Garland.

Kalb, Jonathan. 1989. *Beckett in Performance.* New York: Cambridge University Press.

Katz, Daniel. 1999. *Saying No More: Subjectivity and Consciousness in the Prose of Samuel Beckett.* Evanston, Ill.: Northwestern University Press.

Kelly, Lionel. 1992. "Beckett's *Human Wishes*." In Pilling and Bryden, eds.

Kennedy, Sighle. 1971. *Murphy's Bed.* Lewisburg, Pa.: Bucknell University Press.

Kenner, Hugh. 1968. *Samuel Beckett: A Critical Study.* Berkeley and Los Angeles: University of California Press.

———. 1974. *A Reader's Guide to Samuel Beckett.* New York: Farrar, Straus and Giroux.

Knowlson, James. 1986. "*Ghost Trio/Geister Trio*." In Brater, ed.

———. 1996. *Damned to Fame: The Life of Samuel Beckett.* New York: Simon and Schuster.

Knowlson, James, and John Pilling. 1979. *Frescoes of the Skull: The Later Prose and Drama of Samuel Beckett.* New York: Grove.

Kroll, Jeri L. 1977. "The Surd as Inadmissable Evidence: The Case of the Attorney-General v. Henry McCabe." *JOBS* 2.

Lake, Carlton, ed. 1984. *No Symbols Where None Intended.* Austin, Tex.: Harry Ransom Humanities Research Center.

Lawley, Paul. 1980. "*Embers*: An Interpretation." *JOBS* 6.

———. 1983a. "Counterpoint, Absence, and the Medium in Beckett's *Not I*." *Modern Drama* (December); reprinted in Gontarski, ed.

———. 1983b. "Samuel Beckett's 'Art and Craft'. A Reading of 'Enough,'" *Modern Fiction Studies* 29, no. 1 (spring).

———. 1988. "The Difficult Birth." In Davis and Butler, eds.

———. 1997. "Samuel Beckett's Relations." *JOBS* 6/2.

Lawlor, Sean. 1998. "New Sources for *Dream of Fair to Middling Women*." *Beckett Circle* (spring).

Laws, Catherine. 1998. "Morton Feldman's 'Neither.'" In Bryden, ed.

Lecercle, Ann. 1984. "*Echo's Bones*: Le redoutable symétrie de l'oeuf pourri ou Une poétique de la suture." In Rabaté, ed.

Lee, Heath. 1983. "*Watt*: Music, Tuning, and Tonality." *JOBS* 9.

Levy, Eric. 1980. *Beckett and the Voice of Species: A Study of the Prose Fiction.* Totowa, N.J.: Barnes and Noble.

Libera, Antoni. 1980. "Structure and Pattern in *That Time*." *JOBS* 6.

Little, Roger. 1984. "Beckett's Mentor, Rudmose Brown: Sketch for a Portrait." *Irish University Review* (spring).

Lowe, Fred. 2001. "Sam's Love for Sam: Beckett, Dr. Johnson and *Human Wishes*." *SBT* 8.

Martel, François. 1972. "Jeux formels dans *Watt*." *Poétique* 10.

Mayoux, Jean-Jacques. 1957. "Le Théâtre de Samuel Beckett." *Etudes anglaises.* Oct.–Dec.

———. 1972. *Samuel Beckett.* Paris: Aubier.

———. 1988. "*Molloy:* Un evènement littéraire Une oeuvre." In *Molloy,* by Samuel Beckett. Paris: Minuit.

Mays, J. C. C. 1977. "Mythologized Presences: *Murphy* in Its Time." In Ronsley, ed.

———. 1982. "*Murphy* and the Question of Apmonia." *Gaéliana* 4 (July).

McCarthy, Gerry. 1990. "On the Meaning of Performance in Samuel Beckett's *Not I.*" *Modern Drama* (December).

McCarthy, Patrick A., ed. *Critical Essays on Samuel Beckett.* Boston: G. K. Hall.

McCormack, W. M. 1992. "Samuel Beckett and the *Negro Anthology.*" *Hermathena: Quatercentenary Issue.*

McMillan, Dougald, and Martha Fehsenfeld. 1988. *Beckett in the Theatre.* London: Calder.

McMullan, Anna. 1993. *Theatre on Trial: Samuel Beckett's Later Drama.* London: Routledge.

McQueeny, Terence. 1977. "Samuel Beckett as Critic of Proust and Joyce." Ph.D. diss., University of North Carolina.

McWhinnie, Donald. 1959. *The Art of Radio.* London: Faber.

Mercier, Vivien. 1977. *Beckett/Beckett.* New York: Oxford University Press.

Minihan, John. 1995. *Samuel Beckett: Photographs.* London: Secker and Warburg.

Mitchell, Breon. 1976. "Art in Microcosm: The Manuscript Pages of Beckett's *Come and Go.*" *Modern Drama* (September).

———. 1999. "Six Degrees of Separation: Beckett and the *Livre d'Artiste.*" In Oppenheim, ed.

Mood, John J. 1971. "The Personal System—Samuel Beckett's *Watt.*" *Publications of the Modern Language Association* (March).

Moorjani, Angela B. 1982. *Abysmal Games in the Novels of Samuel Beckett.* Chapel Hill: North Carolina Studies in Romance Languages and Literature.

———. 1998. "*En attendant Godot* on Michel Pôlac's *Entrée des Auteurs.*" SBT 7.

Morot-Sir, Edouard. 1976. "Samuel Beckett and Cartesian Emblems." In Morot-Sir, Harper, and McMillan, eds.

Morot-Sir, Edouard, H. Harper, and Dougald McMillan, eds. 1976. *Samuel Beckett: The Art of Rhetoric.* Chapel Hill: North Carolina Studies in Romance Languages and Literature.

Morrison, Kristin. 1982. "The Rip Word in *A Piece of Monologue.*" *Modern Drama* (September).

Murphy, P. J. 1990. *Reconstructing Beckett: Language for Being in Samuel Beckett's Fiction.* Toronto: University of Toronto Press.

Murphy, P. J., Werner Huber, Rolf Breuer, and Konrad Schoell, eds. 1994. *Critique of Beckett Criticism: A Guide to Research in English, French, and German.* Columbia, S.C.: Camden House.

O'Brien, Eoin. 1986. *The Beckett Country.* London: Faber and Faber.

O'Hara, J. D. 1997. *Samuel Beckett's Hidden Drives.* Gainesville: University of Florida Press.

Oppenheim, Lois, ed. 1999. *Samuel Beckett and the Arts.* New York: Garland.

Oppenheim, Lois, and Marius Buning, eds. 1996. *Beckett on and on . . .* London: Associated University Presses.

Paine, Sylvia. 1981. *Beckett, Nabokov, Nin: Motives and Modernism.* Port Washington, N.Y.: Kennikat.

Perloff, Marjorie. 1981. "Beckett and the Poetry of Absence." In *The Poetics of Indeterminacy*. Princeton, N.J.: Princeton University Press.

———. 1996. "Witt-Watt." In *Wittgenstein's Ladder*. Chicago: University of Chicago Press.

Pilling, John. 1976. *Samuel Beckett*. London: Routledge and Kegan Paul.

———. 1982. "Company." *JOBS* 7.

———. 1986. "Criticism of Indigence: *Ill Seen Ill Said*." In McCarthy, ed.

———. 1997. *Beckett before Godot*. Cambridge: Cambridge University Press.

———. 1998. "New Sources for *Dream of Fair to Middling Women*." *Beckett Circle* (spring).

———. 1999a. *Beckett's Dream Notebook*. Reading: Reading International Foundation.

———. 1999b. "A Mermaid Made Over." In Stewart, ed.

———, ed. 1994. *The Cambridge Companion to Beckett*. New York: Cambridge University Press.

Pilling, John, and Mary Bryden, eds. 1992. *The Ideal Core of the Onion*. Bristol: Longdun Press.

Pountney, Rosemary. 1988. *Theatre of Shadows: Samuel Beckett's Drama, 1956–1976*. Totowa, N.J.: Colin Smythe.

Praeger, Michèle. "Self-Translation as Self-Confrontation: Beckett's *Mercier et/and Camier*." *Mosaic* 25, no. 2.

Rabaté, Jean-Marie, ed. 1984. *Beckett avant Beckett*. Paris: PENS.

Rabinovitz, Rubin. 1984. *The Development of Samuel Beckett's Fiction*. Urbana: University of Illinois Press.

———. 1992. *Innovation in Samuel Beckett's Fiction*. Urbana: University of Illinois Press.

Restivo, Giuseppina. 1991. *Le soglie del postmoderno: Finale di partita*. Bologna: Il Mulino.

———. 1994. "The Genesis of Beckett's *Endgame* Traced in a 1950 Holograph." *SBT* 3.

Robinson, Michael. 1969. *The Long Sonata of the Dead: A Study of Samuel Beckett*. London: Rupert Hart-Davis.

———. 1979. "Beckett and Dante Revisited." *JOBS* 5.

Ronsley, Joseph, ed. 1977. *Myth and Reality in Irish Literature*. Ontario, Canada: Wilfred Laurier University Press.

Schneider, Alan. 1969. "On directing *Film*." In Samuel Beckett, *Film*. New York: Grove.

Segrè, Elizabeth Bregman. 1977. "Style and Structure in Beckett's *Ping*." *Journal of Modern Literature* (February).

Sherzer, Dina. 1976. *Structures de la trilogie de Beckett*. The Hague: Mouton.

Simon, Bennett. 1988. "The Imaginary Twins: The Case of Beckett and Bion." *International Review of Psychoanalysis* 15:331–52.

Smith, Frederik, n.d. "Beckett's 'Johnson Fantasy.'" In *Beckett's Eighteenth Century*. Unpublished ms.

Solomon, Philip H. 1980. "Purgatory Unpurged: Time, Space, and Language in *Lessness*." *JOBS* 6.

Stein, William Bysshe. 1975. "Beckett's 'Whoroscope': Turdy Ooscopy." *ELH*.

Stevenson, Kay Golliland. 1986. "Belacqua in the Moon: Beckett's Revisions of 'Dante and the Lobster.'" In McCarthy, ed.

Stewart, Bruce, ed. 1999. *Beckett and Beyond*. Gerrards Cross: Colin Smythe.

Strauss, Walter A. 1959. "Dante's Belacqua and Beckett's Tramps." *Comparative Literature* 11 (summer).

Stuart, Malcolm. 1981. "Notes on Place and Place Names in *Murphy*." *Recherches anglaises et américaines,* no. xiv.

Thomas, Dylan. 1938. "Recent Novels." *New English Weekly,* March 17.

Thomas, Yves. 1993. "Traduire l'effacement: Notes sur la traduction de *Comment c'est*." *SBT* 2.

Tophoven, Erika. 1994. "Beckett et l'Allemagne." *TransLittérature* (spring).

Topia, André. 1984. "*Murphy* ou Beckett baroque." In Rabaté, ed.

Tritt, William. 1976. "Statistics on Proper Names in *Murphy*." In Morot-Sir et al., eds.

Tubridy, Derval. 1998. "Vain Reasonings: *Not I*." In Jeffers, ed.

Van der Weel, Adriaan, and Ruud Hisgen. 1993. "Unheard Footfalls Only Sounds: *Neither* in Translation." *SBT* 2.

Verdicchio, Massimo. 1989. "Exagmination round the Fictification of Vico and Joyce." *James Joyce Quarterly* 26, no. 4.

Wagner, Steven. 1997. "A Note on *The Unnameable*." *Beckett Circle* (fall).

Wheatley, David. 1995. "Beckett's *Mirlitonnades*: A Manuscript Study." *JOBS* 4/2.

Wolosky, Shira. 1991. "The Negative Way Negated: Samuel Beckett's *Texts for Nothing*." *New Literary History* 22, no. 1 (winter).

Wood, Rupert. 1993. "Murphy, Beckett; Geulincx, God." *JOBS* 2/2.

Worth, Katharine, ed. 1975. *Beckett the Shape Changer*. London: Routledge and Kegan Paul.

———. 1999. *Samuel Beckett's Theatre: Life Journeys*. Oxford: Clarendon Press.

Zaccaria, Paula. 1990. "*Fizzles* by Samuel Beckett." In Butler and Davis, eds.

Zeifman, Hersh. 1975. "Religious Imagery in the Plays of Samuel Beckett." In Cohn, ed.

———. 1976. "Being and Non-Being: Samuel Beckett's *Not I*." *Modern Drama* (March).

———. 1982. "*Come and Go*: A Criticule." In Beja et al., eds.

———. 1987. "'The Core of the Eddy': *Rockaby* and Dramatic Genre." In Friedman, Rossman, and Sherzer, eds.

Zilliacus, Clas. 1976. *Beckett and Broadcasting*. Abo, Finland: Abo Akademi.

———. 1999. "*All That Fall* and Radio Language." In Oppenheim, ed.

Zurbrugg, Nicholas. 1988. *Beckett and Proust*. Gerrards Cross: Colin Smythe.

Index of Works by Beckett

Abandonné, 314
Acte sans paroles I (Act Without Words I), 218–19
Acte sans paroles II (Act Without Words II), 248–49
"À elle l'acte calme," 100–101
"Ainsi a-t-on beau," 102
"Alba," 24–25
All Strange Away, 286–89
All That Fall, 232–36
"Antipepsis," 127–28
"Arènes de Lutèce," 102–3
"Ascension," 96–97
Assez (Enough), 296–97
Assumption, 5–7
As the Story Was Told, 324–26
"Au bout de ces années perdues," 203–4
Au loin un oiseau (Afar a Bird), 250

Bing (Ping), 298–301
"Bois seul," 101
"Bon bon il est un pays," 160
Breath, 298
. . . but the clouds . . . , 342–43

Le Calmant (The Calmative), 147–51
"Calvary by Night," 41–42
The Capital of the Ruins, 140–41
"Cascando" (poem), 85–87
Cascando (radio play), 271–74
A Case in a Thousand, 67–68
"Casket of Pralinen for a Daughter of a Dissipated Mandarin," 10–11
Catastrophe, 372–74

Ceiling, 371–72
Censorship in the Saorstat, 69–70
"Ce n'est au pelican," 28
Che Sciagura (What a misfortune), 7
Christmas Reviews, 68–69
Come and Go, 290–92
Comment c'est (How It Is), 254–62
"Comment dire" (What is the word), 382–83
Company, 349–55
Le Concentrisme or Jean du Chas, 21–22
"Coups de Gong" (Strokes of the gong), 207–8

Dante and the Lobster, 45–47
Dante . . . Bruno . Vico . . Joyce, 2–5
"Da Tagte Es," 61
Le Dépeupleur (The Lost Ones), 308–14
Les Deux Besoins, 97–99
Devlin's Intercessions, 94–95
"Dieppe," 95
Ding-Dong, 50–51
"Dortmunder," 33–34
"The Downs," 372
Draff, 55–57
"Dread nay," 327–28
Dream of Fair to Middling Women, 37–40

"Echo's Bones" (poem), 60
"Echo's Bones" (story), 58–60
Eh Joe, 294–96
Eleutheria, 152–53

415

Embers, 244–48
En attendant Godot (*Waiting for Godot*), 176–82
"Enueg I," 26–27
"Enueg II," 25–26
"Ernest et Alice," 220
Esquisse radiophonique (*Rough for Radio I*), 270–71
"Être là sans mâchoires sans dents," 101
L'Expulsé (*The Expelled*), 141–43

F_ , 155–57
"F1 et F2," 321–22
La Falaise, 328–29
Faux départs, 285
Film, 278–80
La Fin (*The End*), 128–33
Fin de partie (*Endgame*), 225–32
Fingal, 49–50
Footfalls, 334–37
"For Future Reference," 7–8
Fragment de théâtre II, 242–43
From an Abandoned Work, 214–17
"From the Only Poet to a Shining Whore: for Henry Crowder to sing," 16–17

"The Gloaming," 236
Ghost Trio, 337–40
"Gnome," 66

Happy Days, 262–68
"Hell Crane to Starling," 12–13
Henri Hayden, homme-peintre (Henri Hayden, man-painter), 208
"Home Olga," 42–43
Hommage à Jack B. Yeats (*Homage to Jack B. Yeats*), 210
Horn venait la nuit (*Horn came always at night*), 251
"Hors crâne," 326
"Hourah je me suis repris," 204
Humanistic Quietism, 66
Human Wishes, 105–7

Imagination morte imaginez (*Imagination Dead Imagine*), 292–93
An Imaginative Work!, 85

"Ici, personnne ne vient jamais," 206–7
Il est tête nue . . ., 212–14
L'Image (*The Image*), 253–54
L'Innommable (*The Unnamable*), 184–94
J'ai renoncé avant de naître (*I gave up before birth*), 250–51
"Je suis ce cours de sable qui glisse," 158
"Je voudrais que mon amour meure," 157–58
"J.M. Mime," 276–77
"Les joues rouges" (Red cheeks), 99–100
"Jusque dans la caverne ciel et sol," 103

"Kilcool," 280–81
Krapp's Last Tape, 238–41

"Last Soliloquy," 241
Letter to Axel Kaun, 88–89
"Lightning Calculation" 70–71
Long after Chamfort, 343–44
"Long Observation of the Ray," 341–42
Love and Lethe, 51–52

"Malacoda," 60–61
Malone meurt (*Malone Dies*), 168–76
Mal vu mal dit (*Ill Seen Ill Said*), 363–69
"Medical Monologue," 302–3
Mercier et Camier, 133–40
Mime du rêveur A (*Mime of Dreamer A*), 210–12
Mirlitonnades, 345–47
Molloy, 161–68
"Mongrel Mime," 277–78
"Mort de A.D.," 159–60
"La Mouche," 97
Murphy, 73–85
"Musique de l'indifférence," 97

Nacht und Träume, 374–75
Neither, 340–41
Not I, 316–19

Ohio Impromptu, 362–63
"On le tortura bien," 204–6
"Ooftish," 90–94

Peintres de l'empêchement (Painters of impediment), 154–55
La Peinture des van Velde ou le monde et le pantalon (The painting of the van Velde brothers, or the world and the pair of trousers), 125–26
A Piece of Monologue, 355–58
Play, 281–84
Pochade radiophonique (*Rough for Radio II*), 274–75
Poems by Rainer Maria Rilke: Translated from the German by J.B. Leishmann, 65
The Possessed, 23–24
Pour Avigdor Arikha, 301
Pour finir encore (*For to end yet again*), 329–31
Premier Amour (*First Love*), 144–47
Proust, 17–20
Proust in Pieces, 65

Quad, 370–71
"Que ferais-je sans ce monde sans visage sans questions," 158–59
Quoi où (*What Where*), 377–78

Recent Irish Poetry, 68
"Return to the Vestry," 9–10
Rockaby, 360–62
"Rue de Vaugirard," 102

"Saint-Lô," 124
"Sanies I," 49
"Sanies II," 35
Sans (*Lessness*), 305–7
Schwabenstreich (Swabian tricks), 64–65
Sedendo et Quiescendo, 28–30
"Serena I," 44
"Serena II," 44–45
"Serena III," 57–58

Se Voir (*Closed Place*), 303–5
The Smeraldina's Billet-Doux, 30
Un soir, 358–59
"Something there," 326–27
"Sonnet—At last I find," 15–16
Sounds, 322–23
"Spring Song," 36
Still, 319–21
Still 3, 323–24
Stirrings Still, 379–82

"Text" (poem), 11–12
"Text" (prose poem) 34–35
Textes pour rien (*Texts for Nothing*), 194–202
That Time, 331–34
"They come . . . ," 95
Three Dialogues by Samuel Beckett and Georges Duthuit, 182–83
"Tristesse Janale," 20–21

Ur-Watt, 109–13

Verbatim, 347–48
Vieille terre, assez menti (Old earth, no more lies), 252–53
"Vive morte ma seule saison," 160
"The Vulture," 62–63

Walking Out, 31–32
Was Wo (*What Where*), 378–79
Watt, 113–23
The Way, 369–70
A Wet Night, 48–49
What a Misfortune, 52–54
"Whoroscope," 13–15
Words and Music, 268–70
Worstward Ho, 375–77

Yellow, 54–55
"Yoke of Liberty," 24